"I applaud Joseph Holden and Steven Collins for the publication of *The Harvest Handbook of Bible Lands*. Study of the lands and history of the Bible has been of special interest to me for nearly three decades and I have numerous books relating to this interest, but I was surprised with the uniqueness, organization, and scope of their book. Readers who want to understand the culture, chronology, history, geography, and archaeology relating to the Bible will not be disappointed. I know of no book that accomplishes this task as well."

—H. Wayne House, ThD, JD
Distinguished Research Professor of Biblical and Theological Studies,
Faith International University and Faith Seminary

"This is a comprehensive and scholarly volume by two scholars with extensive field experiences. Written in a conversational tone, it incorporates current scholarship that makes it extremely valuable as an up-to-date and reliable guide to biblical study that covers the span of Bible history from Neolithic times to the earliest Christian church discovered at Dura-Europos in Syria in post-biblical times. Especially useful is their firsthand confirmation of the biblical account of the existence of the 'cities of the plain' and the destruction of Sodom."

—William E. Nix, PhD
Director of Master of Arts in Theological Studies,
Professor of Historical and Theological Studies,
Veritas International University

"Joseph Holden and Steven Collins's *The Harvest Handbook of Bible Lands* is certainly an important resource to the Christian community. You should buy one for yourself, your pastor, your church library, and your best friend."

—Terry L. Miethe, PhD, PhD, DPhil (Oxon. Cand.)
Adjunct Professor of Philosophy and Religion,
Veritas International University

The

HARVEST
HANDBOOK™
OF
BIBLE LANDS

STEVEN COLLINS
JOSEPH M. HOLDEN
GENERAL EDITORS

HARVEST HOUSE PUBLISHERS
EUGENE, OREGON

The Harvest Handbook™ of Bible Lands
Copyright © 2019 by Steven Collins and Joseph M. Holden
Published by Harvest House Publishers
Eugene, Oregon 97408
www.harvesthousepublishers.com

ISBN 978-0-7369-7542-1 (hardcover)
ISBN 978-0-7369-7543-8 (eBook)

Library of Congress Cataloging-in-Publication Data

Names: Holden, Joseph M., author. | Harvest House Publishers.
Title: The Harvest handbook of Bible lands / Joseph M. Holden.
Description: Eugene : Harvest House Publishers, 2019.
Identifiers: LCCN 2019005722 (print) | LCCN 2019016965 (ebook) | ISBN
    9780736975438 (ebook) | ISBN 9780736975421 (hardcover)
Subjects: LCSH: Bible—Antiquities.
Classification: LCC BS621 (ebook) | LCC BS621 .H568 2019 (print) | DDC
    220.9—dc23
LC record available at https://lccn.loc.gov/2019005722

Printed in China

19   20   21   22   23   24   25   26   27 / FC-SK / 10   9   8   7   6   5   4   3   2   1

Acknowledgments

In a complex work like this one, which consists of several moving parts, it is difficult to acknowledge everyone who contributed in their own unique way. When Harvest House presented us with this project it seemed simple and straightforward—*we thought.* After all, we have had long careers, collectively, in the fields of biblical studies, ancient Near Eastern history, and Levantine archaeology, respectively. Between us we have written tens of thousands of pages of research, books, and articles on these subjects, as well as more than twenty-five field seasons excavating sites in Israel and Jordan, not to mention having led dozens of study tours to the Holy Land. So how difficult could it be to produce a book about the Bible Lands?

When we sat down to storyboard the project in detail and came to realize the full complexity of what we wanted to accomplish, we quickly realized that one thing was certain—we would need a good team of scholars and researchers to make the project possible!

Our team of scholars is listed in the Contributors section, and all deserve our deepest thanks for their expertise and contributions. Though our team members have their own thoughts on the various details and minutia presented in the book, to be sure, we are united on the point that the Bible presents the modern reader with an authentic and historically reliable record from the ancient Near East.

A few individuals went above and beyond the call of duty and warrant special recognition here. We want to thank Dr. John Moore for staying with the project from start to finish, providing research, text, and photos, along with creating base maps from which each subject map was built from scratch. In this regard, our sincerest appreciation goes to those at Accordance Bible Software—a registered trademark of Oak Tree Software, Inc.—for providing the underlying cartographic material required to make fresh, new maps.

Photos were also provided by James Barber, Daniel Galassini, Dr. David E. Graves, Michael Luddeni, Dr. Carl Morgan, and Alexander Schick. Thanks to each one for taking the time to pour through personal archives for the photographs we needed.

The intense effort expended during the production of this book took a toll on our wives. We wish to express our gratefulness to Danette Collins and Theresa Holden for their support and love during this process. Dr. Collins—who shouldered much of the project, particularly in the final months—owes a huge debt of love and gratitude to his wife Danette for her patience and willingness to "put life on hold" until the book was finished.

Many thanks to Harvest House President Bob Hawkins Jr. and senior editor Steve Miller for their belief in the project and their continued attention to the needs of the reader. Without them this book would have never made it to the press.

Finally, praise and glory are due to God Almighty and the Lord Jesus Christ for the blessing of the Word of God, the Bible. It is our prayer that this little volume will, for many, illuminate the study of the Holy Scriptures by immersing it in the reality of the history from which it arose.

Contents

ABBREVIATIONS

ANE	Ancient Near East
BA	Bronze Age
DSS	Dead Sea Scrolls
EBA	Early Bronze Age
EBA3	Early Bronze Age 3
IA	Iron Age
IA1	Iron Age 1
IA2	Iron Age 2
IA3	Iron Age 3
IBA	Intermediate Bronze Age
IBA1	Intermediate Bronze Age 1
IBA2	Intermediate Bronze Age 2
LBA	Late Bronze Age
LBA1	Late Bronze Age 1
LBA2	Late Bronze Age 2
LXX	Septuagint
MBA	Middle Bronze Age
MBA1	Middle Bronze Age 1
MBA2	Middle Bronze Age 2
MT	Masoretic Text

General Editors

Steven Collins, PhD
Director, Professor of Archaeology & Biblical History,
VIU School of Archaeology,
Veritas International University;
Director, Chief Archaeologist, Tall el-Hammam
Excavation Project, Jordan

Joseph M. Holden, PhD
President, Professor of Theology and Apologetics,
Veritas International University

CONTRIBUTORS

WILLIAM ATTAWAY, PhD
Lead Pastor, Southview Community Church, Herndon, VA

GARY A. BYERS, PhD
Dean, College of Archaeology, Trinity Southwest University;
Senior Archaeologist, Tall el-Hammam Excavation Project and Shiloh Excavations

MARK W. CHAVALAS, PhD
Professor, History and Archaeology of Mesopotamia, University of Wisconsin–La Crosse

ARNOLD FRUCHTENBAUM, PhD
Director, Ariel Ministries; author and researcher;
Adjunct Professor of Old Testament, Veritas International University

DAVID E. GRAVES, PhD
Assistant Professor/Subject Matter Expert for Archaeology, Rawlings School of Divinity, Liberty University

H. WAYNE HOUSE, ThD, JD
Distinguished Research Professor of Biblical and Theological Studies, Faith International University, and Faith Seminary;
Adjunct Professor of Biblical Studies and Apologetics, Veritas International University

JOHN WITTE MOORE, PhD
Professor, Historical Geography, College of Archaeology, Trinity Southwest University;
Visiting Lecturer, VIU School of Archaeology, Veritas International University

CARL MORGAN, PhD
Director, Senior Curator, Museum of Archaeology and Biblical History, Woodland, CA;
Visiting Lecturer, VIU School of Archaeology, Veritas International University

CRAIG OLSON, PhD
Dean, College of Biblical Studies, Trinity Southwest University

AMANDA PAVICH, PhD
Independent researcher; Lecturer, Eastlake Leadership College, San Diego, CA;
author and creator, 5oclock-dock.com Online Apologetics Community

J. RANDALL PRICE, PhD
Distinguished Research Professor Biblical & Judaic Studies, Rawlings School of Divinity, Liberty University

PHILLIP J. SILVIA, PhD
Professor, Archaeology and Biblical History, Trinity Southwest University;
Director, Scientific Analysis, Tall el-Hammam Excavation Project, Jordan

SCOTT STRIPLING, PhD
Provost, Director of the Archaeology Institute, The Bible Seminary;
Director, Shiloh Excavations, Southern Samaria

EDWIN M. YAMAUCHI, PhD
Emeritus Professor of History, Miami University–Ohio

The following graduate and doctoral students also contributed to the research and writing of this book: James Barber, Jeannine Bulot, Angela Everett, B.J. Fink, Brandy Forrest, Harry Gullett, Wesley Husted, Esther Lovato, Larissa Lusko, Brian Maggard, and Frank Policastro.

FOREWORD

Walter C. Kaiser Jr.

The ancient world of the Bible lands is one that continues to expand each year as more and more excavations uncover artifacts and inscriptions that often continue to exhibit enormous bearing on our understanding of the Bible. This fact can be seen in archaeological recoveries from the region of Mesopotamia to the areas surrounding and within the Mediterranean Sea itself.

Quality interpretations of both the Old and New Testaments more often than not call for an understanding of the geography, lifestyle, history, archaeology, and general culture of the times to which the biblical text points. Placing a text of Scripture in its proper context can be a critical move for the one who wants to be faithful to what is being said. It is often in these areas where some of the greatest insights can be gained for our interpretation of the Bible.

Frequently the sustained absence of confirming archaeological data is suddenly reversed when a random find is announced as having been uncovered in one or another excavation. It may then happen that what turns up is the precise evidence that had been sought for decades, if not a century or two. Thus, for example, there was much denial about the reality of an Old Testament people named the Hittites until about 1900, when their capital and a huge collection of their writings turned up in modern Turkey. Likewise, we had a list of all the kings from Assyria, but only Isaiah 20:1 referred to a King Sargon. That name, however, was missing from the list of all the Assyrian kings. But suddenly Sargon's palace was discovered—all twenty acres not far from the Tigris River, and immediately the Bible's version of history was once again confirmed and interpreters were helped as they taught this portion of the Word of God.

Therefore, with *The Harvest Handbook of Bible Lands*, you have right at your fingertips a wealth of information that is available in a most handy form. The maps in this *Handbook* are especially clear and easy to follow. Be sure to read the "Breakouts" in each of the sections, for they contain a load of helpful information for the exegete of Scripture.

May the joy of discovery be yours as you frequently consult this textbook in your exegetical studies. The scope of your learning and practical challenges will be unlimited and enhanced by leaps and bounds as you use this wonderful tool in the interpretive process.

Walter C. Kaiser Jr., PhD
President Emeritus, Gordon-Conwell
Theological Seminary
Hamilton, MA

Bringing Life to the Ancient Near East

The Bible lands have been a source of awe and wonder for millions of travelers who seek a glimpse of the ancient biblical past. To walk where Abraham, Moses, and Jesus walked, and to experience a slice of God's redemptive plan, has fascinated tourists and scholars alike. This has been made possible over the last 150 years by men and women who have dedicated their lives to research aided by disciplines such as archaeology, geography, cultural anthropology, history, linguistics, and other crucial fields of study.

The modern advances these disciplines have contributed to Near Eastern studies have been instrumental in rooting the biblical narratives in the space-time world, with real geography, persons, places, and artifacts of material culture. As a result, critical arguments marshalled against the authenticity of the Bible are no longer allowed to roam unchecked without strong counterarguments challenging the very presuppositions on which the criticism is based. Far from adopting a view that understands the biblical narratives as simply products of the fertile imagination of a Jewish mind or stories emerging from late Judahite priests, the narratives have taken on a life and vitality of their own—and are grounded in reality!

The Harvest Handbook of Bible Lands seeks to bring the reader into the epochs of the biblical world through well-written narrative-style text, maps, photographs, illustrations, timelines, and breakout articles. It brings to life the ancient Near East in the clearest and most concise terms possible. Though it incorporates current ancient Near Eastern studies and archaeology, this *Handbook* takes advantage of the most recent information from all the biblical and scientific disciplines upon which it touches. In the process, not a few traditional-but-erroneous views are dismissed and replaced by more accurate information. The logic of design and presentation keeps the needs of the reader in mind so that they experience ease in discovering the information they seek. It is, at the same time, both an exciting read and a reference book. It is a marvelous tool for all ages as well as a faithful representation of the ancient Near Eastern biblical world for serious Bible students, pastors, and scholars.

Jesus's words are instructive when we consider the important link between history and doctrine, "If I have told you earthly things and you do not believe, how can you believe if I tell you heavenly things?" (John 3:12). The doctrines of Scripture, along with their spiritual benefits, flow out of historical bedrock (Romans 4:25). If this material helps you see the world of the ancient Near East ("earthly things") more clearly, then we have successfully achieved our goal of building confidence in the Bible ("heavenly things").

Steven Collins, PhD
Joseph M. Holden, PhD
General Editors

PART 1

A SURVEY OF THE WORLD OF THE BIBLE

CHAPTER 1

AN INTRODUCTION TO THE BIBLICAL WORLD

The Bible is the divinely inspired and inerrant Word of God. This unique (Latin, *sui generis*) collection of Scripture was delivered to, through, and by human authors across millennia. The books of the Old and New Testaments trace the history of the universe from the acts of creation, through the origins of humanity, to a surviving family, through multiplying clans, tribes, and nations, to a focal ancestor and his promised son, to a people wielding the name of Yahweh, through a chosen tribe and royal lineage, to a Judahite maiden and the virgin-born Word-made-flesh, through the Messiah's earthly career, his death, burial, and resurrection, to visions of his triumphant return. No other book equals this book—his Book.

But this *Handbook* isn't about how all the above themes figure into Christian thought. Neither is it about individual Bible books, spiritual themes, or theological perspectives. These are expounded in countless sources from children's books to scholarly tomes. But not here. This *Handbook* is about physical reality—in particular, the Bible's physical reality.

While we can't help touching upon spiritual and theological themes, the goal is to set both the Hebrew Scriptures and the Ultimate Covenant in their respective *physical* worlds that reflect tangible and three-dimensional reality.

In the following pages, you have at your fingertips concise yet exacting descriptions of the biblical world. This information is brought together from the latest and best historical, archaeological, anthropological, geographical, and textual research. This means some old ideas must move aside to make room for new, more precise conceptions about Bible characters, when and how they lived, and what they saw, heard, touched, tasted, and smelled on a daily basis. And let's not forget things like peoples and politics!

FROM THEM TO US

Once the biblical writers had penned their books, which were later compiled into collections we call the Old and New Testaments, how did they get to us? This process is called *textual transmission*.

Figure 1.01—Example of an Egyptian papyrus document (photo: Alexander Schick)

Many cultures in the ancient Near East (ANE) had writing systems and literature. Their many texts, both secular and religious, were often kept "alive" by copying and recopying. Before the invention of writing (after c. 3300 BC), stories were passed along from

Figure 1.02—Cuneiform tablet of a student, Mesopotamia, eighteenth century BC (photo: Daniel Galassini, courtesy of Museum of Archaeology, Trinity Southwest University)

Figure 1.02) (see *Breakouts 3.11, 3.12*). An official class of specially educated scribes developed in all literate cultures. Keeping texts—especially sacred ones—"in print" was a major scribal responsibility.

From the time the Old and New Testament texts were written down, Hebrew and later Christian scribes maintained rigorous and meticulous methods of replacing old, worn copies with fresh, new ones. But, on average, manuscripts (MSS) did last for a long time: clay tablets (basically, forever!), papyrus (200–300 years), parchment (300–500 years). Because documents lasted for so long, 1,000 years could easily be spanned by only two or three generations of MSS (see *Figure 1.03*). Thus, the idea that hundreds of "generations" of copying biblical texts obscured the original meanings is simply an urban myth!

The discovery of the Dead Sea Scrolls (see *Figure 1.04*; *Breakouts 8.13, 8.14*) gave us copies of biblical books in Hebrew well over 1,000 years older than previously known Old Testament MSS. And, yes, the scribes did their job accurately! But preserving ancient texts, including the Bible, was not simply about copying manuscripts. Languages evolve and diverge over time, and accommodating language change was always an important part of textual transmission (that is, copying).

one generation to the next by memorization and recitation. Without writing, such oral tradition was the only means of preserving knowledge of the past. When writing became available and societies advanced, much of their oral tradition was committed to papyrus (Egypt; see *Figure 1.01*) and clay tablets (Mesopotamia; see

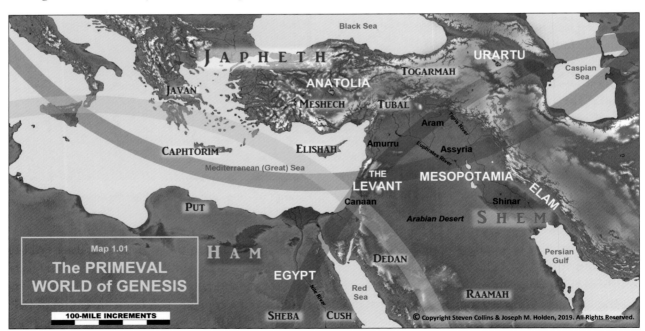

Map 1.01
The PRIMEVAL WORLD of GENESIS

100-MILE INCREMENTS

JAPHETH

URARTU

TOGARMAH

ANATOLIA

Caspian Sea

JAVAN

MESHECH   TUBAL

Aram

Tigris River

CAPHTORIM   ELISHAH

Amurru   Assyria

Euphrates River

Mediterranean (Great) Sea

THE LEVANT   MESOPOTAMIA   ELAM

Canaan

Shinar

Arabian Desert   S H E M

PUT

Persian Gulf

H A M

DEDAN

EGYPT   Red Sea

RAAMAH

Nile River

SHEBA   CUSH

Black Sea

BREAKOUT 1.01

PRONOUNCING BIBLE NAMES AND PLACES

The pronunciations of Bible names and places are typically butchered by almost everyone who attempts to read them out loud. But if you have a desire to pronounce them more correctly, there is a way to do it with relative accuracy.

Because all languages change through time, there really is no such thing as uniformity of pronunciation, as much as dictionary publishers would like us to think! Generally speaking, if any language is spoken for hundreds of years, it will undergo enough changes to make it virtually unintelligible to individuals using the same language but separated in time. For example, speakers of Old English (before AD 1200) would not be able to converse very well with speakers of Middle English (after AD 1200 to about AD 1500). And if someone speaking Middle English tried talking with you today, you would probably not understand a single word he or she said. All languages change dramatically in this way, eventually becoming entirely "new" languages.

This basic principle of language evolution also applies to the biblical world. If somehow a Hebrew-speaking Moses (fifteenth/fourteenth century BC) met face to face with a Hebrew-speaking King David (eleventh/tenth century BC), their conversation would not go very well! They might catch a word here and there, but their pronunciations—as well as word meanings and idioms—would be so different that they would need an interpreter. And the prophet Isaiah probably would not understand much of what King David said, should they find a way to communicate across time.

The same is true of Greek from the New Testament era. No one—not even a top linguist—knows what Koine (common) Greek sounded like in Jesus's and Paul's day. Admittedly, the New Testament Greek taught today is mostly pronounced like English, but some try to use today's Greek as a model. Plato would be lost in modern-day Athens except for recognizing (maybe!) some printed words on signs. And Plato (fifth/fourth century BC) would find it hard to figure out what the apostle Paul was saying in Greek. This is simply what happens to languages over long periods of time. Geographical isolation also adds to this process of change.

Even though we don't know precisely how Hebrew and Greek sounded in antiquity, there are some basic linguistic rules that can lead to a more accurate pronunciation of biblical names and places. Because most of these are *transliterated* (an English rendering of foreign letters/words) and not *translated* (meanings of foreign words), a few guidelines can help avoid some of the worst mispronunciations. These guidelines work for both anglicized Hebrew and Greek words:

- *ch* is always a *k* sound, as in *ch*emical (Chedorlaomer is *K*edorlaomer; cherubim is *k*erubim; Chinnereth is *K*innereth).

- There is no long *i* sound in Hebrew or Greek (always *i* as in it or magazine; never *i* as in idle; Isaiah is not pronounced **eye**saiah!).

- There is no *j* sound as in jump; *j* is actually *y* (Hebrew, *yod*), and is pronounced like the *y* in yellow; Jacob is *Y*acob; Joshua is *Y*oshua; Jesus is *Y*esus (Greek) or *Y*eshua (Hebrew).

- Overall, if you pronounce biblical words as you would in Spanish, you will always be close to a correct pronunciation; unlike English, Spanish has a just *one* vocal sound for each consonant and vowel, and this works very well for a more authentic pronunciation of Bible names and places.

The more accurate your pronunciation of Bible names and places is, the less people are likely to look at you as if you are from another planet. Have fun with your pronunciations!

S. Collins

The dynamics of keeping ancient texts understandable from generation to generation is called *textual contemporization*. Over the course of hundreds of years, word meanings can drift, new words are invented, idioms and manners of speaking change, place-names are updated, dialects develop, and often "daughter" languages emerge. We experience this in the English language every day! It was no different in ancient times. Thus, scribes often replaced archaic terms with contemporary ones, sometimes inserting explanatory "notes" marking their alterations. This happened a lot with geographical names. For example, in the Middle Bronze Age (MBA) story of Abraham,

the town of Laish is called Dan. Later readers would only have known Dan and not Laish, so Dan is used. But the name wasn't changed until much later, during the time of the Judges (Genesis 14:14; cf. Judges 18).

While the present Hebrew text of the Old Testament has a distinctive Iron Age (IA) flavor because it was transmitted during the tenth through the sixth centuries BC, many linguistic features of Genesis through Judges—the Bronze Age (BA) scriptures—preserve authentic cultural "artifacts" from the MBA (time of Abraham, Isaac, and Jacob; see *Breakout 2.05*) and Late Bronze Age (LBA; time of Moses and Joshua; see *Breakouts 3.02, 3.05, 3.11*).

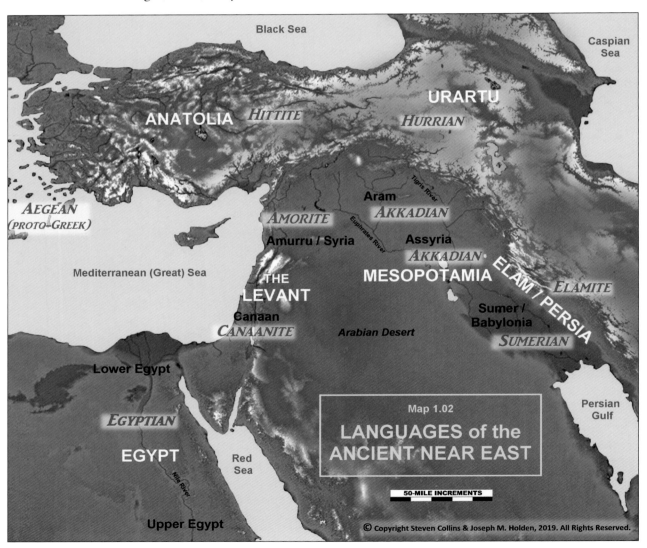

Map 1.02

LANGUAGES of the ANCIENT NEAR EAST

50-MILE INCREMENTS

Figure 1.03—Example of a parchment scroll
(photo: Alexander Schick)

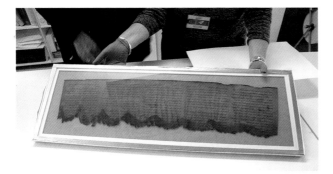

Figure 1.04—Dead Sea scroll (photo: Alexander Schick)

While the physical and mental processes of transmitting and contemporizing biblical texts have produced for us a Hebrew Old Testament and Greek New Testament that are remarkably accurate to their ancient originals, one step remains: *translation*. Most of the currently available English translations of the Bible are reasonably good. Some may even be classed as excellent. But using several translations for comparison purposes is always a good idea.

KEEPING THE BIBLE
IN THE REAL WORLD

Every biblical text is organically connected to the era of its writing. Whether looking back to the past, recording the present, or projecting into the future, every Bible passage or book is linguistically, historically, and culturally a product of its day. Here is a hard-and-fast rule of interpreting any part of the Bible: Never project present ideas onto ancient texts! Also,

avoid superimposing later biblical ideas on earlier ones. Remember, the time and culture of King David was a far cry from that of Abraham's day, and Daniel's epoch was a world away from King David's. Not to mention the historical and cultural distance between Daniel and the apostle Paul! And beware when you hear it said, "Take the Bible literally." What does that mean anyway? *Literal* is a slippery concept. Most often it winds up being what somebody *thinks* a biblical passage "literally" says "to them." This approach is dangerous when we seek to interpret the Bible accurately.

The proper way to understand the Bible is *authentically*. As far as possible, this means seeing it in its original historical context. An *authentic* interpretation is one that respects an author's language, culture, and history without superimposing elements that are foreign or anachronistic to the time of writing. While we may not be able to know every detail of an author's historical setting, getting as much accurate information as possible will always enhance our understanding of the text.

This is where a discipline like archaeology proves invaluable. The worlds of the biblical characters were real worlds. Sights, sounds, and smells. Blood, guts, and grime. Cities, towns, and villages. Houses, temples, and palaces. Swords, spears, and arrows. Jars, bowls, and lamps. A significant portion of the Bible deals with the accoutrements and objects of material culture. Such things are accessible only by the trowels and brushes

Figure 1.05—Tuthmosis III Battle of Megiddo Inscription
(photo: Alexander Schick)

of archaeological excavations. While ancient history is pieced together mostly from written texts and inscriptions (see *Figure 1.05*), the finer details and nuances of societies and cultures are best illuminated from the physical remains buried in the eroding sediments of past civilizations. Indeed, archaeology has a lot to say on the subject of biblical interpretation!

Unfortunately, there are two extreme views on the subject of the Bible and archaeology. On the far left are scholars who want the Bible eliminated from ANE archaeology altogether. Archaeology should not be done with a biblical "agenda," they say. They want archaeology for archaeology's sake, without a biblical bias attached to it. For these so-called biblical minimalists, the Bible gets little or no voice in the pursuit of archaeology.

On the far right are those who think the exact opposite. They disallow archaeology a place in studying the Bible. Put more accurately, they reject any

Map 1.03

SOME IMPORTANT BRONZE AGE CITIES & TOWNS of MESOPOTAMIA

50-MILE INCREMENTS

© Copyright Steven Collins & Joseph M. Holden, 2019. All Rights Reserved.

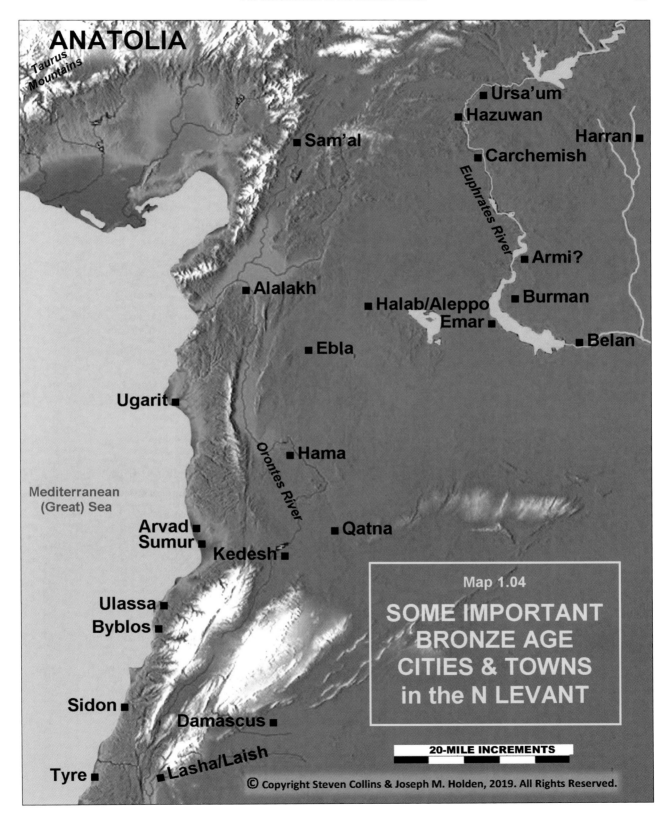

ANATOLIA

Taurus Mountains

Ursa'um

Hazuwan

Sam'al

Harran

Carchemish

Euphrates River

Armi?

Alalakh

Halab/Aleppo

Burman

Emar

Belan

Ebla

Ugarit

Orontes River

Hama

Mediterranean (Great) Sea

Arvad

Sumur

Qatna

Kedesh

Ulassa

Byblos

Map 1.04

SOME IMPORTANT BRONZE AGE CITIES & TOWNS in the N LEVANT

Sidon

Damascus

20-MILE INCREMENTS

Tyre

Lasha/Laish

BREAKOUT 1.02

A THUMBNAIL SKETCH OF
MESOPOTAMIA AND THE BIBLE

Geography. Ancient Mesopotamia—"the Land Between Rivers"—is generally the territory between the Euphrates River in the west and the Tigris River in the east, roughly equivalent to modern Iraq (see *Maps 1.02, 1.03, 1.06*). The Euphrates River started in the mountains of east Anatolia (east Turkey). The Tigris (Akkadian, *idiglat* = "arrow"; cf. Hebrew, *hiddekel*), as its name implies, was a swifter river flowing from the western slopes of the Zagros Mountains. The two rivers came close to each other near ancient Babylon. They merged into a single river, the Shatt al-Arab, before entering the Persian Gulf.

The rivers were useful for irrigation and were interconnected by canals. The hot, dry climate in Mesopotamia caused evaporation that deposited salts on the soil's surface, affecting especially the growth of wheat. Barley was hardier. The main trees were date palms. Lacking timber, the Mesopotamians from the second millennium BC coveted the cedars of Lebanon. They lacked metal and needed to trade for it. The primary building material was clay.

History. Mesopotamia is known as "the Cradle of Civilization," as writing in cuneiform (wedge-shaped) script was developed there beginning c. 3300 BC. The earliest cities were in lower Mesopotamia and developed by the Sumerians. Their cuneiform script was adopted by Semitic Akkadians, Assyrians, Babylonians, Hurrians, Hittites, and even Levantine peoples. During the Neo-Assyrian period (910–612 BC), the Assyrians began an aggressive military expansion against Urartu to the north and Syria to the west. The Assyrians were defeated by a coalition of Medes and Chaldeans in 612 BC. The latter formed the Neo-Babylonian Empire, whose great King Nebuchadnezzar (605–562 BC) built the famed Hanging Gardens of Babylon.

The Old Testament. The Tigris and Euphrates Rivers were two of the four rivers that flowed from the Garden of Eden (Genesis 2:10-14). The Tower of Babel (Genesis 11:1-9) seems to reflect a very early version of what was later, in Babylonia, called a ziggurat. God directed Abraham from Ur in southern Mesopotamia to Haran in northern Mesopotamia (Genesis 11:31), before he migrated to Canaan. Later Abraham sought a bride for Isaac from that region (Aram Naharaim); Jacob also sought refuge in Haran (Genesis 27:43). The Assyrian king Tiglath Pileser III destroyed the Aramean

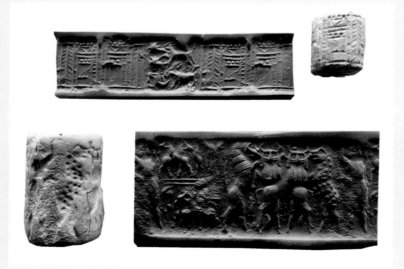

Bronze Age Mesopotamian cylinder seals with impressions (photo: James Barber, courtesy of Bible Lands Museum, Jerusalem)

state of Damascus in 732 BC. After the capture of Samaria in 722 BC, Sargon II deported leading Israelites and replaced them with people from Mesopotamia. Sennacherib invaded Judah in 701 BC, capturing Lachish. He failed to capture Jerusalem but exacted tribute from Hezekiah (2 Kings 18–19; Isaiah 36–37). After the fall of Nineveh in 612 BC (cf. Nahum),

Nebuchadnezzar attacked Judah, destroyed the temple in 586 BC, and deported Judean captives like Daniel. The Jewish exiles were not enslaved but were settled in Mesopotamia and prospered (see Ezekiel). After Cyrus captured Babylon in 539 BC, he allowed the exiles who wished to return to Judah to do so. About 50,000 returned (Ezra 2; Nehemiah 7).

The New Testament. At the day of Pentecost among the pilgrims in Jerusalem were residents from Mesopotamia (Act 2:9). Peter's mention of Babylon (1 Peter 5:13) is an obvious metaphorical reference to Rome, as are also the numerous references to Babylon in the book of Revelation.

E. Yamauchi

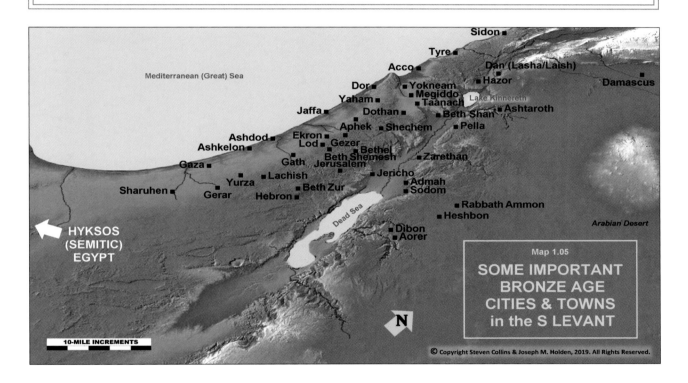

archaeological data that casts doubt on their own interpretation of the Bible (for example, see *Breakouts 2.04, 3.07*). In their minds, because archaeology seems to contradict many of their traditional interpretations of the Bible, they would just as soon steer clear of both archaeology and ANE scholarship. For them, archaeology has no right to speak to biblical interpretation.

Neither of these extreme views is valid. Because the Bible and archaeology arise from the same soil, from

the same worlds, both the text and the ground must be allowed to speak. Both are components of the same reality. They belong together in a mutual conversation—a *dialogical* approach to the Bible and archaeology.

The worlds that gave rise to biblical stories are the same worlds that left behind a wealth of material remains in the stratified ground. They are all part of the same reality. One is the same as the other, whether by word or by physical object. Because this is so, a text

A THUMBNAIL SKETCH OF THE LEVANT AND THE BIBLE

Geography. The Levant, a word derived from Italian meaning "the rising of the sun or the east," refers to the area to the east of the Mediterranean (see *Maps 1.02, 1.04, 1.05, 1.06, 1.07*). Ancient Syria had a coastal region watered by the Orontes River. Its principal city, Antioch, was situated on the Orontes, 20 miles from the coast. It provided a gateway into Mesopotamia to the east. Ancient Phoenicia occupied the area of modern Lebanon. Its mountains came close to the shore, which left little arable land. This area was known for its cedars and other coniferous trees. It also had excellent harbors, such as Byblos, Sidon, and Tyre. Palestine is a very small area, only a little larger than the state of Vermont in the USA. It is 150 miles from Dan to Beersheba, and about 50 miles from Jaffa to Jericho. Palestine's importance lay in its central location connecting Egypt with areas to the north. Melting snows from Mount Hermon (9,000+ feet) fed the headwaters of the Jordan River, which flowed into the Sea of Galilee, situated in a depression 600+ feet below sea level. The Jordan then meandered into the Dead Sea, the lowest spot on earth. Jerusalem is located about 2,500 feet above sea level. Because the prevailing winds are from the west, rain falls on the western slopes of the hills, leaving an arid "rain shadow" in the Judean desert. Valuable copper was mined in the Arabah Valley south of the Dead Sea. Palestine was noted for its grapes, olives, and figs.

History. As early as 2500 BC, Egypt was acquiring cedars from Byblos. Texts from Mari in Mesopotamia (eighteenth century BC) mention trade with Hazor. The Amarna correspondence (fourteenth century BC) between Amenhotep III and IV with kings in Mesopotamia mention a number of cities in Phoenicia and Palestine, including Jerusalem. The city of Ugarit in Syria, destroyed c. 1200 BC, yielded texts that illuminate Canaanean religion. The Phoenicians brought the Semitic alphabet—invented by Semitic peoples living in Egypt and brought into Canaan by the Hebrews and others—to the Greeks. The Phoenicians established trading colonies throughout the Mediterranean. The Assyrians, Babylonians, and Persians added the Levant to their empires. After Alexander the Great died, his successors—the Seleucids in Syria and the Ptolemies in Egypt—fought numerous wars over Palestine. With the Maccabean Revolution against the Seleucids in 165 BC, the Jews enjoyed a century of independence before the conquest of the Romans under Pompey in 63 BC. Judea was ruled by Herod (37–4 BC), then by Roman governors.

The Old Testament. After the conquest of Canaan, Israel enjoyed but a century of independence under Saul, David, and Solomon (tenth century BC). At first Israel's main rival was

Head of an Iron Age figurine from Abel Beth Maacah, Israel; beard on chin digitally restored (photo: courtesy of Tel Abel Beth Maacah Archaeological Project)

the Aramean state of Damascus in Syria. But the Assyrians destroyed Damascus in 732 BC, and then Samaria in 722 BC. Judah was conquered by the Babylonians in the sixth century BC, then ruled by the Persians during the fifth century BC.

The New Testament. Jesus was born c. 5 BC in Bethlehem but raised in Nazareth. A significant portion of his ministry took place at Capernaum on the Sea of Galilee, and he also ventured to the Phoenician coast (Mark 7:24; Luke 4:26). He was tried and crucified in AD 30 or 33 in Jerusalem. The gospel spread to Antioch, where followers of Jesus were first called Christians. Antioch became the center from which Paul spread the gospel throughout the Mediterranean region.

E. Yamauchi

can illumine ancient objects by setting them within a historical framework of peoples and individuals and narratives. In a corresponding manner, artifacts can illumine biblical texts because they contain references to, descriptions of, and allusions to objects of material culture—everything from monumental city gateways to the smallest stone weights.

Think of reality as a scene with infinitely high resolution. The scene is a man seated next to a small table, with a Chihuahua on his lap, and on the table a stack of five books next to a vase of daisies. Now, take a picture of it. The photo is made up of thousands of tiny pixels. On the whole, the original photo represents the reality pretty well. All the details are vivid. But now ask your computer to cut the resolution (the dots per inch, or dpi) in half. At the lower resolution, you can still make out the five books on the table, but the titles on the spines are blurred out. The flowers might still look like daisies, or perhaps not. Now reduce the resolution by three fourths. The dog might still look like a Chihuahua, or maybe it appears to be a small terrier. There is a vase of something, but you're not sure whether they are flowers or lollipops. The man could be in his forties or eighties. You get the idea.

Reality is infinitely hi-res. History is not. Not any kind of history. Not ancient Near Eastern history. Not

Figure 1.06—Melted pottery (L) and mudbrick (R) from Sodom's destruction (photo: Daniel Galassini, courtesy of Tall el-Hammam Excavation Project)

biblical history. What we know about the history of the ANE represents a tiny percentage of the reality behind it. Let's be extremely generous and say 10 percent. The Bible focuses on its narrow subjects (as diverse as they are!), but also represents only a small fraction of the larger reality. Let's say 5 percent. So between ANE and biblical history we have a picture with 15 percent resolution. In terms of tighter "shots," such as a single story line in ANE history (like Tuthmosis III's battle of Megiddo) or one in biblical history (like Joshua's conquest of Jericho), the local resolution might be much higher—perhaps as much as 25 or 50 percent of the reality they represent.

For the purposes of the authors, the percentage of resolution serves its purpose. Within the scope of the

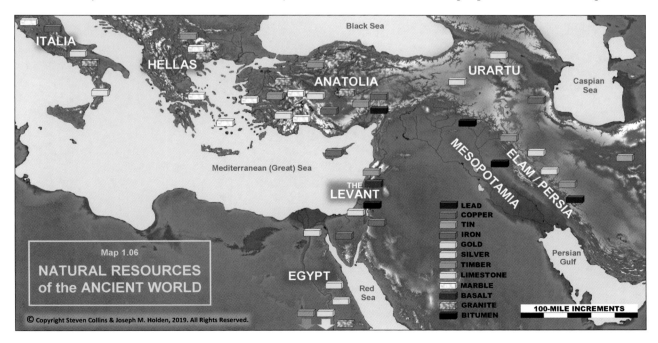

Map 1.06

NATURAL RESOURCES of the ANCIENT WORLD

LEAD
COPPER
TIN
IRON
GOLD
SILVER
TIMBER
LIMESTONE
MARBLE
BASALT
GRANITE
BITUMEN

100-MILE INCREMENTS

authors' intent, the stories are adequate, even perfect. There was no pretense to represent the entire scope of reality at that moment—only a desire to communicate relevant information and make a point.

Let's look at a biblical narrative from this perspective: Joseph's career as top administrator in Egypt, second only to pharaoh. The biblical narrative specifies neither the period of Egyptian history nor the reigning king. Rather, it very simply tells the story the way it happened, and in only enough detail for the account to make sense. Let's say the narrative represents 15 percent of the reality in which the story resides. As it is, it's a great story! But now let's bring in the Egyptian history and archaeology, which adds, say, another 25 percent to the resolution. These additional "pixels" place the story in a specific period of Egyptian history (see *Breakout 2.05*), when chariots were all the rage and a Semitic Asiatic, like Joseph, could actually be embraced by a (yes!) Semitic pharaoh. When we add the biblical "pixels" and the Egyptian "pixels" together, the resolution really makes the Joseph story pop. We catch things that were not possible to see from

the biblical text alone. But the inverse is also true. Egyptian history is clearer because of the biblical story.

By integrating both the biblical data and ANE data, we still may not have captured a 100-percent view of history, but we do have a clearer, more detailed understanding of their common reality. The picture is better with both together rather than separate. And ANE history and biblical history are more colorful for it!

Proper dialogue between the biblical text and archaeology can help correct distortions in our comprehension of both. Errors in our understanding can move closer to the truth. The distance between extreme and often contradictory points of view can sometimes be reduced. In the process, a cause-and-effect relationship between biblical narratives and attempts to write ANE history become valuable in both disciplines.

THE STORY BEHIND THE STORY: DATA VS. INTERPRETATION

The Bible often focuses on *outcomes*, not the means

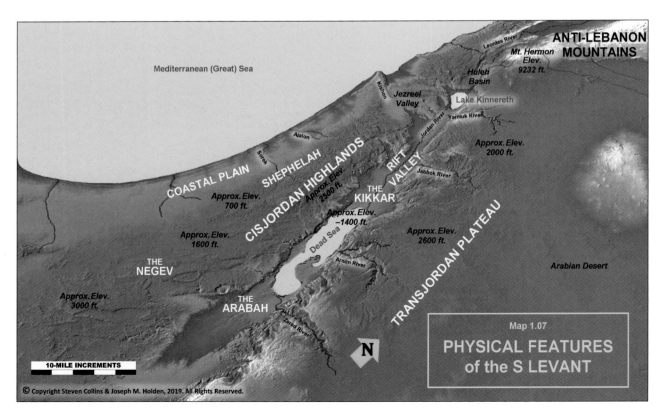

or processes involved. This is also true for most of our "knowledge" of ANE history. For example, an army with superior numbers and equipment loses a key battle, and that is the extent of what the historical record tells us. They suffered defeat, and history marched on to the beat of the victor. But if we could somehow peer into the reality of the scenario, we might discover that on the morning of the engagement our superior army suffered from sudden acute attacks of dysentery and fever. They lost because of illness! But that fact never entered the field books.

It is worth noting, however, that in not a few biblical stories we get interesting insights into the causes behind the effects. Not merely "God did it," but *how* God did it." Recall from 1 Samuel 5 (see *Breakout 4.05*) how the Philistines were "encouraged" to return the Ark of the Covenant to the Israelites because Yahweh inflicted them with "tumors" (the King James "emerods" = hemorrhoids of 1 Samuel 5:9 is more accurate, and fun!— "they had emerods in their secret parts").

In some instances, where the Bible does not specify the physical phenomena associated with accounts as we have them, ANE archaeology and historical sources can sometimes supply explanations or descriptions. One prominent example is the destruction of Sodom and Gomorrah. Genesis 19:24 says, "The LORD rained on Sodom and Gomorrah sulfur and fire from…out of heaven." This clearly describes a cosmic event, but its exact nature eluded scholars until recently. Before the actual location of Sodom was confirmed northeast of the Dead Sea at Tall el-Hammam in Jordan (see *Breakout 2.07*), all sorts of unverifiable theories were suggested— from volcanism to explosions of natural gas triggered by an earthquake. Years of sampling from the MBA destruction layer at Tall el-Hammam and the surrounding area now confirm that Sodom and its satellite towns—300 square miles in all—were obliterated in the super-hot fiery blast of a meteoritic airburst event (see *Figure 1.06*). Even the object's approximate mass, velocity, trajectory, and plasmic temperature index have been calculated from the archaeological and astrophysical evidence at the site. In this case, the biblical scenario of Sodom's destruction is not only confirmed, but also given minute details as a result of archaeological and astrophysical science.

The Bible and archaeology, when an appropriate dialogue is established, can have profound hermeneutical value in both directions. This is a far cry from the anti-Bible sentiment that has dominated ANE archaeology over the past few decades. Good biblical hermeneutics and good archaeology are, in fact, highly complementary. Archaeology and ANE studies must have their proper place in biblical interpretation. Likewise, the Bible must be allowed its appropriate place in constructing an understanding of ANE history.

GETTING COMFORTABLE WITH BIBLICAL AND ANE CHRONOLOGY

The outline of biblical epochs and events from the time of David, Solomon, and afterward accords well with the known history of the ANE. As a result, there are very few arguments among scholars about the general historicity of what we might call the Iron Age Scriptures. It is regarding the millennia prior to the IA—touching on time periods before c. 1200 BC— that scholars wrangle back and forth about the dating of important Bible characters and events. These are the BA Scriptures—Genesis through Judges. Even conservative Bible scholars share little agreement about when Moses and Joshua lived, not to mention the controversy over dating the Hebrew patriarchs.

The heart of the controversy over the earliest portions of biblical chronology is mainly the result of the "work" of Irish archbishop James Ussher in the mid-seventeenth century AD. Others have come away with slightly different numbers, but using the same basic "Ussherian" method: treating the Genesis patriarchal life span numbers as literal base-10 arithmetic values, and simply crunching the numbers. Such calculations result in a creation date of c. 4000 BC, a Noah's flood date of c. 2400 BC, and a birthdate of Abraham of c. 2166 BC (see *Breakout 2.04*). The controversy arises from the fact that because the Ussherian dates fall within the BA, they are woefully out of sync with the well-established chronologies for Mesopotamia, Egypt, and the Levant (Canaan) (see *Breakout 2.05*). Liberal critics of the Bible use such disconnects to deny the Bible's historical credibility.

Some have understood the Genesis life span numbers in their ANE context as Mesopotamian-style, base-60 honorific formulas (see *Breakout 2.04*). When taken in this fashion, the biblical and ANE chronologies are effectively linked by telltale sequences of historical events, cultural practices, and physical objects common to both (see *Breakouts 2.05, 3.02, 3.04,*

3.05). By using this method, the world of the Genesis patriarchs and the careers of Moses and Joshua integrate remarkably with ANE history. Indeed, they are one and the same history! The *Handbook* Timeline (at the back of this book) will give you a good feel for this.

Here are the ANE archaeological periods with some historical characters inserted to help show how all this works out:

ANCIENT NEAR EAST ARCHAEOLOGICAL PERIODS		
Neolithic Age	Before 4900 BC	Post-Flood era
Chalcolithic Age	4900–3900 BC	*Chalcolithic* literally means "copper" and "stone" due to the advances in creating objects made of stone and metal. This period ends with Tower of Babel episode.
Early Bronze Age	3900–2500 BC	Increased settlements and urbanization that included fortification of outer walls, table of nations, first cities.
Intermediate Bronze Age	2500–2100 BC	Pre-Abram patriarchs; urban centers had declined and nomadic lifestyle begins. Natural factors (rain, weather, farming, warfare, etc.) lead to highly transient culture.
Middle Bronze Age	2100–1550 BC	Patriarchal period of Abraham, Isaac, Jacob, and Joseph and his brothers.
Late Bronze Age	1550–1200 BC	Moses, Joshua, and early judges; period of the Israelite exodus from Egypt and conquest of Canaan by Joshua.
Iron Age	1200–332 BC	Reign of the kings of Israel and Judah from Saul to Zedekiah; building and destruction of Solomon's temple; conquest of Jerusalem in 586 BC.
Iron Age 1	1200–1000 BC	Period of the later judges, King Saul, and beginning of the Davidic Dynasty. End of New Kingdom in Egypt.
Iron Age 2	1000–587 BC	Period of David, Solomon, and the Judahite kings. Divided kingdom; the Assyrian and Babylonian sieges of Israel and Judah.
Iron Age 3	586–332 BC	Judah enters Babylonian captivity; fall of the Babylonian Empire and the reign of the Medes/Persians; Jews freed to return to Jerusalem and build the city wall and temple.
Hellenistic Period	332–63 BC	Intertestamental period (between the Old and New Testaments); rise of Greece and Alexander the Great.
Early Roman Period	63 BC–AD 180	Period of Jesus and the apostles with the spread of early Christianity; destruction of Jerusalem and the temple in AD 70, dispersion of the Jews.

GETTING COMFORTABLE WITH BIBLICAL AND ANE GEOGRAPHY

In many ways, Old Testament historical narratives are what we might call *serial geographies*. Virtually no person or event is brought into the text without establishing *place* and *movement* across the landscape. Stories take us "from place to place" (Genesis 13:3 NIV). Rarely do we not have at least a general idea where biblical events happened. Often event locations are specific and detailed. Without a doubt, the biblical books are the most valuable geographical source documents preserved from the ANE.

Simply put, you can't navigate through the Bible without knowing the geography! *Breakouts 1.02* through *1.06* provide thumbnail sketches of the major geographical regions of the Bible—Mesopotamia, Egypt, Anatolia, Persia, and the Levant—and the biblical connections to each region. These *Breakouts* and their associated *Maps* (see *Maps 1.01–1.07*) will help you get oriented to biblical geography. *Breakout 1.07*

provides a geographical glossary with descriptions of each term. *Breakout 1.01* offers helpful suggestions on how to pronounce biblical names and places.

GETTING TO KNOW THE HANDBOOK TIMELINE

The *Handbook* Timeline is arranged not only chronologically, but also geographically. Think of it as *geography stretched through time*. Egypt is on the bottom because it's in the south. Moving north and east, Canaan is next, followed by Syria, then Anatolia (Asia Minor), and Mesopotamia. The thicker the line, the stronger the kingdom or empire relative to others. A broken line represents city-states with no centralized government. Not all kings and historical figures are named, but the most important ones are included. Key events and artifacts are also included. At the bottom, the biblical books are inserted to show their approximate time of writing.

BREAKOUT 1.04

A THUMBNAIL SKETCH OF EGYPT AND THE BIBLE

Geography. The Greek historian Herodotus described Egypt well as "the Gift of the Nile" (see *Maps 1.02, 1.06*). Both in antiquity and today, 95 percent of the population have lived by the Nile, which is formed in Sudan by the confluence of the White Nile from central Africa and the Blue Nile from Ethiopia.

The Nile floods annually from June to September. Too high or too low a Nile could mean years of famine like those recorded in the story of Joseph. A broad delta

has been formed where the Nile meets the Mediterranean. It once had seven branches, including the Rosetta branch, where one of Napoleon's soldiers found the inscription that led to the decipherment of hieroglyphics in 1822 by Jean Champollion. Among Egypt's resources have been sandstone, limestone, gold, wheat, barley, cattle, fish, birds, and papyrus.

History. Egyptian history is divided into some 30 dynasties. The Archaic Era (c. 3100–2700 BC = First and Second Dynasties)

saw the unification of Upper and Lower Egypt. The Old Kingdom (c. 2700–2000 BC = Third through Sixth Dynasties) was the Pyramid Age. During this time the capital was Memphis (near Cairo), and the leading deity was the sun god Re. The Middle Kingdom (c. 2000–1700 BC = Eleventh and Twelfth Dynasties) had its capital in the south at Thebes, and Amon was the dominant god. After the occupation of Lower Egypt by the Hyksos (Semitic invaders from Palestine;

c. 1800–1550 BC), the Egyptians established an empire (c. 1550–1100 = Eighteenth and Nineteenth Dynasties) that included Palestine.

The Old Testament. In the Table of Nations (Genesis 10:6), the people of Mizraim (Egypt) are listed as descendants of Ham. Abraham moved to Egypt during a time of famine (Genesis 12). Hagar, who bore Ishmael, was an Egyptian (Genesis 16). During the Hyksos period, Joseph was sold into slavery and later rose to second in command in Egypt (Genesis 37–50). He was able to invite his family to dwell in Goshen in the Nile Delta. Their descendants lived peacefully until a new pharaoh ("Great House") arose to enslave them (Exodus 1). Moses, who had been adopted by the pharaoh's daughter, was chosen by Yahweh to lead his people out of Egypt in the great exodus. About 500 years later, one of Solomon's wives was the daughter of a pharaoh (1 Kings 3:1). In the following reign of Rehoboam, Shishak attacked Jerusalem and removed gold from Jerusalem (1 Kings 14:25-26). The Cushite pharaoh Tirhakah intervened in vain when Sennacherib invaded Judah in 701 BC (2 Kings 19:9; Isaiah 37:9).

The New Testament. After the massacre of the baby boys in Bethlehem, Joseph and Mary fled to Egypt with infant Jesus (Matthew 2:13). On the day of Pentecost there were Jewish pilgrims from Egypt (Acts 2:10). Coptic Christians claim that Christianity had its start in Egypt through the evangelist Mark—but this is a legend first reported by Eusebius (fourth century AD). The so-called Ethiopian eunuch came from the Sudan, as he was an official of Candace (Acts 8:27), the queen of the kingdom of Meroe. In the Egyptian city of Alexandria on the Mediterranean coast, two of the five districts were occupied by Jews. Apollos, a learned Jewish convert, came from Alexandria (Acts 18:24).

E. Yamauchi

Serabit el-Khadim, Temple of Hathor, Egyptian influence in the southern Sinai region (photo: Michael Luddeni)

A Thumbnail Sketch of Anatolia and the Bible

Geography. Ancient Anatolia is roughly equivalent to modern Turkey (see *Maps 1.02, 1.06*). The name is derived from the Greek *anatolē*, or "the rising" (of the sun, or the east). The region has also been known as Asia Minor. Anatolia is a large peninsula, bounded on the west by the Aegean Sea, on the north by the Black Sea, on the south by the Mediterranean, and in the east by the Caucasus Mountains. The population was concentrated in the south and especially in the west, where a number of rivers gave access to the interior. The north-central Anatolian Plateau, the land of Hatti, was the homeland of the Hittites.

History. In the early second millennium BC, Indo-European peoples migrated to central Anatolia, where they took on the name of that region, Hatti. They were then "sons of Hatti/Heth"—that is, Hittites. Their capital was at Hattusha (also Hattusas; modern Boghazköy), where an archive of cuneiform documents was discovered when the area was excavated in 1906. Their Old Kingdom (c. 1800–1600 BC) was a period of consolidation. The New Kingdom (c. 1600–1200) saw an expansion that led to a clash with Egypt in northern Syria. Ḥattusili III later signed a peace treaty with Ramesses II. After the collapse of the Hittite kingdom, invading Mushki (Phrygians) from Thrace in the west occupied central Anatolia. A wave of Greeks occupied Ionia in west Anatolia after 1100 BC, establishing key cities such as Miletus, which became a center of pre-Socratic philosophy. The kingdom of Lydia, with its capital at Sardis, flourished in the seventh–sixth centuries BC. Gyges invented coinage (c. 650 BC). Cyrus, the Persian king, defeated Croesus in 546 BC and soon occupied Ionia. Alexander the Great liberated the Greek cities. After his death, Pergamum became dominant. Its last king bequeathed his realm to the Romans in 133 BC.

The Old Testament. There is now ample evidence to equate the biblical Hittites (sons of Heth) with the Anatolian Hittites, given clear indications in the archaeological record that migrants from the land of Hatti were residing in the Southern Levant 1,000 years before Abraham. Solomon imported horses from Kue—that is, Cilicia in southeastern Anatolia (1 Kings 10:28). References in Ezekiel 38:2 to Meshech and Tubal are not prophecies about Moscow and Tobolsk, but to the Mushki and to Tabal, a region in eastern Anatolia. Sepharad (Obadiah 20) may be a possible reference to Sardis.

The New Testament. On the day of Pentecost in Jerusalem there were pilgrims from several areas of Anatolia: "Cappadocia, Pontus and Asia, Phrygia and Pamphylia" (Acts 2:9-10). Peter addressed the exiles of the Jewish Diaspora in parts of Anatolia: "Pontus, Galatia, Cappadocia, Asia, and Bithynia" (1 Peter 1:1). Paul, who was proud

Anatolian model of a chariot, fifteenth century BC (photo: James Barber, courtesy of Bible Lands Museum, Jerusalem)

of his city of Tarsus in Cilicia, preached in Anatolia on three mission trips: (1) he evangelized in Galatia (Acts 13–14); (2) he revisited this area, and from Alexandria Troas advanced to Greece (Acts 15–18); (3) on his third trip Paul remained for three years at Ephesus, the metropolis of the province of Asia (Acts 19). On Paul's journey as a prisoner to Rome, his ship stopped at Myra (Acts 27:5) on the southern coast. Paul wrote epistles to churches in Galatia, Ephesus, and Colossae, and the risen Lord addressed letters to the seven churches of western Anatolia: "Ephesus, Smyrna, Pergamum, Thyatira, Sardis, Philadelphia and Laodicea" (Revelation 1:11 NIV).

E. Yamauchi

Breakout 1.06

A Thumbnail Sketch of Persia and the Bible

Geography. Ancient Persia was centered in what is now the modern country of Iran (see *Maps 1.02, 1.06*). At its height (sixth–fifth centuries BC) the Persian Empire stretched from Egypt and the Sudan to the Indus Valley (Esther 1:1) and included Turkey, Syria, and Palestine. The natural boundary that divided Persia from Mesopotamia was the Zagros Mountains range. The long southern coast was arid and devoid of good harbors, and the vast interior was an uninhabitable desert region.

History. The earliest recorded history (c. 2300 BC) concerned Elam in the southwest with its key city of Susa. The Elamites carried off from Mesopotamia the Code of Hammurabi (eighteenth century BC), which was found by a French excavation at Susa. During the end of the second millennium BC, Indo-European Iranian tribes migrated from Russia into the Iranian plateau. Both the Medes and Persians are first noted in Assyrian records (ninth century BC). The Medes settled in the northwest with their capital at Ecbatana (modern Hamadan). The Persians settled in southwest Iran near the head of the Persian Gulf. They were at first subordinate to the Medes. Then Cyrus, who was half Median and Persian, overthrew the Median king in 550 BC. He then defeated Croesus,

the king of Lydia in west Anatolia, and conquered Babylon in 539 BC. His son, Cambyses, conquered Egypt in 525 BC. After overthrowing a Magian usurper, Darius fought about 20 battles, which he recounted in a trilingual (Old Persian, Elamite, Akkadian) inscription on a cliff at Behistun in the Zagros Mountains. Henry Rawlinson copied this inscription in the 1830s and provided the key to the decipherment of cuneiform scripts. In 490 BC Darius's forces invaded Marathon to punish rebellious Greeks, where they were defeated by Athenians. His son Xerxes later launched an invasion of Greece with an enormous army and navy. The Persians defeated the Spartans at Thermopylae, but their fleet was destroyed in the bay of Salamis in 480 BC and their army defeated at Plataea in 479 BC. Artaxerxes I, who reigned from 464–424, had to suppress a revolt in Egypt.

The Old Testament. The Achaemenid kings played key roles in the lives of Jews who had been exiled by the Babylonians. Isaiah proclaimed Cyrus Yahweh's "anointed" servant (Isaiah 45:1). After the capture of Babylon, Cyrus allowed the Jews (who wished to do so) to return to Palestine (Ezra 1). His magnanimous policy has been confirmed by the Cyrus Cylinder. Darius permitted

Persian and Median servants, Persepolis in the time of Xerxes I (photo: James Barber, courtesy of Bible Lands Museum, Jerusalem)

the rebuilding of the temple under Zerubbabel in 520 BC (Ezra 5:2). After winning a beauty contest, Esther became the queen to Ahasuerus (Xerxes). Under Artaxerxes I, Ezra led a company of returning exiles to Palestine in 458 BC (Ezra 7). The king's cupbearer, Nehemiah, returned in 445 BC to rebuild the walls of Jerusalem and to serve as the governor over Judea.

The New Testament. On the day of Pentecost in Jerusalem there were Jews present from various areas of Persia: "Parthians and Medes and Elamites" (Acts 2:9).

E. Yamauchi

BREAKOUT 1.07

A GLOSSARY OF SOME KEY GEOGRAPHICAL TERMS

Anatolia—Asia Minor; bounded north by Black Sea, south by Mediterranean Sea, east by Mesopotamia, west by Aegean Sea; generally the area of modern-day Turkey.

Arabah—means "uninhabited land," thus "wilderness" or "desert," but not necessarily in the classic sense of aridity; bounded on the north by the Dead Sea, south by the Sinai Wilderness, east by the southern Jordan Desert (of Paran), west by the Negev; mostly populated by nomadic tribes.

Aram—the area generally occupied by modern Syria and northern Iraq; bounded north by east Anatolia, Urartu, and Hurrian lands, south by the Euphrates River or Arabian Desert and the Anti-Lebanon Mountains (depending on the period), east by central Mesopotamia and Media, west by the Euphrates River or southwest by the Anti-Lebanon Mountains (depending on the period); most strictly, the area of northern Mesopotamia.

Asia Minor—Anatolia; bounded north by Black Sea, south by Mediterranean Sea, east by Mesopotamia, west by the Aegean Sea; generally the area of modern-day Turkey.

Assyria—a Semitic kingdom most strictly occupying central or north-central Mesopotamia; eventually spread its control over most of

the ANE during the eighth century BC.

Babylonia, Kassite—kingdom with an Indo-European ruling class (from the east) with Semitic populace; most strictly south or south-central Mesopotamia; ruled over most of Mesopotamia from the late sixteenth to the early fourteenth centuries BC.

Babylonia, Old—Amorite/Semitic kingdom; most strictly south or south-central Mesopotamia; ruled over most of Mesopotamia by the late eighteenth century BC.

Babylonia, Neo—Amorite/Semitic kingdom; most strictly south or south-central Mesopotamia; ruled over most of the Fertile Crescent by the late seventh to sixth centuries BC.

Cisjordan (Central) Highlands—the "spine" or "heights" of Canaan (later Israel and Judah); bounded north by the Jezreel Valley, south by the Negev, east by the Rift (Jordan and Dead Sea) Valley, west by the Shephelah foothills; the main highland cities in Old Testament times were Shechem, Jerusalem, and Hebron.

Dead Sea—also known as **Sea of the Arabah, Salt Sea, Lake Asphaltitus** (Roman times); at about 1,300 feet below sea level, the surface of the lake is the lowest elevation on Earth's surface; a

subtropical micro climate in this Rift Valley where the African and Arabian tectonic plates meet; the sea allowed for year-round agricultural production, as it does today; bounded north by the Kikkar of the Jordan, south by the Arabah, east by the Transjordan Plateau, west by the Cisjordan highlands; lies in a geological "bowl" of anhydride salt deposits, causing its poisonous waters always to be at maximum salinity (its saltiness has zero to do with the fact that it has no outlet!); deep northern basin is 31 miles long, 9 miles wide, and 1,000 feet deep on average; lake levels fluctuated over 300 feet up and down throughout antiquity, causing the shallow southern basin to disappear from time to time.

Egypt, Lower (according to the direction of the Nile flow)—the northern half of the Nilotic lands; basically the Nile Delta region down to Herakleopolis in the Fayum area; bounded on the north by the Mediterranean Sea, south by Upper Egypt, east by the Sinai Peninsula (Wilderness), and west by the Libyan Desert.

Egypt, Upper (according to the direction of the Nile flow)—the southern half of the Nilotic lands; basically the Nile Valley south of Herakleopolis and the Fayum area;

bounded on the north by Lower Egypt, south by Nubia, east by a stretch of desert and the Red Sea, west by the Libyan Desert.

Elam—later Persia; Indo-European kingdom; bounded north by Media and Urartu, south by the mountains east of the Persian Gulf, east by Parthian, Sagartian, Carmanian, and Utian tribal territories, west by Mesopotamia; roughly the same area as modern-day Iran.

Fertile Crescent—the swath of arable lands arching from southern Mesopotamia through central and northern Mesopotamia (Aram), then south through the Levant; some scholars include the Nile Valley occupied by Egypt, while others keep it separate; essentially the lands occupied by modern Iraq, southeast Turkey, Syria, Lebanon, Israel, and Jordan.

Galilee—generally the contiguous areas north and west of the Sea of Galilee; bounded north by the hills of Syro-Phoenicia (southern Lebanon), south and southwest by the Jezreel Valley, east by the Rift (Jordan) Valley and Sea of Galilee, west by Syro-Phoenicia.

Hatti—Indo-European kingdom with its homeland in the north-central plateau of Anatolia; in the fourteenth century BC Hatti spread its control over east Asia Minor, Aram to the southeast, the Northern Levant, even into stretches of northeastern Mesopotamia; its empire generally spread over the area now occupied by modern Turkey, Syria, and northern Iraq.

Holy Land—the Southern Levant (modern Israel and Jordan); ancient Canaan.

Jordan Valley—the section of the Rift Valley between the Sea of Galilee (Lake Kinnereth) and the Dead Sea; starting with several spring-fed streams coming from the base of the Lebanon mountains (such as Mount Hermon), the Jordan (means "the descending" of fresh/living water) flows 156 miles from its origins to its termination at the Dead Sea, filling the Sea of Galilee along the way; rich with fish in antiquity; while the river is only a trickle today, in ancient times even its dry-season flow could exceed a quarter of a mile wide; at its delta north of the Dead Sea it overflowed to several miles wide in the springtime (a Nile in miniature!); the valley cities thrived in their well-watered subtropical environment.

Kikkar (Disk) of the Jordan—the widened and roughly circular alluvial plain north of the Dead Sea; roughly the southern third of the Jordan Valley, about 25 miles in diameter; *Kikkar* means "circle" or "disk" (erroneously translated "valley" or "plain"), nongeographically translated as "talent" (a disk-shaped ingot of gold or silver) or "flat bread" (like a pita or tortilla), thus alluding to its wealth and breadbasket nature; in Genesis, a sociopolitical entity called "the Land of the Kikkar" (Genesis 19:28), anchored by the city of Sodom.

Kinnereth, Lake (Sea of)—also called the Sea of Galilee or Sea of Tiberias; a freshwater lake at the north end of the Rift (Jordan) Valley, created by flows from snowmelt and rainfall in the mountains of Lebanon to the north; measures 13 miles north/south and 8.1 miles east/west, with a depth of 150 feet (fluctuating according to rainfall in the region); lake surface is, on average, 690 feet below sea level; in antiquity the lake had several species of commercial fish in abundance, particularly tilapia ("St. Peter's fish"); usually placid, but stormy weather could produce violent seas and waves, particularly along the eastern shoreline.

Levant, Northern—the area generally occupied by modern Lebanon, Syria, and parts of eastern Turkey west of the Euphrates River.

Levant, Southern—the area generally taken up by modern Israel and Jordan, ancient Canaan; the Holy Land.

Levant, the—bounded north by the Euphrates River, south by the

Sinai Peninsula, east by the Arabian Desert, west by the Mediterranean Sea; the biblical Promised Land; essentially the lands occupied by modern Syria, Lebanon, Israel, and Jordan.

Levantine Coast—also known as the coastal plain or plains; bounded north by the mountains of southeast Anatolia, south by the coast of the north Sinai Peninsula, east by the foothills of the various Levantine mountain ranges, west by the Mediterranean Sea; a natural, mostly flat corridor for overland commerce, collectively called the Via Maris (Way of the Sea), linking Egypt with Anatolia and northern Mesopotamia; large port cities dotted the coastline from Anatolia to the Southern Levantine coast.

Mediterranean Sea—a subset of the Atlantic Ocean; comparatively calm compared to more open ocean; highly productive for fishing; created a mild climate around its perimeter; was the primary commercial "highway" connecting the civilizations of southern Europe, coastal Asia Minor, the Levant, and north Africa.

Mesopotamia—the area generally held by modern Iraq; bounded north by eastern Anatolia and Urartu, south by the Persian Gulf, east by Elam/Persia and Media, west by the Arabian Desert and the Northern Levant.

Mittani—Late Bronze Age (LBA) kingdom occupying Aram; most strictly northern Mesopotamia; spread its influence west to the Northern Levantine coastal region during the fifteenth and fourteenth centuries BC; Indo-European Hurrian ruling class with a Semitic general population.

Negev—the region bordered north by the central (Cisjordan) highlands, south by the Sinai Wilderness, east by the Arabah, west by the coastal plain; becomes higher in elevation than even the central highlands, thus it cools off significantly at night, even in the summer; arable, but surface water is scarce; inhabitants relied on springs and cisterns that filled during the rainy season (winter).

Nile Delta—the delta-shaped area of Lower Egypt where the Nile River split into numerous channels as it flowed north to the Mediterranean Sea; in antiquity annual Nile inundations deposited layers of highly fertile silt that allowed remarkable agricultural production; however, both high and low Nile flows could be disastrous; abundant water was managed by a complex system of canals.

Persia—ancient Elam; bounded north by Media and Urartu; south by the mountains east of the Persian Gulf; east by Parthian, Sagartian, Carmanian, and Utian tribal territories; west by Mesopotamia; roughly the same area as modern-day Iran.

Sea of Galilee—also known as Lake (Sea of) Kinnereth or Sea of Tiberias; a freshwater lake at the north end of the Rift (Jordan) Valley, created by flows from snowmelt and rainfall in the mountains of Lebanon to the north; measures 13 miles north/south and 8.1 miles east/west, with a depth of 150 feet (fluctuating according to rainfall in the region); lake surface is, on average, 690 feet below sea level; in antiquity the lake had several species of commercial fish in abundance, particularly tilapia ("St. Peter's fish"); usually placid, but stormy weather could produce violent seas and waves, particularly along the eastern shoreline.

Sharon Plain—a name given to the Levantine coastal plain adjacent to the lands occupied by Israel.

Shephelah—the swath of foothills between the central (Cisjordan) highlands and the Mediterranean coastal plain; bounded north by the Jezreel Valley, south by the Negev, east by the central highlands, west by the coastal plain; cut east/west by several important valleys, in north-to-south order the Aijalon Valley (leading up to Jerusalem; guarded by Gezer), the Sorek Valley (leading up to Jerusalem; guarded by Beth Shemesh), the Elah Valley (leading up to Jerusalem and Hebron; guarded by Azekah), the north Guvrin Valley (leading up to Hebron; guarded by

Mareshah), and the south Guvrin Valley (leading up to Hebron; guarded by Lachish).

Sinai Wilderness—also known as Wilderness of Sin; the triangular region bounded north by the Mediterranean Sea, Negev, and Arabah, south by the Red Sea, east by the Gulf of Aqaba, west by the Gulf of Suez; arid and incapable of sustaining sedentary villages, much less towns or cities; it was a vast area traversed by nomadic herding tribes; full of rugged mountains of substantial elevation; little vegetation with occasional springs and oases; copper mines in west Sinai were operated by the Egyptians.

Sumer—southern Mesopotamia; the same area known later as Babylonia; bounded on the north by Assyria, south by the Persian Gulf, east by Elam, west by the Arabian Desert; generally the area occupied presently by southern Iraq.

Sumer(ia)—non-Semitic(?), non-Indo European(?) group of city-states (kingdom?), speaking a language (Sumerian) unrelated to all other languages in the ANE; occupied southern Mesopotamia in the fourth and third millennia BC.

Transjordan—the region east of the Dead Sea and Jordan River; bounded north by the Anti-Lebanon Mountains, south by the Arabah and Desert of Paran, east by the Arabian Desert, west by the Rift Valley; essentially modern Jordan; south to north the main Old Testament territories/kingdoms were Edom, Moab, Ammon, and Gilead.

Transjordan Plateau—the nearly flat region east of the Rift Valley out to the Arabian Desert; excellent farmland given adequate rainfall; its famous north/south route was the King's Highway.

CHAPTER 2

THE WORLD OF THE
GENESIS PATRIARCHS

WELCOME TO THE MIDDLE BRONZE AGE (2100–1550 BC)

Upon the collapse of the Early Bronze Age (EBA) urban centers about 2500 BC, the majority of the Levantine population adopted a nomadic to seminomadic lifestyle during the Intermediate Bronze Age (IBA) (see *Timeline*). A significant drop in regional rainfall disallowed farming on a scale large enough to support the concentrated populations of cities and towns. Although there were many open villages during this time, occupations were often seasonal and only semisedentary.

One notable exception to this was the city-state anchored by massive Sodom (known today as Tall el-Hammam in Jordan), which occupied the fertile, well-watered lands immediately northeast of the Dead Sea (see *Map 2.04*). The geological strata of the Transjordan region are configured in such a way that most of the underground fresh water flows into the area northeast of the Dead Sea, surfacing via innumerable springs. Thus, Sodom and its neighbors flourished throughout the IBA. However, because the inhabitants of other areas in the Southern Levant (Canaan) were not so fortunate in terms of water resources, the period from 2500 BC to 2100 BC was a difficult one.

Dramatic changes began to take place about 2100 BC. This marked the official beginning of the Middle Bronze Age (MBA) and the establishment of what is widely considered to be the high-water mark of Canaanean culture (a reference to the geographical region, as opposed to ethnic Canaanite tribes). Once again, large urban centers developed throughout the Southern Levant (see *Map 2.02*). Monumental fortifications even more massive and complex than those of the EBA were constructed around nearly every city and town, especially those on important military and trade routes. The Genesis accounts of Abraham, Isaac, and Jacob take place during the hustle and bustle of the MBA2 period, which is the second half of the MBA (see *Timeline*).

During the twentieth and nineteenth centuries BC, the so-called Amorite dynasties in Mesopotamia had set the stage for constant interchange of ideas, knowledge, and political protocol. International relations were extensive (see *Map 2.01*). General prosperity prevailed. But while the Twelfth Dynasty of Egypt (c. 1991–1782 BC) expanded during this time, the Second Intermediate period (c. 1782–1570 BC) that followed was one of serious decline and instability in Egypt, during which the Semitic Hyksos of the Fifteenth Dynasty ruled over the Nile Delta and contiguous areas (see *Map 2.03*).

The MBA ended with the widespread destruction of many of its major city-states, particularly in the land of Canaan. The possible culprits are numerous, but none are certain. Most scholars agree that the Egyptians, angered and vengeful at what they certainly would have termed "the Hyksos debacle" (during which the Semite peoples entered Lower Egypt in large numbers and assumed power for 200 years), likely applied their hand in order to thwart any resurgence of the Semitic Asiatics who had ruled over Lower Egypt for more than 200 years.

Moses's depiction of this era consists of stories collated from existing texts, together with his own writing, to produce the book of Genesis. The stories were already ancient before Moses ever saw them. They provided snapshots from historical periods of the distant past, providing an "organic" bridge to his own world (see *Breakouts 2.01, 2.02, 2.03, 2.04*) and a foundation for every avenue of biblical history and theology for all future time.

GEOGRAPHY

The stories of Abram (hereafter, Abraham), Isaac, Jacob, and Joseph play out essentially over the entire Near East: Mesopotamia, Anatolia, the Levant, and Egypt (see *Maps 1.02, 2.01*). The historical synchronisms and elements of material culture embedded in the narratives of these patriarchs places them in the MBA, specifically MBA2, after c. 1900 BC (see *Breakout 2.05* and *Timeline*). Because we now have a well-established date for the destruction of Sodom (c. 1700 [+/–50 BC]) during Abraham's lifetime (see *Breakout 2.07*), linking the lives of these biblical "headliners" to the regional powers and politics of the MBA2 world is relatively simple.

In Mesopotamia, the Old Babylonian Kingdom was at its peak of power (see *Timeline* and *Map 2.01*). It is possible that Abraham and the famous Hammurabi of Babylon were contemporaries, at least for a while. Because Hammurabi died c. 1750 BC, it is also not out of the question to identify "Amraphel king of Shinar" (Genesis 14:1) with the famous codifier of Babylonian law, Hammurabi, since the events of Genesis 14 took place well before the destruction of Sodom (c. 1700 BC; Genesis 19).

In c. 1700 BC, a coalition of warlike Indo-European tribes collectively called the Hittites conquered the Central Anatolian Plateau (which is the land of Hatti; the name *Hittite* derives from the territory they conquered, Hatti; see *Map 2.01*). This marked the beginning of what would eventually become the Hittite Empire under warrior-king Hattusilis I (Hattusili), c. 1650. Thus, Ephron the Hittite (Hebrew, *hahitti*; Genesis 23) could have been

Figure 2.01—Anatolian Ware (L) and Khirbet Kerak Ware (R) (photos: Steven Collins)

a refugee from the land of Hatti who fled when his homeland was overrun by the conquering Hittites. Archaeology clearly demonstrates that Anatolian (Hattian) ceramic artisans had taken up residence in the Southern Levant as early as Early Bronze Age 3 (EBA3) (c. 2800 BC), producing specialized, Anatolian-style pottery known as Khirbet Kerak Ware (see *Figure 2.01*). So having Hittite migrants in Canaan at the time of Abraham is simply reflective of a well-documented BA reality.

The MBA2 Levant was a land of diverse terrain—coastline, Cisjordan, and Transjordan Plateaus separated by a deep Rift Valley, with high mountains in the north (see *Map 1.07*). Politically, it was carved up by modest city-states (see *Map 2.02*) taking advantage of what commerce they could generate with Mesopotamia and Egypt. Although not without some elements of sophistication, the Southern Levant was a cultural backwater compared to the high cultures of their more successful neighbors to the southwest, north, and east. The Levant (Canaan/Syria) was Abraham's Promised Land.

During early MBA2, Egypt's *Middle Kingdom* was on its last legs (see *Timeline*). By the time Abraham arrived in Canaan, the Thirteenth Dynasty had already succumbed (c. 1782 BC) to the will of a horde of Semitic Asiatic migrants, the so-called Hyksos (see *Map 2.03*). A variety of factors—all likely precipitated by a negative climate fluctuation in the Levant—drove masses of immigrants from Syria and Canaan into Lower Egypt (the Nile Delta region). Their leaders became the Semitic pharaohs of the Fourteenth and Fifteenth Dynasties (see *Map 2.03*). They ruled the Nile Delta region until their expulsion from Egypt c. 1550 BC (see *Breakouts 2.05, 3.01, 3.04*).

BREAKOUT 2.01

ORIGINS: PRIMEVAL HISTORY

The Genesis creation narratives (Genesis 1, 2) factually state that the singular, infinite God (Hebrew, *Elohim*), Yahweh, brought into existence all that exists. The stories are intricately constructed in a manner authentic to the ancient Near Eastern Bronze Age, defying the notion of so-called critical scholars that they were the imaginative musings of late-Iron Age Judahite priests after c. 700 BC. Whether the "nothing" prior to "speaking" physical reality into existence, or the universe itself, all was and is the product of Yahweh's infinite intelligence, power, and creativity.

Humankind rebelled against Yahweh, resulting in a fallen world in need of divine redemption. This is the theme of the primeval literature (Genesis 1–11). It serves as the source from which the stream of redemptive history flows. It records the reality of God's judgment against sin for both the individual and humanity collectively. It reinforces that the solution for sin lay not in the hands of fallen human beings, but in the grace and mercy of Yahweh. The seemingly simple sin of the first man and woman brought the ensuing world to spiritual ruin. And God, who is holy, intervened. In a global watery judgment, humankind was reduced to a single family of eight.

After the great catastrophe represented in the flood narratives (Genesis 6–9), humankind faced the daunting task of reestablishing societies in a harsh, untamed, and unfamiliar world. In spite of the practical and technological skills people no doubt possessed, it took substantial time to set into place the local populations required to access and process the natural resources necessary for constructing higher civilization. Thus families, developing clans, and emerging tribes utilized the resources most readily available—wild flora and fauna, surface metals, and stone. Natural caves provided an immediate housing solution. Huts and

Neolithic goddess figurine; the proliferation of fertility figures throughout ANE history attests to the importance of fertility religion (photo: James Barber, courtesy of Bible Lands Museum, Jerusalem)

Neolithic tower, Jericho (photo: John Witte Moore)

more elaborate stone dwellings followed.

It is no coincidence that the Fertile Crescent, which stretches from the Levant on the west to Mesopotamia on the east, was the cradle of civilization, for the families of Noah and his sons had begun settling their new territories from its northernmost reaches—the mountains of Urartu (Ararat). Tribes eventually found their way into Mesopotamia, the Nile Valley, the mountain plateaus of Anatolia, and the bordering desert regions (see *Map 1.01*). Collectively, we know this region as the Near East.

These are the lands that gave rise to the most advanced cultures and civilizations of the ancient world. This is also the world of the Bible.

Once people were locally established with natural resources identified in their diverse geographical areas, a cultural phenomenon commonly known as the Neolithic Revolution began with amazing vigor throughout the Near East (see *Map 1.06*). By the latter part of the Neolithic Period, remarkable advances in agriculture, water management, settlement planning, animal domestication, pottery making, and

public architecture abounded. As sedentary villages worked ever-larger farms and nomadic hunting/herding groups continued to live alongside localized tribal villages, both symbiosis and periodic conflict occurred—a complex relationship that endured for the balance of ancient Near Eastern history.

Following on the heels of the Neolithic Revolution, an explosion of cultural, artistic, and technological innovation ensued—the Chalcolithic Period (copper/stone; CLP; see *Breakout 2.02*).

S. Collins

These five biblical regions (see *Map 2.01*) are, in fact, the ANE world which, when *properly synchronized* with the narratives of Genesis, provides accurate and remarkable confirmations of the historicity and sociocultural authenticity of the stories from Abraham to Joseph.

CHRONOLOGY

Past attempts to connect the Heptateuch—the first seven books of the Bible, which comprise Genesis through Judges—to what is known of ANE history have met with difficulty (see *Breakout 2.04*). This has made it easier for liberal critics of the Bible to class the Torah, Joshua, and Judges as "pious" fiction. But there is only one factor prohibiting the proper linkage between the first seven biblical books and the BA from which they claim to originate: unbending adherence to the Ussherian "biblical chronology."

For hundreds of years, sincere Bible readers have calculated that the Genesis patriarchs lived at the end of the IBA (c. 2200) into Middle Bronze Age 1 (MBA1; c. 2100–1900 BC). However, archaeological discoveries throughout the region disqualify this time

frame because the cities visited by the patriarchs were not in existence during that time.

If you take the Genesis life spans as base-10 arithmetic values with no possibility of some gaps in the genealogies or the possibility of honorific ages, dates are derived that cannot be synchronized with the well-documented flow of Mesopotamian, Anatolian, Levantine, and Mesopotamian history—that is, ANE history. But the discrepancies are effectively solved either by making a few reasonable adjustments to the Ussher-style traditional chronologies (see *Breakout 2.04*), or by understanding the Genesis life spans as number-formulas in their BA cultural contexts designed to attribute honor to important ancestors (see *Breakouts 2.04, 2.05*).

Ancient Mesopotamians (as Abraham was) commonly used large numbers—even thousands of years!—as a way to honor their most ancient ancestors. Whether the Genesis numbers are understood as literal, base-10 numbers in the modern sense, or as numerical formulas often used by ancient Mesopotamians to attribute honor to ancestors, we find that the archaeology, social customs, and events in the patriarchal

BREAKOUT 2.02

THE PRE-BABEL WORLD

The Chalcolithic Period (CLP; late fifth to early fourth millennia BC) accelerated the cultural developments of the Neolithic Period, including significant advancements in settlement planning, agriculture, pottery making, woolen and linen textiles, ritual art, stonework, and metallurgy. The most significant innovation of the CLP was a highly sophisticated copper industry (see *Map 1.06*). Their technology included the earliest known use of the lost-wax casting process. The knowledge and skill of the Chalcolithic smiths were quite astonishing, by which they produced some of the finest cast-metal objects—such as ceremonial mace heads, crowns, and axes—of any historical period.

Chalcolithic settlements were numerous and widespread across the ANE, including areas that are presently arid to semiarid. Paleoenvironmental studies for the Levant reveal that annual precipitation during the CLP was higher than in later epochs. As a result, Chalcolithic farmers were successful in raising wheat, barley, olives, dates, garlic, onions, pomegranates, lentils, and nuts. The presence of linen cloth in the Cave of the Treasure in Nahal Mishmar (on a cliff face north of Masada) indicates the growing of flax and the existence of sophisticated textile manufacturing technologies. The earliest-known wall paintings are the fresco murals of Tuleilat Ghassul, a large CLP settlement slightly north and east of the Dead Sea.

The relative stability of Chalcolithic society came to an abrupt end. Archaeological evidence suggests that their settlements were not destroyed, as if by an invading army, but were abandoned. It seems that the people vacated their broadhouse settlements in confusion and fear, never to return. In addition to climate change, the ethnolinguistic phenomenon represented in Genesis 11:1-9 may have contributed to this mysterious diaspora. The Tower of Babel incident sent clan and tribal populations in search of new territories and lands in which to settle. Indeed, the archaeological record reveals that CLP societal collapse was followed by several centuries during which nomadism dominated the ANE. It was a time of migrants and refugees.

S. Collins

Chalcolithic Period copper objects, Nahal Mishmar, Israel (photo: Steven Collins)

narratives all fit comfortably in MBA2 (c. 1900–1550 BC; see *Timeline*).

When we examine the historical synchronisms and elements of material culture embedded in the patriarchal narratives, remarkable links between the Bible and ANE history emerge (see *Breakouts 2.04, 2.05, 2.07,* *3.04, 3.05*). And while those involved in contributing to this volume may not all agree on the exact nature of the patriarchal life spans or the patriarchal chronology described here, connecting the chronological "dots" via history, archaeology, anthropology, and climatology (even astrophysics!) yields organic cause-and-effect relationships between the second half of the MBA and the biblical world of Abraham and his "immediate" descendants—after c. 1900 BC. The *Timeline* reflects the latest relevant data.

HISTORY

The biblical stories describing the origin of the universe, the earth, and human beings (see *Breakouts 2.01, 2.02, 2.03*) provide a bridge connecting the creation of all things with God's selection of Abraham as the father of his chosen people. Genesis chapters 1 through 11 give us a thumbnail "pedigree" for everything that exists. Every story is concise and to the point. Each pericope—of Creation, Fall, Flood, Tribes, Kingdoms, Nations, and Babel—codifies historical "moments" in a manner analogous to describing the history of pre-Columbian North America in a single page, or the history of the United States in a single paragraph. While the number of millennia through which these stories unfolded is indeterminate (see *Breakout 2.04*), their focus is to identify who we are (in the image of God), what our problem is (sin), the impact of sin on individuals and humankind collectively (fall, catastrophe, death), and setting a pathway to redemption (the genetic trail leading to the Messiah). Abraham is the pivotal figure joining the primeval past to the redemptive future.

The EBA, IBA, and first half of the MBA are the historical context of Abraham's Semitic ancestors (Genesis 10–11; see *Timeline*). After the demise of the Southern Levantine EBA urban centers c. 2500 BC—likely due to a climate downturn—and the ensuing cultural meltdown in the Southern Levant known as the IBA, the onset of a wetter climate once again precipitated the building of great walled cities beginning c. 2100 BC (see *Breakout 2.03*). While most true cities had ceased to exist in the Southern Levant during the IBA, the great biblical city of Sodom and its satellite towns and villages (Genesis 10:19) continued to thrive unabated and thus had a significant head start in the rise of MBA urbanism.

The massive and complex fortification systems of Tall el-Hammam/Sodom—located in the heart of the Holy Land eight miles northeast of the Dead Sea—were likely among the first such MBA1 defensive architecture of the period, providing a template copied by other MBA cities and towns throughout the region (see *Figure 2.02* and *Breakout 2.07*).

MBA2 (after c. 1900 BC) marked the high point of civilization in Canaan. Large urban centers thrived. By c. 1800 BC, already-prosperous Sodom, Gomorrah, Admah, and Zeboiim in the south Jordan Valley were joined by cities that hadn't existed since the end of the EBA c. 2500 BC—Shechem, Bethel, Jerusalem,

Figure 2.02—Tall el-Hammam/Sodom, overlooking the Kikkar of the Jordan (photo: Michael Luddeni, courtesy of Tall el-Hammam Excavation Project)

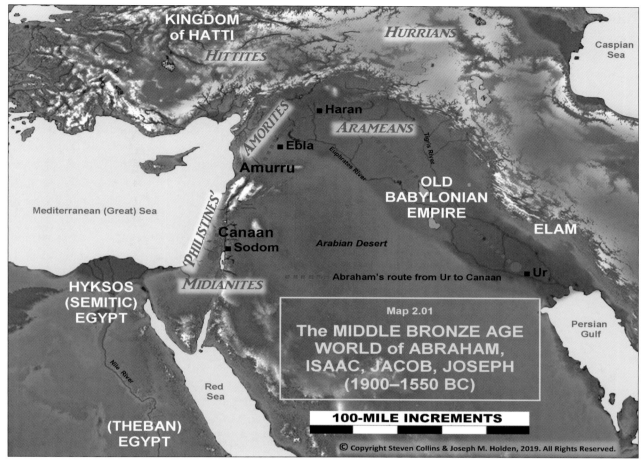

KINGDOM of HATTI

HITTITES

HURRIANS

Caspian Sea

AMORITES

■ Haran

ARAMEANS

Tigris River

Euphrates River

■ Ebla

Amurru

OLD BABYLONIAN EMPIRE

ELAM

Mediterranean (Great) Sea

PHILISTINES'

Canaan
■ Sodom

Arabian Desert

■ Ur

MIDIANITES

Abraham's route from Ur to Canaan

HYKSOS (SEMITIC) EGYPT

Nile River

Red Sea

Persian Gulf

Map 2.01

The MIDDLE BRONZE AGE WORLD of ABRAHAM, ISAAC, JACOB, JOSEPH (1900–1550 BC)

(THEBAN) EGYPT

100-MILE INCREMENTS

Mediterranean (Great) Sea

Dan (Lasha/Laish)

Hazor ■

Damascus ■

Dor ■

■ Megiddo

Lake Kinnereth

Jaffa ■

Dothan ■

■ Beth Shan

■ Ashtaroth

Ekron ■

Ashdod ■

Shechem ■

■ Pella

Ashkelon ■

■ Zarethan

Gath ■

Jerusalem ■

■ Jericho

■ Sodom

Hebron ■

Dead Sea

Arabian Desert

HYKSOS (SEMITIC) EGYPT

N

Map 2.02

CITY-STATES of the MIDDLE BRONZE AGE S LEVANT (CANAAN) (1900–1550 BC)

10-MILE INCREMENTS

Hebron, Dothan, Damascus, Lasha/Laish (Dan). These were the cities of Abraham's story (see *Breakout 2.05*). Monumental fortifications even more substantial than those of the EBA were constructed around nearly every city and town, especially those on important military and trade routes (see *Figure 2.03*).

During the Old Babylonian Kingdom in Mesopotamia, long-distance migrations were common. Old

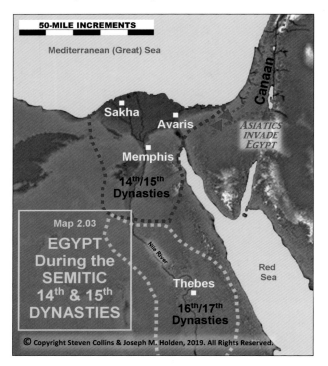

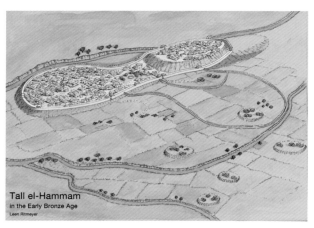

Figure 2.03—Sodom in the Early Bronze Age, surrounded by perennial streams and springs (drawing: Leen Ritmeyer, courtesy of Tall el-Hammam Excavation Project)

Babylonia was ruled by *Ammuru* (Amorites, "westerners"). Terah and his son Abraham—also of Ammuru extraction—set out from the environs of Ur in southern Mesopotamia sometime during the waning years of the great Hammurabi's reign (see *Timeline*). They were headed back west to Canaan (Genesis 11:31), their ancestral homeland. They were not city dwellers, but neither were they Shasu/Bedouin nomads who stayed mostly to themselves and their sheep. Terah and Abraham were Habiru/Hebrew—societally marginalized rabble allied for survival, "marauding nomads" as the city folk called them (see *Breakout 2.06*). A multiethnic band of mercenaries—princes, herders, farmers, tradesmen, warriors—Terah's band of Hebrews probably had a defensive-frontline contract with the city of Ur. So why leave? Perhaps they got a better offer to serve as mercenary protectors of the Haran city-state.

But Abraham had set his eyes on Canaan. Soon after Terah's death, Abraham moved his band of Hebrews from Haran in northern Mesopotamia to Canaan (south Levant) (see *Map 2.01*). He found a land of scattered cities and numerous city-states at the apex of Canaanite culture (see *Map 2.02*). But not all was rosy. Rainfall was intermittently diminishing. Surpluses were dwindling. The ANE climate fluctuation cycle had, once again, caught up with sprawling agricultural operations and a burgeoning population in the Southern Levant. Periodic and often localized famines were made worse by waves of migrants from the north. So Abraham kept moving until he finally wound up in the Nile Delta, in Lower Egypt.

Whether or not Abraham was surprised to learn of it, Delta Egypt had a population dominated by Asiatic Semitic peoples—Ammuru like himself!—with an Egyptianized Canaanite pharaoh on the throne. Decades before Abraham showed up in Egypt, migrants from Canaan had wrested control of Lower Egypt from the Theban Thirteenth Dynasty, initiating the Semitic Fourteenth Dynasty (c. 1797 BC) and the Semitic Fifteenth Dynasty (c. 1640). In fact, the northeast territory of both the Fourteenth and Fifteenth Dynasties was Canaan itself. As the biblical story affirms, Lower Egypt during the Fourteenth Dynasty was a place where

BREAKOUT 2.03

IN THE MILLENNIA BEFORE ABRAHAM

In the wake of the post-Chalcolithic diaspora (see *Breakout 2.02*), tribes and clans were set afoot seeking new homelands. The events described in Genesis 11:1-9 are set parenthetically within the larger story of Genesis 10–11 to provide a backdrop for the scattering of humanity "over the face of all the earth" (11:9). In other words, the Tower of Babel narrative provides a reason for the people movements described in Genesis chapters 10 and 11 and prefigures them.

The period following the CLP societal collapse, the Early Bronze Age (EBA), began with several centuries dominated by human migrations. But this nomadic transition period eventually gave way to what the EBA is known for: the rise of urbanism. The building of fortified cities during the EBA is clearly reflected in Genesis 10. By mid- to late fourth millennium BC, much of the ANE population—formerly set to wandering by the collapse of Chalcolithic culture—began to coalesce into cities. But why fortified cities? Evidently a once-cooperative human collective was now divided into countless groups hostile to each other. And they constructed massive defensive systems—primary and secondary walls, sloping ramparts, towers, and gates—for fear of their neighbors!

Large core cities annexed— usually by conquest—surrounding towns and agricultural fields, becoming city-states. In regions like Mesopotamia, Egypt, and Anatolia, the more powerful city-states gobbled up lesser ones, and kingdoms were born. Larger nation-states also emerged. In time, nation-states would annex other kingdoms and states to become empires.

In Egypt and Sumerian Mesopotamia, great literary civilizations developed. Characterized by complex systems of government and by religious, administrative, and social hierarchies, these cultures flourished by organizing great numbers of people to service large-scale public works projects to utilize the water resources of the Nile (Egypt) and the Tigris and Euphrates Rivers (Mesopotamia). Both Egypt and Sumer developed systems of writing—hieroglyphics and cuneiform, respectively—together with monumental architecture and art.

Between these two cultural centers throughout the Levant and northwestern Mesopotamia, smaller city-states dominated. The EBA and subsequent Intermediate Bronze Age (IBA)—generally corresponding to the pre-Abrahamic patriarchal period of the Bible— saw the rise of the great merchant empire of Ebla in the Northern Levant. Ebla, with its thousands of clay cuneiform tablets, provides us with remarkably detailed accounts of daily operations in an EBA/IBA city-state. These tablets also reveal that much of the patriarchal world of Genesis is consistent with this early period.

Early Bronze Age chalice; probably a cultic vessel (photo: Steven Collins)

In c. 2334 BC, the Semitic dynasty of Sargon established the Akkadian Empire, which encompassed virtually all of Mesopotamia and northern Syria. Sargon's grandson, Naram Sin, destroyed Ebla's great palace. While Ebla was "queen" of the Northern Levant, the EBA/IBA powerhouse in the Southern Levant was the city-state anchored by biblical Sodom (Tall el-Hammam, Jordan; see *Breakout 2.07*). In Egypt, the Old Kingdom pharaohs—the pyramid builders—laid the foundation for the next 2,000 years of Egyptian civilization. Egypt's lack of specialized agricultural products (particularly olive oil and wine), timber, and other raw materials forced the Egyptians into relations with the Levantine city-states.

In the Southern Levant, by about 2500 BC, climate change and shifts in regional commerce resulted in the collapse of virtually all its fortified cities and towns—including well-known sites like Jerusalem, Hebron, and Hazor. With severe drops in rainfall, the Southern Levant, between 2500 BC and 2100 BC, became a landscape full of ghost towns. That is, except for one hardy city-state: Sodom, in the Land of the Kikkar, northeast of the Dead Sea (see *Map 2.04*). Because of abundant rivers (including the Jordan) and springs, Sodom and its satellites thrived during this dry period known as the IBA.

Beginning c. 2100 BC, the climate cycled back into a wetter phase, supporting the rise of a new generation of city-states in Canaan. The Southern Levant coast and Jordan Valley sites were the first to reappear. But it took much longer for settlements to resume in the Canaan highlands (see *Map 2.02*). Sites like Jerusalem, Hebron, Shechem, and Hazor didn't recover from their 400+ years of inoccupation until after 1900 BC. By c. 1800 BC, all the important cities of Canaan were up and running full bore, thus setting the stage for the story of Abraham.

S. Collins

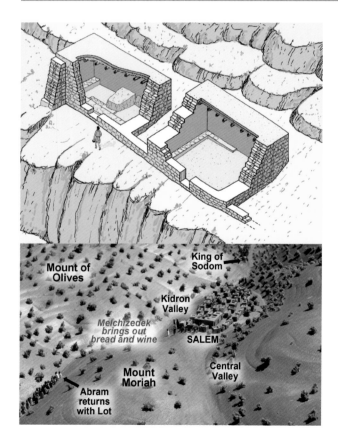

Figure 2.04—Jerusalem in the Middle Bronze Age (bottom) with city wall removed; MBA Jerusalem houses (top) (drawings: Leen Ritmeyer)

a band of Habiru mercenaries led by warlord Abraham the Habiru could be welcomed with open arms (Genesis 12), along with their flocks. The native Egyptians despised sheep and shepherds with a passion, so no such scenario could have played out with a native Egyptian pharaoh of the Middle Kingdom or with a Theban Seventeenth Dynasty (contemporaneous with the Semitic pharaohs of MBA2 Lower Egypt).

Once back in Canaan, Abraham decided to settle into the central highlands of Canaan. His city-state of choice: Salem—that is, Jerusalem (see *Map 2.03*). According to the Bible, Jerusalem was a Jebusite city, a Canaanite clan of uncertain origin (see *Figure 2.04*). The archaeological record reveals that Jerusalem had been unoccupied since its abandonment c. 2500 BC, but by the nineteenth century BC it was back in business. By c. 1800 BC it stood strong once again as the core of a city-state. The massive stone foundations of the fortifications surrounding its water source, the Gihon Spring, testify to the strength of Jerusalem's defenses. While only a fraction of the size of its neighbor to the east, Sodom, it was nevertheless a political powerhouse controlling lands north to Bethel and south to Hebron.

It was with the city-state of Jerusalem under King Melchizedek that Abraham negotiated a mutually beneficial contract (covenant). While the details of that agreement are not specified, its provisions are visible from several details in the narrative of Genesis 14: (1) Abraham and his band of Habiru were living on Jerusalem city-state lands (the reason for the treaty); (2) he had a highly mobile guerilla army of more than 300 warriors providing first-line protection for Melchizedek's lands and royal city (in trade for land use and grazing rights); (3) when he collected war spoils, including slaves ("the people"; see *Breakout 2.12*), he paid a tenth to Melchizedek (also in trade for land use and grazing rights); (4) he refused payment

of war spoils from the king of Sodom, Bera, citing what was obviously a conflict of interest (his contract with Melchizedek was formal and exclusive).

Abraham's mercenary covenant with Melchizedek was one of his many sources of wealth (Genesis 13:2; see *Breakout 2.10*). The scope of Abraham's affluence—which included silver and gold in abundance, along with herds, flocks, and servants—was possible only during the height of the Canaanite civilization in which he lived. Prior to this—that is, during IBA2 (c. 2300–2100 BC) and MBA1 (c. 2100–1900)—there were no cities or towns in the Canaan highlands, much

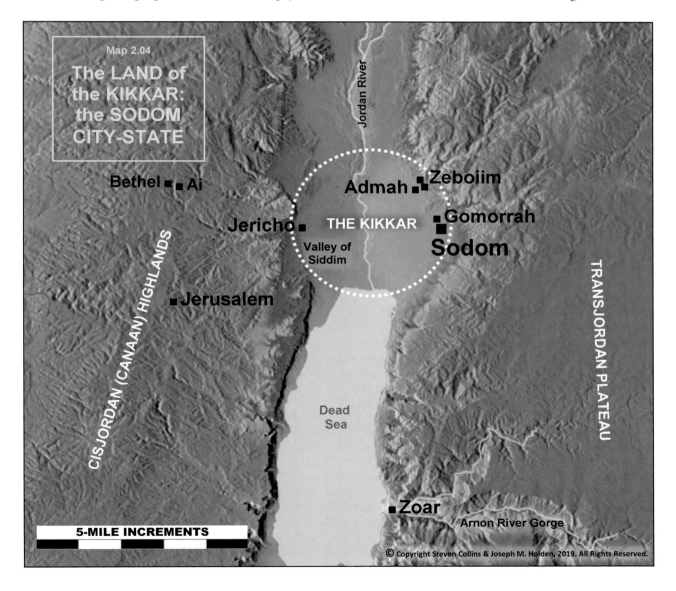

CHRONOLOGY AND THE PATRIARCHAL LIFESPANS

The subject of the Genesis patriarchal life span numbers remains one that is often fraught with controversy. A more traditional view is that the numbers are "face-value" arithmetic values and can be used to build a chronology of the ancient patriarchal world. This is what Irish bishop James Ussher did in the seventeenth century, and some Bible scholars have continued this line of thinking. Using this approach puts the creation of the universe around 6,000 years ago, places the Noah flood around 2500 BC, and marks the birth of Abraham at c. 2166 BC. Taking the Genesis life spans in this manner (as base-10 literal numbers) is, however, not without its problems.

Among the many lines of evidence that contradict the traditional biblical chronology is the ANE chronology worked out over the past 150 years by archaeologists and historians. These data reveal an uninterrupted sequence of ANE civilizations going back to at least 10,000 BC. In most traditional chronologies, the time of Noah's flood is placed at the middle of the third millennium BC, but in ANE chronology that's at the height of both the Old Kingdom in Egypt and the Akkadian Empire in Mesopotamia. As a result, many scholars have viewed the Genesis numbers simply as part of a mythological fabric and have dismissed the book as "pious fiction."

On the surface, harmonizing the traditional patriarchal chronology with the ANE chronology seems difficult at best. But there are, in fact, three reasonable ways to resolve the issue, each of which preserves the divine inspiration and inerrancy of Scripture while being consistent with the flow of ANE history.

The first approach makes three simple modifications: (1) adjust the date of the exodus to the fourteenth century BC (see *Breakouts 3.04, 3.05*); (2) adopt a short Israelite sojourn in Egypt (215 years instead of 430 years), which is consistent with the Septuagint, the apostle Paul in Galatians 3:16-17, Josephus, and several other lines of evidence (see *Breakout 2.05*); and (3) recognize that gaps may exist in the Genesis genealogies that could raise the dates of the creation and flood high enough to accommodate the archaeological chronology of the ANE. These alterations lower Abraham's career from the twenty-second and twenty-first centuries BC to the nineteenth and eighteenth centuries BC, and put the times of Abraham, Isaac, Jacob, and Joseph in their proper cultural context (see *Breakout*

Sumerian King List, nineteenth century BC (photo: Steven Collins)

2.05)—all this while adhering to the face-value literal, longer Genesis life spans.

The second approach is similar to the first but uses a late date for the exodus (mid-thirteenth century BC) and a long (430-year) Israelite sojourn in Egypt. This also puts the Abraham–Joseph sequence in the proper cultural context of MBA 2 (c. 1900–1550 BC; see *Breakout 2.05*).

The third approach for harmonizing patriarchal life spans and ANE chronology holds that a proper literal interpretation of Scripture is the one that makes the most sense within the culture of its origin. Because no ancient culture made a chronology of its history, it is anachronistic to assume that the writer of Genesis did so. Instead, it was common practice in the ANE Bronze Age—including during the times of Abraham and Moses—to use numerical formulas for life spans or reigns for the purpose of attributing honor to significant ancestors. We know that ancient Sumerian and Babylonian genealogies memorialized real people, and we also know that the life spans or regnal numbers of their most ancient ancestors were comprised of schematic or symbolic values that did not relate to actual ages or reigns. The Sumerian King List, for example, celebrates kings who reigned for tens of thousands of years, which readers, both then and now, recognize as honorific, and not actual reign spans.

This view recognizes that the base-10 numbering system of later Iron Age Israel and Judah

Sexagesimal counting tablet, c. 3300 BC; in the Uruk tradition (photo: Daniel Galassini; courtesy of Museum of Archaeology, Trinity Southwest University)

does not fit the Bronze Age cultural context of Abraham and his immediate Hebrew descendants. In this third view, the Genesis life spans cannot, then, be used to construct an "absolute" chronology. The original author(s) did not intend the life spans to be understood in this manner. Therefore, the chronological placement of the patriarchs in the ANE can be best accomplished by using historical and cultural synchronisms (see *Breakouts 2.05, 2.07,*

3.04, 3.05). The approach also unshackles the creation and the Noah flood narratives from the chains of "traditional" chronology, allowing them to be dated based on the best evidence of geology and paleontology.

All three approaches to the Genesis patriarchal life spans allow for the same conclusion: Abraham, Isaac, Jacob, and Joseph belong to the second half of the Middle Bronze Age. This conclusion harmonizes all the relevant cultural and historical data from the Bible and the ANE, and affirms the Genesis text as actual history.

This short explanation of the three approaches is not meant to resolve the controversy over the nature of the Genesis life span numbers, but hopefully it offers expanded perspective and thinking on the subject.

C. Olson, S. Collins

less city-states amid which Abraham could amass such riches.

Of course, the most famous story among the Abraham narratives is that of Sodom and Gomorrah (see *Breakout 2.07*). The Cities of the Kikkar were located on the east side of the Kikkar of the Jordan. The *Kikkar* (Hebrew, meaning "disk") of the Jordan is the roughly circular area immediately north of the Dead Sea, c. 25–30 miles in diameter (see *Map 2.04*). Mentioned in Genesis 10—along with the great city-states of Mesopotamia, Sodom, Gomorrah, Admah, and Zeboiim—they collectively comprised the largest continuously operational BA city-state in the Southern

Levant. It thrived for more than 2,000 years until its destruction in the time of Abraham, c. 1700 BC. It is called the Land of the Kikkar in Genesis 19:28 ("land of the plain" [NIV], Hebrew, *kikkar* = "plain"). Archaeological excavations at Tall el-Hammam confirm that Sodom itself was heavily fortified (see *Figures 2.05, 2.06, 2.07* and *Breakout 2.07*) and seemingly never suffered a military defeat.

The Cities of the Kikkar were wealthy and famous. It is no wonder, then, that Kedorlaomer of Elam (Genesis 14) had tried to maintain the Land of the Kikkar as a vassal state. When the tribute stopped flowing, Kedorlaomer came calling. However, before paying a

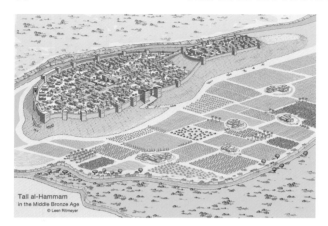

Figure 2.05—Sodom in the Middle Bronze Age with fortified upper and lower cities (drawing: Leen Ritmeyer; courtesy, Tall el-Hammam Excavation Project)

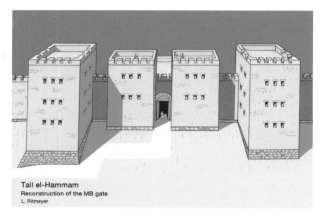

Figure 2.06—Middle Bronze Age gateway exterior, Sodom (drawing: Leen Ritmeyer, courtesy of Tall el-Hammam Excavation Project)

set on intercepting some of these copper shipments before leaving the southern regions. He battled Amalekites at Kadesh, then turned back north to the west shore of the Dead Sea, targeting the Amorites at Hazazon Tamar (En Gedi) along the way. After spending time in the heat of the desert during their copper run, the abundant springs and waterfalls of En Gedi offered the perfect place to refresh and recoup before continuing north toward their final target—Sodom and Gomorrah.

As was typical of ANE warfare, the collective forces of Sodom and the Cities of the Kikkar attempted to engage Kedorlaomer's coalition army away from their doorstep. The plan was brilliant—albeit ill-fated. Facing a much larger army, the Cities of the Kikkar chose to meet Kedorlaomer along a narrow beach front near modern-day Qumran (recall a similar strategy by the Greeks against the Persians at the Battle of Thermopylae). When Kedorlaomer's forces broke through, routing the Cities of the Kikkar army, some of the fleeing warriors fell into "tar pits" (Genesis 14:10 NIV). These were sinkholes that form along the western and northeastern shores of the Dead Sea when the lake level is low, as it was in the time of Abraham and MBA2 (see *Timeline*). Hidden from view until they collapsed under the weight of unsuspecting soldiers, these sinkholes claimed numerous victims as the Cities of the

visit to the Cities of the Kikkar, the Elamite king and his allies from around the region—Amraphel of Shinar, Arioch of Ellasar, and Tidal of Goiim—rushed toward the desert south of Mount Seir (later, Edomite territory; see *Map 2.05*). Their route was the King's Highway south from Damascus along the west edge of the Transjordan Plateau, with a single target in mind: the copper mines and smelting works of El Paran (Wadi Faynan in south Jordan; see *Figures 2.08, 2.09*).

Likely sporting carts loaded with copper ingots, Kedorlaomer headed for En Mishpat (Kadesh) (see *Map 2.05*) through which copper from south Timna passed on its way to Canaan proper. Obviously he was

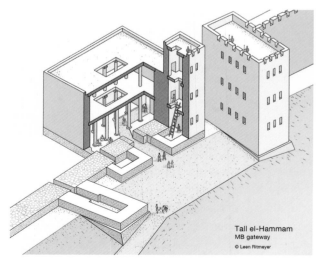

Figure 2.07—Middle Bronze Age gateway interior, Sodom; note the columns and light-wells (drawing: Leen Ritmeyer, courtesy of Tall el-Hammam Excavation Project)

Kikkar army fled across a widening section of beach north and northeast toward Sodom (see *Map 2.05*). (Sinkhole warnings are presently posted for hikers in the area because the lake level is as low today as it was during MBA2.)

Kedorlaomer plundered Sodom and Gomorrah before mounting up to the Transjordan Plateau, connecting once again with the Kings' Highway leading north to Damascus. Once Abraham got word that his nephew, Lot, and family had been taken captive, he immediately set his guerilla warriors in motion (see *Breakout 2.06*). The Amorite brothers Mamre, Eschol, and Aner also probably sent troops (Genesis 14:13). Moving north up the east side of the Jordan Valley ensured that they wouldn't be detected by Kedorlaomer's rear guard. Once they reached Dan (Lasha/Laish), they divided their forces for a night maneuver and defeated Kedorlaomer near Hobah, north of Damascus (see *Map 2.05*).

We are spending time on these little historical details to make a point: The biblical history and geography are often detailed and always accurate. And when you know the ANE history, geography, and chronology,

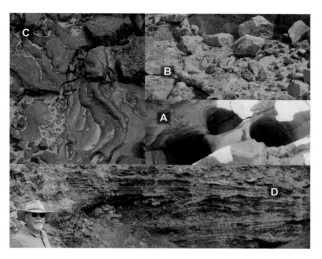

Figure 2.08—Copper mining operations in Wadi Faynan, southern Jordan; mine shafts (A), copper ore (B), slag (C), and excavated slag pile (D) (photos: Daniel Galassini)

you can follow the action! Sometimes, because of the many "holes" in the ANE written records, it is difficult to identify biblical characters in extrabiblical sources. In the case of the four allied kings of Genesis 14, it is unnecessary to assume that any of them—except perhaps Kedorlaomer himself—personally participated

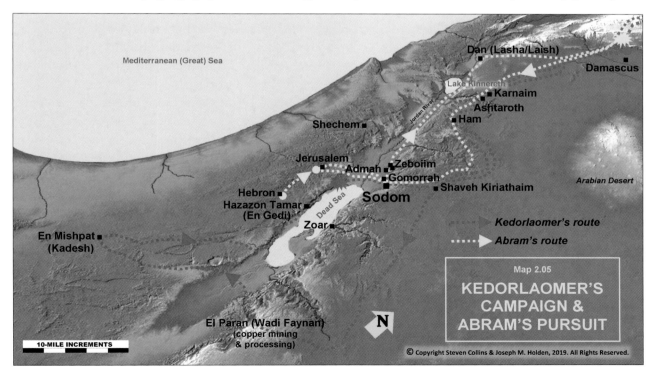

Mediterranean (Great) Sea

Dan (Lasha/Laish)

Damascus

Lake Kinnereth

Karnaim

Ashtaroth

Ham

Shechem

Jordan River

Jerusalem

Admah

Zeboiim

Gomorrah

Shaveh Kiriathaim

Arabian Desert

Hebron

Hazazon Tamar (En Gedi)

Dead Sea

Sodom

Zoar

En Mishpat (Kadesh)

Kedorlaomer's route

Abram's route

El Paran (Wadi Faynan) (copper mining & processing)

N

Map 2.05

KEDORLAOMER'S CAMPAIGN & ABRAM'S PURSUIT

10-MILE INCREMENTS

Figure 2.09—Miners' village, Wadi Faynan (photo: Daniel Galassini)

in this Southern Levantine campaign any more than King Bera of Sodom and his allied kings did in the Battle of the Valley of Siddim against them. But can we know anything about them?

If Amraphel is identified as Hammurabi of Babylon (see *Figure 2.10*)—who was a Semitic Amorite—then it is reasonable that he contributed mercenary troops to Elamite (proto-Persian) king Kedorlaomer, as did the others two kings. It was, after all, Kedorlaomer's offensive (Genesis 14). But it was easier for him to pick up troops along the way as he crossed over the Fertile Crescent toward the Levant than to launch a much larger force all the way from Elam. While the kingdoms (perhaps city-states) of Ellasar and Goiim are presently unidentifiable, both Arioch and Tidal are Indo-European names from either the Hittite or Hurrian realms (see *Map 2.01*). Since the Elamites were also of Indo-European extraction, it is logical that Arioch and Tidal contributed mercenary troops at Kedorlaomer's request—as did Amraphel—with the promise of dividing the spoils and captives with them on the return trip. Such long-distance alliances and campaigns were common during the MBA, but not before or after.

Sodom was wealthy to the point of arrogance (Ezekiel 16:49-50; see *Figure 2.11*). After all, the people had

thrived there as the Southern Levant's most important city-state for more than 2,000 years without a single military defeat, as the archaeological record shows. But while Sodom was able to "pay off" Kedorlaomer and send him on his way, a fiery destruction was looming. Archaeology confirms that the 350-square-mile Sodom city-state, the Land of the Kikkar (Genesis 19:28), was destroyed by a catastrophic, meteoritic airburst event, precisely as described in Genesis 19:24-25 (see *Breakout 2.07*). The area remained uninhabitable for the next 700 years.

The story line of Lot incorporates at least two mysteries that have long remained unsolved: the pillar of salt and the location of Zoar. But now they are solvable. How did Lot's wife become a "pillar of salt" (Genesis 19:26)? The cosmic object God used to destroy the Cities of the Kikkar streaked in from the southwest and exploded into a super-heated plasma over the north end of the Dead Sea (see *Breakout 2.07*). This displaced a huge quantity of Dead Sea water with its poisonous salts and vaporized it, all of which was pushed over the Kikkar. Lot's wife stopped to look back toward Sodom while she was still on the margin of the blast zone, while Lot and their daughters obviously kept moving. The hot, vaporized brine precipitated out over the area where Lot's wife stood, coating the landscape

ABRAHAM, ISAAC, JACOB, AND JOSEPH: CITIZENS OF THE MIDDLE BRONZE AGE

Biblical antiquity—the ANE—is chronologically divided into segments commonly called periods, ages, eras, or epochs. Each period differs from the preceding and succeeding ages in terms of peoples, cultures, societal structures, technologies, and even climate.

Even though there is controversy over the nature of the life span numbers in Genesis (see *Breakout 2.04*), the stories of Abraham and his immediate descendants are full of historical and cultural synchronisms connecting them to the MBA2 period (c. 1900/1800–1550 BC)—not earlier or later.

The EBA ended about 2500 BC because of climate change and drought. At that time, all but a handful of cities and towns in the Southern Levant (Canaan) ceased to exist (Sodom and the Cities of the Kikkar were the notable exceptions). By about 2200 BC the rains returned, which gradually led to the refounding of towns, cities, and city-states in Canaan. All the patriarchs from Abraham to Joseph dealt with droughts and famines, which doesn't fit with the wet climate of the late IBA and MBA1, before 1900 BC.

But the Southern Levant did suffer periodic droughts after 1900 BC, which eventually drove

the Semitic Asiatic peoples by the tens of thousands into the Nile Delta, where they eventually took over (the "Canaanite" Fourteenth and Fifteenth Dynasties of Egypt, c. 1800–1550 BC). Abraham and Isaac dealt with these intermittent famines, and drought caused Jacob's family to relocate to the Nile Delta during the Hyksos period when the Semitic pharaohs of the Fifteenth Dynasty ruled Lower Egypt (the Nile Delta region).

Heddle pulley for separating threads on a loom, Middle Bronze Age (photo: James Barber, courtesy of Bible Lands Museum, Jerusalem)

It is a notable fact that *none* of the cities and towns in the Abraham narratives (except Sodom and the Cities of the Kikkar)— Bethel, Hebron, Jerusalem, Dan (Lasha/Laish), Damascus, Beer-

sheba—were occupied from c. 2600/2500 BC to c. 1900/1800 BC (see *Map 2.02*). In other words, Melchizedek's Jerusalem couldn't have existed until after 1900/1800 BC. It is also important to realize that the city of Sodom itself was destroyed by a fiery cataclysm "from Yahweh out of the heavens" c. 1700 (+/–50 BC). This is confirmed by numerous radiocarbon dates from the excavations at Tall el-Hammam, the site of biblical Sodom (see *Breakout 2.07* and *Map 2.04*). Without a doubt, the geography of Genesis 12–25 fits no other period but MBA2.

Genesis recounts Abraham's covenant with Yahweh (chapters 15 and 17) and also his treaty with Abimelech (chapter 21). The covenants and treaties of the EBA (c. 3600–2500 BC), IBA (c. 2500–2100 BC), MBA (c. 2100–1600 BC), LBA (c. 1600–1200 BC), and IA (c. 1200–332 BC) differ radically. Abraham's covenant with Yahweh and treaty with Abimelech match one era only: MBA2.

In Genesis chapter 37, Joseph was sold into slavery for 20 shekels of silver (see *Breakout 2.11*). An examination of trade documents reveals that the average price of a slave during MBA2 was, in fact, 20 shekels. We can compare this with the cost to replace a slave according to the Mosaic Law during the LBA: 30 shekels (Exodus 21:32)—the average price of a slave during the LBA. The Bible even gets the inflation curve correct!

The MBA2 Hyksos period saw the first chariots in Egypt. When Joseph attained administrative power second only to pharaoh himself, he was introduced to the Egyptian populace through a royal parade in which he and pharaoh rode in chariots. This scene could have happened only in the Hyksos period, after c. 1650 BC.

These and many other historical synchronisms place Abraham, Isaac, Jacob, and Joseph squarely during MBA2 and demonstrate the historicity of the Genesis narratives that tell their stories.

S. Collins

BREAKOUT 2.06

ABRAHAM: BEDOUIN HERDSMAN OR HABIRU WARLORD?

The Sunday-school version of Abraham is far from the reality presented in the Genesis narratives. He was anything but a mild-mannered saintly sort who passively herded sheep across an idyllic, pastoral landscape. Abraham was a tough cookie!

While most scholars have interpreted Abraham as a Bronze Age Bedouin pastoralist (known as Shasu in the ANE), he simply doesn't fit this profile. The Shasu Bedouin clans that tended their flocks across the Fertile Crescent (see *Map 2.01*) were typically monoethnic (usually Semitic), tending their flocks across limited home ranges and moving seasonally to take advantage of better pasture lands. They kept mostly to themselves and only occasionally interacted with city folk to whom they sold milk, yogurt, cheese, meat, and wool. The Shasu Bedouin were very much a natural

part of regional landscapes and played a significant role in local economies. They were the "milk" in "the land of milk and honey," while "honey" represented the agricultural economy of sedentary folk living in cities, towns, villages, and hamlets. The Bedouin had a relatively self-sustaining and stable lifestyle but were by no means a wealthy class. While they certainly would defend their interests, warfare wasn't the Bedouin way of life.

By contrast, Abraham—likewise Isaac and Jacob—was a long-distance traveler. He ran with a large and ethnically diverse entourage. He was multilingual. He maintained a standing guerilla force with more than 300 well-trained and equipped fighting men. He provided mercenary frontline protection for the city-state of Jerusalem (thus his contract with Melchizedek, and King

Bera of Sodom tried to hire him). Abraham bought property, owned flocks and herds (likely employing Shasu!), and likely grew grain. He owned slaves and had servants. He entered into contracts with a variety of sociopolitical entities. He was extremely wealthy. He frequented palaces and maintained relationships with the upper echelons of society, including kings and aristocrats. Abraham was no Bedouin!

But if Abraham, Isaac, and Jacob weren't Bedouin pastoralists, what were they? There is only one class of ancient Near Eastern society that fits the career of Abraham and his descendants: the Habiru (Akkadian; *'Apiru* in Egyptian). The Habiru have been variously described as marauding nomads, nomadic mercenaries, societal castoffs, and warring rabble. What we know for sure is that throughout the Bronze Age, Habiru bands were known to exist across the

Near East, from Mesopotamia to Egypt. These groups were multi-ethnic and included people from all sectors of society, often joined by exiled royals, nobles, and military leaders. Habiru bands were also led by warlords who were well equipped to wage war and could take down even a large city, especially in regions like Canaan when the area was not controlled by a major kingdom or empire. The Habiru often allied themselves with city-state kings, providing a frontline of defense in trade for running their flocks and herds on city-state lands. They were the disenfranchised of ancient Near Eastern society who banded together

to do whatever it took to live a prosperous life. Hello, Abraham!

A looming question exists regarding the relationship between the terms *Habiru* and *Hebrew*. We must realize that Habiru was a name given by city folk to marauding bands of brigands (as they saw them). Local Bedouin, as a historic and integral part of local economies living symbiotically with cities and towns, were never called Habiru. Nor did Bedouin clans ever pose a threat like Habiru bands did. Whether or not *Habiru* and *Hebrew* are the same linguistically, they certainly shared virtually identical characteristics. At no point in the Bronze Age portion

of the Old Testament (Genesis through Joshua) would city folk not have styled the patriarchal Hebrews as marauding Habiru. They fit the bill perfectly. Of course, not all ANE Habiru were biblical Hebrews (such a claim misses the point). It is, however, highly probable that *habiru / ʿapiru* and biblical *ʿbr* (with the article, *hʿbr*) are linguistically identical. This lends a richness of meaning and cultural context to "Abram the Hebrew" (Genesis 14:13) and all other references to Hebrews in the Old Testament.

S. Collins

and her with it. Instant death, along with a white coating of anhydride salt! Meanwhile, Lot and his daughters fled to Zoar (see *Breakout 2.08*).

A recurring theme throughout the stories of Abraham, Isaac, and Jacob is famine that results from drought. Abraham lived during the second half of the MBA2, at the height of Canaanite civilization. The population of cities and towns was at an all-time high. The more people there are, the more agricultural production is required. In this scenario, even modest fluctuations in seasonal rainfall amounts puts stress on food production systems. MBA2 Dead Sea levels were near a historic low, revealing that rainfall amounts were trailing off from what they were during IBA2 and MBA1.

However, most cities and towns had springs that they could rely on for irrigation when the rains diminished. In this way, they could endure moderate drought conditions. But when grain surpluses dwindled, nomadic groups like the Hebrews could have a difficult time buying the food they needed. This usually meant relocating

to a region with enough agricultural production to support locals plus a substantial migrant population. For nomads living in the Southern Levant (like Lot), the Land of the Kikkar—"well-watered…like the land of Egypt" (Genesis 13:10)—had been a convenient solution. But the Kikkar of the Jordan was now a wasteland in the aftermath of its annihilation (Genesis 19:24-25, 28). Lower Egypt was then the nearest and best solution. So when famine once again threatened Canaan, Jacob and his family wound up in Egypt's Nile Delta.

The career of Joseph authentically belongs to the waning decades of the Hyksos period in Egypt (see *Timeline* and *Breakout 2.05*). At least three elements of the story confirm this. First is the ease of relocation to Egypt of Semitic Asiatics, like Jacob. Because the native Egyptians generally hated nomadic Semites and their sheep, the time of the Semitic "Canaanite" pharaohs in Lower Egypt—the so-called Hyksos period—was the ideal cultural climate for Joseph and his family.

Second, Joseph's introduction as Egypt's chief administrator—second only to pharaoh—via a chariot

Figure 2.10—The Great Hammurabi (standing) receiving laws from Shamash, god of justice (photo: Alexander Schick)

processional (Genesis 41:43) cannot have happened before the Hyksos period because it was the Hyksos who introduced the chariot (see *Figure 2.12*) into Egypt in the first place.

Third, after Joseph's death "there arose a new king over Egypt, who did not know Joseph" (Exodus 1:8). This obviously refers to the rise of the heavily anti-Asiatic (anti-Semitic) Eighteenth Dynasty that expelled the Hyksos from Lower Egypt (see *Timeline*). Its first king, Ahmosis, set in motion a policy and protocol that would last the duration of the Eighteenth Dynasty: an institutional hatred for and enslavement of Asiatic Semitic peoples (see *Breakouts 2.12, 3.01, 3.04*). From this point on, Egyptian slave raids into Canaan eventually lowered the population of the south Levant by 75 percent—a calculated measure taken to prevent a repeat of the Hyksos debacle. Exodus 1:10 (and following) is surely a reflection of early Eighteenth Dynasty politics and paranoia.

PEOPLES AND KINGDOMS

AMORITES—A Semitic people living in the north Levant and northwest Mesopotamia (see *Map 2.01*).

Their name (Akkadian, *Ammuru*) means "Westerners." Most of the central hill country tribes of this period were of Amorite extraction, such as the Perizzites, Girgashites, Jebusites, etc. According to Mesopotamian documents, any group living in the Levant was Ammuru, even the Canaanites. Biblically, while the Canaanites lived in the coastal areas and in the Jordan Valley north of the Dead Sea (Genesis 10:19; cf. Joshua 11:3), the Amorites occupied the Transjordan highlands (Joshua 2:10) and the Cisjordan hill country (Genesis 14:13). However, any attempt to draw strict boundaries for Southern Levantine people groups during this highly mobile era of refugees, migrants, and mercenary groups (MBA2) is difficult at best.

ARAMEANS—Abraham spent time in Haran, in the upper Euphrates (northwest Mesopotamia) in the region of Aram Naharaim or Paddan Aram (Genesis 24:10; see *Map 2.01*). Part of the family stayed there (Nahor, Bethuel, Laban) as Arameans (Genesis 25:20), and both Isaac and Jacob's wives came from there. In fact, the Israelites declared themselves descendants of "a wandering Aramean" (Deuteronomy 26:5). Some scholars think this region may well have been the location of "Ur of the Chaldeans" instead of the much larger and culturally different Sumerian/Akkadian Ur.

Figure 2.11—Decorated pottery from the Middle Bronze Age palace at Sodom (photos: Daniel Galassini; drawing: Steven Collins, courtesy of Tall el-Hammam Excavation Project)

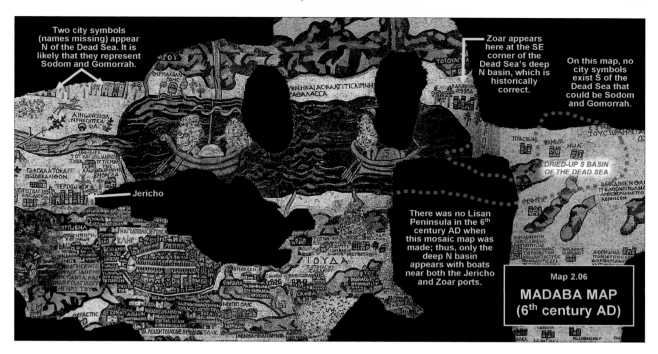

Two city symbols (names missing) appear N of the Dead Sea. It is likely that they represent Sodom and Gomorrah.

Zoar appears here at the SE corner of the Dead Sea's deep N basin, which is historically correct.

On this map, no city symbols exist S of the Dead Sea that could be Sodom and Gomorrah.

DRIED-UP S BASIN OF THE DEAD SEA

Jericho

There was no Lisan Peninsula in the 6th century AD when this mosaic map was made; thus, only the deep N basin appears with boats near both the Jericho and Zoar ports.

Map 2.06
MADABA MAP (6th century AD)

BABYLONIA—The region around the city-state of Babylon was situated on what used to be the Euphrates River, about 50 miles south of modern-day Baghdad (see *Map 2.01*). There is evidence of civilization in this region going back to at least 3000 BC. Its first dynastic period began around the nineteenth century BC (see *Timeline*). The greatest king of the eighteenth century BC was unquestionably Hammurabi (ruled c. 1792–1750 BC). At the height of his reign the empire spanned the Mesopotamian region, including the Persian Gulf and Upper Tigris regions. He was responsible for collecting large quantities of legal documents, instituting massive legal reforms, and codifying written law. His law codes were a marvel of the ancient world. He was succeeded by his firstborn son, Samsuiluna.

EGYPT (HYKSOS)—The Old Kingdom (c. 2613–2181) pyramids of kings Khufu, Khafre, and Menkaure were already ancient history and deteriorating by the time Abraham was born sometime after 1800 BC. By the time of the weakening Thirteenth Dynasty, internal problems and corruption allowed a Semitic Asiatic population called the Hyksos ("foreigners" from Canaan) to gain power in Lower Egypt. They ruled from Avaris (see *Map 2.03*). By the eighteenth century BC, the

contemporary Theban Dynasty had become a Hyksos vassal. The Hyksos introduced into Egypt the composite bow, the horse, the chariot, and advances in bronze and ceramics technology. Efforts to drive out the hated Hyksos failed until Ahmose of Thebes unified the country in the mid-sixteenth century BC, after the death of Joseph.

HATTI (HITTITES)—Some of the earliest records of the Hittites mention a king by the name of Pamba in the twenty-second century BC, but little can be nailed down for the ruling succession until Tudhaliya, grandfather of Hattusilis I, in the late seventeenth century BC. So we know that Hittite kings were ruling their homeland, Hatti (see *Map 2.01*), through the entire MBA (c. 2100–1550 BC), even though we do not know all of their names (see *Figure 2.13*). But the Hittites had no sociopolitical presence in the Levant during the time of Abraham. The Genesis Hittites were migrants from the Land of Hatti (central Anatolia) who had been setting up business in the Northern and Southern Levant since at least 2700 BC (see *Breakout 2.05*). Anatolian cultural influences are found in the Levant all through the MBA as well.

PHILISTINES (Sea Peoples)—Critics of the Bible are fond of attacking the appearance of the Philistines

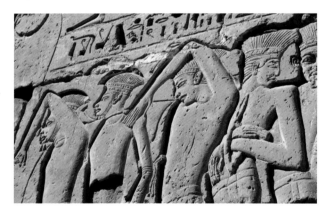

Figure 2.12—Chariot, Egypt (photos: Alexander Schick)

Figure 2.13—In the land of Hatti; Lion Gate of Hattusa, Hittite capital (photo: David E. Graves)

Figure 2.14—Philistines in Egyptian art; note the "feathered" headdress (photo: Alexander Schick)

in the book of Genesis as anachronistic because the Aegean group called Peleset doesn't appear by name until the reign of Rameses III in the twelfth century BC (see *Figure 2.14*). But such criticism is entirely unwarranted. There were many families and/or tribes migrating from the Aegean region to the Levant from at least the early third millennium BC. This continued through the MBA, as evidenced by the work of

Minoan artisans appearing in coastal palaces of the Southern Levant and in the southern Jordan Valley, along with Minoan-inspired architecture. The Minoan and Cycladic cultures of the Aegean realm evolved into the Mycenaean civilization of the LBA and Iron Age 1 (IA1), groups of which appeared in droves in the eastern Mediterranean, eventually settling along the south Levantine coast. The Bible writers lump all the so-called Sea Peoples under the term *Philistines* for reasons of simplicity. For the biblical authors, Philistines are Aegean peoples regardless of their tribal names, just like the way North Americans call the hundreds of Native American tribes who reside there *Indians*.

Shasu-Bedouin—The Bedouin (Egyptian, *Shasu*) were nomadic Semitic tribes whose lives centered on the herding of sheep and goats. They moved from pasturage to pasturage seasonally. They were economically and socially self-contained, although they provided a range of sheep/goat-related products for sale to city and town folk. The Shasu tended to stay to themselves and were nonmilitaristic, peaceful people who lived off the land. They could, however, protect their own interests when required to do so.

Habiru/ʿApiru—The term *Habiru* (Egyptian, *ʿApiru*) has a range of meanings, including "marauding nomads," "outcasts," "invaders," "mercenaries,"

BREAKOUT 2.07

THE DISCOVERY AND EXCAVATION OF SODOM

Controversy over the existence and location of Sodom and the so-called Cities of the Plain has raged for more than a century. In recent decades, liberal scholars have declared the fabled "sin cities" to be pure legend, thus believing that any attempt to locate them is futile. Most nineteenth century explorer-scholars accepted their existence, locating them either northeast of the Dead Sea or toward the south end of the Dead Sea. Many, following the lead of twentieth-century archaeologist W.F. Albright, put them underneath the waters of the Dead Sea's shallow south basin. Bible-respecting scholars today are still divided between the suggested north and south Dead Sea locations for Sodom. However, recent research, discoveries, and excavations are successfully overturning previous inadequate theories about the existence, location, and destruction of Sodom and its neighbors.

Given that the traditional Ussher chronology for the Genesis patriarchs is invalid (see *Breakout 2.04*), and that on historical and archaeological grounds Abraham belongs to the MBA2 period (after c. 1800 BC; see *Breakout 2.05*), a solid identification of biblical Sodom has emerged from the excavations at Tall el-Hammam in Jordan. Tall el-Hammam

Excavating in the Sodom palace, Middle Bronze Age (photo: Daniel Galassini, courtesy of Tall el-Hammam Excavation Project)

is the site of the largest continuously occupied Bronze Age city in the Southern Levant (Canaan). It also has numerous cities/towns within an eight-mile radius. It, along with all its satellite cities/towns, was destroyed by a violent, high-heat catastrophe during the MBA2. The entire area remained without any human settlements for the next 700 years.

The biblical "map" of Sodom's location found in Genesis 13:1-12, which says that Sodom and its city group were located in "the Kikkar of the Jordan." The Hebrew term *kikkar* simply means "circle" or "disk" (not "plain"!) and refers to the widened alluvial plain of the southern Jordan Valley immediately north

of the Dead Sea (see *Map 2.04*). The eastern half of this 25-mile disk of well-watered territory—called the Land of the Kikkar in Genesis 19:28—is clearly visible from the area just east of Bethel/Ai, from which Lot could see "the whole plain [*kikkar*] of the Jordan" (Genesis 13:10 NIV), the location of Sodom. Only the northern tip of the Dead Sea is visible from Bethel/Ai, so the south Dead Sea area was definitely not in view—and not the location of Sodom.

Tall el-Hammam and its associated cities/towns occupy the precise geographical location described in Genesis 13:1-12. They also flourished continuously as a city-state from at least 3300 BC

(Sodom, Gomorrah, Admah, and Zeboiim of Genesis 10) down to the moment of their obliteration by a meteoritic airburst event— "sulfur and fire from the LORD out of heaven" (Genesis 19:24)— in the time of Abraham (c. 1700 [+/–50] BC), all of which is confirmed by the archaeological record unearthed by the Tall el-Hammam Excavation Project.

By contrast, we now know that the southern Dead Sea sites proposed for Sodom and Gomorrah were all extinct by c. 2500 BC, centuries before the time of Abraham, and that no settlement ever existed in the oft-inundated area of the Dead Sea's south basin. These points, together with the fact that a southern location for the Cities of the Kikkar completely contradicts the geography of Genesis 13:1-12, require that such outdated theories about Sodom's location be rejected.

Now well into its second decade, the excavation of the massive site of Tall el-Hammam/Sodom has unearthed a large temple complex, domestic areas, and sophisticated fortifications replete with a monumental gateway system, sloping ramparts, and a surrounding lower-city wall (with towers) nearly two miles in length. The site also has a separately fortified upper city with a large palace (see *Figures 2.05–2.07*).

The discovery and excavation of Tall el-Hammam/Sodom is one of the most important archaeological discoveries to date not only because of its biblical importance, but also for its significant contribution to our understanding of the BA in the Southern Levant.

S. Collins

"foreign rabble," and "raiders." They were seen in various ways by different people. In essence, they were multiethnic bands of people from diverse backgrounds living on the margins of society, generally transient, who did whatever it took to survive. Their ranks could include individuals from every imaginable class and profession, even including exiled princes, government officials, and warriors who had fallen out of favor with others in their former positions. The Habiru tended to be warlike and were often hired by city-states as mercenary protectors. The term *Hebrew* (*'ibri*) is derived directly from Habiru/'Apiru (see *Breakout 2.06*).

MIDIANITES—A nomadic Semitic group that lived south and east of Edom in the northwest Arabian Peninsula and east Sinai Peninsula (see *Map 2.01*). During the patriarchal era some traveling Midianites captured and sold Joseph. Apparently they later assimilated the little-known Ishmaelites (Genesis 37:28; Judges 8:24).

PEOPLES OF THE SOUTHERN LEVANT—The mix of peoples coming into the south Levant show signs of Canaanean, Amorite, Aegean, Anatolian, Urartian, Mesopotamian, and Egyptian roots (see *Maps 2.01, 2.02*). The biblical record has names for many of them—Hivites, Girgashites, Perrizites, Jebusites, Ludites, Anamites, Naphtuhites, Pathrusites, Casluites, Caphtorites, Arkites, Sinites, Arvadites, and Zamarites, to name a few! While it is virtually impossible to trace the origins of many of these groups, the Bible makes it abundantly clear that the Levant was, through all its primeval and BA history, a swirling melting pot of migrants and refugees from lands both near and far. This is also confirmed by the archaeological record.

SOCIETIES AND CULTURES

SOCIAL STRATIFICATION—A MBA city-state was ruled by a societal father figure, with the populace serving the "king" in what is best described as a feudal system. City-state lands were "owned" by the king, with a portion of the agricultural production "paid" to families who worked the fields. Society was highly stratified. The "royal" family got the top jobs—officials, administrators, priests. Top-level military "officers" were high on the social ladder. Below them were the various trades. Generally, clans, families, and/or guilds plying the smellier, grittier trades— things like brick making, construction, pottery making, and metal working—were on the lower rungs of society. City and town dwellers tended to stay away from nomadic herders except to purchase their products.

Tribalism—Tribes, made up of families and clans, existed in both urban and nomadic contexts. They tended to occupy traditional lands or ranges and could often be at odds with other tribal groups. More powerful tribes that became sedentary agriculturalists were the basis for villages growing into towns and towns into cities. Dominant tribes became the ruling classes. They usually had their own patron deities, which, in the case of the stronger tribes, emerged as "city gods."

City-States—Large, fortified urban centers often annexed or built towns strategically located within the circumference of the lands they controlled, becoming city-states. This also included villages and hamlets of people working the agricultural fields and specialty trades living in isolation (because of the smoke they produced) like metalsmiths and potters. The centralized government exercised control of all aspects of commercial activity and enterprise, building monumental architecture and public buildings designed to reinforce overall community identity.

Inheritance—The customs and/or laws of inheritance permeated every level of society. At the top, inheritance traditions created expectations of hereditary rule. The concept of firstborn or primal son meant that whichever male in the family held this right would inherit the most or all ("double portion"), be it a pottery shop, city-state, kingdom, or empire. Generally, women were not given any inheritance, but were themselves inherited.

Women's Roles—Throughout antiquity, whether queen or slave, the average woman died between age 25 and 30 from complications of her tenth to twelfth pregnancy. Rarely did women (or men) live beyond age 40. If a woman reached age 50 or 60, she was very old and probably honored. A very small percentage (probably less than 10 percent) lived beyond age 70. The primary function of women in ancient societies was to give birth to and raise children. They also managed most or all of the home and kitchen operation, from cooking fuels to food storage to food preparation to cooking. Young children of both sexes probably helped with domestic chores. They may also have participated in textile production, basket weaving, making handmade cooking vessels, and helping with house or tent maintenance.

Men's Roles—Men typically worked the agricultural fields and/or trades as beer producers, metalsmiths, potters, weapon makers, flintknappers, woodworkers, brick makers, stone and brick masons, plasterers, toolmakers, and fishermen. There were countless other jobs as well. The men of nomadic tribes were shepherds and likely shared a wide range of tasks with women. Men were also warriors and soldiers when contracted or conscripted. Only the largest kingdoms and empires had standing armies with professional soldiers. Elite positions included administrators, scribes, priests, and supervisors of trade groups.

Political Climate—The time of Abraham, his sons, and grandsons was one of general prosperity, both in Mesopotamia and in the Levant (see *Timeline*). Although the native throne of Egypt was in decline while Semitic Asiatic kings ruled Lower Egypt, the so-called Hyksos pharaohs had a thriving kingdom and economy, politically amenable to people like Abraham the Hebrew. Long-distance political alliances were common. People were also migrating to the Levant from faraway lands like Crete (Minoans) and Anatolia (Hittites).

LANGUAGES AND WRITING

Akkadian—This was the principal Semitic language (a branch of Afro-Asiatic) of the third and second millennia BC. It was the dominant language in Mesopotamia (see *Map 1.02*) and was the language of international trade and correspondence throughout the Near East. Early dialects of Akkadian were spoken during the EBA and IBA (see *Timeline*). The early second millennium Babylonian dialect of Akkadian is considered classic Akkadian. It was also Abraham's birth language. It was written in cuneiform (*cuneus,* meaning "wedge") script on clay tablets (see *Figure 2.15*).

Sumerian—Spoken in Sumer (south Mesopotamia; see *Map 1.02*) from at least the fourth millennium into the third millennium BC. A language *isolate*, Sumerian is not related to any other known language.

It was perhaps one of the original post-Babel language groups. It became a dead language after Sumer was subsumed by the Akkadian Empire of Sargon the Great (c. 2300 BC; see *Timeline*). However, the Sumerian language survived for centuries as a scholar's language for the study of religious and literary texts. It was written using cuneiform script on clay tablets (see *Figure 2.16*).

AMORITE—The dominant Semitic language of the north Levant beginning in the third millennium BC (see *Map 1.02*). It had migrated into the south Levant and Mesopotamia by the early second millennium BC, brought by Amorite (*Ammuru*, meaning "Western") migrants. The Hebrew patriarchs were certainly familiar

Figure 2.15—Lexical cuneiform tablet with parallel columns of professions given in both Sumerian and Akkadian (photo: Daniel Galassini, courtesy of Museum of Archaeology, Trinity Southwest University)

Figure 2.16—Sumerian cuneiform tablet (photo: Daniel Galassini, courtesy of Museum of Archaeology, Trinity Southwest University)

Figure 2.17—Canaanean cuneiform tablet (photo: Daniel Galassini, courtesy of Museum of Archaeology, Trinity Southwest University)

Figure 2.18—Hittite cuneiform tablets (photos: Steven Collins, David E. Graves)

with this language, if not fluent in it. It was often written in cuneiform script on clay tablets (see *Figure 2.15*).

Canaanite—A language of the northwest Semitic group, closely related to Amorite. It probably existed as multiple dialects among the numerous tribal groups in Canaan (south Levant) during the second millennium BC (see *Map 1.02*). It is a direct forerunner of Phoenician and Hebrew. Abraham learned Canaanite when he relocated to the Southern Levant. Canaanite was the birth language of Isaac, Jacob, and Joseph. It was written in cuneiform script on clay tablets (see *Figure 2.17*).

Hittite—An Indo-European language of Anatolia. It was the language of the second millennium Hittite Empire (see *Map 1.02* and *Timeline*). Anatolian migrants brought strands of the language into the Levant during the third and second millennia BC. The earliest forms of Hittite were written using a system of hieroglyphs, but eventually it was written in cuneiform script on clay tablets (see *Figure 2.18*). Abraham probably heard the Hittite language now and then from his Anatolian associates.

Egyptian—Belongs to a branch of the Afro-Asiatic languages. It was spoken in Egypt from at least the fourth millennium BC and remained the principal language of Egypt down to the Early Roman period (see *Map 1.02* and *Timeline*). It was commonly written in *hieroglyphics* with ink on papyrus (paper) using various kinds of pens and was, of course, inscribed in stone on monuments and tombs (see *Figure 2.19*). It could also be painted on plaster. All visitors to Egypt, including the Hebrew patriarchs, would have been surrounded by hieroglyphic inscriptions. A cursive *hieratic script* was also developed, written on papyrus with a reed pen (see *Figure 2.20*). This easier-to-use script was invented

Figure 2.19—Three Egyptian writing systems: hieroglyphics, hieratic, and demotic (photos: Steven Collins, Alexander Schick)

during the third millennium, in parallel with hieroglyphics, for producing longer documents and "books."

BELIEFS AND RELIGIONS

Animism—Attributing spirit or soul to inanimate objects, plants, animals, and natural phenomena. An underlying belief in all tribal religions, animism is usually practiced by means of rituals—from simple

LOCATING ZOAR

The traditional location of Zoar at es-Safi near the southern tip of the Dead Sea is at least casually accepted by most Bible scholars. The location of Zoar is one of the key components of the theory of a southern Dead Sea location for Sodom and Gomorrah and is consistently used as an argument against locating the Cities of the Kikkar northeast of the Dead Sea.

However, there is a Bible passage that seems definitive in eliminating the southern end of the Dead Sea as a viable area for Zoar: Deuteronomy 34:1-4. A straightforward reading of the passage identifies Zoar as a southern border-marker of the Israelite tribal allotment of Reuben at the Arnon River—a point seemingly ignored by most Bible scholars.

Deuteronomy 34:1-4 gives a sweeping panorama of the six geographical areas shown to Moses that comprise the Promised Land (see *Map 3.08*), moving in a counterclockwise direction from Pisgah, north through the Transjordan, across to the Cisjordan north of Lake Kinneret, south through the Cisjordan to the Negev, then north once again to the southern Jordan Valley below Pisgah (see *Map 2.04*). The panorama begins and ends at Pisgah (less than a quarter mile north of Mount Nebo). Following the text of Deuteronomy

34:1-3, the Promised Land's six-part geography looks like this (writer's translation):

"…Yahweh showed him the whole land,"

1. "(תא־) the Gilead unto (דע) Dan"

2. "and (תאו־) all of Naphtali"

3. "and (תאו־) [the] land of Ephraim and Manasseh"

4. "and (תאו־) all of [the] land of Judah unto (דע) the western sea"

5. "and (תאו־) the Negev"

6. "and (תאו־) the Kikkar of the Valley of Jericho, City of Palms, unto (דע) Zoar"

Notice that there is a large geographical disconnect moving from "the Negev" (5) to "the Kikkar of the Valley of Jericho…unto Zoar" (6). The writer jumps from the Negev all the way to the southern Jordan Valley, with the addition of "unto (דע) Zoar." Why this jump? When we recall the promises about the descendants of Esau (the Edomites) and Lot (the Moabites), the answer is clear and reflected on all Bible maps: *Edom and Moab were off-limits to the Israelites* (Deuteronomy 2:4-5, 9). Looking at any good map of the Israelite tribal allotments, "the Negev" (5) represents the

allotment to Simeon. The area represented by "the Kikkar of the Valley of Jericho…unto Zoar" (6) is none other than the allotment to the tribe of Reuben, the southern extent of which was the Arnon River, the border of Moab.

The extent of the Reubenite territory is clearly laid out in Joshua 13:9-10 (writer's translation): "...from Aroer on the rim of the Arnon Gorge, and the town in the middle of the gorge, and [the] whole plateau of Medeba unto Dibon, and all the towns of Sihon, king of the Amorites, who ruled in Heshbon unto [the] border of [the] sons of Ammon…" If in Deuteronomy 34:3 "the Kikkar of the Valley of Jericho…unto Zoar" defines the same Reubenite territory as presented in the Joshua passage above—it likely does—then Zoar marks the southern border of Reuben and is possibly identified in Joshua 13:9 as "the town in the middle of the gorge" (NIV).

Regardless of whether Zoar was "the town in the middle of the [Arnon] gorge" (but what else could it be?), the fact that it is listed with the geographical areas and locations comprising the Promised Land in Deuteronomy 34:1-4 places Zoar at the southern border of the Israelites in the Transjordan—the Arnon River

Gorge. The entire region south and southeast of the Dead Sea from below the Arnon and west to the Negev was occupied by Moab and Edom and was not a part of the land promised to the Israelites. The traditional site of Zoar (es-Safi) is in the far southern part of the Moabite kingdom, perhaps in Edom, far from Israelite territory.

The famous sixth-century AD Madaba Map depicts the Dead Sea as it was during the Byzantine period. At that time the Dead Sea level was at or near a historic low, with the entire shallow south basin completely dried up. The Madaba Map has no Lisan Peninsula either! It only shows what existed in the sixth century AD:

the capsule-shaped deep northern basin (see *Map 2.06*). Roman/Byzantine Zoar was a deep-water port at the southeast corner of the *northern* basin, slightly south of the Arnon Gorge. This reinforces the location of the much earlier Zoar in the same area.

S. Collins

to complex—by which the surrounding world (environment) is manipulated to human advantage. Professional animistic practitioners—shamans, healers, magicians, wizards, priests—are often consulted. However, animism is intimately personal in most cultures. The "higher" religions are almost always layered over animistic beliefs. The family line of Abraham was comprised of tribal animists. Animism dominated the Hebrews and Israelites for most of their history.

Mesopotamian Religion—Our understanding of Mesopotamian religion in the MBA is limited to literary texts found in city archives. Thus, we are essentially looking at the "formal" religion of royals and elites who commissioned the preservation of myths, hero tales, and legends, often copied from earlier Sumerian works of the third millennium. There is no sense of logic to the polytheistic amalgam that is Mesopotamian religion. It was ever a moving target, always changing and developing, and quite different from one city-state to the next. A few of the more popular deities were *An* (*Anu*), sky god and father of the gods; *Enki* (*Ea*), god of fresh water, rivers; *Inanna* (*Ishtar*), goddess of love, fertility, and war; *Nanna* (*Sin*), god of the moon; and *Utu* (*Shamash*), god of the sun, justice. As in most cultures, Mesopotamian gods were deified necessities or features of nature (see *Figure 2.21*). But at the level of everyday people, we have no idea what religion was like beyond the Euphrates River during the MBA. Because most tribal peoples, then and now, are fundamentally animistic, it is a safe estimation that the average

Mesopotamian farmer or tradesman was an animist regardless of his "higher" religious beliefs, if any.

Canaanite Religion—The picture of Canaanite religion during MBA2, the time of Hebrew patriarchs, is difficult to determine for two simple reasons. The book of Genesis does not say much about it, and almost no Canaanite texts are known from this period. Our knowledge, therefore, depends on the archaeological record interpreted in the light of later biblical

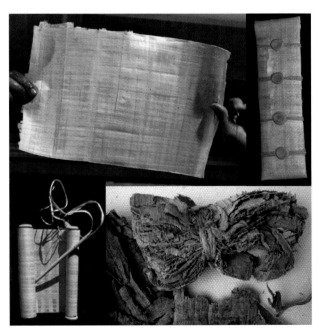

Figure 2.20—Papyrus, pen, and ink; note the document tied closed with string, bearing daubs of clay with seal impressions (photos: Alexander Schick)

and extrabiblical texts. In general, the religious pantheon in Canaan looked like this when Abraham entered the land: *El, 'Il, Elyon,* the unapproachable creator god; *Athirat* (later *Asherah*), mother goddess, consort of El; *Ba'al,* variously storm god, fertility god; *Ba'alit,* female counterpart of Ba'al; *Dagon,* fertility god of grain; *Eshmun,* goddess of healing; *Horon,* god of the underworld; *Kotharat,* goddess of marriage, pregnancy; *Kothar-wa-Khasis,* god of skilled craftsmen; *Moloch* (*Molech, Melqart*), god of fire; *Mot,* god of death; *Nikkal-wa-Ib,* goddess of orchards and fruit; *Qadeshtu,* goddess of "holy" (sacred) prostitutes; *Resheph,* god of disease and healing; *Shachar* and *Shalim,* twin mountain gods of dawn and dusk, and peace (Shalim); *Shapash* (*Shemesh*), sun goddess; *Sydyk,* god of righteousness, justice; *Yam,* god of rivers and sea; *Ya,* leader of the gods; *Yarikh* (*Yareah*), god of the moon. There were many more! How these gods and goddesses related to one another and what their duties were varied widely from region to region, even city to city. (See *Figure 2.22.*)

CANAANITE WORSHIP PRACTICES—There was no standardization in Canaanite religion. Some gods became patron deities of cities and towns. These are variously identified in the Bible. A few examples are *Jerushalim* (Jerusalem), after Shalim; *Ba'al Gad,* after Ba'al; *Jericho,* after Yarikh; *Beth Shemesh* after Shemesh. Rituals included offerings of things like grains, olive oil, fruits and nuts, sheep, donkeys, horses, and humans. Child sacrifice is well known from foundation deposits (jar burials) found beneath the floors of MBA houses. Copulation with sacred male and female temple prostitutes and animals was also considered an act of worship (becoming "one" with the god or goddess). These

Figure 2.21—A variety of Mesopotamian deities (photos: Steven Collins, Alexander Schick, David E. Graves)

Figure 2.22—Canaanean deities (photos: David E. Graves)

Figure 2.23—Dolmen ("table top") monument from Bronze Age (photo: Steven Collins)

practices were later specifically mentioned and forbidden in the Mosaic Law. Open-air shrines topped hills across the south Levant and included standing stones (menhirs; Hebrew plural *masseboth*), stone stacks, menhir alignments, circles of standing stones (henges), "dancing" circles marked by stones, and poles (phallic representations) set in holes drilled into bedrock. The Canaanites also planted sacred trees and groves. Much religious energy was spent on ancestor worship in the building of megalithic landscapes filled with dolmens (stone, "tabletop" monuments; see *Figure 2.23*), and other stone features (as described above).

TEMPLES—Temples during this period were usually *tripartite*; that is, they had a courtyard, outer sanctuary, and inner sanctuary (see *Figure 2.24*). Each city and town had at least one sacred precinct and an associated temple (see *Figure 2.25*). Just how public these sacred areas were is open to question. Most temples had associated administrative rooms or buildings surrounding them. Inside the "holy of holies" (the inner sanctuary) were standing stones representing the key deities worshipped there. There was usually at least one altar (square, rectangular, or circular). The size of a temple generally corresponded with the size of the city or town.

YAHWISM AND THE HEBREW PATRIARCHS—Abraham was born into a world dominated by animism and polytheism. The one true God, *Yahweh* by name, began dealing with Abraham in Haran. From that point forward, Yahweh remained the principal deity of the Hebrew patriarchs. In this light, Exodus 6:3 must be translated "I appeared to Abraham, Isaac, and Jacob as El Shaddai, and did I not by my name Yahweh make myself known to them?" Abraham, his sons, grandsons, and great grandsons were beneficiaries of Yahweh's revelation of himself as *the* singular creator God (*El, Elohim*). Because both El and Yahweh were generally known in the south Levant as "members" of the Canaanite pantheon, there can be little doubt that this caused confusion for the early Hebrews who, for the most part, saw Yahweh as the chief Hebrew God but not necessarily the *only* God (see *Figure 2.26*). Pure, classic monotheism did not emerge until the giving of the Law to Moses. But even after Moses, Yahwistic monotheism

Figure 2.24—Middle Bronze Age temple, Tell Tayinat, far northwestern Levant (drawing: Leen Ritmeyer)

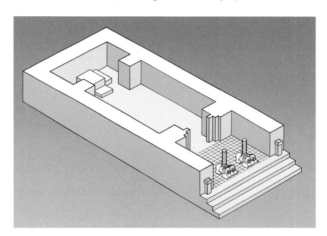

Figure 2.25—Isometric drawing, Middle Bronze Age temple, Tell Tayinat (drawing: Leen Ritmeyer)

did not "win" the Israelite or Judahite mind until the Babylonian captivity in the sixth century BC.

EL, ELOHIM—*El* was always recognized as the superlative, ultimate, creator God. *El* was also the generic Canaanite term for deity. The plural *Elohim* could simply mean "gods," or even "lesser gods" like angelic beings. From the get-go, Genesis identifies Yahweh as Elohim—Yahweh is his personal and only name; Elohim is simply "God," the designation of deity. But why use the plural *Elohim* and not singular *El* when connecting Yahweh with "God"? While theologians have wrangled over this question for centuries, the answer may be quite simple. With the fall of the first human pair, the image of God that they represented was, as it were, fractured into countless pieces. Each of these pieces came to represent a particular attribute of deity, whereby individual attributes, in time, were considered to be deities in and of themselves—creator god, fertility god, fertility goddess, god of war, god of peace, god of storms, god of seas, and such endlessly. Each god was a focus of human need. Yahweh declared that he, and he alone, was the Elohim (pantheon!), uniquely meeting all human needs. Thus, his progressive revelation ultimately affirmed Elohim (Yahweh alone) as the one true God, keeping the plural Elohim but always using it with a singular verb, reinforcing his singularity!

Figure 2.26—Canaanite standing stones (or menhirs; Hebrew, singular *massebah*, plural *masseboth*), Gezer (photos: Alexander Schick)

Figure 2.27—Lower (L) and upper (R) Middle Bronze Age Hazor, a great city "erased" by time (photo: John Witte Moore)

ARCHITECTURE AND INFRASTRUCTURE

CITIES, TOWNS, AND VILLAGES—The size of settlements in the Levant during the MBA can be divided according to the number of hectares or acres (2.47 acres per hectare): *large cities*, 50-plus acres; cities, 20-plus acres; towns, 10-plus acres; villages, 3-plus acres; hamlets, less than 3 acres. (In the Bible, they are all simply called cities.) The scale of settlements in Mesopotamia is much greater, with large cities exceeding as much as 200 to 500 acres and more. In many ways, Canaan (south Levant) was a backwater land where the scale and quality of cities and towns was meager compared to those in Egypt or Mesopotamia. Although of lesser quality, south Levantine cities and towns were built in the same way as in the rest of the Near East—mudbrick superstructures on stone foundations. They were almost always fortified. City planning often included central temple precincts, with radial streets connecting the center of the city with a ring-road just inside the city wall. Houses and public buildings were located in between (see *Figure 2.27*).

FORTIFICATIONS—The key feature of MBA fortifications in Mesopotamia and the Levant was a sloping, earthen *rampart* system ringing the city. The city wall was often built on top of the rampart (freestanding rampart; see *Figure 2.28*). A rampart could also be built against the outside of the city wall (supplemental; see *Figure 2.29*). City walls were usually 10 to 20 feet thick and 25 to 45 feet high. Gateway systems could be simple passageways with flanking chambers, or they could be complex combinations of flanking defensive towers, gate passageway, gatehouse, and guiding walls to control foot traffic. Main gateways of larger cities were designed as "killing zones" to discourage direct assault (see *Figure 2.06*). Many MBA gate passageways were arched (see *Figures 2.30, 2.31*).

MONUMENTAL AND PUBLIC ARCHITECTURE—Gateways, palaces, temples, administrative buildings, and other kinds of public architecture were usually *monumental* in nature (see *Figure 2.32*). This simply means that they were designed on a grander scale than domestic structures for the purpose of impressing citizens and visitors alike. They represented the power and authority of the city or city-state ruling administration. Monumental buildings had more robust foundations and walls (three to six feet thickness is typical) than houses. The sizes of their foundations suggest that they were multistoried buildings, accessed by ladders and stairs (rare). The thicker the foundation, the taller the building. Construction was mudbricks on stone foundations, coated with a mud-sand plaster. Ceilings/roofs used wooden beams with crossing wattle and daub (sticks and mud), topped by mud plaster with lime and crushed limestone.

HOUSES—MBA houses (see *Figure 2.33*) consisted of several rooms built around a central, open courtyard used for cooking. They were built of mudbricks on stone foundations. Wall thickness was usually one to two feet. Houses were often two stories, usually

accessed by ladders, less frequently by external stairways. Walls were finished with mud-sand plaster. Beam-and-stick ceilings/roofs were covered with a mud-sand-lime mix, which became very hard when dry. Such structures needed constant maintenance, especially during the rainy season (October through March).

SACRED ARCHITECTURE—The focal point of city life was the sacred precinct that contained at least one temple, several shrines, and related administrative structures used by priests and support personnel (see *Figure 2.34*). Temples were generally tripartite; that is, having three rooms of increasingly holy function. The innermost was a holy of holies, where representations of the city's patron god(s) were enshrined.

SACRESCAPES—These were landscapes designed with worship-related features and structures. The Bible calls them high places. In these locations there were

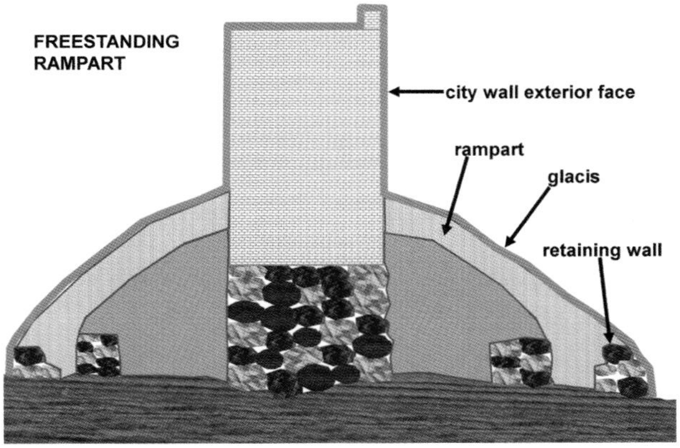

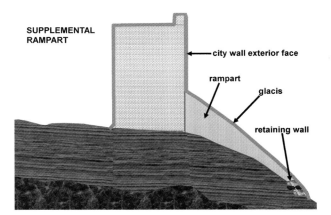
Figure 2.28—Freestanding rampart with city wall, Middle Bronze Age (drawing: Steven Collins)

Figure 2.29—Supplemental rampart with city wall, Middle Bronze Age (drawing: Steven Collins)

Figure 2.30—Middle Bronze 2 arched city gate, Tel Dan (entrance enhanced) (photo: John Witte Moore)

Figure 2.31—Middle Bronze 2 gateway at Tel Dan (photo: courtesy of Israel Museum; drawing: Leen Ritmeyer)

Figure 2.32—Excavation of a Middle Bronze Age monumental structure (photo: Daniel Galassini, courtesy of Tall el-Hammam Excavation Project)

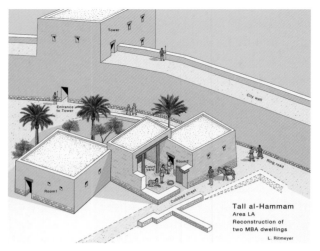

Figure 2.33—Reconstruction drawing of a Middle Bronze Age house (drawing: Leen Ritmeyer, courtesy of Tall el-Hammam Excavation Project)

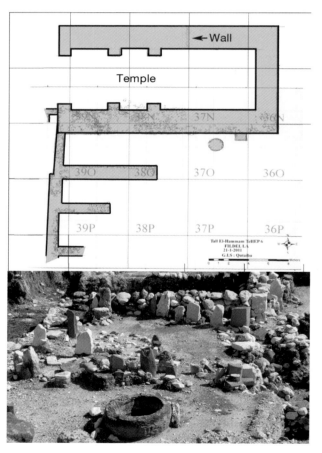

Figure 2.34—Above, temple complex, Sodom; below, Middle Bronze Age temple, Hazor (drawing: courtesy of Tall el-Hammam Excavation Project; photo: Alexander Schick)

standing stones (menhirs), Asherah poles (phallic symbols), sacred trees, and sacrificial altars (see *Figure 2.35*). Standing stones (Hebrew, *masseboth*; *massebah* singular) represented deities and may have been painted. More extensive sacred landscapes included stone (dancing?) circles and stone alignments with astronomical orientations, all connected by ritual avenues. Most often sacrescapes included a necroscape devoted to the dead.

NECROSCAPES—A portion of a sacrescape, including cemeteries and various monuments, devoted to the remembrance of the dead. Shaft and cave tombs, cairns (stone piles over graves), and memorial structures like dolmens were common during the MBA (see *Figure 2.36*).

INFRASTRUCTURE—Also called infrascape, this is the alteration and use of the landscape in support of a city-state—roads, water management, stone gathering, brickworks, walls dividing agricultural fields, terracing, watchtowers. These are the elements of the city-state shared by each community, from the central city to the outlying villages and hamlets servicing farms, groves, and vineyards (see *Figure 2.37*).

WEAPONS AND WARFARE

REASONS FOR WAR—There were several reasons for war in the ANE. Most common was the "need" to acquire additional territory. If the expansionist army met resistance, warfare ensued. City-states could expand their lands by conquest, eventually becoming a kingdom. In time, with much wider conquests, they could become an empire. But warfare could also be a local affair, with one city attacking another rival city for nothing more than bragging rights. Times of famine might mean launching attacks to capture food and resources. Nomadic groups might pillage caravans and vulnerable, unwalled villages and hamlets for survival or even sport. In the ANE, springtime was "the time when kings go out to battle" (2 Samuel 11:1), after crops were planted and houses and buildings were refurbished from winter rain damage. After all, your farmers and workmen were also your soldiers!

BATTLE TACTICS—In the time of the Hebrew patriarchs—the MBA—the technologies of siege warfare had become enough of a threat to require a shift in defensive architecture. The use of siege towers and offensive tactics like sapping (tunneling under walls) led to an effective "cure": massive earthen ramparts from 50 to 100 feet thick at their base, with a 25- to 40-degree facing slope (called glacis) (see *Figure 2.38*). With a city thus fortified, it could take months to get the population within to succumb to starvation. A well-watered and stocked city might even succeed in outlasting an invading army. But allowing an army to camp on your doorstep was not always the best approach. Often, cities would link up with regional allies in order to attack a large military threat at a distance, in open battle. Such was the Cities of the Kikkar engagement against the army of Kedorlaomer (Genesis 14).

WEAPONRY—Weapons during the MBA were the product of a long history of development (see *Figure 2.39*). The first "mass produced" weapon in the BA arsenal was the war club, or mace, used mainly for denting skulls. The answer to this was a helmet of leather and copper or bronze. In order to puncture helmets, a small, slender battle axe was introduced. The fenestrated (epsilon) axe and related duckbill axe were the mainstays of close combat. Assorted bronze blades and points were

Figure 2.35—Pagan 'personal' shrines (photos: Alexander Schick, David E. Graves)

used on daggers, spears, and lances (pikes). The longer sword was yet to appear, even though Moses used the idiom from his day, "with the sword," in Genesis 34:26. Surprisingly, the most common weapon of all was the sling and sling-stone. It was accurate, particularly at short range (10 to 30 yards), as well as lethal and cheap.

DEFENSIVE GEAR—Archaeological evidence exists for MBA helmets, plate armor, leggings, and shields (see *Figure 2.40*). However, using a complete set of defensive armor was not as common as we might think. It seems that flexibility and mobility were preferred by Egyptian and Levantine armies who wore minimal armor, in comparison to Mesopotamian forces, whose soldiers chose to go with heavier armor.

Figure 2.36—Dolmens in the Hammam Megalithic Field; they were not tombs, but monuments memorializing ancestors (photos: Michael Luddeni, courtesy of Tall el-Hammam Excavation Project)

BREAKOUT 2.09

ORIGINS OF YAHWEH WORSHIP

The daily practice of Israelite religion developed mainly in Canaan (the Promised Land) during the many centuries between the eighteenth and sixth centuries BC. The revelation of the Mosaic Law in the fourteenth century BC was one thing. The adoption of Mosaic monotheism by the average Israelite was quite another. We must not think that the earlier versions of Yahwism were the same as the ultimate form that emerged during the Babylonian captivity of Judah during the sixth century BC (see *Timeline*).

In Canaan, in Ugaritic literature, El was the head of the pantheon of the gods. The term *El* probably means "mighty" and was used in the Levant (Canaan) by several cultures (including the Hittites) at least by the MBA. It was also the generic term meaning "deity"—singular *el*; plural *elohim*. Every religion surrounding Abraham and later Israel was animistic and polytheistic, and depictions of gods (*elohim*) were usually that of powerful humans or physical elements like rivers, oceans, earth, or celestial bodies (animism). Joshua 24:2 makes it clear that Abram's family was polytheistic. Abra[ha]m, however, was directed to focus on Yahweh.

Yahweh said to Abram, "I am the God [*Elohim*] who called you out of Ur" (Genesis 15:7; author's paraphrase). From this familial connection to Yahweh the family emerged out of Egypt as a people who eventually established a nation-state. Yahweh demanded singular worship, which was *unique for the time and culture*. Yahweh, as the recognizable God of the Old Testament, gradually became more known through a process of progressive revelation.

Unlike other national deities of the ANE, Yahweh was self-identified, without need, and declared Himself sovereign over all of reality (Psalm 90:2), not merely over the family of Abraham, his offspring, and later the nation of Israel. The name *YHWH* (the tetragrammaton revealed to Moses and defined as "I AM WHO I AM" Exodus 3:14) derives from the Semitic verb of being. He is the "self-existent" One. Yahweh, who brought Abram out of Ur and would take his descendants out of Egypt, was/is the one true God (Psalm 115).

By Genesis 4, Yahweh Elohim had already instituted a system of worship and required Cain and Abel to bring the first fruits of their labors as an offering to him. Sometime between Cain and Abel and Noah, God further required not only an offering, but the building of an altar. Genesis 8:20 records that the first task Noah carried out upon disembarking from the ark was to build an altar and offer burnt sacrifices to the Lord.

The altar, early on, became a symbol of Yahweh worship. The altar allowed humans to approach God and offer sacrifices for sins, and it gave Yahweh a place to commune with humans. This was very similar to the way other ancient deities were worshipped, and early altars were usually constructed of natural stone. Altars to Yahweh continued to be built throughout the Patriarchal Age. There are numerous references in Genesis to Abraham, as well as Jacob, worshipping Yahweh by sacrificing burnt offerings upon altars.

Exodus records Moses building altars for the worship of Yahweh. In Exodus 20:24-26 God instructed Moses about how he wanted his altar constructed. In Leviticus 1 Yahweh gave instructions to Aaron and the Levitical priests about how to worship him, with specific guidelines about how to build an altar and the types of sacrifices to be offered upon it.

Worship altars and their accompanying sacrifices, whether Yahwistic or pagan in nature, were sacred meeting places that allowed for interaction between the human and the divine.

B. Maggard, S. Collins

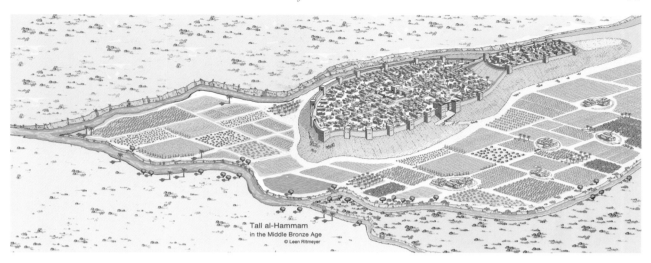

Figure 2.37—Agricultural fields, Middle Bronze Age, Sodom; large cities required large quantities of food (drawing: Leen Ritmeyer, courtesy of Tall el-Hammam Excavation Project)

INDUSTRIES AND OBJECTS

AGRICULTURE—Agriculture was the mainstay of every ANE hamlet, village, town, city, kingdom, and empire. In the Levant, staple crops were various kinds of wheat, barley, millet, and emmer (also known as wheat). Barley was, by far, the go-to crop during the MBA (see *Figure 2.41*). Other crops included sesame, flax (for linen), lentils, and chickpeas. Figs, pomegranates, apples, almonds, dates, and pistachios were specialty crops. Honey production was perhaps from wild hives, but the early domestication of bees is not out of the question. For the south Levant, two agricultural commodities were widely prized as the finest in the ANE: olive oil and wine. The olive tree was indigenous to Canaan (in time, transplanted all over the Mediterranean world), and the climate was perfect for growing a variety of wine grapes. Had it not been for the abundant olive oil and wine production, the kings of Egypt and Mesopotamia probably would have paid little attention to Canaan.

HERDING—While Canaanite city-states likely had some cattle grazing on their lands, such herds were maintained on a small scale compared to Egypt, for which cattle were a priority. The south Levant was sheep and goat country. Sheep and goats were tended by nomadic Bedouin (Shasu) herdsmen in every corner of Canaan; they moved their flocks seasonally to pasturage and water (see *Figure 2.42*). This created the millennia-enduring symbiotic relationship between the Levant's nomadic herders (symbolized by milk) and sedentary farmers (symbolized by honey). Shepherds provided themselves and the sedentary folk with milk, yogurt, cheese, meat, sheep and goat skins, wool and goat hair, and bone ("poor man's ivory"). There

Figure 2.38—Upper City rampart constructed of mud bricks, Middle Bronze Age, Sodom (photo: John Witte Moore, courtesy of Tall el-Hammam Excavation Project)

Figure 2.39—ANE bronze weapons of the Middle Bronze Age: spear points (A), ceremonial axe (B), "epsilon" axe (C), duckbill axe (D), fenestrated axe (E), slim battle axe (F) (photos: Daniel Galassini, Steven Collins, courtesy of Museum of Archaeology, Trinity Southwest University and Bible Lands Museum, Jerusalem)

Figure 2.40—Armored tunic, Middle Bronze Age; sewn into this wool cloth are plates of bronze, the corrosion of which helped preserve the fabric (photo: Michael Luddeni, courtesy of Tall el-Hammam Excavation Project)

Figure 2.41—Jars of barley, Middle Bronze Age (photo: Daniel Galassini, courtesy of Tall el-Hammam Excavation Project)

Figure 2.42—Taking flocks to pasture (photo: Michael Luddeni)

was also a related and profitable sideline to herding sheep and goats. Each animal was a masticular-gastrointestinal "machine" for producing organic fuel pellets—sheep and goat droppings! Because dried dung was a primary fuel for cooking stoves, and because each adult animal could eat from 4 to 6 pounds of *dry* forage per day (20+ pounds fresh forage), a modest flock of 200 sheep and goats could make more than 1,000 pounds of *dry* fuel pellets each day. That's at least 180 *tons* of dry fuel pellets per year from a single flock! The sheep and goat pellets were probably collected by Bedouin children, then sold in the city/town markets.

FISHING—In Canaan, fishing industries flourished along the Mediterranean coast, providing a valuable protein source to the diet of people who lived in cities like Ashkelon, Ashdod, and Jaffa (see *Map 2.02*). Fish oil was also an important commodity and, in coastal areas, was often used as a lamp fuel instead of the standard olive oil. The fishing industry of Lake Kinnereth was modest and probably did not produce surplus beyond the need of local lakeshore cities and towns like Zer/Zed (later Bethsaida).

KITCHENS AND COOKING—For three millennia, the focal point of the Levantine kitchen was the handmade holemouth cooking pot. The hearth consisted of a ring of cobble-sized stones 2 to 4 feet in diameter. The 18- to 24-inch-tall cooking pot sat on its base within the hearth, and a fire was built around it so that the flames and heat were directly against the vessel. The holemouth jar's wide shoulders and narrower flat base created a pear shape that helped in heating it (see *Figure 2.43*). But this old, traditional way of cooking was dying out by the time of Abraham. The fast potter's wheel brought in a new class of vessels: rounded-bottomed cooking pots, with or without handles (see *Figure 2.44*). This advancement paralleled the development of the beehive oven (archaeologically, *tabun* or *tannur*). The new oven was built of clay on a ring of stones, had an arch-shaped opening, and a 4- to 6-inch hole at the top, where a cooking pot would sit. This

Figure 2.43—Holemouth jar, a cooking standard in the millennia before Abraham (photo: Michael Luddeni, courtesy of Tall el-Hammam Excavation Project)

design enclosed the cooking coals, allowing bread to be baked inside on a ceramic tray.

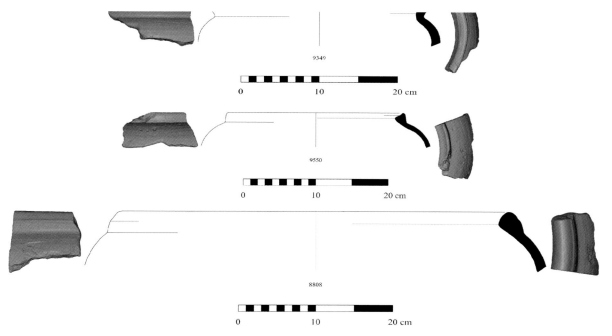

Figure 2.44—Cooking pots, Middle Bronze Age; 3-D scans of sherds and resultant drawings (photo: courtesy of Tall el-Hammam Excavation Project).

ECONOMICS, MONEY, AND WEALTH

The accumulation of personal wealth traces back to the earliest known civilizations. In the ANE, the most valuable possessions were land and livestock—fertilized, irrigated, arable land on which herds of goats and flocks of sheep could thrive. Land was typically held by families or by the king, who granted the land as a gift to secure the loyalty of important people, especially senior government officials.

As the land produced crops or supported herds and flocks, the landowner could exchange these to acquire goods, services, and other objects of value, such as tin, copper, silver, barley, and even art. Economies grew from these exchanges as craftsmen, traders, and landowners became more successful. Alluvial valley locations with few natural resources, such as Mesopotamia (see *Map 1.06*), could acquire materials like metals and varieties of stone by trading agricultural surpluses with peoples in mountainous regions where such natural resources were readily available but arable land was scarce. Thus, trade and trade routes were born.

As wealth increased and economies grew, caravans became an integral part of the system of trade. Importing and exporting allowed the produce and hard goods of one region to be enjoyed by another.

Spices, dyes, and perfumes from the Far East made their way into Mesopotamian societies through large caravans, while dates, olives, olive oil, wool, and precious metals made their way east. Trade caravans carried large amounts of bitumen and cedar, which were highly valued as construction materials.

Bracelet ending in a gold lion's head, Anatolia, Middle Bronze Age (photo: James Barber; courtesy of Bible Lands Museum, Jerusalem)

Accompanying the caravans were herds of goats and flocks of sheep, as well as donkeys for working in the copper mines. Caravans also transported lapis lazuli and other jewelry items such as gold bracelets and earrings, as well as cosmetic oils and perfumes. From the Aegean region, ships brought pottery and objects of art and returned with cargos of olive oil, sesame oil, spices, and wool.

Exchange rates for products and services were established early on as trading "currency." For centuries, currencies were meted out by means of weights and measures. Barley, copper, tin, and silver were used in measured and weighted amounts. One shekel of silver equaled 8 grams, a mina of silver equaled 60 shekels, and 1 ephah was the equivalent of a bushel. Coinage did not become a currency until the sixth century BC (first in west Anatolia) and was adopted gradually because most societies generally preferred silver and weights and measures as currency rather than hard coins and other metals.

Many references to ANE economies, the accumulation of wealth, and exchange-rated currencies can be found in the Bible. In Genesis 37:28, we read that Joseph was sold for 20 shekels of silver. Ruth 2:17-18 describes how Ruth gleaned, gathered, and threshed an ephah of grain. Genesis 12:16, 13:2, and 20:14-16 provide insight into the great wealth accumulated by Abraham and the use of wealth by kings to earn favor with important individuals.

The New Testament describes how Judas betrayed Jesus for 30 pieces of silver (shekels), and in his parables, Jesus mentioned the talent, a unit of measurement for weighing precious metals, as well as the widow's mite, a small bronze lepton coin worth half the value of the quadran, a bronze Roman coin of low value.

W. Husted, S. Collins

A Middle Bronze Age Recipe: Mersu
(see *Figure 2.45*)

*(This recipe dates to MBA2;
adapted from the Mari tablets, Syria.)*

Ingredients (makes about 20 pieces)
½ pound (8 oz.) dried, pitted dates, finely chopped
½ cup water
¼ cup (1 oz.) pistachios, shelled and finely chopped
3 cups wheat flour (use barley flour for authenticity)
1 cup chilled butter, cut into small cubes
5 tablespoons milk

Instructions

Put the dates in a small pan and add water. Cook over medium heat until a thick paste forms, stirring often (about 5 to 8 minutes). Mix in pistachios. Set this aside to cool. Mix flour and butter together until it resembles coarse crumbs. Add milk slowly until dough holds together. Cover dough and cool it down (no refrigerators in the MBA, but go ahead!) for 30 minutes. Break off a 2-inch piece of dough and roll it in your hands until it becomes pliable. Shape into a ball. Make an indentation in the ball's center using your thumb and pinch the sides between your thumb and index finger to enlarge the indentation. Take some of the cooled date paste and fill it three-quarters full. Pinch the edges of the dough together and roll into a ball. Place on a baking sheet. Repeat with the rest of the dough and bake for 25 minutes in an oven preheated to 325° F.

CONSTRUCTION—The building trade was important—indeed critical—across the entire ANE. The nature of the construction materials, stone and mudbricks, created not only the industries of stone gathering, mining, and cutting, but also the intensive production of mudbricks (see *Figure 2.46*). Structures built entirely of stone were rare. Ninety-five percent of every building project consisted of mudbricks. Thus, mudbrick manufacturing was one of the primary industries for every civilization at every level—from the simplest farmhouse to the most elaborate palace. Wall surfaces of mudbrick and stone were always covered in thick coats of mud-sand

Figure 2.45—Mersu—Bronze Age sweets (photo: Wes Husted)

plaster (sometimes with lime added). These kinds of buildings required continuous maintenance, especially during and after the winter rainy season. But thick mudbrick walls—18 to 24 inches for houses, and 3 to 10 feet or more for palaces and temples—kept building interiors warm in the winter and cool in the summer.

POTTERY—Although potters in earlier times pursued their profession with skill and artistry, the invention of the fast potter's wheel toward the end of the third millennium BC changed things dramatically. With the fast wheel, MBA potters attained greater levels of delicacy and aesthetics, along with increased technical precision (see *Figure 2.47*). The fast wheel also allowed the development of ceramics factories that could produce great numbers of vessels with considerable uniformity. The potter's wheel allowed more imaginative rims and bases to be made and permitted a decrease in the overall thickness of vessel walls. Ring and disc bases became common. Rims often took on elaborate "rolled" and "stepped" profiles. Sharp profile curves in vessel walls, called carinations, gave a new flair to the bowls, chalices, and goblets of the period. Burnished dark red slip became a favorite decorative treatment, while incising and geometric painting continued their popular appeal. Pinched-bowl oil lamps, using from 1 to 4 wicks, proliferated, as did wide-mouth kraters and large storage jars (with or without handles), often painted with wavy and straight lines around the neck and shoulders.

METALLURGY—There was very little, if any, true bronze during the so-called EBA (the Hebrew word for copper and bronze is the same). It was in the MBA that

Breakout 2.11

Weights and Measures

Since the beginning of humanity there have always been people who take advantage of the weak and naive. Human nature is oftentimes not pretty, fair, equitable, or just. The Bible records in 1 Timothy 6:10 that "the love of money is a root of all kinds of evils." Yahweh knew that money was a great tempter and that oftentimes humans would resort to dishonorable, unscrupulous, and even evil means to gain it. That is why, in the Mosaic Law, he warned his people over and over again to have honest weights and measures, as in Leviticus 19:36: "You shall have just balances, just weights, a just ephah, and a just hin: I am the LORD your God, who brought you out of the land of Egypt." In Proverbs 11:1 we read, "A false balance is an abomination to

Hematite balance-scale weight, Middle Bronze Age (photo: Daniel Galassini, courtesy of Museum of Archaeology, Trinity Southwest University)

the LORD, but a just weight is his delight," and Micah 6:11 says, "Shall I acquit someone with dishonest scales, with a bag of false weights?"

Below is a short list of weights and measures used in Israel under the Law of Moses and into the New

Testament period. Yahweh has always been a God of order, integrity, and fairness, and he expected his people to be too. Understanding biblical weights and measures is an important part to the understanding of the Hebrew Bible.

Weights

Hebrew	English Translation	Equivalence	US Measures
kikkar	talent	60 minas	75 pounds
maneh	mina	50 shekels	571 grams
sheqel	shekel	2 bekas	11 grams
pim	pim	0.67 shekels	8 grams
beqa	beka, half a shekel	10 gerahs	6 grams

Dry Measures

Hebrew	English Translation	Equivalence	US Measures
homer	homer	2 lethechs	6.5 bushels
ephah	ephah, measure	3 seahs	21 quarts
omer	omer	2 kabs	2 quarts
bat	bath	6 hins	6 gallons

Length Measures

Hebrew/Greek	English Translation	Equivalence	US Measures
topah, tepah (H)	handbreadth	4 fingers	3 inches
etsba (H)	finger	¼ handbreadth	0.75 inches
zeret (H)	span	3 handbreadths	9 inches
amah (H)	cubit	2 spans	18 inches
orguia (G)	fathom	4 cubits	6 feet
stadion (G)	stadion/furlong	1/8 Roman mile	606 feet
milion (G)	Roman mile	8 stadia	4,854 feet
mahalak (H)	day's journey		20 miles
sabbatou hodos (G)	Sabbath day's journey	6 stadia	3,637 feet

Note: Measurements have been rounded to the nearest whole number.

The Human Body

The *cubit*, mentioned more than 100 times in the Bible, was the length of a man's forearm from the elbow to the tip of the middle finger, or approximately 18 inches. Not everyone's arm was the same length, so over time there developed a regular cubit of about 18 inches and a royal cubit of 20 to 21 inches in length.

Other body parts were also used for measuring purposes, including *fingers*, *palms*, and *spans* from the tip of the little finger to the tip of the extended thumb. The people of the Bible used their fingers, hands, and arms to determine measurements.

Donkeys and Daughters

The *homer*, the Ugaritic word for donkey, referred to the normal load placed on a donkey. Other units of measurement for solids and liquids were the *ephah* (one-tenth of a homer), a *hin* (one-sixth of an ephah), the *omer* (one-tenth of an ephah), and the *seah* (one-third of an ephah).

For wet measurements, water pots called *baths* (the biblical word for daughter, *bat*) were used. A *bath* was equal to an *ephah*. Some believe this measure came from the size of the pot that daughters in a household could carry. The smallest unit was the *log* (one-seventy-second of an *ephah*).

Larger Measures of Area

Taken from the word *yoke*, an *acre* was the amount of land a yoke of oxen could plow in a given amount of time. Another method was to describe an area in terms of how much seed it took to sow it.

Weights for Precious Metals

The balance scale, usually made of bronze, was used primarily to measure precious materials such as gold and silver. To "weigh" comes from the word *shekel*, which was the basic unit of weight. The *gerah*, a word for grain, was the smallest unit of weight, or one-twentieth part of a shekel. A *beka* was equivalent to one-half shekel. One *mina* was equivalent to 50 shekels. A *talent* (*kikkar*) was the largest weight and equal to 3,000 shekels.

C. Morgan

one or more metallurgical geniuses figured out that adding 10 to 15 percent tin to copper made a much stronger metal and could take a sharper and more durable edge. MBA peoples continued to use copper for everyday items, while bronze production was favored for military applications. Most of the copper in Canaan came from the mines of Wadi Faynan (see *Map 2.05*).

Tool Making—The old anthropology adages "necessity is the mother of invention" and "form follows function" combine in the BA to produce a vast array of tools and implements that are fundamentally the same throughout history. A shovel looks like a shovel, a rake looks like a rake, an axe looks like an axe, an awl looks like an awl, a spoon looks like a spoon, a

Figure 2.46—New mudbricks laid over in situ MBA mudbricks (photo: Daniel Galassini, courtesy of Tall el-Hammam Excavation Project)

comb looks like a comb, and a safety (toggle) pin looks like a toggle pin! Artisans mass-produced the tools and implements of daily life and sold them at marketplaces usually located at or near the main city gates.

TEXTILES—Sheep wool and flax fibers (linen) were the main threads of the ANE (see *Figures 2.40, 2.48*). Generally, wool was warmer in winter and linen was cooler in summer. In their hot climate, Egyptians preferred linen almost exclusively. The variable seasons of the Levant saw both wool and linen in widespread use—in Mesopotamia too. In the Levant, textile production was heaviest in the north (around Ebla in Syria; see *Map 2.01*) and in the south Jordan Valley (the Sodom city-state).

COMMERCE AND CARAVANS—For the dynamic economies of Mesopotamia and Egypt, moving surplus goods and commodities to markets in often-faraway places was critical. Thus, commercial sea lanes and overland routes were the veins and arteries of the Fertile Crescent (see *Maps 1.02, 2.01*). The Levant (Syria and Canaan) contained the crossroads connecting all the major kingdoms and empires with each other and with the larger Mediterranean world (MBA Canaanite storage jars and juglets were even found at Minoan Akrotiri on the Island of Santorini). Caravans mostly used donkeys, but camels were also employed in limited numbers (statements that camels were not domesticated until the IA are simply untrue). The caravan trade was operated by dedicated nomadic groups, which could also include the Habiru/'Apiru/Hebrews.

Figure 2.47—Pottery of the Middle Bronze Age (photos: Daniel Galassini, courtesy of Museum of Archaeology, Trinity Southwest University)

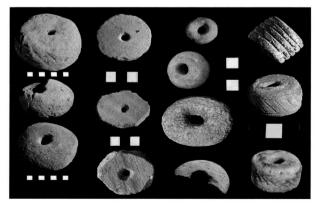

Figure 2.48—Tools for textile production: spindle whorls, loom weights (photos: Michael Luddeni, courtesy of Tall el-Hammam Excavation Project)

BREAKOUT 2.12

THE INSTITUTION OF SLAVERY

We know that slaves were an integral part of the economies of every major culture and society in the ancient world, but we often wonder why. How did people become enslaved? The most common way this happened was when prisoners of war were sold into slavery. Other ways include being born into the household of a slave, or being convicted of a crime, including indebtedness. The concept of slavery, especially in Mesopotamia, may also have included the necessity of working for another (in essence, being an employee) for the sake of providing for one's self and family. Not being a person of independent means identified you as a brand of slave.

Slaves served in varying capacities from the earliest civilizations in Egypt, Sumer, and Mesopotamia. Large-scale building projects and the development of arable land required farmhands, laborers, masons, brick makers, and foremen—work done primarily by slaves. In homes and cities, slaves served in domestic capacities as well as in administrative and civic positions.

Palace complexes and temples required slaves who could till the land and grow the crops that supplied their needs. Slaves were also employed as skilled craftsmen who built and maintained temple facilities.

The ancient Egyptian, Greek, and Roman Empires utilized vast numbers of slaves in their major building projects. These projects, in turn, drove the need for larger mining operations, which also required vast numbers of slaves. By the time of the Christian era, the average number of slaves in the Roman Empire equaled three to five slaves for every free citizen, depending on the region. Other empires, however, had fewer slaves, such as the Persian Empire, whose rulers found it more economical to hire people to do the work.

In the Old Testament, there are numerous examples of slaves as servants. Genesis 14:14 records Abraham's ability to field an army of 318 men from his many servants, and in Genesis 39:1-4, Joseph's role as a slave/servant of Potiphar, an Egyptian official, is documented.

The Old Testament cites specific laws concerning slaves owned by Israelites, including their humane treatment, the process for freeing slaves, the redemption of slaves by a relative, and the penalties for not following these laws (Exodus 21:1-11; Leviticus 25:39-55; Deuteronomy 15:12-18).

Male slaves of Israelites were to be freed by their owners after six years of work or at the next jubilee year, and given livestock, grain, and wine as a parting gift. Despite this commandment, Israelite slaves were often enslaved longer than six years. As punishment, God gave the kingdom of Judah into the hand of its enemies, the Babylonians, as described in Jeremiah 34:8-22.

During Roman times, slaves who were skilled craftsmen and had a means of earning an income could purchase their freedom, which led to a large class of citizens known as *freedmen* in the Christian era. Other slaves could be freed by their owners or purchased by a relative.

Early Christians saw themselves as slaves and servants of Christ and did not condemn slavery—probably because it was an entrenched part of society in the ANE. Paul and Peter urged the humane treatment of slaves and encouraged believers in the early church to treat slaves fairly, but slave trading was condemned by Timothy (1 Timothy 1:10).

W. Husted, S. Collins

CHAPTER 3

THE WORLD OF MOSES AND JOSHUA

WELCOME TO THE LATE BRONZE AGE 1 AND 2A (1550–1300 BC)

The transition from the Middle to the Late Bronze Age (LBA; see *Timeline*) is fuzzy at best, both in terms of dating and cultural elements. And there is the additional issue of the time frame of the Israelite conquest of Canaan—namely, did Joshua's exploits occur toward the end of the LBA (c. 1250 BC, as in the movie *The Ten Commandments*) or much earlier?

Archaeological evidence militates against a mid-thirteenth century BC date for the Israelite exodus and conquest (see *Breakouts 3.04, 3.05*), as does the biblical record, which seems to place these events in the late fifteenth to fourteenth century BC. Archaeologically speaking, the end of LBA1 (fifteenth century BC) does not very well support such a sequence of events. A few scholars see problems with the traditional MBA/LBA chronology and have even suggested moving the end of the MBA down to 1400 BC, which, for them, synchronizes the Israelite conquest with the widespread collapse of the MBA city-states. However, overwhelming archaeological evidence from excavations in the south Jordan Valley, particularly at Tall el-Hammam, makes this view absolutely impossible.

It is more likely that the period of the Israelite conquest of Canaan corresponds with the beginning of the Egyptian Amarna period of the fourteenth century BC. Indeed, the collapse of Egypt's powerful Eighteenth Dynasty was, in all likelihood, caused by the exodus events (see *Breakouts 3.04, 3.05*). All the cities listed in the biblical conquest narratives were disrupted or destroyed at that time. All—so it seems to many scholars—except one: the town of Ai. The traditional site of Ai, Et-Tell, was not occupied during the MBA or LBA, causing many critics to dismiss Joshua's conquest of Ai as an etiological legend. However, the recently identified and excavated site of Khirbet el-Maqatir, less than one mile away, has both MBA and LBA strata, making it a convincing candidate for the "garrison" of Ai destroyed by Joshua (see *Map 3.06*).

The LBA reveals a remarkable and systematic absence of occupation on the east Kikkar of the Jordan northeast of the Dead Sea (see *Map 2.04*), the once-well-watered Land of the Kikkar (Genesis 19:28) formerly occupied by the infamous Sodom and Gomorrah and the cities of the Jordan Plain ("Plain" is Hebrew *Kikkar*, which means "Disk"; see *Breakout 2.07*). This area—which had a rich and unbroken occupational history from the Chalcolithic Period through the Middle Bronze Age—was obliterated toward the end of the MBA (Abraham's time), followed by a conspicuous absence of cities, towns, and villages for the next seven centuries. This 700-year LBA gap on the east Kikkar marks the aftermath of the destruction of the Cities of the Kikkar in Genesis 19. When Moses and the Israelites arrived in this same location centuries later—the Plains of Moab—it was both biblically and archaeologically unoccupied and described as the wasteland below Pisgah (see Numbers 21:20 NIV).

The LBA is also known for the arrival of a major wave of Sea Peoples. Biblically and archaeologically, the most prominent of these were the Philistines. Philistine origins trace to the Aegean region (see *Breakout 4.04*). Having abandoned their Aegean—Mycenaean and Minoan—homelands, the Philistines (generic Old Testament term for peoples of Aegean origin)

BREAKOUT 3.01

HOW LONG WAS ISRAEL'S SOJOURN IN EGYPT?

It would seem that Exodus 12:40 provides an answer to this question: "The length of time the Israelites lived in Egypt was 430 years" (NIV). Whatever the nature of this span—literal or formulaic (see *Breakout 2.04*)—it represents the time span from Jacob's entrance into Egypt (Genesis 47:7) until the time of the exodus. But the apostle Paul seems to throw a monkey wrench into our understanding of the subject by stating, "Now the promises were made to Abraham...the law...came 430 years afterward" (Galatians 3:16-17). Paul clearly says that 430 years passed from the giving of promises to Abraham until the exodus, after which the law was delivered—from Abraham to the exodus, not Jacob to the exodus! While at first this seems to be a glaring contradiction, the discrepancy is easily resolved by the convergence of five facts.

First, the traditional reading of Exodus 12:40 is from the *Masoretic Text* (MT) as represented by its primary exemplar, the Leningrad Codex. The MT dates from around the tenth century AD and is the Hebrew text that stands behind most English Bible translations.

Second, Paul's Bible was the Greek translation of the Old Testament, the *Septuagint* (designated by the Roman numerals LXX, meaning "seventy"), which originated in the third century BC. In it, Exodus 12:40 reads, "Now the length of time the Israelite people lived in Canaan and in Egypt was 430 years" (some manuscripts reverse this order to "Egypt and Canaan"; the inclusion of Canaan with Egypt is also found in the *Samaritan Pentateuch*).

Third, when a reading in the MT (represented in the current Hebrew Bible) differs from the LXX (Paul's Bible), the reading of the Dead Sea Scrolls (DSS; second to first centuries BC) almost always sides with the LXX against the MT. In other words, the earliest surviving versions of Exodus 12:40—the third century BC LXX and the second to first centuries BC DSS—have an Israelite Egyptian sojourn of 430 years, spanning a period from the time of Abraham until the exodus. It is only the tenth century AD MT that has Egypt without Canaan.

Fourth, the objection of those who might say, "But Abraham wasn't an Israelite!" is solved in the ancient Near Eastern concept of descendants being "in the loins of" an ancestor, which is also common in the Bible. Thus, Abraham, Isaac, Jacob, and Jacob's sons were all collectively sojourners in Canaan, then in Egypt.

Fifth, Josephus understood the "loins" concept, and is adamant on the issue: "[The Israelites] left Egypt...four hundred and thirty years after our forefather Abraham came into Canaan, but two hundred and fifteen years only after Jacob removed into Egypt" (see *Breakout 9.17*).

That the Israelites were in bondage in Egypt for about two centuries under an administration hostile to Semitic Asiatics fits perfectly with the known history of Egypt and the ANE (see *Breakouts 3.04, 3.05*), as well as the overall witness of Scripture.

S. Collins

took up permanent residence in the Southern Levantine coastal areas, often serving as a sophisticated nemesis of the Israelites.

The LBA is generally known as a time of Egyptian domination over the land of Canaan (see *Map 3.02*). Because of the Egyptian yoke of exploitation, the city-states (see *Map 3.04*), as well as other populations of the Levant (Canaan), suffered cultural deterioration during most of this period. Nevertheless, the Canaanites played a significant role on the international cultural stage during the LBA.

After the expulsion of the Hyksos in the

mid-sixteenth century BC (see *Map 3.01*), Pharaoh Ahmose succeeded in reuniting Egypt and forging it into a formidable military and economic power (see *Breakout 3.05* and *Map 3.02*). This included renewed interest in the strategic benefits and products of Canaan (see *Map 1.06*). In the mid-fifteenth century BC, Tuthmosis III consolidated Egyptian control over most of the Levant by defeating 119 (by his count)

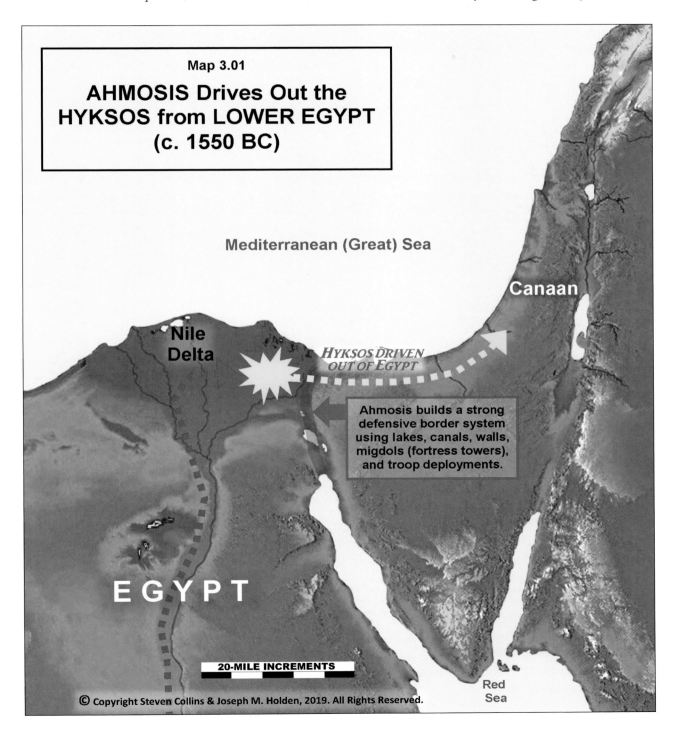

Map 3.01

AHMOSIS Drives Out the HYKSOS from LOWER EGYPT (c. 1550 BC)

Mediterranean (Great) Sea

Canaan

Nile Delta

HYKSOS DRIVEN OUT OF EGYPT

Ahmosis builds a strong defensive border system using lakes, canals, walls, migdols (fortress towers), and troop deployments.

EGYPT

20-MILE INCREMENTS

Red Sea

Canaanite city-state kings at the battle of Megiddo and in subsequent military campaigns.

During the fourteenth century BC, weakness and turmoil in Egypt diminished its ability to control the Levantine city-states. More than 380 clay tablets—written primarily in Akkadian, using cuneiform script—found in the palace of Amenhotep IV (Akhenaten; see *Timeline*) attest to this instability. More than 150 of the tablets are correspondence from Canaanite city-state kings requesting military assistance from Egypt in the face of attacks by the marauding 'Apiru (or Habiru).

The thirteenth century BC saw waves of cultural change in the land of Canaan, brought about by the arrival of the Sea Peoples and the rise of the Israelites as a force to be reckoned with.

GEOGRAPHY

Biblically, there are four ancient superpowers that come into play when setting a historical context for Moses and Joshua (see *Map 3.02*): Egypt, Mittani (north Mesopotamia), Hatti (Anatolia), and Assyria (middle Mesopotamia). But, you might ask, where are Mittani, Hatti, and Assyria mentioned in the stories of the Israelite exodus and conquest of Canaan? They aren't. But they are still important in understanding how the ANE and biblical histories link up during the LBA. As you will see, being familiar with all the ANE players of the time is necessary for understanding the backstories of the exodus and conquest.

Of course, Egypt was the central player during this period (see *Timeline* and *Map 3.02*), especially for the exodus narratives (see *Breakouts 3.04, 3.05*). Particularly, the Eighteenth Dynasty is in focus. Its first king, Ahmosis, ended two centuries of Semitic Asiatic control of Lower Egypt by forcing the Hyksos from the Nile Delta region (see *Map 3.01*). With Upper and Lower Egypt unified once again under native Egyptian control, the "power" pharaohs of the Eighteenth Dynasty—Ahmosis, Amenhotep I, Tuthmosis I, Tuthmosis II, Hatshepsut, Tuthmosis III, Amenhotep II, Tuthmosis IV—brought Egypt into its Empire period.

The times of these kings has become known as the era of the Egyptian domination of the Levant. Egypt extended its eastern border up to the Euphrates River (see *Map 3.02*).

The next important regional power during this period was Mittani (also Mitanni, but Mittani is the better spelling; see *Timeline* and *Map 3.02*). The Mittani kingdom occupied northern Mesopotamia (Aram), and consisted of a Hurrian (Indo-European) ruling class dominating an Akkadian-speaking Semitic populace. The Egyptians called Mittani *Nahrima* (Hebrew, *Naharaim* is north Mesopotamia). They also controlled a corridor running west from the Euphrates River to the north Levantine coast, giving them access to the lucrative Mediterranean commerce. Kings Artatama I and Tushratta were particularly important players during the careers of Moses and Joshua.

The Indo-European Hittites of the central Anatolian Plateau (see *Maps 3.02, 3.03*) were also an important factor in Moses and Joshua's world. Even though they receive only an "honorable mention" in the Pentateuch as one of the major groups occupying the Promised Land (Genesis 15:18-21; Exodus 3:8; Joshua 3:10), how they got there and the regional role they played is central to understanding the exodus and conquest stories. Their land, nation, and eventual empire was called Hatti. Migrant families from the land of Hatti were clearly present in the north and south Levant from at least 2800 BC onward, as confirmed by both archaeology and the biblical text. But it was warrior-king Suppiluliuma I (or Suppiluliumas; see *Timeline*) who annexed the north Levant to the Hittite Empire in the aftermath of the exodus events, after which Egypt went into a tailspin (see *Breakout 3.05*).

Assyria was gaining power but remained a vassal-state of Mittani as long as Mittani's Hurrian royal house was bonded with Egypt via the Egypto-Mittanian alliance (see *Breakouts 3.04, 3.05* and *Map 3.02*). When Egypt, staggered by the devastating events of the exodus, abandoned its long-held Levantine territories (see *Map 3.03*), the Hittites crushed Mittani, releasing Assyria to rise as an international powerhouse in its own right (see *Breakout 3.05, Map 3.03,* and *Timeline*).

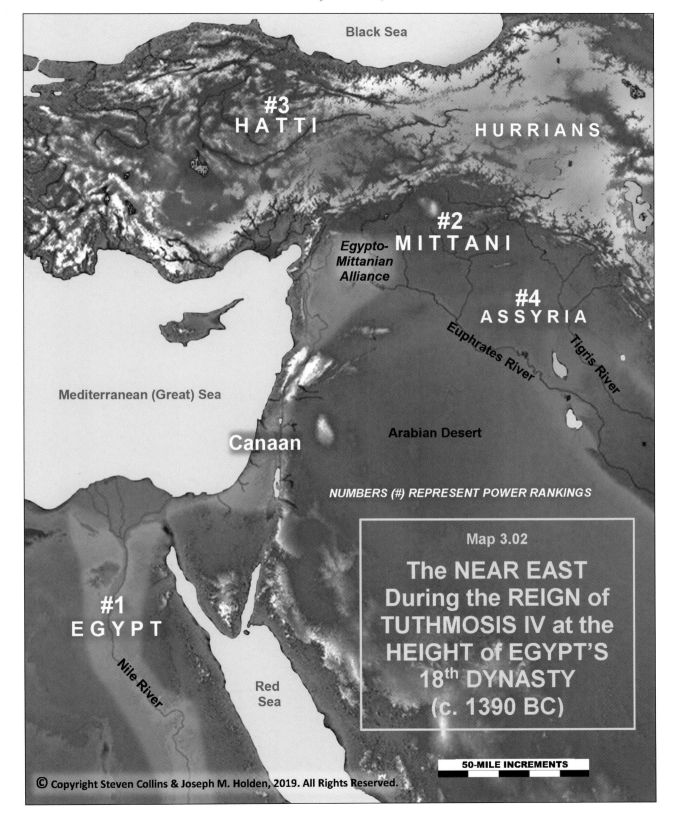

Black Sea

#3
HATTI

HURRIANS

#2
MITTANI

Egypto-Mittanian Alliance

#4
ASSYRIA

Euphrates River

Tigris River

Mediterranean (Great) Sea

Canaan

Arabian Desert

NUMBERS (#) REPRESENT POWER RANKINGS

Map 3.02

The NEAR EAST During the REIGN of TUTHMOSIS IV at the HEIGHT of EGYPT'S 18th DYNASTY (c. 1390 BC)

#1
EGYPT

Nile River

Red Sea

50-MILE INCREMENTS

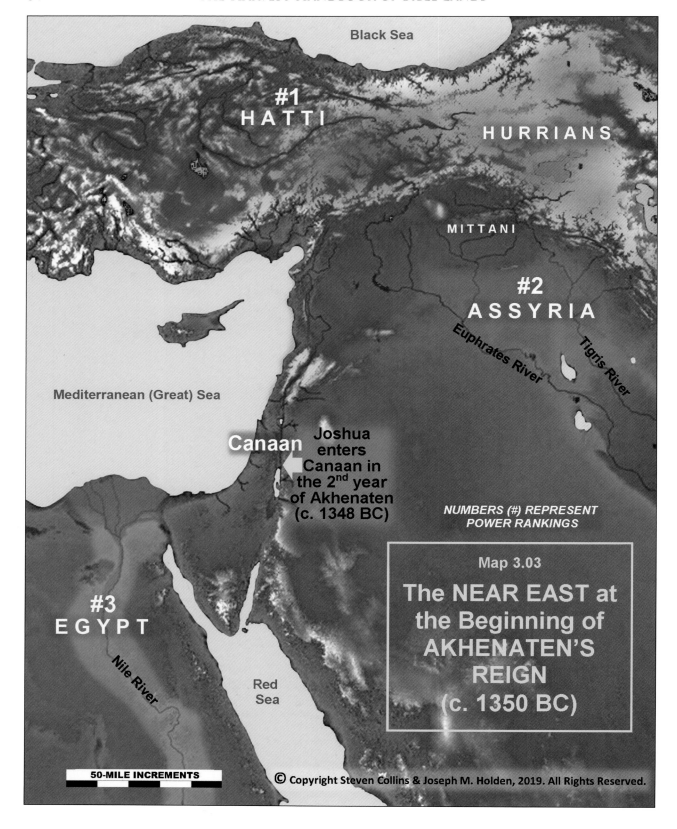

Black Sea

#1
H A T T I

H U R R I A N S

M I T T A N I

#2
A S S Y R I A

Euphrates River

Tigris River

Mediterranean (Great) Sea

Canaan

Joshua
enters
Canaan in
the 2nd year
of Akhenaten
(c. 1348 BC)

*NUMBERS (#) REPRESENT
POWER RANKINGS*

Map 3.03

**The NEAR EAST at
the Beginning of
AKHENATEN'S
REIGN
(c. 1350 BC)**

#3
E G Y P T

Nile River

Red
Sea

50-MILE INCREMENTS

BREAKOUT 3.02

MOSES'S ROYAL CAREER AND HITTITE CONNECTION

Current ANE scholarship recognizes that the Mosaic Law follows a pattern found in Hittite suzerainty treaties of the LBA. It is also known that elements of Israelite culture show more affinity to the Hittite sphere than, say, Egypt or Mesopotamia. On the surface, this seems to be a mystery not easily solved. However, with the exodus events placed into their proper historical context (see *Breakouts 3.04, 3.05*), connections and scenarios come into view and provide insights into possible links between Moses and the land of Hatti.

Egypt's mighty Eighteenth Dynasty (c. 1550–1320 BC) began with a "great house" (the meaning of *pharaoh*) who "did not know Joseph" (Exodus 1:8). In addition to observing an official policy reinforcing the hatred and enslavement of Asiatic Semitic peoples, including the Israelites, the mid-Eighteenth Dynasty pharaohs—Tuthmosis II, Hatshepsut, Tuthmosis III, Amenhotep II, and Tuthmosis IV—entertained the idea of treaty alliances with the two other powerhouses of the ANE at the time: Mittani of northern Mesopotamia and Hatti of Asia Minor (see *Map 3.02*).

Although Mittani's capital, Washukanni, and the bulk of its kingdom lay in northern Mesopotamia, Mittani also controlled a corridor westward to the Mediterranean coast and its lucrative maritime commerce. Hatti desperately wanted to control this same coastal corridor but was shut out by Mittani. During the reign of Tuthmosis I, Egypt began attempts to annex the entire Levant, declaring the Euphrates River as Egypt's new northern border. This didn't sit well with Mittani because it effectively interfered with its route to the Mediterranean coast. Egypt's encroachment also resulted in perennial military conflict between Mittani and Egypt. All the while, landlocked Hatti salivated at the thought of negotiating a treaty with Egypt that would give them, not Mittani, access to the Mediterranean trade routes. During this period, both Hatti and Mittani entered into negotiations with Egypt—a diplomatic "war" in which Egypt entertained both options, a century-long process that lasted until the reign of Tuthmosis IV.

At this point, the stage is set for a speculative exercise that reveals a logical connection between Moses and Hittite law and culture. Four points form the possible (probable?) link.

First, Moses was raised in Egypt's royal house as the son of one of pharaoh's daughters, likely during the second half of Tuthmosis III's reign (see *Breakout 3.04*). He spent his first 40 years (also symbolic of a generation) living as a member of the royal elite.

Second, royals got the cushy jobs in Egypt—high priests, high administrators, military commanders, ambassadors, and high-level diplomats.

Third, Moses's adult career played out during a time when Egyptian diplomats were negotiating with both Hatti and Mittani on potential treaties that would lead to a "brotherhood" alliance in which either the Mittanians or the Hittites (not both!) would, with Egypt's blessing as a treaty guarantor, allow goodwill access to the northern Mediterranean coast and its sea trade.

Fourth, in the ANE, it was typical for diplomats to spend years or even decades in a foreign capital working on behalf of their kingdom or empire. If Moses had spent his royal life as a high-level career diplomat—perhaps even an ambassador—working on draft documents for an Egypto-Hattian alliance, this would explain his familiarity with Hittite treaty structures, life, customs, and worldview.

Certainly, all the necessary elements existed during the midstretch of Egypt's Eighteenth Dynasty to explain how Moses could have come under the Hittite influences that colored his law code, as well as subsequent Israelite culture.

A historical footnote is in order. During his reign, Tuthmosis IV (c. 1401–1391; the Exodus Pharaoh; see *Breakouts 3.04, 3.05*) ended 100 years of Egyptian negotiations with Mittani and Hatti by enacting a treaty with King Artatama of Mittani. The ratification of the Egypto-Mittani alliance immediately made Hatti a sworn enemy of Egypt. After the death of Tuthmosis IV, during the reign of his son Amenhotep III, the great Hittite warrior-king Suppiluliuma I focused with impunity the wrath of Hatti against Egypt's ally Mittani. He had no worries about Egyptian interference, and with good reason. Suppiluliuma knew that Egypt's once-great Eighteenth Dynasty was imploding from a host of catastrophic problems (attributable to the exodus events; see *Breakout 3.05*). The Hittites now had what they had always wanted: control of the Northern Levantine coast and access to the Mediterranean sea-lanes.

S. Collins, J. Holden

During the high-stakes chess game that was the political and military climate of the LBA, the Levantine city-states were merely pawns (see *Map 3.04*). With no strength individually or collectively to resist the will of the regional power players who tromped through the Levant to engage one another, the Syrian and Canaanean cities and towns were always at the mercy of whatever imperialist army was in the vicinity. And during a specific stretch during which the "big boys" had left the neighborhood, Joshua moved in to wreak havoc (see *Breakout 3.16* and *Map 3.07*).

CHRONOLOGY

As for placing the exodus and conquest scenarios at a definite point in Egyptian history, arriving at any kind of consensus—even among conservative scholars—is near impossible. But arguably, this is because of faulty approaches to the issue and not a lack of historical evidence. Most have simply picked their favorite Egyptian chronology (high, middle, or low) and stuck that together with their favorite biblical-exodus chronology (high, middle, or low) to come up with some sort of match. But never do these kinds of methods yield satisfactory results—simply because they ignore the critical lines of necessary evidence (see *Breakouts 3.04, 3.05*).

The proper way to find the right exodus pharaoh—

and thus the correct chronology—is to begin by asking the right question. The all-important question is this: *If the terrible events associated with the exodus actually occurred as the Bible describes them, what would have happened to Egypt?* The answer is obvious: *The reigning dynasty would have suffered serious decline, if not out-and-out collapse.* When you ask this question and follow it with a rigorous historical analysis based on the exodus events in the relevant biblical narratives, the result is remarkable (see *Breakouts 3.04, 3.05*).

What we find is that the exodus events occurred toward the end of Tuthmosis IV's reign, and the exodus itself in the year of his death—c. 1415 BC (high chronology); c. 1400 (middle chronology); c. 1390 (low chronology). The correct exodus "year" is tied not to some formula (biblical or otherwise) of absolute dates, but to historical synchronisms linking biblical events (causes) with Egyptian events (effects). What we discover is that in the 200-year stretch of dates proposed for the exodus (fifteenth through thirteenth centuries BC), there is only *one* dynastic collapse. And that is none other than the demise of the greatest dynasty in all of Egyptian history—the magnificent Eighteenth Dynasty (see *Breakout 3.05*).

When the exodus is placed correctly, what follows is an amazing sequence of historical synchronisms between ANE history and the conquest narratives. It all happened during the fourteenth century BC.

HISTORY

Virtually all historical sources—including the apostle Paul in Galatians 3:16-17—confirm that the approximate time span from Jacob's entrance into Egypt to the exodus was on the order of 215 years (see *Breakouts 2.04, 3.01*), about half of the 430 years from God's promise to Abraham (Genesis 12; 15; 17) until the giving of the law. Jacob and Joseph lived in Egypt during the final decades of the Semitic Fifteenth (Hyksos) Dynasty (see *Timeline* and *Breakout 2.05*). The Hyksos introduced the chariot into Egypt, and Joseph's story has a chariot parade to match (Genesis 41:42-43). After the Hyksos were finally expelled from Lower Egypt by Eighteenth Dynasty (Theban) military might (see *Map 3.01*), what followed was exactly as described in Exodus 1.

From its inception, the Eighteenth Dynasty was viciously anti-Semitic. Its first king, Ahmosis, established a set of Egyptian policies specifically designed to prevent a repeat of what he surely saw as the Hyksos debacle. Nearly 1,500 years of native Egyptian pharaohs had given way to what was, for them, an unimaginable humiliation: the crown of Lower Egypt on the head of a Semitic Asiatic from Canaan. By c. 1800 BC, the whole of the Delta was overrun by Asiatics. And it did not take long for them to take advantage of the situation (see *Map 2.03*). The Semitic Fourteenth Dynasty led into the equally Semitic Fifteenth Dynasty (Hyksos) after c. 1700 BC. For much of this period the Asiatics also extracted tribute from Upper Egypt, adding insult to injury.

The so-called Hyksos ("foreign rulers") introduced two important technologies to the Black Land (Egypt's name for itself): the *composite bow* and the horse-drawn war *chariot*. These two inventions helped them gain the upper hand in the Nile Delta, which they exercised for the better part of two centuries. The resulting native Egyptian hatred for the Hyksos cannot be overstated.

With the Hyksos defeated and chased back into Canaan—sometime between 1550 BC and 1530 BC—Ahmosis put his hatred of Semitic peoples into action with a vengeance. This was the pharaoh (or "Great House") who "did not know Joseph" (Exodus 1:8). One of his first actions was to turn the large Asiatic

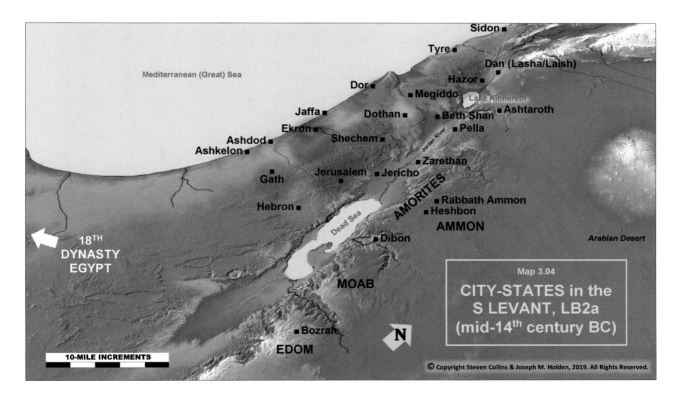

Map 3.04
CITY-STATES in the S LEVANT, LB2a (mid-14th century BC)

BREAKOUT 3.03

THE PASSOVER

The origin of the biblical *Pesach* (Passover) is found in Exodus 12, where we find the rules that were intended only for the first Passover (such as placing blood on the lintel and doorposts) as well as those intended for all subsequent yearly observances (such as partaking of roasted lamb with bitter herbs and unleavened bread).

The purpose of the yearly observance was so the Jewish people could remember how God had brought Israel out of Egypt with a strong hand and an outstretched arm, and to cause the children to ask about the reason for the observance ("and you shall tell your son") so that the remembrance would be passed down to subsequent generations, and so it has. The Hebrew/Jewish calendar is divided between feasts and fasts, and the most important feast is that of Passover.

Biblical law required only three things for the yearly observance: roasted lamb, matzah (unleavened bread), and bitter herbs. However, rabbinic laws and traditions have added many other elements. These include the drinking of four cups of wine, with each cup given its own name. The first cup is the *Cup of Thanksgiving*, which inaugurates the observance. The second cup is called the *Cup of Plagues* in remembrance of the

ten plagues that fell upon Egypt. The first two cups are partaken of before the Passover dinner. Following dinner comes the third cup, the *Cup of Redemption*, in remembrance of the physical redemption of the Jewish firstborn from the last plague. Finally, toward the end of the service comes the fourth cup, the *Cup of Praise*, which includes the singing of certain psalms.

Another rabbinic custom is that of reclining toward a left-handed position at certain points of the ceremony, including the drinking of the four cups of wine and the eating of the first piece of the unleavened bread. Yet another rabbinic innovation is that of a single bag with three compartments, and within each compartment a loaf of unleavened bread is placed. At some point the middle loaf is removed from its compartment and broken in half. One of those halves is then wrapped in linen cloth and hidden somewhere. Later, in connection with the third cup of wine, that half is removed from its hiding place, unwrapped, and distributed to all those around the table.

The Passover service is called the *seder,* a term that means "order"—the ceremony follows a very specific order, with much of it having Messianic significance.

Kadesh (benediction)—The longer of four blessings and partaking of the first cup of wine.

Rachatz (washing)—The first washing of the hands before partaking of the first item to be eaten.

Karpas (dipping)—The dipping of a piece of vegetable, usually parsley, into salt water and eating of it to commemorate that in the springtime of Israel's nationhood God rescued the people by the salt waters of the Red Sea.

Yachatz (breaking)—The breaking of the middle loaf of unleavened bread.

Rachtzah (washing)—The second washing of hands in preparation for the eating of two ceremonial items and the Passover meal.

Maggid (telling)—The telling of the whole Passover story, the singing of certain songs, and the ceremony and drinking of the second cup of wine.

Maror (bitter herb)—The eating of the bitter herb, which entails dipping a piece of unleavened bread into horseradish.

Koreich (sandwich)—A small sandwich is made using two pieces of unleavened bread that "sandwich" a mixture of horseradish and *charoset* (comprised of chopped apples, nuts, honey, cinnamon, and wine, symbolizing the brick mortar that Jews had to use to build the cities of pharaoh).

Shulchan Orech (table meal)— The eating of the Passover meal.

Tzafun (afterward)—The eating of the middle matzah, which had been hidden.

Bareich (grace)—The grace after meals and the drinking of the third cup.

Hallel (praise)—The singing of praise psalms and the drinking of the fourth cup.

Nirtzach (acceptance)—Asking God to accept the service upon its conclusion.

A. Fruchtenbaum

population of Lower Egypt into slaves (see *Breakouts 2.12, 3.04*). Further, he reinforced Egypt's eastern border from the Gulf of Suez to the Mediterranean Sea (see *Map 3.01*) with lake-connecting canals, stretches of wall, and a string of towering fortresses, each a *migdol* (see Exodus 14:2) with associated Egyptian troops. All of this was designed to keep the Nile Delta slaves *in* and the rest of the Asiatic Semites in Canaan *out*.

But Egypt's anti-Asiatic paranoia (cf. Exodus 1:8-22) ran even deeper than slavery and a strong eastern border. As the Eighteenth Dynasty pharaohs worked on rebuilding their administration, infrastructure, key cities, economy, and military capabilities, they needed even more slaves. They also figured out that keeping Canaan's Semitic Asiatic population low was proactive in the light of recent history. And they quickly saw that acquiring more slaves and controlling the population of Canaan went hand in hand. This resulted in systematic slave raids into Canaan, particularly during the reigns of Hatshepsut, Tuthmosis III, Amenhotep II, and Tuthmosis IV.

It also meant that the young children of Asiatic slaves in the Nile Delta, Hebrews included, were useless as labor and thus a waste of food resources. Besides, there was a constant flow of useful older children and young adults coming from Canaan via slave campaigns. There was, therefore, no economic reason to allow large numbers of slave-infants to grow up in Egypt. In this context, pharaoh's order in Exodus (1:15-22) to kill male Hebrew infants is consistent with the known history of the mid-Eighteenth Dynasty. Moses's basket was probably fished from the Nile (Exodus 2:1-10)

during the last few years of Tuthmosis III's reign, at a time when his son, Amenhotep II, was coregent with his father (see *Timeline*).

Egypt's Eighteenth Dynasty set its sights on annexing the entire Levant—Canaan and Syria—beginning in the reign of Tuthmosis I (see *Map 3.02*). By the reign of Hatshepsut, this was becoming a reality. During the reign of warrior-pharaoh Tuthmosis III, it was ironclad (more appropriately, bronze-clad!). Thug-in-chief Amenhotep II reinforced Egypt's Euphrates border with the blood of numerous Syrian kinglets who tried to rebel against him (he personally beheaded them in a ceremony at the Luxor Temple in Upper Egypt). Egypt's seemingly unlimited wealth—supported in part by its Nubian gold mining operations (see *Map 1.06*)—made unending military campaigns into the Levant a kind of obligatory "sport" for the Eighteenth Dynasty kings (while in Syria, they also hunted Asian elephants). Their military presence in the Levant was also a perennial necessity. Both Canaanite and Syrian city-state kings looked for every opportunity to foment rebellion against Egypt.

But Tuthmosis IV thought the constant fight for its Euphrates border was a waste of national resources. Because the Mittani kingdom of north Mesopotamia had carved out a corridor to the north Levant coastal ports, Egypt was always at war with Mittani. An Egyptian border at the Euphrates River meant that the Egyptians had to cross over Mittani's Mediterranean trade routes to maintain it. It was a messy situation, and expensive. Tuthmosis IV had a flash of brilliance that could solve the problem: diplomacy.

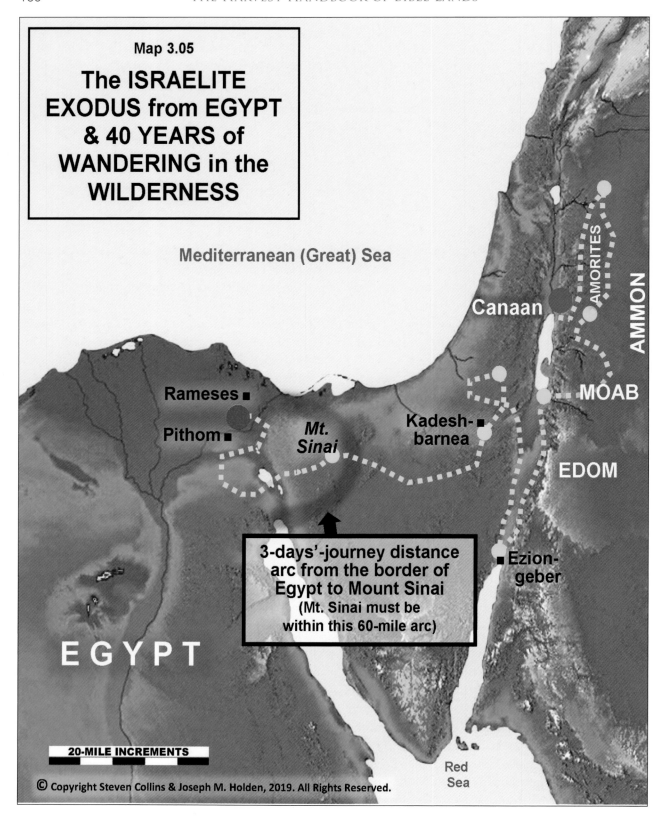

Map 3.05

The ISRAELITE EXODUS from EGYPT & 40 YEARS of WANDERING in the WILDERNESS

Mediterranean (Great) Sea

AMORITES

AMMON

Canaan

MOAB

Rameses ■

Pithom ■

Mt. Sinai

Kadesh-barnea ■

EDOM

3-days'-journey distance arc from the border of Egypt to Mount Sinai (Mt. Sinai must be within this 60-mile arc)

■ Ezion-geber

EGYPT

20-MILE INCREMENTS

Red Sea

BREAKOUT 3.04

THE PHARAOH OF THE EXODUS

There is no shortage of Egyptian kings who have been tagged as the pharaoh of the exodus. Of those who ruled during the Eighteenth Dynasty, Tuthmosis III, Amenhotep II and III, and Akhenaten all have devotees. The most famous of all is Rameses II of the Nineteenth Dynasty (thanks, in part, to the classic movie *The Ten Commandments*). The issue is complicated by divergent biblical and Egyptian chronologies, and a lack of rigor in approaching the problem logically and systematically.

Dates for the exodus range from *early* (mid-fifteenth century BC), *middle* (mid- to late-fourteenth century BC), and *late* (thirteenth century BC)—a 200-year spectrum! Egyptian history also has high, middle, and low chronologies that can vary from 30 to 50 years at any given point. Herein lies the problem: Which chronologies do you use? High biblical with high Egyptian? High biblical with low Egyptian? Low biblical with middle Egyptian? Middle biblical with low Egyptian? Confused yet?

The fact that not even conservative scholars can agree on who the pharaoh of the exodus was is perhaps indicative of inadequate methodology, even something as simple as not asking the right question(s). It certainly is *not* possible to find the correct exodus pharaoh simply by

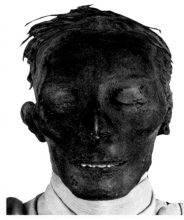
Mummy of Tuthmosis IV (photo: Steven Collins)

picking your favorite biblical and Egyptian chronologies and sticking them together! But this is the approach most have taken, and thus we have more exodus pharaohs than you can shake a stick at! But there is a better way: using *historical synchronisms* to find reasonable cause-and-effect associations between biblical and Egyptian history.

An adequate approach for selecting this specific "bad boy" pharaoh must begin by asking the right question. *The* key question for identifying the exodus pharaoh is one that almost no one has bothered to ask. It's this: *If the five major events accompanying the exodus actually occurred, what would have happened to Egypt?*

Here are the five core events of the exodus in a nutshell: (1) ten plagues; (2) plundering of Egypt; (3) catastrophic loss of labor; (4)

severe military losses; and (5) death of pharaoh. According to the biblical narrative, the ten plagues alone were enough to inflict serious chaos upon Egypt. Add to these the calamitous economic and military losses of the next four core events, and Egypt would have had a dynasty-threatening crisis on its hands. In other words, look for a *dynastic collapse* within the two-century range of possible exodus dates, and that will pinpoint this unique historical moment and the pharaoh who tempted the wrath of Yahweh.

Was there a dynastic collapse during or at the end of Rameses II's rule (late-thirteenth century BC)? No. What about the fifteenth century BC? Did the Eighteenth Dynasty suffer collapse during or at the end of Tuthmosis III's reign? No. Amenhotep II? No (in fact, Egypt got stronger!). Tuthmosis IV? Yes! While Egypt's golden age arguably gained momentum during his short time on the throne, around the time of Tuthmosis IV's death the Eighteenth Dynasty began a downward spiral that eventually led to catastrophic failure. This is the historic moment detailed in the exodus text, the reality of which was reflected in the demise of the greatest dynasty in the history of Egypt—Dynasty Eighteen (see *Breakout 3.05*).

S. Collins

3.08). There, Moses wrapped up his work on the five Torah books (see *Breakouts 3.07, 3.11, 3.12*), while Joshua prepared the army and the people to cross the Jordan.

The Jordan crossing (Joshua 3) took place in about the second year of Pharaoh Akhenaten's reign, at a time when Canaan was devoid of Egyptian influence and troops (see *Breakout 3.16*). Joshua set up his command camp in an area called Gilgal just east of Jericho, from which the central, southern, and northern campaigns were launched (see *Map 3.07*). Jericho was Joshua's first target (Joshua 6; see *Breakout 3.15*). Next on the list was Ai, which also brought about the defeat

of nearby Bethel (Joshua 7, 8; see *Maps 3.06, 3.07*). Ai—probably the site of Khirbet el-Maqatir—was a fortified garrison associated with Bethel, marking the north border of the Jerusalem city-state (see *Maps 3.04, 3.06*). Beth Aven—probably located at modern Beitin, across the valley from Bethel/Ai—seems to have been a fortified defensive town on the south border of the Shechem city-state (see *Map 3.04* and *Breakout 3.16*).

Archaeology reveals that Jerusalem and Shechem were, in fact, the two main city-states in the Canaan highlands during the fourteenth century BC (LBA2a), as witnessed in the Amarna Archive (see *Breakout 3.16*). But while Jerusalem and its territories were

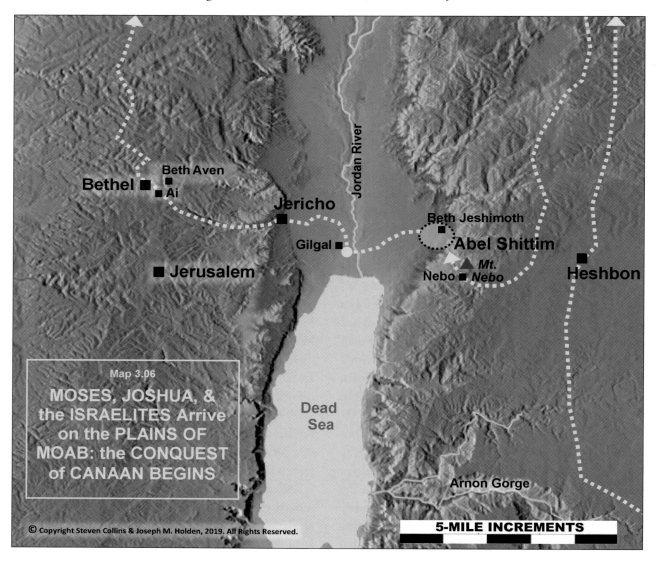

Map 3.06

MOSES, JOSHUA, & the ISRAELITES Arrive on the PLAINS OF MOAB: the CONQUEST of CANAAN BEGINS

Bethel Beth Aven Ai Jericho Jordan River Beth Jeshimoth Abel Shittim Gilgal Jerusalem Nebo *Mt. Nebo* Heshbon Dead Sea Arnon Gorge

5-MILE INCREMENTS

targeted by the Israelites, Shechem seems to have been an ally. Joshua never attacked Shechem. However, he did take the Israelites up to Mount Ebal and Mount Gerizim (Joshua 8:30-35). Shechem was located between these two mountains. This, along with the general chaos in Canaan that Joshua contributed to at a time when Egypt was no longer controlling the Levant, is reflected in more than 150 of the 382 Amarna Letters (see *Breakout 3.16*).

Joshua's campaign against the south hill country was launched from Gilgal (Joshua 9–10; see *Map 3.06, 3.07*). In the process, he defeated an Amorite coalition allied against him, a remarkable military feat. The famous "long day" of Joshua contributed to the victory (see *Breakout 3.17*). The northern campaign, also launched from Gilgal (Joshua 11), targeted another Canaanite coalition headed by the king of Hazor. Engaging a foreign army with troops from multiple cities and towns at a predetermined location is authentic to the LBA, as seen in Tuthmosis III's recounting of his Battle of Megiddo (see *Breakout 3.20*). In fact, all of Joshua's battle accounts are written in an Egyptian style, reflecting the fact that both he and Moses grew up in Egypt during the height of the Eighteenth Dynasty (see *Breakout 3.20*).

Joshua's three campaigns in Canaan left the Promised Land considerably "tenderized" by the edge of the sword (see *Breakout 3.14*), but not entirely conquered (Joshua 13:1-7). The remaining work was left to the individual tribes, whose territories were parceled out in Joshua 13–21 (see *Map 3.08* and *Breakout 3.18*). Although the land was not entirely subdued, from this point forward the Israelites were certainly a force to be reckoned with, a fact confirmed by Pharaoh Merneptah in c. 1210 BC, when the people of Israel succeeded in making the top-nine list of Egypt's perennial enemies (see *Breakout 3.19* and *Timeline*).

PEOPLES AND KINGDOMS

AMALEKITES—A nomadic tribe living mostly in the Negev, for which we have no extrabiblical data. They are said to be descendants of Esau (Genesis

36:12), but they became Israel's mortal enemy. They attacked the Israelites without provocation during the exodus as they were nearing Mount Sinai (Exodus 17:8-16; see *Map 3.05*), for which the Amalekites received divine condemnation and were to be completely wiped out (Deuteronomy 25:19). King Saul carried this out (1 Samuel 15). But the name of the Amalekite king—Agag—lived on as a tribal name into the Persian era (Esther 3).

AMMONITES—Lived in the Transjordan Plateau north of both the Moabites and Edomites (see *Map 3.08*). The Arnon River marked the boundary between Moab and Ammon. Their capital was Rabbath Ammon, where Amman, the capital of Jordan, sits today. According to Genesis 19, the Ammonites and Moabites were descendants of Lot from incest with his daughters, which conferred on them the status of inferior relatives of Israel. Moses was commanded not to battle the Ammonites because they were related (Deuteronomy 2:9). There were numerous encounters between the Israelites and Ammonites (both good and bad) during the time of the Judges, the Israelite monarchy, and after the exile.

AMORITES (OR AMMURITES)—A Semitic people group mentioned in Mesopotamian texts as early as EB2 (see *Map 3.08* and *Timeline*). The name comes from the Akkadian word *Ammuru*, meaning "Westerners," since they lived to the west of Mesopotamia in Syria. They relied on herding sheep and goats over large distances but lived as communities rather than as nomads. In the Bible, *Amorite* is sometimes used as a synonym for *Canaanite* (Genesis 15:16; Joshua 7:7) because they were one of the larger people groups within Canaan (Exodus 3:8; Deuteronomy 7:1). Most of the "-ites" in Canaan were of Amorite stock anyway. But how and when the Amorites moved to Canaan is not entirely clear.

Earlier archaeologists hypothesized that an invasion/migration of Amorites had led to or helped propel the collapse of the EBA culture. However, there is a growing consensus that there is little biblical or archaeological evidence to support this theory. It seems more likely that Amorite communities emerged during (or shortly after) the end of the IBA (see *Timeline*),

BREAKOUT 3.06

THE LOCATION OF MOUNT SINAI

The actual location of Mount Sinai remains a mystery. However, a rigorous geographical analysis of the relevant biblical texts can set a distance-arc beyond which proposed locations for Mount Sinai become doubtful, even ludicrous. In the pursuit of this famous mountain's whereabouts, the biblical text, and not traditions, must guide the search.

The quest must begin with a detailed understanding of what the pertinent texts *do* and *do not* say. The salient information from the book of Exodus can be summarized in 13 points (see *Map 3.05*):

1. Moses flees Egypt and goes to Midian, the seasonal territories of a far-ranging nomadic group, including the northern Sinai Peninsula and the southeast Levant (2:15);

2. from Midian Moses grazes his flock to the backside of the Sinai Wilderness, that is, *westward* toward Egypt (3:1);

3. while in the western part of the Sinai Wilderness, Moses encounters Horeb, Mount Sinai (3:1);

4. Yahweh instructs Moses to bring the Israelites from Egypt to worship him at Horeb, a "three-days' journey" from Goshen/Egypt (3:12, 16, 18);

5. Moses returns to Midian (4:18);

6. Moses heads back toward Egypt (4:19), staying at an inn along the way (4:24);

7. Moses returns to Mount Sinai and Aaron travels from Egypt to meet him there (4:27);

8. Moses and Aaron go back to Egypt to meet with the elders of Israel (4:29);

9. Moses and Aaron deliver to pharaoh Yahweh's command to let the Israelites go three-days' journey into the wilderness to Mount Sinai to offer sacrifices (5:1-3);

10. Moses returns to Yahweh at Mount Sinai (5:22);

11. Moses goes back to Egypt to speak once again to the Israelite elders (6:9);

12. back at Mount Sinai, Yahweh speaks to Moses and Aaron (6:10, 13);

13. for the first time, Yahweh reiterates his instructions to Moses in Egypt, not at Mount Sinai (6:28ff).

Exodus 6:28 marks the first time Yahweh spoke to Moses in Egypt. Before that, all communications between Moses and Yahweh occurred either at Mount Sinai or in Midianite territory. The fact that Moses—Aaron, too—traveled back and forth between Horeb and the Egyptian Delta (Lower Egypt) so many times suggests that the distance from the Israelite enclave in Goshen (Exodus 8:22) to Mount Sinai was reasonably short.

And so it was. Several times, the distance from pharaoh's country to Mount Sinai is described as "three-days' journey" (Exodus 3:18; 5:3; 8:27)—that is, from the border of Egypt to Horeb. In the ANE, a day's journey represented the *distance* that a moderately equipped army (or caravan) could travel in a single day. Estimates range from 18 to 28 miles. Using a high-rounded average of 25 miles, a three-days' journey was no more than 75 miles (if anything, probably less). Whether such a distance was traveled in 3 or 30 days, it was still a three-days' journey.

The three-days' journey was specified by Yahweh himself in his marching orders to Moses. Thus, the allowable distance from the border of Egypt to Mount Sinai is no more than 75 miles. Drawing a 75-mile distance-arc from the Egyptian border creates a boundary beyond which Horeb cannot be found. The traditional location in the southern Sinai Peninsula lies far beyond the three-days' journey limit, as does the off-the-wall location in Saudi Arabia.

Which of the many mountains within an acceptable distance-range from Egypt is the actual Horeb/Mount Sinai remains an unsolved mystery.

S. Collins, J. Moore

BREAKOUT 3.07

CRITICAL THEORY AND MOSAIC AUTHORSHIP OF THE PENTATEUCH

The first five books of the Old Testament form the most seriously challenged section of the Bible—in particular, Moses's authorship of the Pentateuch (the five books of the Law) through what has been called the *documentary hypothesis* or *JEDP theory*. Challenges to Mosaic authorship have been an issue since the seventeenth century AD, when Benedict Spinoza voiced his denial of it in his *Theological-Political Treatise* (1677). Jean Astruc, in his 1753 attempt to refute Spinoza, was the first to propose a primitive version of the documentary theory.

Soon after, in the nineteenth century, many critical scholars adopted this theory. Astruc limited his analysis to Genesis. Johann Gottfried Eichhorn was the first to apply this theory to the entire Pentateuch, with a series of publications beginning in 1780. Wilhelm M.L. de Wette also made a significant contribution to this discussion in positing that Deuteronomy was its own independently constructed source in his *Dissertation Critico-Exegetica* in 1805; a year later, this hypothesis was repeated in his *Beitraege zur Einleitung*. De Wette went so far as to say that none of the Pentateuch was composed prior to the time of David! However, it was Julius Wellhausen who popularized (not created—a common misconception) the idea that the Pentateuch was written by various persons whom he called *Jehovist* (J, also known as Yahwist), *Elohist* (E), *Deuteronomist* (D), and *Priestly* (P), each one supposedly distinguished by their literary characteristics. Thus, the name *JEDP theory* refers to the various sources hypothesized.

However, the JEDP theory has come under increasing attack by scholars in recent years for many reasons, including the fact there have been no JEDP "documents" ever found—no traces can be seen in the hundreds of biblical texts found in the DSS or anywhere else. Yale scholar William W. Hallo points to the paucity of the theory:

The literary-critical study of the Hebrew Bible has had a checkered history. The [JEDP] documentary hypothesis with which it began over two centuries ago remains to this day a hypothesis, the [JEDP] documents which it reconstructed [are] beyond recovery; their precise extent, their absolute and relative dates, and their changes over time [are] all matters of dispute; and the applicability of the hypothesis beyond the Pentateuch [is] severely limited...Given such disparate and even desperate reactions to two centuries of modern Biblical scholarship, it is perhaps not surprising that much of the most exciting work...has been...from...epigraphic [archaeological] discoveries.*

There also exist further independent reasons for rejecting the JEDP theory and affirming Mosaic authorship.

First, *Scripture itself attributes authorship of the Pentateuch to Moses.* Within the Pentateuch itself it is repeatedly stated that Moses wrote down the words of the law given directly to him by Yahweh (Exodus 17:14; 24:4, 7; 34:27; Numbers 33:1-2; Deuteronomy 31:9, 11). Books within the rest of the Old Testament also give witness to this fact.

The book of Joshua attests to Mosaic authorship in 1:8 and 8:31-32, identifying them as the "book of the law" or the "book of the law of Moses." The title "law of Moses" is used by David in 1 Kings 2:3 to refer to the first five books written by Moses, while 2 Kings 14:6 gives the same title, quoting from Deuteronomy 24:16. Again, 2 Kings refers to the same title of the Pentateuch.

Other references to the Mosaic authorship are found in Ezra 6:18, Nehemiah 13:1, Daniel 9:11-13, and Malachi 4:4. The authorship of the Torah is always attributed to Moses throughout the Old Testament and even into the New Testament. The Gospels refer to the writings of the Torah as "Moses" in John 5:46-47 and 7:19 as well as Acts 3:22. Other passages in the New Testament refer to Moses as the author of the Torah, such as Romans 10:5. It is also interesting to note that Mark 12:26 states that God himself uttered the words written in Exodus 3:6 to the historical Moses.

Second, upon further investigation, *other internal evidences attest to Moses's authorship of the Pentateuch.* Independent investigations of the historical events recorded, of the contemporary issues of Moses's day, of the descriptions of the plants and wildlife, and of the conditions of geography and climate have led scholars to believe that the author was originally a resident of Egypt and not of Israel. Research also confirms that the author of the Pentateuch was an eyewitness of the exodus and wilderness wanderings, and someone who possessed a very high degree of education, literary skill, and familiarity with Egypt and the Hebrew way of life. Moses is the most reasonable choice as author because he appears to have possessed all the qualities and training necessary to fulfill the role of author.

The many geographic details recorded in passages such as Exodus 15:27 suggest that the author was an actual participant in the events themselves. Genesis and Exodus show the author's familiarity with the land of Egypt and with Egyptian names, expressions, customs, and culture. In addition, the unity of arrangement and harmony that underlies the Torah also points to a single author of the text. And taking into account that the Pentateuch was written over a period of about four decades through progressive revelation given by God, we would expect differing writing styles.

Third, *the late date many critics assigned to Deuteronomy (the seventh century BC) has been thoroughly discredite*d by the research of Meredith Kline and the archaeological data. In his landmark work *The Treaty of the Great King*, Kline demonstrates that Deuteronomy follows the form of the typical Hittite suzerainty treaty of the second millennium BC. This is the very time during which Moses would have written Deuteronomy.

J. Holden

* William W. Hallo, *The World's Oldest Literature: Studies in Sumerian Belles-Lettres* (Leiden, the Netherlands: Brill, 2010), 677.

including groups in the hill country of Canaan (Genesis 48:22; Numbers 13:29) and in the Transjordan (Numbers 21:21-34; 32:33). Egyptian records corroborate the biblical text in portraying a diverse population of several people groups in the Levant during the MBA and LBA. Of these groups, Amorites were one of the most significant.

EDOMITES—Lived to the south of the Zered River and south of the Dead Sea on both sides of the Arabah (see *Map 3.08*). Their capital was in Petra (at least in this area), and they are associated with Mount Seir (meaning "hairy"). The Bible describes the Edomites as descendants of Jacob's brother Esau (whose nickname, Edom, means "red"). Moses addressed the Edomites as brothers even though the Edomites refused to let the Israelites pass through their land (Numbers 20:14-21).

EGYPT (EIGHTEENTH DYNASTY)—The start of the New Kingdom was initiated by Ahmose I. He consolidated power with a strong central government (see *Timeline*). Tuthmosis I attempted to expand Egyptian hegemony to the Euphrates River, an action reinforced by succeeding "Queen Pharaoh" Hatshepsut. By the end of Tuthmosis III's reign, the Egyptian Empire was the most powerful player in the ANE (see *Map 3.02*). After the death of Tuthmosis IV, Egypt began to collapse. Although there were building projects continuing for 30 or more years, Egypt lost its territories in the Levant (see *Map 3.03*). In 1351 BC, Amenhotep IV became king and changed his name to Akhenaten ("blessed of the Aten") and abandoned the traditional Egyptian deities. His monotheism angered the priest-class and his moving of the capital from Thebes to Amarna did not sit well with the high administration. This took place during the heart of Egypt's Amarna period.

Hatti (Hittites)—The Hittite homeland was in central Anatolia (see *Map 2.01*), the land of Hatti. These people were Indo-Europeans. The Old Testament calls them sons of Heth (Genesis 10:15). Hattusilis, king of Kussara, began a southern and eastern expansion of his kingdom. The Hittite armies followed, and fighting soon climaxed in Aleppo and the kingdom of Yamhad. The Hittites kept marching east and didn't stop until they took Babylon and the Amorite kingdom of Hammurabi (see *Map 2.01*).

But eventually they shrank back inside Anatolia (see *Map 3.02*). The Hittite Empire period (see *Timeline*) appears to have originated with a Hurrian family from the region around Kizzuwatna, but the Mittani Hurrian ruling class of northern Mesopotamia eventually carved out a kingdom that also managed to control a corridor to the Mediterranean through the Northern Levant (see *Map 3.02*). This cut Hatti's access to the Northern Levant coastal ports. When Eighteenth Dynasty Egypt began to collapse (see *Breakout 3.05*), the Hittites took advantage, changing the ANE map once again (see *Map 3.03*).

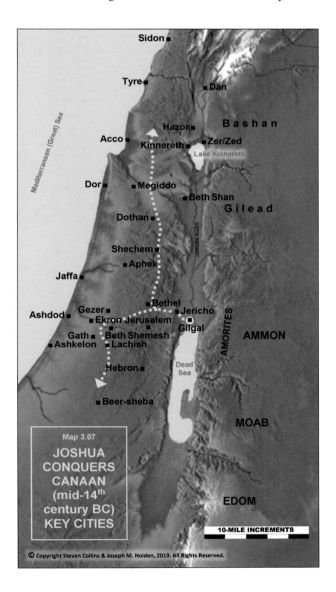

Map 3.07
JOSHUA CONQUERS CANAAN (mid-14th century BC) KEY CITIES

10-MILE INCREMENTS

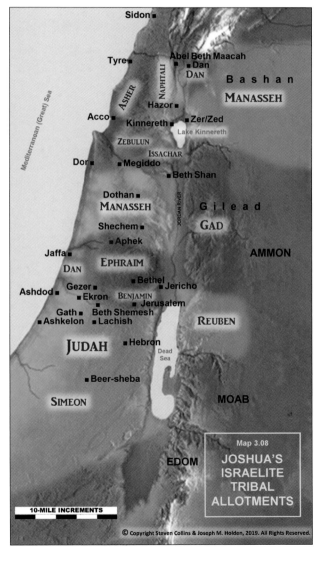

Map 3.08
JOSHUA'S ISRAELITE TRIBAL ALLOTMENTS

10-MILE INCREMENTS

BREAKOUT 3.08

ISRAEL ON THE PLAINS OF MOAB

After almost 40 years of wandering, Moses led the Israelites to an area in the southern Jordan Valley called the Plains of Moab (Numbers 33:48-49), opposite Jericho (see *Map 3.05*). Numbers 33:49 says they camped "along the Jordan from Beth Jeshimoth to Abel Shittim" (NIV). Traditionally, the identification of these two places has been speculated upon, but with little or no archaeological data in support. That is, until recently.

Many current scholars have suggested that Abel Shittim is Tall el-Hammam. This is probably correct. It makes geographical and military sense that Moses would place the Israelite encampment in the most strategically advantageous location in this area northeast of the Dead Sea. This leaves little doubt that Tall el-Hammam is, in fact, Abel Shittim. It is, by far, a superior location on account of water, an elevated and defensible flat ground, a 360-degree view of the entire region, and a direct line of sight to Jericho across the Jordan. It would certainly be a military strategist's first pick (it has been used in modern times by the Jordanian army!). But what about Beth Jeshimoth?

It is remarkable that the Israelite army had been fighting its way across the Transjordan Plateau before they set their eyes toward the southern Jordan Valley. All the relevant biblical narratives make it clear that the Plains of Moab was a textbook staging area for the next step in their campaign: crossing the Jordan. It was ideal because no one was home! And it was the perfect location at which to rest from many battles, reorganize, and reconnoiter the next target: Jericho.

Excavations at Tall el-Hammam and data from surrounding sites indicate that this entire area east of the Jordan opposite Jericho was uninhabited from c. 1700 BC until c. 1000 BC. When Moses and the Israelites arrived there c. 1350 BC, no one was home. It was unoccupied because about 350 years earlier, the entire 300-square-mile area was destroyed by a violent, meteoritic airburst event (see *Breakout 2.07*). After all, Tall el-Hammam was also the location of Sodom itself!

Indeed, what had been the greatest of the Cities of the Kikkar (see *Breakout 2.07* and *Map 2.04*) was, in Moses's day, a massive mound of ruins. But ancient Sodom's topography was still strategic and its rivers and springs still flowed. And, as was the case with all the surrounding area, there was no settlement there during the fourteenth century BC (LBA2a). Well, almost. During recent excavation seasons at Tall el-Hammam, on the acropolis of what had been Sodom's upper city during the MBA (prior to c.

1700 BC), excavators found a single freestanding structure dating to fourteenth century BC. It dated to the precise historical moment when Moses and Joshua moved onto Abel Shittim (Tall el-Hammam).

What was this building? To be sure, it wasn't large (no more than 15x15 feet), nor was it a typical domestic structure. It had huge ceiling beams (10-12 inches diameter), doorposts and lintels, storage facilities, wooden furniture, painted pottery, a huge widemouth water jar, and jewelry. It also had another telling assortment of objects: a set of bronze balance-scale pans. What was this lonely, isolated, "upscale" building doing sitting atop this massive pile of ruins with its 360-degree view, sitting astride the intersection of the region's main north-south and east-west trade routes? The answer seems clear: It was a customs or tariff office, likely operated by Jericho, thus placed to collect road-usage fees from passing caravans.

What would you call a government building sitting atop the charred ruins of an enormous city that is surrounded by the ruins of other cities and towns? Would "House of the Desolation" be an appropriate nickname? This is the meaning of Beth Jeshimoth! And it was the ideal spot for Moses's command camp because it offered panoramic views in all directions. The

Levitical camp with the tabernacle at its center would have occupied the almost-circular platform of the lower portion of the Tall el-Hammam site to the west and immediately below the "House of the Desolation."

It's inconceivable that Moses would have destroyed the building at first. Rather, it's much more

likely he used it as his Moab Plains command center (then demolished it upon leaving). Thus, the Israelite camp spread from "Beth Jeshimoth [Moses's lofty headquarters] to Abel Shittim [the lower tall and immediate area bounded on the north and south by perennial rivers, with the Jordan River a short march to the west]" (Numbers 33:49).

And yes, the structure was burned down and left as a smoldering pile of ruins during the fourteenth century BC, matching the date of the only Jericho that Joshua could have faced: LBA2a Tell es-Sultan (see *Breakout 3.15*). There was no LBA Jericho before or after the fourteenth century BC.

S. Collins, J. Moore

HURRIANS—This Indo-European people group is mentioned in early Hittite texts. Their homeland lay north of Mesopotamia (see *Maps 2.01, 3.02*), but coalesced into a short-lived political entity—the kingdom of Mittani—in the middle of the second millennium BC (see *Timeline*). Their territory was in northwest Mesopotamia and the north Levant; thus they alternately clashed with and influenced the Hittite Empire. Their identification with the biblical Hivites (Genesis 34:2; Joshua 9:7; 11:3; Judges 3:3; 2 Samuel 24:7) seems plausible but remains unconfirmed.

MOABITES—A Transjordan Semitic people group living between the Ammonites to the north and the Edomites to the south (see *Maps 3.05–3.08*). Their capital was in Dibon. Genesis identifies them as descendants of Lot and one of his daughters. There are many interactions between the Israelites and Moabites throughout the Hebrew Scriptures. When Moses sought a route to the Promised Land, he had to deal with the Moabites (Numbers 22:1-3).

MIDIANITES—Moses lived among the Midianites and married one—Zipporah, the daughter of Jethro (Exodus 2:21). But after the exodus, the Midianite women and Moabite women led the Israelite men into sexual sin and idolatry (Numbers 25). At this point, at least some of the Midianites must have moved north past Edom and were living among the Moabites. For leading the Israelites astray, the Midianites were condemned and slaughtered, except for the unmarried girls (Numbers 31). However, this cannot

have completely wiped out the tribe as they reappeared during the time of the Judges.

MITTANI—The Mittani kingdom flourished c. 1500–1340 BC (see *Timeline*) and consisted of an Indo-European Hurrian ruling class and a Semitic populace. Their capital was Washukanni, destroyed in 2 attacks about 20 years apart by the Hittite warrior-king Suppiluliuma in the mid-fourteenth century BC. Mittani had formed an alliance with Egypt, but when Egypt's control of the north Levant began to wane during the early part of Amenhotep III's reign, the Hittites attacked Mittani, destroyed its capital city, and wrested away the control of the entire north Levant (see *Map 3.03*).

ASSYRIA—Old Assyria (see *Timeline*) was a vassal state of Old Babylonia and later of the Mittani kingdom during most of the second millennium BC (see *Map 3.02*). Assyria finally emerged as an independent state in the fourteenth century BC, after the fall of Mittani, but had few dealings with the Levant.

ISRAELITES—From Mesopotamian stock (see *Map 2.01*), the Israelites were a Semitic people who went back to the time of Abraham, Isaac, and Jacob—*Israel* derives from when Jacob's name was changed (Genesis 32:38), and the people of Israel from his sons. They had moral and treaty/covenant structures similar to those of the Hittites. Their language was first Akkadian, then Canaanean/Amorite, and eventually Hebrew (Canaanite "cooked" in isolation in Egypt).

Having escaped from bondage in Egypt, they first

appeared en masse in the Southern Levant in the mid- to late fourteenth century BC (see *Map 3.08*). They were entirely nomadic until the late fourteenth and thirteenth centuries BC. Eventually they settled down, moved into conquered towns and cities, and built new communities. Archaeologically speaking, for a long while, they can hardly be distinguished from the Canaaneans. But by the twelfth and eleventh centuries BC, a true Israelite culture becomes visible. The Israelites had a literary tradition and were likely a literate people.

Peoples of the Southern Levant—Before Joshua's conquests, Canaan (south Levant) had many city-states (see *Map 3.04*) and vast numbers of related and unrelated tribes occupying the landscape. Canaan was a melting pot of peoples from the Fertile Crescent, Anatolia, the Indo-European arc, and even the Aegean region, not to mention a tapestry of locals. The bulk of the groups in Canaan were Semitic and spoke languages related to Amorite (Ammurite).

SOCIETIES AND CULTURES

Social Stratification—Whether in Kassite Babylonia, Mittani, Hatti, Egypt, or the Levant, social stratification was an ever-present reality. But as witnessed from time to time even in the larger kingdoms and empires, a "regular" could, given the right circumstances, rise to power as king. Many new royal houses were launched in such a fashion. The first few pharaohs of the Eighteenth Dynasty were little more than military buddies of the previous king, and not hereditary rulers. The Nineteenth Dynasty started similarly, with a military coup and subsequent military commanders appointed as pharaoh by an old-army-comrade-king. But eventually each royal house settled into the standard pattern of hereditary succession (firstborn or primal son). In this way, political hierarchies were more fluid than the general social order of a given culture. All of society was stratified, from the trade guilds down to households. Slaves—most often war captives from despised people groups—were common at all levels, if one could afford them.

Tribalism—Because it is difficult to perceive given the paucity of relevant preserved city archives and the fact that nomadic groups left few if any written documents at all, understanding tribalism in the ANE relies heavily on ethnographic research done in modern times. Such studies do provide fair analogies, however. Tribal structure was basic to all ancient societies regardless of the level or complexity of a culture. Tribal heads (chieftains) were the highest-ranking elder and maintained that position until death. Other men and women in the tribe (or clan, as it were) existed ultimately for the good of the collective. Families could vie for rank in a clan, and clans could compete for influence in or control of a tribe. This was the social application of human nature!

City-States—During the 500-year period preceding the MBA (see *Timeline*), the south Levant had only a single city-state: Sodom (see *Breakout 2.07*). All the others collapsed due to a severe downturn in the climate. But beginning around 2100 BC, the rains increased and the stage was set for the Canaanean city-states to rise again. And rise they did! Slowly at first, along the coast and in the south Jordan Valley. By 1900–1800 BC, towns and cities began to appear in the Canaanean central highlands (Jerusalem, Hebron, Shechem), the Galilee region (Hazor), the north Jordan Valley (Lasha/Laish/Dan), and the Jezreel Valley (Megiddo). With the emergence of the Southern Levantine city-states (see *Map 3.04*), the MBA2 period became the pinnacle of Canaanean civilization.

Inheritance—Generally ruled by laws of primogeniture, the hereditary head of a family, clan, tribe, kingdom, or empire was most often the father's choice (firstborn or primal son). Of course, exceptions happened by intrigue, coups, and open rebellions. But eventually the hereditary right to rule came back into play. Women had no inherent hereditary rights, which made laws of levirate marriage critical. Levirate (Latin, meaning "husband's brother") marriage was the custom or law that a man should marry the wife of his deceased brother. In Egypt, the pharaonic throne was legitimized by marriage to the "god's wife" (principal queen; or her daughter, blood daughter) of the previous king.

BREAKOUT 3.09

THE TABERNACLE

After the exodus, God chose Bazalel and Oholiab to construct his sacred dwelling, known in the Hebrew Bible as the *mishkan* (Exodus 31:3-7; 38:21-23). This tabernacle, made from animal skins and measuring approximately 45 x 10 feet (170 x 85 feet including the outer court), served as a *temenos* (Greek, "a sacred temple enclosure") for the Israelite cultic system. The sanctuary was divided proportionally 2:1 between the Holy Place, where Levites officiated the sacrificial system, and the Holy of Holies, which housed the Ark of the Covenant. Sacrifices enabled the Hebrew nation to expiate sin, thereby restoring fellowship with God. Likewise, sacrifices facilitated the restoration of fractured interpersonal human relationships. The propitiation process called for strict adherence to the written requirements of the Torah. In fact, everything pertaining to the tabernacle had to be done "according to the pattern" (Exodus 25:40 NIV).

Throughout the Jewish people's 40 years in the wilderness, the tabernacle functioned as the nucleus of Israelite society. The 12 tribes camped around this structure in a prescribed manner. Eventually the nation crossed into Canaan and, following a 7-year conquest, the Israelites arrived at Shiloh in the mid- to late-fourteenth century BC. There, according to Joshua 18:1, they erected the tabernacle, in the heart of the tribal territory of Ephraim, the tribe of Joshua, their new leader.

According to the *Seder Olam* 8, it remained there for 369 years; however, the biblical date is closer to 300 years. Renewed archaeological excavations at Shiloh (S. Stripling, director) have yielded an abundance of evidence that the site was occupied during the Late Bronze Age (c. 1480–1180 BC) and Iron Age 1 (c. 1180–980 BC), the timeframe that the Bible indicates the tabernacle rested at Shiloh (see *Timeline*).

An eleventh-century BC Philistine incursion into the central hill country motivated Eli, the high priest, to send the ark to the Battle of Ebenezer (modern Izbet Sartah). After the ark's capture by the Philistines (see *Breakout 4.05*), it never returned to Shiloh. Instead of judging Israel from Shiloh, Samuel meted out justice from the cities of Bethel, Gilgal, and Mizpah, as well as from his home at Ramah (1 Samuel 7:16-17). Nob became the tabernacle's new home for two generations (1 Samuel 21–22) before it moved to Gibeon (modern el-Jib). From there, it disappears from the biblical narrative. However, tabernacle imagery and symbolism play an important role in John's writings in the New Testament (John 1:14; Revelation 21:3), and many aspects of the tabernacle foreshadow Christological concepts.

S. Stripling

Tabernacle, side view, Holy of Holies (model, photo: Leen Ritmeyer)

Women's Roles—Bearing children was paramount, thus women were expected to marry at a young child-bearing age, usually within a few months after the onset of puberty. She almost always moved to the home of her husband's family—this was true for royalty too! In some cultures, dowries were paid to the groom or his family. Among nomadic peoples, the would-be husband might have to provide something of value to the bride's father to compensate for the loss of a working hand.

Men's Roles—Men "ruled" their families within the structure of a patriarchy. The patriarch (chief elder) in a family, clan, or tribe remained such until death, when the customs of patrimony kicked in to determine a new patriarch. Within the agricultural and trade guilds, masters "ruled" in a hierarchy of experience and expertise. Professional warriors were trained up by a system of mentorship (see *Breakout 5.02*). Practically every man was a trained warrior (to some extent) who could be called upon—or even conscripted—to fight when needed.

Political Climate—This was perhaps the headiest time in the ANE. Powerful kingdoms existed in every region of the Fertile Crescent and beyond (see *Timeline* and *Map 3.02*). Egypt reached the pinnacle of its wealth and prestige. Hatti was strong and getting stronger. Mittani had reached its apogee. Assyria

Figure 3.01—One of the Amarna Letters, Akkadian in cuneiform on clay, Late Bronze Age (photo: Michael Luddeni, courtesy of Cairo Museum)

was coalescing into a regional threat. And the Levant was in the geographical pathway of everyone's aggressions. The entire Near East was positioned to experience some explosive changes—all, as it turned out, in the wake of Yahweh's dealings with Egypt's Eighteenth Dynasty (see *Breakout 3.05*).

LANGUAGES AND WRITING

Akkadian—Akkadian had now flooded the ANE as the *lingua franca* of international commerce and diplomacy. So much so that even the Egyptians used this Semitic tongue, written with cuneiform script on clay tablets, to correspond back and forth with their neighbors. The Amarna Letters found in the ruins of Akhenaten's palace (see *Breakout 3.16*) attest to the almost-universal use of Akkadian, although some of the letters coming from the Southern Levant were written in a "Canaanized" version of it. Akkadian remained the dominant everyday language of Mesopotamia (see *Figure 3.01*).

Amorite—People in the north Levant still spoke Amorite dialects, but this Semitic language was now being influenced by Indo-European Hittite and Hurrian because both groups were pressing their interests in the region. Upper-class Hurrians were already ruling over the Akkadian and Amorite speaking groups of north Mesopotamia, and the Hittites, by the mid- to late fourteenth century BC, had taken control of the north Levant (see *Breakout 3.05*). Amorite as a distinct language was losing ground in the melting-pot context of the LBA Levant.

Canaanite—The tribes of the south Levant were still speaking the various local dialects of Canaanite. The Phoenicians—local Canaanites focused on maritime commerce—had taken this language to classical literary heights, the best examples of which come from the coastal city of Ugarit (see *Map 1.04*). The Ugaritic literature is helpful for understanding many features of biblical Hebrew. The Canaanite dialect spoken by the Hebrew tribes, which had moved from Canaan to Lower Egypt in the time of Jacob, was "cooking" in isolation. It became the Hebrew of Moses and the Israelites (see *Breakout 3.11*).

BREAKOUT 3.10

EGYPTIAN MAP LISTS

The cities and locations mentioned in the books of Numbers and Joshua—through which the Israelites are said to have traveled (see *Map 3.05*)—are confirmed by Egyptian "map lists" from New Kingdom pharaohs, such as Tuthmosis III, Amenhotep III, and Rameses II (fifteenth through thirteenth centuries BC). Interestingly, the biblical lists (Numbers 33: Iyyin, Dibon-gad, Almon-diblathaim, Nebo, Abel-shittim, Jordan; and Joshua 15: Janum-Apheqeh-Hebron) are virtually identical to these Egyptian lists of the same period and present the same cities/locations in the exact same order!

Clearly, these matching biblical and Egyptian map lists derive from the ancient Egyptian practice of identifying routes to and through various regions by listing the cities and locations along those routes in a specific geographical orientation or direction of travel *from Egypt*. And the Egyptian map lists solidly refute the claims of some scholars that certain biblical cities, such as Dibon in Numbers 33 and Hebron in Joshua 15, did not exist during the Late Bronze Age.

If the Torah books were late Iron Age compositions as the negative higher critics insist, one might ask: Why would late Iron Age Jewish writers be interested in such Egyptian-like geographical precision? They weren't, because they didn't *have to* go to that much trouble to create simple fictional stories about Israelite origins. These precise details exist in the exodus and conquest stories because they are accurate and, therefore, they're authentic to the Late Bronze Age in every way.

S. Collins

BREAKOUT 3.11

MOSES AND THE SEMITIC ALPHABET

While writing systems were developing in Egypt (*hieroglyphics*) and Mesopotamia (*cuneiform*) around 3300 BC, a true *alphabet* did not appear in the ANE until after 1800 BC. Writing systems like hieroglyphics and cuneiform were complex, with hundreds of characters. Their signs had values ranging from pictograms (a fish meant "fish"), to logograms (single signs reflected whole words or phrases, usually archaic), to syllables (consonant plus vowel, like *ba*), to sound-signs (as in *t* for "t"). Words could be "spelled" by using virtually any combination of the above, which made learning these writing systems difficult. As a result, writing was reserved for the educated elite, such as scribes, administrators, priests, and royals.

When hieroglyphics and cuneiform reigned, there was no such thing as public literacy. And as we all know, information is power. Therefore, in the Bronze Age, power lay in the hands of kings and their administrations. A nonliterate populace was a distinct advantage for the ruling class. Thus, during the first 1,500 years of writing, there was no easily learnable alphabet.

An alphabet is a set of signs—usually 20 to 30—representing the basic range of human vocalization. It is easy to learn. It is easy to write and read. It can be adapted to almost any language, although it was never used in Mesopotamia or Egypt until late in the Iron Age.

There were ancient attempts at alphabetic writing, but without long-term success. In the Bronze Age Aegean world of the Minoans, Mycenaeans, and early Greeks, alphabets like Phaistos script (not deciphered), Linear A (not deciphered), and Linear B struggled to gain hold. At places like Ugarit on the Northern Levantine coast, an alphabet using cuneiform-style characters lasted barely a century. But one alphabet enjoyed great success, eventually replacing them all: the Semitic alphabet, which gave rise to most of the alphabets in the world, such as Hebrew, Phoenician, Moabite, Aramaic, Arabic, Greek, Latin, Russian, German, English, and dozens of others. Indeed, most of the world's alphabets are derived from the original Semitic alphabet.

But why an alphabet? Certainly the kings and aristocrats of the ancient world did not sanction this! For the first time in history, common people had the opportunity to read and write. The Semitic alphabet seems to have started in Egypt, adapted from 20 or so of the simpler hieroglyphic signs, at a time when Semitic people from the Levant were flooding into the Nile Delta during the latter part of the Middle Bronze Age and first part of the Late Bronze Age (c. nineteenth through fifteenth centuries BC), the sons of Israel among them. But why at this particular moment in history?

In Deuteronomy 27:2-8 (cf. Joshua 8:32), God commanded Moses to set up in the Promised Land what amounted to stone "billboards" upon which were written the words of the law (likely the Ten Commandments). These plastered, inscribed stone monuments were for public viewing.

This assumes public literacy among the Israelites (otherwise, what was the point?). The wandering Israelites were commoners, former slaves. They entertained no international diplomats. They had neither royalty nor upper-class elites. Yet they were expected to be able to read the law for themselves as they entered into the Land of Promise. In essence, God desired a literate people!

It seems more than a coincidence that an easily learned alphabet had developed just in time for Moses to write the books of the Torah and for the Israelites to be able to read the laws of Yahweh for themselves as they came into the Promised Land in the fourteenth century BC.

S. Collins

BREAKOUT 3.12

WRITING MATERIALS

By 3300 BC, people were writing in both Egypt and Mesopotamia and made use of specific surfaces on which to express their ideas—mineral (stone, clay, and metal), vegetable (papyrus or wood), and animal (parchment or vellum).

Mineral. Early in Egypt, the face of natural rock formations, constructed stone walls, and carved stone monuments (*stelae*) were inscribed in hieroglyphic script. Job 19:24 speaks of engraving words on stone with a metal stylus. In Egypt, smooth, flat stone flakes or chips (*ostraca*) were drawn or written upon with ink—like ancient scrap paper. Meanwhile, early in Mesopotamia, the standard writing surface for government records, religious texts, and official legal transactions was unfired clay tablets impressed with cuneiform script created by using a stylus. Isaiah's reference to writing on a tablet may mean inscribing a clay tablet (Isaiah 30:8). Texts were also engraved on thin metal sheets, but this was an expensive process that required significant craftsmanship and thus are very rare. Two tiny silver scrolls (known as the Ketef Hinnom Silver Scrolls) found in a Jerusalem tomb were inscribed with the priestly benediction from Numbers 6:24-26 and apparently worn as amulets. These unique scrolls date to the beginning of the sixth century BC, which make them our oldest copy of a biblical text. In addition, the Copper Scroll, a thin copper sheet that was discovered among the Dead Sea Scrolls, bears an account of hidden treasure (though this account is not a biblical text). Ancient coins are the best-known examples of inscribed (stamped) metal, originating in wealthy southern Anatolian kingdoms by the end of the sixth century BC. The Persian Empire (fifth century BC) popularized gold and silver coins as a medium of exchange and a means to communicate governmental propaganda.

Animal. Parchment or vellum was specially prepared sheepskin or goatskin—frequently sewn together to create sheets of a scroll and written upon in ink. These were more expensive yet lasted longer than papyrus, and among the Jews, they were the medium of choice for sacred texts. The only clear biblical reference to parchment is 2 Timothy 4:13 (NIV), where Paul mentions "my scrolls"

Writing pens and ink, Egypt (photo: David E. Graves)

(Greek, *biblia*; presumably papyrus) and "the parchments" (Greek, *membranas*), likely Old Testament texts.

Vegetable. Papyrus (officially *Cyperus papyrus*; Hebrew *gome* ["bulrushes"—Exodus 2:3 KJV]) was Egypt's writing medium of choice—at least by the mid-third millennium BC. Ten-foot tall papyri grew prolifically in the marshy areas of the Nile Delta. The stems were cut into long, wet strips and arranged side by side to create a sheet, with the edges slightly overlapping. A second layer was placed directly above at a right angle, and the sheet was pounded smooth while still wet. Left to dry flat under pressure and afterward polished with a stone or shell, the sheet

was then ready to serve as a writing surface. Papyrus was the Mediterranean region's writing material of choice during New Testament times; the apostle John's desire to not communicate with "paper [Greek, *chartes*] and ink" (2 John 12) would indicate he wanted to use papyrus. Ink (Greek, *melanos*; "black") was a mixture of carbonized (burned) material, water, and oil (or gum), and was written using a reed pen. The oldest-known New Testament text is the John Rylands Papyrus (p52)—the leaf of a codex (book) with John 18:31-33 on one side and John 18:37-38 on the other, possibly dating from between AD 125–150.

G. Byers

HITTITE—The Indo-European Hittites were controlling the Northern Levant by c. 1365 BC but had little impact on the linguistic situation in Canaan (south Levant). However, Moses's intimate familiarity with LBA Hittite law codes—the Mosaic Law is structured as a Hittite suzerainty treaty—reinforces the likelihood that he was fluent in Hittite (see *Breakout 3.02*).

EGYPTIAN—Because of its relative geographical isolation, the Egyptian language continued unabated, bolstered by administrative texts, literary works, and the fact it was "plastered" across Egypt on thousands of public monuments. Obviously, Moses was fluent in Egyptian and could read both hieroglyphic and hieratic scripts (see *Figure 3.02*).

BELIEFS AND RELIGIONS

EGYPTIAN RELIGION—Egyptian religious practices of the LBA, corresponding with the Eighteenth and Nineteenth Dynasties, grew out of an understanding of a great pantheon of gods (more than 2,000!) and the vital roles they played in every aspect of life and abundant afterlife. These highly anthropomorphic and zoomorphic gods were the focal point of both personal and civic practice. Their characteristics changed over time to fit new worldviews, political agendas, and international relations (see *Canaanite Religion* next).

The most well-known gods include Isis, Osiris, Horus, Amun-Re, Hathor, Heka, Bastet, Thoth, and Anubis (see *Figure 3.03*). The lesser-known gods were localized to specific regions or performed specific services or functions. Because the prosperity of Egypt depended upon the yearly flooding of the Nile River, many of these gods were imbued with agricultural, fertility, and life-sustaining themes. During the New Kingdom, the priesthood of the composite god Amun-Re held the most power, and the worship of him sometimes bordered on monotheism. The Egyptian king, or pharaoh, was seen as the manifestation of a deity on earth—such as Amun-Re. Because of his deific status, a pharaoh's rule and decisions were absolute, his actions and annals flawless.

CANAANITE RELIGION—Egypt's renewed interest in the land and resources of Canaan during the LBA period meant that religious influences arrived via diplomatic correspondence—and its armies. The rigidity of the Canaanite religious culture was on the decline but continued to include El and his consort, Asherah, as well as ritual sacrifices and prostitution on behalf of the gods with agricultural themes—the thunder/rain god Baal and his female consorts, the fertility goddess Astarte, and the warrior goddess Anat (see *Figure 3.04*). Interestingly, some of these gods were accepted into the Egyptian pantheon with temples and monumental presence.

The interrelationship between Canaanite and Egyptian religious practices is also seen in burial items like scarabs and anthropoid clay coffins (see *Figure 3.05*). Cultic amphorae (ritual vessels) began to be produced with handles in the Canaanean fashion, and the Canaanean sickle sword (see *Breakout 3.14*) came

Figure 3.02—Egyptian texts, Late Bronze Age (photos: James Barber, David E. Graves)

Figure 3.03—Egyptian deities (photos: Alexander Schick)

BREAKOUT 3.13

GIANTS IN THE LAND

The Bible speaks of "tall" (Hebrew *midah* or *rum*) individuals and people groups. Goliath of Gath's (1 Samuel 17:4) "height [*gobah*] was six cubits and a span" (9'9" or 3 meters) according to the Masoretic Text and some editions of the Septuagint. Josephus (*Antiquities* 6.171), Dead Sea Scroll fragment *4Qsam*ᵃ, and other Septuagint (LXX^BL) editions say "four cubits and a span" (6'9" or 2 meters). An unnamed Egyptian soldier—a "tall [*midah*]" man of "five cubits" (7'6" or 2.25 meters)—was killed by Benaiah, son of Jehoiada (1 Chronicles 11:23).

Among Philistine soldiers at Gath was an unnamed "man of great [*midah*] stature" who was "descended from Rapha" (2 Samuel 21:20; 1 Chronicles 20:6 NIV). King Saul was "from his shoulders upward…taller [*gaboah*] than any of the people" (1 Samuel 9:2).

Nephilim/Nephilites, which is translated *gigantes* in the Septuagint, Vulgate, and Josephus (*Antiquities* 1.73), were related to the Anakim/Anakites (Numbers 13:28, 33)—the only biblical reference to Nephilim/Nephilites being tall (*midah*, verse 33). Anakim/Anakites are first mentioned associated with the Nephilim/Nephilites (Numbers 13:33). Described as

"tall" (*rum*) (Deuteronomy 2:11, 21; 9:2), they were also equated with the Rephaim/Rephaites (Deuteronomy 2:11).

Hieratic-inscribed Egyptian Middle Kingdom Execration Texts in Berlin's Egypt Museum are bowls inscribed inside and out with curses against Egypt's Levantine enemies. Ceremonially breaking and burying these bowls was to hurt those named on the bowls. The bowl incantations against Iy Aneq have been suggested as early references to the Anakim/Anakites.

People in Canaan, possibly Amorites (Deuteronomy 1:27), were "taller" (*rum*, verse 28), although Anakim/Anakites were also noted (verse 28). Rephaim/Rephaites (called Emites by the Moabites and Zamzummim by the Ammonites [Deuteronomy 2:11, 20]) were associated with the Anakim/Anakites and also "tall" (*rum*; Deuteronomy 2:10-11, 20-21). Rephaim/Rephaites may also be sons "descended from the giants"—including the "tall" (*rum*) man with six-digited hands and feet (1 Samuel 21:20; 1 Chronicles 20:6)—who, like Goliath of Gath, were Philistine soldiers.

Og, the king of Bashan with the 13-foot-long and 6-foot-wide iron bed ("sarcophagus"?) was of the Rephaim/Rephaites

(Deuteronomy 3:11). Sabeans were "men of stature [*midah*]" (Isaiah 45:14). Men of Cush were "tall" (*mashak*) people (Isaiah 18:2, 7).

Egyptian Pharaoh Ramesses II's victory over the Hittites at the Battle of Kadesh in 1274 BC was among his crowning achievements, carved in relief (image or text) 15 times in his temples. The battle's turning point came through information from two captured Shasu (Levantine Bedouin) soldiers. While Egyptian reliefs regularly depict pharaohs as larger than all others, in this scene the Shasu are shown as having greater stature than the Egyptians.

Papyrus Anastasi I (British Museum) is a nineteenth-century BC hieratic text, purportedly a letter from Egyptian army scribe Hori to a fellow scribe named Amenemope. Amenemope's infamous ambush by Shasu warriors in Canaan—displaying poor judgment and character—is recounted in this letter. Some among the Shasu were noted as four to five cubits tall (6'8" to 8'6" according to the Egyptian royal cubit). While this may have a satirical literary composition and not official correspondence, the image suggests taller men from Canaan.

G. Byers

BREAKOUT 3.14

THE SICKLE SWORD

Throughout the books of Exodus, Numbers, Deuteronomy, Joshua, and Judges, we find the common idiom "the edge of the sword." In this phrase, the word translated "edge" is always singular (Hebrew, *peh*; literally means "mouth"). During the times of Moses, Joshua, and the Israelite judges, the expression "to smite with the edge of the sword" was a favorite way to describe killing one's enemies in battle. In later periods, including the books of Samuel, Kings, and beyond, the term all but disappears—except in a few vestigial cases—even though there was a lot of smiting going on. This change in terminology clearly demonstrates just how historically accurate and authentic the biblical text is.

When we examine what the archaeological record says about military weapons during the LBA and IA, this change comes clearly into focus. During the MBA (2100–1550 BC), the battlefield weapons of choice were axes of one sort or other—like the duck-billed axe and epsilon axe. Toward the beginning of the LBA (c. 1500 BC), the epsilon axe, with its single curved edge, eventually became a more elegant and powerful weapon known as the sickle sword (indeed, it looked much like a sickle). The sickle sword, with its long, curved,

single-edged blade, was a formidable weapon. In a tight marching rank, it could be held by the handle with only two fingers while the dull side of the blade curved upward and fit snugly around the arm. As a one- or two-fisted weapon, it was capable of lopping off arms and heads with ease.

The Egyptians made the sickle sword standard military issue, and this weapon is frequently depicted in their art. There is no doubt that when the Israelites departed Egypt under Moses, their fighting men were armed with the finest sickle swords of Egyptian manufacture. Later, when the Israelites marched into the cities of Canaan under the leadership of Joshua, their single-edged bronze sickle swords glistened in the bright Near Eastern sunlight. The phrase "smite with the edge of the sword" is a direct, specific reference to the single-edged sickle sword.

By the time of David and Solomon, nobody had ever seen what was, by then, an ancient bronze sickle sword. Swords had become double-edged and were made with iron. And the idiom "smite with the edge of the sword" disappeared after the LBA, a fact reflected in the text of the Old Testament itself. Is it merely coincidence that this idiom appears in

Egyptian-style sickle sword (photo: James Barber, courtesy of Bible Lands Museum, Jerusalem)

Bible stories from the LBA when the single-edged sickle sword was the weapon of choice, but quickly disappears during the IA, when swords had become double-edged? No, it is not a coincidence at all. The stories of Moses, Joshua, and the Israelite judges contain eyewitness elements of the events they describe. Writers in later times would not have documented such specific details from earlier times.

S. Collins, J. Holden

Figure 3.04—Baal, Astarte, Anat—Canaanean deities (photos: James Barber, Alexander Schick; courtesy of Bible Lands Museum, Jerusalem)

Figure 3.05—Clay anthropoid coffins, Late Bronze Age (photos: Alexander Schick)

Ammonite texts by similar names. The most noted practice of Molech worship was child sacrifice by burning (see *Figure 3.07*). In the book of Leviticus we find many prohibitions against sacrificing children to Molech. The practice is well documented in the archaeological record.

HITTITE WORLDVIEW—The Hittite culture (Anatolia; modern Turkey/Asia Minor) flourished during the second millennium BC, growing from a prosperous local city-state to a regional powerhouse able to overtake large parts of Syria and Mesopotamia and eventually causing problems for the mighty Rameses II of Egypt. Success of the kingdom depended heavily on agrarian pursuits, and the two primary deities—storm god Taru and sun goddess Arinniti (see *Figure 3.08*), among 1,000 gods—reflect that complex interrelationship. The Hittite king acted as chief priest and steward over lands "owned" by the gods, thus his sacred duty as Great King and Hero was twofold: (1) perform religious rites, and (2) expand the kingdom. Because the king's anointing was believed to be divine, he acted as judge in civil matters and believed

into use as an Egyptian symbol of power, a gift from the gods as an assurance of victory. In cultural pockets where the Sea Peoples appear, the pantheon included Dagon (although originally from Mesopotamia), and cultic complexes often used mudbrick rather than stone altars. The marrying of Canaanite deities with the religious practices of the Sea Peoples (forefathers of the Philistines) may have been the precursor to the more well-known Greek pantheons from the Hellenistic period. Canaanite high places, sacred groves, and elaborate temples (see *Figure 3.06*) continued to be used for worship throughout this period.

MOLECH—Molech (Moloch; Milcom) is a difficult god to nail down. The name is a variant of the Hebrew consonantal spelling *mlk*, simply meaning "king." He appears as a sun or fire god in Phoenician and

Figure 3.06—Canaanite Late Bronze Age temple, Hazor (photos: John Witte Moore)

Figure 3.07—Sacrificial installation, Megiddo (photo: Joseph Holden)

Figure 3.08—Hittite deity, Teshub (photo: Steven Collins, courtesy of Museum of Anatolian Civilizations, Ankara)

himself to be the final authority in negotiations and treaties, even over the rulers of other kingdoms. Upon death, Hittite kings enjoyed the status of gods.

YAHWISM—During this period we see a marked shift in the Hebrew understanding of God—the codification of Israelite religion as belief in *the* singular deity, Yahweh (Deuteronomy 6:4). The comparatively simple patriarchal worship practices—burnt offerings, prayer, meditation, and solitude—suggesting direct access to Yahweh without a mediating priesthood transitioned to a ritual system of atonement, behavioral objectives, and a formal (though portable) worship center with sacred objects. While the fundamental understanding of *atonement*—the idea that when a moral or cosmological crime has been committed, a death must occur to atone, or pay with blood, for the wrong—continued to be the central idea. The rightness or wrongness of behavior was divinely given at a central gathering, to be lived out both at the local and regional levels. The Hebrew people and a mixed multitude of others entered into a covenantal relationship with Yahweh, wherein they became his personal and sacred possession. The patriarchal idea of possessing an area or territory on behalf of Yahweh continued in the biblical account of Joshua training up an army to conquer Canaan (Joshua 7–8).

MOSAIC LAW—The moral, religious, and legal code given by Moses in covenant (treaty) form to the followers of Yahweh is found in the Mosaic Law (most notably Deuteronomy 19–20). The purpose of the law was to define a group of people as separate from the religious and cultural practices of the ANE during the time of Moses and Joshua. The Mosaic Law also established a formal priesthood and system of theocratic governance, setting the stage for the Hebrews to become a nation—Israel. This law was in stark contrast to the Canaanite religious culture, in which there was no indication of any moral code to be followed. Whereas devotees of the Canaanean religions might only be as good as the behavior of the gods they followed, a follower of Yahweh's law was seen as reflecting the goodness inherent in the Creator of that law.

ARCHITECTURE AND INFRASTRUCTURE

CITIES, TOWNS, AND VILLAGES—The state of Canaanean civilization in the LBA south Levant was very different from what it had been during the MBA, the time of Abraham. Many of the larger cities had been targeted and destroyed by the Egyptians after they chased the Semitic Hyksos from Egypt, c. 1550 BC. During the first 150 years of the LBA (see *Timeline*), Egypt systematically raided Canaan to capture slaves and to purposefully keep the population of the Southern Levant low. Thus, the cities met by Joshua were smaller and not as well defended as in the previous period. The LBA peoples of Canaan generally reused the old, ramparted fortifications from the MBA, refurbishing them, and in some cases built new city walls. A handful of cities—like Jerusalem, Shechem, Megiddo, and Hazor—managed to gather satellite towns and villages around them and operate as city-states.

FORTIFICATIONS—Rampart-based fortifications

BREAKOUT 3.15

JOSHUA AND JERICHO

From his excavations at Tell es-Sultan/Jericho during the 1920s, John Garstang declared that he had discovered the famous city walls of Jericho that "fell down flat" (Joshua 6:20) during Joshua's campaign against the city. Bible scholars rejoiced! Then in the 1950s, as a result of her excavations at Jericho, Kathleen Kenyon concluded and published that Garstang had misdated the city wall to the fifteenth–fourteenth century BC, and that it actually belonged to the end of the MBA (c. 1550 BC). She also announced that there was no walled city at Jericho during the LBA (1550–1200 BC)—the alleged time of Joshua. This became the new conventional wisdom in archaeology and still dominates most scholars' thinking on the subject.

This did not sit well with some conservative archaeologists. One response was to "down-date" the end of the MBA from 1550 BC to 1400 BC. This approach proved to be archaeologically unworkable. Another slant was to insist that Kenyon misread the Jericho pottery as MBA when it actually was LBA, as Garstang thought. But this did not (and does not) square with the pottery evidence from other Jordan Valley sites, which clearly show that the pottery associated with Jericho's MBA destruction is just that—MBA, not LBA. Yet another way to counter Kenyon's assessment is to suggest a massive amount of erosion at Tell es-Sultan/Jericho that all but "erased" the city Joshua conquered. But in the light of the latest archaeological evidence, none of these scholarly gyrations is necessary.

Continuing excavations at Jericho over the past several decades confirm that there was, in fact, a LBA2a walled town at the site dating to the fourteenth century BC (whether Kenyon missed it or ignored it is an ongoing discussion). So both Garstang *and* Kenyon were wrong about Joshua's Jericho!

The archaeological evidence is now clear: There was no occupation at Jericho during LBA1 (c. 1550–1400 BC). This eliminates the early date for the exodus (1446 BC) and conquest (1406 BC). There was no occupation at Jericho during LBA2b (c. 1300–1200 BC), which disqualifies the late date for the exodus (c. 1250 BC) and conquest (c. 1210 BC). The only Jericho that existed during the LBA was during LBA2a (c. 1400–1300 BC)—and it was fortified! This confirms that the exodus occurred around the beginning of LBA2a (c. 1400 BC or after), with the conquest occurring in mid to late LBA2a (after c. 1350 BC) (see *Breakouts 3.04, 3.05*).

S. Collins

Figure 3.09—Modern reconstruction of a Hittite city fortification, Late Bronze Age, Hattusa (photo: Alexander Schick)

Figure 3.10—Monumental construction; bastion entrance to Late Bronze Age Megiddo (photo: John Witte Moore)

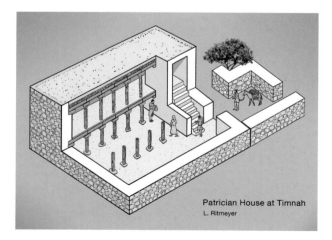

Patrician House at Timnah
L. Ritmeyer

Figure 3.11—House, Late Bronze Age, Timnah (drawing: Leen Ritmeyer)

still dominated. All the old MBA ramparts, even some city walls, were still standing throughout the LBA. The LBA inhabitants of Canaan refurbished and rebuilt many of the already-existing defensive systems with their monumental gateways and towers. To the Israelites who saw these fortifications for the first time, they appeared impressive, even intimidating (see *Figure 3.09*).

MONUMENTAL AND PUBLIC ARCHITECTURE— The tradition of monumental architecture continued in the south Levant during this period, although on a more modest scale. Temples remained a central focus of city planning, and some were impressive, as at Hazor (see *Figure 3.10*). Construction was of mudbrick on stone foundations, all coated in a mud-sand plaster (sometimes with lime added). Local oak and cedar from Lebanon were commonly used for roof beams and door and window frames. Walls were thick and provided excellent insulation. The extent of window use is mostly a mystery, but it is believed they were used to bring light into public buildings. It is also possible that some ceiling light-wells were used.

HOUSES—LBA houses continued the traditions of the MBA, with multiple rooms arranged around a courtyard used for cooking. Mudbrick construction was standard, along with beam-wattle-daub roofs finished with clay-sand-lime plaster (see *Figure 3.11*).

SACRED ARCHITECTURE—The tripartite temple was still the most popular form. It reinforced the mystery and holiness of sacred spaces by limiting access increasingly as one moved toward the interior and most separated shrine. The Israelite tabernacle (see *Figure 3.12*) and, later, Solomon's temple followed this same basic design.

NECROSCAPES—By this time, most of the extensive megalithic sacrescapes of earlier periods had been abandoned. What remained were cemeteries of cave and shaft tombs that housed single or multiple interments (see *Figure 3.13*). Grave goods buried with males often included daggers and other bronze weaponry, causing some to believe these males had been warriors. However, such burials are now interpreted generally as simply male in nature.

INFRASTRUCTURE—During this period the Egyptians maintained an elaborate system of Levantine highways and roadways, mainly for purposes of moving troops, including chariot forces, quickly from Egypt up through Canaan and into Syria (see *Map 3.02*). This system also included fortresses and garrisons in key locations. Those who lived in cities and towns in the Levant maintained critical water resources by digging wells, access tunnels, and cisterns inside their defensive walls. The stockpiling of surplus grain was also important, so they used in-ground silos for bulk storage and built warehouses in which to place large grain jars (see *Figure 3.14*).

WEAPONS AND WARFARE

SICKLE SWORDS—The shift away from the battle axe was nearly complete with the appearance of the sickle

Figure 3.13—Tomb painting, Late Bronze Age, Egypt (photo: James Barber, courtesy of Bible Lands Museum, Jerusalem)

Figure 3.14—Storage facilities, Late Bronze Age customs house (photo: Daniel Galassini, courtesy of Tall el-Hammam Excavation Project)

Figure 3.12—Overhead view of the Israelite tabernacle (drawing: Leen Ritmeyer)

sword. The name comes from the sword's shape, and the sharpened edge was on the outside curve of the blade. It was still a close-combat weapon used for hacking at people, like its battle-axe predecessors, but with a much longer cutting edge. Sizes vary from quite small (16 inches) to large (24 inches) (see *Figure 3.15*). The double-edged straight sword did not yet exist in the Near East.

BRONZE TO IRON—While the vast majority of weapons during the LBA were made of bronze, a few iron weapons are known from this period, such as the iron dagger from King Tut's tomb. It was, however, not made of smelted iron, but of meteoritic iron.

BREAKOUT 3.16

JOSHUA AND THE AMARNA LETTERS

With the exodus linked to the death of Tuthmosis IV—which marked the onset of the once-great Eighteenth Dynasty's collapse (see *Breakouts 3.04, 3.05*)—the Israelite conquest of Canaan would have begun during the second year of Pharaoh Akhenaten's bizarre reign. In the decades of Egypt's implosion after the catastrophic exodus events that forced Tuthmosis IV to release Israel from bondage, Egypt had to withdraw its military presence from Syria and Canaan (see *Maps 3.02, 3.03*). Now in dire straits, Egypt was forced to abandon its long-held Asiatic territories, leaving its former Levantine subjects to their own devices. The Hittites filled the void in Syria, while Canaan itself descended into chaos. By the time the "heretic" king Akhenaten took the throne, Egypt was long gone from the Southern Levant.

Thus, Joshua and the Israelites entered an Egyptian-less Canaan, exactly as the book of Joshua describes the situation. In the Amarna Letters—discovered among the ruins of Akhenaten's palace at Tell el-Amarna—we find the kings of Canaan beseeching the pharaoh to at least send a few troops to ease their fears about the deteriorating situation caused by

Egypt's withdrawal. The Amarna archive also confirms Akhenaten's failure to provide an Egyptian military response to alleviate the bedlam. But Akhenaten didn't merely refuse assistance; he *could not* act because Egypt itself was in crisis and things were getting worse.

Chaim Herzog and Mordechai Gichon assess and describe the state of affairs perfectly:

> Joshua also had to reckon with the prospect of interference by the Egyptians, as Canaan was [technically] still part of the Pharaonic Empire. We now know from the archives of King Amenhotep IV [Akhenaten]... that most calls for aid from the Canaanites...had been put off with empty promises. And Joshua, though certainly not privy to the Egyptian diplomatic correspondence, did gauge the actual situation correctly. The time was ripe for a strike, and there was little danger of Egyptian interference as long as the Israelites kept to the mountains and away from the plains, the site of the Via Maris (Way of the Sea)...

(Herzog and Gichon, *Battles of the Bible* [London: Greenhill Books, 2002], 49).

After defeating Jericho, Bethel,

and Ai, Joshua marched northward to Shechem, located between Mount Gerazim and Mount Ebal (Joshua 8). It is at this point that a remarkable connection between Joshua and the Amarna correspondence occurs.

In the Amarna Letters, King Lab'ayu of the Shechem city-state was accused by other Canaanite city rulers of aligning himself with the Habiru (or 'Apiru; see *Breakout 2.06*). Lab'ayu's sons were accused of the same offense. Evidently a large group of Habiru—"marauding nomads"—had encamped around Shechem and were on friendly terms with Lab'ayu and his family. And by what other term would Canaanite city-dwellers have referred to Joshua's Israelites, since they had all grown up as nomads in the wilderness and would have been perceived as nothing more or less than the raiding rabble called Habiru? Although some scholars have disallowed—on quite flimsy grounds—a relationship between the terms *Habiru* and *Hebrew*, there is no doubt about the linguistic similarity of the two terms.

It is also worth noting that, according to the biblical text, the Israelites never attacked Shechem or any town belonging to the Shechem city-state (see *Map*

3.07). And might not the Akkadian name Lab'ayu—which in Hebrew is *Leba'-Ya* = "lion of Yahweh"—suggest that the king of Shechem was, in some fashion, a worshipper of Yahweh, the God of Joshua (Hebrew, *Yehosua* = "Yahweh saves")? After all, the Shechem territory was a former stomping ground of the Israelites' Hebrew ancestors!

Although written from radically different points of view, the biblical story of Joshua's association with Shechem and—as reflected in the Amarna Letters—the Canaanite accusation of Habiru ties to King Lab'ayu of Shechem seem far more than coincidental.

S. Collins, J. Holden

BREAKOUT 3.17

JOSHUA'S LONG DAY

Joshua 10:12-15 appears to claim that the sun stopped in Gibeon, and the moon in the valley of Aijalon. This is how it has been interpreted by ancient Jewish and Christian scholars, who also argued that the purpose of the miracle was to allow the Israelites more daytime to defeat their enemies. If taken literally, one would think this miracle would have significant cosmic consequences, to say the least; however, one must first interpret the Bible in its ancient context.

According to Joshua 10, the Israelite leader Joshua made a mad dash to get to Gibeon to protect that town against a coalition of Amorite kings. Like any good military leader in antiquity, Joshua inquired of God about his chances in battle. God guaranteed victory, which was all Joshua needed know.

The lyric poetry of Joshua 10:12 states that the sun halted in Gibeon, and the moon in Aijalon. This signifies that the sun was in the east and the moon in the west, meaning it was morning, not evening. Joshua was certainly not asking for more sunlight (after all, the day had just begun). Furthermore, the event was considered unique not because of any astronomical abnormalities, but because God listened to the voice of a man and fought for Israel (verse 14).

So what was Joshua asking for? Let me explain. While I am not an astronomy geek, I am a Mesopotamia geek. The phraseology in Joshua 10:12-13 sounds suspiciously like vocabulary used in Mesopotamian celestial omen texts. In fact, it is clear that the relative positions of the sun and moon played a role in determining military movements. Kings consulted omen priests who told them whether or not a particular solar/lunar juxtaposition was favorable for victory.

For example, one omen states, "When the moon and sun are seen with one another on the 14th [that is, the fourteenth day since the last full moon], the land will be satisfied." This was a good omen. Another omen states, "When the sun and moon are seen with each other on the 15th day, a powerful enemy will raise his weapons against the land"—clearly a bad omen.

To be clear, Joshua was not asking or searching for an omen, but in the eyes of his enemies the juxtaposition of the sun and the moon in the sky meant a terrible omen for them, causing Israel's enemies to flee in a panic.

M. Chavalas

BREAKOUT 3.18

TRIBAL ALLOTMENTS

God assured Abraham (Genesis 15:18-19) that his descendants would inherit the land of the Canaanites and other tribal groups in the Southern Levant. Centuries of Egyptian slavery tested the veracity of this covenant promise. After the exodus and nearly four decades of wilderness wanderings, Moses turned his attention toward righteously dividing the land that lay before the people of Israel. Only through land inheritance would the nation successfully transition from a nomadic lifestyle to a sedentary lifestyle.

Moses blessed the tribes but did not specify the boundaries of their allotments. While camped at Abel Shittim (Numbers 25:1) and after conquering the Transjordan kingdoms of Sihon and Og, the tribes of Ruben and Gad petitioned Moses to allow them to inherit the lands of these vanquished kings. With restrictions, Moses consented, and he included half of Manasseh's tribe in the arrangement. Thus two-and-a-half tribes settled east of the Jordan River. Twenty percent of the priestly tribe of Levi joined them to ensure that the worship of Yahweh remained a top priority for those tribes. Thus, parts of four tribes settled in the Transjordan, providing a buffer from border invasions from the east.

After Moses's death, Joshua led a six-year military campaign in the Cisjordan region (see *Maps 3.06, 3.07*). Thus, in the mid to late fourteenth century BC, with Israel clearly in control of the highlands from Shechem to Hebron, Joshua turned his attention to matters of land inheritance (see *Map 3.08*). At Gilgal, in consultation with Eleazar the high priest and the heads of the tribal clans, Joshua established boundaries for several more of the tribes: Judah, Ephraim, and the other half of Manasseh (Joshua 14–17). As with the Transjordan tribes, 20 percent of the Levites shared in the inheritance of these two-and-a-half tribes. Thus, five tribes received their allotments before Joshua ordered that the sacred tabernacle be erected at Shiloh, a site occupied by the Amorites for hundreds of years.

The remaining seven tribes received their inheritance at Shiloh (Joshua 18:1). Joshua commissioned three men from each tribe to conduct a survey and to divide the remaining land into seven parts. He then cast lots at the entrance of the tabernacle (Joshua 19:51) to determine which territory would belong to the tribes of Benjamin, Simeon, Zebulun, Issachar, Asher, Naphtali, and Dan.

Two of the allotments proved particularly problematic. Dan received an inheritance in the coastal plain but failed to rout the powerful native inhabitants (Judges 1:34). As a result, the Danites relocated to the northern region of the city of Leshem/Laish (Joshua 19:47-48). Simeon also received a difficult allotment that was landlocked within Judah's boundaries. Centuries later, when the nation of Israel was divided into the northern and southern kingdoms during the reign of Rehoboam, the people of Simeon could not join Jeroboam's new northern kingdom without forfeiting their land inheritance. The Bible never addresses this dilemma, but it seems likely that Judah absorbed Simeon, yielding a nine-to-three division of the tribes instead of the traditional ten-to-two division between Israel and Judah respectively

To keep the numbers straight, it is important to remember that Levi did not receive a regular inheritance because it served as the priestly tribe. However, Joseph received a double portion, reflected in the lands of Ephraim and Manasseh. Hence, the number of tribes remains 12. The tribal allocations occurred in three phases: Transjordan (2.5), Gilgal (2.5), and Shiloh (7). Moses oversaw the first phase, and Joshua oversaw the subsequent phases.

S. Stripling

Although extensive use of iron would not begin until the twelfth century BC, in Iron Age 1 (IA1), smelted iron blades are known from Anatolia as early as 2500 BC. Smelted iron objects are known from Anatolia, Mesopotamia, and Egypt during the fifteenth century BC.

Chariots of Iron—The mention of iron in the book of Joshua, and particularly iron chariots (Joshua 17:16-18), is often criticized by scholars as anachronistic (iron is also mentioned throughout the books of the Torah). But such criticism rises from an ignorance of the archaeological facts. Smelted iron is known to have been present in Anatolia in the mid-third millennium BC, and in Mesopotamia, Egypt, and Anatolia in the mid-second millennium BC. But more importantly, nobody in the ANE made chariots entirely of iron in any period! "Chariots of iron" simply refers to chariots with structural or armor components made of iron. Iron finds are rare (even in the Iron Age!) for the simple reason that iron was extremely expensive to produce. Thus, as much as possible, every bit of iron was recycled over and over again.

Slings and Slingers—Slingstones are common in the archaeological record of this period, even though not mentioned in the Bible until the book of Judges. Slingers were used in attacks on cities to lay down cover fire over city walls and gate towers while soldier crews ripped off metal sheathing and set the city gates on fire (see *Figure 3.16*).

Figure 3.15—Sickle sword, standard weapon of the Late Bronze Age (photo: Daniel Galassini, courtesy of Museum of Archaeology, Trinity Southwest University)

INDUSTRIES AND OBJECTS

Agriculture—Even though the LBA was a wet period in the Levant, the low-Canaanite-population policies of Egypt's Eighteenth Dynasty did not support surplus-level agricultural production, at least not to the level of the previous MBA. But for the Israelites, it was "a land flowing with milk and honey." *Honey* was representative of farming because of the importance of bees as primary pollinators. Cereal crops remained staples, supporting bread baking and beer production. A variety of fruits and nuts were also enjoyed, especially dates, figs, pistachios, and almonds. The main exportable commodities were Canaanean olive oil (see *Figure 3.17*) and wine, both of which were in great demand

Figure 3.16—Sling stones were popular military projectiles throughout the Bronze Age (photo: Alexander Schick)

Figure 3.17—Olive press installation (drawing: Leen Ritmeyer)

around the Mediterranean basin and transported by Phoenician merchant ships.

Herding—Shasu Bedouin herders were mostly unimpeded by the Egyptian military presence in the Levant (mainly from c. 1500 BC until c. 1380 BC). Unlike their sedentary counterparts, they could move easily to remain unaffected. Besides, the Egyptian army probably relied on shepherds to provide meat to their troops (even though Egyptians had an intense dislike for sheep because of their destructive grazing habits).

Kitchens and Cooking—Cooking remained a courtyard activity in homes across the south Levant. The rounded cooking pot now dominated. Beehive-style ovens (tabuns) made of clay were for baking (inside), while cooking pots were nestled in the hole at the top (outside). Porridges and stews were common. Meat was probably cooked and served only on festive occasions.

Tah'u Stew
(see Figure 3.18)

This Babylonian stew recipe stretches from the MBA to the LBA and was found written in Akkadian on a clay cuneiform tablet (no. 4644 from the Yale Babylonian Collection).

Ingredients
1 lamb shank
3 cups water
2 tablespoons olive oil
Salt to taste
2 cups beer (probably wheat beer)
1 large onion, chopped
1 teaspoon coriander
1 teaspoon cumin
3 beets, cooked, peeled and chopped
4 cloves garlic, chopped
1 leek, sliced
Coriander to taste

Instructions
Wash and prepare all the vegetables for the stew.

Figure 3.18—Tah'u stew; a tasty Bronze Age meal (photo: Wes Husted)

Chop the onion and beets. Sear lamb shank on all sides with olive oil in a large pot. Add water, salt, beer, onions, coriander, cumin, and beets. Let ingredients cook for 10 minutes on medium heat. Chop the garlic and leeks. Add the garlic and leeks to the stew and bring to a boil. Reduce heat to low and let the stew simmer for an hour, stirring occasionally. Take lamb out of the pot and pull or cut the meat off the bone; then return the meat to the pot. Sprinkle with coriander and enjoy a bowl of Tah'u stew!

Fishing—Joshua 19:35-38 mentions what are known as "the cities of the fishermen" around Lake Kinnereth (Sea of Galilee). This implies that the towns encircling the lake had fishing as their main industry and is supported by the archaeological record of the area. Boat anchors, net needles, and fishing implements have been found in almost every excavation of every period (see *Figure 3.19*). Of course, this is expected because Lake Kinnereth supported large fish populations in antiquity. The Levantine coastal cities also had major fishing industries that supplied the entire region.

Metallurgy—The copper mines of Wadi Faynan (modern-day south Jordan; see *Map 2.06*) continued their production, as did the Egyptian copper works in the Sinai Peninsula. To make bronze, you needed to add 10 to 15 percent tin to a copper base. Extremely rare and not native to the ANE, tin had to be imported all the way from northern or western Europe. This indicates the existence of vast trade networks across Central Asia and Europe (see *Map 1.06*).

Stone—ANE structures were almost always built on foundations of unworked field stones. Foundation stones (boulders) were often "mined" from the ruins of previous periods or gathered from the surrounding

BREAKOUT 3.19

ISRAEL ON THE MERNEPTAH STELA

The famed Merneptah (or Merenptah) Stela is one of the many important pieces of artifactual evidence in Near Eastern archaeology. It is also highly controversial in terms of its biblical implications. While its exact date has yet to be agreed upon, most scholars, based on more recent evidence, place Merneptah's campaign against the Southern Levant in the fifth year of his reign (c. 1208 BC). This particular stela is constantly in the spotlight

Stele of Pharaoh Merneptah (photo: Michael Luddeni)

because it mentions Israel. It is the earliest extrabiblical reference to any people group by that name. Along with the carved reliefs in the temple at Karna—reliefs that depict Merneptah's campaigns—this stele sheds light on the transition from the LBA to the early IA, of which little is known.

Merneptah, who ruled for a short time—roughly ten years—was the fourth pharaoh of Egypt's Nineteenth Dynasty. He took the throne at about age 50 and was eager to set off on a military campaign, as was customary for Eighteenth and Nineteenth Dynasty kings. He was the first pharaoh to encounter the newly arrived Sea Peoples (biblical Philistines), and his stela from 1208 BC mentions the various groups with which he came into contact during his Southern Levantine incursion.

A key component of the text on the Merneptah Stela is a reference to Israel not as a city-state or kingdom (as is the case with others on the inscription), but simply as a people group that was present in Canaan during Merneptah's campaign. Some scholars argue that this may not be a reference to biblical Israel at all, but

to a formidable tribe with a similar-sounding name. But this group had managed to rank as one of the perennial enemies (Nine Bows) of Egypt, and it occupied lands distributed to Israel after Joshua's conquests in Canaan in the mid to late fourteenth century BC. Certainly, in the 100-plus years after Joshua's conquests were finished, the Israelites had plenty of time to establish themselves as a group to be reckoned with, even though they were without a king or centralized government. As the saying goes, if it looks like a duck and quacks like a duck, it just might be a duck! Thus the mention of Israel on the Merneptah Stela is, in all likelihood, biblical Israel.

This period was a "dark age" in the Southern Levant, and documentation is sparse. Because it is one of the few written texts depicting the geopolitical scene of that time, the Merneptah Stela is a pivotal piece of the Levantine puzzle. With its discovery, archaeologists have a record and anchor point from which to decipher the history of Israel during its formative years under the judges.

B.J. Fink, S. Collins

landscape. This was an industry in itself. Stone quarrying was another important industry during this time, producing worked and cut stone for use in monumental buildings and as stairs. Limestone was most prominent. Basalt was used for special applications requiring extra durability (see *Figure 3.20*).

FLINT—Flint and the lower-grade chert was an enduring material because it offered a super-sharp edge. While replaced in the BA by copper and bronze for use in weaponry, flint remained the material of choice for surgical applications (such as circumcision among the Israelites). Slingstones were also knapped from flint/chert, as were grindstones and hammer-stones, and the replaceable blade "inserts" for scythes (sickles) for harvesting grain (see *Figure 3.21*).

TEXTILES—Sheep's wool, goat hair, and flax fibers continued to be the raw materials of the textile industry. Spindle whorls and loom weights have been found by the thousands in excavations across the Levant, attesting to the importance of textile production in every sector of the region (see *Figure 3.22*). Purple dyes were produced from several species of sea snails of the Muricidae family. Reds came from the dried, powdered bodies of kermes scale insects. Blacks, reddish-browns,

Figure 3.20—Basalt used at Hazor, Late Bronze Age (photo: Alexander Schick)

browns, oranges, yellows, greens, and blues came from a variety of vegetables, fruits, herbs, barks, and roots.

POTTERY—If the making of pottery during the MBA marked an explosion of technical and artistic improvements, then the pottery of the LBA was a revolution in decoration and design (see *Figure 3.23*). The primary influence for the painted ceramics of the Levant was the Mycenaean pottery brought by the Sea Peoples from their Aegean homeland (see *Map 1.02* and *Timeline*). The general trends in form were obviously continuations from the MBA, but monochrome- and bichrome-painted vessels were much greater in abundance in the LBA, reflecting Mycenaean motifs.

The LBA was a period of vigorous international trade, as seen in the material culture of the major commercial centers of Greece, Egypt, and Canaan. During the LBA, Canaanite pottery found its way all over the Mediterranean world and into Egypt. Canaanite commercial jars have been found in great numbers in the Aegean and Mycenaean areas and in major Egyptian centers, indicating a high level of demand for Canaanite oil and wine. These large jars have handles attached to wide shoulders and taper down nearly to a point at the bottom. Obviously, they were not made for storage—they do not stand on their own—but were made for shipping purposes. Their shape maximized cargo space efficiency and prevented shifting while in transit. Some of the most beautiful pottery of LBA Canaan was bichrome ware crafted by a school of master potters

Figure 3.19—Egyptian faience bowl featuring tilapia, a popular fish (photo: James Barber, courtesy of Bible Lands Museum, Jerusalem)

Figure 3.21—Flint sickle blades (photos: Michael Luddeni, courtesy of Tall el-Hammam Excavation Project)

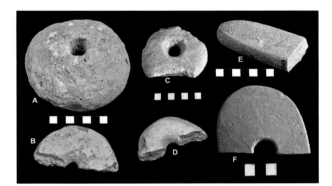

Figure 3.22—Weaving tools, Bronze Age (photos: Michael Luddeni, courtesy of Tall el-Hammam Excavation Project)

Figure 3.23—Pottery of the Late Bronze Age; several of these forms show Aegean motifs (photos: Daniel Galassini, Steven Collins; courtesy of Museum of Archaeology, Trinity Southwest University)

working in one of the coastal centers of greater Canaan. Another significant invention of the LBA was the pilgrim flask (see *Figure 3.23*).

TRADE—The LBA marked the pinnacle of Mediterranean maritime trade, as well as overland trade, with civilizations located in far-flung places (see *Map 1.06*). Tin was imported into the Levant from as far away as Spain and northern Europe. Copper and bronze moved from the Levant to Europe and Mesopotamia. Canaanean olive oil and wine, shipped by the Phoenicians, moved throughout the Mediterranean world. Exotic spices and incense came from southern Arabia and Punt (Somalia), and various woods from Africa through Nubia. Lebanon cedars found their way to every corner of the ANE. Not only goods but also artisans from the Aegean, Anatolia, Egypt, and Mesopotamia came to the south Levant to ply their skills.

BREAKOUT 3.20

JOSHUA AND EIGHTEENTH DYNASTY BATTLE ACCOUNTS

Everyone loves a good war story, and the epic tales from ancient battles are no exception. Who isn't familiar with the deceit of the Trojan horse? While it can be difficult to separate factual records from mythical saga in these later (c. 710–760 BC) Greek-style poetic compositions, the great BA battle accounts of Egypt's Eighteenth Dynasty do not leave much to the imagination. They contain exhaustively detailed records of battle objectives, troop maneuvers, topographical movements, and celebratory actions. In other words, with the right geographical starting point, you could almost recreate Thutmose III's Battle of Megiddo (c. 1457 BC) from the Karnak Temple inscriptions alone.

Although some dating variations exist for the magnificent era of the Eighteenth Dynasty, there is significant confidence among Egyptologists regarding the precision with which the dates are assigned. This is *not* the case during the same period in the Southern Levant, where there can be significant swings from one scholar's chronology of biblical events to another's.

There are three reasons for this: (1) the similarity of pottery forms from the MBA/LBA transition can be chronologically confusing; (2) the inability to separate local Canaanite culture from (possible) Israelite culture; and (3) the lack of written materials found in the area. The desire to create a cohesive historical record has led scholars to look for outside indicators, especially within the narratives of ancient Egypt, to corroborate biblical accounts. Given a fourteenth-century BC date for the conquest (see *Breakouts 3.04, 3.05, 3.15*), it is no surprise to see the same literary formula used by an ancient chronicler to describe the siege of Megiddo *also* being used to detail another war story of the same time period, Joshua's battle at Ai.

The Ai battle account, recorded in Joshua chapters 7 and 8, contains thematic elements specific to Eighteenth-Dynasty war stories, and in similar order: battle objectives, troop movements, terrain challenges, and post-victory celebrations (thanksgiving). In fact, this particular biblical narrative offers so many topographical details that with the correct starting point (Khirbet el-Maqatir), it is possible to recreate the entire attack.

The biblical narrative of Joshua's battle at Ai fits right in with the geography-heavy journalistic style used by Eighteenth Dynasty Egyptian writers to describe their battles. After all, Joshua did grow up in Egypt! This is a good example of how cultural synchronisms, highlighted by literary style, can demonstrate the historical integrity of the Bible.

A. Pavich

BREAKOUT 3.21

THE *'ELEPH* IN THE ROOM

God had promised Abraham many descendants, and the number of Israelites had increased significantly in Egypt. However, the number of 600,000 able-bodied fighting men (Exodus 12:37; Numbers 1:46; 26:51) at the time of the Exodus has led some to believe the Bible is in error in light of known demographic profiles of ANE cultures, including Egypt and Canaan. The answer to this challenge turns on the Hebrew word *'eleph* (or *'elep*) and how people in the Late Bronze Age used it and understood it. Admittedly, the subject is, by no means, a simple one.

Understanding this problem, and the challenge it presents to archaeologists and the ammunition it supplies to skeptics, we need to consider this large number in light of what we know about the size of both ancient and modern armies. An army of 600,000 (= 600 *'eleph*) men is larger than the military forces of almost every country in the world today, including the United Kingdom. The largest army in the history of the ancient world, that of the Persians, was about half this size. So 600,000 would be a very large army in modern terms, and unprecedented in

the ancient world. By comparison, the Egyptian army during the New Kingdom—the time of Moses—numbered about 25,000, according to Egyptian monumental inscriptions (and the ancient Egyptians are known for their frequent exaggerations!). One might ask, then: Why would 600,000 Israelite fighting men be the slightest bit worried about being pursued by a force of only 25,000 Egyptian troops? Such a massive horde of Israelite soldiers, even on foot, could easily have overwhelmed Pharaoh's army.

The problem is further clarified when we recognize that the 600,000 number implies a total Israelite population of at least 2.5 million people, a difficult number to imagine given the archaeological data. That is to say, the collective Canaanite population during the Late Bronze Age (Moses's time) was approximately 75 percent lower than it had been during the Middle Bronze Age (time of Abraham) when the population is estimated to have been around 350,000 in the entire Southern Levant (Canaan). Because of frequent (and calculated!) Egyptian slave raids into the region during the first part of the Late Bronze Age, the population of Canaan

was reduced to less than 100,000 in Moses's day. And in Deuteronomy 7:1, Yahweh said he would bring the Israelites into a land (Canaan) where there were "seven nations stronger and more numerous than you." Indeed, at the time, the total population of mighty Hazor—"the head of all those [Canaanite] kingdoms" according to Joshua 11:10—is generously estimated to have been between 3,000 and 5,000. As a result, some have inferred that if Joshua's army was 600,000 strong, the Israelites wouldn't have needed Yahweh's help, as they would have exponentially outnumbered the collective size of all the armies in Canaan.

There are additional difficulties with this large number: (1) the two midwives in Exodus chapter 1 could not have handled their workload (unless they supervised an army of midwives); (2) it would be impractical for the people to have gathered around to hear Moses and Aaron (Exodus 16:8-12); and (3) Israel was *smaller* than any of the seven nations then living in Canaan (Deuteronomy 7:1, 7). If "600 *'eleph*" is translated 600,000, it appears to create disagreement with other scriptures. For example, Joshua 4:13 lists 40,000 equipped for war, not 600,000. The number of firstborn males counted by Moses in the wilderness was 22,273 (Numbers 3:43). Since there is only one firstborn male per family, this must be an accurate count of the number of families. But to sustain a fighting population of 600,000 men, this relatively small number of families would need to average 25 sons (or 50 children).

Those who claim that the 600,000 number is somehow a mistake or scribal exaggeration have failed to consider the range of meaning encompassed by 'eleph. There are at least two ways to approach this:

First, textually speaking, the Hebrew text preserving this "large" number is correct. It is not some kind of embellishment or overstatement. The problem isn't the number in the Torah text. The issue is, most certainly, the *translation* and *interpretation* of the number.

So how can we begin to understand what seems to be an extremely large number that appears to contradict archaeological findings?

Can it be reconciled with a literal, authentic, normal reading of the text, and harmonized with what is known from the archaeological record? It is hard for us *moderns*, with our "science influenced" mindset, to shift toward authentically *ancient* ways of thinking, but such an adjustment can help with this issue. After all, we are dealing with a Late Bronze Age text. At the very least, we should not be surprised if Moses's use of 'eleph in such contexts appears puzzling at first.

We can move toward a solution by understanding that ancient Bronze Age people didn't always use numbers the same way we do. For us, it's easy: Just do the math! But ancient "numbers" are not that simple. The Hebrew 'eleph can mean "thousand." But it is also the first letter of the Hebrew alphabet (originally a stylized bull's head), which, when spelled out ('eleph or 'aleph), also means "cattle," "herd," or "group" with no numerical meaning implied. In a military context, it could have meant "company," "battalion," or "squad" with no specific number ("thousand") intended. For example, it is possible that Moses could be referring to 600 companies, battalions, or squads, and not thousands.

Second, perhaps 'eleph, in this context, referred to the *eligible* fighting men from a family, clan, or tribe, regardless of the actual number. Some ancient cultures also had a practice of multiplying "counts" by ten when those "numbers" were associated with kings or deities. It was their way of saying that a king or deity was worthy of far greater than what they could, in reality, offer. Seems odd to us, but to ancient minds it made perfect sense. Another example of this is 1 Samuel 18:7: "Saul has struck down his thousands, and David his ten thousands."

There can be no doubt that the original readers of the Pentateuch had no problem comprehending the meaning of 'eleph as applied to the Israelite military and people collectively. For our understanding, the Hebrew term 'eleph works best if taken in an authentic ANE manner. This approach not only introduces harmony with other biblical passages (see above), but also with the best archaeological data from the Late Bronze Age world.

With these alternatives in mind, there is absolutely no reason to view this and related passages as historical error.

S. Collins, C. Olson

CHAPTER 4

THE WORLD OF THE ISRAELITE JUDGES

WELCOME TO LATE BRONZE AGE 2B AND IRON AGE 1 (1300–1000 BC)

By the end of the thirteenth century BC, Pharaoh Merneptah had already recognized Israel as one of the perennial enemies of Egypt, naming the nation as one of the "Nine Bows" or enemies of Egypt (Merneptah Stela; see *Breakout 3.19*). This clearly indicates that the coalescing of the Israelite nation was well under way long before the beginning of the Iron Age (IA). But it was in IA1 (see *Timeline*) that the Israelites began to gain the momentum that culminated in the rise of the Israelite monarchy and the Davidic Dynasty.

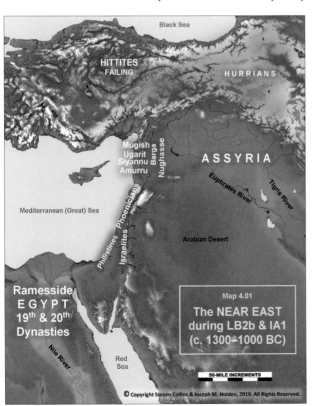

Of course, as both the Bible and archaeology attest, Israel was not the only important player on the Levantine stage during this period. The Philistines and other related Sea Peoples controlled the southcoastal plains while the Phoenicians dominated Canaan's northern coast. The remnants of the indigenous Canaanite population were ever present. In Transjordan, along with the Israelites, there were the Ammonites, Moabites, Edomites, and Arameans (see *Maps 3.08, 4.01, 4.02*). The biblical period of the Judges accurately represents the sociopolitical situation during IA1, as confirmed by archaeology.

The clear "full bore" beginning of the IA occurred in the mid-twelfth century BC. It was marked by a severe decline in Egyptian control and the destruction of the last Canaanite strongholds by the Philistines and the Israelites. With the defining cultural dominance of the Israelites in the Cisjordan Highlands and Philistines on the coastal plains (see *Map 1.07*), the stage was set for one of the most active and interesting periods, biblically and archaeologically, in the history of the region.

From their Aegean homeland, the Philistines and other Sea Peoples continued to arrive in great waves during the early IA (see *Timeline, Map 4.02, and Breakout 4.04*). The Sea Peoples in Egyptian records—Peleset (Philistines), Weshesh, Tjekker, Danuna, and Sheklesh—are generally known as Philistines in the Bible, probably because they were allied together in what some have called the Philistine Confederation. Cultural and linguistic indicators from both archaeological and biblical sources reveal that the Sea Peoples (generically, Philistines) came from Crete, the Aegean region, Sicily, Italy, the southern coast of Asia Minor, and Cyprus. Minoan and Mycenaean elements abound in the sophisticated material culture of the Philistines. Their five greatest cities—Gaza, Ashkelon, Ashdod, Ekron, and Gath (see *Maps 1.05, 4.02*)—are well known from both archaeology and the Bible.

GEOGRAPHY

In the three or so centuries between Joshua and King Saul (see *Timeline*), the ANE was generally in turmoil. In the waning decades of the Late Bronze Age (LBA), Mittani ceased to exist and the Hittite Empire was crumbling. Hatti was all but extinct by 1200 BC. Egypt's Nineteenth Dynasty collapsed c. 1190 BC, and the Twentieth Dynasty was out of

ANATOLIA

Mycenae

Knossos

CAPHTOR

ELISHAH

Mediterranean (Great) Sea

LEVANT

LIBYA

Map 4.02
The SEA PEOPLES ARRIVE in the S LEVANT (c. 1200–1100 BC)

EGYPT

Nile River

50-MILE INCREMENTS

BREAKOUT 4.01

THE RELATIONSHIP BETWEEN JOSHUA AND JUDGES

Reading the military history of another nation can be enlightening and enjoyable, and Joshua is no exception. But like any military history, Joshua's account mentions its share of death and destruction, as well as poor decisions and collateral damage. For modern readers, the book of Joshua presents two difficult problems. First, Joshua seems to be an unrealistically rosy account of the conquest, one that appears to be contradicted by the book of Judges (for example, Joshua 10 vs. Judges 1). Second, God's command to make war against and slaughter the Canaanites seems to contradict God's loving nature.

Regarding the seemingly unrealistic optimism of the book, a close look at Joshua reveals that it is a much more complex work than a casual reading reveals. The book was written using rhetorical techniques such as hyperbolic language (Joshua 11:23), selection (Joshua 15–18), summary (Joshua 11:12-23), and stereotypical elements (Joshua 10:1-15) to convey its message. The writer used *absolute language* to describe the conquest in black-and-white

terms instead of shades of gray. He described a complete victory, even while he acknowledged that the victory was only partial (for example, Joshua 11:16 versus Joshua 13:1).

The command to completely destroy a nation, including the slaughter of all the inhabitants, seems harsh and offensive to many people today. It portrays Yahweh's character in an unflattering light. Critical scholars attempt to deal with this problem by recasting the *ḥāram* command (that is, "utterly destroy") as historical fiction or a ritual festival. While this removes the actual practice of *ḥāram* from the Israelite people, it remains a celebrated ideal. Thus, other objections aside, these proposals do not provide an adequate solution to the problem.

Other scholars have noted that there are many similarities between these commands and common military tactics employed by all nations in the ancient ANE. The Mesha Inscription and Mari Letters show this. In addition, Norbert Lohfink (1986) reminds us that "wars in the Ancient Near East, even

when they are better not termed 'holy wars,' always had a religious dimension."[*] The conquest by Israel represents nothing worse than the common military tactics of the time.

Peter C. Craigie helpfully points out that "war is a human activity; furthermore, it is a sinful human activity, revealing man's inhumanity to his fellow man…To state it another way, God employs, for his purpose of bringing salvation to the world, the very human beings who need salvation."[**] Yahweh had already prophesied judgment on the Canaanites and Amorites when the time was right (Genesis 15:16; Leviticus 18:24-30). The instrument inflicting the judgment (Israel) was not culpable for the Canaanite sins that brought about the judgment.

C. Olson

[*] Norbert Lohfink, "ḥāram" and "ḥērem," in G. Johannes Botterweck, and Helmer Ringgren, eds., *Theological Dictionary of the Old Testament* (Grand Rapids: Eerdmans, 1986), Volume 5, 180-99.

[**] Peter C. Craigie, *The Problem of War in the Old Testament* (Grand Rapids: Eerdmans, 1978), 41-43, 96.

business by 1077 BC. For all intents and purposes, the greatness of Egypt was gone forever. Only in Mesopotamia did the Old Assyrian and Middle Assyrian kingdoms have any real degree of success (see *Map 4.01*).

The latest arrivals in the Levant (Canaan) were the so-called Sea Peoples, the group we know from the Bible as the Philistines (see *Timeline* and *Breakout 4.04*). They settled the coast and adjacent areas of the south Levant (see *Map 4.02*). Also in play during the biblical Judges period were the nomadic Midianites and Amalekites, the city-dwelling Moabites and Ammonites of Transjordan, and the Canaanite cities and towns led, once again, by Hazor (see *Map 3.04*).

CHRONOLOGY

Joshua's campaigns were finished toward the end of the fourteenth century BC (see *Breakout 3.07*). Whether you use a high, middle, or low Egyptian chronology affects the absolute dating of the exodus and conquest (see *Breakouts 3.04, 3.05*), and thus of the first judge (see *Breakout 4.01*). Also, there are many uses of the symbolic number 40 in the book of Judges, which makes phrases like "40 years of peace" simply a reference to a generation. The important point to remember is that the world of the judges spans all the time between the book of Joshua and the crowning of King Saul c. 1052 BC (see *Timeline*). An approximate chronological breakdown of the judges and the ensuing periods of oppression takes the following form:

CHRONOLOGY OF JUDGES AND OPPRESSION	
Judge/Oppression	Approximate Dates
Joshua's Conquests Finished	c. 1340 (+/–20) BC
Mesopotamian Oppression	*c. 1340–1332 (+/–20) BC*
Othniel	c. 1342–1302 BC (1 generation)
Moabite Oppression	*c. 1302–1284 BC*
Ehud	c. 1284–1204 BC (2 generations)
Philistine Oppression	*?*
Shamgar	?
Canaanite Oppression	*c. 1204–1184 BC*
Deborah and Barak	c. 1184–1144 BC (1 generation)
Midianite Oppression	*c. 1144–1137 BC*
Gideon	c. 1137–1097 BC (1 generation)
Abimelech and Ammonite Oppression	*c. 1097–1094 BC*
Jephthah	c. 1094–1088 BC
Philistine Oppression	*c. 1088–1048 BC (1 generation)*
Samson	c. 1074–1054 BC
Samuel	c. 1094–1014 BC (2 generations)

The above scheme is only one of many ways to slice the chronology of the book of Judges. It is even possible that some of the oppressions and judges were localized, meaning that they could have overlapped to some extent. One fact is certain: The time of the judges was a veritable free-for-all (Judges 21:25) in the south Levant, a characterization supported by the archaeology of the region.

BREAKOUT 4.02

POPULATION INCREASE IN THE SOUTHERN LEVANT

As scholars work to determine the many shifts and changes in the course of history, they divide the past into distinct periods based on numerous criteria. Toward the end of the Late Bronze Age (c. 1200 BC), the Near East was thrown into chaos. In contrast to other historical shifts in the Levant, this period did not experience a decrease, but rather a significant growth in population—specifically in the Southern Levant. As economies collapsed and migrant populations roamed the Mediterranean regions, the Southern Levant became a unique mix of opportunity and growth for many local groups, including the Israelites.

Whether it be nomadic invasion, climate change, economic distress, or a combination of reasons, the major powers of the ANE faltered or collapsed, leaving a power vacuum in the contested Levant. It was this gap in political oversight that allowed unprecedented population growth for such a small region.

As the LBA came to an end, the first major migrant groups to appear were the Sea Peoples.

A conglomeration of tribes from the Aegean region, they came in large numbers by ship, while others came by land through Anatolia. After losing a major sea battle to the Egyptians in an attempt to land on the northern coast of Egypt, several groups of Sea Peoples traveled east to settle along the Southern Levantine coast (see *Map 4.02*). The most powerful of these warrior groups, the Peleset (Philistines), quickly cemented control of the area with military superiority. With their penchant for urban living, their population rose quickly and grew to include several large cities. Their territory, known biblically as Philistia ("land of the Philistines"), was challenged by other migrant groups that soon added to this population boom.

While the Sea Peoples arrived and conquered from the west and north, wide-ranging militant groups called Habiru/ʿApiru also plagued the Southern Levant. The most notable of these were the Israelites, who conquered Canaanean settlements from the east. The Israelites settled in cities and towns from the Cisjordan

highlands to the Negev, and rural areas between Philistia and the kingdoms of Moab and Edom in the Transjordan. As the Philistines (Israel's generic term for all Sea Peoples) and Israelites pushed their way through the heart of the Southern Levant, many of the remaining Canaanean tribes moved north, increasing the population of Phoenicia.

With these influxes of migrant and nomadic groups, the population of the Southern Levant grew rapidly. With the help of Philistine and Phoenician maritime trade, the cultural spheres of these groups flourished and the population of what had been Canaan increased dramatically throughout the twelfth and eleventh centuries BC. The Israelites settled in the central hill country, and the Transjordan kingdoms extended their borders as well. While these groups often clashed with each other, they all prospered, augmented by continuous migrations and the absence of oppressive foreign powers.

B.J. Fink, S. Collins

HISTORY

The association of the late LBA and IA1 with the Israelite judges is recognized by most scholars (see *Timeline*). Not only was it a time of upheaval in the south Levant as described in the book of Judges, but it was also a very difficult epoch for most of the ANE.

Although Rameses II (the Great) and the early kings of Egypt's Nineteenth Dynasty had done their best to resurrect the glory days of the empire (mid-Eighteenth Dynasty), the best they could accomplish was modest control of the Levantine coast up to Acco, and southeast down the Jezreel Valley to Beth Shan. They also ran into interference from the Hittites, who had annexed the north Levant in the wake

50-MILE INCREMENTS

HATTI

ARZAWA

Ugarit

Kadesh

Mediterranean (Great) Sea

Canaan

EGYPT

Nile River

Map 4.03
The BATTLE of KADESH (Qidd-su) (c. 1274 BC)

of the exodus events and the resulting collapse of the Eighteenth Dynasty (see *Breakout 3.05*). Eventually the Egyptians and Hittites fought to a stalemate at the Battle of Kadesh (see *Map 4.03*), which finally led to an Egypto-Hittite treaty. But by c. 1200 BC, the Nineteenth Dynasty was collapsing right along with the BA—likewise, Hatti.

Meanwhile, the Assyrians—since their former suzerain master, Mittani, no longer existed—were gobbling up city-states across the whole of Mesopotamia. This land grab and attempt at empire-building was a long process but kept Assyria busy putting its own house in order. For the time being, the Assyrians had no interest in the Levant (see *Map 4.01*).

A new wave of Aegean migrants—mostly Mycenaeans, but also related groups—had packed up and headed for the Levant. Although called Sea Peoples, they came mostly by land across Anatolia and down into the Levant from the north. They were warriors, and many cities and towns fell to their military prowess. They were likely a contributing factor in the collapse of the Hittite kingdom. But they were settlers too. Their cultural influences are seen in excavations from Anatolia and south through the Levant.

Some of these Aegean groups did come in their warships by sea. One well-known wave of Aegean warrior-migrants tried to land on the coast of Egypt during the reign of Rameses III. The Egyptians rebuffed them. However, it looks as if Egypt agreed not to interfere with them if they would settle along the Southern Levantine coast, and that is what they did. Their tribes were known by many names, preserved in Egyptian and other ANE records—Dananu or Denyen, Eqwesh, Lukka, Karkisa, Shekelesh, Tjekker, Sherden, Teresh, Weshesh, and Peleset. But *Peleset* is the name with which we are most familiar—*Philistines* (see *Breakout 4.04*). Although the Bible picks up on other Aegean place names in describing Sea People groups—the most common is Caphtor/Caphtorim (Crete—Genesis 10:14; Deuteronomy 2:23), an ancient reference to the Minoan civilization that laid the foundation for all subsequent Aegean cultures—*Philistines* became a catch-all term for the entire population of Aegean migrants and refugees.

BREAKOUT 4.03

CUSHAN OF MITTANI

One potentially serious problem for late-date exodus theorists (those who believe the exodus occurred during the late thirteenth century BC) comes from the book of Judges, which reports that the Israelite judge Othniel defeated "Cushan-Rishathaim king of Aram Naharaim" (Judges 3:8-10 NIV). C. Billington (2001) argues convincingly that Cushan was a vestigial ruler of the Mittani kingdom (see *Maps 3.02, 3.03*). If this is so, then Othniel's defeat of Cushan must have occurred prior to the ultimate demise of Mittani in the late fourteenth century BC. Thus, the Othniel story strongly supports a late-fifteenth- or early-fourteenth-century BC date for the exodus, during Egypt's Eighteenth Dynasty (see *Timeline* and *Breakouts 3.04, 3.05*).

With Tuthmosis IV as the pharaoh of the exodus (see *Breakout 3.04*), a remarkable historical synchronism arises from the book of Judges, linking a Mittani king in Judges 3:7-11 to a brief window of time toward the end of the Amarna period in Egypt. With the exodus occurring proximate to the death of Tuthmosis IV, there are three keys to this synchronism: (1) the identification of Cushan-Rishathaim king of Aram Naharaim as a Mittani ruler; (2) the

demise and virtual nonexistence of the Mittani kingdom toward the end of the fourteenth century BC; and (3) the death of the well-known Mittani king Tushratta shortly after the end of Akhenaten's reign (c. 1334 BC).

On the first point, Cushan of Judges 3:7-11 was a Mittani king on the basis of both geographical and linguistic evidence. There can be little doubt that the name *Cushan* is not Semitic but of Indo-European origin, as was the Mittani ruling class. Further, the term *Rishathaim* is directly related to *Reshet/Reshu* (in Egyptian texts), *Rishim/Rish/Urshu* (in Ugaritic texts), *Urshu* (in Eblaite texts), and *Urshu* (in Hittite texts) and refers to locations in northern Mesopotamia, the region controlled by the Mittani kingdom during its existence. The biblical term *Naharaim* (meaning "between the rivers") is obviously equivalent to the Egyptian term for Mittani, *Naharin* (or *Nakh(ri)ma'* as it appears in EA 75 of the Amarna correspondence.

On the second point, the final destruction of the Mittani kingdom by the Hittite warrior-king Suppiluliuma toward the end of Akhenaten's reign (see *Breakout 3.05*) sets a historical limit for military action into Canaan

(or anywhere for that matter) by a Mittani ruler. Once Tushratta had fled his capital, Washukanni (see *Map 3.03*), and was subsequently murdered, the kingdom of Mittani lasted only a few more years. By the end of the fourteenth century BC, the Mittani kingdom and its Hurrian ruling class was all but extinct.

On point three, it is clear that Tushratta died shortly after the end of Akhenaten's reign as a direct result of the military onslaught of Suppiluliuma against Mittani. Unless a case could be made that biblical Cushan is Tushratta (a Cush/Tush relationship could certainly be entertained), the death of Tushratta limits the timeframe of a Cushan engagement against the Israelites. This makes even more sense when you realize that Tushratta, who had ruled since the days of Amenhotep III, had inherited the Egypto-Mittanian treaty initially negotiated during the reigns of Tuthmosis IV and Artatama (see *Breakout 3.04*). Although Egyptian control of Syria and Canaan had, for all practical purposes, ended during the reigns of Amenhotep III and Akhenaten, Tushratta had tried repeatedly, without success, to maintain his "brotherhood" with Akhenaten, especially in the face of continued Hittite expansion. Tushratta wanted help from Egypt against the Hittites and when none materialized, his attitude toward Akhenaten turned cold. His three known Amarna Letters demonstrate this increasing animosity toward the pharaoh.

With Egypt out of the Levant (Canaan), Tushratta dead, the Egypto-Mittanian alliance defunct, and the Mittani kingdom itself on the verge of extinction, it is entirely plausible that a remaining Mittani prince or city-state king could have made forays into Canaan, thereby becoming the oppressor of Israel mentioned in Judges 3:7-11. With no fear of any Egyptian reprisal, such an incursion into Israelite territory by a Hurrian ruler from northern Mesopotamia (Aram-Naharaim) or from former Mittani territory in the Northern Levant makes sense.

The potential time frame for Cushan's oppression of the Israelites in Canaan is blocked on the early end by Tushratta's death and on the late end by the demise of the Mittani kingdom toward the end of the fourteenth century BC. This accommodates an exodus—at least 47 years earlier—at the end of the reign of Amenhotep II, or even better, Tuthmosis IV. The Indo-European (Hurrian) Cushan as a king of Aram Naharaim (Egyptian, *Naharin* or *Nakh(ri)ma'* = "Mittani") does not fit a post-1300 BC date for the exodus.

S. Collins

In a nearly topsy-turvy Levant, the Israelites, tribe by tribe, tried to carve out territories for themselves according to the tribal allotments designated by Joshua. Sometimes it worked; sometimes it didn't. Seven years of often-heavy fighting during the Joshua campaigns had taken its toll on the Israelite tribes. It was their responsibility to finish the job Joshua started (see *Breakout 4.01*). Simply put, they did not.

It has often been observed, and rightly, that orthodox Yahwism as captured by the Law of Moses had little place in the book of Judges. It did not take long for the Israelites to do what other occupying conquerors had done. The Akkadians had adopted Sumerian culture. The Hyksos had adopted Egyptian culture. And the Israelites now adopted Canaanite culture. In a very short period of time, the Hebrews became as Canaanite as the Canaanites themselves. This is certainly the witness of the archaeological record (see *Breakout 4.02*). During the thirteenth, twelfth, and eleventh centuries BC, it is hard to tell an Israelite from a Canaanite!

By c. 1210 BC, a stela commissioned by Pharaoh Merneptah (son of Rameses II) lists Israel as one of the "Nine Bows," or perennial enemies, of Egypt (see *Breakout 3.19*). This is telling. It signals that, at the very least, the Israelite tribes had done a good enough job distinguishing themselves as a force to be reckoned with to justify such recognition. Their conquest of Canaan had begun only 130 years earlier. In four or five generations, the Israelites had managed to subjugate much of the south Levant and to control it well enough to be classed by Egypt as a people. And the population of the south Levant was growing by leaps and bounds (see *Breakout 4.02*). The climate was steadily becoming wetter, and the Israelite-dominated land of Canaan was now beginning to produce surpluses worthy of regional attention.

The sin-oppression-repentance-deliverance sequence repeated over and over again through the book of Judges notwithstanding, the foreign raiders did not come into Canaan merely for the purpose of harassing the Israelites or treating them harshly. They came to steal the land's abundance by pillaging, exacting tribute payments, or both.

One of the more interesting oppressors of Israel was Cushan-rishathaim, the king of Aram Naharaim (Judges 3:7-11). Quite a title! Who was he, and where was he from? Cushan was a Hurrian from

BREAKOUT 4.04

PHILISTINES AND SEA PEOPLES

Originating in the Aegean region, the Sea Peoples—of Minoan, Cycladic, and Mycenaean extraction—began showing up in the Southern Levant (Canaan) during the EBA (3900–2500 BC). Their artistic and cultural influences are seen along the Levantine coast, even in the Transjordan, throughout the MBA (2100–1550 BC). One of the heaviest Sea People migrations came from the Mycenaean (proto-Greek) culture during the thirteenth and twelfth centuries BC, among which was a tribe named *Peleset* by the Egyptians. The term *Philistine* derives from Peleset and became the generic biblical word for all Sea Peoples—understandably so because the many Sea People tribes (Peleset, Tjekker, Shekelesh, Denyen, Weshesh, Sherden, and others) congealed together when they arrived along the Southern Levantine coast and built city-states joined in a confederation collectively (and conveniently) called Philistia (land of the Philistines) (see *Map 4.02*).

With their earliest mention appearing during the reign of Pharaoh Merneptah, the arrival of the Sea Peoples represents the chaos that enveloped the ANE at the end of the LBA and into the early

Ceramic horse, Philistine; Israel Museum reproduction (photo: Daniel Galassini, courtesy of Museum of Archaeology, Trinity Southwest University)

centuries of the IA (see *Timeline*). Due to systematic economic collapse around the northern Mediterranean region, migrants fled from the crumbling Mycenaean states to islands like Cyprus before making their way to toward Egypt and the Southern Levant.

With conflict between Merneptah and a Libyan alliance that included the peoples of the sea, the culmination of the carnage came in battles recorded by Rameses III (c. 1176 BC). Rameses documented a great land battle followed by a massive naval engagement

from which Egypt emerged victorious. However, Egyptian dominance would never again reach its previous threshold, which would allow smaller cultural spheres to develop within the Levant. As seen in the pottery uncovered from the Southern Levant all the way up to eastern Anatolia (modern Turkey), the Philistines were of Greek (Aegean) origin. On one hand, this shows that the Sea Peoples (Philistines) were not the cause of the economic instability of the time, although they certainly took advantage of it. On the other, it provides historical credibility to the well-established cities of the biblical Philistines encountered in the book of Judges and beyond.

With the growing numbers of Sea Peoples inhabiting the coastal region of the Levant, Philistine centers of power began to pop up. Within the same monumental stela (c. 1208 BC), Pharaoh Merneptah described both the Sea Peoples and Israel. With their mercenary fighting abilities, both the Israelites and Philistines quickly carved out territory for themselves—thus clashes between the two emerging Levantine powers were inevitable.

B.J. Fink, S. Collins

the Indo-European arc north of Mesopotamia. He belonged to the Rishi people (also *Rishathaim*). He ruled in Aram Naharaim, which is northern Mesopotamia. This is a perfect description of a Hurrian king/prince ruling over a Mittanian city or city-state and poking his nose into the south Levant after the collapse of the Egypto-Mittanian alliance. By 1300 BC, Mittani was extinct, with Aram swallowed up by Assyria. Every indication is given that Cushan was a vestige of the Mittani kingdom before it was decimated by the Hittites and northern Mesopotamia was subsumed by Assyria (see *Breakout 4.03*).

Although the Israelite tribal territories had been designated by Joshua (see *Map 3.08*), the tribes' situation remained fluid. Some still felt dispossessed—such as the Danites (Judges 17–18). And there was intertribal warfare (Judges 19–21) among the Israelites themselves. There were border skirmishes with the Philistines throughout the period, although Samson's anti-Philistine pranks were more on the order of personal vendetta (Judges 13–16; see *Breakout 4.06*).

By far the most interesting, even humorous, Philistine story of this era is their theft of Israel's Ark of the Covenant (1 Samuel 4–7). Because of this, the God of Israel set his hand against the Philistines. Many were dying. Others experienced plagues with tumors or boils. The two Hebrew words used to describe the afflictions experienced by the Philistines probably refer to hemorrhoids (the KJV rendering is the archaic "emerods"). No doubt, stealing the Ark of the Covenant was not a comfortable experience for the Philistines! The ritual return of Yahweh's ark has an interesting parallel in Homer's *Iliad* (see *Breakout 4.05*).

The period of the judges closes in the first eight chapters of 1 Samuel, whose career extended well into the kingship of Saul (see *Breakout 4.07*). The situation in the Levant just prior to Samuel's anointing of Israel's first king, Saul, was, to a degree, chaotic. But that was always true of the Levant, particularly Canaan, because of the fact the area was a melting pot of diverse peoples. It had been, and would always remain, a crossroads land sandwiched between the ANE superpowers (see *Map 4.01*).

PEOPLES AND KINGDOMS

EGYPT—Amenhotep IV succeeded to the throne and changed his name to Akhenaten ("blessed of the Atun"). His monotheism angered the priest-class along with his move to Amarna. This is the start of the Amarna period (1351–1323 BC; see *Timeline*) during the collapse of the Eighteenth Dynasty. This was a period of withdrawal for Egypt. The Levantine territories were largely ignored, and plagues still ravaged the entire region. The Nineteenth Dynasty sported Rameses II (the Great), who brought Egypt back into prominence—but not to the same level of strength that the Eighteenth Dynasty had exhibited. After the Nineteenth Dynasty, the remaining dynasties were comparatively weak.

NAHARAIM—The destruction of the Mittani (Naharaim) capital, Washukanni (c. 1368, then c. 1341 BC), put an end to the Mittani kingdom, but local chieftains remained for a short period. The name Cushan Rishathaim King of Aram Naharaim was a vestige of the old Mittani order (see *Breakout 4.03*).

AMMONITES—The Semitic Ammonites (see *Map 4.01*) were closely related to Moab and had one major city called Rabbah (Rabbath Ammon). The Israelites were forbidden to fight them, as they were, like Moab, descendants of Lot. They were left alone during the Israelite conquest. Later the Ammonites attempted to expand their territory by conquest yet failed (Judges 11:13).

MIDIANITES—The Midianites (see *Map 4.01*) were Semitic nomads who, by the time of Moses, had amassed great wealth. God commanded Moses to conquer the Midianites (Numbers 25:16-18). During the time of Gideon, the Midianites allied themselves with Moab and subjugated Israel for seven years. Gideon finally defeated the Midianites and killed their leaders.

AMALEKITES—The Semitic Amalekites (see *Map 4.01*) were nomadic enemies of Israel and sided with Midian, Moab, and Ammon. They dwelled mainly in the Negev. God decreed their obliteration in Exodus 17:8-16.

MOABITES—Moab (see *Map 4.01*) was situated on the Transjordan east of the Dead Sea, occupying a plateau between the Arnon Gorge and Zered River, north of Edom. The Moabites were presented in the Bible as the descendants of Lot from an incestuous relationship with his oldest daughter (Genesis 19:30-38). Judges 3:12-14 says Israel was subject to Eglon, king of Moab, for 18 years. He was defeated by the left-handed judge of Israel, Ehud (Judges 3:30).

HAZOR/CANAANITES—The Bible designates Canaanites as those living west of the Rift (Jordan) Valley (see *Map 1.07*) and up to Syria. They were Semitic in origin. They existed in the Levant with their chief city-state, Hazor, extending dominance in the region. The Israelite campaigns (see *Map 3.07*) never succeeded in wiping out the Canaanite population, and the constant influence of Canaanite religion and intermarrying caused infiltration of polytheistic pagan ideas into Israel. Hazor was finally conquered by Deborah and Barak, and later fortified by Solomon.

PHILISTINES—The five Philistine (see *Breakout 4.04*) cities of the coastal plain (see *Maps 1.05, 4.02*) were a perennial problem for Israel. First Samuel speaks of Philistine oppression and fierce fighting to subdue the region with the Battle of Mizpah. The Egyptians, under Ramses III (in 1191 BC), defeated the invading Philistines using fellow-Philistine mercenary troops that must have offered their services to the Egyptian military prior to the battle.

SOCIETIES AND CULTURES

SOCIAL STRATIFICATION—With Canaan reeling from the campaigns of Joshua, the final years of the Bronze Age (LBA2b) and the initial decades of the Iron Age (IA1; see *Timeline*) saw a collapse of urban culture across the south Levant. With new waves of migrants, cities and towns across the region faced hard economic times, with attacks not only by marauding Habiru (including the Israelite tribes), but also by Sea People groups. This affected what had been the higher echelons of society more than any other level. The common people still plied their trades and worked the farms, but exactly who controlled the agricultural production, and to what extent, is difficult to tell. The

Philistines (Sea Peoples) were solidifying their hold on the Levant's southern coastal region, and the Phoenicians to the north still dominated the Mediterranean shipping lanes. But the highlands of Canaan were in flux.

TRIBALISM—In times of social upheaval and economic distress, tribalism is reinforced. With the larger political systems breaking down, smaller social units like tribes and clans were even more important. Localism became the focus of Canaan's population, including the Israelite tribes who were trying to carve out a place for themselves in their assigned territories. Tribes mingled and intermarried—the new with the old. Once again, Canaan proved to be a melting pot of diverse ethnicities.

CITY-STATES—During this difficult period, the larger city-states of the Northern Levant fared better than the cities and towns of the Southern Levant. Warfare seems to have been the rule rather than the exception, and agricultural settlements were vulnerable targets. But this crumbling of the old feudal social order would, by the end of the eleventh century BC, lead to a new change for the Southern Levant: the emergence of kingdoms and nation-states.

INHERITANCE—Still family-based in the laws of primogeniture, the inheritance of an entire estate, whether flocks and tents or an absolute monarchy, belonged to the firstborn or primal son.

WOMEN'S ROLES—Although the ANE had intermittent royal females who played dominant roles, they were few and far between. In Israel, a few women, like Deborah in the book of Judges, rose to meet military and political challenges. Home and hearth remained the primary focus of women in every societal class. When given in marriage, the wife would leave her parents and become a part of her husband's family. There she would join in the communal raising of children, including her own.

MEN'S ROLES—It was a warrior's world. Regardless of social rank or lack thereof, being a warrior was paramount. In this regard, young men, beginning at puberty, were often apprenticed into the formal warrior class by a military mentor (see *Breakout 5.02*)

for a period of several years. It is likely that tradesmen and farmers also received similar military training, but not to the extent of professional soldiers. Boys and young men were probably trained in their family trades through guild apprenticeships, whether by their fathers, uncles, or other masters.

Political Climate—After the resurgence of Egypt during the reigns of Seti I and Rameses II (the Great) (see *Timeline*), the Nineteenth Dynasty began to unravel. By the late eleventh century, the Hatti Empire was history and Egypt was in serious decline, allowing the Levantine coastal city-states—the Philistines and the Phoenicians (see *Map 4.02*)—to pursue their own fortunes without Hittite or Egyptian interference (see *Breakout 4.04*). The "Wild West" that was the central highlands of Canaan was burgeoning with a growing population of Israelites (see *Breakout 4.02*) who were on the verge of coalescing into a kingdom.

BREAKOUT 4.05

HOMER, HEMORRHOIDS, AND THE RETURN OF THE ARK OF THE COVENANT

After the Philistines captured the Israelite Ark of the Covenant as a trophy of war (1 Samuel 5–6), the Israelite God Yahweh sent a severe, uncomfortable plague upon them (tumors, actually *hemorrhoids*!). In order to appease the anger of Yahweh, an assembly of the people and Philistine chiefs was held in each city. They also called for priests and diviners. The Philistines determined that the ark must be returned with guilt offerings. They fashioned hemorrhoidal tumors and mice out of gold. The ark and gold offerings were then placed on an ox-drawn cart and driven toward the land of the enemy (Israel). Philistine chiefs followed it on its journey. Upon arrival, the oxen were sacrificed to Yahweh. All in all, these goings-on seem rather bizarre! But a careful study of the biblical text and archaeology reveals that the original homeland of the Philistines was the Aegean region, including several island locations such as Caphtor (Crete). Indeed, archaeology shows that a large wave of Philistines came from the Aegean area during the Homeric Bronze Age and settled on the southern coast of Canaan (see *Breakout 4.04*).

And herein lies the connection. From the *Iliad* (lines 10-446; as summarized by N. Bierling, 1992) we read that the Achaeans captured the daughter of Cryses, a priest of the god Apollo, and took her from her island home. In response, Apollo inflicted a deadly plague on the Achaeans. To assess the situation, an assembly of Achaean troops and chiefs was convened. They called for a priest/prophet or an interpreter of dreams. They decided that the daughter of Cryses must be returned with holy offerings. Apollo was also known as Smintheus, the mouse god. Oxen were placed aboard a ship (remember, Cryses lived on an island) along with the daughter and offerings to Apollo. A chief and select crew accompanied Cryses's daughter. Upon arrival, the oxen were sacrificed.

It is astounding to realize that the Bible preserves this ancient Aegean protocol for appeasing an angry god that is documentable, point by point, from Homer's *Iliad*. It stretches the seams of credulity to suggest—as many scholars do—that Judahite priests living in the latter years of the Iron Age could have invented such a story. And why would they go to so much trouble to insert this authentic tidbit from the ancient Aegean culture? The most straightforward explanation is this: The biblical story is historically accurate *because it happened*!

S. Collins, J. Holden

BREAKOUT 4.06

SAMSON AND THE PHILISTINE TEMPLE

The author(s) of the book of Judges lived within an oil-and-water-like mixture of cultures that, although stirred together, maintained separate and competing religious and social ideologies. Despite holding different views from their neighbors, the Israelite writer(s) were familiar with Philistine socioreligious practices as well as the architecture of Philistine temples.

Among the large and diverse Canaanean pantheons, the principal deities of the Philistines were Baal, Astarte, and Dagon (borrowed from Mesopotamia), the latter perhaps being one of their chief gods. Dagon (from Hebrew, meaning "fish"; cf. Ugaritic and Samaritan Hebrew versions of the same root word meaning "grain") is mentioned 15 times in the Bible in the context of the conquest of Canaan through the pre-Davidic Israelite monarchy, all within the period of the Judges.

Biblical references to Dagon are no surprise because he was worshipped throughout the entire Fertile Crescent from Mesopotamia into the Southern Levant over a period of millennia. Dagon worshippers peppered the landscape of ancient Israel with temples erected and consecrated to him. The temple cult of Dagon is mentioned several times throughout

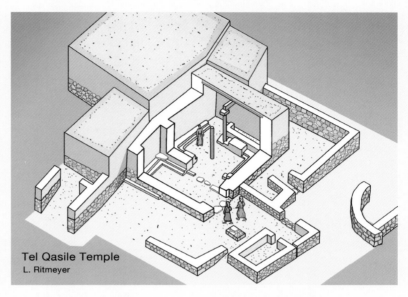

Tel Qasile Temple
L. Ritmeyer

Two-columned Philistine temple design (drawing: Leen Ritmeyer)

the Old Testament (see Joshua 15; 19; Judges 16; 1 Samuel 5; 1 Chronicles 10). In addition to the Hebrew Scriptures, the apocryphal book of 1 Maccabees (widely considered to be an excellent historical record of the intertestamental period) also makes mention of a Philistine temple of Dagon (1 Maccabees 10:82-85).

Just as Baal and Asherah were well known to the Israelites (and often co-worshipped alongside Yahweh), the cult of Dagon was similarly familiar to them, along with all of the trappings of its ritual practices.

Temples were centrally located within ancient settlements so that the sacred and the secular were intimately related. Thus, the particulars of the various local religious sects were well known to all members of the community, regardless of an individual's ethnic or religious background. Not only was the architectural design of Philistine temples known to ancient Israelites who lived contemporaneously alongside them, but, thanks to archaeological excavations throughout Israel, they are becoming familiar to us as well.

Looking back to the story of Samson in Judges 16, the remains of grain-grinding tools have been discovered in the same ruins as Philistine temples at locations like Kiryat Gat and Tel Qasile, Israel, near the modern coastal city of Tel Aviv.

The temple excavations at Tel Qasile reveal an eleventh-century BC (time of Samson) Dagonic temple measuring 26 by 48 feet. Notably, the structural design featured well-crafted twin stone-column bases that were centrally located and cylindrical. Upon them were a pair of cedar pillars, seven feet apart, which supported the roof. It is likely that the temple destroyed by Samson at Gaza had a similar design. Such twin pillars in close, central proximity explains how Samson, once maneuvered into position between them, was able to "bring down the house" of Dagon (Judges 16:29-30):

> Samson grasped the two middle pillars on which the house rested, and he leaned his weight against them, his right hand on the one and his left hand on the other. And Samson said, "Let me die with the Philistines." Then he bowed with all his strength, and the house fell upon the lords and upon all the people who were in it. So the dead whom he killed at his death were more than those whom he had killed during his life.

J. Barber, S. Collins

But it wouldn't happen without first an internal struggle in true ANE fashion—the House of Saul against the House of David.

LANGUAGES AND WRITING

Akkadian—The principal language of the Old Assyrian dynasties and Middle Assyrian kings (see *Timeline*), Akkadian, continued its domination of Mesopotamia and as the international language of commerce and correspondence throughout the ANE. Often carved in cuneiform script on stone monuments (see *Figure 4.01*), the daily writing of Akkadian was done on clay tablets.

Canaanean Dialects—Throughout the south Levant, the general population spoke a variety of Canaanean and Amorite dialects, with a new addition emerging: Hebrew. The Israelites brought their version of "Canaanite" with them into the Promised Land. Having spoken it in Egypt for several centuries in isolation from Canaan, the Israelite language developed its own distinctions. We call it proto-Hebrew, or early Hebrew. In time, as the Israelite tribes began to settle into their allotted territories, Hebrew grew in popularity. By the tenth century it was well on its way to becoming the Israelite national language (see *Figure 4.02*).

Alphabet to the Levant—The Semitic alphabet emerged in Egypt during the centuries that the Israelites—and other Semitic Asiatics—were living

Figure 4.01—Assyrian monumental inscription (photo: Joseph Holden)

Figure 4.02—Eleventh-century BC Semitic script (photo: David E. Graves)

in the Nile Delta, much of the time as slaves of the Eighteenth Dynasty (see *Breakout 3.11*). With their alphabet, the Israelites were generally a literate people as they now began to expand into the south Levant. The term *alphabet* refers to a limited number of letters (usually 20 to 30) listed in a fixed order. However, the value of each letter is not necessarily limited to a single phoneme (sound), whether a consonant or a vowel. Alphabetic writing can also include syllabic values that include both a consonant and a vowel sound together (such as ba, la, ta, etc.). The Greek alphabet had signs for both consonants and vowels. The Western Semitic alphabets, such as those used for writing Phoenician, Hebrew, and Aramaic, were primarily consonantal in nature. Today, modern Hebrew writing, a derivative of Aramaic square script, is also consonantal.

CUNEIFORM ALPHABET—The earliest known list of letters in alphabetical order (known as an *abecedary*) is from Ugarit (see *Map 1.04*) and dates to about 1350 BC. Its invention may have been sparked by contact with the recently arrived linear Semitic alphabet by way of the Israelite entrance into the south Levant in the same time frame (see *Breakout 3.11*). This particular alphabet consists of 30 cuneiform-style characters, each with a single vocal value, thus making it a true alphabet. The language of the Ugaritic texts has been classified as Canaanean (Phoenician) or Ammurite (Amorite), both in the north/northwest Semitic family. The cuneiform alphabet (see *Figure 4.03*) was short-lived. Before the end of the twelfth century BC it was replaced by the Semitic linear alphabet.

CUNEIFORM—Still the dominant script in Mesopotamia during this period (fourteenth to eleventh centuries BC), the cuneiform system was the means of writing Assyrian documents on clay tablets. It was also the script carved onto Assyrian stone monuments.

EGYPTIAN—The Egyptian language continued throughout LBA2b and IA1 (see *Timeline*) and was written both in hieroglyphics and hieratic script. Hieratic was common for texts written on papyrus, while hieroglyphics dominated monumental inscriptions.

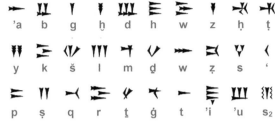

Figure 4.03—Cuneiform alphabet; Late Bronze Age abecedary, top (photo: Daniel Galassini)

Figure 4.04—Standing stone, Iron Age, Dan (photo: Alexander Schick)

BELIEFS AND RELIGIONS

SACRIFICES—The sacrifice of animals and humans was a ritual reality of all ANE religions. In the Southern Levant, offerings also included libations (such as wine, olive oil, perfumes) and food items (such as grain, fruit, cooked meat). Human sacrifice was less frequent, but not rare. Most identifiable human sacrificial offerings

Figure 4.05—Inscribed jar: "Yahweh and his Asherah"; ancient cartoonish Bes-like portrayal of the central Israelite deity and consort (photos: Steven Collins)

were infants, often found in jars buried beneath floors and inside mudbricks. In this light, Jephthah's commitment of his daughter as a human sacrifice (Judges 11) was typical of the Canaanite religion he and the Israelite tribes had embraced—that is, Jephthah's Yawhism was corrupted.

CANAANITE RELIGION—Baal, Ashtoreth, and Asherah were the dominant deities in Canaan during this era. For a Canaanean family, religion was life itself. Every aspect of human existence was influenced by ritual, and always with sacrifice—whether agricultural produce, animal, or human. Temples, shrines, and high places (hilltop, open-air sanctuaries) abounded. Deities were represented mainly by standing stones (Hebrew, *massabah/masseboth*) in all worship contexts. At open-air shrines Asherah poles (phallic symbols), held in "female" niches carved into exposed bedrock, symbolized sexual union and fertility (see *Figure 4.04*). This was all part of the Canaanean psyche. The Israelites embraced the local religion with enthusiasm—to their peril.

BAALISM—Baal was both a storm god ("he who rides the clouds") and a fertility god. Without a doubt, he was the most revered god in Canaan, with his name linked to many cities and the names of individuals.

The Hebrew word *ba'al* means "lord" or "sovereign." For many Canaanites, Baal was the king of the gods.

YAHWISM—Both biblically and archaeologically, the worship of Yahweh during this period was cloudy to say the least. We must not confuse revealed Mosaic Yahwism with the Yahwism of the Israelite tribes. They had abandoned the Mosaic Law early on. The Israelites were mixing with the local Canaanean tribes and tended to be syncretistic in their approach to religion. Thus, according to the biblical texts describing this period and the archaeological record, it is very difficult to tell the difference between a Canaanite and an Israelite in terms of material remains, including religious objects and architecture. For many Israelites, Yahweh even had a wife/consort, Asherah (see *Figure 4.05*). During this era, pure, revealed Yahwism was hard to come by.

ASHTORETH—A foreign goddess, Ashtoreth (later, Astarte; in Mesopotamia, Ishtar) is not to be confused with Asherah, consort of the Canaanite god El and known as the consort of Yahweh. She was the Sidonian/Phoenician goddess of fertility, sexuality, and war (see *Figure 4.06*).

FOREIGN GODS—They were foreign in the sense that they were not Yahweh, the exclusive God of Israel

(Judges 10:16; 1 Samuel 7:3). As much as the Israelite tribes attempted over and over to rid themselves of polytheistic influences, they returned to them quickly and often. Because common Yahwism was mixed with polytheistic elements, it is sometimes difficult to determine, for example, from which perspective the book of Judges was written. There is a difference between the true Yahwistic monotheism of Moses and having Yahweh as Israel's principal deity. While some biblical personalities like Samuel may have understood and practiced the true monotheism of Yahweh (Hebrew, *YHWH*), it is easy to make the case that when Israel periodically returned to Yahweh (usually translated "the Lord") after wholesale religious apostasy, they simply reoriented their focus, once again, on Yahweh as their national deity. And it never took them long to reembrace the foreign gods.

ARCHITECTURE AND INFRASTRUCTURE

Four-Room Houses—In the twelfth century BC, what was known as the Israelite four-room house began to appear in settlements throughout the central hill country of the south Levant (see *Figure 4.07*). This type of house was also found in Egypt and was not exclusively an Israelite invention. The term is also a misnomer because these houses could have less or more than four rooms! The structure consisted of a central courtyard where meals were prepared and cooked, surrounded by two, three, four, or more rooms. Often there would also be one or more rooms on a second floor. Village houses were often connected around a perimeter, creating a protective "wall." Thus, animals could be kept within the enclosure at night. The basic design was a functional matter that incorporated agricultural and social elements.

Figure 4.06—Ashtoreth figurine, Iron Age (photo: James Barber, courtesy of Bible Lands Museum, Jerusalem)

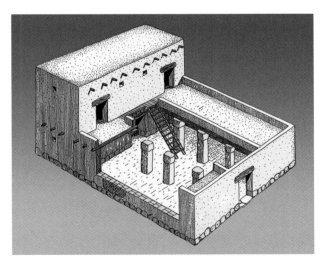

Figure 4.07—Israelite four-room house, Iron Age (drawing: Leen Ritmeyer)

THE CAREER OF SAMUEL

Think of the tremendous changes brought about by Samuel. When he was born, the Israelites were at one of the lowest points in their history. They were divided by tribes and defeated by foreign powers. By the end of his life, Samuel had overseen the transition to a monarchy and had anointed Israel's greatest King—David. The nation was united, was repelling foreign nations, and was well on the way to its greatest strength and prosperity.

Samuel's story begins with a little family in a small town. In fact, it begins with an ignored and insignificant woman. Her name was Hannah. Facing impossible odds, Hannah chose to trust in Yahweh alone and was rewarded by becoming an author of Scripture. First Samuel 2 is a psalm written by Hannah. But her influence was even greater. Where did Samuel get his integrity (1 Samuel 12)? It certainly was not from his 'mentor,' the corrupt priest Eli. Hannah's story reminds us never to underestimate the influence of a praying mother!

The Roman philosopher Seneca said: "Luck is what happens when preparation meets opportunity!" First Samuel 2–3 outlines Samuel's preparation. God revealed himself to Samuel (1 Samuel 3:21) and gave him words to speak (1 Samuel 3:19), so that Samuel gained a strong reputation throughout the land (1 Samuel 3:20). When Eli and his sons died at the Battle of Aphek (1 Samuel 4), young Samuel's preparation met his big opportunity.

It may not have seemed like a great opportunity. The people of the land were at their lowest ebb spiritually—"everyone did what was right in their own eyes" (Judges 21:25). They had lost faith in the priesthood and sacrifices due to the abuses of Eli's sons. They were under the occupation of the Philistines, and the Ark ("the glory of Yahweh"—1 Samuel 4:21) had departed. The text is silent about what Samuel did for the next 20 years (1 Samuel 7:2), but the fruit of his ministry speaks volumes.

Just 20 years later the entire nation repented, publicly confessed their sin, and removed all their false gods (1 Samuel 7:3-6). Samuel was recognized as the leader/judge over all Israel (1 Samuel 7:6, 15). The people trusted in Yahweh when confronted with enemies rather than trusting in their own strength or their false gods (1 Samuel 7:7-9). Yahweh defended his people, and they were victorious over the Philistines. They were able to live in peace, and even retake cities that had been taken from them (1 Samuel 7:10-14). And Samuel continued to lead Israel as a circuit judge (1 Samuel 7:16-17).

What was Samuel doing for those significant and fruitful years? Some speculate that he spent that time re-energizing the Levitical priesthood (of which he was a part) and training up a school of prophets (1 Samuel 10:5-10; 19:20). But that was not all. Samuel's integrity (1 Samuel 12) gave him the authority necessary to unite the nation under a king—first the fearful King Saul, then the godly King David.

God told Samuel, "People look at the outward appearance, but Yahweh sees the heart" (1 Samuel 16:7). This was not only true of the young shepherd whom Samuel was anointing. It was also true of Samuel himself—the greatest unsung hero of the Old Testament.

S. Stripling

ROADS AND FOOTPATHS—The entire land was crisscrossed with roadways and pathways interconnecting every city, town, village, hamlet, water source, hilltop sanctuary, and cemetery. This was true in every period, but the importance of such connectivity was enhanced by the demise of city-states and a cultural shift to village life driven by agricultural and pastoral production.

CITIES, TOWNS, VILLAGES, AND HAMLETS—The vast feudal estates of the south Levant were a thing of the past. During the twelfth century BC much of the agricultural production lay in the hands of local families and clans forming cooperatives that networked across the region. This eventually led to the rise of larger towns and urban settlements—often fortified—coalescing around the production of local commodities like cereal grains, olive oil, wine, and textiles (from wool and flax/linen). But these were not the old-style city-state economies controlled by a centralized government. It seems that the ownership of agricultural lands lay in the hands of the farmers or farming families. Some important city-states would rise again toward the end of the eleventh century, but with a more open approach to government and economics.

WEAPONS AND WARFARE

SICKLE SWORDS VS. STRAIGHT SWORDS—The concept of a straight two-edged sword was new. The sickle sword (see *Breakout 3.14*) had dominated since the fifteenth century BC, but it was mostly a hacking weapon in the old battle-axe tradition. The iron double-edged sword was a superior and multidimensional weapon that could, when wielded by a trained warrior, cut in any direction, with the additional advantage of a sharp tip that could be used for a thrust-kill. The bronze sickle sword was now a liability and obsolete. While the transition to the straight sword was not instant, it became the dominant weapon by the end of the eleventh century BC (see *Figure 4.08*).

BRONZE TO IRON—By the end of the twelfth century BC, iron production was widespread enough that most weaponry was made of this extremely durable material. An iron sword could cut through a bronze sword. Iron dominated in every way—including iron

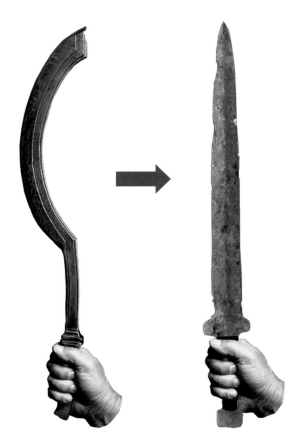

Figure 4.08—Sickle sword (Late Bronze Age) to straight sword (Iron Age) (photos: Daniel Galassini, courtesy of Museum of Archaeology, Trinity Southwest University)

Figure 4.09—Iron Age tools (photos: Alexander Schick)

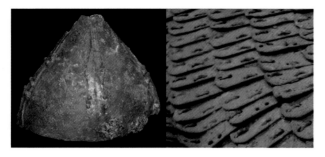

Figure 4.10—Personal armor: Iron Age helmet; scale armor from a later period but fundamentally unchanged since the Early Bronze Age (photos: Alexander Schick)

Figure 4.11—Fishing scene, Egypt; multiple species of fish are depicted (photo: David E. Graves)

sheathing on gates and shields, iron plating on helmets and armor, iron arrow and spear points, iron nails and tools, and iron plough blades (see *Figure 4.09*). The Iron Age (IA) had arrived in full force (see *Timeline*).

WEAPONRY—By this time chariots were widely used (where practical), and siege machinery—battering rams with iron tips on wheeled platforms and siege towers (raising archers and slingers to eye level with their counterparts on the city wall)—were becoming even more lethal. With more and more iron being used for weapons and defensive gear, soldiers were becoming less mobile on the battlefield (see *Figure 4.10*). A heavily armored warrior was less able to maneuver (or run!) than one who was lightly outfitted. Thus, two well-armored soldiers would fight until one killed the other. Some armies, or divisions of armies, preferred less (or no) armor in favor of more freedom of movement or retreat. In the closing years of the eleventh century (see *Timeline*), young David chose the latter.

INDUSTRIES AND OBJECTS

AGRICULTURE—The localized arrangement of farming (as opposed to the earlier feudal system) was reinforced by the Mosaic Law among the Israelites—that is, whenever they bothered to reference it. Each man to his own field (Exodus 22)! Agricultural fields, even larger farming estates, were worked by families and clans, which became an Israelite norm. Olive oil and wine production was ramping up during this period, and the same was true of the cereal and specialty crops (like dates, figs, and pomegranates).

HERDING—Always the most unchanging and stable element of the ANE, nomadic shepherds continued to provide wool, milk products, and meat for the sedentary population. They also provided sacrificial animals for religious rituals. With a growing Israelite population, this meant an increasing need for sheep. Business was good!

FISHING—Fresh and dried saltwater fish were important foods for the coastal cities of Philistia and Phoenicia. Freshwater fish from the Kinnereth Lake (Sea of Galilee) included musht (a type of tilapia), biny, and sardines ("small" fish) (see *Figure 4.11*). The commercial fishing industry at Kinnereth supplied mostly the local markets.

KITCHENS AND COOKING—The open courtyards of houses served as kitchens, with grinding stones, mortars and pestles, and one or more clay ovens (tabuns; see *Figure 4.12*). The main cooking fuel was the dung of foraging animals (sheep and goats) augmented by sticks and occasional wood gathered from the countryside. The smoke of cooking fires was a nuisance but tolerated for obvious reasons.

METALLURGY—Copper production continued at places like Wadi Faynan and Timna (see *Maps 1.06, 2.05*), with tin imported to make bronze. Copper was still big business, and the metal of choice for a wide range of applications. In the Levant, iron was an imported material and very expensive, but object production was done locally. Only weapons and heavy-wear items like plough blades and door hinges were fashioned of iron.

BUILDING MATERIALS—In the Levant, everything

from houses to temples to palaces to city walls was constructed of mudbricks on stone foundations (see *Figure 4.13*). Stones could be brought in from the surrounding hillsides or "mined" from the ruins of past civilizations. Cannibalizing old stone foundations was usually more convenient. Mudbrick manufacturing was a perennial industry for every settlement, regardless of size. Plasterers working with mud-sand and mud-lime mixes were kept busy all year around. Local pine and oak had regrown in the south Levant during IA1 (twelfth century BC; see *Timeline*), but higher demand from the increasing population began the deforesting process once again during the eleventh century BC. When the local lumber became scarce, builders turned to Lebanon and the north Levant for timber. Recycling old lumber was a common practice.

FLINT—The super-sharp cutting edge of a flint blade (see *Figure 4.14*) kept flint in demand for surgical procedures, the skinning of animals, and as blade inserts on sickles (scythes).

TEXTILES—Clothing never goes out of fashion! As a result, the weaving of cloth remained a critical

Figure 4.12—Tabun (oven), Iron Age (photos: Daniel Galassini, courtesy of Tall el-Hammam Excavation Project)

Figure 4.13—Iron Age walls—mudbricks on stone foundations, Beer-Sheba (photo: John Witte Moore)

Figure 4.14—Flint blades, Iron Age (photos: Michael Luddeni, courtesy of Tall el-Hammam Excavation Project)

industry. It is hard to know whether textiles were produced by households, contract labor, or mass production facilities. Archaeological evidence seems to support all three sources. Spindle whorls and loom weights have been found in domestic and in what seem to be public contexts (see *Figure 4.15*). Wool for the cold months, linen for the hot months, and wearer's choice for the mild months!

POTTERY—Generally speaking, the pottery of IA1 is cruder than that of LBA2 and IA2 (see *Timeline*). Red burnished slip was a favorite finish on many vessels, from jugs and juglets to bowls and kraters. While

Figure 4.15—Weaving in a household, Iron Age (photo: Alexander Schick)

many of the LBA pithoi (large storage jars) did not have handles, most of the IA1 pithoi had handles and bore a collar just below the rim (see *Figure 4.16*). These collar-rimmed storage jars are often viewed as typical for IA1, but evidence for the collar-rimmed style traces back to the LBA and even the MBA.

TRADE—International trade was not as aggressive during IA1 (see *Timeline*) as it had been in the days of Egypt's Nineteenth Dynasty. The Hittite Empire had crumbled, Egypt was in the doldrums, and the militarily aggressive Sea Peoples were coursing across the eastern Mediterranean world by land and in ships, intent on finding new territories to inhabit. While this period was one of general social upheaval and dramatic changes, goods still flowed through traditional trade routes all over the ANE and the Mediterranean world. Times were tough, but people did what they had to do to survive and, if possible, thrive.

Figure 4.16—Pottery of the early Iron Age (photos: Daniel Galassini, Carl Morgan, Steven Collins; courtesy of Museum of Archaeology, Trinity Southwest University and Museum of Archaeology and Biblical History, Woodland, CA)

CHAPTER 5

THE WORLD OF DAVID AND SOLOMON

WELCOME TO IRON AGE 2A (1000–900 BC)

During Iron Age 2 (see *Timeline*), the Israelite culture expanded from its strongholds in the central hill country (see *Map 5.01*)—cities like Bethel, Shechem, Jerusalem, and Hebron—into surrounding areas due to the expansion policies of both King David and King Solomon (see *Map 5.02*). Although many alliances were formed with surrounding nations, border conflicts inevitably arose, particularly with their perennial enemy, the Philistines (see *Breakouts 4.4, 5.01* and *Map 4.02*).

Before the recent discovery of ancient extrabiblical references to the House of David—such as the Tel Dan Stela and the "Heights of David" reference among the inscriptions of Pharaoh Soshenq I—the historical reality of David, and even Solomon, was questioned by some scholars (see *Breakout 6.04*). But as more and more artifacts relating to the great IA temple of Yahweh and other aspects of the stories of David and Solomon come to light, it is increasingly difficult for critics of the Bible to deny the historicity of these characters.

The Old Testament's portrayal of the events of IA2 and IA3—the exploits of the Israelite and Judahite kings and the Assyrian, Babylonian, and Persian Empires—represents the finest historical writing of the period.

GEOGRAPHY

With Egypt in serious decline, the Philistines and Phoenicians mostly content with their coastal territories, and the Assyrians minding their own business in Mesopotamia, the stage was set for the rise of a Levantine kingdom (see *Timeline* and *Map 5.01*). That is, given just the right mix of circumstances—and so it was.

Saul's kingdom was more in name than in hard-held boundaries. It was King David who, by war and treaty, solidified his hold on much of the south Levant (Canaan) (see *Map 5.02*). He managed to subdue Edom, Moab, and Ammon in the Transjordan, making them vassals. He also made vassals of the Arameans and welcomed Geshur as a treaty partner. During David's rule, Jerusalem became the capital city.

The extent of Solomon's kingdom expanded on what he inherited from David, mainly to the north. He accomplished this by taking on Hamath as a vassal state.

CHRONOLOGY

We are now in IA2a (c. 1000–900 BC; see *Timeline*). Saul's reign lasted for about 40 years (c. 1050–1010 BC). David's reign lasted from c. 1010 BC to c. 970 BC, also 40 years. Solomon for 40 years as well, from c. 970 BC to c. 931/930 BC. The number 40 is, of course, the length of a "formulaic" generation. Therefore, one could argue that the actual lengths of Saul's, David's, and Solomon's reigns are uncertain. On one hand, by using the number 40 for each reign, it may be that the biblical writer was simply affirming that each had a long and successful rule over his generation. On the other hand, the numbers could be literal, and they do fit in with the ANE chronology of this period. Either way, the time frame of these kings is well established.

BREAKOUT 5.01

DAVID AND THE PHILISTINES

The Philistines were Aegean Sea Peoples who invaded the land of Canaan, finally settling along the coast of the Southern Levant during the thirteenth–twelfth centuries BC (see *Breakout 4.04*). Their famous Pentapolis in the southwestern Levant was comprised of five city-states, including Gaza, Ashkelon, Ashdod, Ekron, and Gath. Archaeological excavations at many of these sites reveal that the IA Philistine culture had its origins in the world of Mycenaean Greece. The Mycenaeans had also established themselves on the island of Crete (biblical Caphtor).

For several centuries, the Philistines were Israel's sworn enemies. However, they were used by God to chasten the Israelites for their idolatry (Judges 10:7-8), and to test and teach later generations how to fight in battle (Judges 3:1-3). David was a young shepherd when he was anointed to become the second king of Israel. However, his appointment as king was delayed for 15 years. During that time, David became a refugee and was himself tested and tried. His life often in peril because of King Saul, David spent some of his time as an exile in Philistine territory.

The relationship between David and the Philistines was anomalous. David's early encounters with the Philistine confederacy, including his victory over Goliath, resulted in him gaining a reputation among the Philistines as a mighty warrior (1 Samuel 21:11; 29:5). Due to his numerous Philistine victories, David was well known throughout the land (1 Samuel 18:30). At one point while David was in exile, he formed a quasi-alliance with Achish, king of Gath. This arrangement benefited both men. King Achish gained a skilled mercenary whose reputation preceded him, accompanied by a small army of mighty men dedicated to David's cause. David's shrewd decision to dwell among the Philistines caused King Saul to cease his tenacious hunt for him because following David into Philistine territory with a large army might have been interpreted as an act of war.

David used his time as a fugitive to carry out the will of God while living among the Philistines. As the anointed king-elect, David continued to conquer cities that Joshua and the Israelites failed to subdue when they had entered the Promised Land.

The short-lived alliance between David and King Achish ended when the Philistines went to war against the nation of Israel, and King Saul and his three sons were killed in battle. This set the stage for David's appointed time as king.

Not long after, David became king of Judah, and eventually over the entire nation of Israel. When David became king of the Israelite nation, he eventually subdued the Philistines (2 Samuel 8:1). Battles continued between the Israelites and Philistines until the Assyrians annihilated the Philistines around 700 BC. Philistia ceased to exist, and the remaining Philistines assimilated into the surrounding cultures.

L. Lusko, S. Collins

HISTORY

Even if the Bible did not exist, archaeologists and historians would predict—given the political situation in the ANE beginning in the late eleventh century BC—that if the Levant was ever going to have a kingdom or nation-state, this was the time (see *Map 5.01*).

Egypt was in no shape to mess with anyone (see *Timeline*), including those in the Levant. Neither the Philistines nor the Phoenicians were interested in gaining inland territory. The Geshurites were happy with their little kingdom, as were the Arameans. Assyria had no interest in the Levant yet. The Israelite tribes were well established in the central hill country and in part of the Transjordan. The nomadic Amalekites to the south were happy wandering within their traditional ranges. The Edomites were busy guarding their copper mines and running ingot caravans in all directions. The Moabites had vast farmlands on the Transjordan Plateau and were generally content inside their geographically discreet territory. Ammon also had sprawling plateau farmlands yet held their territory firmly with strategic defensive systems and a network of guard towers throughout their kingdom.

The time was indeed ripe for a Levantine kingdom, and it was Israel's loose coalition of tribes that had more of the "right stuff" in place than anyone else. What Israel "needed" was a king and central government to help pull it all together. Historically speaking, if the people had not pressed Samuel for a king and gotten one, someone else would have (as least eventually) stepped in to fill the political void. Timing is everything; Israel now had a king.

As adequate as King Saul was for starters, he was neither aggressive nor savvy enough to whip Israel into a true national entity. He was a king, but barely more than a tribal warlord or chieftain. That was how he lived, and that was how he died. Saul's story is painfully authentic to the late eleventh century BC, as is David's rise to the throne. With Saul still ruling but discredited, David was anointed king by Samuel. There was then war between the two houses (2 Samuel 3:1).

In the ANE, when one competing royal claimant vied against another, levels of palace intrigue and

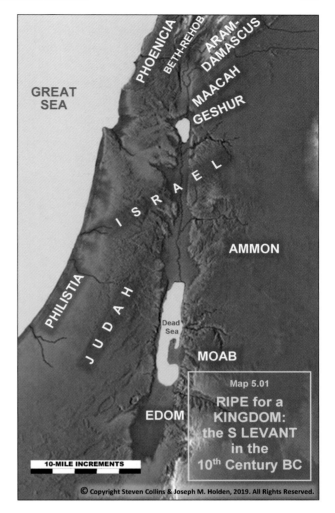

Map 5.01

RIPE for a KINGDOM: the S LEVANT in the 10th Century BC

10-MILE INCREMENTS

© Copyright Steven Collins & Joseph M. Holden, 2019. All Rights Reserved.

Figure 5.01—Tel Dan Stela; *byt dvd* "House of David" circled (photo: David E. Graves)

murderous plots rose until one got the upper hand. This invariably meant death not only to the loser, but to everyone related by blood and loyalty. The transition from Saul to David was a complicated and bloody affair in true ANE fashion! All the royal players in the story—Saul, Jonathan, Ish-bosheth, David—were warriors first and foremost (see *Breakout 5.02*). Essentially, fighting and war were the way to get things done.

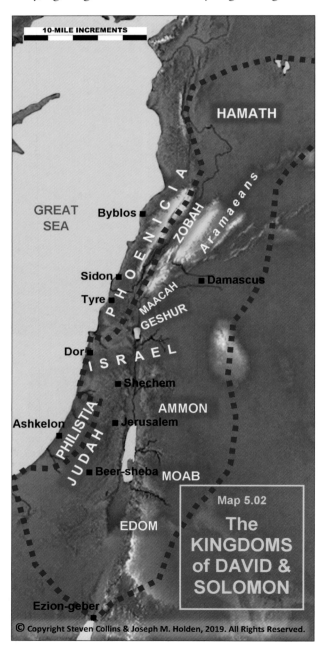

10-MILE INCREMENTS

HAMATH

GREAT SEA

Byblos

PHOENICIA

ZOBAH

Aramaeans

Sidon

MAACAH

Damascus

Tyre

GESHUR

Dor

ISRAEL

Shechem

PHILISTIA

AMMON

Ashkelon

Jerusalem

JUDAH

Beer-sheba

MOAB

Map 5.02

The
KINGDOMS
of DAVID &
SOLOMON

EDOM

Ezion-geber

Diplomacy was rare. Rivals and enemies, and even mere insulters, were engaged by murder or in battle, not in conversation!

David spent many years as a mercenary fighter, at times even working for the Philistines (1 Samuel 27; 29; 30; see *Breakout 5.01*). Disenfranchised by King Saul, David led the life of a Hebrew (*Habiru*; see *Breakout 2.06*) along with his fighting men (1 Samuel 23:13; 27:2; cf. 1 Chronicles 11–12). Eventually the House of David was victorious over the House of Saul. Once King David was in full control of the Israelite military, he set about putting together a kingdom. It did not take him long to figure out that the most logical location for the capital city of his budding nation-state was Jerusalem (see *Breakout 5.04*). The centuries-old Canaanite-Jebusite city had defensive walls with massive stone foundations built back in the time of Melchizedek (MBA2), and in David's day it was still well fortified. Jerusalem also had a marvelous water supply, the Gihon Spring, and a system of associated water channels for getting water where it was needed.

The problem was, Jerusalem's defenses were so good that neither Joshua's army nor subsequent Israelite forces had been able to take the city. In the early days of David's rule, it was still a Jebusite stronghold (2 Samuel 5:6). But David discerned that the key to taking the city was its water system (2 Samuel 5:8; 1 Chronicles 11:5-7; see *Breakout 5.03*). It worked. The next thing we know, David had taken up residence in Jerusalem (see *Breakout 5.04*) and began building his palace (see *Breakout 5.05*; David's palace is currently being excavated immediately south of the Temple Mount).

His many sins aside, David's career was, in a word, brilliant. His skills as a warrior and commander served him well, both before and after he ascended to the Israelite throne. He also possessed administrative skills, using them to build a nation-state well recognized in the region. Indeed, if your kingdom touched on David's, you were either fighting him or becoming a vassal. While we have precious little extrabiblical material from IA2, several discoveries reinforce King David's biblical reputation, one of which is the Tel Dan Stela (see *Figure 5.01*).

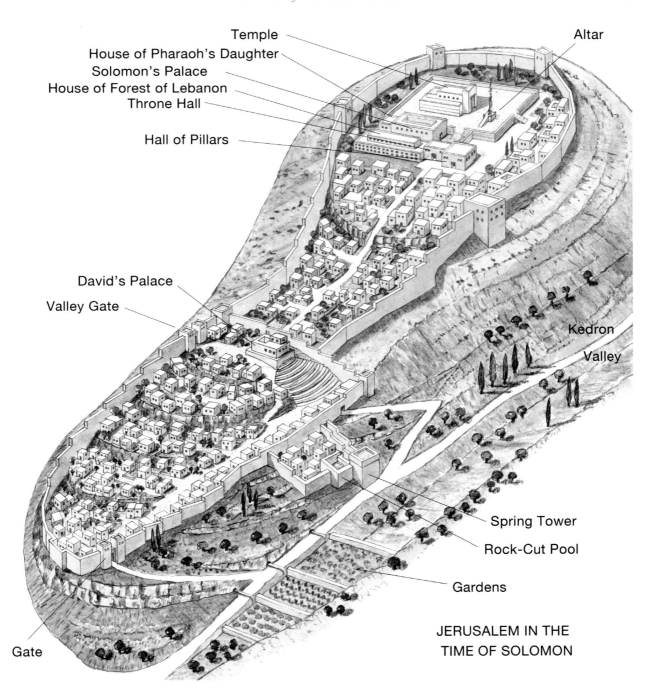

Temple

House of Pharaoh's Daughter

Solomon's Palace

House of Forest of Lebanon

Throne Hall

Hall of Pillars

Altar

David's Palace

Valley Gate

Kedron

Valley

Spring Tower

Rock-Cut Pool

Gardens

Gate

JERUSALEM IN THE
TIME OF SOLOMON

Figure 5.02—Solomon's Jerusalem (drawing: Leen Ritmeyer)

During the ninth century BC, the Tel Dan Stela inscription was issued by Hazael of Aram-Damascus. On it he boasted of victories over Israel and its ally, the king of the "House of David" (Judah). The stela was found in pieces, in secondary use as wall stones at Tel Dan in northern Israel. Enough pieces of the inscription survive to corroborate the events recorded in 2 Kings 8:7-15, 28 and 9:15-16. Before the *byt dvd* (meaning "House of David") reference in this Aramaic inscription came to light, not a few scholars doubted the historical authenticity of King David, the father of the Judahite Dynasty referred to in the Old Testament as the "House of David" (1 Samuel 20:16; 2 Samuel 3:1, 6).

BREAKOUT 5.02

MILITARY MENTORSHIP

There were no boot camps in the BA or IA. Boys were trained into military readiness through a lengthy process of one-on-one mentoring. In the ancient world, all civilizations had a male military-culture in which experienced warriors adopted apprentices who were, over several years, trained in all manner of fighting skills and personal disciplines—everything from swordsmanship to wrestling, cultural protocols to social graces, personal hygiene to sexual conduct. The training was long and involved an intimate bond between the warrior and his young apprentice.

The earliest evidence of this practice comes from the Minoan civilization of BA Crete. For the Minoans, the male mentor/apprentice relationship was culturally universal. Every boy was trained into manhood through this process. On Crete it was inaugurated by a prearranged "kidnapping" in which a boy was ritually abducted from his mother by a "gang" sent from a would-be mentor. As the custom of military mentorship spread beyond Crete into the Aegean region and Greece, the rite of ritual abduction was abandoned. However, all the other elements remained. This process became the foundation of military training across Europe, the Near East, Middle East, and Far East. It was adopted by virtually every warrior-culture from the Roman army to the Samurai of Japan.

In general terms, the ancient process of military mentorship followed a well-established process. Male children were raised by their mothers until age 12. At that time the boy, now to become an *eromenos* (Greek, "beloved"), was given over to a 22-year-old mentor (*erastes*, meaning "lover") in a formal, intimate relationship for a period of 8 years. After the 8 years, usually followed by a 2-year hiatus, the now-32-year-old warrior/mentor was eligible to take a wife or take on another apprentice. The now 20-year-old graduate (*ephebe*) then lived alone for 2 years, after which he took on his own military apprentice.

Of course, each warrior-culture developed its own adaptations of the military mentorship process. However, such intimate training relationships were fundamental to all ancient military systems. These mentorships also involved sexual relations and, among equine warriors, bestiality with horses, shared between warrior and apprentice. Such detestable sexual practices were specifically prohibited by the Mosaic Law: "You shall not lie with a male as with a woman; it is an abomination. And you shall not lie with any animal and so make yourself unclean with it…it is perversion" (Leviticus 18:22-23; cf. Exodus 22:19; Leviticus 20:15).

In the Bible, terms like "armor-bearer," "shield-bearer," and "attendant" generally refer to military apprentices and reflect the ancient practice of warrior mentorship.

S. Collins

With this discovery, the existence of the Davidic Dynasty and its namesake king became the stuff of history, not merely legend. Since the Tel Dan inscription began turning heads in the 1990s, scholars have recognized additional ancient references to King David and the Judahite Dynasty bearing his name. An Egyptian monumental inscription—from about the same period as the Tel Dan Stela—mentions the "heights of David." The Mesha Stele (ninth century BC), which mentions the Israelite king Omri, likely also refers to the House of David (*bytd--*).

As extrabiblical physical evidence of David's existence continues to mount, it is clear that the House of David—the Israelite kingdom of David and Solomon and the later kingdom of Judah—is a cultural necessity for a complete picture of the Near East during IA2.

By the reign of Solomon, Israel was "the big kid on the block." Solomon even took an Egyptian princess as a wife in an alliance with Egypt (1 Kings 3:1)—the lesser giving his daughter to the greater. He pushed the borders of Israel to their greatest extent (see *Map 5.02*). Unlike his father, Solomon was not a warrior according to the old Hebrew custom. His modus operandi was opulence in the best (or worst!) tradition of ANE kings. He amassed remarkable wealth (see *Breakout 5.09*). He entertained international dignitaries (see *Breakout 5.08*). And he made Jerusalem his showplace (see *Figure 5.02* and *Breakout 5.06*).

According to the Bible, Solomon's two crowning achievements were his Jerusalem palace and the temple of Yahweh (see *Figures 5.03–5.05* and *Breakout 5.07*). He spent far more time constructing his palace (13 years) than he did building the temple complex (7 years). The adorning of his palace was lavish, if not outlandish. He was also wise (intelligent) in the extreme (1 Kings 4:29-31). He was a man of letters and music (1 Kings 4:32). He could expound on trees and herbs. He could lecture on all kinds of mammals,

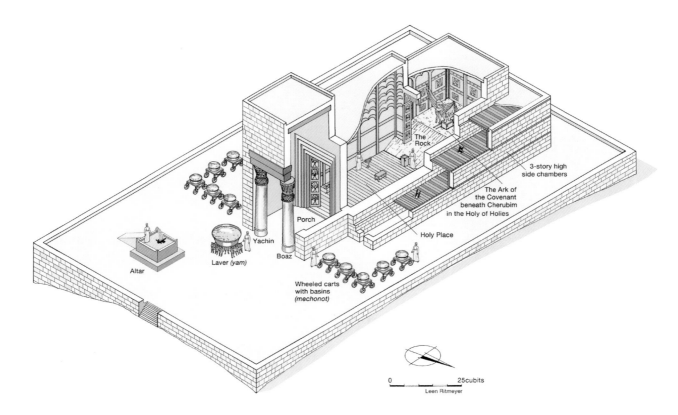

Figure 5.03—Solomon's temple (drawing: Leen Ritmeyer)

BREAKOUT 5.03

JOAB, THE TSINOR, AND THE CONQUEST OF JERUSALEM

After the Battle of the Elah Valley, in which David, a young shepherd boy, was able to defeat the Philistine champion Goliath, King Saul took David into his household and trained him as a soldier. Within several years, David had become a famous warrior in his own right, incurring the wrath and jealousy of the aging Saul. David was forced to flee for his life and was accompanied by a troop of loyal men. Eventually he sought refuge with the Philistines by pretending to be a traitor to Saul and Israel.

Saul was killed fighting a Philistine army at Mount Gilboa, after which David returned to the tribe of Judah and was acclaimed as their new king. Ish-bosheth, a surviving son of Saul, ruled in the north for two years after the death of Saul, but when he was assassinated, the northern tribes accepted David as their king.

As king of all the tribes of Israel, David determined to make Jerusalem his capital, it being well fortified and centrally located. No details of the attack are provided in the Bible other than a statement by David that "whoever would strike the Jebusites, let him get up the water shaft [Hebrew, *tsinor*] to attack" (2 Samuel 5:8). This has traditionally been understood to refer to some sort of tunnel that provided secret access to a city that had proved impregnable to the Israelites ever since the days of Joshua.

The water supply to the Jebusite city in the time of David was provided by the Gihon Spring located in the Kidron Valley outside of and below the walls of the city. While most Canaanite cities of that time had tunnels or fortifications around their water supply, many have assumed that there was no such protection to the Gihon Spring at the time of David (however improbable that would be). But in 1867, Sir Charles Warren, a British engineer, discovered a tunnel running through the hillside above the spring, as well as a vertical shaft from that tunnel down to the spring itself. It has been argued that Warren's Shaft was the means by which David gained access into the city. Yet research has since shown that the shaft is a late geological arrival and was not present at the time of David.

In the early 2000s, excavations at the Gihon Spring revealed the foundations of a massive enclosure that surrounded and protected the spring (in contradiction to the idea that no such protection existed). There has also been found a previously unknown older tunnel (built in the MBA) that ran alongside the city walls and was covered with stone slabs and camouflaged outside the city confines. This newly discovered tunnel was connected

Canaanite water channel, Jerusalem; "roof" blocking stones (R) were perhaps a point of entry if removed (photos: John Witte Moore)

to the Gihon Spring and seems to have served as an early irrigation system to the agricultural terraces along the slopes above the Kidron Valley. The tunnel, large enough to allow a man to walk upright, allowed exterior access to the spring located within the fortified walls of the city.

It is probable that Joab or other of David's men had observed maintenance being performed on the outer extent of the tunnel, during which one or more of the covering stone slabs had been temporarily removed (perhaps replaced). This meant removing the camouflaging soil and overgrowth from that section of the tunnel, revealing an external means of entry into the city. Probably under the cover of night, a small group of Israelite warriors removed a few blocking stones, entered the water channel, and got into the city. They then overpowered guards at a nearby gate and opened it, allowing more Israelites to enter and conquer the allegedly impregnable Jerusalem.

This tunnel, currently dubbed the Canaanite Dry Tunnel, appears to provide an acceptable answer to the question of the location of Joab's water shaft.

J. Moore

birds, reptiles, and fish (1 Kings 4:33). He showered his friends with gifts of cities and land and built a fleet of commercial ships at the port city Ezion-geber (1 Kings 9:26; see *Map 5.02*). In all these ways, Solomon was a typical ANE monarch.

But Solomon had a dark side. Very dark, indeed. It is said that during his reign he loved Yahweh, but that he also had a taste for ancient religious practices like sacrificing at the outdoor shrines of the high places (1 Kings 3:3-4). Solomon also had a large number of foreign wives for whom he built all manner of pagan shrines and high places (1 Kings 11). He also descended into worshipping gods and goddesses like Ashtoreth, Milcom/Molech, and Chemosh (see *Breakout 5.10*).

Because of these things, his life had an ugly ending and he left a sad legacy. Solomon had so reinforced pagan worship practices among his own people that they would struggle with apostasy against Yahweh for the next three centuries.

PEOPLES AND KINGDOMS

ASSYRIA—The Assyrian people had lived in northern Mesopotamia since the Early Bronze Age (EBA) but were subjects of the Sumerian, Akkadian, and Babylonian dynasties (see *Timeline*). Assyria emerged as an independent kingdom in the fourteenth century BC (LBA) as the Kassite Babylonian dynasties were in decline. They continued to expand their power and reach throughout the IA with a combination of ruthless military campaigns (see *Breakout 6.06*) and the pursuit of trade. However, the Assyrians were minding their own business in Mesopotamia and immediately adjacent areas. They were not threatening the Levant—not yet.

PHILISTIA—Saul was unsuccessful in defeating the Philistines, and they overran most of the region to the west of the Jordan, occupying Beth Shan in the Jezreel Valley (see *Breakouts 4.04, 5.01*). David defeated them decisively after his reign at Hebron, and they were confined to smaller peaceable areas without incident until the time of the divided kingdom (see *Map 5.02*). The Philistines had a presence in the south

Figure 5.04—Solomon's temple, detail (drawing: Leen Ritmeyer)

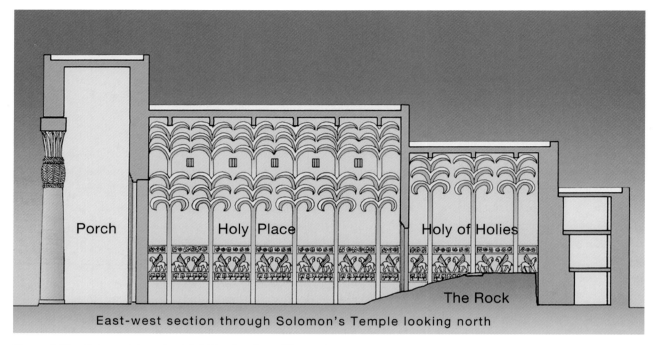

Porch   Holy Place   Holy of Holies

The Rock

East-west section through Solomon's Temple looking north

Figure 5.05—Solomon's temple, detail (drawing: Leen Ritmeyer)

Levant simultaneously with the Judahites, and whatever was left of the Philistines by the fifth century BC eventually became Hellenized with the conquest of the Levant by Alexander the Great.

PHOENICIA—With the growing instability of Egypt's reign during the Amarna period (fourteenth century BC), the entire region revolted, and the Phoenicians prospered (see *Maps 3.07, 5.02*). Every kingdom in the Fertile Crescent relied on the Phoenician maritime trading empire for the importation and exportation of myriad commodities (see *Figure 5.06*). Hiram, king of Tyre, made a profitable trade alliance with King David that extended into Solomon's reign. They allied themselves with the House of Omri in the northern kingdom of Israel during the period of the divided monarchy. King Ahab's wife, Jezebel, was Phoenician.

GESHUR—A kingdom that occupied the northeast part of the Golan Heights above Lake Kinnereth (see *Map 5.02*). David's wife Maacah was the daughter of Talmai, king of Geshur (2 Samuel 3:3). The people known as Geshurites were never driven from the land, as instructed in Joshua 13:11. Their capital city, Zer (or

Figure 5.06—Phoenician ship restoration (photo: Alexander Schick)

BREAKOUT 5.04

SOLOMON'S TEMPLE

There were three successive temples built on the historic site identified in Jerusalem as Mount Moriah (2 Chronicles 3:1). Solomon built the First Temple, and it was dedicated around 960–950 BC (1 Kings 6:38).

The temple was built to replace the tabernacle commissioned by Yahweh in Exodus 25. The temple-like tabernacle was fashioned to be a place for God to dwell among his people. The temple dimensions were 90 feet long, 30 feet wide, and 45 feet high (1 Kings 6:1-10). This temple structure no longer exists, but similar three-chambered (tripartite) temples can be observed at comparably dated sites like Tell Tayinat and Tel Arad.

Solomon's temple consisted of an outer porch, the inner Holy Place, and the Holy of Holies. Physically, the temple was made of quarried limestone covered with panels of cedar wood and overlaid in places with gold (1 Kings 6).

At the front of the temple were two hollow bronze pillars, one on each side the entrance, individually named Boaz and Jachin (1 Kings 7:21). Two gold-overlaid doors led from the porch or vestibule to an interior nave or Holy Place.

Inside the Holy Place was the golden altar of incense and the golden table for the bread of presence, and ten golden lampstands, five on the north side and five on the south (1 Kings 7:48-49).

Inside the Holy of Holies stood two massive fifteen-foot-tall golden cherubim, with the Ark of the Covenant resting between them (1 Kings 6:23-28; 2 Chronicles 5:1-14).

The first temple was destroyed when Jerusalem fell to the Babylonians in 586 BC (2 Kings 25:8-9). The Jewish return from Babylonian exile, made possible by the decree of Cyrus around 538 BC, allowed for the rebuilding of the temple, which was undertaken by Zerubbabel. This structure was completed c. 515 BC but reflected little of its past splendor (Haggai 2:3). Apparently, this temple did not have the ark or many of the previous "glories" (1 Esdras 1:54).

The second (actually, third) temple construction began during the reign of Herod the Great, c. 20 BC, and according to Josephus, was initiated at least in part because the old foundations were unstable. Herod's much larger temple was made of white marble with gold-overlaid doors. This expansion project also included a massive temple complex with porches and numerous courts. The entire complex was destroyed when Jerusalem fell to the Roman army in AD 70.

B. Maggard, S. Collins

Zed—Joshua 19:35; the site of New Testament Bethsaida), was destroyed by the Assyrians in the eighth century BC (see *Figure 5.07*).

MOAB—Moab was a regional power (see *Map 5.02*), and David took his parents there for protection against Saul (1 Samuel 22:3-4). Moab was subjugated by Judah and forced to pay tribute (2 Kings 3:4). King Mesha of Moab finally rebelled against Judah, but the Moabites were conquered for good by Jehoshaphat, after which they declined into oblivion in fulfillment of Amos's prophecy (Amos 2:1-3).

EDOM—The capital city of Edom was Ezion-geber (see *Map 5.02*), of which the land initially belonged to the Horites (or "cave dwellers"; Genesis 14:6). The Edomites intermarried with Esau and his tribe eventually absorbed the Horites. In time, an Edomite kingdom emerged and is mentioned in Numbers 20:14-21. David eventually subdued the Edomite people and garrisoned the entire region. Solomon had a seaport at Ezion-geber.

AMMON—The people of Ammon were a warlike and fierce enemy of Israel. Ammon was briefly allied with David under Nahash (2 Samuel 10:2), but most of the time the Ammonites were bitter enemies. During the time of Moses, they had secured Balaam's services in an attempt to curse Israel. The Ammonites also allied themselves with Sanballat to undermine the work of restoring Jerusalem (Nehemiah 2:10-19; see *Breakout 7.10*). They were defeated, as predicted by Ezekiel (Ezekiel 25:1-7), by the forces of Judah Maccabee (1 Maccabees 5:6) in the second century BC.

AMALEKITES—Saul failed to destroy the Amalekites during his reign, as instructed (1 Samuel 15:8-9). David finally defeated them after a raid on Ziklag (1 Samuel 30:18). The Amalekites lived in the Negev southwest of the Dead Sea and in the Sinai from Rephidim to Egypt (see *Map 3.07*). They often joined with the Canaanites and Moabites against Israel.

ARAMEANS—Early on the Arameans were seminomadic and rivaled the Assyrians during the ninth century. They were later made up of several small kingdoms or city-states occupying the region around Damascus and extending toward Phoenicia. Aram-Damascus was the prominent Aramean kingdom in this period (tenth and ninth centuries BC). David defeated a smaller Aram of Zobah, along with Damascus (2 Samuel 8:3-7), and Aram Naharaim (Aram of Mesopotamia). During the reign of Solomon, Aramean influence waned.

EGYPT—The Twenty-first and Twenty-second Dynasties of Egypt were a low ebb for Egypt. The kingdom was often weak and divided into regional factions, even ruled by foreigners at times. Solomon was strong enough to take an Egyptian princess in a diplomatic marriage—in such unions, the weaker gave the daughter in marriage to the stronger. But under Shoshenq I, Egypt went on to plunder Jerusalem in the days of Solomon's son Rehoboam (see *Breakout 5.09*).

SOCIETIES AND CULTURES

SOCIAL STRATIFICATION—Although the turmoil of IA1 (see *Timeline*) had taken its toll on the upper classes of what had been the larger urban centers, the Southern Levant was poised for a reordering of society and politics at the hands of a growing population of Israelite tribes, the borders of which had become blurred, even indistinct. Much of the Israelite population had remained nomadic to seminomadic, but by the time of Saul, a kingdom, with a definable royal class, was beginning to emerge in the central highlands (see *Map 5.02*). But not without conflict.

TRIBALISM—Local society in the ANE was, and remained, tribal to the core. Whether you were a pauper or a king, pedigree was everything—that is, unless you could usurp position or control by intrigue or force, or both. Under the right circumstances, a tribe could dominate other tribes, or a family or individual might rise to take control of a people. Tribal warfare often resulted. Thus was the story of Saul and David.

CITY-STATES—The large Levantine cities were no longer operating in the old feudal sense. If anything, they were centers of economic power and influence drawing their local resources together for the benefit of their city, satellite towns, and villages. In essence, they were collectives. Of course, the king of the city-state had reasonable power, but more as a formidable CEO than an absolute monarch. The five great Philistine cities—Gath, Gaza, Ashkelon, Ashdod, and Ekron—remained independent of each other, but economically,

Figure 5.07—Geshur gate and patron deity Hadad (photo: John Witte Moore; inset photo: James Barber)

BREAKOUT 5.05

DAVID'S JERUSALEM

King David and his army captured the city of Jerusalem, and it became known from this point onward as the City of David. It was the capital of his kingdom and served as the religious and governmental center for the 12 tribes of Israel.

At the time of David, Jerusalem occupied about 10-12 acres on the eastern hill or ridge of what is modern-day Jerusalem, with a population in the city proper of approximately 2,000 people. Jerusalem was surrounded on three sides by valleys, and the Gihon Spring provided a consistent source of water for the city's inhabitants. The main defenses and city structures had been built and rebuilt by local Canaaneans (Jebusites) for more than 800 years—since the time of Abraham and Melchizedek.

After capturing the city, David installed additional fortifications and began to refurbish and expand the city through building projects paid for with ever-increasing taxes and conscriptions of workers. This situation would continue and worsen through the reign of his son Solomon. David's reign from Jerusalem saw a dramatic expansion of centralized government and a significantly robust economy due to his military conquests and, no doubt, international trade.

It was David's desire to build a permanent structure, a temple, in Jerusalem for the worship of Yahweh. This would centralize Israel's national worship—as opposed to the use of outlier shrines and the portable tabernacle, which had been in multiple locations during Israel's history in the land. This desire, according to the biblical text, came from David's concern that he lived in a palace of cedar, but Yahweh's ark dwelt in a tent.

It is also likely that David saw a permanent worship center in Jerusalem as advancing his goal of centralizing power, both religious and administrative, for the entire kingdom of Israel. Bringing the Ark of the Covenant to Jerusalem was the first step in this process. However, God made clear to David that the temple would not be his project to carry out, but instead, that his son Solomon would build it.

W. Attaway

BREAKOUT 5.06

DAVID'S PALACE

In 2005, on the eastern slope of the City of David, south of the Temple Mount in Jerusalem, Eilat Mazar uncovered the remains of a monumental, palatial building known as the Large Stone Structure (or Fortress of Zion), supported by the well-known Stepped Stone Structure (built between LBA2 and IA1; possibly the Millo of 1 Kings 9:15-24; 2 Chronicles 32:4-5). The Large Stone Structure dates to the time of David and Solomon (tenth–ninth centuries BC).

Mazar believes this to be the remains of the palace of King David, which dates to the early tenth century BC, although she has taken strong criticism for her claim. Mazar's evidence consists of the following: (1) the monumental size of the structure compared with other contemporary buildings demonstrates that it had a significant royal or public usage; (2) it is located outside the Jebusite city walls; (3) the occupational strata of the Large Stone Structure and the Stepped Stone Structure, based on pottery and radiocarbon analysis, date both structures to the Iron Age 2a (tenth–ninth centuries BC); (4) a fine black-on-red Cypriot juglet (IA2a) and several ivory inlays demonstrate a Phoenician connection and luxurious lifestyle; and (5) the discovery of several bullae (seal impressions) also supports the use of the building by royalty.

Among the names on some 51 seals (bullae) recovered so far are the names of two ministers of King Zedekiah's court and Hezekiah, king of Judah. "Yehuchal [English, Jehucal] Ben Shelamayahu,

son of Shovi" (587/6 BC, discovered in 2010) and "Gedaliah Ben Pashchur" (587/6 BC, discovered in 2008) were two of the four officials who plotted to kill the prophet Jeremiah (Jeremiah 37:3; 38:1). Another bullae name, "Gemaryahu ben Shafan," is also mentioned in the Bible as King Jehoiakim's scribe toward the end of the first temple period (Jeremiah 36:10).

The discovery in 2012 of the earliest alphabetic text ever identified in Jerusalem also supports the administrative use of the structure. It was discovered on the broken shoulder of a large storage jar (IA2a, tenth century BC). While

Mazar claims that the letters *m, q, p, h, n,* possibly *l,* and *n* do not spell out any known words, Gershon Galil and Douglas Petrovich suggest that it could possibly read: "[In the firs]t [(regnal) year]: pseudo-[wi]ne from [the garden of ...]." Based on the paleo-Hebrew script (mainly the formation of the two *yods*) and date, it may belong to the first regnal year of an unnamed king shortly after Jerusalem was taken by the Israelites, suggesting that Judah was, by this time, ruled by a substantial central authority such as a sole monarch.

D. Graves

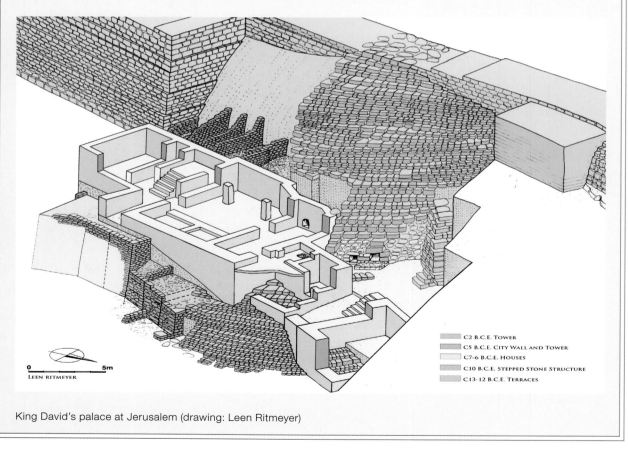

0   5m
LEEN RITMEYER

☐ C2 B.C.E. TOWER
☐ C5 B.C.E. CITY WALL AND TOWER
☐ C7-6 B.C.E. HOUSES
☐ C10 B.C.E. STEPPED STONE STRUCTURE
☐ C13-12 B.C.E. TERRACES

King David's palace at Jerusalem (drawing: Leen Ritmeyer)

socially, and militarily cooperative. The Phoenician cities were run in a similar fashion. The highland cities were comparatively small (more town than city) and more vulnerable. David took advantage of the independent nature of the Philistine cities.

INHERITANCE—As relates to families, clans, and tribes, not much had changed by the time of David. There was one notable exception: Samuel, the king-maker. David rose not by right of hereditary succession, but by divine selection at the hands of the prophet/judge Samuel. Otherwise, the laws of primogeniture still applied in this IA world.

WOMEN'S ROLES—In David's and Solomon's world of royal and international dignitaries, women could occasionally rise to prominence. One way for this to happen was to be the favored queen of a ruling monarch. While there were no females in the succession of Israelite or Judahite rulers, there were prominent queens and international personalities. Common women still raised children and managed households.

MEN'S ROLES—Men pursued all manner of trades and, when called upon, took up arms as trained soldiers. The Israelite tribes were a society of warriors with all the obligatory protocols of ANE warrior culture. But war was the exception rather than the rule, so most men had a "day job" that paid the bills. David's mighty men (1 Chronicles 11) may have been an exception. They served as his enforcers, personal army, and royal guard.

POLITICAL CLIMATE—The Philistines were not particularly interested in the central highlands, so tensions between them and the emerging kingdom of Israel were primarily limited to border skirmishes (see *Map 5.02*). Aram-Damascus and Geshur were solidifying their own territories with little or no interference from Assyria. Assyria was strong and getting stronger but was not yet a threat to the Levant. Egypt was in no position to bother anyone. The Canaanite highlands were available for the taking, and that's exactly what David did. Solomon expanded Israel's territory mainly through diplomacy from a position of relative strength.

Figure 5.08—Iron Age 2 ostracon; writing on a pottery sherd (photo: Steven Collins)

LANGUAGES AND WRITING

HEBREW—The Semitic Canaanean language that had accompanied the Israelite tribes into and out of Egypt had, by this time, become enough of a distinct dialect to be called Hebrew.

HEBREW ALPHABET—From the beginning of the IA (see *Timeline*), the inhabitants of Canaan, including the ancient Israelites, used similar alphabetic scripts. Because of the ease of learning a short alphabet, literacy increased dramatically at all levels of society. During the IA, ostraca became common—pieces of broken pottery upon which were written brief notes or correspondence written by everyday people and not trained scribes or priests (see *Figure 5.08*).

PHILISTINE/GREEK—The Philistines brought their early Greek language and alphabet with them from their Mycenaean homeland. Very few Philistine inscriptions exist, but what survives makes it clear that their language was transplanted from the Aegean sphere. It is possible that much of their population learned local dialects like Hebrew and Phoenician, which was typical of people migrating to new lands.

Egyptian—The native Egyptian Twenty-first Dynasty was hanging by a thread during the time of King David and King Solomon, and the Libyan (Meshwesh) Twenty-second Dynasty was founded by Soshenq I (biblical Shishak) in the final decade of Solomon's reign. The Egyptian language continued to be used for inscriptions and texts, but it is possible that an ancient Libyan tongue was also used by the non-Egyptian royal house.

Akkadian—The Assyrian dialect was a later version of the Akkadian language that had dominated Mesopotamia for more than 1,000 years. Although Akkadian was still spoken over all of Mesopotamia, never in its history had it been so isolated from the Levant and Egypt. The Western Semitic languages like Phoenician, Hebrew, Moabite, and Ammonite covered most of the Levant, with Aramaic on the rise in north Mesopotamia.

BELIEFS AND RELIGIONS

Yahwism—The emerging nation of Israel had descended to a low ebb religiously by the time the prophet/judge Samuel arrived on the scene. Saul was a miserable failure as king of Israel and never solidified his hold over all the tribes. With Samuel's anointing of David as king, things began to turn around. Samuel himself restored Israel's faith in the Torah of Moses, and King David was committed to keeping the laws of Yahweh. The process by which this change took place is fuzzy at best, but somehow Israel, under David, recommitted itself to following Yahweh's statutes. The priesthood was restored to credibility in the eyes of the people, and the tabernacle was restricted to its proper use. Prophets of Yahweh once again appeared across the landscape.

Tabernacle/Temple Worship—The tabernacle was a portable shrine (see *Breakout 3.09*) incorporating

---

BREAKOUT 5.07

SOLOMON'S JERUSALEM

When Solomon was crowned king, the united kingdom of Israel was undergoing a profound period of economic and military success. In fact, the reigns of David and Solomon are known as the golden age of Israel's history. Solomon's Jerusalem was the shining capital city of what had become an internationally known mini-empire.

Following the example of his father David, Solomon continued with more building projects and expansions. His greatest accomplishment in this area was the temple, making Jerusalem the permanent spiritual center of the kingdom of Israel. The temple took seven years to construct and involved expanding the city's dimensions to include the present-day Temple Mount.

Solomon instituted administrative reforms during his reign, perhaps expanding on what his father had begun. Dividing the land into 12 administrative districts, he intended to provide for the needs of the military and the palace. This also served to weaken the old tribal identities and loyalties as he replaced them with a strong, centralized national government and identity. Each district was ruled by a governor who was appointed by Solomon and who would be loyal to him.

Solomon's building projects, including the temple, became a bone of contention for the people of Israel. His decisions to fund the building projects with even heavier taxes than his father had imposed, as well as to expand conscription of forced laborers, caused his popularity to diminish as the people grew increasingly resentful. These decisions also alienated the northern tribes of Israel, which contributed to the splitting of the kingdom after Solomon's death. What had been a strong, united kingdom under David would be a nation divided and in decline after the death of Solomon.

W. Attaway

Figure 5.09—The Holy of Holies, Solomon's temple (drawing: Leen Ritmeyer)

Figure 5.10—Arad Sanctuary, Iron Age 2a; a worship center in Judahite territory (time of Solomon) depicting two deities with standing stones in the holy of holies (photo: Steven Collins)

ARCHITECTURE AND INFRASTRUCTURE

TEMPLES—Across the Levant, temples were built for local gods in every city and town. Philistine temples had a particular design unique to that culture (see *Breakout 4.06*). The tripartite temple was known across the entire ANE, and Solomon's temple was built similarly (see *Breakout 5.07*). While the inner shrines of other temples contained representations of gods (usually standing stones), Solomon's temple had no representation of Yahweh, as stipulated by the Mosaic Law. However, Solomon did build outlier shrines at various locations, including his southern garrison at Arad (see *Map 5.02*), which included two standing stones (one larger than the other) likely representing Yahweh and Asherah (see *Figure 5.10*).

all the accoutrements for the corporate worship of Yahweh as laid forth in the Mosaic Law. Similar portable structures are known from antiquity. The tripartite arrangement of the tabernacle was transferred to Solomon's temple, with all the fixtures rendered on a larger scale and with permanent materials (see *Breakout 5.07*). The Holy of Holies was reserved for the manifest presence of Yahweh himself (see *Figure 5.09*).

DAVID AND IDOLATRY—While the Bible affirms over and over that David was fully devoted to Yahweh, there are indications that he became lax in his practice of the Mosaic Law from time to time. For example, why was there an idol in close proximity to David's bedchamber (1 Samuel 19:13)?

SOLOMON AND IDOLATRY—Although a superlatively wise person who started off on the right path with Yahweh at the beginning of his reign, Solomon eventually degenerated into the most severe levels of pagan religion (1 Kings 11:3-8; see *Breakout 5.10*).

ADMINISTRATIVE STRUCTURES—All urban centers possess administrative structures, often monumental in nature, and this period is no exception. Cities needed space for administrative functions, and this was true for both David's and Solomon's palaces (see *Figure 5.11* and *Breakouts 5.05, 5.06*). The temple complex also had associated administrative buildings (see *Figure 5.12*).

HOUSES—The so-called four-room house was still the standard of the day. However, when built on sloping terrain (like the perimeter of the City of David), houses had to be modified to hug the hillside. They were stacked together to avoid collapse and minimize erosion (see *Figure 5.13*).

GATES—The six-chambered gateway was the standard for IA2 cities and towns (see *Figures 5.14, 5.15*). Side chambers perhaps stored weapons and provisions. How many sets of hinged doors were present is a matter of debate. Two sets seems to be a maximum. Often there was an outer and inner gateway.

FORTIFICATIONS—Walls were generally from 9 to 18 feet thick (see *Figure 5.16*), and from 20 to 40 feet high. Foundations consisted of numerous courses of stone topped by a mudbrick superstructure. During this period, city walls were often built using an inset-offset design with towers and bastions (see *Figure 5.17*).

STORE-CITIES—Kings like David, and particularly Solomon, relied on district agricultural production that needed to be processed and stored prior to distribution. They featured silos for storing raw harvested grain (see *Figure 5.18*) and warehouses for storing threshed grain in pottery storage jars (see *Figure 5.19*). Such "store cities" (1 Kings 9:19; 2 Chronicles 8:4-6; 16:4; 17:2) were heavily fortified towns located in each of Solomon's 12 administrative districts.

PROTO-IONIC/AEOLIC COLUMN CAPITALS—The proto-Aeolic (or proto-Ionic) column capital was a standard architectural feature throughout the kingdom of Israel (see *Figure 5.20*). It was used mainly in palaces and administrative buildings.

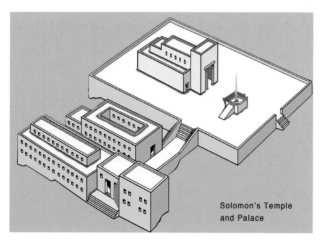

Figure 5.11—Solomon's palace adjacent to the temple (drawing: Leen Ritmeyer)

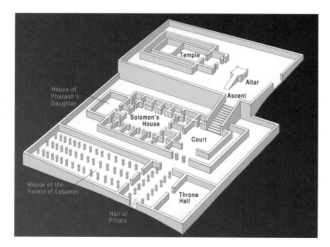

Figure 5.12—Temple administration buildings (drawing: Leen Ritmeyer)

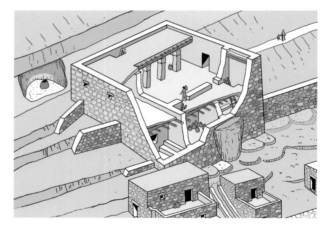

Figure 5.13—Terraced houses, David's Jerusalem (drawing: Leen Ritmeyer)

Figure 5.14—Gateway, Iron Age 2a, Megiddo (photo: Joseph Holden)

Figure 5.15—Iron Age 2 gateway, Gezer (photo: John Witte Moore)

WEAPONS AND WARFARE

WEAPONRY—By this time the straight double-edged sword was standard military issue, along with daggers and various kinds of axes and clubs (many of personal manufacture). Slings and slingstones were also extremely common, along with the composite bow and iron-tipped arrows (see *Figure 5.21*).

ARMOR—Higher-ranking warriors probably wore scale or plate body armor, armlets, leggings, and a helmet fashioned from leather and bronze or iron (see *Figure 5.22*). But the heavier armor limited speed and mobility, and thus could sometimes have been a liability. Shields were generally round(ish) and faced with leather and perhaps iron studding intended to dull a striking sword (see *Figure 5.22*).

Figure 5.17—City wall, inset-offset style, Tel Dan (photo: John Witte Moore)

Figure 5.16—Megiddo; model showing city walls, Iron Age 2a (photo: John Witte Moore)

Figure 5.18—Iron Age 2 grain silos in a store city of Israel (photo: Michael Luddeni, courtesy of Tall el-Hammam Excavation Project)

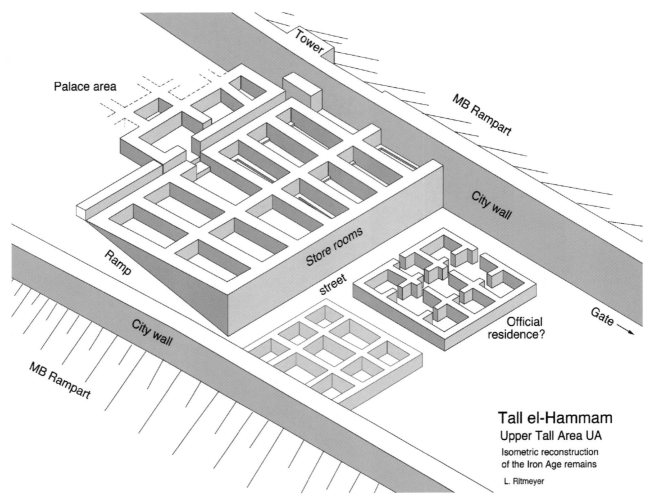

Figure 5.19—Grain warehouse, Iron Age 2a (drawing: Leen Ritmeyer, courtesy of Tall el-Hammam Excavation Project)

Figure 5.20—Proto-aeolic column capitals; a standard in Israelite monumental buildings (photo: Alexander Schick)

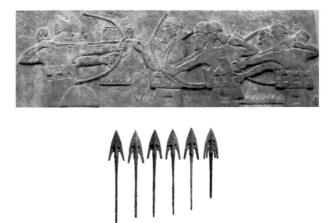

Figure 5.21—Composite bow, iron arrow points, Iron Age 2 (photos: David E. Graves)

BATTLE TACTICS—Open warfare remained typical. Opposing armies would amass opposite one another with the battleground between. When the trumpet sounded the charge, both armies would run headlong into a violent, clashing, slashing melee. Commanders watching the battle would sound the trumpet for a further advance or retreat, depending on what they observed. The main combat was hand-to-hand. The carnage was always ghastly. If the battlefield was mostly flat terrain, chariots could be used as firing platforms for arrows. If such an approach could be avoided by "champion-against-champion" combat, that would save lives. But this "calmer" approach was used only when the prize was of lesser value, as in the border disputes that arose between the Israelites and Philistines.

All-out siege warfare was reserved for attaining major conquests of cities and their territories. Sieges took a lot of time, energy, and material, with the goal of defeating the target through starvation and thirst. The attacking army might spend months building a siege ramp upon which they could move troops to the top of the city wall (see *Figure 5.23*). Once this happened, it was all but over for the inhabitants. Cities and towns would often capitulate to demands of annexation and vassalship early on to avoid the more negative consequences of resistance.

INDUSTRIES AND OBJECTS

AGRICULTURE—Cereal crops, fruit-producing trees, and a host of specialty crops were all part of the agricultural scene during the second half of the IA. The best archaeological attestation of beekeeping and honey production comes from this period (see *Figure 5.24*). Grain surpluses were housed in store-cities for processing and distribution to support the royal administration. Such surpluses could also be used to mitigate any production losses due to drought or crop failures.

HERDING—Oh, the ubiquitous shepherds! Bedouin and other herding nomads generally worked their own flocks. They might also be hired by city/town-dwelling entrepreneurs who owned flocks and herds but needed herdsmen to pasture their animals. The

"dung trade" was also important for supplying fuel for cooking fires in cities, towns, and villages.

FISHING—Saltwater fishing was a big industry for the coastal settlements of the Phoenicians and Philistines. The bones of species both large and small have been found in coastal sites and even as far inland as Tall Hisban in Jordan. Coastal rivers were inhabited by Nile perch and other species. Inland freshwater rivers and lakes (particularly Lake Kinnereth) served mainly local populations. The Jordan River had numerous fish species, including types of perch, tilapia, catfish, and carp (see *Figure 5.25*).

KITCHENS AND COOKING—The round-bottom cooking pot came in a variety of sizes and styles. It could be placed either on coals in an open hearth or in the draft-hole at the top of a tabun (beehive-style clay oven; see *Figure 5.26*). Stews of vegetables, with or without meat, were always on the menu, as well as flatbreads.

Figure 5.22—Armor, shield, Iron Age 2 (photo: James Barber, courtesy of Bible Lands Museum, Jerusalem)

Figure 5.23—Remains of the Assyrian siege ramp, Lachish (photo: Alexander Schick)

Lentils, onions, leeks, chickpeas, barley, wheat, and various kinds of beans were made into a variety of dishes. Olives and olive oil were basic ingredients. Sweets were made from barley flour with date paste, fig paste, and many kinds of fruits and nuts. Meat (sheep, goat, doves/pigeons, and occasionally wild game) was probably eaten on special occasions like festivals and feasts.

Metallurgy—Wadi Faynan and Timna (see *Map 2.05*) were the two main locations that provided copper ore, still the principal metal for common objects. Bronze (copper and tin) was cheaper than iron and easier to work. Iron ore came mainly from Anatolia (see *Map 1.06*) and was expensive. Various kinds of bellows were used (see *Figure 5.28*) to create adequate heat (from charcoal) both to smelt the raw material and to forge objects with hammer and anvil. The process was very similar to modern-day metalsmithing.

Stone and Stoneworking—From building foundations to column capitals to food-preparation vessels, stone of various kinds was common in all periods. It was the most-widely available building material in the south Levant. Limestone, hard sandstone, and basalt (see *Figure 1.06*) in unworked condition were good foundation material. Cut stone (ashlars) were used in some construction applications in monumental buildings like temples, palaces, and an occasional

Figure 5.24—Clay beehives, Iron Age 2a, Tel Rehov (photos: Alexander Schick)

Figure 5.25—Kinds of fish in Kinnereth Lake (Sea of Galilee), Iron Age 2a (public domain)

Figure 5.26—Contemporary clay ovens reflect ancient cooking traditions (photo: David E. Graves)

BREAKOUT 5.08

SOLOMON AND THE QUEEN OF SHEBA

First Kings 4:21 says, "Solomon ruled over all the kingdoms from the Euphrates to the land of the Philistines and to the border of Egypt. They brought tribute and served Solomon all the days of his life." Solomon's diplomacy and trade with other nations is unrivaled in Israel's history. He was one of the great rulers of this region and was visited by numerous heads of state. One of these visitors was the queen of Sheba (1 Kings 10:1-3). She visited Solomon likely with the purpose of strengthening their commercial relationship.

During his reign, Solomon controlled two major trade routes: the King's Highway in Transjordan and the Via Maris, which led to Mediterranean ports (see *Map 5.02*). These were lucrative avenues of income for the nation of Israel.

Sheba was probably located in the southwestern corner of the Arabian Peninsula. The merchants from this region were known far and wide, including in Israel, as traders in gold, gems, incense, and myrrh.

Hearing of Solomon's great wisdom, the queen came to test him with difficult questions, which he handled deftly one after another. In response she expressed amazement and praised God, "who has delighted in you and set you on the throne of Israel" (verse 9). The biblical text records that upon seeing all of his prosperity and hearing all of his wisdom, "there was no more breath in her" (verse 5). The sheer magnitude of all this greatness took her breath away! Her gifts to Solomon of gold, spices, and precious stones were significant. The biblical writer records that "never again came such an abundance of spices such as these that the queen of Sheba gave to King Solomon" (verse 10).

W. Attaway

gateway (see *Figure 5.29*). Unlike in Mesopotamia and Egypt, architectural elements of carved stone were relatively rare in the Southern Levant during the BA and IA. Grinding stones were generally made of basalt gathered from the Galilee and Golan areas, and at some places along the eastern shore of the Dead Sea.

Figure 5.27—David's raisin cakes (photo: Wes Husted)

King David's Raisin Cakes (see Figure 5.27)

This is an adapted IA2 recipe mentioned in 1 Chronicles 12:40 that is called "sacred" in Hosea 3:1 (NIV).

Ingredients

1 cup raisins
2 cups water
½ cup butter
¾ cup honey
½ teaspoon salt
½ teaspoon ground cinnamon
½ teaspoon ground nutmeg
1¾ cups whole wheat flour

Instructions

Preheat oven to 350° F or 175° C. Lightly grease one 10x10-inch baking pan (recommend a mini-loaf pan that makes 8 small loaves). In a large saucepan, boil the raisins with the water for 10 minutes. Add the butter and melt in the boiling raisins, then add the honey and stir until it's mixed in. Remove the pan from the heat and allow the mixture to cool. In the same pan add the whole wheat flour, salt, cinnamon, and nutmeg. Mix well, and pour batter into baking pan. Bake at 350° for 35 minutes.

BRICKMAKING—The superstructures of most houses and buildings in the IA Levant were made from mudbricks. Mostly they were sun-dried, but at some locations evidence of fired bricks has been found. Still, sun-dried mudbricks comprised better than 98 percent of construction material across the ANE. House walls averaged 1.5 to 2 feet thick. The walls in monumental buildings were 3 to 6 feet thick. City walls were 10 to 40 feet thick (see *Figure 5.30*). Mortar was made of mud/clay or mud/clay/ash. All mudbrick and stone surfaces were covered with clay/sand or clay/sand/lime plaster (see *Figure 5.31*). While generally durable and strong, mudbrick construction needed constant maintenance, especially following a rainstorm.

FLINT—Still the best material for getting a super-sharp edge, flint (and the lower grade chert) never went out of style for certain kinds of cutting implements. Surgical applications like treating wounds and circumcision required a fine flint edge. Harvesting tools, such as the sickle/scythe, had flint blades set into a curved wooden bow (see *Figure 5.32*). Flint was also superior to a metal blade when it came to skinning an animal or fine-cutting meat.

TEXTILES—Making cloth was always a major industrial endeavor as well as a cottage industry. Spindle whorls and loom weights (made of every imaginable material) have been found throughout virtually every IA archaeological site (see *Figure 5.33*).

POTTERY—Definite changes in pottery forms accompanied the consolidation of the Israelite kingdom beginning around 1000 BC. Israelite pottery forms began to dominate in the hill country of Canaan and significantly influenced the pottery of surrounding areas, including the coastal regions and the Transjordan. IA2 pottery was a much better product than that of the previous period. Firing was generally good and forms were made with great care, even for the common wares (see *Figure 5.34*).

TRADE—With the mini-empire of David and Solomon growing in the Southern Levantine hill country and with stable kingdoms and/or confederations—Edom, Moab, Ammon, Geshur, Aram-Damascas, Phoenicia, and Philistia—in all the surrounding areas,

Figure 5.28—Pipe bellows, ancient Egypt (photo: Herve Champollion/akg-images)

Figure 5.29—Quarrying ashlars (well-worked stones), Iron Age 2 (drawing: Leen Ritmeyer)

Figure 5.30—Mudbrick city walls, Beer-sheba (photo: John Witte Moore)

Figure 5.31—Preserved plaster on Iron Age 2 walls (photo: Michael Luddeni, courtesy of Tall el-Hammam Excavation Project)

Figure 5.32—Sickle (scythe) with flint blades inserted, Egypt (photo: Michael Luddeni)

the benefits of regional and international trade were once again experienced in the eastern Mediterranean Basin. Levantine olive oil and wine were coursing around the Mediterranean on Phoenician vessels. The availability of every possible commodity soared—copper, tin, iron, gold, silver, precious stones, exotic woods, spices, incense, and ivory. And, for the first time, a new product began to appear in Mesopotamia, Egypt, and likely the Levant: silk from the Far East.

Figure 5.33—Clay loom weights (photo: Alexander Schick)

BREAKOUT 5.09

SOLOMON'S WEALTH

According to 1 Kings 10, Solomon collected more than 20 tons of gold annually. Shortly after Solomon's death, Shishak, king of Egypt, plundered Jerusalem during the reign of Rehoboam. "He took away the treasures of the house of the LORD and the treasures of the king's house" (1 Kings 14:26). Shishak's forces included 1,200 chariots, 60,000 horsemen, and troops of Libyans, Sukkites, and Cushites. He captured the fortified cities of Judah, including Jerusalem (2 Chronicles 12).

Critics have groaned over the masses of wealth said to belong to Solomon, but archaeology confirms that the amount of gold attributed to him is commensurate both in use and extent with what is known of ANE kings during the IA. And this very biblical story is confirmed by Egyptian inscriptions in an interesting historical twist: Pharaoh Shoshenq I (biblical Shishak) plundered Jerusalem (c. 925 BC) and died within a year of the conquest. After Shoshenq's death, his son, Osorkon I, took the throne. Osorkon, after ruling just over three years, made spectacular gifts to the gods and goddesses of Egypt, including more than *383 tons of silver and gold.* Osorkon later buried his coregent son, Shoshenq II, in fine fashion, in a solid silver coffin (in Egypt, silver was more valuable than gold!).

How did a mediocre Egyptian king, during a relatively depressed era of Egyptian history, get that kind of wealth? Egyptologist K.A. Kitchen provides the answer:

Shoshenq's financially lucrative campaign against Judah/Israel—recorded on his triumphal relief at the Karnak temple of Amun in Thebes—put large quantities of gold and silver into the coffers of Egypt. When Shoshenq died, all that wealth passed into the hands of his son, Osorkon, thus providing the wealth to support Osorkon's generous gifts to Egyptian temples. The Solomon/Osorkon connection testifies to the accuracy of the Bible as a historical record.

S. Collins, J. Holden

Figure 5.34—Pottery of Iron Age 2a (photos: Michael Luddeni, Daniel Galassini, Steven Collins; courtesy of Museum of Archaeology, Trinity Southwest University)

BREAKOUT 5.10

SOLOMON'S SPIRITUAL FAILURES

In the ANE, it was common for treaties and trade agreements to be formalized by the marriage of the daughter of one king to the son of the other. Solomon instituted many such treaties, including a treaty with the pharaoh of Egypt, which involved Solomon marrying the pharaoh's daughter. First Kings 11:1-3 recalls,

King Solomon loved many foreign women, along with the daughter of Pharaoh: Moabite, Ammonite, Edomite, Sidonian, and Hittite women, from the nations concerning which the Lord had said to the people of Israel, "You shall not enter into marriage with them, neither shall they with you, for surely they will turn away your heart after their gods." Solomon clung to these in love. He had 700 wives, who were princesses, and 300 concubines. And his wives turned away his heart.

Solomon, whose father David had been described as a man after God's own heart (see Acts 13:22), in his later years turned away from the one true God, Yahweh. He followed his wives into the worship of "Ashtoreth the goddess of the Sidonians, and of Milcom the abomination of the Ammonites" (1 Kings 11:5).

How did the wisest man who had ever lived up to that point in history fall prey to such a temptation? How could a man whose unselfish prayer resulted in God granting him unparalleled wisdom end his life praying to false gods and leading others to do the same by his example?

Solomon's spiritual failures are a warning to all who read about them. Even the wisest are not exempt from Satan's schemes to turn our hearts away from God. Even Solomon, a wise king who was the talk of the nations, was a fallible human who followed his lusts and abandoned his God. May we learn from his example and never think ourselves incapable of the same.

W. Attaway

Altar, worship center, Arad, a Solomonic southern border fortress; Yahweh was worshipped here along with a goddess consort (photo: John Witte Moore)

THE WORLD OF ISRAEL AND JUDAH

WELCOME TO IRON AGE 2B–C (c. 900–586 BC)

After the death of Solomon, two kingdoms resulted: Israel in the north and Judah in the south (see *Timeline* and *Map 6.01*). Neither was strong enough to resist the rising Libyan Dynasty in Egypt nor the formidable Assyrians dominating Mesopotamia and eying the Levant (Canaan). But in spite of this sandwich of threats, trade was vigorous and politics were dynamic. It didn't take long for Babylon to thrust itself into the mix. As always in the ANE, sociopolitical change was the rule, not the exception.

GEOGRAPHY

The geographical shifts from the beginning to the end of this period are dramatic (see *Maps 6.04, 6.06, 6.09*). It starts with Mesopotamia dominated by a growing Assyrian Empire eyeing the rest of the Near East. It ends with no Assyrian kingdom at all, replaced by the Neo-Babylonian Empire. It begins with a united Israelite monarchy in the Levant, which shortly split into two separate kingdoms, Israel and Judah, and ends with Judah alone. After a brief Egyptian resurgence, Babylon subsumes the Levant.

CHRONOLOGY

We have now reached the waning decades of Iron Age 2a through 2b-c (IA2a–IA2b-c; c. 900–586 BC; see *Timeline*). By far the best chronology of the Israelite and Judahite kings is that of Edwin R. Thiele. The following list of kings and their regnal dates is adapted from Thiele's work with a few minor adjustments.

Figure 6.01—Shoshenq I wall relief (photo: David E. Graves)

187

KINGS OF ISRAEL	
Saul c. 1050–1010 BC	
David c. 1010–970 BC	
Solomon c. 970–930/31 BC	
KINGS OF THE DIVIDED KINGDOM	
Kings of Judah/Dates BC	Kings of Israel/Dates BC
Rehoboam/930–913	Jeroboam I/930–909
Abijah/913–910	Nadab/909–908
Asa/910–869	Baasha/908–886
Jehoshaphat/872–869 (coregent w/Asa) Jehoshaphat/872–848 (total reign)	Elah/886–885
Jehoram/853–848 (coregent w/Jehoshaphat)	Zimri/885
Ahaziah/841	Tibni (rival of Omri)/885–880
Athaliah/841–835	Omri/885–874
Joash/835–796	Ahab/874–853
Amaziah/796–767	Ahaziah/853–852
Azariah (Uzziah)/792–767 (overlaps Amaziah) Azariah (Uzziah)/792–740 (total reign)	Joram (Jehoram)/852–841
Jotham/750–740 (coregent w/Azariah) Jotham/750–735 (official reign) Jotham/750–732 (total reign)	Jehu/841–814
Ahaz/735–732 (overlap w/Jotham) Ahaz/732–715 (official reign)	Jehoahaz/814–798
Hezekiah/715–686	Jehoash/798–782
Manasseh/696–686 (coregent w/Hezekiah) Manasseh/696–642 (total reign)	Jeroboam II/793–782 (coregent w/Jehoash) Jeroboam II/793–753 (total reign)
Amon/642–640	Zechariah/753
Josiah/640–609	Shallum/752
Jehoahaz/609	Manahem/752–742
Jehoiakim/609–598	Pekahiah/742–740
Jehoiachin/598–597	Pekah/740–732
Zedekiah/597–586	Hoshea/732–723/722

* Adapted from Edwin R. Thiele, *The Mysterious Numbers of the Hebrew Kings* (Grand Rapids, MI: Kregel Academic, 1994).

HISTORY

The death of Solomon occurred shortly after the beginning of Egypt's Twenty-second Dynasty in what is called the Third Intermediate period. By this time, the native-Egyptian Theban pharaonic line was all but extinct. Shoshenq I, founder of the Twenty-second Dynasty, was of Meshwesh Libyan lineage (ruled c. 943–922 BC). This dynasty of Libyan pharaohs ruled from Tanis (see *Maps 6.02, 6.03, 6.04*). The prior Twenty-first Dynasty was a period of serious decline and chaos in Egypt. With Shoshenq I (see *Figure 6.01*) came a modest reunification of Egypt and an era of relative stability. He also had his eyes on Solomon's Israelite kingdom in the Levant.

But for the moment, Shoshenq I—biblical Shishak—knew that attacking Solomon was a bad idea. Israel had already demonstrated significant military might in subduing numerous surrounding kingdoms and in bringing others to the negotiating table. So Shishak waited for an opportune moment. In about the thirteenth year of his reign, such a moment arrived.

But let's back up a bit. Late in Solomon's reign, Jeroboam, one of his administrators (1 Kings 11:26-28), rebelled against the aging king. Solomon sought to kill him, but Jeroboam fled to the court of Shishak (Shoshenq I) in Egypt (1 Kings 11:40). Shortly thereafter, Solomon died, c. 931/930 BC, and was succeeded by his son Rehoboam. On hearing of Solomon's death, Jeroboam returned to Israel from Egypt, maneuvering himself to represent the northern tribes before King Rehoboam. Their request was simple: "Go easier on the people than your father did" (see 1 Kings 12:4). Rehoboam's tough-guy response effectively split the kingdom (see *Breakout 6.01*), leaving him to rule over Judah only. Jeroboam, now Jeroboam I, reigned over the northern kingdom of Israel (see *Map 6.01* and *Breakout 6.03*).

Map 6.01 — The ISRAELITE MONARCHY SPLITS in TWO

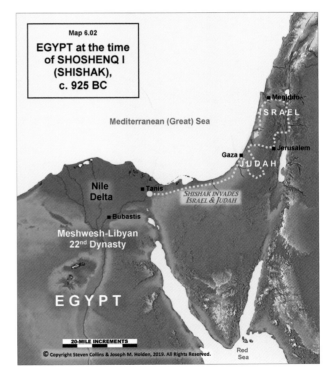

Map 6.02 — EGYPT at the time of SHOSHENQ I (SHISHAK), c. 925 BC

In the fifth year of Rehoboam (ruled c. 930–913 BC), Shishak of Egypt made his move against the Levant—both Judah and Israel (1 Kings 14; 2 Chronicles 12). In the process he plundered from Jerusalem the riches accumulated by Solomon (1 Kings 14:25-26; 2 Chronicles 12:9). Thus, much of Solomon's wealth was transferred to Egypt. According to Egyptian records, within a year after returning from his campaign against Judah and Israel, Shoshenq I (Shishak) was dead. He son, Osorkon I, thus became the beneficiary to Solomon's wealth (see *Breakouts 5.09, 6.04*).

From the first moments of the divided kingdom (see *Timeline* and *Breakouts 6.01, 6.02*), Israel easily fell into the idolatry modeled publicly by Solomon. It was an effortless transition given Israel's long history of following pagan religious traditions. Jeroboam I purposefully paganized the Yahwism of the northern tribes (1 Kings 12; 13; see *Breakout 6.03*). Yet the religious practices of Judah in the south were not much better. Throughout the remaining history of both Judah and Israel (see *Breakouts 6.02, 6.03*), Mosaic Yahwism rarely got a second thought. Judgment was on the horizon.

Given that the Assyrians had been solidifying their grip over the Mesopotamian region for the better part of 500 years, the time was ripe for a move on

Map 6.03

The TIME of REHOBOAM & JEROBOAM

Figure 6.02—Shalmaneser III image (photo: David E. Graves)

the Levant. By the ninth century BC, Assyria was the only superpower remaining in the Near East (see *Map 6.06* and *Timeline*). For many scholars, this was the first true empire in the ANE, perhaps even the world. In time, not only did the Assyrians control all of Mesopotamia, but also much of Elam to the east, Urartu to the north, Anatolia, the Levant, and, for a short while, Egypt (see *Map 6.06*). The Assyrians also developed the fiercest fighting force the ANE had ever seen (see *Breakout 6.06*).

In 853 BC, an important event occurred that is not recorded in the Bible, and it sheds light on Israel's relationship with Aram/Damascus in opposition to Assyria. Shalmaneser III (see *Figure 6.02*) invaded Syria, where he was opposed by a coalition of kings led by Hadadezer (biblical Ben-hadad II) of Damascus and Ahab of Israel, at the Battle of Qarqar (see *Breakout 6.05* and *Map 6.05*). It appears that Assyria did not win the battle and may have been beaten back. Shalmaneser III returned to Syria several times after that, and Assyria eventually succeeded in controlling the entire Levant during the reign of Tiglath Pileser III

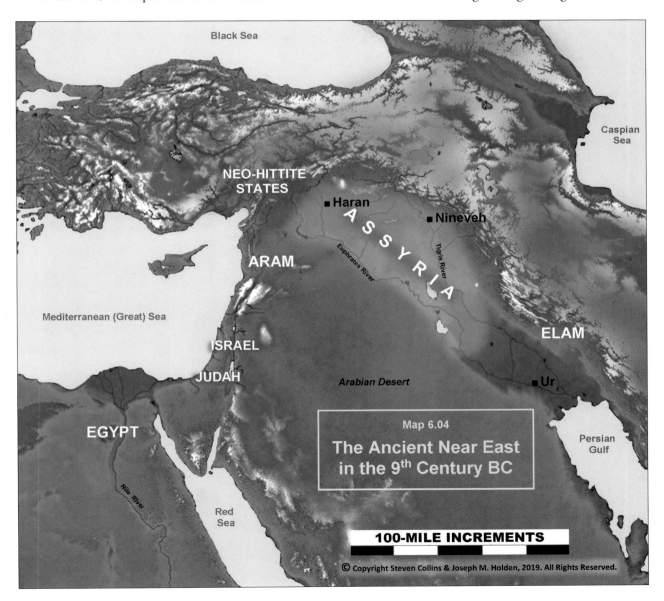

Map 6.04

The Ancient Near East in the 9th Century BC

100-MILE INCREMENTS

(c. 745–727 BC; see *Maps 6.06, 6.07* and *Figure 6.03*). Aram and Israel were decimated during the reigns of Shalmaneser V (c. 727–722 BC; see *Figure 6.04*) and Sargon II (c. 722–705 BC; see *Figure 6.05*).

In 722/721 BC, Assyria (see *Breakout 6.08* and *Map 6.07*) destroyed the northern kingdom of Israel (2 Kings 17), which had located its capital in Samaria (see *Map 6.06*), a new city built by King Omri of Israel. The Assyrians exiled the surviving population of Israelites to places in Assyria and repopulated the area around Samaria with pagan groups deported from Mesopotamia. These peoples eventually mixed with the remaining local Israelites and later became known as the Samaritans (see *Breakout 9.08*). The new population of Samaria created a blend of pagan and Jewish theologies and, as a result, was never truly Jewish. For this reason, they were regarded by the Jews of Judea as a corrupted and blasphemous people to be avoided. This state of affairs is well documented in the various New Testament references to Samaritans.

During the reign of Hezekiah in Judah (c. 715–686 BC), Jerusalem expanded to the west hill (see *Figure 6.06*). In order to supply water to this new part of the city, Hezekiah's workmen dug a tunnel through solid

Figure 6.03—Tiglath Pileser III image (photo: David E. Graves)

Figure 6.04—Shalmaneser V image (public domain; later imagined image)

Figure 6.05—Sargon II image (photo: David E. Graves)

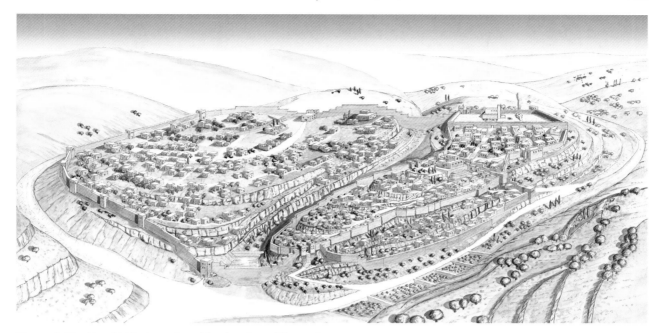

Figure 6.06—Hezekiah's Jerusalem (drawing: Leen Ritmeyer)

rock from the Gihon Spring to what became known as the Pool of Siloam (2 Kings 20:20; see *Breakout 6.07*). Hezekiah was also aware of the ever-present Assyrian threat. In preparation for a likely Assyrian attack, Hezekiah reinforced Jerusalem's northern defenses with a massive wall more than 22 feet thick, called the Broad Wall (Nehemiah 3:8; Isaiah 22:9-10; see *Figures 6.07, 6.08*).

Around 701 BC—20 years after the destruction of Samaria—the Assyrian army of Sennacherib (see *Figure 6.09*) attempted to conquer Jerusalem. However, Sennacherib did not take the city. The biblical version of the event is found in 2 Kings 18:14 and 19:35-36: "The king of Assyria required of Hezekiah king of Judah three hundred talents of silver and thirty talents of gold...the angel of the Lord went out and struck down 185,000 in the camp of the Assyrians...Then Sennacherib king of Assyria departed and went home."

Sennacherib's own version of his assault on Jerusalem is recorded on a six-sided clay prism known as the Prism of Sennacherib (see *Breakout 6.04* and *Figure 6.10*). It contains the accounts of the first eight military campaigns of Sennacherib (705–681 BC). It also includes information that, when combined with the

Figure 6.07—Hezekiah's broad wall (photo: John Witte Moore)

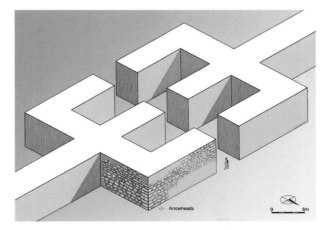

Figure 6.08—Hezekiah's broad wall with "middle gate" (drawing: Leen Ritmeyer)

Figure 6.09—Sennacherib image (photo: David E. Graves)

Figure 6.10—Sennacherib's Prism (photo: Joseph Holden)

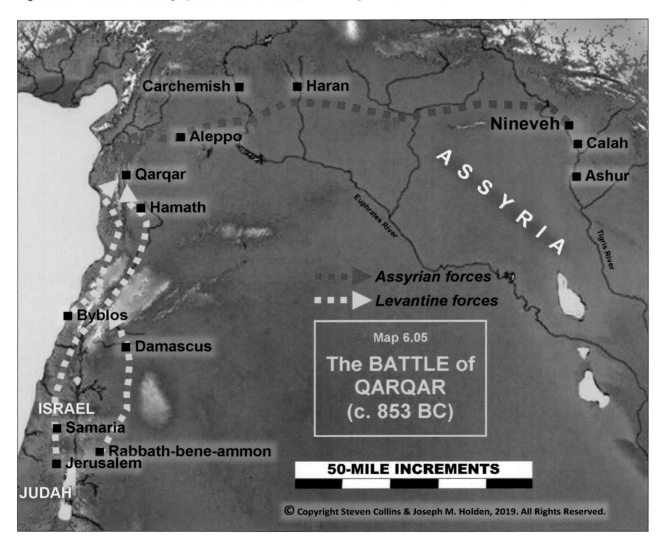

Carchemish ■   ■ Haran

Nineveh ■

A S S Y R I A

■ Aleppo   ■ Calah

■ Qarqar   ■ Ashur

■ Hamath

Euphrates River   Tigris River

▶ **Assyrian forces**

▶ **Levantine forces**

■ Byblos

■ Damascus

Map 6.05

The BATTLE of QARQAR (c. 853 BC)

ISRAEL
■ Samaria
■ Rabbath-bene-ammon
■ Jerusalem

JUDAH

50-MILE INCREMENTS

biblical data, provides a clearer picture of Sennacherib's exploits. In the account of his third campaign (701 BC), Sennacherib described his march to the west, where he defeated several Levantine kingdoms, after which he encountered the Egyptian army. The Egyptian commander is not identified in Sennacherib's *Annals*, but he is identified in the Old Testament as Tirhakah (2 Kings 19:9; Isaiah 37:9), a Nubian ruler who later became Pharaoh Taharqa of Egypt (690–664 BC; see *Timeline*).

The Prism recounts the siege of 46 fortified Judean cities, including Jerusalem, which was under Hezekiah. As quoted above, the biblical account (2 Kings 18:13–19:36; also Isaiah 36:1–37:37) concludes with the statement that the Assyrian army was struck down by the angel of Yahweh, whereupon Sennacherib broke camp and returned to Nineveh. In typical Near Eastern fashion, Sennacherib's Prism does not record that major setback for the Assyrians, but it does tacitly agree with the biblical version by making no claim that he took Jerusalem (see *Breakout 6.04*). His account refers only to tribute taken from Hezekiah. Sennacherib's

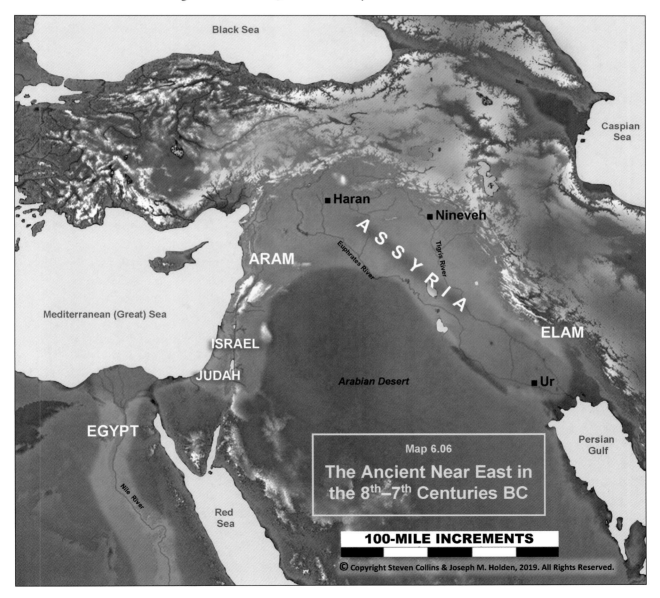

Map 6.06

The Ancient Near East in the 8th–7th Centuries BC

100-MILE INCREMENTS

BREAKOUT 6.01

THE DIVISION OF THE KINGDOM

Solomon was blessed by Yahweh and was given all that a man could wish for: wealth, fame, power, and unparalleled wisdom. Yet in spite of these great blessings, at the end of his life he betrayed the one true God and entered into the vilest of pagan worship. In punishment by Yahweh, most of the kingdom was taken from the line of Solomon and given to a scoundrel named Jeroboam. Rehoboam, the son of Solomon, retained rule over only the tribe of Judah (1 Kings 12; 2 Chronicles 10).

The breakup of the Israelite kingdom followed the death of Solomon in 930/31 BC. It was, to some degree, the result of a display of great hubris on the part of Rehoboam while he was attending a convocation of the tribal leaders at Shechem. When confronted with a request by the northern tribes that he ease the burdens imposed by Solomon, his response was that he intended to continue ruling as his father had—and be, if possible, even tougher. That angered the northern tribes, who attempted to kill him, and

he was forced to flee for his life. The people installed Jeroboam as their ruler and the kingdom of Israel was divided into two parts. The northern kingdom retained the name *Israel*, and the newly-formed southern kingdom was called *Judah* after the name of the primary tribe of the region.

After the temple had been constructed by Solomon, the worship of Yahweh became temple-based. With the temple located in Jerusalem, Jeroboam I was concerned that many of his subjects would wish to continue worshipping there and reject him as king. To remedy the problem, he formed his own version of Israelite religion, building two temples with golden calves in which to worship—one in Dan at the northernmost point of the new Israel, and another in Bethel, north of Jerusalem and inside the southern border of Israel. This syncretistic, pagan worship "became sin to the house of Jeroboam" (1 Kings 13:34) and persisted throughout the time of the divided kingdom and beyond.

The separate monarchies were

formed at a time of great political vulnerability, a circumstance that led to their ultimate destruction. Through the ninth century BC, Israel was challenged by the rise of the Arameans. The Assyrians rose to their greatest strength during the eighth century BC and eventually destroyed the Arameans and the northern kingdom of Israel. The Assyrians also reduced the southern kingdom to impotence as a vassal state (see *Timeline*). In the late seventh century BC, a resurgent (Neo-) Babylonian kingdom overthrew the Assyrians, gaining control of the Fertile Crescent. They went on to destroy Jerusalem and carried many of the people of Judah into a generation of exile in Babylon (see *Breakout 7.01*). It is unlikely that a united Israel would have been able to survive the rise of the Mesopotamian superpowers, but the fact that they were continually fighting with their neighbors and had abandoned Yahweh left them in a greatly weakened state and susceptible to conquest.

J. Moore

descriptions of the other sieges of Judean cities specify that he had destroyed them—but not Jerusalem, which stands in perfect agreement with the Bible.

In Egypt c. 664, the Twenty-sixth Dynasty of Pharaoh Necho II (or Neco; see *Figure 6.11*) of the Bible (2 Kings 23 NIV; 2 Chronicles 35 NIV; Necho II, 610–595 BC) replaced the Nubian Twenty-fifth Dynasty. Necho II set his mind on conquering the Levant as a preventive measure against a rising Babylonian kingdom that was already threatening Assyria (see *Timeline*). Necho II attempted to support Assyria against Babylonia, while King Josiah of Judah was seemingly siding with Babylon against the Assyrians. At Megiddo, Josiah tried to block Necho's advance into the Levant and was

killed (2 Kings 23:29 NIV). The Babylonians drove back the Egyptians and, in 609 BC, defeated a crumbling Assyria (see *Timeline*). In c. 605 BC, Nebuchadnezzar of Babylon defeated Necho II at Carchemish, then proceeded to conquer Judah (see *Maps 6.08, 6.09*).

PEOPLES AND KINGDOMS

ISRAEL—The northern kingdom included the ten tribes that rebelled under Jeroboam I against Solomon's son Rehoboam (see *Timeline*). This split caused a civil war in Israel (see *Breakouts 6.01, 6.02*), and the northern tribes under Jereboam I (ruled c. 930–909 BC) founded a separate kingdom (see *Map 6.01*). Under King Omri,

Map 6.07
The NEO-ASSYRIAN EMPIRE at its APEX (early 7th Century BC)

100-MILE INCREMENTS

© Copyright Steven Collins & Joseph M. Holden, 2019. All Rights Reserved.

Figure 6.12—Siege of Lachish Reliefs (photo: David E. Graves)

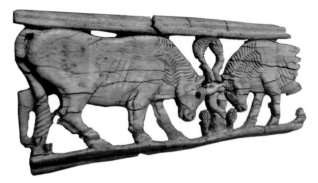

Figure 6.13—Neo-Assyrian art object; ivory furniture inlay (photo: James Barber, courtesy of Bible Lands Museum, Jerusalem)

was established under David and Solomon—resulted from the split between Jeroboam I to the north and Solomon's son Rehoboam to the south, who continued the dynasty (House) of David (see *Map 6.01*). Judah had a series of good and bad kings (see *Timeline*) along with infighting and political pressure from the northern kingdom of Israel and foreign adversaries. Judah's capital city, Jerusalem, was destroyed in 586 BC by the Neo-Babylonians (see *Breakout 7.01*), and its elite citizens were forcibly removed to Babylon.

SYRIA/ARAMEANS—Solomon was unable to capitalize on his father David's victories over the Arameans, and thus they grew as a military power (see *Map 6.04*). King Asa (910–869 BC) allied the southern kingdom of Judah with Syria, which led to an invasion of the northern kingdom of Israel by the Arameans. The House of Omri allied itself with Phoenicia. King Rezin

Figure 6.11—Necho II image (photo: Steven Collins)

the capital was moved to Samaria. The House of Omri was a northern dynasty that overshadowed its descendants until it was destroyed (see *Breakout 6.04*). They were usually under threat of invasion from Syria, and later the Assyrians (see *Breakout 6.06*) utterly destroyed the northern kingdom of Israel (Samaria) in successive attacks that climaxed in 722 BC (see *Breakout 6.08*).

JUDAH—the southern kingdom of Judah—which

of Aram came to power c. 750 BC and formed an alliance with Israel, after which they attacked Judah. A panicking King Ahaz allied with the Assyrians in spite of the warning from Isaiah not to do so (see *Map 6.06*).

ASSYRIA—Assyrian records and artwork glorify their efficient, vicious war machine as a major factor in keeping conquered nations from rebellion (see *Figure 6.12* and *Breakout 6.06*). And their military ferocity is what they're mostly noted for. At the same time, Assyrian society and culture was highly sophisticated (see *Figure 6.13*), with numerous sprawling urban centers (see *Figure 6.14*) within major city-states such as Nineveh (the capital city), Calah, and Ashur, to name a few. The Assyrians controlled the

Figure 6.14—1850s photo, excavation of Assyrian city ruins, Nineveh (public domain)

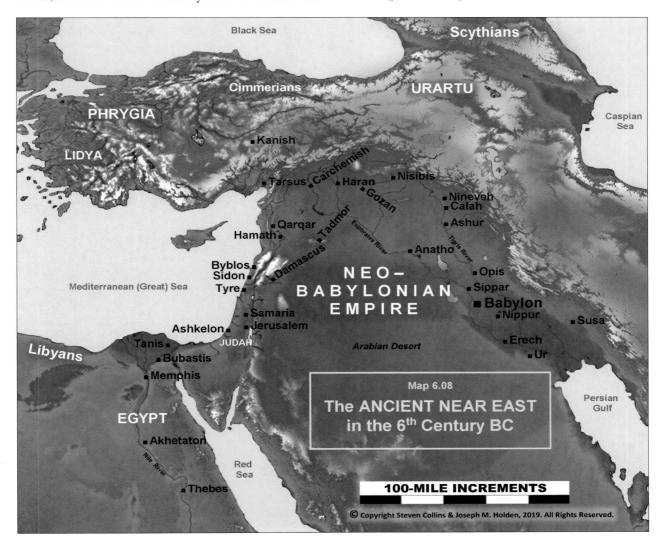

Map 6.08
The ANCIENT NEAR EAST in the 6th Century BC

100-MILE INCREMENTS

entirety of Mesopotamia (see *Map 6.07*) from the Persian Gulf, the north Levant (Aram and Syria), down into the south Levant, even becoming a threat to Egypt. Nineveh was captured in 612 BC by Babylon, and the Assyrian army was crushed at Haran in 609 BC, which marked the end of Assyria as an independent state (see *Timeline*).

MOAB—By this time Moab (see *Map 6.04*) was an off-and-on vassal of Israel and often forced to pay heavy tribute (2 Kings 3:4). The Moabite Stone (Mesha Stela; see *Breakout 6.04*) recorded the Moabite version of their battles and skirmishes by King Mesha (cf. 2 Kings 3). Shalmaneser of Assyria and his successor defeated and destroyed Moab as predicted by Isaiah (Isaiah 15).

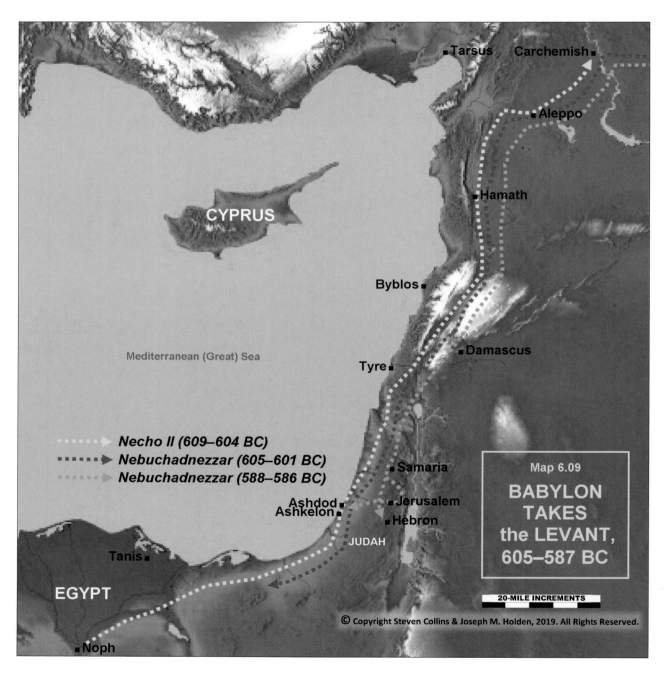

Necho II (609–604 BC)
Nebuchadnezzar (605–601 BC)
Nebuchadnezzar (588–586 BC)

Map 6.09

BABYLON TAKES the LEVANT, 605–587 BC

20-MILE INCREMENTS

EDOM—Edom revolted against Judah c. 847 BC, and 50 years later, King Amaziah conquered them again. In 735 BC, King Rezin of Syria captured Edom. Assyria demanded and received tribute from Edom as early as the seventh century BC, from Asa-Nirari III to Ashurbanipal. Edom took over the southern regions of Judah after the Babylonians destroyed Jerusalem in 586 BC.

EGYPT—This time in Egypt (tenth–sixth centuries BC; see *Timeline*) is called the Third Intermediate period, following the demise of the New Kingdom. Power was held by Tanis (secular) and Thebes (religious); the two cities ruled jointly with different agendas (see *Map 6.02*). Eventually civil war caused Egypt to splinter between Tanis, Hermopolis, Thebes,

---

BREAKOUT 6.02

THE KINGS OF ISRAEL AND JUDAH

The division of Israel into two smaller entities created two separate lines of kings. The kings of Judah were of the Davidic Dynasty and, with only one brief exception, continued to rule in an uninterrupted line until the Babylonian exile. By contrast, the northern kingdom of Israel was a pagan nation surrounded by hostile neighbors, and it experienced considerable internal turmoil. Many of the kings in the northern kingdom took the throne by force, and their successors survived only a generation or two.

The first few kings of Israel fought with Judah, attempting to reclaim the southern lands. By the middle 850s BC things had stabilized somewhat, and a king named Omri built the city of Samaria as his capital. Ahab, his son, was a strong and successful king from a political perspective, and is even mentioned in Assyrian archives. However, he and his pagan wife, Jezebel, were terrible tyrants who were challenged by

the prophet Elijah. Ahab died in battle and Jezebel was killed by Jehu, a successor king who had been anointed by the prophet Elisha. Jehu went on to destroy the entire extended family of Ahab.

After the time of Ahab, political conditions worsened rapidly for the northern kingdom. Samaria, the capital city, was destroyed by the Assyrians c. 722 BC (see *Timeline*), with the survivors carried off into exile and lost to history.

The southern kingdom of Judah avoided the worst depredations of the Assyrians, but after the fall of Samaria to the north, Hezekiah, the king of Jerusalem, participated in a rebellion against the Assyrians c. 705 BC. In punishment, the Assyrians sent an army against Judah, and only the intervention of Yahweh prevented the destruction of that city as well (see *Breakout 6.04*). Isaiah the prophet lived in Jerusalem and counseled Hezekiah during those terrible times.

The kings of Judah submitted to Assyrian domination for another century after the fall of Samaria. However, the Assyrians fell to the Babylonians in 612–609 BC, who then extended their rule over Judah as well. In the face of the Judean kings' continued resistance to Babylonian rule, the Babylonians destroyed Jerusalem in a terrible siege in 586 BC. Many of the survivors were carried off in what is known as the Babylonian captivity (see *Breakout 7.01*). The prophet Jeremiah lived in Jerusalem at that time and had counseled against resistance to Babylon. He survived the siege but eventually died in exile in Egypt.

After the fall of Jerusalem, the Holy Land remained under a succession of foreign powers to and beyond the time of Christ. The only exception to foreign rule was the time of the Hasmonean kings, who controlled the land for a century before the arrival of the Romans in 63 BC (see *Breakout 8.08*).

J. Moore

Memphis, and Sais. The Nubians invaded from the south but could not prevent the Assyrian advance under Esarhaddon (see *Timeline*).

SOCIETIES AND CULTURES

Social Stratification—No matter how the politics played out and what kingdoms rose and fell, society at the street level was a ladder not easily climbed. Because families, clans, and tribes tended to work in focused trades, the class assigned to those trades was where a person's life was spent. The "dirty" trades—pottery making, metalsmithing, brickmaking, mining—were low on the social ladder. However, even within these social contexts, subcultures existed in which status was determined by age and experience. The higher echelons of national and city government had their own ranks. This little affected the average person. Life was lived in the context of one's own line of work and family dynamics. After all, life was short (55 years on average), and life at any level could be full and, with family and friends, enjoyable!

Tribalism—Neither Israel nor Judah ever lost their tribal mentality, which was their primary identity. Cultures surrounding Israel were no less tied to their tribal roots. As much as the united monarchy had tried to blur or deemphasize tribalism in favor of nationalism, tribal dynamics were not erased. The tribes were the fabric of society. They were the structure that supported national entities wherever they existed in the ANE. Empires and kingdoms could crash and disappear, but the tribes—the people—remained.

Nation-States—There were always town and city "kings," or kinglets, if you like. Functionally, we would call them mayors or city managers. But in this period, very few cities and towns were independent—arguably, none of them were. Every local polity was subsumed into a larger political entity, either a kingdom or empire. If they were located in a border area, their allegiance might shift back and forth as advantage dictated. It was all about economics. Connectivity with regional and international markets and trying to figure out which political alignments could

best suit one's own purposes sometimes made for strange bedfellows.

Inheritance—Primogeniture (patrimony), as a general rule of thumb, influenced succession and inheritance from the family level all the way to the king of, say, the Assyrian Empire. In a way, this was a means of preventing societal chaos and preserving social order. Everyone recognized that this was cultural reality, the unspoken law that said, "You belong here, but not there." In this regard, the Mosaic Law was the most elaborate in all of Near Eastern antiquity.

Women's Roles—The northern kingdom of Israel produced some interesting and influential women. But the average woman in any IA society was still focused on having and raising children and running a household. Certainly, the female subculture produced its own matriarchs and women of influence. Household weaving was probably the women's responsibility, which had its own kind of hierarchy. Women may also have helped with harvesting various crops and drying fruits for household use and for selling at the local market. There was less division of labor between men and women in nomadic herding societies.

Men's Roles—Beyond their responsibilities as farmers or tradesmen, males were prepared as warriors from puberty. While standing armies were rare for city-states, the larger kingdoms, and certainly every empire, maintained full-time professional armies. When potential conflicts arose or territories needed to be annexed, kings would often draft conscripts to fill out their military ranks. Men raised sons in their chosen trades. It is not clear whether there was any flexibility in choosing one's own trade. Even the Israelite tribe of Levi mentored its sons in the priesthood, their assigned profession.

Political Climate—The Twenty-second (Libyan), Twenty-third (Libyan), Twenty-fourth (local/Saite), Twenty-fifth (Kushite/Nubian), and Twenty-sixth (local/Saite) Dynasties of Egypt were minor in comparison to those of earlier periods. Nevertheless, they played a role in regional politics. Some of these pharaohs are even mentioned in the Bible (biblical names in italics): Soshenq I (*Shisak*; Twenty-second;

BREAKOUT 6.03

ISRAELITE WORSHIP

What later became Israelite religion and worship (*Yahwism*) began to emerge during the MBA (see *Timeline*) in the region known as Canaan (see *Map 2.02*). At its inception, early Yahwism had animistic and polytheistic elements, but was balanced by devotion to its primary deity, Yahweh, at least by the main patriarchs like Abraham, Isaac, and Jacob (those in the direct stream of divine revelation). Across the ANE, the connection between the divine and geography was a powerful component in defining both the national deity and state religion. Israel was no exception.

ANE religions typically had both animistic and polytheistic elements. Spirits inhabited inanimate and animate hosts (*animism*), and pantheons of deities (*polytheism*) were an integral part of everyday life. There was no demarcation between religious and secular reality. All was inextricably integrated. Historically, there were only two movements toward *monotheism*. The first followed the revelatory line beginning with Abraham and reaching its pinnacle with Moses—yet was not adopted nationally until after the Babylonian captivity of Judah. The second, that of Pharaoh Akhenaten (see *Breakout*

3.05), was arguably a response to Mosaic monotheism and the failure of Egyptian deities in the face of Yahweh's wrath.

"Ideal" Yahwism focused on the worship of a single, universal God with ultimate moral authority. This was a unique worldview particular to ancient Israel alone. The intricacies of the Mosaic Law (c. fourteenth century BC) and its "militaristic" monotheism was, however, almost systemically lost on the general Israelite populace. More often than not, the Israelites—even the later Judahites—pursued animistic and polytheistic cultic beliefs and practices as readily as their Canaanean neighbors. (Indeed, Yahweh was patient!)

During the late IA (see *Timeline*), Israelite worship generally centered on one God, Yahweh, while at the same time acknowledging the existence of other deities. Pagan temples abounded in the Levant. The divine was often viewed through the lens of holiness, with temples being "holy houses" allowing the deities to "live" within their walls. Worship traditionally occurred in a cultic complex, with the main focus on a central temple in which an image (idol) was "physically" inhabited by the deity. Rituals were

complex and absolute, almost always involving sacrifices of animals and, in certain cases, humans. The Israelites were surrounded by such cultic practices and were naturally drawn to them. Archaeology reveals that among the Israelites, the goddess Asherah was often viewed as Yahweh's consort.

Mosaic monotheism specifically prohibited the people from making any images of Yahweh. Thus, the tabernacle and Solomon's temple had only a "seat" of presence inside the Holy of Holies, but no image or idol. Mosaic Yahwism also restricted the worship of the singular God to a single temple and demanded the removal of alternate shrines and cult centers from the land. But this religious cleansing of the land of Israel never fully happened. Ingrained animism and a penchant for polytheism plagued the Israelites perennially. The syncretistic religion inaugurated by Jeroboam—first king of the northern kingdom of Israel following the death of Solomon—shows just how easy it was for the Israelites to fall into idolatry.

The temple and sanctuary at Tel Dan is an example of an Israelite worship center during the time of the divided monarchy (see *Timeline*). In order to discourage pilgrims from traveling to the temple in Jerusalem, King Jeroboam constructed two large border sanctuaries, at Bethel on his southern border and Dan on his northern border. The Tel Dan sanctuary—the only surviving monumental temple complex of its kind—was comprised of a large podium with an immense flight of stairs adjoining a three-room sanctuary. Archaeologists have unearthed evidence for a large ashlar-constructed horned altar, as well as a smaller stone-horned altar, indicative of cultic activity. The presence of the bull motif at Tel Dan and other surrounding sanctuaries reflects the linking of Yahweh with elements of Baalism, wherein people attributed to him the characteristics of pagan deities. Additional evidence for this is seen in a bronze plaque unearthed in the temple area at Tel Dan, which depicts a deity perched atop a bull. In the northern kingdom, the bull was viewed not only as an earthly manifestation and a means of communion with Yahweh, but also served as a divine "throne" for his presence. The horns on the altars purposefully imitated their counterpart at Solomon's temple in Jerusalem.

B. Forrest, S. Collins

1 Kings 11; 14; 2 Chronicles 12), Osorkon IV? (*So*; Twenty-second; 2 Kings 17), Taharqa (*Tirhakah*; Twenty-fifth; 2 Kings 19; Isaiah 37), Necho II (*Neco*; Twenty-sixth; 2 Kings 23; 2 Chronicles 35–36; Jeremiah 46), and Apries (*Hophra*; Twenty-sixth; Jeremiah 44). Some of these dynasties overlapped because they were ruling either Upper or Lower Egypt, or both, intermittently (see *Map 6.02*). By the late eighth century BC (see *Timeline*), Assyria had pushed into the Levant and was threating the kingdom of Israel. Just over a century later, Babylonia crushed Assyria (c. 609 BC), then the kingdom of Judah (c. 605–586). Both Israel and Judah had a hard time figuring out who to side with against whom. Sometimes they chose poorly.

LANGUAGES AND WRITING

HEBREW—By this period the Hebrew dialect that we know from existing manuscripts was fully formed, but it was still being written in the old-style Semitic script (see *Figure 6.15*).

AKKADIAN VS. ARAMAIC—Neo-Assyrian Akkadian was slowly but surely being replaced by Aramaic in northern Mesopotamia (Aram Naharaim) and was moving through Assyria. It became a language of high status among Assyrian scribes and administrators. By the end of the seventh century BC, Aramaic had virtually replaced Akkadian in most of Mesopotamia. It became the *lingua franca* of the Babylonian Empire. A northwestern Semitic language similar to Hebrew, Aramaic was quickly adopted by the captive population of Jews in Babylon. The alphabetic writing known as Aramaic

Figure 6.15—Late Iron Age Phoenician inscription (photo: James Barber, courtesy of Bible Lands Museum, Jerusalem)

Figure 6.16—Aramaic script, Late Iron Age (photo: Joseph Holden)

Figure 6.17—Moabite and Ammonite script on seals bearing the name of the god Chemosh (photos: James Barber, courtesy of Bible Lands Museum, Jerusalem)

Figure 6.18—Egyptian hieroglyphs, Iron Age 2b–c (photo: Steven Collins)

square script became the means of writing the Hebrew language from that point forward (see *Figure 6.16*).

OTHER SEMITIC LANGUAGES—In the second half of IA2 (see *Timeline*), the Edomites, Moabites, Ammonites, Israelites, Judahites, Arameans, and Phoenicians all spoke Semitic dialects and used similar alphabetic scripts (see *Figure 6.17*). Even the Philistines had given up their Indo-European proto-Greek language in favor of a dialect of Hebrew or Phoenician.

EGYPTIAN—Even though the Libyans and Nubians ruled Egypt for much of this era, they still wrote their monumental inscriptions in native Egyptian with hieroglyphic script (see *Figure 6.18*). The power of Egyptian culture and language had a profound influence even on these conquerors of the Black Land. They seemed to relish being "Egyptians"!

BELIEFS AND RELIGIONS

ISRAEL—The corruption of Yahwism into a syncretistic jumble with Baalism and other local religions made the kingdom of Israel fundamentally no different than the Canaanean cultures that Moses and Joshua faced when they first entered the Promised Land. True Mosaic religion was nowhere to be found in the northern kingdom (see *Breakout 6.03*). Elements of Yahwism in Israel are evident in both archaeology and the biblical text, but vestiges only.

JUDAH—Although the kings of the Davidic Dynasty (House of David) retained their hereditary grip on the throne of Judah, their religious practices were, more often than not, very little different from those of their Israelite cousins to the north (see *Breakout 6.03*). Periodic attempts to return Judahite religion to the old ways of Mosaic Yahwism were short lived.

SYRIA—Hadad, the storm god, was the principal god of Aram/Syria during this period (see *Figure 6.19*). Of course, other deities accompanied him. Hadad was known as far back as the third millennium BC in Ebla (*Hadda*). He was Adad in Mesopotamia, Teshub to the Hurrians, and often linked with Baal of the Canaanites. Many biblical, Aramean, and Mesopotamian city and personal names invoke him.

Figure 6.19—Hadad, Syrian deity (public domain)

Figure 6.20—Terrace farming, Israel (photo: Michael Luddeni)

Figure 6.21—Iron Age 2b–c gateway, Geshur (photo: John Witte Moore)

ARCHITECTURE AND INFRASTRUCTURE

CITIES, TOWNS, AND VILLAGES—Settlements tended to remain in the same locations for the same reasons century after century: defensible high ground, adequate land for farming, and readily accessible water resources. Sloping ramparts left over from the Bronze Age (BA) provided a perfect platform for building city walls. Old stone foundations meant a ready supply of building material for new construction. In the Levantine hill country, stone terraces were already in place, with little fixing needed (see *Figure 6.20*). Thus, terrace farming came easily. Local "kings" did their part in administering their territories in service to the central Judahite or Israelite governments at Jerusalem and Samaria (*Shamron*), respectively. Towns guarded outlying agricultural fields, and worker villages dotted the agriscape.

ROADS AND HIGHWAYS—Roads were a major convenience for moving goods by caravan from one city or town to another and for local travel. But well-traveled roadways were also used for moving armies from one location to another. The Assyrians and Babylonians took full advantage of road systems.

FORTIFICATIONS—Many of the fortified settlements of late IA2 were now in their final phase. Most were set behind heavy defenses, and for good reason. Israel and Judah were not usually on good terms. Egypt (in one form or other) was always a reasonable threat for Judah. Aram-Damascus was beating up on Israel periodically. And the Assyrians were capable of crushing them all at any time. The city of Zer/Zed (later, Bethsaida), the capital of Geshur (see *Map 6.04*), had a perimeter defensive wall that was almost 20 feet thick! It didn't help. The Assyrians blew through the gates of Zer/Zed before the end of the eighth century BC (see *Figure 6.21*).

GATEWAYS—The six-chambered gate continued

BREAKOUT 6.04

EXTRABIBLICAL REFERENCES TO ISRAELITE AND JUDAHITE KINGS AND THRONES

Archaeological excavations are adding to a growing number of extrabiblical references to Israelite and Judahite kings. This means that many elements of biblical narrative can be tied directly to ANE history.

There are numerous extrabiblical media by which Israelite and Judahite kings were recorded throughout the Levant (Canaan) and Mesopotamia. These appear across the region in the form of monumental inscriptions, palace records, correspondence written on clay tablets, as well as seals and ostraca (writing on pottery sherds or pieces of stone). These media come from Israel itself and its enemies.

In the northern portion of Israel, the *Tel Dan Inscription* was unearthed in 1993/94 in three pieces (found in secondary use as wall stones). In its original state, it was a sizeable basalt monument with an old Aramaic inscription from the mid-ninth century BC. The inscription includes a reference to the "House of David" (Dynasty of David), confirming the existence of King David and the royal line bearing his name. The Tel Dan Inscription is also noteworthy for mentioning King Jehoram of Israel and King Ahaziah of Judah. It was written by an enemy of Israel, probably Hazael of Aram-Damascus.

In addition, King Hezekiah's name is found outside the Bible several times. His royal seal appears on two bullae (hardened clay seal impressions), and some of his servants are mentioned on three additional bullae. Hezekiah is also mentioned by Sennacherib of Assyria on the *Taylor Prism*, which was written to commemorate Sennacherib's raid on Jerusalem in 701 BC. It reads, "But as for Hezekiah, the Jew who did not bow in submission to my yoke…"

Another ruler likely represented is King Jehu of Israel (2 Kings 9:1). He is shown on the six-foot-high *Black Obelisk* of Shalmaneser III (858–824) with this accompanying statement: "I received tribute from Jehu of the House of Omri." Omri's dynasty is recorded in 1 Kings 16:15-28. He, along with the "House of Judah," is also mentioned on the *Moabite Stone* (Mesha Stele) discovered in 1868.

King Manasseh of Judah (687–642/41) is mentioned by Esarhaddon in 676 BC, and by Assurbanipal in 666 BC. Tiglath Pileser III names Menahem of Samaria and Pekah of Bit-Khumri (Israel). In addition to

Mesha Stela (photo: Alexander Schick)

the previously mentioned bullae of Hezekiah there are a wide variety of ancient bullae and seals bearing the impressions of kings like Jotham and Ahaz, as well as servants of Azariah/Uzziah.

When you consider that archaeology has touched only a tiny fraction of the ANE, the fact that extrabiblical media mentioning biblical kings and characters are almost commonplace attestations to the organic connections between biblical and ANE history.

B. Maggard, S. Collins

THE BATTLE OF QARQAR

Often when we read history, the characters can seem flat, like actors in a melodrama: the hero, the villain, the damsel. This is particularly true of the period of the divided kingdom (c. 931–586 BC) with its laundry list of IA kings labeled "good" or "bad." But is there more to the story?

The first direct, contemporaneous reference to a king of Israel or Judah is an entry in the annals of Shalmaneser III of Assyria. This monolith inscription was discovered in southeastern Turkey while archaeology was in its infancy (around 1861). The Battle of Qarqar (in Syria; see *Map 6.05*) took place in the sixth year of his reign (c. 853 BC), and was fought against a coalition of Levantine kings that included Ahab of the northern kingdom of Israel (ruled c. 874–853 BC).

Even though seven chapters are devoted to Ahab in biblical narratives (1 Kings 16:29–22:40; 2 Chronicles 18), we do not know much from these records other than that he did some purging of the previous administration, was the husband of notorious Phoenician princess Jezebel, and was an idolatrous bad king.

Coalition warfare, specifically practiced in the ninth century BC Levant, allied several smaller nations or city-states for the common purpose of defeating a larger enemy. Once the battle was over, each army went back to its respective territory—or picked on each other, depending on who was ripe for a double-cross!

King Shalmaneser saw the territorial influence of Egypt's Twenty-second Dynasty waning after the death of Shoshenq I (Shishak of the Bible; 1 Kings 14:25) and used it to his advantage. Shalmaneser's empire-expansion record contains references to the essential strength of his campaign's enemy leaders, known as the Big Four and the Little Seven. Ahab of Israel was included in the Big Four due to the large numbers of ground troops and chariots he contributed.

It is interesting to note that when the site chronology of Megiddo was estimated, archaeologists dated the equine stables (Strata IVB and IVA) to the Solomonic era, while Stratum IVA was determined to belong to the time of Ahab. Although some scholars disagree with the use of the term *stables*, the structures with the capacity to house hundreds of horses seem to have been in continuous use from the time of Solomon to the time of Ahab. This further corroborates the history in the annals of Shalmaneser and the existence of the biblical King Ahab as a person with significant power and socioeconomic impact in and out of the area.

Perhaps this is why the biblical writers chose to omit this battle: It was too far outside the territory of Israel and the scope of what was considered important to communicate. Perhaps this speaks to Ahab's overinvolvement in the affairs and religious practices of other powers. We can be confident, though, that each piece of the story—the early discovery of the monolith, the biblical narrative, and the emerging evidence from current digs—fits together to create a nuanced historical picture of a biblical king who might otherwise be seen as one-dimensional.

A. Pavich

to be the standard for this period, but other configurations have also been unearthed in excavations across the Levant (see *Figures 6.22, 6.23*).

HOUSES—Houses with central courtyards, generally two stories, were the norm. Each room was directly accessible from the courtyard. Upper rooms were reached by ladders or, in some cases, stairs (see *Figure 6.24*). Mudbricks on stone foundation were

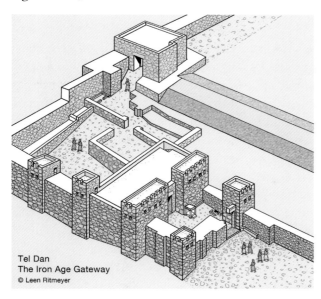

Figure 6.22—Iron Age 2b-c gateway, Dan (drawing: Leen Ritmeyer)

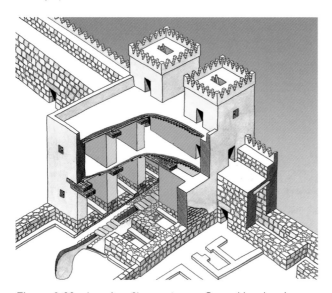

Figure 6.23—Iron Age 2b–c gateway, Gezer (drawing: Leen Ritmeyer)

typical, although in this period we find more and more houses made almost entirely of stone, particularly in the Transjordan.

TEMPLES—Temples and outlier open-air shrines were public spaces, except for inner sanctuaries, where priests and priestesses performed rituals. Temples of the Canaanean gods were attended by sacred prostitutes (both male and female) whose acts of copulation with humans and animals represented the divine realm of the gods they served. Sacrifices of grain, animals, and humans (mainly infants) were common (see *Figure 6.25*) in the hopes of attaining successful crops, herds, and families. Failures were attributed to a lack of precision in the performance of the relevant rituals. This reinforced the urgency of making sure the ritual was done right the next time.

WEAPONS AND WARFARE

ASSYRIANS—Infantry, archers, slingers, charioteers, cavalry, siege towers and ramps, battering rams— these were used brilliantly by the Assyrian army (see *Breakout 6.06*). They were notorious for their brutality. Resistance of any kind usually meant that the town leaders were impaled on poles, pulled apart by horses, or flayed alive (see *Figure 6.26*).

SIEGE EQUIPMENT—Wheeled battering rams

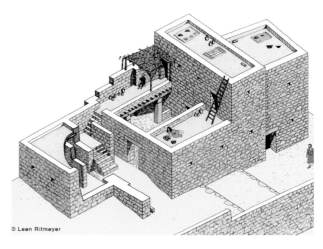

Figure 6.24—Iron Age House with stairs (drawing: Leen Ritmeyer)

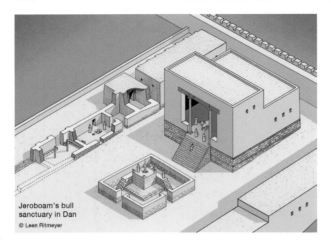

Figure 6.25—Jeroboam's worship center at Dan (drawing: Leen Ritmeyer)

with pointed iron tips took down gates in a hurry. Siege towers were assembled on site to raise archers to the height of the city walls (see *Figure 6.27*). Siege ramps of earth and rubble were constructed for the inevitable final rush to take the city. These tactics were systematic. They were well rehearsed, and rarely did they fail.

ARMOR—Assyrian infantry were more heavily armored than most warriors in the ANE. They wore conical helmets of iron, a layered leather shirt with iron plates or chain mail, leather/iron leggings, and armlets of iron. Their shields were either disk-like or full-body for archers and slingers. Officers were more armored than regulars (see *Figure 6.28*).

WEAPONRY—Spears with double-edged points and double-edged thrusting swords were the main

weapons of the Assyrian infantry. Slingers were prominent, as they were in all ANE armies. The composite bow was a lethal addition, often fired from chariots and horseback. In close combat, all manner of knives, battle axes, and clubs (maces) were used by conscripts fighting alongside better-armed professional warriors (see *Figure 6.29*).

INDUSTRIES AND OBJECTS

AGRICULTURE—The mainstay of all ANE civilizations, agricultural production was the key to economic and social stability. With the Assyrian army as specialists of the siege, the early spring planting of crops became the foundation on which the siege was organized. This is why spring was the time of going to war. With crops beginning to grow, laying siege to a city meant hemming it in for three, four, or even six to eight months. The besieging army would use the ripening crops for food while the city inhabitants eventually starved.

HERDING—Bedouin shepherds had a delicate choice to make when a large army came into a region like the Levant. The Assyrian army numbered in the tens of thousands. It was the largest army the world had ever known. Warriors needed protein. But would the Assyrians round up sheep and goats and take them by force with their cavalry, or would they purchase what

Figure 6.26—Torture on the Lachish Reliefs; impaling on pikes and flaying captives alive (photos: David E. Graves, Steven Collins)

Figure 6.27—Depiction of the Assyrian siege of Lachish (public domain)

Figure 6.28—Assyrian personal armor, weapons, and battering ram; Lachish Reliefs (photo: Steven Collins)

Figure 6.29—Weapons and armor, Iron Age 2b–c (photo: James Barber, courtesy of Bible Lands Museum, Jerusalem)

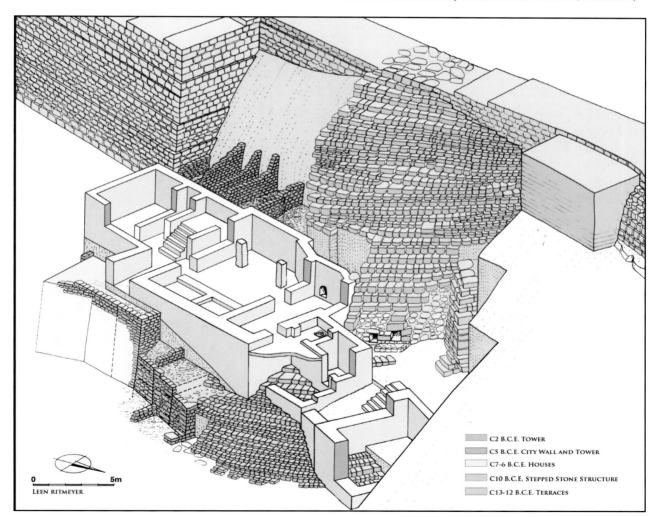

C2 B.C.E. TOWER
C5 B.C.E. CITY WALL AND TOWER
C7-6 B.C.E. HOUSES
C10 B.C.E. STEPPED STONE STRUCTURE
C13-12 B.C.E. TERRACES

LEEN RITMEYER

Figure 6.30—David's palace, Iron Age 2, is representative of palatial buildings of that period (drawing: Leen Ritmeyer)

BREAKOUT 6.06

THE ASSYRIAN WAR MACHINE

The Assyrians existed for more than 1,000 years. Based in northern Mesopotamia, they rose and diminished several times before they were finally destroyed. In the nineteenth and eighteenth centuries BC, they were traders with routes from their main city, Ashur, to a series of trading colonies in Anatolia. They fell first to the Old Babylonians, and later to the kingdom of Mittani (see *Timeline*).

From the fourteenth century to the tenth century BC the Assyrians rose once again as the Middle Assyrian Empire. They expanded across the Fertile Crescent as far as Phoenicia. They deported conquered peoples and demanded tribute from captured territories. The arrival of warring Aramaean bands constantly attacking and finally devastating Assyrian agriculture resources caused their decline once again.

The Neo-Assyrians rose to power 20 years later (see *Timeline*). This is the empire that comes to mind when we think of the Assyrians. Once again, they expanded their territories across the Fertile Crescent. This time they developed into the most effective military force the ANE had ever seen. Their army became the model for later empires such as Neo-Babylonia and Persia.

The Assyrian army had four main combat branches: infantry (foot soldiers), artillery (archers and slingers), cavalry (mounted warriors), and chariotry. Artillery units using weapons such as slings and bows were the first to confront the enemy. Slingers had a lethal range up to 100 yards. In combination with infantry, an archer, a spearman, and a soldier carrying a large shield often worked together as a functioning entity within an auxiliary unit.

Heavy infantry, the fighting core of the army, followed the artillery and auxiliary units. They used close-combat weapons such as swords, pikes, daggers, and maces. Mounted troops consisted of both cavalry and horse-drawn chariots. Both platforms were used primarily for firing arrows. Chariots were lightweight, two-wheeled, and usually drawn by a pair of horses.

Engineer units built and operated siege machines and oversaw siege tactics. They used battering rams, dug "sapper" tunnels under walls, and built siege ramps and towers.

Assyrian armor was leather for the enlisted troops, and scale for officers.

Traditionally, soldiers were conscripted from the population, but Tiglath Pileser III (744–727 BC) created a standing army of trained professionals.

The Assyrians tried to avoid long sieges by using psychological warfare, hoping to persuade enemies to surrender sooner rather than later. They often destroyed the surrounding crops and countryside. Besieged cities were made examples of when conquered. Towns were often leveled. Captives were flayed and butchered alive. Corpses were impaled on poles for all to see, and left to rot. These warfare tactics and practices are documented in graphic relief carvings that appear on Assyrian monuments.

The Neo-Assyrians swept across the Fertile Crescent with ferocity. They destroyed the Arameans, including their city-state of Damascus in 732 BC. They conquered Israel in 722 BC, and threatened Judah during the reign of King Hezekiah (680s BC). They expanded their empire to the north and east as well.

As the empire grew, veterans were given homes in new territories. The conquered were deported and absorbed into populations elsewhere.

Assyria met its end shortly after Babylon and the Medes formed an alliance in 612 BC. The "new kids on the block" systematically destroyed Assyria town by town until the empire was obliterated, never to rise again.

J. Bulot, S. Collins

BREAKOUT 6.07

HEZEKIAH'S TUNNEL

The Assyrian war machine, which had been expanding across Mesopotamia during the eighth century BC, destroyed the city of Samaria, the capital of the northern kingdom of Israel. At that time, King Hezekiah was heir-apparent to the throne in Jerusalem, capital of the southern kingdom of Judah. Ahaz, father of Hezekiah and the king in Jerusalem, followed a policy of appeasement toward the Assyrians, and thus avoided any Assyrian reprisals against Jerusalem after the fall of Samaria.

Upon the death of Ahaz, Hezekiah ascended the throne. He modified the foreign policy of his father, openly rebelling against the Assyrians in 705 BC. This action resulted in a punitive campaign by the Assyrians against Judah.

In preparation for this anticipated invasion, Hezekiah undertook changes to ensure the water supply to the city in the event of a siege. The population of the city had increased dramatically with refugees from the north, as well as through normal population growth. Many of the new inhabitants were living on the hill west of the old Solomonic city, while the Gihon Spring (the primary water source) was located on the far eastern side of Jerusalem. Thus, the Gihon waters were nearly inaccessible to the inhabitants of the western hill.

It has been theorized that Hezekiah and his engineers noticed that a fissure in the limestone stratum beneath the city allowed water to trickle from the Gihon Spring into the central valley at the south end of the city. Hezekiah accomplished an astonishing engineering feat by following this fissure. His workers

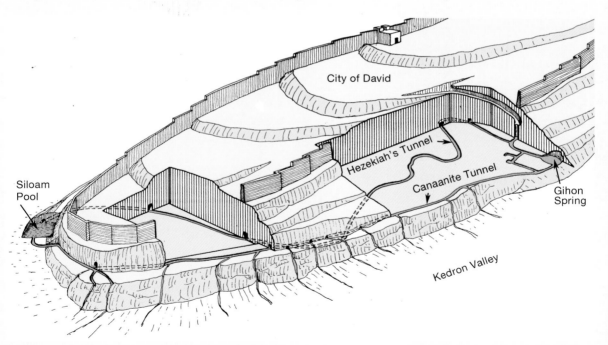

Details of Hezekiah's Tunnel (drawing: Leen Ritmeyer)

tunneled from both ends, met in the middle, enlarged the fissure as needed, and created a proper grade for drainage. Water from the Gihon Spring was then able to flow out from the newly created tunnel into the lower end of the central valley. Hezekiah then extended the city wall across the mouth of the central valley, creating a reservoir that was accessible to the inhabitants of the western hill. Problem solved!

The new reservoir was named the *Pool of Siloam* as early as the time of Nehemiah and was the pool to which Jesus sent an invalid to bathe and be healed of his blindness. Water from the Gihon still flows into the pool today, and a walk through this astonishing tunnel is one of the greater experiences that visitors enjoy during a trip to the Holy Land.

J. Moore

Siloam Inscription reproduction describing the completion of Hezekiah's Tunnel (photo: Joseph Holden)

they needed from local herdsmen? Probably the latter. It makes more sense that the Assyrian tacticians would want to keep a ready supply of meat "on the hoof" in every area they planned to annex. They were masters at stocking masses of provisions along their routes, but meat is better fresh, and live animals keep multiplying. Thus, shepherds were of equal benefit to both their city-folk neighbors and to an invading army!

FISHING—The coastal Levant had spectacular fishing. Fish could be salted and dried and kept for long periods. It could be shipped long distances with no spoilage. Fish oil was used for cooking and for lamps. It is likely that most people living in coastal towns ate fresh catches sold in the local markets daily.

KITCHENS AND COOKING—Food and meal preparation remained physically at the center of the household, with the central, open-air courtyard kitchen as the hub of the architectural arrangement. The round-bottomed pot (in many sizes), by this time, had been the main cooking vessel in the Southern Levant for 1,000 years. The beehive-shaped clay oven had also been around for at least that long (see *Figure 5.26*).

Dried sheep and goat dung, augmented with dried twigs and occasional larger pieces of wood, remained the principal cooking fuel.

METALLURGY—Weapon and implement production was localized, using iron ore mined mainly in Asia Minor and copper mined in the south Levant, Sinai, and Elam/Persia. Tin (added to copper to make bronze) came either from the eastern Mediterranean region or east of the Zagros Mountains (see *Map 1.06*).

STONE—Stone vessels and working implements like grinders and mortars/pestles were fashioned from a wide range of stone-types: alabaster and gypsum (for fine objects such as sculptures and architectural elements), limestone, basalts, and others. Granite was common in Egypt.

BUILDING MATERIALS—More stone was used in monumental buildings than in domestic structures. Cut stone had many applications in temples and palaces (see *Figure 6.30*). Mudbricks were the material of choice for most superstructures built on stone foundations. Roofs could be thatch or wattle/daub covered with clay/sand/lime plaster. Room sizes were limited to

Figure 6.31—Columned building, Iron Age, Hazor (photo: John Witte Moore)

the length of available timber. Columns (usually wood in the Levant; stone in Egypt and Mesopotamia) were used to create larger rooms (see *Figure 6.31*).

FLINT—Still the sharpest cutting edge available for precision work, like shaving. It was also used for harvesting implements and for making handheld hammer stones and slingstones (see *Figure 6.32*).

TEXTILES—The kingdoms of Israel and Judah had many textile production centers. In fact, almost every excavated city and town of this period has an abundance of loom weights, often made of clay (see *Figure 5.33*). Raw wool was provided by nomadic herdsmen and flax for linen was grown by local farmers—the "milk and honey" of the land, representing shepherds and farmers, was even evident in producing cloth!

POTTERY—In the latter part of IA2 (see *Figure 6.33*), many commercial jar handles were stamped with seal-impressions bearing the names of various cities such as Hebron, Mamshit, Socoh, and Ziph (see *Figure 6.34*). They also contained the designation lamelekh ("to the king [of]"), indicating that the contents of the jars were destined for use by the ruling administrators of specified cities. Pottery making continued with few innovations until the end of the Persian period (IA3). The next major transformation

Figure 6.32—Ancient hammer stones for food preparation (photo: Daniel Galassini, courtesy of Museum of Archaeology, Trinity Southwest University)

in pottery types in the Levant occurred around 800 BC, with the decline of Phoenician influence and the increase of Assyrian intervention. There are also clear differences between the pottery types of Israel (north) and Judah (south). Generally speaking, the pottery of IA1 is cruder than that of LBA2 and IA2. Many vessels were decorated with red burnished slip, from jugs and juglets to bowls and kraters. While many of the large LBA storage jars (*pithoi*; singular, *pithos*) had no handles, IA pithoi tended to have handles, and often

included a collar around the neck just below the rim. While such collar-rimmed jars are interpreted as typical for IA1, the collar-rimmed style has its roots as far back as the LBA, even the MBA.

TRADE—Even with the periodic disruptions of war, commercial trade networks were the framework of all national economies. Local populations were quite capable of sustaining their own lives from their fields and flocks. But commercial surpluses of commodities, and the ability to move those products to buyers in

BREAKOUT 6.08

THE FALL OF SAMARIA

Solomon died c. 931 BC. With his death, the united monarchy ended as well (see *Timeline*). The northern kingdom of Israel was established under the reign of Jeroboam, who rebelled against Solomon's son Rehoboam. The kingdom of Judah was in the south, and the royal line of David was established in the capital city of Jerusalem. The ten tribes to the north made up what was to become Samaria, alternately called Ephraim or Israel. This northern region, along with its capital city, was known as Samaria.

King Pekah, usurper of the Samarian throne, made unwise alliances with King Rezin of Damascus, Syria, and invaded Judah to the south when the people refused to align with the north against Assyria. These events are recorded by Isaiah. Judah, under the authority of evil King Ahaz and against the advice of Isaiah,

appealed to the Assyrian ruler Tiglath Pileser III, who put down the rebellion in Damascus. Pekah, who was from the north, was himself assassinated, and Hoshea was installed as king of Israel in his place.

Hoshea immediately sued for peace with Assyria and, for a time, kept the throne. Tiglath Pileser was busy in Babylon, and King Hoshea tried to form an alliance with Egypt. After Tiglath Pileser died, his son Shalmaneser V (c. 727–722 BC) ascended the throne. Hoshea decided to withhold Israel's annual tribute money to Assyria, which resulted in a final, decisive invasion by Assyria. This was the end of the rebellion, but previous Assyrian resettlement campaigns had already done significant damage to Israel/Samaria.

Samaria was conquered by Sargon II in 722/721 BC (see

Timeline). This destruction was the fulfillment of Micah's prophecy (Micah 1:1) and was recorded in 2 Kings 17. Sargon II, son of Shalmaneser V, may have been involved directly as general of the Assyrian forces, co-conquering with his father. According to the likely exaggerated Khorsabad annals, Sargon II directly claims, "I besieged and captured Samaria, carrying off 27,290 of the people who dwelt therein…" He then reintroduced peoples from other conquered regions of the Assyrian Empire into the Samarian lands in an effort to prevent future problems with the area. This intermingling of Gentiles and Israelites caused the lineages of the northern tribes to blur, and the so-called "ten lost tribes" were, in essence, absorbed into what became the Samaritan people and region.

B. Maggard, J. Holden

neighboring and distant lands, were the key to national economic success. With Egypt in a slump and Assyrian and subsequent Babylonian interference in the Levant, times were tough for caravaners plying overland routes. Only the Phoenicians, with their emphasis on the Mediterranean Sea trade, were enjoying unhindered success. Their master craftsmen made glass and luxury goods that were in demand from kingdoms far and wide. Phoenician-produced items found their way even to the British Isles! They were also expert shipbuilders. Their purple dye was prized by Mesopotamian rulers. For the Assyrians or Babylonians to mess with the Phoenicians (the name means "purple Tyrian dye") would essentially be the same as cutting off your nose to spite your face.

Figure 6.33—Pottery of Iron Age 2b–c (photos: Daniel Galassini, Steven Collins, Carl Morgan; courtesy of Museum of Archaeology, Trinity Southwest University)

Figure 6.34—*lmlk* handles, Iron Age 2b–c (photos: David E. Graves and Alexander Schick)

CHAPTER 7

THE WORLD OF THE EXILE AND RETURN

WELCOME TO IRON AGE 3 (586–332 BC)

Iron Age 3 (IA3) began with the Babylonian conquest of the Fertile Crescent and ended with the rise of Alexander the Great in the late fourth century BC. Assyrian control of the Levant (Canaan) had lasted just over 100 years before they were conquered by the Babylonians (see *Timeline*). How quickly things changed in the ANE! The northern kingdom of Israel was absorbed by the Assyrians, while the southern kingdom of Judah was snuffed out by the Babylonians. Nebuchadnezzar's policy of deporting to Babylon the crème-de-la-crème of conquered populations, however, turned out to be a blessing to the Judahites (Jews) in the long term. After Babylon fell to the Medo-Persians in 539 BC, the Persians allowed the Jewish captives an opportunity to return to their homeland. The Persians even covered much of the cost to rebuild Jerusalem's defenses and the temple of Yahweh!

GEOGRAPHY

Even with all the territory that the Neo-Babylonian Empire was able to dominate (see *Maps 6.09, 6.10*), it did not last long. Within 70 years of conquering the Assyrians, Babylonia was subsumed by the Medo-Persian Empire (see *Maps 7.01, 7.02* and *Timeline*). This is an example of how the ANE could almost change in an instant! Persia's kings supported the return of Babylonian captives to their homelands, including the Judahites (Jews).

CHRONOLOGY

By 586 BC, King Nebuchadnezzar of Babylon had initiated a deportation agenda for the conquered peoples of the Levant—that is, for the best, brightest, and most skilled. This included untold numbers of Judahite captives. Their "employment" in the Babylonian regime lasted about 70 years. In c. 539, the Persian monarch Cyrus the Great permitted the Jews to return, if desired, to their homeland in Judah and rebuild their temple (see *Timeline*). Later, c. 445 BC, Artaxerxes I issued a decree for the restoration of Jerusalem and its city walls, and additional Judahites returned with Nehemiah to what had been the territory of Judah.

HISTORY

After the Battle of Carchemish (605 BC), in which Babylonia, with the help of the Medes, defeated the combined armies of Egypt and Assyria, Nebuchadnezzar II of Babylon marched south and besieged Jerusalem. King Jehoiakim (aka Eliakim) paid tribute to Nebuchadnezzar (2 Kings 24; 2 Chronicles 36). Emboldened by Egypt's defeat of Nebuchadnezzar in 601 BC, Judah rebelled against Babylon. In response, the Babylonian army once again lay siege to Jerusalem, during which time Jehoiakim died. The city fell in March of 597 BC during the reign of Jehoiakin (aka Jeconiah; 2 Kings 24; 2 Chronicles 36). Nebuchadnezzar plundered Jerusalem and the temple and carted off Jehoiakin and other prominent citizens to Babylon (see *Breakout 7.02*). Jehoiakin's uncle, Zedekiah, was appointed king in Jerusalem by Nebuchadnezzar.

Zedekiah (aka Mattaniah) revolted against Babylon, making an alliance with Pharaoh Hophra of Egypt (2 Kings 24:20; 25; 2 Chronicles 36; cf. Jeremiah 44). Nebuchadnezzar stormed back to the area in 587/586 BC, defeated the Egyptians, and demolished Jerusalem and its temple with a vengeance. Zedekiah was captured and made to witness the execution of his

sons, after which he was blinded and taken to Babylon (see *Figure 7.01*) along with additional captives (Jeremiah 52). Jerusalem lay in ruins and Judah became the Babylonian province of Yehud. The Babylonian captivity of Judah had begun (see *Breakout 7.01*).

Babylon appointed a native Judahite, Gedaliah, as governor of Yehud/Judah (2 Kings 25). Many Jews had fled to Edom, Moab, and Ammon in the face of Babylonian aggression in the area, and Gedaliah now encouraged them to return to Judah and help bring

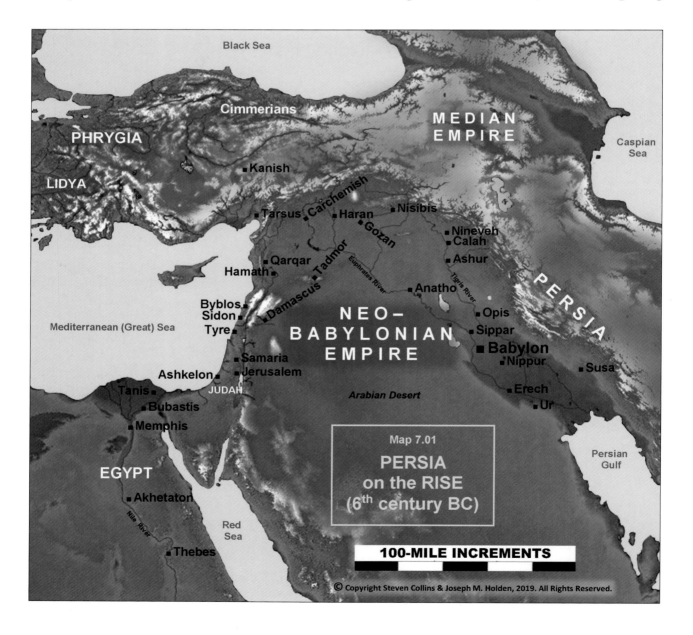

Map 7.01

**PERSIA
on the RISE
(6th century BC)**

100-MILE INCREMENTS

the country back to prosperity. But soon he and his Babylonian advisors were assassinated by a member of the royal family, which caused many Judahites to flee to Egypt because they feared a military response from Babylon (2 Kings 25:25-26).

Back in Babylonia, the Jewish captives thrived, building a large and successful community and taking advantage of a booming Babylonian economy (see *Breakout 7.02*). The great prophet Daniel (see *Breakout 7.03*), with his remarkable administrative abilities, prospered through a long and stellar career in service to Nebuchadnezzar II (605–562 BC), Amel-Marduk (562–560 BC), Neriglissar (560–556 BC), Labashi-Marduk (556 BC), Nabonidus (556–539 BC), and Belshazzar (?–539 BC). When Babylon was captured by the Medo-Persians in 539 BC, Daniel was thereafter retained in a high-level administrative position into the period of Darius the Mede and Cyrus the Persian (aka "the Great"; ruled 559–530 BC; see *Breakout 7.05*)—at least three years beyond the fall of Babylon (Daniel 10:1).

Darius the Mede is known only from the Bible. Some scholars have identified him as Cyrus himself (see *Figure 7.02*), or Ugbaru, Cyrus's general who captured the city of Babylon in 539 BC. It is more likely that Darius the Mede was a king (Hebrew, *melek*) appointed by Cyrus to rule concurrently over the newly acquired Babylonian territories in the year or two following the fall of Babylon—in essence, an administrative front man.

The Hebrew word for king, *mlk*, has many applications throughout the Bible. A *mlk* can be the king (emperor) of an empire, the king (monarch) of a city-state, the king (prince/governor) of a city or town, even the king (commander) of a military garrison. And because the Medes were allied with the Persians when Babylon was captured, it makes sense that the Persian King Cyrus would designate a Median like Darius to rule as king over Babylon in the transition. Cyrus's palace in his capital city, Pasargadae, was 500 miles southeast of Babylon, as the crow flies (see *Map 7.02*). Thus, having a temporary administrative king over the newly annexed Babylonian region makes abundant sense.

We have many written documents and inscriptions corroborating the accounts of the Jews' return from

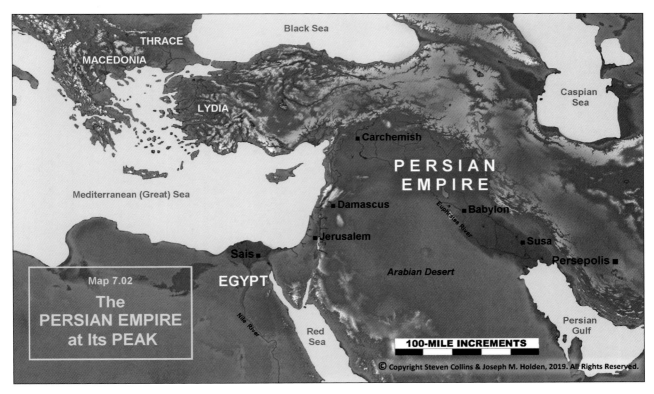

captivity in Babylon, as recorded in the book of Ezra (also noted in 2 Chronicles 36:22-23; see *Breakouts 7.06, 7.07*). Cyrus the Great was a pivotal figure in these developments. He supported the return of peoples previously displaced from their homelands by the Babylonians; this included the Judahites (Jews). Cyrus also wanted returning peoples to reestablish their temples and worship practices in their homelands. And the bulk of this was accomplished with Persian funds. The rebuilding of Jerusalem and its city walls is recorded in the book of Nehemiah (see *Breakout 7.09*).

Only a fraction of the Jews living in Babylon during this time returned to their hometowns in Judah (see *Breakout 7.02*). Significant populations of Jews living in

Figure 7.01—City of Babylon, model (photo: Alexander Schick)

Figure 7.02—Cyrus the Great image (photo: Steven Collins)

Egypt also remained there. Back in Judah, the rebuilding efforts of Ezra and Nehemiah were not always welcomed by Jerusalem locals (see *Breakout 7.10*). Although they were now back in their land, the Jewish people faced an uncertain future (see *Breakout 7.08*).

PEOPLES AND KINGDOMS

JUDAH—Judah was defeated by Babylon and Jerusalem was sacked and burned in 586 BC. Large numbers of high-ranking captives were taken from the cities and sent to Babylon for reeducation and service to the empire. Judah was useful for farming and livestock, with the people subjugated and heavily taxed. Local satraps administered the kingdom for Persia, but not without difficulties from local dispossessed peoples who had been introduced by Assyria.

BABYLONIA—Babylon was one of the greatest empires of this time. It had fantastic public and private zoos, gardens, colorful monumental gateways, palaces,

Figure 7.03—Ishtar Gate, Babylon; modern reproduction (photo: Alexander Schick)

BREAKOUT 7.01

THE BABYLONIAN DEPORTATION OF JUDAH AND CAPTIVITY

Under the rule of Nebuchad-nezzar II, the Babylonian Empire invaded Judah and conquered Jerusalem in 587/86 BC. This was the final blow to the southern kingdom of Judah. For many generations the regions of both Israel and Judah had been under persistent attack—first by civil war and infighting, followed by invasions from Aram-Damascus and Assyria. Both Aram-Damascus and Assyria, like Egypt before them, had depopulated the Levant (Canaan) just enough to prevent uprisings of local peoples while still allowing for pastoral-rural growth and food production.

The Babylonian Chronicles detail many invasions of the Levant. After Babylon's victory over Egypt at the battle of Carchemish in 605 BC, the Babylonians became the sole rulers in the Levant.

Nebuchadnezzar had to return to the region known as Hattu-land (the Levant, because of its long-time connection to the land of Hatti) to put down a rebellion and levy taxes. According to 2 Kings 24, he removed the appointed vassal king Jehoiachin (Jehoiakim's son) in 597 BC and deported more of the population (this was the deportation that included the prophet Ezekiel). Babylon then appointed King Zedekiah and made repeated forays to Jerusalem to collect tribute. Jehoiachin was exiled to Babylon under Awel-Marduk (biblical Evil-Merodach, 2 Kings 25:27; Jeremiah 52:31, 34). There are cuneiform tablets that record the rations and allowances given to Jehoiachin and his five children, with some kind of limited freedom in the area of the royal palace in Babylon.

Ignoring the advice of Jeremiah, King Zedekiah rebelled against Babylon. He apparently aligned himself with Egypt's King Hophra—in a secret treaty—against Babylon c. 589 BC. Nebuchadnezzar, who already had troops in Syria besieging the city of Tyre, marched to Jerusalem, where the then-active rebellion was put down. Zedekiah was blinded and imprisoned until his death in Babylon (2 Kings 25), and the deportation of Judahites began in earnest.

The Babylonian lists of peoples and classes of people removed into exile reads quite strangely and includes every conceivable profession, including soldiers, sailors, craftsman, musicians, carpenters, guards, and even a "keeper of monkeys"! The Babylonians, like the Assyrians before them, were brutal, sweeping through the region with little regard for people and places. But deportation "Babylonian style" often meant opportunities in a new land. Those left behind in Judah had a difficult road ahead in a homeland decimated by war.

Babylon was most certainly the largest and most advanced city of the ANE during the time of Nebuchadnezzar II (c. 605–562 BC). There are many Semitic names recorded in the annals of Babylon during this time of captivity, indicating that the best and brightest of the captives took advantage of opportunities for political and social advancement within Babylonian society.

B. Maggard, J. Holden

and vast residential areas. All manner of peoples with influence and wealth lived there (see *Figure 7.03*). They had recently thrown off the yoke of Assyrian domination under the administration of Naboplassar (c. 626–605 BC) and established the great Chaldean city-state of Babylon. This was a powerful metropolis. The city known as Babylon during the reign of Nebuchadnezzar II (605–562 BC) was probably the most advanced city of the ancient world.

PERSIA—Cyrus defeated Media, Lydia, and Babylon, founding the Persian (Achaemenid) Empire in 550 BC. The Persians had many similarities with the Medes and unified together with them to form a powerful empire. The Persian capital city of Persepolis (see *Figure 7.04*) was in southern Mesopotamia (modern Iran). The empire, at its height, extended to modern-day Ukraine, throughout Asia Minor, to the Indus River Valley (India), and southwest to Egypt. It was

---

BREAKOUT 7.02

LIFE IN BABYLON FOR THE CAPTIVES

The captivity of the Jewish people under Babylon began with raids on Jerusalem, then the final destruction of Jerusalem by Nebuchadnezzar in 587/6 BC. The numbers of deported Israelites (2 Kings 24:14-16 and Jeremiah 52:28-30 for a total of 12,600) found in Scripture appear consistent with the earlier deportations of the Assyrians. Evidence from the Bible indicates that the prisoners were the "urban elite," while the people left behind were mostly farmers and shepherds.

Jeremiah told the people that they would be in captivity for 70 years, and then Yahweh would punish the Babylonians (25:11-12). Jeremiah instructed the Judahites to build houses and live in them, plant gardens, and seek the general welfare of Babylon for the good of the Babylonian people and also the exiles themselves (Jeremiah 29:5-7).

When Cyrus issued a decree (c. 539) that the captives should be set free to return to their own lands and cities, some went back, but many remained. One Judahite settlement in Babylon where Jews continued to live was known as al-Yahudu. Life in Babylonia could be prosperous, and many Jews flourished in postexilic communities as they had during their captivity. They became active members of the larger cities and regions.

More than 100 Babylonian clay tablets have been found that document events and daily life among the Babylonian exiles. These documents indicate active trade, payment of taxes, and various kinds of debts owed. Exiled Judahites maintained their Hebrew language, and much of their ethnic identity. It is believed that the concept of the synagogue took shape during the exile. Synagogues were a place of worship and gathering together. Because the Jerusalem

temple was now far away and in ruins and the temple services and sacrifices had come to an end, synagogues provided places of teaching and community through which the spiritual life of the Jewish people could be sustained.

Other clay cuneiform documents from Babylonia reveal rations and allowances given to Jehoiachin and his five children, along with a modicum of freedom in the palace precincts. The books of Esther and Daniel were written during the time of the exile. The book of Daniel begins in the third year of Jehoiakim, king of Judah (Daniel 1:1), and ends in the third year of Cyrus (Daniel 10:1). Esther was composed during the reign of Ahasuerus (Xerxes) about 50 years after Cyrus's edict. The biblical books of Jeremiah, Ezekiel, and Isaiah also deal, in part, with the period of the Babylonian captivity.

B. Maggard, S. Collins

Figure 7.04—Persian capital, Persepolis (photo: David E. Graves)

the largest empire ever in the ancient world (see *Map 7.02*) until the rise of Rome. Its collective armies probably exceeded 500,000 men. On more than one occasion the empire put 250,000 to 350,000 soldiers on a battlefield. Their cities were every bit as impressive as those of Babylonia. Cyrus the Great was responsible for the return of the Jews from exile, a policy reiterated later by Artaxerxes I, allowing the rebuilding of Jerusalem.

MEDIA—In the seventh century BC the Medes were absorbed by the Persians. Generally, the geographic region occupied by the Medes was west and south of the Caspian Sea, and south to the Zagros Mountains and Elam (see *Map 7.02*). The Medes were warlike and known for great horsemanship. They were similar to the Persians in many respects.

EGYPT—Under Esarhaddon, the Assyrians invaded Egypt and conquered it by 666 BC. Egypt was in a rebuilding mode only to be defeated by Cambyses II of Persia in 525 BC. This was the state of Egypt until the coming of Alexander the Great (see *Breakout 8.02*). In 332 BC, Alexander, with a smaller but technically superior army, conquered the Persian Empire.

After Alexander's death, his general Ptolemy founded the Ptolemaic Dynasty (323–30 BC) in Egypt (see *Breakout 8.04*).

SOCIETIES AND CULTURES

SOCIAL STRATIFICATION—A rigidly stratified society was always the rule in the ANE. But for the Judahites (Jews) of this period, the turmoil and chaos created by the Babylonian conquest of the Levant went a long way toward leveling their society. Survivors remaining in their home territories after the Babylonian conquest had to band together to endure as communities. They were forced to stand side by side regardless of what their previous social status had been. The need to survive trumped social hierarchy! That happened as well to the captives carted off to Babylonia. From that point on, the Jews became a community not ordered by societal standing but bound together by a collective identity. The epicenter of that collective identity was their religion.

TRIBALISM—Israelite tribalism had continued for more than a millennium, and it was not overturned

The Career of the Prophet Daniel

Daniel was the son of a prominent family in Judah, born about 620 BC. In 604 BC, King Jehoiakim of Judah surrendered the city of Jerusalem, agreeing to pay tribute to Nebuchadnezzar, who was the crown prince of Babylon. Daniel and three friends—Hananiah, Mishael, and Azariah—were deported to the Chaldean capital in the first wave of captives. The Babylonian policy was to take sons of the royal family and princes as hostages and indoctrinate them in the Babylonian language (Aramaic), culture, and religion with the intention of returning them to their native land to be loyal administrators for the empire.

Daniel, while a teenager, distinguished himself in his dedication to Yahweh through intellectual prowess and by refusing to eat non-Kosher food at the "cadet academy." When King Nebuchadnezzar had a disturbing dream, he used it to test his priests, requiring a demonstration of their ability to divine an interpretation. But beyond that, he required that they tell him the content of the dream first! The ancients believed dreams were communication from the gods. The usual interpretive protocol was for the priests (diviners) to be told the dream, after which they consulted an extensive dream-interpretation document that "revealed" its meaning to the dreamer—with a good dose of subjectivism on the part of the priests!

Nebuchadnezzar gave his cabinet of spiritual advisors—magicians, astrologers, diviners/seers, and exorcists—a single day to meet his demands or be executed. They were shocked at this breach of divining protocol! But young Daniel, a student advisor with deep devotion to Yahweh, was already gaining a reputation as an extraordinary dream-solver. He was able to reveal the details of Nebuchadnezzar's dream and its interpretation. This event catapulted Daniel to prominence. His loyal, diligent work for the Babylonian administration kept him at the highest levels of government for more than 60 years, during which he served 4 kings—Nebuchadnezzar and Belshazzar (son and coregent to King Nabonidus) of Babylon, and the Medo-Persian kings Cyrus and Darius.

Daniel's book resides in the Writings (*K'Tuvim*) portion of the Hebrew Bible. Throughout his Mesopotamian career he remained a rigorously pious follower of Yahweh, experienced visions, and publically interpreted dreams and visions for his royal bosses on at least three occasions.

His main career, however, was in civil administration. While Daniel was an honored author of a canonical work, his book does not appear in the collection of Old Testament prophets (seers). Nevertheless, Jesus, in the Olivet Discourse (Matthew 24:15), identified Daniel as a prophet.

Bible critics challenge the authorship and date of Daniel's book (written in the 530s BC), claiming it must have been written during the Hellenistic or Hasmonean period (332–63 BC). This is because Daniel chapters 10 and 11 contain prophecies detailing the history of wars between the Seleucid and Ptolemaic dynasties, who ruled Judah as a small province from 320–167 BC. On one hand, if we accept that God can provide authentic revelation to his prophets, then the visions of Daniel describe political and military events that affected Judah c. 248–160 BC. On the other hand, if we do not believe that God can provide information about the future, then we must explain how the book of Daniel was translated from Hebrew to Greek, the Septuagint (LXX) version, early in the reign of Ptolemy II (285–246 BC) when the events described by Daniel occurred between 248 and 165 BC.

H. Gullet, S. Collins

by the Babylonian conquest of Judah and captivity in Babylon. Tribal identification remained an important component of personal image. However, on the social and religious levels, the disruption of Israelite/Judahite culture during this period had a homogenizing effect that reinforced the people's collective identity as Jews.

CITY-STATES—Even the great empires of Assyria, Babylonia, and Persia were composed of city-states (each with its own territory) melded together by royal administrations wielding enough military might and organizational acumen to forge a national unity. In essence, city-states functioned as states or counties within a larger, centralized political system.

INHERITANCE—Inheritance laws and traditions remained virtually unchanged throughout all of ANE history. But among the remaining Judahites (Jews) and scattered Israelites, the territorial tribal allotments originally laid out in the days of Moses and Joshua ceased to exist.

WOMEN'S ROLES—Among the Jews in Babylon, the female subculture increased in importance (see *Breakout 7.02*). In their attempt to maintain their Jewish identity in a land foreign to everything they had ever thought or experienced, the community of women evolved a matriarchal system that became the "blood" of Jewish life from this time forward. (To be truly Jewish, one must have a Jewish mother!) While not as outwardly visible as the male societal structure, women were the warp and weft of the cultural tapestry.

MEN'S ROLES—In this era, the male subculture of the Judahite captives developed two new wrinkles: the *synagogue* and the *rabbi* (see *Breakout 8.01*). With the temple in ruins, along with the priesthood that had maintained it, Judaism in captivity sought ways of keeping some semblance of its worship system alive. The answer lay in teaching the Hebrew Scriptures, especially the Torah (Law). It was not necessary for a learned teacher (rabbi) to be of the Levite tribe. The purpose of the newly emerging rabbinical Judaism was to educate young men in the structures and details of the faith as a means of keeping Jewish communities pure and free from the pagan influences that surrounded them on every side.

POLITICAL CLIMATE—Aside from periodic clashes between Babylonian paganism and Jewish monotheism (as seen in the book of Daniel), many Jews distinguished themselves within the political structure of Babylonia and Persia. So well did the Jewish community fare in its Mesopotamian "home" that, when they had the opportunity to return to the land of Judah, most chose to stay in Babylon. Back in Judah, political wrangling often made the lives of the local inhabitants difficult. Rebuilding was not as easy as the returnees expected (see *Breakout 7.10*).

LANGUAGES AND WRITING

HEBREW—No doubt the learned Judahite men in captivity kept their Hebrew language alive by studying and teaching from the Hebrew Scriptures. By this time, Hebrew had attained its classical form, written in Aramaic square script (see *Figure 7.05*).

ARAMAIC—The Babylonian *lingua franca*, Aramaic became the everyday spoken language of the Jews living in Babylon (see *Figure 7.06*). It mixed with Hebrew to eventually become the Aramaic spoken in Judea in New Testament times.

PERSIAN—Old Persian belongs to the Indo-Iranian branch of the Indo-European language family. (The modern version is Farsi, or P[h]arsi.) It was written in an alphabetic cuneiform script of 36 characters along with a few logograms (a sign representing a word or phrase) (see *Figure 7.07*).

Figure 7.05—Late Iron Age Hebrew script (photo: Steven Collins)

Figure 7.06—Aramaic inscription (photo: Joseph Holden)

Figure 7.07—Farsi (Pharsi) script (cuneiform alphabet) (photo: Joseph Holden)

BELIEFS AND RELIGIONS

JUDAISM—While captive in Babylon, the Jews, for the first time in their history, fully embraced the true monotheism of Moses. It blossomed in their hearts and minds, erasing more than 1,000 years of flirting with, and often wallowing in, the mire of syncretistic paganism. Embedded in a land of idols, the "Sons of Jacob" finally comprehended the true nature of their God. Yahweh was indeed One.

PERSIAN RELIGION—The most prominent religions of the ancient Persians were Mithraism and Zoroastrianism. Mithraism was an ancient polytheistic religion in which the god Mithra was chief. Mithra (a Mittani/Hurrian deity as early as the fifteenth century BC; later, Mithras to the Romans) was the sun god, the god of pure light. As such, Mithra was invoked in contracts and treaties as "the one from whom nothing is hidden." Zoroastrianism was founded by Zarathustra (Zoroaster) around 600 BC. It was a functional monotheism centered on the god of wisdom, Ahura Mazda (see *Figure 7.08*). (Actually, it was a henotheistic religion focused on one deity, but not denying that other gods might exist.) The most prominent feature of Zoroastrianism is *dualism*, in which reality is sharply divided between good and evil, the spiritual realm and the material realm.

NEO-BABYLONIAN RELIGION—The Babylonian Marduk (see *Figure 7.09*) replaced the long-standing Mesopotamian Enlil as the chief of the gods. The epic

Figure 7.08—Persian deity, Ahura Mazda image (photo: Steven Collins)

myth Enuma Elish was a Babylonian period composition with interesting parallels to the creation accounts in the book of Genesis. Images (idols) of deities were of great importance to the Babylonians. They were washed and cared for according to a strict ritual formula. The gods were believed to inhabit their images as well as the natural phenomena they represented.

ARCHITECTURE AND INFRASTRUCTURE

CITIES, TOWNS, AND VILLAGES—The city of Babylon covered about 2,200 acres. By comparison, the Jerusalem of Solomon was about 20 acres, and the Jerusalem of Hezekiah was around 60 acres. This gives you an idea of the difference of scale between the "backwater" cities of the south Levant and the magnificent civilizations of Mesopotamia and Egypt. Towns, villages, and hamlets sprang up to house agricultural workers and those working in specialty trades, like potters and metal workers.

TEMPLES—While the Jerusalem temple lay in ruins at this time, Neo-Babylonian temples were the religious centers across southern Mesopotamia. They were much larger than their south Levantine counterparts, but still tripartite in form (see *Figure 7.10*). An idol of the god to whom a temple was devoted stood in the most holy place.

ADMINISTRATIVE STRUCTURES—The city of Babylon was massive, with a vast administrative complex teeming with top officials and rank-and-file administrative personnel. Offices existed for every imaginable governmental function: taxation, waterworks, city maintenance, architectural design, food production, trade relations, legal matters, and more (see *Figure 7.11*).

HOUSES—Still typically built of mudbricks on stone foundation, houses in Babylon were little different than those to which the Judahites were accustomed back home.

GATES—Babylon had many gateways, with the most impressive being the Ishtar Gate (see *Figure 7.03*).

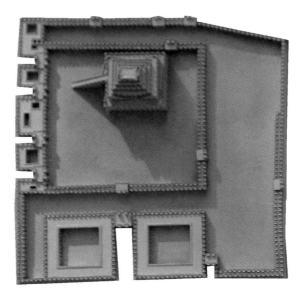

Figure 7.10—Neo-Babylonian temple (photo: Alexander Schick)

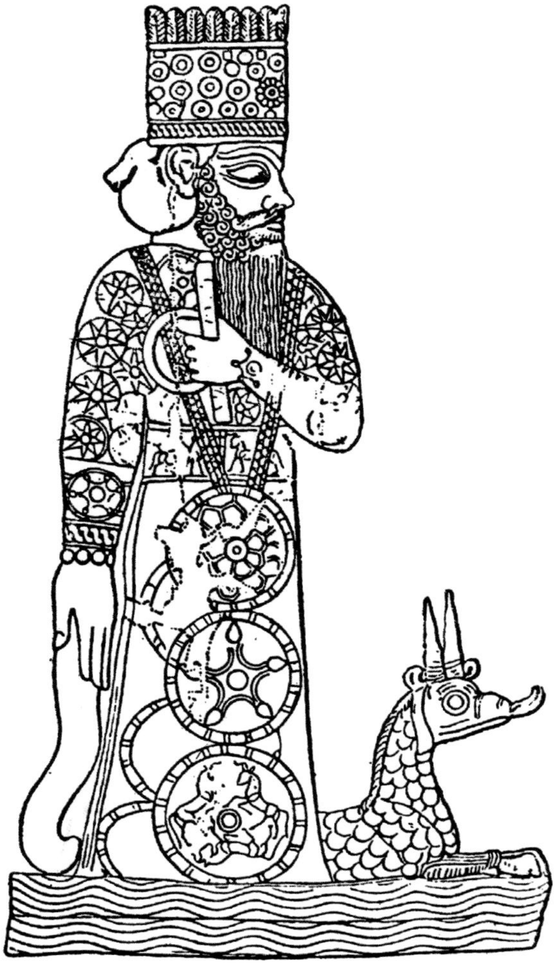

Figure 7.11—Administrative building in Babylon, reconstructed (photo: David E. Graves)

Figure 7.09—Neo-Babylonian deity, Marduk image (public domain; retouched, Steven Collins)

Breakout 7.04

The Fiery Furnace

As elsewhere in the ANE, most permanent Mesopotamian structures were built of sundried mudbricks and mud mortar, and covered with mud plaster. Yet royal Mesopotamian construction projects had sufficient resources to kiln-fire large numbers of mudbricks, hardening and virtually waterproofing them. Excavations at the thirteenth-century BC Elamite ziggurat *Dur Untash* (Iran) found the remains of brick kilns near the tower's still-standing walls constructed with tens of thousands of fired mudbricks.

Fired mudbricks were installed on the exterior faces of thick walls, with sundried bricks filling the interior. Using bitumen (asphalt/tar) as mortar between fired bricks was also known as early as Mesopotamia's Uruk period in the fourth millennium BC (Genesis 11:3 NIV—"they used brick instead of stone, and tar for mortar"). Some 150 years after Nebuchadnezzar, Herodotus (*The Histories*: Book One), who likely never visited Babylon himself, spoke of fired mudbricks in Babylon's defensive walls and hot bitumen for mortar.

Frequently, the exterior faces of already-fired mudbricks were coated with a colored, alkaline, wood-ash-and-sand glaze, then refired. This created a costly and often spectacular result. In addition to weatherproofing a structure's exterior with tiles of gleaming blues and greens, images of animals and mythical beasts were often created in relief across the collective faces of four to five dozen polychrome-glazed fired mudbricks. Remarkable feats of artistry, awe-inspiring decorations, and not-so-subtle royal propaganda—such was Nebuchadnezzar's Babylon.

The exteriors of most of Babylon's public structures—city walls, gates, towers, palaces—were faced with fired mudbricks mortared with bitumen. Even Babylon's canal subsurfaces were paved with fired mudbricks, as were walking surfaces like the Euphrates bridge, major roadways (the Processional Way), and palace floors.

Many bricks were also stamped with a legend: "Nebuchadnezzar, King of Babylon, fosterer of Esagila and Ezida, son of Nabopolassar, King of Babylon." Excavator Robert Koldewey (AD 1855–1925) suggested that there were millions of such stamped bricks throughout Babylon—visual reminders of Nebuchadnezzar's boast: "Is not this great Babylon, which I have built by my mighty power…and for the glory of my majesty?" (Daniel 4:30).

But Babylon's fortunes ebbed and flowed following its capture by the Persians. After Alexander the Great died in Nebuchadnezzar's palace at Babylon (323 BC), the city lost its cosmopolitan status. With the expansion of Islam in the region (after AD 700), Babylon crumbled into a mass of ruins—but remained impressive nonetheless.

During the medieval period, Arab writers knew the site as a source of building bricks for nearby villages. Later, eighteenth- and nineteenth-century European visitors were impressed by the mounds of ruins, not even knowing it was Babylon. They, too, witnessed and lamented how locals were robbing out the fired mudbricks at such a rate that the plans of many buildings were being lost. Only with the year-round German Orient Society's excavations (from 1899 to 1914) directed by Koldewey did this wholesale looting begin to wane.

Today, in museums and through restoration work at the site, these fired, glazed, and relief-casted mudbricks still symbolize the greatness of what was once Nebuchadnezzar's Babylon. They also serve as a reminder of the blazing furnace into which Daniel's three Hebrew friends were cast (Daniel 3), undoubtedly one of the royal brick kilns Nebuchadnezzar employed to honor himself.

G. Byers

Faced with glazed bricks (tiles), this spectacular entrance to Babylon was like nothing the Judahites had ever seen.

FORTIFICATIONS—Some ancient sources tell us that the walls of Babylon were 80 feet thick, more than 300 feet high, and encircled the city for more than 50 miles. While archaeology shows that these figures are exaggerated (on average by a factor of two), it is possible that, depending on the topography, the wall height and thickness could have come close to these proportions in certain sectors.

BUILDING MATERIALS—As elaborate and sophisticated as the great Mesopotamian cities were, their construction was still mainly mudbricks on stone foundations. This tells us just how good these materials really were. They were strong, durable (with maintenance!), and made it relatively easy to put up structures of any size. The one-up brick technology of the Babylonians was the extensive use of fired mudbricks, mainly for wall surfaces, and the glazing of brick surfaces in vibrant colors for monumental applications, with the addition of glazed reliefs of animals and mythical beasts (see *Breakout 7.04* and *Figure 7.12*).

WEAPONS AND WARFARE

BABYLONIANS—The Babylonian army was very similar to that of the Assyrians they defeated. They used infantry, chariotry, archers and slingers, cavalry, and perhaps camelry. They were trained in a variety of tactics and strategies, depending on the terrain and circumstances in which they were fighting. Given the many city-states within their empire, the Babylonians could easily muster large numbers of both professional soldiers and conscripts—in the tens of thousands, if necessary.

PERSIANS—The Persians had the largest army in the history of the ANE up to that time. While estimates vary in different ancient sources, once adjustments are made for exaggerations it seems that the Persians were capable of putting 300,000-plus men on a battlefield, if necessary, with another 30,000 to 50,000 on horseback, plus archers, slingers, and chariots. Thus, if you went up against the Persians, you could be facing a force numbering around half a million.

BATTLE TACTICS—In general, archers using composite bows or longbows would send waves of arrow-fire into enemy ranks, killing as many as possible before actual engagement. Then a shock-charge of heavy cavalry would attempt to separate the enemy troops from their commanders and cause chaos. This was followed by a mass wave of infantry to engage the now-flummoxed enemy warriors in hand-to-hand combat. Chariots could also be sent to fire on enemy ranks from the perimeter of the melee. Slingers could provide cover fire over any enemy position as needed. The Persians could also use elephants (both Asian and African) sporting mobile firing platforms for multiple archers. Both the Babylonian and Persian armies could strike fear into their opposition by their sheer numbers and superior matériel (see *Breakout 7.05*; *Figure 7.13*).

Figure 7.12—Detail of glazed tiles, Ishtar Gate (photo: Steven Collins)

Figure 7.13—Battle scene, Persian army (public domain)

ARMOR—Professional soldiers were generally better outfitted than conscripts. Chainmail or scale-plate shirts were worn by archers and some infantry. All used shields, often borne by shield-bearers. Many warriors wore only helmets and minimal or no armor in favor of mobility and speed with their weapons. Full-armored infantry were less mobile but used in stand-one's-ground situations while less-armored soldiers ran and maneuvered to assist their less-mobile comrades with spears, swords, and battle axes (see *Figure 7.14*).

WEAPONRY—Double-edged swords, pikes, spears, daggers, clubs, and battle axes were used by infantry in close combat (see *Figure 7.15*). The Babylonians used mostly composite bows, while the Persians preferred the longbow. Slings and slingstones were always useful for cover fire but were also accurate and lethal up to 30 yards. Chariots were mobile firing platforms (the ancient equivalent of fighter planes).

INDUSTRIES AND OBJECTS

AGRICULTURE—Vast agricultural estates and state-owned lands produced the cereal crops required to feed an empire. Babylon alone had a population of around 200,000. The south Mesopotamian sector of the Babylonian Empire (Babylonia proper) had a population of two to two-and-a-half million people, not including nomadic groups. The subsequent population of the entire Persian Empire (see *Map 7.02*) was on the order of 50 million people. This required agricultural production on a massive scale.

HERDING—Once again, herding was important for all the same reasons: milk products, meat, and wool. Oxen (cattle) and pigs were also part of the picture, but these were not raised by nomads. These more sedentary animals had to be fenced or penned, and so were part of the agricultural scene run by cities, towns, and villages. It is not known to what extent the governments of the Babylonian Persian Empires owned their own herds of cattle, pigs, sheep, and goats. But there is textual evidence that they did control some aspects of animal husbandry on state-owned lands.

FISHING—The Tigris and Euphrates Rivers and their tributaries contained a large number of fish species. Several kinds of carp and trout, catfish, and eels were caught commercially. Raising fish in fishponds was also a widespread practice in Mesopotamia.

METALLURGY—Iron and copper were available from the Caucasus region, Asia Minor, and the Zagros Mountains. Tin also came from the Zagros Range or via trade routes from the western Mediterranean region. Iron was harder and wore well in more rugged applications. Copper and bronze (copper + tin) were still in wide use.

STONE—In Mesopotamia and Persia, specialty stone was used for decorative purposes. Wall reliefs were typically done with gypsum-alabaster. Marble or near-marble (hard limestone) was brought from the Caucasus Mountains and the Zagros Range (see *Map 1.06*) and used to make large sculptural elements like column capitals and other architectural features (see *Figure 7.16*).

Figure 7.14—Armor and weapons of Persian soldiers, Susa; glazed tiles (photo: Steven Collins)

Figure 7.15—Weapons, Babylonian and Persian (photo: Alexander Schick)

BREAKOUT 7.05

PERSIAN EMPIRE 101

The Persian Empire was founded by Cyrus II of Anshan (part of Elam). He reigned c. 559 to 530 BC. During this time he conquered most of the territory stretching from Iran to western Asia Minor. His son, Cambyses, became king in 530 BC and added Egypt to the empire. Toward the end of Cambyses's reign, his brother usurped the throne, prompting a civil war (stories vary in detail). In 522 BC Darius I, an officer in the army and distant relative of Cyrus, put down the revolt. Cambyses died of an illness, and Darius took the throne. Darius documented the civil war—along with his legitimate claim to the throne and praise to the god Ahura Mazda—with a large, multilingual, cliffside relief-carving known as the *Behistun Inscription*.

Darius continued to expand the Persian Empire during his reign, but he also organized it for efficient management. There were five imperial cities: Ecbatana, Susa, Babylon, Pasargadae (refurbished and expanded by Cyrus), and Persepolis (built by Darius). Darius and his royal entourage moved from city to city depending on the season and various state events.

Cyrus set up regions (similar states or provinces) and appointed governors (satraps), but their roles were not well defined. Satraps were usually nobles loyal to the crown. The areas under their jurisdiction were called *satrapies*, of which there were about twenty. A *medinah* (plural *medinot*) was a sector within a satrapy, perhaps a cluster of towns and villages similar to a county. Each medinah had a local administrator. For example, Judah was a medinah governed by Nehemiah within the satrapy of Ebernari (Aramaic for "land beyond the river"). Satraps had two main responsibilities—they collected imperial taxes, and they supplied conscriptions of soldiers from their satrapy when necessary.

Tribute payments were standardized, and eventually Persia began minting coins. Communication across this vast empire (see *Map 7.02*) was maintained by a messenger service over an extensive network of roads. There were transfer stations for messengers every 15 to 20 miles, as well as rest stops for travelers. Armed forces kept the highways safe, and travelers were required to have passports fashioned from leather.

Subsequent kings increased imperial taxes so much that farmers and tradesmen had a hard time paying them. Many people had to borrow to pay their taxes, then lost their farms to wealthy banking families. Often these people remained on the farms as tenants, working the land they once owned. Temples were also taxed heavily, with most of the money going to the Persian central government. Banking archives from wealthy families in Babylon document a steady increase in the number of unpaid mortgages. In Judah the situation was much the same. The people cried out for relief to their governor Nehemiah (Nehemiah 5:1-5). They resented supporting the Jerusalem temple and felt abandoned by Yahweh, as reflected in the book of Malachi.

The Persian Empire came under attack by Alexander the Great in 334 BC. By 330 BC, the last Persian king was killed, and Persia fell to Greece.

J. Bulot, S. Collins

BREAKOUT 7.06

CAPTIVITY ENDS

The captivity of the Judahites (Jews) started with multiple raids by the Babylonians that culminated in the destruction of Jerusalem by Nebuchadnezzar in 587/86 BC. Jeremiah instructed the people that, while in Babylon, they were to build houses, cultivate gardens, and practice good citizenship for the benefit of all (Jeremiah 29:5-7). This they did. They flourished in places like Babylon and al-Yahudu, managed stable ethnic communities (evidenced by the retention of traditional Yahwistic names), and became part of the fabric of the larger cities and regions. Archives of clay tablets document life inside exilic Babylonia, providing insights into the structure and life of Judahite communities that preserved their Hebrew roots.

The Jewish exile ended under Persian rule, when the Hebrews were given the right to return to Judah. This occurred by a decree of Cyrus c. 538 BC. Cyrus II had defeated the Babylonians and was engaged in a campaign of restoration predicted by the prophet Isaiah. Cyrus not only permitted the Jews to return their homeland and capital city, Jerusalem—he also allowed, and helped fund, the rebuilding of the Jerusalem temple by Zerubbabel. This rebuilt temple lacked the splendor of Solomon's masterpiece (Haggai 2:3), but it reestablished an important focal point for Jewish religious life.

Nehemiah chapter 4 speaks to the political climate of Jerusalem at that time. At first, there were local Samarians and dignitaries interested in helping build the temple. But they became enemies after they were turned away. Notable among them was the appointed governor Sanballat the Horonite, of whom there is extrabiblical evidence from excavations at Elephantine (modern Aswan, Egypt) in a papyrus dating to the reign of Darius II, c. 407 BC. Despite factions of opposition, work on the Jerusalem temple was completed around 515 BC.

B. Maggard, S. Collins

BREAKOUT 7.07

IMPORTANT EXTRABIBLICAL INSCRIPTIONS FROM THIS PERIOD

The northern kingdom of Israel fell in 722/21 BC to the Assyrian onslaught of Shalmaneser or Sargon II. This event is recorded in 2 Kings 17 and on the inscribed *Prism of Sargon II* found at Nimrud (modern Kalhu, Iraq).

Subsequently, the Babylonians conquered Assyria, then turned their attention toward Judah. There is substantial archaeological evidence at Jerusalem of massive destruction that took place there during the sixth century BC, and at other sites around the Southern Levant such as Hazor, Megiddo, and in the Beersheba Valley.

After the fall of Jerusalem to Babylon in 587/86 BC, deportations under King Nebuchadnezzar resulted in some of the Judahite

Sargon Prism (photo: Joseph Holden)

Nabonidus Cylinder, reproduction (photo: Steven Collins, courtesy of Museum of Archaeology, Trinity Southwest University)

Cyrus Cylinder, reproduction (photo: Steven Collins, courtesy of Museum of Archaeology, Trinity Southwest University)

population being forcibly relocated to Babylonia. In Babylon, Nebuchadnezzar's throne, then in the hands of Nabonidus and coregent son Belshazzar, fell to Cyrus II (c. 539 BC). Belshazzar was the last ruler in the city of Babylon when it fell to the Medes and Persians and is confirmed by several clay cylinder documents commissioned by his father Nabonidus.

Cyrus founded the Achaemenid Dynasty of Persia. He decreed that peoples who were in captivity had the right to return to their homelands. This is recorded in the biblical book of Ezra as well as in cuneiform script on a clay cylinder, the *Cyrus Cylinder*, which now resides in the British Museum.

Nehemiah returned to Judah during the reign of King Artaxerxes I, whose tomb has been found at Naqsh-e Rustam, about 12 miles from the ancient capital city of Persepolis (in Iran). Excavations at Elephantine (Aswan, Egypt) have unearthed papyrus evidence (dated to c. 407 BC) of opposition to Nehemiah (Nehemiah 2), notably governor Sanballat the Horonite. Also in Nehemiah 2 is Tobiah the Ammonite, reflected in an established family name discovered in the Transjordan west of Rabbath-Ammon. Nehemiah's third enemy, Geshem the Arabian, was a king of Qedar in northwest Arabia. His name is recorded in Wadi Tumilat (eastern Nile Delta). The *Behistun Rock*, located in present-day Iran, shows the rise of Darius I (521–486 BC) and his family line. Mentioned in Ezra 6:1-12, he succeeded Cyrus II and was a friend of Judah, the remaining people of Israel.

B. Maggard, J. Holden

TEXTILES—As in the rest of the ANE, wool and linen garments were worn across Mesopotamia and Persia. Vegetable and mineral dyes in a wide range of colors were used to create royal and upper-class clothing. The clothes of the common classes were generally left natural for everyday use.

POTTERY—Populations across the Fertile Crescent were burgeoning, and pottery production began to make big leaps in terms of mass production. Kilns were larger and firing techniques were better. But gains in quantity and overall quality affected the aesthetics of common wares, especially in the artistry of attaching handles. Fine wares were still beautifully crafted and decorated (see *Figure 7.17*).

TRADE—The needs of empires also drove the success of local industries by connecting them to international markets. By the late sixth and early fifth centuries BC, commercial routes literally connected the Persian Empire to the entire Eastern Hemisphere—China, India, Afghanistan, Egypt, Nubia, the Levant, Anatolia, Greece, Italy, Spain, and North Africa.

Figure 7.17—Pottery and objects from the Persian period (Iron Age 3) (photos: Steven Collins, James Barber, Alexander Schick, David E. Graves, Carl Morgan)

Figure 7.16—Architectural features, Babylonia and Persia (photos: Alexander Schick, James Barber, David E. Graves)

EZRA AND THE NEW JUDAISM

Ezra had set his heart to study the Law of the LORD, and to do it and to teach his statutes and rules in Israel" (Ezra 7:10). The returning exiles comprised a people known for striving against their God. Although Yahweh had steadfastly proved himself faithful as Provider and Deliverer, the Israelites had, for centuries, proved themselves an obstinate people. They resolutely lived out a painful cycle of obedience and backsliding, which often degenerated into outright rebellion. Even so, when they repented, Yahweh rescued them.

As Yahweh had warned decades earlier, Judah's disobedience resulted in the Babylonian exile and subjugation under a succession of Mesopotamian kings. Now, in order to show himself faithful and to fulfill the promises he had made to Abraham more than 1,000 years earlier, Yahweh raised up three men as rebuilders of the nation of Israel. They led the Jews in three successive exoduses out of Mesopotamia and returned them to the Promised Land.

The Persian kings Cyrus and Artaxerxes commissioned Zerubbabel, Ezra, and Nehemiah to lead the Judahites back to their homeland and give them a new beginning. The rebuilding of the Jerusalem temple by Zerubbabel reestablished the centralized, national worship of Yahweh. Ezra's restoration of the Torah as Yahweh's covenant reaffirmed their national identity as God's people. Nehemiah's faithfulness to ensuring that Jerusalem's city walls were rebuilt helped to reinstate the people's physical presence in the land by granting them security inside their Holy City. These various efforts had the cumulative effect of reinstituting the authority of Yahweh in the minds of the returned exiles. But the question remained: Would they obey their God with willing hearts?

To ensure the faithfulness of the people and the survival of the nation, Ezra focused on God's Torah commands and introduced reforms not found in the Torah. In addition to enforced general obedience to the Law of Moses, Ezra imposed a tariff—in addition to Torah-mandated tithes and offerings—to raise funds for the temple. Further, and most remarkably, Ezra forbade marriage to non-Israelites. He insisted that those already thusly wed divorce their spouses and that foreign women and their children be sent away. Many agreed to his demands. Ezra's new Judaism had a demonstrable effect on the general behavior of the people of Judah.

As harsh as his ultimatums seem to modern readers, the reality was that Judah/Israel was not ready to assert itself above its covassal neighbors of Samaria, Edom, and Ammon, much less the likes of Egypt or Persia, which ruled over them. Ezra's reforms helped to assure the former exiles' survival as a fledgling nation.

However, Ezra's attempts to solidify and purify the people were not entirely successful. Without wholehearted devotion to Yahweh, their situation remained desperate. Indeed, these children of Abraham who had returned to their homeland and possessed the promises of God still languished in spiritual exile. Although Yahweh's judgment had passed, large numbers of the Jewish people remained dispersed in far-flung places. And a long, difficult road lay ahead for them.

J. Barber, S. Collins

BREAKOUT 7.09

NEHEMIAH: JERUSALEM AND ITS WALL

Born in Babylon during the Judahite captivity, Nehemiah had never been to Jerusalem. He was cup-bearer to the king of Persia. In the twentieth year of King Artaxerxes, his comrade Hanani and others had just returned from Judah. Nehemiah questioned them about the Jews who had escaped captivity and the state of affairs in Jerusalem. Hanani reported that Jerusalem was in ruins and the people were in great despair. Its city walls were heaps of rubble and char.

Nehemiah was heartbroken. Upon hearing of Jerusalem's deplorable conditions, he "sat down and wept and mourned for days" (Nehemiah 1:4). Nehemiah immediately turned to Yahweh and "continued fasting and praying before the God of heaven." The king had never seen him so distraught. Artaxerxes asked what was wrong, and Nehemiah told him about Jerusalem and the condition of his people. The king responded with genuine concern, whereupon Nehemiah sought permission to go and rebuild the city of his fathers. Artaxerxes agreed.

As with previous attempts to rebuild Jerusalem, enemies who inhabited the area went to great lengths to distract, accuse, mock, conspire against, intimidate, and attack the Jews in attempts to hinder them from completing the building project. But Nehemiah was focused and determined. Because of his organizational skills, the project proceeded at fever pitch, to the point that work continued 24 hours a day with two sets of crews. While one worked, the other, outfitted with armor, stood guard with spears, shields, and bows.

In spite of nagging adversity, Nehemiah and the local Jews continued work unabated by the shenanigans of their enemies. Prayers were offered up as well, and Nehemiah's trust in Yahweh was their protection. Yet trouble came not only from the outside, but the inside as well. The people had been laboring tirelessly, working so intensely that the only time they changed their clothes was to wash them. Informants from within tried to trick Nehemiah into paying a visit to his enemies. But they only meant him harm, and he knew it. Relentlessly, the construction continued. Finally, Jerusalem had risen from the rubble. The job was finished.

Despite all the difficulties, the city walls were completed in just 52 days. New doors were hung at the gateways. Jerusalem was again a fortified city. Excavations by Kathleen Kenyon in the 1960s revealed a section of Nehemiah's wall located above the City of David. Nehemiah had mostly rebuilt the previous city walls, but the excavations revealed a new section that was built north of the City of David because the original wall foundation was so badly destroyed and pilfered that it was better to start from scratch.

E. Lovato, S. Collins

BREAKOUT 7.10

LOCAL OPPOSITION TO THE WORK OF EZRA AND NEHEMIAH

Both Ezra and Nehemiah were born in Babylon. There are many parallels between them. They both set out from Babylon to help rebuild Jerusalem. Ezra was a priest and scribe from the line of Aaron who wrote scrolls of the Torah. Nehemiah was King Artaxerxes's cup-bearer—a high "office" given only to a most-trusted individual whose service of tasting the food and drink of the king guarded the monarch from potential assassination attempts. Both set out to do the work of Yahweh in Jerusalem, and each encountered local opposition.

Like Nehemiah, Ezra was active in Babylon and was well known as a teacher and scholar. But his heart was always with those in Jerusalem. Each man, in his time, had the full support of the reigning king of Persia to return to Jerusalem to rebuild the temple of Yahweh, which had not stood since the Babylonian conquest of Judah almost three generations before.

The Assyrians began, and the Babylonians continued, the practice of deporting populations from their homeland and resettling them in the distant reaches of their empires. This being the case, non-Judahite "foreigners" had occupied Jerusalem and were claiming the land. This created a difficult situation for the Jews returning from exile. Upon arriving at Jerusalem, both Nehemiah and Ezra stirred up anger among the local inhabitants, who feared the returning Jews would flood in and take over (see *Breakout 7.09*).

After Ezra and his group of returnees arrived, the temple foundations were laid in the second month of the following year (536 BC), all under priestly supervision. This done, the assembly burst out in praise to Yahweh, singing the very hymn that David had composed on the occasion of housing the Ark of the Covenant in its new tabernacle on Mount Zion (1 Chronicles 16). Because of their excitement, everyone in the area could hear the sound of praise, which angered the non-Jewish locals. Fearing what the locals might do, Ezra and Nehemiah prayed to God for protection. Each had set out to accomplish the work of God—Ezra to reinstate the Law of Moses and temple worship, and Nehemiah to restore the fortifications that protected the Holy City. Both succeeded.

E. Lovato, S. Collins

CHAPTER 8

THE WORLD BETWEEN THE OLD AND NEW TESTAMENTS

WELCOME TO THE PERSIAN AND HELLENISTIC PERIODS (539–63 BC)

The invasion of Greece by Xerxes in 481–479 BC foreshadowed the eventual demise of the Persian Empire some 150 years later. In 334 BC, Alexander of Macedon—soon to be known as Alexander the Great—launched an invasion of the Persian Empire following the same route, in reverse, traversed by Xerxes. In 332 BC, Alexander marched over the Fertile Crescent, subduing everything in his path. By 327 BC, he had reached the Indus Valley (modern east Pakistan and northwest India), but his troops refused to go any further. He died soon thereafter (see *Breakout 8.02*).

Alexander's legacy, Hellenism, was the most powerful cultural influence of the *intertestamental period* (the historical gap between the Old and New Testaments). After much political and military maneuvering, two of Alexander's generals, Seleucus and Ptolemy, carved up most of the Near East between themselves. Seleucus, based in Babylon, controlled the northern and eastern territories, while Ptolemy took Egypt. Eventually the Seleucid Dynasty wrested control of Syria and Palestine from the Ptolemies. One Seleucid ruler, Antiochus IV Epiphanes (215–163 BC), attempted to eliminate traditional Jewish culture (see *Breakout 8.01*) in Palestine (Southern Levant or Canaan). His reign of terror against the Jews was ended by the Maccabean Revolt, whereby the Jews were able to regain control of Jerusalem and the surrounding region until the Romans came in 63 BC.

GEOGRAPHY

Until the coming of Alexander the Great, Judea remained under the hegemony of the Persian Empire, along with the entire Near East (see *Map 7.02*). With Alexander's conquests, the political map changed once again. The south Levant passed from Alexander, to Ptolemy, and later to Seleucus (see *Map 8.02*). The Maccabees eventually wrested control of Judea, which remained in Jewish hands until the coming of the Romans (see *Map 8.03*).

CHRONOLOGY

For biblical purposes, the chronology of the Southern Levant (Palestine) is our focus. It can be divided up like this (see *Timeline*):

CHRONOLOGY OF THE SOUTHERN LEVANT (PALESTINE)	
539–332 BC	Persian Empire
332–323 BC	Alexander's Empire
323–198 BC	Under the Ptolemies
198–157 BC	Under the Seleucids
167–142 BC	Maccabean Revolt
142–63 BC	Hasmonean Judea
63 BC onward	Roman Control

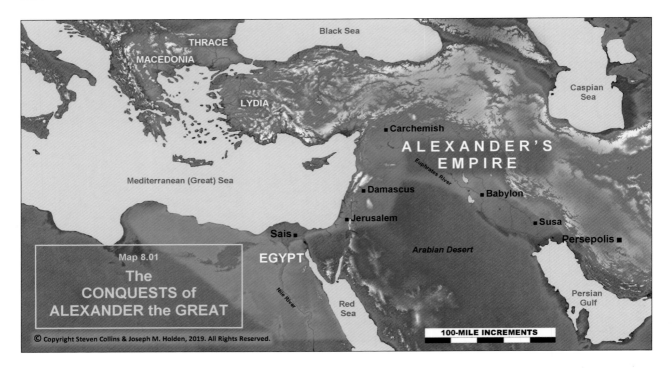

HISTORY

The book of Nehemiah contains the last identifiable historical references of the Old Testament. In the New Testament, additional datable events begin with the birth of Jesus and the death of Herod the Great. This leaves a gap of about 450 years that is covered by neither Old nor New Testament and is called the intertestamental period. However, these four-and-a-half centuries contain some of the most important events in Western history, including the unification of the ANE by the Persians, the conquest of the Persian Empire by Alexander the Great, the imposition of the Hellenistic culture on the Western world, and the *Pax Romana* (Roman Peace) enacted by the ascendancy of the Roman Empire. These events prepared the way for the rapid spread of the Christian gospel—all were prophesied in the writings of the prophet Daniel.

The Persians, early in their rise to empire status, attempted to regain control of the coast of Asia Minor, which was populated by Greek colonies. Athens interfered with these Persian attempts and incurred the wrath of the Persian kings, who twice attacked the Greeks. The first attack, initiated by Darius I in 490

BC, ended in disaster for the invading Persians at the Battle of Marathon.

Xerxes (known as Ahasuerus in the book of Esther) orchestrated a second attack in 480 BC. His enormous expedition of combined land and naval forces broke through a small Greek force that held the Thermopylae Pass, then burned the city of Athens, an event never forgiven by the Greeks. Later, the Persian navy was destroyed by the Greek navy in the Bay of Salamis, and the rest of the Persian land forces were defeated the following spring. Persia never again seriously threatened the Greeks, although hostilities between the two empires persisted for another 150 years.

ALEXANDER THE GREAT

In 334 BC, Alexander of Macedon (who would go on to become Alexander the Great; see *Figure 8.01* and *Breakout 8.02*), launched an invasion of the Persian Empire (see *Map 8.01*). He defeated three Persian armies, including two that were commanded by then-current Persian king Darius III. In 333–331 BC, Alexander marched over the Fertile Crescent, subduing

everything in his path. After arriving at the Indus Valley in 327 BC, Alexander had to stop because his troops refused to do further battle. Turning back to Babylon, Alexander pondered additional conquests, but died from a fever (or poison?). Though this man of many excesses was dead, the collective Greek influence (Hellenism; see *Breakout 8.03*) imposed upon the Near East by his conquests was profound.

Alexander had left behind the largest empire in the world without a chosen successor. His generals fought among themselves for the next 25 years and, when the dust settled, two men emerged as the primary successors to Alexander: Seleucus and Ptolemy (see *Breakout 8.04*). They carved up most of the Near East region between themselves. Ptolemy, a senior general in the army of Alexander, occupied Egypt almost immediately upon Alexander's death, heading off any similar action by his rivals (see *Map 8.02* and *Breakout 8.05*). Seleucus, a somewhat junior officer in Alexander's army, took control of most of the rest of Alexander's conquered regions, including what today comprises Syria, Iraq, Iran, Afghanistan, and Pakistan, as far east as India.

Figure 8.01—Alexander the Great (photo: David E. Graves)

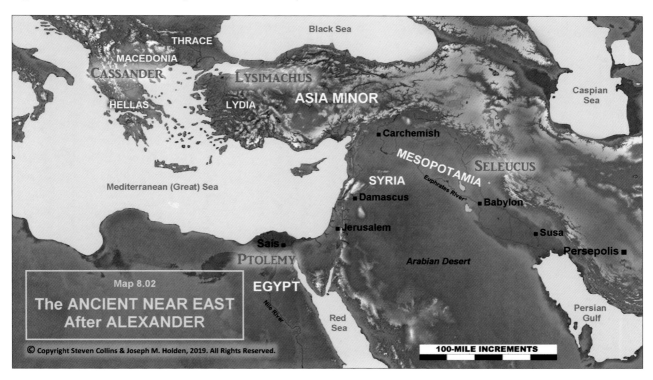

BREAKOUT 8.01

THE JEWISH SYNAGOGUE

There is no mention of synagogues anywhere in the Hebrew Bible. They appear frequently in the four Gospels and in the book of Acts. The concept of the synagogue originated in Babylon during the exile. There were two major reasons for the 70 years of Babylonian captivity: first, for the people's failure of observing the sabbatical years; and second, the people's involvement in idolatry. So God brought Israel right into the world epicenter of idolatry: Babylon. There, the Jewish people were finally cured of their tendency toward embracing false gods, which, in turn, led to the establishment of the synagogue.

The initial purpose of synagogues was not to serve as centers of worship, but as schools to teach the truths of the Mosaic Law and the prophets. When the people returned from Babylon, synagogues were introduced into the land of Israel. But exactly when this happened is not clear. There is no mention of synagogues in the post-exilic historical books of Ezra and Nehemiah, nor in the post-captivity prophetic books of Haggai, Zechariah, or Malachi. The earliest records of synagogues in the land come from the Greek/Hellenistic era in the second century BC. As the Gospels and Acts show, by the first century AD, synagogues were found all over the land of Israel, Babylonia, Europe, and Asia Minor.

Before AD 70, the synagogue's purpose remained the same as it was in Babylonia. Furthermore, the Torah, the five books of Moses, were divided into 54 sections, and each Sabbath the same section was read at every synagogue everywhere in the world. Following the reading of the Law came a reading from the *Nevi'im*, the Prophets. However, not all the prophets were read, only selections. The reading was then followed by a message from the rabbi based on what had been read either from the Law or the Prophets. Moreover, only portions from the *K'tuvim* were read—not every Sabbath, but on special occasions, such as the reading of the Song of Solomon during Passover, or the reading of Jonah during Yom Kippur, the Day of Atonement.

After the destruction of the Jewish temple in AD 70—at the rabbinic council of Yavneh where the Sanhedrin was then operating—the synagogue replaced the temple as the center of Jewish spiritual life, and rabbis replaced the priests as spiritual leaders. In time, the synagogue became more than a school and included worship meant to imitate the worship that

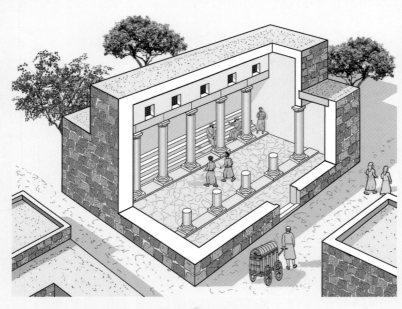

The Capernaum synagogue (drawing: Leen Ritmeyer)

took place at the temple. Thus, the daily morning and evening sacrifices led to the daily morning and evening synagogue services. There had also been Sabbath services in the temple, so additional services were scheduled in the synagogue for the Sabbath. For the Day of Atonement there are now five services in the synagogue, as there were in the temple.

With the rise of less-orthodox synagogues, the format described above is not necessarily followed, but for those who practice Orthodox and ultra-Orthodox Judaism, the above pattern continues.

A. Fruchtenbaum

In 198 BC, Antiochus III ("the Great"), a descendant of the first Seleucus, wrested control of the Levant (Canaan) from the Ptolemies. His son, Antiochus IV (Epiphanes), cruelly oppressed the Jews in his attempt to eliminate their faith and replace it with Greek religion and philosophy—a severe attempt at Hellenization (see *Breakout 8.06*).

MACCABEAN REVOLT AND HASMONEAN RULE

The oppression of Antiochus IV led to rebellion by the Jews, dubbed the *Maccabean Revolt*, which lasted from 167 until 142 BC (see *Breakout 8.08*). The insurgency was initiated by the five sons of Mattathius Hasmon, an elderly village priest. Judah (Judas), the leader of the rebellion, had the nickname Maccabee (meaning "Hammer"), and the name was appended to the revolt. One of the key victories was regaining control of the temple in Jerusalem from the Seleucids, along with its subsequent cleansing and purification in 165 BC. This event was the first *Hanukkah*, celebrated annually since that time.

When the revolt finally wound down, four of the Hasmon (thus, Hasmonean) brothers were dead, but the Jews had attained independence (see *Map 8.03*). Simon, the last surviving brother, ascended the throne of the newly independent kingdom. For nearly a century after the Maccabean Revolt, the area of Palestine was ruled by Simon and his descendants—that is, until the Romans arrived in 63 BC. The Hasmoneans were every bit as corrupt and tyrannical as any of the foreign leaders of the previous 500 years, so there was little change in the daily lives of the Jewish people.

Two Hasmonean brothers—Hyrcanus II and Aristobulus II—battled for the positions of king and high priest. When civil war was about to break out between the two, they both appealed for assistance from Pompey, a Roman general stationed in Syria at the time who was annexing Syria to the Roman Empire. The end result of their appeals to Pompey was the Roman annexation of Palestine as well in 63 BC. The Roman legions quickly dominated Egypt, the Levant, and northern Mesopotamia (see *Breakout 8.09*).

HELLENISM AND THE TRANSLATION OF THE HEBREW SCRIPTURES

The Greeks prized learning, and the Romans prized Greek culture. The great Greek centers of culture at Cyrene, Tarsus, Rhodes, the islands of Cos and Samos, and Syracuse (on Sicily) fostered the Hellenization process at great distances from its epicenter at Athens. But the highest concentration of Greek scholarship was in Alexandria, Egypt. Ptolemy I Soter (c. 323–283 BC) founded the famed Library of Alexandria, the largest library in the Greek world, and Ptolemy II Philadelphus (c. 283–246 BC) was its greatest patron.

During the Early Roman period, great strides were made in the areas of historical writing, poetry, prose, philosophy, science, and medicine. However, Greek cultural influences were not confined to intellectual pursuits. Greek city planning and architecture brought a new organization and look to the cities of the Near East. The widespread use of the Greek language helped launch a new era of vigorous trade and commerce throughout the Mediterranean

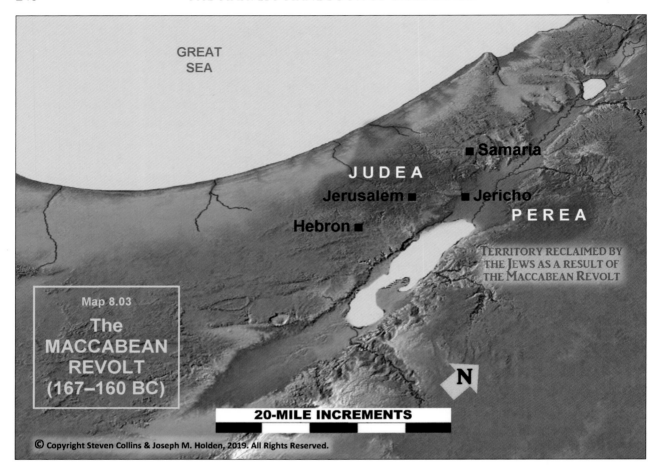

GREAT
SEA

■ Samaria

JUDEA

Jerusalem ■   ■ Jericho

PEREA

Hebron ■

TERRITORY RECLAIMED BY
THE JEWS AS A RESULT OF
THE MACCABEAN REVOLT

Map 8.03

The
MACCABEAN
REVOLT
(167–160 BC)

N

20-MILE INCREMENTS

world, even as far as eastern Mesopotamia. Educated Romans were expected to read and understand Greek as well as Latin.

Hellenism also had a profound influence on Judaism, especially for Jews of the Diaspora (those dispersed from the Holy Land). Thus, a Greek translation of the Hebrew Scriptures was needed. This work was done in Alexandria during the mid-third century BC under the patronage of Ptolemy Philadelphus and became known as the Septuagint (LXX; see *Breakout 8.07*).

The incorporation of most of the Near East into the Roman Empire brought about a new era of stability. Although the famed *Pax Romana* and rule of law was enforced with an iron hand, local rulers were often left in place as a matter of appeasement and regional control. In Judaea, the Hasmonean/Herodian rulers were thus subsumed and used by the Roman government.

RISE OF HEROD THE GREAT

In 40 BC, Herod ("the Great")—an Idumean and the son of an assassinated governor of Judea who also had contacts within the Nabatean sphere (see *Breakout 8.12*)—sponsored by Octavian and Mark Antony, was appointed by the Roman senate to take the throne of Judea as king of the Jews (see *Breakout 8.10*). He was, of course, merely a Roman appointee, along the lines of a governor/procurator, but was permitted to bear the title of king. Herod was given enormous latitude in how he governed his subjects. Part of the arrangement for him to become king was that he would drive out the Parthians who had attacked and occupied Jerusalem in 40 BC. Herod retook the land with great brutality and was finally able to sit on the throne in Jerusalem in 37 BC.

Herod was a tyrannical monster who ruled with

BREAKOUT 8.02

ALEXANDER THE GREAT

Alexander the Great (Alexander III; 356 BC–323 BC) ruled the Greek kingdom of Macedon (331–323 BC). As a youth he was tutored by Aristotle (384–322 BC) until he was 16. At the age of 20 he ascended to the throne following the assassination of his father, Philip II. Alexander is most famous for launching a military campaign that stretched his control from Greece to northwest India, resulting in one of the largest empires of the ancient world. He was just 30 years old at the time!

In 334 BC, Alexander invaded the Persian (Achaemenid) Empire. This was a ten-year campaign that ended in the defeat of Persia's King Darius III and the looting and destruction by fire of their capital, Persepolis, in 330 BC. In Orosius's words, "…after this he [Alexander] headed for India [326 BC], in order to make the Great Outer Ocean and the ends of the East the bounds of his empire." He was victorious at the Battle of the Hydaspes but was forced to turn back due to the demands of his homesick troops. Preparing to invade Arabia, Alexander was struck by an illness while in Babylon and died in June of 323 BC. Today he is considered one of history's greatest military commanders, undefeated in battle.

Alexander, following his father's goals, imposed Greek culture, religion, and language (Hellenism) on the territories he conquered. The Greek language promoted by Alexander the Great became the *lingua franca* across his conquered territories, for both business and political purposes. Known as Koine Greek, it remained in use until about AD 500. This fostered a merging of Greek culture and practices with local cultural elements that, in many areas, has lasted into modern times.

Hellenism (see *Breakout 8.03*) created a marked distinction between Hellenized Jews (who kept their Jewish identity but without the strict religious adherence, and adopted Greek culture) and non-Hellenized Jews. After Alexander's death, because Israel was located between the Hellenistic Seleucid and Ptolemaic kingdoms, it experienced civil instability and conflict as non-Hellenized Jews resisted the dominant culture.

D. Graves

Silver coin of Alexander (photo: Steven Collins)

BREAKOUT 8.03

THE INFLUENCE OF HELLENISM

Hellenism refers to the adoption of Greek culture—including art, architecture, language, lifestyle, and philosophy—by non-Greek peoples. After Alexander the Great conquered the eastern Mediterranean lands (332 BC), which included Judea, he attempted to syncretize the Greek and Asian populations (see *Breakout 8.02*). Alexander organized mass marriage ceremonies between his Greek officers and local women, identified local gods with Greek deities, founded and named new cities with Greek names, sponsored Greek athletic games, and maintained the Greek language as the official language of government.

After his death in 323 BC, Alexander's generals divided the empire into four parts and continued the process of Hellenization. Judea both resisted and adopted the growing Greek influence. One result of adoption was the Septuagint (designated by Roman numerals for 70, LXX), the Greek translation of the Old Testament, produced by 70 Jewish scholars in Alexandria, Egypt. By the time of Jesus, the people of Judea spoke a dialect of Aramaic, but Greek continued as the international language of the Roman Empire. The New Testament authors used Greek as the original language of the New Testament, rather than the ancestral Hebrew or the colloquial Aramaic.

Many of the people of Judea resisted the rush to Hellenize. Active resistance brought about the Maccabean Revolt and the subsequent independent state of Judea. It also influenced the decision of the Essenes to move from Jerusalem into the wilderness at Qumran, where they lived separated from the "polluting" influence of Jerusalem and produced the Dead Sea Scrolls.

Examples of Hellenization in Judea are found in *The Antiquities of the Jews* by the Jewish/Roman historian Flavius Josephus. He shows the extent of Hellenism when he recounts that a candidate for the Jewish high priesthood, Joshua, changed his name to Jason, while his brother, Onias, who was awarded the high priesthood, changed his name to Menalaus. Both very-Greek names were extraordinary for a Jewish high priest, unless the position had become highly politicized by the influence of Antiochus's Greek government. Josephus further records that Menalaus informed King Antiochus that leading Jewish families in Jerusalem desired to fully practice a Greek lifestyle and requested permission to build a gymnasium in Jerusalem. Gymnasia were facilities where Greek sports like wrestling and boxing were practiced in the nude. Josephus also informs us that many of the Jewish gymnasium participants sought to hide the fact they were circumcised. Such was an affront to all religious Jews.

The Hellenization of Judea lasted from 332 BC, when Alexander the Great visited Jerusalem, to 63 BC, when power shifted to Rome with the coming of the Roman general Pompey. However, the effects of Hellenization endured long after the Roman destruction of Jerusalem in AD 70.

F. Policastro, S. Collins

an iron hand. His many excesses were tolerated by the Romans because he was a personal friend of Octavian. Octavian became Caesar Augustus (see *Figure 8.02* and *Breakout 8.11*), the first emperor of Rome, about four years after his victory at Actium in 31 BC. Cleopatra VII, the last Ptolemy to sit on the "Egyptian" throne, had joined forces with Mark Antony in a naval engagement against Octavian—known as the Battle of Actium, off the western coast of Greece. Octavian won. Cleopatra committed suicide, as did her lover, Mark Antony. Egypt was subsequently annexed into the Roman Empire.

Herod the Great had as many as ten wives and numerous children, most of whom were raised and educated in the household of Caesar in Rome. As a result, many of the later Herods were also politically powerful men because of their personal friendships with the first four Roman emperors. King Herod executed several members of his own family, accusing them of treason (either real or imagined). Thousands of his subjects were also executed during his bloody reign.

The enlargement of the Temple Mount—with its enormous supporting platform—is just one of the many major construction projects commissioned by Herod the Great during his reign (see *Breakout 9.06*), and the expansion and refurbishing of the temple and surrounding buildings continued after he died in c. 4 BC. His death was celebrated throughout the Roman province of Judaea (Judea), including several destructive, celebratory riots. His kingdom was divided among three of his sons—Archelaus, Antipas, and Philip.

As a result of the political and religious situation in Judea/Palestine during the closing decades of the intertestamental period, Jewish life was complicated. The synagogue system, operated by local rabbis, was the foundation of every Jewish community (see *Breakout 8.01*). But there were many religious factions, and each had its political leanings. Some linked up with the Roman-controlled Herodians. Others wanted to throw off the Roman yoke. A few abandoned what they perceived as a corrupt Judaism and sought geographical isolation (see *Breakout 8.13*). Thus, the stage was set for the New Testament era.

PEOPLES AND KINGDOMS

PERSIA—Persia conquered Babylon in 536 BC. This gave conquered peoples the right to return to their homelands, the Jews included. Persia had a vast geographical area to control, and under the rule of Cyrus, and later Darius (see *Breakout 7.05*), instituted local governing *satrapies* controlling regions on behalf the central government. The empire was sectioned into provinces, and generally local religious, political, and cultural institutions functioned with a degree of autonomy. Darius III (Codomannus) was overthrown by Alexander in 330 BC (see *Breakout 8.02*), but the underlying structure of what had been the Persian Empire helped to facilitate his ability to control his own empire.

GREECE/MACEDONIA—Greece proper occupied the southern part of the Balkan Peninsula—with Macedonia just to its north—and the islands of the Aegean Sea (see *Map 8.01*). In the fifth century BC,

Figure 8.02—Caesar Augustus image (photo: David E. Graves)

Athens was the seat of one of the greatest golden ages of civilization. Athenian thought would lead to what would later become the Hellenism fostered by the conquests of Alexander the Great (see *Breakout 8.03*).

NABATEANS—An Arab tribal people living east of Edom (see *Breakout 8.12*). After the dissolution of Edom they migrated west, forcing the weakened Edomite population to move west into the southern part of Judah. The Nabateans took over the Edomite capital of Petra and, because they controlled vital trade routes, were able to build a prosperous commercial empire. Known for elaborate structures carved into the rock cliffs at Petra, they were conquered by the Romans in AD 106. The Nabateans and their "Rose City" (Petra) gradually declined after trade was diverted through Palmyra during the second century AD. They are not mentioned in the Bible, but the Nabateans converted to Christianity during the Byzantine era.

EGYPT—When Alexander died, Ptolemy took control of Egypt. The Ptolemaic kingdom battled with the Seleucids over control of the Southern Levant. In 198 BC, Egypt was defeated in the battle of Panion, after which Judea was annexed to the Seleucid kingdom based in Syria. While the "royal" Ptolemaic line of rulers—including several Cleopatras (see *Breakout 8.11*)—were thoroughly Greek and not Egyptian, they adopted the local Egyptian culture lock, stock, and barrel. But, of course, they spoke Greek.

STATUS OF THE LEVANT—The Levant during the intertestamental period was ruled by successive kingdoms and empires: the Persians (to 332 BC; see *Breakout 7.05*), the Greeks of Alexander (332–323 BC; see *Breakout 8.02*), the Ptolemies (323–198 BC; see *Breakout 8.04*), the Seleucids (198–165 BC; see *Breakout 8.04*), the Maccabees (165–63 BC; see *Breakout 8.08*), and finally the Romans (63 BC onward; see *Breakout 8.09*).

ROME—Rome (probably an Etruscan name) came from a mixed ethnic group around the Tiber River on the Italian Peninsula. As the Etruscans faded into history, most of Italy was Roman by the middle of the third century BC. The three Punic wars between Rome and Carthage started in 264 BC and ended in 146 BC, with the Romans prevailing. Rome defeated Greece at the battle of Corinth in 146 BC, effectively ending the Greek city-states. By the first century AD, Rome controlled the entire Mediterranean world and beyond (see *Breakout 8.09* and *Map 9.01*).

HASMONEANS/MACCABEES—A Jewish family (the Hasmons) given the nickname Maccabee initiated a revolt against the Seleucid kingdom and its ruler Antiochus IV Epiphanes. The revolt started in 168 BC. The eventual leader, Judah Maccabee, cleansed the temple, which had been defiled by Antiochus, giving rise to the festival of Hanukkah. Judah/Judas was at first politically stalemated due to religious disagreements, but eventually the causes became unified. After a good bit of political intrigue and battles against the Seleucid army, Judea gained its independence in 141 BC (see *Breakouts 8.06, 8.08*).

SOCIETY AND CULTURE

GREEKS—It was Hellenism that captured the Roman mind (see *Breakout 8.03*). The Greek language dominated the Roman world as the *lingua franca* of commerce. During this period, literature, philosophy, science, and medicine made great strides. Greek culture influenced everything from academics to architecture, giving a different look to cities across the eastern part of the empire, including in the Levant.

ROMANS—Beginning about 63 BC, the incorporation of most of the Near East into the Roman Empire brought about a new era of stability. With the Roman Peace, tens of thousands of miles of primary and secondary roads, Koine Greek (used to write the New Testament), law-reinforcing military legions, trained architects and engineers and builders, advanced architectural and infrastructure technologies, and a vast reservoir of slaves, the Romans built what became the greatest empire in the history of the world prior to the modern era (see *Breakout 8.09* and *Map 9.01*).

JUDEA—The situation here was complicated—really complicated! Jewish factions irritated each other

BREAKOUT 8.04

THE HELLENISTIC STATES: SELEUCIDS AND PTOLEMIES

Hellenization is the name given to the policy of Alexander the Great to unite his empire through Greek influences (see *Breakout 8.03*).

The Greeks divided the known world into two parts—*Hellenes* (Greeks) and *barbarians* (foreigners whose "ugly" languages sounded like "bar bar bar bar bar" to the Greek ear). Nonetheless, Alexander realized the importance of encouraging local cooperation. In the early years, when he set out to crush Persian resistance, he knew that anything done on his part to garner support from a native population was paramount. Following this protocol, Alexander made sacrifices at the temple in Jerusalem and participated in the temple rituals in Egypt.

Alexander conquered key ports from Issus (Turkey) to Alexandria (Egypt), securing lines of communication back to Macedonia, where he hired Greek heavy infantry (hoplites) to replace the casualties of his continuing wars of conquest. In addition to Greeks, Alexander mustered into service several thousand soldiers from both Samaria and Judea before marching to Egypt in 334 BC.

Alexander's policy of imposing Greek culture on conquered lands was based on his belief that the Greeks were superior to all societies in warfare, learning, language, art, architecture, technology, philosophy, and lifestyle. He established cities, each named Alexandria, along trade routes and at strategic points in the empire. These new cities were garrisoned by mercenary troops and led by Greeks, often wounded veterans from his army. Greek was the official language of these cities. Local elites who wished to retain their influence had to learn Greek and adopt Hellenic styles of dress, worship, and even entertainment. Eventually, almost every city of any size built Greek-style marketplaces, theaters, gymnasia, and bathhouses. They became islands of Greek culture and influence in the conquered lands.

After Alexander's death (323 BC), his empire was divided between his four main generals—Lysimachus, Cassander, Ptolemy, and Seleucus, collectively known as the *Diadochoi* ("successors"). Initially they fought each other to become supreme ruler, but as the civil wars continued into their second and third decades, the empire devolved into four rival kingdoms separated along geographical lines. The two Hellenistic kingdoms that influenced Jews living in the Southern Levant—returnees under Ezra and Nehemiah, c. 444/45 BC—were the Seleucids (based in Antioch of Syria) and the Ptolemies (based in Alexandria, Egypt). Jews were granted citizenship in both kingdoms and even served in their respective armies. Ptolemy II built the library at Alexandria and sponsored the translation of the Hebrew Scriptures into Greek.

The Jews in Antioch and Alexandria spoke Greek, exercised in the gymnasiums, went to the theaters, and dined (*symposia*) with Greeks. Dinners included nonkosher wine, foods, and easy intimacy with the hosts' slaves or paid entertainers—all forbidden by Jewish law. However, for more than 150 years, Judah/Judea's elite families and high priests (appointed by the king) were seduced by the power, wealth, and culture of the Greeks. The wealthier coastal and urban Jews were more Hellenized than the rural populations.

In 198 BC, Antiochus III, the sixth Seleucid king, defeated the army of Ptolemaic Egypt near the headwaters of the Jordan River, annexing Samaria, Judah, and Idumea. The gentle persuasion of Ptolemy was replaced by the enforced Hellenization that took place during the reign of Antiochus IV.

H. Gullet, J. Holden

BREAKOUT 8.05

THE ROSETTA STONE

The discovery of the *Rosetta Stone* in 1799 by Boussard, one of Napoleon's soldiers, was the key to the decipherment of Egyptian hieroglyphics. The stone is named after the town of Rosetta (Rashid) in the Nile Delta region of Egypt, where it was discovered. The stone was moved to Cairo, where Napoleon had it copied. When the French surrendered Egypt to the British in 1801, the inscribed stone then passed into British hands. It is now on exhibit in the British Museum.

The Rosetta Stone, which weighs more a ton, is an irregularly shaped slab of black basalt about 5.7 feet high, 2.5 feet wide, and 9 inches thick. The inscription is comprised of two languages: Egyptian and Greek. The two Egyptian sections are written in *hieroglyphics* (top 14 lines) and *demotic* (Egyptian, "shorthand"; middle 32 lines). The third section (bottom 54 lines) is written in Koinē Greek, making the inscription bilingual and not trilingual. Essentially, the text in each section was the same. Early nineteenth-century scholars who could read the Greek portion were then able to decipher the Egyptian and demotic sections. It may be that the purpose for the great diversity of scripts was to ensure that the message—a high priestly decree—was communicated to as many people as possible.

Before 1800, attempts to decipher the Egyptian scripts on the stone were unsuccessful. The hieroglyphic pictures were believed to be mystical symbols, not a script for writing a language. In 1802, A.I.S. de Sacy and J.D. Akerblad made some progress when they identified several proper names in the demotic text by comparing it with the Greek text.

Further work was carried out by T. Young, an accomplished linguist. He discovered that the royal names were written within ovals (*cartouches*), and he worked out from these a phonetic alphabet. In 1814, he figured out that the eyes of the birds and animals in the pictorial script "faced" the beginning of a sentence. Difficulty came when he failed to recognise that the demotic and hieroglyphic sections were paraphrases and not literal translations. As a result, not all the characters lined up perfectly.

Jean-Francois Champollion continued the work with the discovery that the hieroglyphic text was the translation of the Greek, not the reverse, as had been thought. Working with a meagre alphabet compiled from handwritten notes he had taken in Egypt, and skillfully applying his knowledge of Coptic (Egyptian

Rosetta Stone (photo: Alexander Schick)

written with the Greek alphabet), he successfully deciphered the Rosetta Stone. In 1822 and 1823, he presented his findings before the Academy of Inscriptions in London.

The true significance of the Rosetta Stone is not in its message, but rather in the role it played in helping to decipher Egyptian hieroglyphics. Until 1822, Egyptian history, as told on the walls of tombs and monuments, lay in mystical silence as curious-but-unknowable symbols. Champollion's brilliant work with the Rosetta Stone opened up 3,000 years of written Egyptian history, essential for the study of the humanities as well as the illumination of many biblical texts.

D. Graves

enough for there to be discord (see *Breakout 9.04*). The populace, for the most part, hated the Herodians (see *Breakouts 8.10, 9.02*) and despised Rome's control (see *Breakout 8.09*). Judea was a powder keg waiting to explode, and there were plenty of sparks. Eventually, the Romans would find their patience pushed to the breaking point (see *Breakout 9.16*).

LANGUAGE AND WRITING

GREEK—The Minoans and Mycenaean Greeks had developed both pictographic and linear scripts during the second millennium BC. Linear A script didn't last long (it has never been deciphered). The writing of Greek with Linear B script died out with the demise of the Mycenaean civilization in Greece c. 1100 BC. The Semitic alphabet—used to write all the languages of the Levant—came with Phoenician maritime traders to the Greek world. The Greeks loved it and adopted it (see *Figure 8.03*). By the eighth century BC, the archaic Greek alphabet was well established, generally resembling the letter forms of the West Semitic alphabet of the eleventh century BC. Even though the Greeks had borrowed their script from the Phoenicians—they were well aware of the origin of their alphabet and wrote often about it—they did contribute an important innovation of their own: They added vowel signs. For their vowels, they used Semitic letters not already used for Greek consonants: *aleph* became alpha (A); *he* became epsilon (E); *yod* became iota (I); *'ayin* became omicron (O); *waw* (also adopted for other sounds) became upsilon (U).

LATIN—The Latin or Roman alphabet is derived from the archaic Greek script. The Roman system of writing played a most important role in the history of civilization. During the Roman period, the Latin alphabet had 23 letters. Today there are 26 letters due to the addition of *J, U,* and *W. J* and *U* were invented to allow a visual distinction between them and the sounds of *I* and *V. W* was invented in the eleventh century AD to designate the sound halfway between *V* and *U. Latin script is used for writing most European languages, including French, Spanish, Italian, German, and English.

ARAMAIC—This is a dialect of the Northwest Semitic family of languages that had spread through the Fertile Crescent in the first millennium BC. Aramaic originated with the Arameans, who were located in the region around the Euphrates River and what is now west Syria. As the Assyrians spread westward after 1000 BC, absorbing the Arameans, the language began to penetrate into the Assyrian sphere. By the time the Babylonians conquered the Assyrians in the sixth century BC, Aramaic was so widespread that it became the official language of the Neo-Babylonian Empire. The Jews exiled to Babylon picked up the language there, which was easy for them to learn because Hebrew and Aramaic were closely related. Aramaic followed the Jews back from Babylon to Judea, where it comingled with Hebrew to eventually become the Aramaic of the New Testament era.

HEBREW—Hebrew was always at the core of Jewish life. The language was kept alive by scribes and rabbis in the copying and studying of the Hebrew Scriptures, and it was taught to Jewish boys so they could read the Torah. Even with the availability of the Greek translation of the Old Testament, the Septuagint, the Hebrew Scriptures still had their place in conservative Jewish circles. However, the street language of Palestinian Jews in this and the New Testament era was the related Aramaic dialect that was, to be sure, influenced by Hebrew.

Figure 8.03—Early Greek alphabet on a kylix (L); undeciphered archaic-proto-Greek (Minoan) characters on the Phaistos Disk from Bronze Age Crete (R) (photos: David E. Graves, Steven Collins)

BELIEF AND RELIGION

JUDAISM—The Judaism of the intertestamental period was the final permutation of the Yahwism that had its earliest beginnings in the life of Abraham. Prior to the Babylonian exile, the religious observances of the Israelites and Judahites had been corrupted by local pagan influences. In spite of the revealed Mosaic Law, preexile public Yahwism had no fixed structure or observance. It was, literally, all over the map. However, the exile brought about a 180-degree shift. For the first time in many centuries, the public focus was the Torah, which was taught by rabbis, reinforced by synagogue worship and celebration, and infused into the consciousness of every Jewish child (males more formally). Polytheism in the Jewish community was gone. The monotheistic Yahwism of Moses had—finally!—won the day.

GREEKS—The religion of the ancient Greeks was polytheistic with a huge pantheon of gods that lived on Mount Olympus. They were not omnipotent in their powers or origins and were quite unpredictable. They possessed human virtues as well as human weaknesses such as jealousy, lust, and hatred. There was a concept of an afterlife, with post-death realms ranging from Tartarus, a place of punishment, to Elysium, an afterlife of reward. This was the kind of religion practiced by the Gentiles of the Bible (the non-Jews) during the intertestamental period and into the days of the early Christian movement.

ROMANS—The ancient Romans were also polytheistic with a pantheon of gods. The legends and stories of their gods, in many ways, resembled those of the Greeks, from whom they adopted many aspects of their faith. Many Greek and Roman gods were equated. When the Romans became an empire in the first century BC, the people even began deifying some of their political leaders, adding them to the pantheon as well. The Romans were tolerant of all faiths and cultures as long as those people were obedient subjects, but the refusal of the stiff-necked Jews (and later, the Christians) to make offerings to the Roman gods led to the harsh treatment of those religions by Roman leaders.

ESSENES—Along with the Pharisees and Sadducees, the Essenes were a major religious sect in Judea during the first and second centuries BC (see *Breakout 9.04*). They were located in numerous cities and are also believed to have been the occupants of the community of Qumran, which is associated with the Dead Sea Scrolls (DSS) that were discovered in the mid-twentieth century AD (see *Breakouts 8.13, 8.15*). The Essenes lived a religious, communal life of poverty with strict adherence to Jewish law. It is commonly held that they were the copyists of the various scrolls stashed away in caves in the later AD 60s, while others theorize that at least some of the DDS were from the temple in Jerusalem and hidden in the Dead Sea caves to protect them from the arrival of the Roman armies that destroyed Jerusalem in AD 70 (see *Breakout 9.16*).

ARCHITECTURE AND INFRASTRUCTURE

GREEK POLIS—The Greeks were "conscious" Hellenizers. That is, they were purposeful in transforming every land they conquered into a reflection of Greece in as many ways as possible. One way of doing that was to transform cities so that they had the layout and look of a Greek polis (city) (see *Figure 8.04*). This meant building Greek-style buildings, streets, theaters

Figure 8.04—Greek polis features; agora (market; top L), cardo (main north-south street; top R), tetrapylons at the intersection of the decumanus (main east-west street) with the cardo (bottom) (photos: John Witte Moore)

BREAKOUT 8.06

ANTIOCHUS IV

The Hellenic period in the Near East lasted about 250 years, from 323 BC to 63 BC. The Seleucids of Syria and the Ptolemies of Egypt fought each other to control the land bridge between Africa and Asia, an area including the small province of Judah/Judea. By the 190s BC, Rome had reached the borders of the Seleucids in what is now Turkey. The Seleucid king Antiochus III fought but was defeated by Rome in 188 BC. His heir, the future Antiochus IV, was taken as a hostage to Rome, while his brother Seleucus I became king (187 BC). Rome exchanged Antiochus for the new king's heir, Demetrius. Seleucus I was assassinated by a usurper, Heliodorus, who was then eliminated by Antiochus IV (175 BC). Antiochus IV claimed the throne as coregent with his young nephew, another Antiochus.

Antiochus IV invaded Egypt (170 BC), conquering virtually everything except Alexandria. He installed a puppet king, Ptolemy VI. But in 169 BC, the Egyptians rebelled and set up a new (infant) King Ptolemy VII, and sent an appeal to Rome asking that Egypt become a "client" kingdom. In 168 BC, Antiochus IV again invaded Egypt in an attempt to end the Ptolemaic Dynasty and merge the two kingdoms. Outside Alexandria, Antiochus IV's army was met by a small Roman force accompanied by proconsul Gaius Popillius Laenas. Laenas carried a letter from the Roman senate ordering Antiochus IV to withdraw from Egyptian territory or face war with Rome.

Antiochus returned to Antioch via Jerusalem. He sacked Jerusalem, removed the city walls, and erected a garrison to control the temple area. Further, he imposed Greek worship on the Jews, initiating a series of bans to Jewish practices—including no Sabbath worship and no circumcision. He polluted the temple by installing a statue of Zeus in the Holy of Holies, sacrificing a pig on the altar, and seizing the temple treasury.

Further, Antiochus ordered each village leader to make a public sacrifice to the Greek gods. In Modi'in, a priest and his sons refused, killing the Seleucid soldiers and scribe who were to witness the sacrifice. This ignited the Maccabee Rebellion, a civil war in Judea between the Hellenized Jews and the more orthodox rural population. The rebellion was briefly successful (165 BC), and the Maccabees cleansed the temple and restored temple worship and the offering of sacrifices—events celebrated as Hanukkah. The Seleucids were defeated by Parthia in the east, and the Judean rebellion succeeded in founding the Hasmonean Dynasty, a Jewish kingdom ruled by the high priest from Jerusalem.

The career and actions of Antiochus IV were prophesied by Daniel (11:13-35). Antiochus's desecration of the temple—sacrificing swine and erecting a graven image in the Holy of Holies—is called "the abomination that makes desolate" by the Jewish sages, including Daniel (11:31). Jesus, looking back some 200 years to these historic events, warned his disciples that in the future a similar desecration would occur: "When you see the abomination of desolation spoken of by the prophet Daniel...flee to the mountains" (Matthew 24:15). This prophecy is echoed by John in Revelation 13:6ff. Antiochus IV, the brutal Greco-Syrian ruler, is a prefigure of that future ruler.

H. Gullet, S. Collins

and amphitheaters, and public monuments. Cities were laid out with a main north-south street, or the cardo, and a main east-west street, or the decumanus. At the intersection of the cardo and decumanus was often a monumental tetrapylon arrangement—either one structure with four gates, or four separate structures—highlighting the importance of the junction as the city center. The Romans adopted the organization of the Greek polis as their own, with few alterations.

GREEK ARCHITECTURE—There were three orders of Greek architecture: Doric, Ionic, and Corinthian. Simplicity, proportion, perspective, and harmony were basic

to each style. Limestone and architectural-grade marble were the building materials of choice, with wooden trusses holding up a ceramic-tiled roof (see *Figure 8.05*).

EARLY ROMAN ARCHITECTURE—The Romans used all three Greek architectural orders (Doric, Ionic, Corinthian) and added the Tuscan and Composite orders, which were adaptations of the three Greek styles (see *Figure 8.06*). While the Greeks used the

Figure 8.06—Arches became the mainstay of Roman architecture (photos: John Witte Moore, David E. Graves, Joseph Holden)

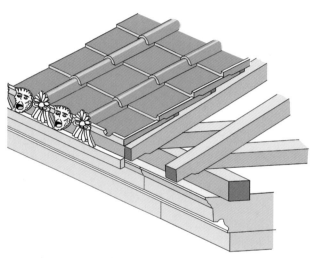

Figure 8.05—Greek roof construction (drawing: Leen Ritmeyer)

Figure 8.07—Domes revolutionized Greco-Roman buildings (photos: John Witte Moore)

arch, the Romans turned it into a major engineering and architectural fundamental. From the arch came the vault (a straight series of arches) and the dome (a circle of arches) (see *Figure 8.07*). Roman buildings used stone walls with rubble fill, or fired clay bricks, overlaid with various kinds of limestone and marble. In cheaper applications, walls were plastered and painted to look like marble (see *Figure 8.08*).

Figure 8.08—Faux marble and painted walls of Herod the Great (photos: John Witte Moore, Joseph Holden, Alexander Schick)

WEAPONS AND WARFARE

GREEKS—The Greek hoplite (foot soldier) used mainly a helmet, shield, and spear. Both double- and single-edged swords were common. But the spear was, by far, the preferred weapon. Soldiers also used catapults that threw ballista (stone balls) of various sizes (see *Figure 8.09*).

PARTHIANS—The Parthians ruled in what is now modern Iran from about 247 BC to AD 224. They clashed with Roman legions as the Roman Republic tried to expand its empire to the east. The Romans never conquered the Parthians (they were overcome by a neighboring people, the Sassanids). Horse warfare was their main military prowess. The "Parthian shot" was an extremely difficult archery maneuver done on horseback. While retreating from an opposing army, Parthian horse-archers would fire backward toward the enemy.

BATTLEFIELD TACTICS—Up until this period, battlefield engagements consisted mostly of chaotic, hand-to-hand combat as armies ran en masse into a headlong clash. The Greeks changed this dramatically with their sophisticated use of the phalanx (a similar formation had been used by ANE armies to some extent for more than 1,000 years, but the Greeks took this tactic to an entirely new level). Phalanx warfare

Figure 8.09—Ballista and catapult (drawings: Leen Ritmeyer)

used tight, rectangular ranks of soldiers trained to maneuver in any direction at marching or running speed (see *Figure 8.10*). The exterior ranks wielded long spears and large shields with which a collective phalanx could literally run over and through a typical opposing infantry. The phalanx's center ranks also had shields that could be held overhead to create a "roof" that provided protection from incoming arrowfire. Multiple phalanxes were a terrifying sight. Used in

Figure 8.10—Greek trireme (public domain)

BREAKOUT 8.07

THE SEPTUAGINT

The *Septuagint* is the Greek translation of the Hebrew Scriptures (Old Testament). The term comes from the Latin word *septuaginta,* which means "seventy" and is based on the tradition that about 70 Jewish translators were involved in the work. Thus, the abbreviation for the Septuagint is LXX, the Roman numeral for 70.

One of the negative influences of the spread of Hellenism was that the Hebrew Bible was no longer understandable in the synagogues. Thus, the Septuagint was the first translation of the Scriptures (280–200 BC) and was the Bible predominantly used by Jesus and the New Testament writers.

There are four ancient legendary accounts of the origin of the Septuagint. One of the stories, told in the Letter of Aristeas (c. second century BC), reports that Demetrius of Phaleron (head of the Alexandrian Library?) was directed by Ptolemy II Philadelphus (285–246 BC) to collect all the books in existence for the library at Alexandria, Egypt. Noticing that the Jewish Scriptures were not found in Greek, he sent word to the Jews at the temple in Jerusalem to convince the high priest to send 72 Jewish scholars to translate their holy book into Greek. According to tradition, the work was accomplished in 72 days on the isle of Pharos.

Complete handwritten copies of the Septuagint date to the early fourth century AD, and these were the basis for the early Latin translations of the Bible. However, fragments of the LXX text have also been found among the Dead Sea Scrolls, which date prior to the time of Christ and predate all existing Hebrew texts. Thus, the LXX is invaluable for studying the Greek of the New Testament era in both the Jewish and Christian communities.

The LXX provides additional light on the original Hebrew Bible. For example, Jewish scholars argue that the Hebrew word *almah* in Isaiah 7:14 should be translated "young woman" and not "virgin," but the translators of the Septuagint understood that Isaiah was speaking about a virgin because they used the Greek word *parthenos* to translate *almah. Parthenos* means "virgin"! In rebuttal, Jewish scholars replied that other Greek renderings of the verse (in Aquila, Symmachus, and Theodotion) used the Greek word *neanis* (= "young woman") when they translated *almah* in Isaiah 7:14. However, these Jewish scholars, who lived after the birth of Jesus, had a motive to disparage the prophecy of the virgin birth. But the Jewish translators of the Hebrew Scriptures from more than 200 years *before* Jesus's birth had no such agenda. They simply translated the term as they understood it as declared by Isaiah.

D. Graves

BREAKOUT 8.08

THE MACCABEES AND HASMONEANS

The family name of the Hasmonean Dynasty originated with the ancestor Asamonaios, according to historian Flavius Josephus. The family was thrust into prominence through the actions of Mattathias, grandson of Asamonaios. After profaning and plundering the temple in Jerusalem, agents of the Seleucid king Antiochus IV came to the village of Modi'in in Judea to compel Greek sacrifices and force Hellenization. Josephus wrote that Mattathias would neither offer sacrifices to Greek gods nor adopt Greek customs. He even killed a fellow Jew who came to offer a sacrifice. With the support of Mattathias's five sons, the Maccabean Revolt began.

Mattathias's sons all had Jewish names: John, Simon, Eleazar, Jonathan, and Judas, who was nicknamed Maccabeus (meaning "hammer"). This is significant in light of the Hellenizing of Jerusalem under the influence of the fully Hellenized high priests Jason and Menelaus. Similar to our own day, the city tended to be more politically liberal and less religiously conservative. However, in the countryside (where Modi'in is located), the people tended to be more conservative in their faith and loyal to their national identity and customs. The Maccabean Revolt, which resulted in an independent state of Judea, was not only a physical war between the followers of the Maccabees and the armies of King Antiochus IV, but also a religious and cultural war of identity between the cosmopolitan city Jews and the conservative Jews of the rural countryside.

The political reasons for the imposition of Hellenism may be traced to abrupt changes in the geopolitical landscape. Antiochus III lost all of his western territories in the Treaty of Apamea following a devastating military loss to Rome in 188 BC. Antiochus IV was confronted by Rome in 169 BC when he decided to invade Egypt. He was turned back by diplomacy, leaving Judea as a contested borderland between the two kingdoms. But the situation could not abide in a vacuum. Antiochus IV stationed troops in Jerusalem and pursued an aggressive campaign of Hellenization, banning Jewish practices, including temple sacrifices. Further, he polluted the temple by observing pagan rituals in it (see *Breakout 8.06*).

When the rural areas of Judea were forced to Hellenize, the people rose up to follow the Maccabees. It is interesting to note that while the modestly successful revolt sought to confront Hellenism and restore the Jewish roots of the population, by the third generation of Maccabees, the Jewish people had compromised their values. When the high priest Alcimus died, the people bestowed the high priesthood on "general" Judas Maccabeus. When Judas died, his brother Jonathan assumed leadership of the army. Jonathan was then made the high priest—not by the Jews, but in a political move by Alexander Bala, a contender for the throne of Antiochus IV.

Upon Jonathan's death, the Jews conferred the priesthood on his brother Simon. Then after Simon's death it passed, as if by dynastic succession, to Simon's son, John Hyrcanus. After John Hyrcanus died, his son, Aristobulus, acceded to both the throne and the high priesthood. Aristobulus went on to wear a crown and turned the government into a kingdom, with himself as king. By this time, Judea had devolved into a perfectly Hellenistic state.

F. Policastro, S. Collins

conjunction with infantry regulars, artillery, and cavalry, the phalanx allowed the army of Alexander the Great to defeat the mighty (and larger) Persian army.

NAVAL WARFARE—Greek warships had both sails and oars. The biggest warship, the *trireme*, had three ranks of oars and could attain average speeds of 7.4 knots (8.5 mph) over long distances. A trireme had up to 180 rowers, one to an oar. Long oars at the stern steered the ship. Ancient warships, including those of the Greek navy, were fitted with bronze rams for broadside attacks against enemy ships (see *Figure 8.11*).

ARTILLERY—Archers remained the standard artillery of the day, but *ballistae* (*ballista*, singular) machinery was now added to the mix. These tension-driven weapons could launch large projectiles significant distances and were mainly used in siege warfare against city walls and towers (see *Figure 8.12*). Large stone spheres and iron rods (bolts) were typical projectiles.

INDUSTRY AND OBJECTS

AGRICULTURE—With increasing populations across the ANE as Greek-style cities dominated the urban scene, food production had to increase dramatically. Thus, both private and large-scale government-controlled farms contributed to the ever-growing demand for grain and cereal crops. Specialty tree and plot crops were also in demand—apples, plums, pomegranates, pears, almonds, dates, figs, grapes, beans,

carrots, cabbages, celery, radishes, leeks, onions, chickpeas, turnips, and many more. Beer and wine production, as always, were mainstays, the alcohol content of which helped against all manner of "bugs" carried by unsanitary water sources.

In the Greek and subsequent Roman worlds, there were several farm management systems. Smaller farms were worked by the owner and his family. Medium-sized farms were run by families as well as slaves under the supervision of foremen. Larger operations applied tenant farming (also called sharecropping), in which the owner and tenant(s) divided up the produce. A private or government-owned farm could also be leased to a tenant. Slaves were critical to the financial success of all larger-scale agricultural production. Farms also managed herds of cattle, swine, and for the first time in history, poultry (see *Figure 8.13*).

HERDING—With massive population expansion throughout the Mediterranean Basin and the ANE, sources of protein and wool were in demand. In areas

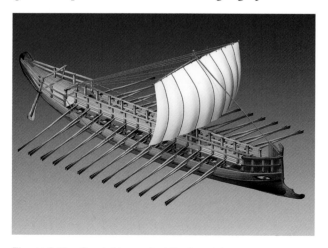

Figure 8.11—Greek bireme (public domain)

Figure 8.12—Ballistae weapons (photos: Alexander Schick)

Figure 8.13—Roman chicken motifs (photo: David E. Graves)

where human populations were spread out or sparse, the ubiquitous local shepherds (Bedouin in the Near East) were adequate for providing lamb and related products. But for large urban centers, herds of cattle and pigs were a growing necessity, as well as the newly introduced jungle fowl (chickens). Cattle, swine, and chickens were generally tended on farms (see above).

Fishing—With the rise of Greek (and later, Roman) culture across Mediterranean world and Near East, the fishing industry became more and more important. Fish and all manner of marine animals were an integral part of the Aegean diet, and this "taste" spread wherever Hellenism took root.

Metallurgy—Greek cities were several orders of magnitude larger than those of the Bronze Age (BA) or Iron Age (IA). Thus the need for metal objects— cooking pots and utensils, architectural pieces, jewelry, farming implements, and of course weapons. This meant one thing: mass production in mining, smelting, and metalworking. Master jewelry makers crafted their goods with gold, silver, and electrum (gold and silver mixed), and sculptors worked with bronze. All these artisans took their pursuits to new heights (see *Figure 8.14*).

Stone—For the first time in history, architects and sculptors used marble extensively as a primary material. Because metamorphosed (high quality) marble was not available in the ANE, the builders of each Greek polis (city) had to import marble from faraway places like Greece, Italy, and Asia Minor (modern Turkey). Marble was available in a variety of architectural and sculptural grades. While it was okay for architectural

Figure 8.14—Greek bronze sculpture (photo: Steven Collins)

Figure 8.15—Greek white marble sculpture depicting armor and shields (photo: Steven Collins)

marble to have grey streaks or be altogether grey, the preference for sculptural marble was that it be as pure white as possible (see *Figure 8.15*). Important Greek buildings, like temples and palaces, often used marble of near-sculptural quality.

BREAKOUT 8.09

THE RISE OF ROME

Many of Jesus's teachings contain references to people, events, or social conditions of his time. To fully understand some of these teachings, it is helpful to understand the political situation in the Holy Land at the time of Christ.

Western civilization in New Testament times belonged to the Romans. People walked on Roman roads, traded on seas patrolled by Roman fleets, traveled through lands protected by Roman legions, and lived or died according to how well they followed Roman laws. However, while the Romans were relatively new arrivals in the Holy Land in Jesus's day, they were simply the latest in a long line of conquerors and occupiers. They followed the Assyrians, the Babylonians, the Persians, Alexander the Great, and the Greek successors of Alexander.

The Roman Empire had its beginnings around 800 BC (the time of the divided kingdom of Israel) as a tiny, crude farming community on the Italian peninsula. The people there had driven out their kings and organized as a republic by c. 500 BC (the time of the Persian Empire), and by c. 300 BC had conquered their immediate Italian neighbors, gaining control of Italy (by that time, Alexander had conquered the Persian Empire and died). Their expansion to the east started c. 200 BC, slowly but steadily absorbing the lands bordering the Mediterranean Sea. The Romans finally arrived in the Holy Land in 63 BC when the Roman general, Pompey the Great, conquered Jerusalem and annexed the region to the empire.

A young man who was present when the Romans arrived was a ten-year-old Idumean by the name of Herod. Young Herod was the son of Antipater, an administrator in the Hasmonean government when the Romans annexed the country. The Romans appointed Antipater as governor of Judea shortly after their arrival, and it was this early introduction to Roman politics that would allow young Herod, in 40 BC, to rise to the throne in Jerusalem as King Herod the Great. This same Herod would become vassal and close personal friend of Mark Antony, and eventually of Caesar Augustus himself. He was also an acquaintance of Cleopatra VII (yes, the notorious Egyptian queen!), but primarily as a political rival.

J. Moore

BREAKOUT 8.10

HEROD THE GREAT

When the Romans, under General Pompey, annexed the Hasmonean kingdom in 63 BC, Herod was the ten-year-old son of Antipater, a high-ranking official of the newly conquered Hasmonean kings. The Romans eventually appointed Antipater governor of Judea, which permitted him to appoint his two sons, Herod and Phasael, to government positions. Herod was serving as a young and already-hated governor of Roman Galilee at the time Julius Caesar was assassinated (44 BC), coincidental with the assassination of his father, Antipater.

In 40 BC, amidst the political confusion following the death of Caesar, the Parthians attempted to wrest control of the region from the Romans. Phasael died in the invasion, but Herod escaped the attack, made his way to Rome, and convinced Mark Antony and Octavius (the two successors to Julius Caesar) to provide him with an army so he could retake Judea/Palestine. Herod asked that they allow him to take the title of king if he was successful. They granted his request, and he was successful, finally seating himself on the throne in Jerusalem in 37 BC.

In the years up to his death in 4 BC, Herod established himself as one of the most powerful, wealthy, favored, and hated men in the Roman Empire. He was the trusted vassal of Mark Antony until Antony died in battle (30 BC) at the hands of Octavius, his rival for political power. Herod then became a close personal friend of Octavius, who became the first emperor of Rome, taking the title Augustus (Caesar Augustus of the New Testament). Herod's sons and grandsons would be educated in Rome while living in the emperor's house. They became the friends and confidants of several successor emperors.

However, Herod's personal life was in shambles. He executed his wife Mariame on account of a false accusation of adultery. Herod had a series of young wives and numerous children, and also executed three of his sons, a mother-in-law, his grandfather-in-law, and a brother-in-law, all under suspicion of treason. Untold numbers of his subjects were executed as well.

A prodigious builder, Herod refurbished many of the cities within his realm and initiated the enlargement of the Jerusalem temple and precinct in 18 BC, a project that would continue for decades.

Herod's friend and patron, Caesar Augustus, had allowed him the privilege of naming his successor(s), and Herod did so, stipulating that he would be followed by three of his sons: Archelaus, Antipas, and Philip. Antipas (not called by this name in the New Testament) was appointed tetrarch of Galilee, and it is this Herod who receives the most attention in the New Testament because of his interaction with Jesus and the disciples. Archelaus, ethnarch of Judea, and Philip, tetrarch in the Gaulanitis (Golan) region, each receive a single mention in the New Testament. To be clear, after Herod the Great, the frequent mention of Herod in various settings in the Gospels are always references to Antipas.

At the time of his death, Herod the Great was a diseased, loathed, and feared man. His death was, no doubt, a huge relief to all of his subjects—and probably to family members as well. He did, however, leave behind a substantial legacy of monumental architecture and infrastructure, a sizeable portion of which is still visible today.

J. Moore, J. Holden

Herod's Temple (model, photo: Leen Ritmeyer)

BREAKOUT 8.11

CAESAR AUGUSTUS

By the middle of the first century BC, Rome, while ostensibly a republic ruled by a senate, had endured decades of political turmoil as well as two civil wars between ambitious generals seeking power. The survivor of the latest war was Julius Caesar, who gained absolute power in Rome from 49 BC until his assassination in 44 BC.

Several men attempted to step into the void left by the death of Caesar, including Mark Antony, one of his top generals. However, Caesar's will designated Octavius, his 18-year-old great-nephew, as his heir. Consequently, Octavius had all the wealth and notoriety attached to Caesar's name. This somewhat sickly and, at first, little-known youth used his newly acquired wealth to purchase the loyalty of Caesar's now-leaderless army, an action that positioned Octavius as a top contender to head the empire.

Antony, Octavius, and Lepidus (a third contender for power who was soon marginalized and exiled to Africa) agreed to share power behind the scenes as a triumvirate. They agreed that Antony would rule the eastern half of the republic and Octavius would govern the western half. However, Antony, in the east, became enamored with Cleopatra, queen of Egypt, and divorced his Roman wife, Octavia, the sister of Octavius. This, along with other perceived crimes, led Octavius to proclaim Antony a traitor and declare war against him. The armies and navies of the two men met in an enormous conflict at Actium in 31 BC, a clash won by Octavius's forces after Antony fled the field of battle. Antony and Cleopatra huddled in Alexandria until an army led by Octavius arrived to arrest them. At that point the lovers committed suicide, leaving the 32-year-old Octavius as the sole power over Rome.

Within a few years, the Roman senate acknowledged Octavius as emperor (historians tend to regard 26 or 27 BC as the official start of his reign), and he ruled with absolute power until his death in AD 14. Octavius reorganized the government, enabling it to control the vast empire Rome had assimilated during the previous century. He then ruled over a period of relative calm and further expansion.

As an aside, in 40 BC, Antony introduced Octavius to a politician from Judea named Herod. Antony, ruling in the east, had become the patron of Herod and, after the invasion of Jerusalem by the Parthians in 40 BC, both Antony and Octavius forced the senate to provide Herod with an army for the purpose of reclaiming Judea. Following the death of Antony in 30 BC, Octavius became a lifelong friend of Herod, a relationship that allowed Herod the freedom to develop into the tyrant we know from historical records.

Finally, we should note that Octavius added the name of Julius Caesar to his own so that he truly was a Caesar. As emperor, he was awarded the title Augustus, thus becoming the Caesar Augustus mentioned in the Bible (Luke 2:1). In generations to follow, however, the title Caesar would be used to refer to the emperors in general.

When Caesar Augustus died in AD 14, he was succeeded by Tiberius, his adopted but now-elderly son, and the slow but inexorable decline of the Roman Empire began.

J. Moore

BREAKOUT 8.12

THE NABATEANS

The Nabateans were a group of Arabian tribes that existed first as nomads, then as a trading empire until about AD 106. Josephus claims that they descended from Ishmael's eldest son Nebajoth (Genesis 25:13). Very little is known about the prehistoric period of their existence. As nomads, their range extended from the Red Sea to the Euphrates, including the area known as Edom, south and east of the Dead Sea. This area was inhabited by the Edomites, the descendants of Jacob's son Esau. In 586 BC, Jerusalem was destroyed and her people exiled to Babylon. The Edomites took this chance to relocate, moving west across the Arabah to the Negev and areas

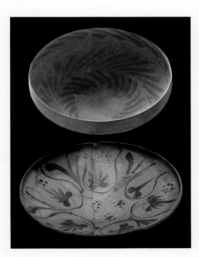

Nabatean pottery (photo: Alexander Schick)

south of Jerusalem. They then became known as the Idumeans. The Nabateans then settled into the area the Edomites had abandoned. This was the beginning of their "caravan empire."

Using camels to cross the deserts, the Nabateans established trade routes for commodities such as incense, spices, and copper from the desert and bitumen from the Dead Sea. The site we know today as Petra became their capital city. It offered passage to the Mediterranean through the Wadi Musa. Gaza became their western seaport. The Nabateans became quite wealthy, charging a 25 percent tax for the use of their routes. We know from graffiti that they spoke Aramaic in the course of their trade dealings, but there are no surviving Nabatean documents, so all our information about them comes from other sources.

The Nabatean trade empire peaked between 100 BC and AD 100. This was when most of the ruins we see in Petra were built. Their architectural style combines Mesopotamian, Egyptian, Hellenistic, and the Nabatean's own unique influences. Roman-style architecture was added when they began trading with Rome. Much of the building was done

In the Nabatean city of Petra, southern Jordan (photo: John Witte Moore)

by King Aretas III Philhellene. He expanded the kingdom and trade routes, built cities, and minted coins. He controlled Damascus for a time, giving him access to the Silk Road trade.

The Nabateans maintained alliances and agreements with Rome and its provinces in the region. Rome wanted incense for use in temples and bitumen for waterproofing ships. Herod Antipas married a Nabatean princess, then divorced her so he could marry Herodias (a situation that led to the beheading of John the Baptist—Matthew 14:1-12). This resulted in a war with the Nabatean king Aretas IV in AD 36. This king also controlled Damascus for a time (2 Corinthians 11:32).

The Nabateans were the Arabs mentioned in the literature of that day, including the writings of Josephus. Their land was called Arabia (Galatians 1:17), an adaptation of the term *Arabah*. During the Jewish wars they worked for Rome as ancillary military units and mercenaries, and they annexed into the Roman Empire c. AD 106. This move allowed them to trade throughout the Roman world.

The Nabateans diminished during the Islamic period because they were no longer on the major trade routes. After a series of earthquakes and the subsequent Crusader invasions, Petra was abandoned and the people became absorbed into other cultures.

J. Bulot, S. Collins

WOOD—The roofs of most buildings were constructed mainly of wood (with ceramic tile, slate, or lead facing). Wood was also used for furniture and shipbuilding. With sprawling urban centers and new towns and villages springing up across the now-Hellenized world, timber was in great demand. This led to the deforestation of vast regions and required suppliers to go farther and farther for the wood they needed. Carpenters were in high demand and could make a reasonable living.

TEXTILES—Textile production reached industrial proportions across the Greek sphere of influence (see *Figure 8.16*). Extensive use of linen required the growth of vast crops of flax. The demand for wool made it necessary to raise large flocks of sheep. In Egypt, cotton

Figure 8.16—Ancient textile patterns; cloth (R) from the later Bar Kochba era shows a pattern used for centuries (photos: David E. Graves, Alexander Schick)

was being made into cloth and traded throughout the Mediterranean world. For those who could afford it, imported silk cloth was also available.

POTTERY—The sweeping changes brought about by Alexander's conquests included a revolution in pottery making (see *Figure 8.17*). Prior to Hellenistic influences, most of the pottery of the region was tempered with coarse grits of sand, ground-up limestone or pottery sherds, mica, or other materials. But the coarse texture of local clays was unsatisfactory to potters familiar with the fine-silt clays used in Greek pottery. With the dominance of Greek culture came the demand for the better clays, production techniques, and firing methods to which the Greeks themselves were accustomed. When potters did use local clays, they employed better preparation techniques to increase the quality of their products. And better firing techniques virtually eliminated the need for temper (also called grog). Among the Hellenistic pottery repertoire are found several distinctive wares. White ware, made from fine whitish clays and well fired, was used for household and commercial applications. Black ware, produced by a paint-and-firing process called sintering, had a glossy black finish. Red and black ware, produced by using the same sintering process, is the kind of ancient Greek pottery familiar to most people today.

SEA TRADE—What the Phoenicians had mastered over the millennium prior to the Hellenistic period, the Greeks, other Aegean peoples, and even the Egyptians now turned into a vast industry for moving goods and services wherever they were desired throughout the Mediterranean Basin. Caravans became the logical extension of the shipping industry, moving products from seaports to inland locations, including the Near East.

Figure 8.17—Diverse kinds of Hellenistic pottery (photos: James Barber, David E. Graves, Joseph Holden, Steven Collins, Carl Morgan; courtesy of Bible Lands Museum, Jerusalem and the Museum of Archaeology and Biblical History, Woodland, CA)

BREAKOUT 8.13

THE DEAD SEA SCROLLS

The accidental discovery of the Dead Sea Scrolls (DSS) by shepherds in the caves around Khirbet Qumran in 1946 and 1947 revolutionized the field of biblical studies and is arguably the greatest archaeological find of the twentieth century. Portions of approximately 1,100 manuscripts were recovered dating from the Hasmonean period (152–63 BC) through the early Roman period (63 BC–AD 68), many of which were pieces of Zealot correspondence from the Bar Kokhba (Second Jewish) Revolt (c. AD 132–136). During this time the settlement of Qumran was occupied by a Jewish religious sect called the Essenes, mentioned by Josephus. The scrolls were discovered hidden in 11 caves near the Qumran settlement along the northwest shore of the Dead Sea in the Jordan Valley, while none of them were found at the Qumran settlement itself.

About 220 of the scrolls are biblical texts, with most books of the Hebrew Bible represented. Up until the discovery of the DSS, no substantial copies of any of the Hebrew Scriptures were known from before the tenth century AD (i.e., Aleppo Codex, AD 935). The DSS dates have been confirmed by archaeology, paleography, and radiocarbon dating.

There were 21 scroll fragments from Isaiah recovered. The most famous, The Great Isaiah Scroll (1QIsa[a]), is the only DSS Old Testament book recovered intact.

It was copied onto 17 sheets of leather stitched together, measuring 23.5 feet long, with 54 columns of text that orthographers date to between 125 and 100 BC. The scrolls of Isaiah were at least 1,000 years older than any previous extant copy and confirm the DSS as the earliest examples of Hebrew writing on parchment and papyrus. The Great Isaiah Scroll strongly confirms the accuracy of later copies, even those of the tenth century AD.

Until the DSS discovery, it was believed that perishable materials such as parchment and papyrus could not survive for two millennia. Since the recovery of the initial scrolls, several others have been discovered in other caves north and south of Qumran along the western scarp of the Jordan River Valley. A twelfth cave (no. 53) once containing DSS was identified in January 2017. A small, unmarked leather scroll was found among broken Qumran-style pottery, together with linen cloth and leather straps to secure the scrolls.

D. Graves

Dead Sea Scroll jar (photo: John Witte Moore)

BREAKOUT 8.14

DEAD SEA SCROLL PARALLELS TO THE GOSPELS

The DSS preceded the writings of the Gospels by more than 100 years, yet there are passages in the Gospels that have close parallels to some found in the DSS. However, there is little evidence that any New Testament author was aware of or used material from the sectarian documents (nonbiblical texts found at Qumran). It's because of this that several texts prove to be so interesting. It's equally true that the Essenes at Qumran shared much in common with the teachings of the New Testament authors, although it is likely that no direct links existed between them. They did, however, share a common knowledge of the Jewish Scriptures, as well as other works, such as the book of 1 Enoch.

One scroll, known as the Apocryphon of Daniel (4Q246)—written in Aramaic—mentions a person similar to the prophet Daniel, who interprets a vision of the Son of God, paralleling Luke 1:32-35, a similarity that cannot be easily dismissed.

Luke quotes the words of the angel Gabriel to Mary regarding the son to be born of her: "He will be great and will be called the Son of the Most High, and the Lord God will give to him the throne of his father David" (verse 32). Moreover, the angel continues that this one will "be called… the Son of God" (verse 35). The title "Son of God" is used of King David (2 Samuel 7:14; Psalm 2:7), but the title "Son of the Most High" is not found in the Hebrew Bible except in plural form (for example, Psalm 82:6). The fact that 4Q246 and Luke use the singular form invites the possibility that Luke had some access to the document (though this is doubtful) or the two may have shared a common source. There is disagreement among DSS scholars over the person mentioned in these DSS texts. Is he a messiah—a reference to the Greek idea of a son of God—or possibly even an antichrist? This is largely dependent on matters such as the deciphering and translation of the Aramaic text. On balance, the Messianic sense seems more likely (a view common to professor J.J. Collins of the University of Chicago and others).

While titles for Messiah are shared by Luke and the Essene author, another DSS document (4Q521), known as the Messianic Apocalypse, mentions the Lord with reference to the Messiah who preaches to the poor and does miracles like healing the sick, raising the dead, and calming the sea. All of these are given by the Gospels (Matthew 11:3-5; Luke 7) as works of Messiah Jesus. Again, there is no clear evidence of a New Testament author's knowledge of these Qumranic texts, but there is a reasonable prospect that they may have shared some traditions or sources.

H. Wayne House

APOCRYPHON OF DANIEL TEXT PARALLELS WITH LUKE 1:32-35	
Apocryphon of Daniel (4Q246)	**Luke 1:32-35**
Will be great	Will be great
Shall be called the Son of the Most High	Shall be called the Son of the Most High
Shall be called Son of God	Shall be called Son of God
His kingdom is everlasting kingdom	He will rule forever

Breakout 8.15

The Geography of Qumran

The Qumran Plateau is a raised terrace located in the Judean Desert on the northwest shore of the Dead Sea. It is surrounded on the north by the Wadi Jafet Zaben and on the south by the Wadi Qumran. Upon this site, several communities may have existed in the biblical period. The first may have been in relation to the City of Salt, one of the six cities in the wilderness of Judah mentioned between Nibshan and Engedi (Joshua 15:62) and a second in connection with the school of the prophets (2 Kings 2:3-6; 4:38-44).

There is also archaeological evidence of both construction at the site and habitation during the late first temple period. During the Hasmonean period (140–37 BC), the site was occupied by a Jewish sect concerned about maintaining strict ritual purity and preparing for the Messianic age. This community, popularly identified with one of the Essene sects, continued under the Herodian Dynasty until they were driven from the site by a Roman invasion in AD 68 in conjunction with the First Jewish Revolt.

The Essenes are most famous for having copied and preserved the oldest known copies of the Old Testament, as well as for commentaries and other sectarian

Cave 4, Qumran (photo: Joseph Holden)

literature they produced that provides a window into the religious, political, and social beliefs and practices of the late second temple period. These documents, known as the Dead Sea Scrolls (DSS), were found hidden in the rugged limestone cliffs located to the north and south of the plateau on its west side. This area contains fault caves, and some 300 caves have been documented and recorded by Israel Antiquities Authority surveys or reported by locals or archaeologists.

In the caves less than a mile to the north of the Qumran settlement were found the first of the

DSS, stored in ceramic jars. These caves were numbered in order of their discovery—caves 1, 2, 3, and 11. Caves located about the same distance to the south of Qumran had evidence that they once contained scrolls, although no scrolls have yet been found. Based on the 1993 Antiquities Authority survey (published in the journal ʾAtiqot in 2002), these new scroll caves have been designated 52, 53A, and 53B. Additional scrolls were found in caves along the Qumran plateau. The site is composed of marl, a soft soil that was covered and deposited by the Dead Sea in remote antiquity. Because this substance is easily carved, numerous man-made caves exist, many from the second temple period. They were carved into the sides of the plateau or on the adjacent plateau that abuts the cliffs on the west side. Here, scroll caves 4, 5, 6, 7, 8, 9, and 10 were identified in the 1950s. Ground-penetrating radar surveys (2012, 2018) may have located at least one additional collapsed cave on the east side.

The east side of the Qumran plateau is bounded by a wall. Beyond this wall, descending over the adjacent hill down to the road, is an ancient cemetery. The cemetery contains at least 1,000 graves of men, women, and children, mostly from the second temple period, but also includes later Bedouin burials. In 2017, a discovery of an additional 60 graves (only males) was made next to the modern visitor's center at the site.

The unique topography of the caves and the natural geographical setting of the plateau invited habitation by those who wanted both a desert retreat and a pivotal position near the roads leading from Jericho and to Jerusalem. It also afforded a landscape with caves for hiding precious documents as well as, later, hiding the Zealots (during the First Jewish Revolt) and the soldiers of Bar Kokhba (during the Second Jewish Revolt).

R. Price

CHAPTER 9

THE WORLD OF THE NEW TESTAMENT

WELCOME TO THE EARLY ROMAN PERIOD (63 BC–AD 180)

We have now entered the Early Roman period (see *Timeline*). No matter what direction you look, Rome dominates (see *Map 9.01*). The famed (infamous!) intertwining of Roman emperors and government officials with the Herodians and local Jewish leaders in Judea was, from the beginning, a political flashpoint. It was also a seething mire of immorality, intrigue, murder, and mayhem. But *the* Light shines brighter in the deepest night. Welcome to the New Testament era!

GEOGRAPHY

By the opening of the New Testament era with the birth of Christ in the final years of Herod the Great, the Roman Empire was in control of the entire Mediterranean world and beyond (see *Timeline* and *Map 9.01*). The Roman province of Judaea (or Judea) was linked tightly to the household of Caesar via personal relationships with members of the Herodian family. The carving up of Herod's kingdom after his death was, as far as the Roman Empire was concerned, unofficial. These puppet kingdoms were tolerated as a means of maintaining peace in the area (see *Map 9.02*). Herod Archelaus was given Judea proper. Herod Antipas got Galilee and Perea. Herod Philip received Gaulanitis and territories to the north and east. After the death of Herod Philip, Herod Agrippa I and II, in turn, took over the lands that had been under his control.

CHRONOLOGY

Note that some of the following dates are approximations, while others are more precise. We have not delineated between them except by occasional question marks to represent a range of uncertainty.

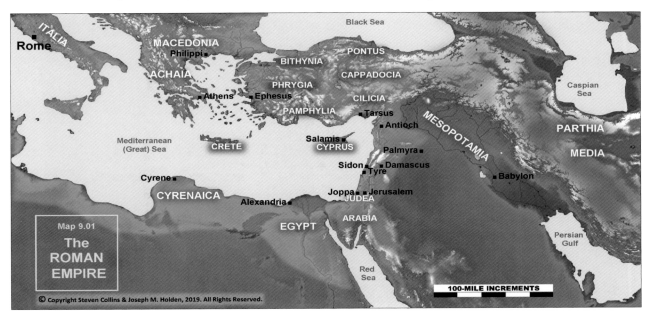

Map 9.01
The ROMAN EMPIRE

100-MILE INCREMENTS

© Copyright Steven Collins & Joseph M. Holden, 2019. All Rights Reserved.

EARLY ROMAN CHRONOLOGY	
Date	**Events**
63 BC	Annexation of Palestine by the Romans (see *Map 9.01*)
40 BC	Herod the Great appointed as king of Judea (see *Breakout 8.10*)
37 BC	Herod takes the throne in Jerusalem (see *Breakout 8.10* and *Map 9.02*)
28 BC	Julius Gaius Octavius Caesar becomes the first emperor of Rome, known in the New Testament as Caesar Augustus (see *Breakout 8.11*)
7–4 (?) BC	Birth of Jesus (see *Breakout 9.03*)
4 BC	Death of Herod the Great and succession of his three sons, Archelaus, Antipas, Philip (see *Breakout 9.02* and *Maps 9.03, 9.04*)
AD 14	Tiberius, adopted son of Caesar Augustus, becomes the second emperor of Rome
c. AD 29	Beginning of the ministry of John the Baptist, and soon after, the start of Jesus's ministry: Luke 3 says, "In the fifteenth year of the reign of Tiberius Caesar...the word of God came to John the son of Zechariah in the wilderness...all the people were baptized, and...Jesus also had been baptized...Jesus, when he began his ministry, was about thirty years of age" (verses 1-2, 21, 23).
AD 32–33 (?)	Crucifixion and resurrection of Jesus (this depends on the date chosen for his birth, the date selected for the interpretation of Luke 3, and the length of time assigned to his ministry) (see *Breakouts 9.13, 9.14*)
AD 35/36 (?)	Paul's conversion to Christianity (see *Breakout 9.15*)
AD 37	Caligula becomes the third Roman emperor
AD 35–69	Writing of the Gospels and the balance of the New Testament
AD 41	Claudius becomes the fourth emperor of Rome after Caligula's assassination
AD 48–49	Paul's first missionary journey (see *Map 9.05*)
AD 50–52	Paul's second missionary journey (see *Map 9.05*)
AD 53–57	Paul's third missionary journey (see *Map 9.05*)
AD 54	Nero becomes the fifth emperor of Rome
AD 59	Paul's trial before Festus and Agrippa II
AD 59–60	Paul's final voyage to Rome (see *Map 9.05*)
AD 64	Deaths of Peter and Paul (?)
AD 66	Beginning of the Jewish revolt against Rome (see *Breakout 9.16*)
AD 67	Arrival of the Roman army under General Vespasian (see *Breakout 9.16* and *Map 9.06*)
AD 68	Death of Paul (alternate date)
AD 68	Death of Nero
AD 69	Vespasian becomes the sixth Roman emperor (after three other generals attempted to take the throne in 68–69 following the death of Nero)
AD 70	Destruction of Jerusalem and second temple by the Romans in response to the First Jewish Revolt (see *Breakout 9.16* and *Map 9.06*).

HISTORY

Many of Jesus's teachings contain references to the people or events or social conditions of his time. To fully understand what he was saying, it is helpful to understand the political reality of the Holy Land (Southern Levant; Palestine) in that era.

In the first century AD, the Western world was Roman. Roman soldiers kept highways and roads safe (see *Breakout 9.09*). Maritime commerce plied the seas, which were patrolled by Roman ships. Overland commerce and travelers coursed through lands protected by Roman legions. Everyone lived (or died) under the protection (or condemnation) of Roman law. And Herod, the local Roman appointee in Judea, was a Roman at heart through and through.

Herod was a ten-year-old of Idumean origin. He

was the son of Antipater, a man who was appointed governor of Judea by the Romans shortly after their arrival in the region (see *Breakout 8.10* and *Map 9.02*). This same Herod would go on to become vassal to, and close personal friend of, Mark Antony and eventually to Caesar Augustus himself (see *Breakouts 8.11, 9.01, 9.02*).

THE CAESARS AND HEROD THE GREAT

At the beginning of the New Testament era, the absolute ruler of the Roman Empire was the emperor in Rome (see *Breakout 9.01*). The first of these emperors was Gaius Julius Caesar Octavius (great-nephew and young heir of the assassinated Julius Caesar), recognized as emperor c. 28/27 BC. Remarkably, he became

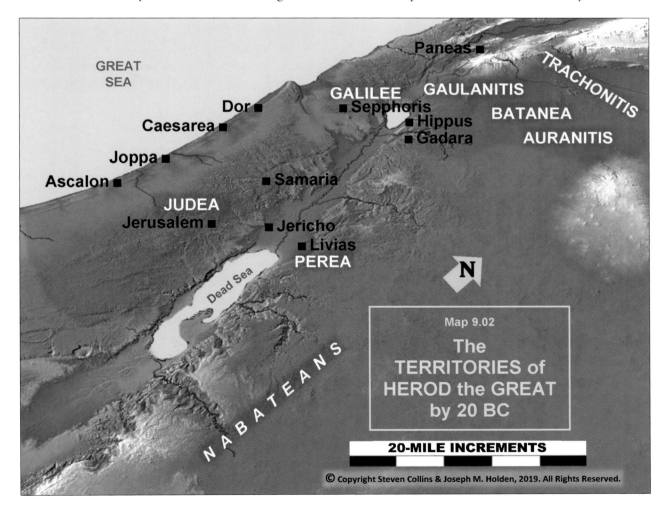

Map 9.02

The TERRITORIES of HEROD the GREAT by 20 BC

20-MILE INCREMENTS

a good friend and supporter of Herod the Great, having helped to arrange the appointment of Herod as the king of Judea in 40 BC. Gaius Julius Caesar Octavius ruled as the first emperor from 28 BC to AD 14 and was on the throne until Jesus was nearly 20 years old.

Upon Caesar's death, he was followed by his aging adopted son, Tiberius (see *Figure 9.01*), who ruled for the next 23 years (AD 14–37). Thus, Tiberius was emperor during Jesus's ministry and crucifixion. And when Jesus taught his followers to "render to Caesar the things that are Caesar's" (Matthew 22:21), he was using the term *Caesar* to mean any secular government, a usage that came into favor after the death of Augustus.

The early years of the Christian movement, as reported in the book of Acts, were overseen by three different Roman emperors. Tiberius was followed by Caligula (see *Figure 9.02*), an insane monster who was the great-nephew of Tiberius. Caligula was assassinated by his personal bodyguards after only four years (AD 37–41).

Claudius (see *Figure 9.03*), the elderly uncle of Caligula, succeeded him on the throne (AD 41-54) and ruled somewhat benignly until his death (possibly poisoned by his fourth wife to allow her young son, Nero, to ascend the throne at age 16).

Nero (see *Figure 9.04*), another arguably insane tyrant, took the throne after Claudius, and then committed suicide in AD 68—perhaps to prevent his arrest and execution by his enemies. Nero was the Caesar to whom Paul would make his appeal as stated in Acts 25:11.

The New Testament begins with the narrative of Jesus's birth (see *Breakouts 9.03, 9.07*) shortly before the death of Herod, the local representative of Roman governance. In lands conquered by Rome, such local supervision and control was provided by Roman appointees of various titles, such as procurator, governor, ethnarch, tetrarch, and king. Normally these appointees served in their positions for a few years and then were replaced, much as modern ambassadors

Figure 9.01—Tiberius image (photo: Joseph Holden)

Figure 9.02—Caligula image (photo: David E. Graves)

serve in their posts. However, Herod had a special relationship with Rome (specifically with Mark Antony and then with Octavius, later to be called Caesar Augustus—Luke 2:1). He was not only designated as king in 40 BC, but also was rewarded by Augustus with the high honor of naming his successors (see *Breakout 9.02*). In other words, his kingship was hereditary (as long as Augustus or his successors permitted it!). Even as powerful as Herod was, he was still a Roman appointee ruling at the behest of the emperor and could be replaced at any time (see *Map 9.02* and *Breakout 8.10*).

While Herod could have been known as Herod the Horrible just as well as Herod the Great, he carried out amazing building ventures throughout his kingdom. They were massive, monumental projects made to impress not only his Roman sponsors but also visitors from around the empire and the local Jewish leaders (see *Map 9.02* and *Breakout 9.04*) and population (see *Breakouts 9.05, 9.06* and *Figures 9.05, 9.06*).

Herod's rule was fraught with challenges from both outside and within his realm. At the time of his death,

he was feared and despised by virtually his entire kingdom. Also, according to the historian Josephus, his last hours were spent in great pain and suffering from a multitude of physical ailments. Herod died shortly after the birth of Jesus, having had at least ten wives and numerous sons and daughters. He had executed several members of his family, including his three eldest sons, for real or imagined acts of treason. As a result, in the final of six wills penned just before his death, he designated his next three eldest sons as heirs, dividing his territories between them. These sons are the various and often confusing Herods who appear in the books of the New Testament (see *Breakout 9.02*).

HEROD: ARCHELAUS, ANTIPATER, PHILIP, AGRIPPA I, AND AGRIPPA II

At the time of his death, Herod controlled numerous provinces at the eastern end of the Mediterranean Sea, including Idumea, Judea, Samaria (see *Breakout*

Figure 9.03—Claudius image (photo: David E. Graves)

Figure 9.04—Nero image (photo: David E. Graves)

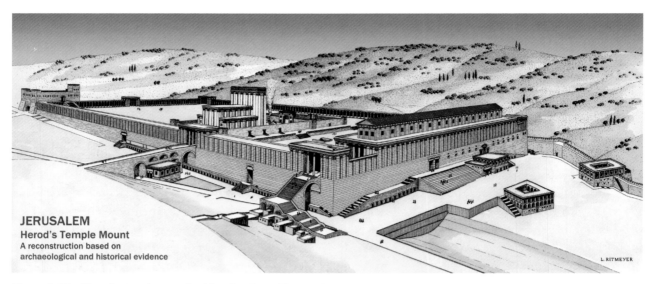

Figure 9.05—Herod's temple complex (drawing: Leen Ritmeyer)

9.08), Galilee, Perea, and areas in the Golan (see *Map 9.02*). These were divided among the three sons named in his will (see *Breakout 9.02* and *Map 9.03*).

The eldest of the three inheriting sons was the 19-year-old Archelaus, who was to rule over Judea and Samaria, a territory that included Jerusalem and Caesarea Maritima (the artificial harbor built by Herod). He was assigned the title of ethnarch, a lesser title than king, and was distressed by this designation. Caesar promised to give Archelaus the title of king if he were to prove himself worthy of such recognition. He didn't.

Archelaus (ruled 4 BC–AD 6) proved to be a tyrant,

Figure 9.06—Masada palaces of Herod the Great (drawing: Leen Ritmeyer)

very much his father's son. This is almost certainly the reason for the detour that Joseph took with his family on his return to Israel after the stay in Egypt. After the citizens of Judea and Samaria appealed to Caesar for relief from Archelaus, the latter was deposed and exiled by Caesar after nine years on the throne. Jesus was about 10 to 12 years old at the time.

The territories ruled by Archelaus were taken from the Herodian family, and from that time forward were supervised by a series of appointees called procurators. The fifth of these, appointed in the AD mid-20s shortly before the ministry of Jesus, was a man named Pontius Pilatus (Pilate; AD 26–36). It was Pilate who was in Jerusalem at the time of Jesus's arrest, and it was he who condemned Jesus to be executed, culminating in the events of Jesus's final days before his crucifixion (see *Breakouts 9.10, 9.11, 9.13*). Jesus's death didn't last (see *Breakout 9.14*).

The second son to inherit territory was 17-year-old Antipas (ruled 4 BC–AD 39), a full brother of Archelaus. He received Galilee and Perea, the region on the eastern side of the Jordan River in what is now modern Jordan (see *Map 9.03*). This was a desirable inheritance because these were fertile and productive regions. He was given the title of tetrarch over his holdings, a reference to the fact that he was governing a territory that was about one quarter the size of the regions governed by his father.

Because Antipas ruled over Galilee, he had contact with Jesus's disciples and was the Herod who beheaded John the Baptist (Matthew 14). Antipas was celebrating the Passover in Jerusalem when Jesus was arrested, and it was this circumstance that caused Pontius Pilate to ask him for help in settling the legal questions surrounding the arrest and punishment of Jesus.

It should be noted that in the Bible, Antipas is not referred to by his given name but is always referred to as Herod or King Herod, which is confusing for some readers. A few years after the crucifixion of Jesus, Antipas was removed from the throne by Caligula, the new emperor at that time, and his territories were given to Agrippa, a grandson of Herod the Great.

The third inheritor of Herod the Great was his son Philip (ruled 4 BC–AD 33/34), the 16-year-old

---

BREAKOUT 9.01

THE ROMAN EMPERORS

The Roman Empire had its beginnings around 800 BC as a farming community on the Italian peninsula, which was governed by kings. Around 500 BC the people overthrew their corrupt rulers and organized as a republic, governed by a senate (essentially the wealthy aristocracy) and two elected leaders (consuls) who served one-year terms and could veto each other and the senate. This chaotic system was no longer able to govern its territories as they expanded. This brought to the fore a series of strong generals who, seeking absolute rule, clashed in bloody civil wars. These included such famous personalities as Julius Caesar vs. Pompey (c. 49 BC) and Mark Antony vs. Octavius (c. 30 BC).

After Octavius (great-nephew of Julius Caesar) defeated Mark Antony and his lover/ally Cleopatra of Egypt, he was finally able to accomplish what no one else had been able to do—assume absolute power as emperor (28 BC). He ruled as the first emperor from 28 BC to AD 14. This means he was on the throne until Jesus was nearly 20 years old. And remarkably, he became a great friend and supporter of Herod the Great, to the point of helping to arrange the appointment of Herod as king of Judea in 40 BC.

Tiberius (AD 14–37), the adopted son of Octavius who followed him to the throne, was a disgusting and dissolute tyrant who ruled for 23 years, including during the time of Jesus's ministry. Thus, when Jesus taught his followers to "render to Caesar the things that are Caesar's" (Mark 12:17), he was using "Caesar" as a generic term for any ruling government.

Tiberius was followed by his great-nephew Caligula (AD 37–41), an insane monster who was assassinated by his personal bodyguards after only four years on the throne. During his brief reign, he nearly bankrupted the empire.

Claudius (AD 41–54), the elderly uncle of Caligula, succeeded Caligula on the throne and ruled during the early years of Christianity's spread through the Roman Empire.

Nero (AD 54–68), the adopted son of Claudius, followed Claudius to the throne at age 16. He was another arguably insane tyrant and was emperor when the apostle Paul traveled to Rome to appeal his conviction.

Governance of the Roman Empire would continue to deteriorate over the ensuing centuries with increasing numbers of inept, corrupt, and tyrannical rulers. The western half of the empire would succumb to barbarian tribes in the AD 400s, and the remaining eastern half of the empire would sink into impotence until the destruction of Constantinople in AD 1453, bringing the Roman Empire to an ignominious end.

J. Moore

half-brother of Archelaus and Antipas (see *Breakout 9.02* and *Map 9.04*). He was given rule over much of the Golan, the region northeast of the Sea of Galilee, and like Antipas, was given the title of tetrarch.

Philip was a decent, fair ruler who administered his territory well until he died in AD 34, about the time that Jesus was crucified (see *Breakouts 9.10, 9.13*). The two major cities in his tetrarchy were Caesarea Philippi and Bethsaida, both economically important to the region and both visited by Jesus. Philip is mentioned only once in the New Testament (Luke 3) in a list of key figures of that day.

Antipas was removed from office shortly after Jesus's crucifixion and resurrection (see *Breakouts 9.13, 9.14*). As the Christian movement began (see *Breakouts 9.11, 9.12*), as related in the book of Acts, the holdings of all three of Herod's sons were eventually granted to a grandson, Agrippa I (ruled AD 37–44). He had

been raised in Rome in the household of Augustus and was the personal friend of young Caligula, who became emperor upon the death of Tiberius. Caligula rewarded Agrippa for his loyalty by granting him rule over the territories of his half uncles, and he was also given the title of king.

This Agrippa, mentioned in the book of Acts, executed James the brother of John and imprisoned Peter. After a short reign, he collapsed and died while giving a speech in Caesarea (Acts 12:21-23). As was the case with Antipas, this grandson of Herod is not referred to by his name, Agrippa, but is called Herod in the New Testament.

After the death of Agrippa (see *Breakout 9.02*), several years passed before any territory was given to his son, also named Agrippa—Agrippa II (AD 53?). He received a rather modest inheritance, the territory in the Golan that had been ruled by Philip (see *Map 9.04*).

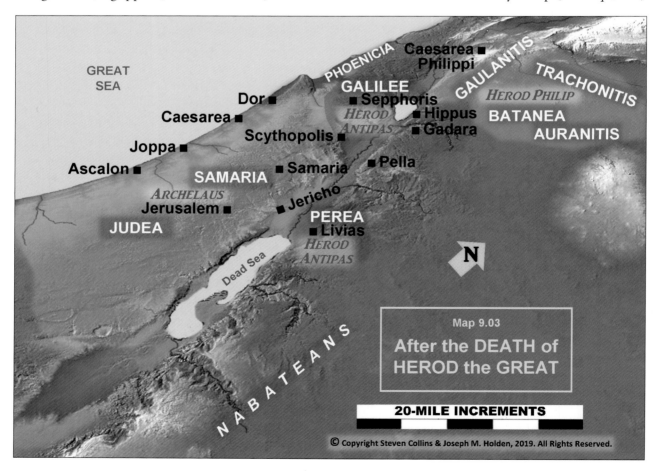

Map 9.03

After the DEATH of HEROD the GREAT

20-MILE INCREMENTS

This Agrippa is referred to by his given name in the book of Acts and is the man who listened to the defense given by Paul in Caesarea before Paul was sent to Rome (Acts 26). This probably occurred around AD 59.

As the years progressed, Agrippa was a vigorous defender of Roman policies. He attempted to prevent the local Jewish revolt staged in Palestine in the late AD 60s, but to no avail. When the Roman legions arrived to put down the revolt, Agrippa II supported them to the fullest. At that point, he disappeared from history (but there are some who argue that he survived into the AD 90s).

BREAKOUT 9.02

THE HERODS

Herod the Great, enabled by his friend Caesar Augustus, was absolute ruler of the Holy Land until his death c. 4 BC. His three sons, a grandson, and a great-grandson would continue to govern various parts of the region as Roman appointees for another 70 years during New Testament times. Herod the Great accomplished this posthumously by having willed the succession of three sons, not just one. Natural brothers Archelaus (19 years old) and Antipas (17 years old) were joined by 16-year-old Philip (half brother to the other two).

Archelaus, appointed as ethnarch of Judea, was certainly his father's son and a natural tyrant. Upon the vigorous complaints of his subjects, Archelaus was deposed by Caesar Augustus in AD 6 after fewer than ten years on the throne. Governance of the province was then provided by a series of procurators, one of whom was a man named Pontius Pilatus (Pilate). Archelaus is mentioned a single time in the New Testament, in Matthew 2:22.

Philip, appointed as a tetrarch in the region of the Golan (Gaulanitis), ruled benignly until after the crucifixion of Jesus. His territory was then taken alternately by Roman-appointed procurators or other descendants of Herod. He is mentioned a single time in the New Testament, in Luke 3:1.

Antipas, who is not mentioned by that name in the New Testament, was appointed tetrarch of Galilee. He receives a lot of attention in the New Testament due to his connection to Jesus and his disciples, and the multiple mentions of Herod throughout the Gospels are mostly references to Antipas.

Shortly after the death and resurrection of Jesus, Antipas was deposed by Caligula, the emperor at that time, and replaced by Agrippa, a grandson of Herod the Great and Caligula's childhood friend. He is not called Agrippa in the New Testament, but is referred to as "Herod the king" (Acts 12:1).

For a short time until his death in AD 44, Agrippa ruled the entire territory that had been governed by his grandfather Herod the Great. The death of Agrippa is described in Acts 12.

After Agrippa died, procurators ruled the various provinces of Roman Palestine. Agrippa II, the son of Agrippa and great-grandson of Herod the Great, was given a small territory to rule, and is the King Agrippa who met with Paul in Acts 25.

There are several other Herodians mentioned in the Bible, including Herodias (half niece of Antipas), the daughter of Herodias (named Salome, a fact mentioned by Josephus), Philip (another half brother of Antipas) the ex-husband of Herodias, and two sisters of King Agrippa, Berenice and Drusilla.

After the Roman destruction of Jerusalem in AD 70, the family of Herod disappeared from history.

J. Moore

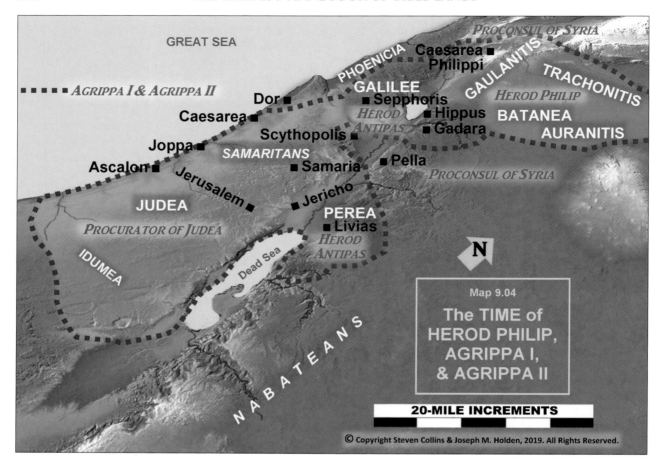

Figure 9.07—Model of city of Rome, first century AD (photo: Alexander Schick)

The historical details of the New Testament end with Paul's departure for Rome (see *Map 9.05* and *Breakout 9.15*). After a harrowing voyage that endured storms and a shipwreck on the island of Malta, Paul arrived in Rome, where he was imprisoned and eventually executed by Nero (although scholars differ on this conclusion, with some traditions suggesting that Paul proceeded on to Spain and continued his ministry there).

THE DESTRUCTION OF JERUSALEM

After Paul's journey to Rome (see *Figure 9.07*), the province of Judea descended into political chaos due to neglect of the region by Rome as well as the incompetence and corruption of the procurators assigned to the area. This reflects on a specific practice mentioned in the New Testament: taxation. The *Pax Romana* (a world peace enforced by Roman power) was funded by taxation. These taxes were collected by local men who competed for the right to impose them. They paid a fixed amount to the state, so whatever they collected beyond that was theirs to keep. This encouraged confiscatory taxation (often collected by strong-arm techniques) and explains the contempt heaped upon tax collectors by local Jews, and the Jews' "righteous" astonishment at Jesus's willingness to associate with such people.

Various political groups such as the Zealots (see *Breakout 9.04*) agitated for rebellion against the Romans and violence increased (see *Breakout 9.16*). A subgroup of Zealots (called Sicarii) arose who were primarily political assassins. They directed their activities not only against the Romans, but also against Jews who collaborated with the Romans. Assassinations were commonplace, along with looting, murder, and the burning and sacking of Jewish villages, as well as attacks against the Romans themselves.

Riots erupted between Jews and Gentiles in most of the major cities, and thousands of people were slaughtered in the streets. As the violence escalated, Agrippa II attempted to defuse tensions but was unsuccessful. When war arrived he sided completely with the Romans, providing troops and money to Vespasian, the Roman general in charge.

The Zealots conquered several fortresses, including Masada (see *Breakout 9.05*), and then were able to eject the Roman garrison from the Antonia Fortress in Jerusalem (see *Figure 9.08*). Some of the region was liberated and freed of Romans, at least for a while, yet violence broke out all over Judea between Greeks

Map 9.05
PAUL'S MISSIONARY JOURNEYS

100-MILE INCREMENTS

and Jews. The ensuing atrocities were usually directed against whichever group was in the minority in a specific area. A Roman expedition sent from Syria to put down the rebellion lost thousands of men, and most of the army was annihilated. The first coins dated to the years of the war were minted at this time (see *Figure 9.09*).

The Sanhedrin (Jewish high court) began preparations for all-out war. They appointed Joseph ben Matthias, a Pharisee and scholar (see *Breakout 9.04*), to organize the Galilean defense. This is the man we know as Josephus Flavius, the Jewish historian (see *Breakout 9.17*).

Nero, the emperor at the time, was in Greece when the insurgency broke out. He sent Vespasian, his finest general (who would follow Nero to the throne in AD 69), to put down the rebellion. Vespasian arrived in Ptolemais (see *Map 9.06*) in AD 67 and began brutally conquering the lands surrounding Jerusalem in preparation for a siege of the city. He was ready to begin the siege in AD 68, but his plans were interrupted by the suicide-death of Nero. After a year of confusion during which three generals attempted to take the throne, Vespasian's troops acclaimed him as emperor, and he departed for Rome. His son, Titus, a fine general in his own right, completed the conquest of Jerusalem in a terrible siege that lasted from early AD 70 until the city fell on September 8 of the same year (see *Breakout 9.16*).

After the heavy hand of Rome had fallen, Judea became an independent Roman province with a fixed occupational army. In the aftermath, many cities and towns were destroyed and much of the country was depopulated. The once-great temple in Jerusalem lay in ruins (see *Figure 9.10* and *Breakout 9.16*). Finally, it is probable that the new emperor, Vespasian, used the looted temple treasures to help finance the building of the Coliseum in Rome.

PEOPLES AND KINGDOMS

ROMANS—Julius Caesar returned to Rome enriched by a long governorship in Farther Spain. He allied himself with the Roman aristocracy and became one-third of a powerful new triumvirate (three simultaneous rulers functioning jointly) together with Crassus and Pompey (see *Breakout 9.01*). Caesar became the powerful governor of Gaul. Crassus was

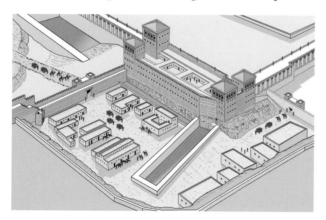

Figure 9.08—Antonia fortress (drawing: Leen Ritmeyer)

Figure 9.09—First Jewish Revolt coins (photo: Alexander Schick)

Figure 9.10—AD 70 Temple Mount destruction; giant architectural stones crashed onto the pavement below the temple platform, which is above (photos: John Witte Moore)

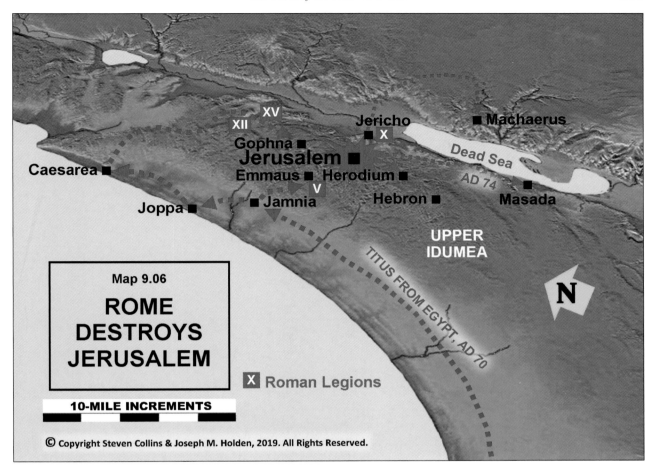

killed in battle, leaving two rivals, Julius Caesar and General Pompey. When Pompey marched into Jerusalem in 63 BC (see *Breakout 8.09*), this ended the brief self-rule of the Jews under the Hasmoneans (see *Breakout 8.08*). Julius Caesar and Pompey involved Rome in a personal civil war that ended when Pompey was murdered in Egypt by Ptolemy XIV, the husband of Cleopatra. Caesar then defeated Ptolemy with the help of Antipater, the Arab father of Herod the Great (see *Breakout 8.10*).

JEWS—The Jews centered in old Judea ruled independently after the overthrow of the hated Seleucid (Syrian) rulers (see *Breakout 8.08*). But that came to an end when the Romans invaded Palestine/Judea in AD 63 (see *Breakout 8.09*). While under Roman-Herodian rule the Jews had relative peace, but there were tensions between various Jewish factions (see *Breakout 9.04*). Synagogues and rabbis provided a powerful influence in local communities (see *Breakout 8.01*).

SAMARITANS—The Samaritans (see *Breakout 9.08*) were a despised mixed-ethnic group of Israelites and foreign peoples who had been part of the northern kingdom of Israel. They had been at odds with the rebuilding of the temple in Jerusalem after the Babylonian captivity. The Samaritans built their own temple atop Mount Gerizim around 400 BC. It was completely destroyed by the Maccabees under the leadership of John Hyrcanus c. 100 BC (see *Breakout 8.08*). The Samaritans rejected all the biblical books except for the Torah and bitterly fought with the Hasmonean kingdom that had destroyed their temple. During New Testament times, they were still hated by the "proper" Jews of Judea.

BREAKOUT 9.03

AWAY IN A MANGER, BUT NOT IN A BARN

Joseph, a descendant of King David, journeyed to Bethlehem, his ancestral home, with espoused wife Mary to participate in a mandatory census (Luke 2:1-3). In the ANE, a family's historic ties to their hometown were of utmost importance. Because Joseph was of the royal line of David, space would have been found for Joseph and family upon arrival in the city. Even in the Roman period, the Davidic connection to Bethlehem was so strong that Bethlehem was still known as the "city of David" (2:4, 11).

Again, the expectation of accommodations for a direct descendant within the Davidic ancestral home was not unreasonable. Furthermore, as Luke noted earlier, Mary had relatives nearby in the "hill country" of Judea (1:39). With Jesus being born "while they were there" (2:6), it seems possible that there may have been time for such alternate arrangements.

Although no barn is mentioned in the text, the "manger" (Greek, *phatna*) is prominent (Luke 2:7, 12, 16). Stone-carved and plastered mangers are known to be on the ground floor of domestic structures in Israel throughout biblical times (Judges 11:31; 1 Samuel 28:24). Historians and anthropologists have noted the practice of keeping animals in the house down through history. While flocks were kept in sheepfolds out in the fields (Luke 2:8), valuable or vulnerable animals—oxen, donkeys, sick or pregnant sheep and goats—would be brought into the house's ground floor domestic stable. Such was the place where the infant Jesus would have been laid in a manger.

Luke records that "there was no place for them in the inn" (Luke 2:7—"inn" is the Greek term *kataluma*). The only other New Testament mention of a *kataluma* is as the upper chamber "guest room" of a house in Jerusalem where the Last Supper was held (Luke 22:11 and its parallel Mark 14:14). There is no reason why Luke's use of the term in 22:11 ("guest room") on the last night of Jesus's life should be different from his use of the same term in 2:7 ("inn") on the first night of Jesus's life. His statement "no place for them in the inn" indicates that the "guest room" of the house where Mary and Joseph were staying was already full. The NIV's 2011 revision acknowledges this fact, changing "inn" to "guest room" (2:7).

Luke knew what a public inn was, using that term in the account of the Good Samaritan at an "inn" (10:34—Greek, *pandocheion*) with an "innkeeper" (verse 35—*pandocheus*). Luke's use of *kataluma* indicates an altogether different kind of space—the "guest room" of a family home. Thus, Luke's nativity account had no barn (or lean-to) in mind, no statement by an innkeeper, nor even the presence of an innkeeper! Instead, on that first Christmas, baby Jesus was placed in a manger on the ground floor of a Bethlehem house—likely among family—because the upstairs "guest room" was already full.

G. Byers

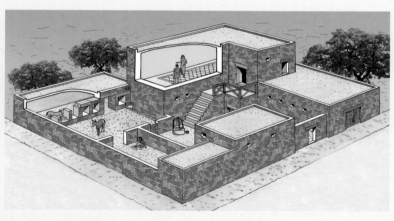

Family home, first century AD (drawing: Leen Ritmeyer)

BREAKOUT 9.04

THE JEWISH SECTS

During the intertestamental period, the Greco-political successors of Alexander the Great lorded over the Jews, their temple, and at times their right to worship Yahweh their God (see *Breakouts 8.04* and *8.06*). If the Jewish people were to avoid physical, cultural, and spiritual extermination, it was imperative that something be done. The Jewish Revolt ensued (see *Breakout 8.08*), and Judah suffered through peace and war for generations. When Rome gobbled up the region in AD 63 (see *Breakouts 8.09, 9.01*), Jewish semi-autonomy came to an end.

Jewish rabbis and scholars began to rethink how they understood the Torah and worshipped God. Different philosophical schools divided the Jews into factious denominations—Pharisees, Sadducees, Essenes, and Zealots—and there were significant theological and political distinctions between them.

The *Sadducees* ("Righteous Ones") claimed legitimacy through their connection to the Old Testament priest Zadok. Despite their theological differences (rejecting the resurrection—Matthew 22:23-34; Luke 20:27-40), by the time of Jesus, the Sadducees had become aristocratic and elitist. Many of them lived in lavish mansions funded, at least in part, by taking advantage of their fellow countrymen in the operation of a profiteering currency-exchange enterprise. The masses entering the temple precinct paid a premium to purchase the Tyrian silver coins required to pay the temple tax.

The *Pharisees* ("Separated Ones") were less interested in personal prosperity and temple matters. Instead, they promoted themselves as scribes and teachers of the law within the network of synagogues (see *Breakout 8.01*).

The *Essenes* were the copyists and librarians of the Dead Sea Scrolls (see *Breakout 8.13*). They referred to themselves as "The Sons of Light" and everyone else as "The Sons of Darkness." Their daily lives were hyper-focused on purity in all forms, particularly through ritual immersion in water. It appears that they considered the operation of the Jerusalem temple illegitimate. As separatists, they participated in a number of temple-like rituals that, in effect, made their Dead Sea community (Qumran) a kind of proxy temple replacing what they viewed as a heretical counterpart in Jerusalem.

Whether or not the *Zealots* were an actual religious sect is debated. They were, however, a notable politicoreligious presence in first-century AD Judea. A subsect of the Zealots, the *Sicarri*, were militant extremists who shrouded themselves in a veil of intrigue and whose terroristic manifesto advanced their aims through violence.

These sects were of human, not scriptural, origin. To be realistic (and ironic!), each believed they could achieve Jewish political sovereignty and righteousness before God through political maneuvering, deception, human works, precise ritual formulas, and by violence if necessary. In stark contrast, John the Baptist and Jesus of Nazareth demanded repentance—changed minds, hearts, and actions.

Preparing the way for Messiah Jesus, John the Baptizer (see *Breakout 9.12*) declared, "Bear fruit in keeping with repentance" (Matthew 3:8). Immediately after John was imprisoned by Herod Antipas, "Jesus came into Galilee, proclaiming the gospel of God, and saying, 'The time is fulfilled, and the kingdom of God is at hand; repent and believe in the gospel'" (Mark 1:14-15).

John and Jesus preached repentance, not rebellion. They emphasized the necessity of simple belief over prescribed behaviors and proclaimed that faith in the true Messiah trumped human goodness. For the spiritually famished Judeans of the first century, this was very good news indeed!

J. Barber, J. Holden

Breakout 9.05

Herodian Fortresses

Although Herod the Great is remembered by many for his brutality and paranoia, he is also regarded as a master builder who could accomplish seemingly impossible projects. Herod was involved in 20 or more sites in Israel and at least 13 beyond its borders. Some of Herod's greatest achievements were his many fortresses, especially his palace fortresses. These, along with their accompanying defenses, help us gain insight into the man and his times.

Several factors contributed to Herod's palace-fortress concept. He enjoyed the finer things and extreme comforts of life even in hostile conditions. He needed a defensive perimeter against his enemies in the east. He was afraid of revolt from the Jews and even his own family. He wanted to demonstrate to Rome his capabilities of building and governing. And build he did!

Herod built three different winter palaces at Jericho, the third being the most extravagant and luxurious. Protection for Jericho was provided by Cypros, a former Hasmonean fortress that overlooked the Wadi Qelt above Jericho. According to Josephus, Cypros was named after Herod's mother.

The Herodium, a volcano-shaped fortress standing seven miles south of Jerusalem and three miles southeast of Bethlehem, rose to a height of nearly 200 feet. The palace was the largest in the Mediterranean world. Relatively well preserved, it contains circular walls, towers, storerooms, extravagant living quarters, gardens, a large bathhouse, and an artificial lake. This structure served not only as Herod's fortress, but also his burial place.

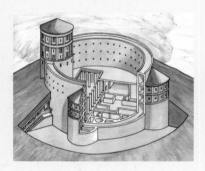

The Herodium near Bethlehem; fortress of Herod the Great (drawing: Leen Ritmeyer)

Herod's Jerusalem projects were among his most important. There was the colossal reconstruction of the temple, which ended up taking decades to complete (John 2:20), as well as two palace-fortresses. Herod's chief residence was a large palace complex on the west side of Jerusalem. A strong fortress with three large towers was built just north of the palace.

The palace-fortress of Machaerus was about five miles east of the Dead Sea at 2,300 feet above sea level in what is now Jordan. Josephus gave the most extensive description of this former Hasmonean fortress, describing towers that were "sixty cubits high" at the four corners of massive walls. He wrote of a palace within that had spacious apartments and numerous cisterns. He also reported that Machaerus was the location where John the Baptist was executed during the time of Herod Antipas.

At Masada, just west of the south end of the Dead Sea, Herod built a large palace-fortress on the ruins of an earlier Hasmonean stronghold. Sheer-faced cliffs that rise hundreds of feet high with access limited to a single "snake" path made this location seem impregnable. Comfort was not neglected. There were two palaces at Masada, one having three terraces. The site had several large cisterns and storerooms that would enable the occupants to withstand an extended siege. This was what the Jewish Zealots had in mind when they withstood a Roman attack in AD 70–73, although ultimately, they were defeated.

C. Morgan

BREAKOUT 9.06

THE HERODIAN TEMPLE

The center of Jewish faith and life, the Jerusalem temple, was built on Mount Moriah, facing the rising sun and overlooking the Kidron Valley toward the Mount of Olives. The second temple—better identified as the third temple—was an expansion of Zerubbabel's version from c. 515 BC. This final temple project was started under Herod the Great in the first century BC. According to Josephus, the massive remodel was initiated at least in part because of the unstable foundations of the previous iteration.

Herod employed 10,000 masons and other craftsmen, along with 1,000 special Levites, to work without disturbing the temple services. Herod's enlarged temple was made of white limestone that was quarried locally. Some of the foundation stones for this massive undertaking weighed up to 50 tons. The platform-retaining walls surrounding the temple complex were at least 15 feet thick, and the western wall was 1,590 feet long. This platform wall had four gates: from north to south they are Warren's Gate, Wilson's Arch, Barclay's Gate, and Robinson's Arch (names of nineteenth-century explorer-scholars who identified them). There were eight gates leading into the temple precincts, and a ninth gate, called the East Gate (Shushan Gate), was said to have been the most magnificent of all. It was the principle gate used by worshippers once they were inside the complex.

Herod extended the temple platform in three directions: north, west, and south. He added the Antonia Fortress at the northwest corner, and a royal stoa (large columned hall) on the south end. The entire complex was one of the largest in the ancient world, occupying about 145 acres. Work on the Jerusalem temple structures was completed 46 years after it began (John 2:20), with some additional work continuing to c. AD 64.

The First Jewish Revolt (AD 66–70) was the culmination of years of skirmishes, and the Jews expelled the Roman forces for a time. But Rome sent Vespasian and Titus to crush the rebellion. The two leaders entered the city with 60,000 troops. These soldiers destroyed the temple by fire and manual demolition when Jerusalem fell in AD 70. They chopped down the olive trees on the Mount of Olives and used them, along with other combustible materials, to create an explosive conflagration in the cisterns next to the temple, blowing the structures' stones apart. The destruction was total.

B. Maggard, S. Collins

BREAKOUT 9.07

THE MAGI

In Matthew chapter 2, we read of magi who came from the east, seeking after one "who has been born king of the Jews" (verse 2). Magi were wise men in eastern cultures, and despite what is proclaimed in many Christmas songs and seen in nativity scenes, they were not kings. They probably did not ride on camels, and most likely there were more than three of them. Early in the magi tradition there were 12, then the number was reduced to 3. The actual number is unknown. Tradition gives them the names Caspar, Melchior, and Balthasar.

Historically, the magi were wise counselors, mainly from Persia and Arabia. They were held in high esteem in the Persian court, were admitted as consultants, and gave advice to kings in times of war and peace. They were Gentiles, a tribe of priests, similar to the Levites in Israel. The magi served as the teachers and instructors of the Persian kings. No sacrifice could be offered unless one of the magi was present. They were men of piety and wisdom, skilled in the philosophy, religion, divining, medicine, and science of their day.

In the book of Daniel, we see that Daniel and his friends Hananiah, Mishael, and Azariah were recruited to be magi in the court of Nebuchadnezzar, with Daniel in charge of all the magi. Daniel and his friends certainly influenced the magi, and we can be certain that they taught them about the one true God, Yahweh, the God of Abraham, Isaac, and Jacob. The teachings of Daniel surely influenced the magi for generations, and Matthew's Gospel seems to indicate that they still remembered Daniel's teaching about the Messiah, the one who was to come, the King of all kings. They were looking for him—likely because of the Messianic math in Daniel 9—and they knew the time had come when they saw his "star" in the heavens. The appearance of a new heavenly object—be it an alignment of planets, a comet, or a supernova explosion—was regarded as an indication that a remarkable event was occurring or about to occur.

The magi probably came to Jerusalem mounted on Persian steeds (horses famous throughout the ancient known world), and likely with troops to guard them as they traveled. Such an official entourage looking for the one "who has been born king of the Jews" made Herod nervous—disturbed, no doubt—playing on his oft-demonstrated paranoia. Herod was not born a king. He was appointed. A rival hereditary king of royal blood—now *that* was a threat Herod might kill for. *And he did.*

W. Attaway

SOCIETY AND CULTURE

ROMAN CULTURE—By the time the Romans arrived in the Levant c. 64–63 BC (see *Breakout 8.09*), the Jewish world had long endured the cultural shock of Hellenism (see *Breakout 8.03*) with its challenges to conservative Jewish beliefs. The Romans further challenged the Jews with the multicultural approach of their conquests. They were polytheistic and willingly enlarged the number of permissible religions so long as they presented no challenge to the Roman State. Roman society was divided between a very wealthy upper class, a thriving middle class of merchants, and a lower class of servants (simply, those who had to work for someone else). There was also a vast multitude of slaves (mostly battle captives). An extensive set of laws governed all aspects of daily life, and the enforcement of those laws was swift and harsh.

JEWISH CULTURE—The Jewish culture of the New Testament era was the result of major changes that occurred during the Babylonian exile (see *Breakouts 7.01, 8.01*). These refinements and reorganizations of Mosaic Yahwism were reintroduced to the Jewish inhabitants of Judea by the return of Ezra in c. 450 BC (see *Breakout 7.08*). Jews lived according to very strict laws derived and interpreted from the Torah, laws that governed every aspect of their lives. They made constant effort to observe rules of hygiene, dietary restrictions, community activities, and religious celebrations. In the face of enormous challenges by the Hellenistic and Roman cultures, Jewish communities often isolated themselves from non-Jewish societies, such as the Gentiles of the Decapolis and the Samaritans (see *Maps 9.02, 9.03*), as well as their Roman overlords. The region of Lower Galilee was an economic center of the time, and it is from this region that Jesus and his disciples first spread their message.

BREAKOUT 9.08

THE SAMARITANS

After King Solomon's death, the kingdom of Israel was divided (see *Timeline* and *Map 6.01*). Jeroboam, representing the northern tribes, rebelled against Solomon's son Rehoboam and set out to rule a separate kingdom. This civil war—mostly of words—caused a division resulting in a kingdom of Israel in the north and a kingdom of Judah in the south. The split was permanent. The Samaria of the New Testament era was a carryover from the days of the divided monarchy when Samaria became the capital of Israel, a name that was often applied to the entire northern kingdom itself. The royal line of David remained in its ancestral territory, with Jerusalem as the capital of the southern kingdom of Judah.

As successive generations ruled, Yahweh sent prophets to both nations. In Israel, the house of Omri (885–874 BC) was established after the suicide of Zimri. Lengthy infighting ensued, focused at the new and well-fortified capital of the north, Samaria (1 Kings 16). The son of Omri, King Ahab, attempted to strengthen the northern kingdom against the Syrian threat and looming invasion. Subsequent kings of Israel obtained the throne mostly through political intrigue, skirmishes, coups, and assassinations. Jehu's Dynasty

was the longest (90 years; 2 Kings 10:30; see also 1 Kings 21).

The northern kingdom finally attempted to make peace with its neighbors, including Judah, but was overtaken by Assyria under the reign of King Sargon II in 721/22 BC (2 Kings 17:5-24). The primary post-conquest tactic of Assyria was forced resettlement. In the case of Israel, peoples from other conquered nations were relocated to the region of Samaria, and the Israelites were moved to distant territories. In this way, ethnic boundaries were blurred through intermarriage and tribal identities were diluted. The mixed population of Israel/Samaria would eventually become the Samaritans of the New Testament era. Nebuchadnezzar came into possession of the former territory of Israel/Samaria (c. 612 BC) after defeating the Egyptians, who had wrested control of these same lands from Assyria.

After the post-exilic return of the Babylonian captivity Jews to the territory of Judah, some Samaritans sought to aid in rebuilding the Jerusalem temple but were turned away. In response, Sanballat, the governor of Samaria (Nehemiah 13:28), tried to obstruct the project (Ezra 4:1-4). The Samaritans built their own temple around 400 BC on Mount Gerizim, just above ancient Shechem.

The Maccabees destroyed the

Samaritan temple under the leadership of John Hyrcanus in the late second century BC. One possible reason for this may have been because of the defiling of the Samaritan temple at about the same time that Antiochus IV Epiphanes despoiled the Jerusalem temple (167 BC; 2 Maccabees 6:2; see *Breakouts 8.06, 8.08*). The "pedigreed" Jewish people thought of Samaritans as tainted and less than Jewish.

Josephus related an episode that further increased Jewish hostility toward Samaritans: A group of Samaritan men entered the temple precinct in Jerusalem at night and defiled it by spreading the ground-up bones of dead people across the temple courtyards. This hostility between Jews and Samaritans is demonstrated in the New Testament in John 4:9, where John included this note concerning the relations between the two during the time of Christ: "Jews have no dealings with Samaritans" (John 4:9).

The first-century AD region of Samaria was loosely a swath from the Mediterranean Sea on the west, as far as the Jordan River to the east, with some southern territory included, encompassing cities such as Sychem (Shechem), Sabaste (Samaria), and Caesarea Maritima (see *Map 9.02*).

B. Maggard, S. Collins

POLITICAL CLIMATE—In the region of and around first-century AD Palestine, the best descriptor of the political situation is *tension*. The collective Jewish memory of their persecution at the hands of the Seleucids (see *Breakouts 8.06, 8.08*) was still raw and memorialized (Hanukkah). So-called Jewish Zealots resisted the idea of any foreign power ruling over what they saw as their Promised Land. The Roman control of Judea/Palestine (see *Breakout 8.09*) stuck in their craw, and they were always looking for an opportunity to foment rebellion locally or on a larger scale if possible.

The Jews themselves were carved up into religious sectarian groups—Pharisees, Sadducees, Essenes—with no love lost between them (see *Breakout 9.04*). The Essenes were mostly separatists (the Qumran community; see *Breakout 8.13*), and the Pharisees and Sadducees (see *Breakout 9.04*) wielded significant political influence in the face of Rome's desire to appease local populations as much as possible. The Herodians (see *Breakouts 8.10, 9.02*), although ruling over Palestinian Jews at the behest of Rome, were not looked upon with favor by the purest Jewish factions. Roman officials, backed by a powerful Roman military presence, kept a close eye on everything. Throughout the Early Roman period (see *Timeline*), Palestine was a powder keg filled with torch-brandishing political opponents.

LANGUAGE AND WRITING

GREEK—Alexander and his Hellenistic posterity had spread the Koine (common) version of the Greek language across the entire stage of his empire. The Romans were keen to keep and even expand it as the *lingua franca* of their empire. Greek remained the principle language of international commerce for the next 600 years (see *Figure 9.11*), and Koine Greek became the language of choice for the writers of the New Testament.

LATIN—Latin was the official language of Roman government (although Greek was used when advantageous). Latin inscriptions were common throughout the Roman Empire, including Palestine (see *Figure 9.12*).

ARAMAIC/HEBREW—The Aramaic adopted by the Jews living in Babylonia and brought back to Palestine during their return from captivity became mixed with Hebrew to create a mongrel language spoken by Jews across the region. Some call it Aramaicized Hebrew, while others describe it as Hebraicized Aramaic. Both languages are very similar, belonging to the Northwest Semitic language group. Both Aramaic and Hebrew inscriptions are known from Roman Palestine (see *Figure 9.13*).

BELIEF AND RELIGION

JUDAISM—In the first century AD, while Judaism was certainly monotheistic, it was certainly not monolithic. The named Jewish sects are well known—Pharisees, Sadducees, Zealots, Essenes (see *Breakout 9.04*). There were many other splinter groups based on

Figure 9.11—Greek text, first century AD (photo: Alexander Schick)

Figure 9.12—Latin inscription, first century AD (photo: Alexander Schick)

either religious or political leanings, or both. Each faction followed one or more central leader-figures, often hailed as messiahs. Some of the messianic fervor was political, some religious. On the religious side, rabbis dominated local communities and synagogues (see *Breakout 8.01*), while some were itinerant. Rabbinic Judaism often departed from or added to the Mosaic Law, seeking definitions and details for righteous living.

ROMAN RELIGION—Borrowing and renaming the gods of the Greek pantheon—Zeus to Jupiter, Athena to Minerva, Aphrodite to Venus, Phoebus Apollo to Apollo, Poseidon to Neptune, and so forth—Roman religion was a syncretistic amalgam of older traditional gods mixed with deities and demons from cultures subsumed by the Roman Empire. Notable among their adopted mystery (for initiates only) religions was Mithraism (originating in India). Other mystery cults followed deities (like Dionysus), famous thinkers (like Pythagoras and Plato), or localized beliefs (like the Eleusinians).

EMPEROR WORSHIP—Emperor worship (also referred to as the Imperial cult) was instituted in Rome after the reign of Caesar Augustus. Other ancient cultures had engaged in the deification of important individuals, so this was simply a continuation of ancient practice. A deceased emperor or family member could be deified as an honor. When this was done, temples were sometimes built to honor the newly deified individual and cults of worship might form. Whether the Roman world truly believed that these individuals had become gods is a matter of some dispute, but the practice persisted until Emperor Theodosius I declared Christianity to be the official religion of the empire in the late AD 300s.

ARCHITECTURE AND INFRASTRUCTURE

ROMAN CITIES—The Romans took Greek city planning and structure to a whole new level and scale. The central crossing streets (north-south cardo and east-west decumanus) remained fundamental. Cities always included market plazas, commercial streets,

Figure 9.13—Aramaic and Hebrew ostraca from Masada, first century AD (photo: Alexander Schick)

Figure 9.14—Roman Appian Way (photo: David E. Graves)

temples, residential areas, palaces, administrative buildings, theaters or amphitheaters, and the obligatory hippodrome for horse racing, chariot competitions, gladiatorial games, and other blood sports. While in the more ancient world of the Bronze and Iron Ages the main criteria for locating a city or town were (1) defensible high ground, (2) arable land, and (3) adequate water resources, the Romans had no such constraints. With aqueducts they could bring water to any location from 100 miles or more, if needed. Food could be easily imported, as required. The Romans

Roman Roads

During the early Roman period, cities were linked by a network of well-built and maintained public roads (Latin, *viae publicae*) that also promoted security (*via militaris*), communication, and trade. These same roads would enable Christians to spread the gospel of Jesus quickly and efficiently over long distances. Rome was the center of the Roman Empire and, literally, the phrase "all roads lead to Rome" was true.

These were among the best-known major roadways leading to and from Rome: the *Via Appia* (Appian Way) to Apulia; the *Via Aurelia* to France; the *Via Cassia* to Tuscany; the *Via Maris* connecting the major trade routes between Egypt, the Levant, Anatolia, and Mesopotamia; and the *Via Traiana Nova*, which passed through the Levant. An estimated 29 major roads went out from Rome to connect with approximately 375 smaller roads in the provinces. The Romans had 56,000 miles of paved highways and 186,400 miles of secondary roads—some paved, some covered with gravel. An example is the road from Heshbon (Latin, *Esebus*, near Mount Nebo) to Livias, then across the Jordan River to Jericho, then up to Jerusalem. This particular Roman road was

Roman bridge/aqueduct (photo: David E. Graves)

surveyed for the first time in February 2010 (Graves and Stripling, "Re-Examination of the Location for the Ancient City of Livias," in *Levant* 43, no. 2 [2011]).

There were three different methods used to construct Roman roads: leveled and packed earth (Latin *viae terrena*); packed earth with a gravel surface (*viae glareata*); and a substantial prepared base paved with cut limestone or basalt blocks (pavers), sometimes with mosaic tiles (*tessera*) or marble (*via munita*). All the roadways were able to be travelled on by foot, horse, cart, or wagon. According to Roman law, roads had to be at least eight feet wide for straight sections and

sixteen feet wide for corners to allow easy passage.

In Italy, during the Imperial period (27 BC–AD 284), construction costs of roads were funded from the public purse (Latin, *aerarium*), while in the provinces they were funded by the local landowners or communities. There were political connections to the building of roads; those who spent a lot of their own money on repairing the roads (*curator*) were often elected to political posts.

Because common travelers did not have the privilege of military escorts, roadhouses (Latin, *mansio*) were located about every 20 miles (a day's journey) as rest stops to provide food and protection for Roman citizens on official business. Roman forts were commonly built close to the roadhouses, and less-reliable inns were situated nearby for noncitizen travelers in need of rest and refreshment. In addition, between the way stations, at intervals of about nine miles, there were horse-changing stations (*mutationes*) with workshops and accommodations.

To indicate the distance between cities, milestone pillars (Latin, *miliarium*; eight feet high by two feet wide) were erected along public roads, bearing inscriptions indicating the distance to the next major destination. The Roman government often included inscriptions identifying who the curator of the road was and when the work was carried out.

D. Graves

Figure 9.15—Roman latrines; Ephesus (L), Scythopolis (Beth Shan) (R) (photos: David E. Graves, John Witte Moore)

were offensively minded and not worried about having elevated cities for defensive purposes. Interestingly, the number one criterion for those involved in the planning and building of cities was good air! Smoke pollution was a perennial problem, and consistent breezes were a necessity for clearing the air.

ROADS—The enormous Roman road network connected every corner of the empire with well-engineered roads that were designed to last. Connected by watchtowers, police posts, and inns, they provided safety and comfort for travelers. Local industry could now be marketed in the farthest reaches of the empire. Most importantly, the roadways allowed for the rapid movement of armies and their materiel, which were the foundation of the Roman Empire (see *Figure 9.14*).

AQUEDUCTS—Improved hygiene in the cities resulted from the flowing water brought in by aqueducts. This provided clean water for drinking, for fountains, and to flush effluent from the public latrines (see *Figure 9.15*). Hygiene was unchanged in the countryside, however, and people continued to suffer from a high infant mortality rate and a wide range of parasites and diseases.

BRIDGES—Well-designed bridges, like the roads, were essential to travel throughout the empire, and the Romans excelled at building them. Arched bridges that spanned valleys could also serve as part of an aqueduct system (see *Figure 9.16*).

SEWAGE SYSTEMS—Sewer systems were common in large Roman cities. They carried off rainwater as well as the waste and runoff from public baths and latrines. In spite of the use of such sewers, the cities were still largely filthy and unsanitary due to the fact that most of the lower-income housing had no access to the city sewers.

HARBORS—The Romans utilized harbors throughout the Mediterranean world and even constructed a remarkable artificial harbor at Caesarea on the coast of Palestine. The harbor at Caesarea Maritima (see *Figure 9.17*) ranks as one of the great engineering accomplishments of the age and, at its height, was a major center of commerce and the equal of the Egyptian harbor at Alexandria.

Figure 9.16—Arched Roman bridge/aqueduct; Roman architects could span deep valleys with arched structures (photo: David E. Graves)

Figure 9.17—Caesarea Maritima harbor, top L of photo (photo: David E. Graves)

WEAPONS AND WARFARE

ROMAN LEGIONS—The Roman army was traditionally composed of groups of men called legions. These were of various sizes through the centuries, but usually came to around 5,000 soldiers. The actual number of fighting men marching into battle, however, varied from conflict to conflict. The largest recorded Roman army was nearly 90,000 strong in the Battle of Cannae against Hannibal in 216 BC (which they lost). On the battlefield,

Figure 9.18—Roman soldier (photo: David E. Graves)

the Romans were effective in their use of the phalanx formation, which they borrowed from the Greeks. The phalanx was used in conjunction with hand-to-hand infantry, artillery (archers and ballistae), chariots, and cavalry.

ARMOR—Roman legionnaires wore torso armor that came in a variety of styles, such as mail shirts and scale armor, greaves to protect the lower legs, helmets, and shields (see *Figure 9.18*). They carried a number of offensive weapons depending upon their duties.

WEAPONRY—The weaponry of Roman legionnaires depended upon their task in the legion. Their shields were long and heavy. They carried one or more of a variety of swords of different sizes. There were bowmen, men with darts, men with slings, and masters of javelins and spears. And behind all these men were those who manned devices that hurled huge arrows, iron rods, and stone balls (ballistae) against the enemy (see *Figure 9.19*).

SIEGE WARFARE—The Romans were superb fighters and this extended to siege techniques. This was gruesomely displayed by their siege of Jerusalem in AD 70, an efficient action that was completed in several months and resulted in the complete destruction of the heavily fortified city. Siege machinery—which included siege towers, battering rams, and catapults for heaving stones and fire-bombs—coupled with a steely and lethal patience, enhanced the ability of the Romans to take almost any target.

Figure 9.19—Roman military gear (photos: Alexander Schick, Steven Collins)

Figure 9.20—Roman leather goods (photo: Steven Collins)

INDUSTRY AND OBJECTS

AGRICULTURE—It is estimated that up to 80 percent of the Roman Empire's population consisted of slaves. A significant number of those slaves served the agricultural industry. Food production was paramount for sustaining large city and town populations, as well as feeding the vast Roman military complex. Practically every kind of crop—grains, fruit, vegetables, nuts—grown in the Mesopotamian Basin and contiguous regions was available in city markets throughout the Empire. Flax fields supported the textile industry. Poultry production expanded exponentially during the Early Roman period, providing a whole new repertoire of cuisine.

HERDING—Wool remained a prized fiber for making cloth and rugs. Thus, shepherds and their products were always in demand. Lamb was a prized meat, along with beef and pork. Milk, yogurt, and cheese were common on Roman dining tables. Animal skins provided leather (see *Figure 9.20*) for a wide range of footwear, clothing items, straps and chords, armor elements, wineskins, waterskins, and parchment (for important documents).

FISHING—With the Mediterranean Sea as a "Roman lake," all manner of seafood was on the menu. One of the most important fish products (or byproducts) was *garum*, a pungent fish sauce used daily across the empire from the modest home hearth to the most

Burial Practices

While the Egyptians embalmed their dead and the Romans and Greeks cremated theirs, during the late second temple period (between 30 BC and AD 70) Jewish burial practices were different and carried out in two stages. First, the body was placed in a cave for a period of about a year, where the flesh would decompose and fall off the bones (Latin, *ossilegium*). Following decomposition, the bones were collected and placed in either ossuaries (bone boxes, which were made of stone during this period), communal graves, or wooden coffins inserted into niches (*loculi*) in cave-tombs or funerary monuments. Ossuaries and coffins often bore the name of the deceased. This two-stage practice was popular during the late Hellenistic and early Roman periods.

In preparation for the two-stage Jewish burial, the body was washed and wrapped in a clean cloth (shroud; Matthew 27:57-60; Mark 15:42-46; Luke 23:52-54). In the Mediterranean climate, bodies decomposed quickly, so spices and perfumes (Greek, *aromata*) were applied to the body and wrappings to mask the odor of decay (John 19:38-42). Lazarus, who was raised back to life, and Jesus, who was resurrected

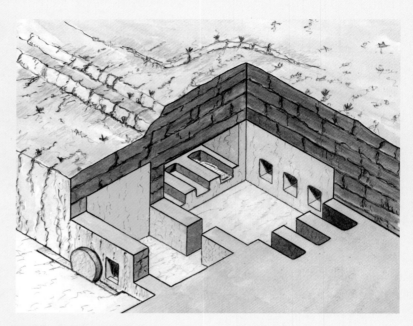

Kokhim tomb of a wealthy family (drawing: Leen Ritmeyer)

from the dead, were in this first stage of burial when they experienced bodily resurrection (John 11:1-44; Luke 24). Even the body of a crucified criminal was buried properly, but not in a place of honor, such as a family tomb. Also, there was to be no mourning for the executed criminal.

There were two types of interiors for first-century rock-cut tombs. The first was a long narrow niche (Latin, *loculus*; Hebrew, *kokh*, pl. *kokhim*) cut at right angles to a central chamber. The second was a low bench cut parallel to the wall and into the chamber wall, creating a canopy (Latin, *arcosolium*, pl.

arcosolia). The latter type of tomb was reserved for the wealthy and people of high standing in society and was likely the kind in which Jesus's body was placed. His was the tomb of a wealthy individual (Matthew 27:57-60; Isaiah 53:9). The so-called Garden Tomb dates to the eighth century BC and has none of the features of a first-century AD tomb. The tomb inside the Church of the Holy Sepulchre, although eroded from centuries of abuse by clerics and pilgrims, is definitely an *arcosolium*. Excellent examples of first-century "rolling stone" *arcosolia* also exist in abundance in a garden tomb area atop

A modest rolling-stone tomb, Jerusalem (drawing: Leen Ritmeyer)

with rectangular or circular stone doors to the chamber.

In 1980, ten ossuaries were discovered in a Talpiot (or Talpiyot) tomb near the Old City of Jerusalem (Nos. 701-709). The names on six ossuaries read *Mariamenou [e] Mara* ("Mary, who is…"), *Yhwdh br Yshw'* ("Judah/Jude, son of Jesus"), *Mtyh* ("Matiyahu" or "Matthew"), *Yshw' br Yhwsp* ("Jesus, son of Joseph"), and *Mryh* ("Mary"). While these names are familiar to any reader of the New Testament and we can easily assume they refer to the biblical figures, these names were very common in the first century, so any connection to the biblical persons is doubtful. Not to mention that the family tomb of the biblical Joseph and Mary would likely have been near Nazareth, not Jerusalem.

D. Graves

the Mount of Olives, although they are not accessible to the public.

Around Jerusalem there are many surviving first-century tombs—hewn into the natural bedrock—that were used for secondary burials. Often in front of larger tombs was a courtyard with an inscribed and decorated cut stone (Latin, *nefesh*) above or next to it, preserving the memory of the interred. Entrances to the more elaborate tombs often resembled a temple or palace,

lavish palace kitchens. Making garum started by filling vats with small fish and fish guts gleaned from processing anchovies, tuna, mackerel, and other species. They were alternately layered with just the right amounts of salt and aromatic herbs, then lidded and placed in a sunny location for several months until the mixture attained the perfect malodorous aroma. When the concoction was fully fermented, it was then strained. The thick, amber-colored oily liquid was the precious and potent garum, which was then barreled and bottled for distribution across the Roman world (see *Figure 9.21*). The thick paste left over from the straining process was *allec*. While not prized or priced like garum, allec was still widely traded.

KITCHENS AND COOKING—Nonskid ceramic cookware was all the rage during the Roman era (see *Figure 9.22*). Iron and bronze pots, pans, and utensils were also common, but expensive. Kitchens were typically in outdoor courtyards and had food-preparation tables, open and covered hearths with spits, baking ovens of brick or stone, and a pantry for keeping ingredients safe from vermin. Water was carried from local sources and stored in large jars. Cooler underground storage was common for olive oil and wine and usually accessible from the courtyard. In principle, Roman cooking was little different from modern cooking, with virtually every imaginable grain, vegetable, fruit, nut, fish, and meat from wide-ranging geographical regions. Garum sauce was widely used to flavor everything from cabbage to meats to wines. Garum, which has high

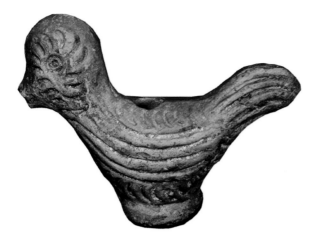

Figure 9.21—Chicken motif garum container, Early Roman period (photo: Daniel Galassini, courtesy of Museum of Archaeology, Trinity Southwest University)

Figure 9.22—Non-skid cooking pot, Early Roman period (photo: Daniel Galassini, courtesy of Museum of Archaeology, Trinity Southwest University)

levels of monosodium glutamate (MSG), is also used as a flavor enhancer in the modern food industry. The following recipe is from the *Roman Cookbook* by Apicius (but no garum!) written c. AD 14–37.

Roman Custard
(makes about 1 cupcake pan; see Figure 9.23)

This is a common Roman recipe from the first century AD.

Ingredients
4 cups milk
½ cup honey
6 eggs
½ tsp nutmeg, plus some for garnish
Berries (or other fruits) for garnish

Instructions
Preheat oven to 325°. Gather all ingredients together. Pour milk into a bowl and mix with honey until blended (a flat plastic spatula works well for this). Whisk egg yolks in a separate bowl; set aside. Pour milk/honey mixture into a small saucepan and heat briefly for around 1-5 minutes, just enough for the milk and honey to combine. Take milk/honey mixture off the stove and let cool for a few minutes.

Once cool, add the well-beaten egg yolks. Add nutmeg and stir thoroughly (it's fine to keep using the whisk here). Pour custard into a baking dish. We suggest using a cupcake pan, as this will allow the custard to cook more evenly. (If you choose to use a large baking dish, you should also increase your baking time. However, in a large dish, the custard might not cook completely and instead may turn out a bit like mush, as happened on one of our failed attempts to recreate this recipe.) Bake 15-20 minutes, or until custard is golden brown. Remove and let sit for about one hour at room temperature. Garnish with berries of your choice and enjoy!

Figure 9.23—Roman custard; modern pan! (photo: Wes Husted)

BREAKOUT 9.11

FROM PASSOVER TO THE LORD'S SUPPER

What is often called the Last Supper should be called the Last Passover, since that is what Jesus was observing when he inaugurated the ceremony of the bread and the cup to be observed by the body of the Messiah (the church) until he returns. In *Breakout 3.03* on the Passover, a number of details were described that have Messianic implications (you should read that *Breakout* in order to fully understand this one). What this *Breakout* does is correlate New Testament references to certain facets of the Jewish observance with Jesus's own Last Passover, concluding with how the church has inherited the ceremony of the bread and the cup, thus observing a mini-Passover.

Matthew 26:20-23. During his Passover, Messiah Jesus announced that one of the 12 men reclining at the table would betray him. Eleven of the disciples wanted to know who it would be, but Jesus named no one. Instead, he gave a clue: The one "who has dipped his hand in the dish with me" will do this (verse 23). This refers to the *karpas* ceremony. With a large number of participants, as was the case here, there would be several saltwater dishes spread across the table, so each dish would be within easy reach

of three to four men. At the point when Jesus dipped his vegetable into the saltwater dish, Judas did the same. However, the others did not catch the clue.

Matthew 26:30. This verse notes that the disciples concluded by singing a hymn. The Greek text more literally reads "they hymned." This refers to the *Hallel* psalms, which includes Psalm 118, a Messianic psalm.

John 13:21-30. Two things should be noted here. First, for the second time, Jesus announced that one of his disciples would betray him. Again, they wanted to know who it was, and again he named no one. But then he gave another clue: "he to whom I will give this morsel of bread when I have dipped it" (verse 26). This refers to the *koreich* ceremony, in which small sandwiches are made of unleavened bread filled with the horseradish and *charoset*. The one who officiates makes the sandwiches for the others and, in this case, it was Jesus. His response was that the one to whom he would give the "morsel of bread" (the first one) was the betrayer. It was given to Judas, at which point Judas left the room. The purpose of the horseradish is to bring tears to the eyes. No doubt this ceremony brought tears to the eyes

of the Messiah because one of his own was about to betray him. The second item to note is the reference to reclining, and one of the times that reclining is practiced is during this very ceremony.

Luke 22:14-20. That this was a Passover service is clearly stated (verses 14-16), as well as the fact this Passover would be the Passover of fulfillment. As Jesus began the service, Luke mentions a cup, which refers to the fourth cup (Cup of Thanksgiving), and so he gave thanks. Then the ceremony began (verses 17-18). Verse 19 refers to the *yachatz* ceremony, which has to do with the middle of the three pieces of bread used for Passover. When Jesus said, "This is my body," such was only true of the Jewish unleavened bread. Three things had to be true of this bread for it to qualify for the Passover. According the Mosaic Law it had to be unleavened, because symbolically, leaven represented sin. The body of the Messiah was unleavened, or sinless, and he proved to be the only Jew who could keep the Mosaic Law perfectly down to every jot and tittle. Rabbinic law added two more requirements: The bread had to be both striped and pierced in order to reduce the danger of leavening. The body of the Messiah was also striped by Roman whips during his scourging, and it was also pierced—by the nails of crucifixion and the spear in his side. Verse 20 focuses on the cup. This was the third cup, the Cup of Redemption. Luke specifies that it was "the cup after supper," which is the third cup. In Judaism this is a symbol of a physical redemption, but for us it symbolizes the spiritual redemption that was provided by means of Jesus's blood.

Thus, when the church celebrates communion, it is an abridged Passover. The bread the church partakes of is the middle of the three loaves, and the cup the church partakes of is the third (Cup of Redemption) of the four cups of wine.

A. Fruchtenbaum

METALLURGY—One of the worst jobs for a slave was working in the iron or copper mines. Essentially this was a death sentence. Slaves, mostly war captives and criminals, were the expendable human machinery that drove the mining economy. The Roman Empire's need for metals of all kinds was insatiable. Iron, copper and tin (to make bronze), silver, and gold were the "big four." And the Romans controlled all the territories where these metals were found (see *Map 1.06*). Being a metalsmith was hard work but a worthy profession, and a necessity! Skilled smiths were in great demand and could lead a decent middle-class life. That is, until they died from inhaling the charcoal smoke, cinders, and chemical fumes associated with their profession.

STONE—Slavery fueled the stone-quarrying industry. Working in a quarry was meant as a death sentence for war captives, convicted criminals, and sometimes political enemies of the Roman State. But Roman builders needed finely cut stone, and lots of it. Foundations, columns (bases, capitals, and drums), pediments, fountains, aqueducts, streets—were all made with stone. Cutters, finishers, and carvers were often skilled paid laborers, although well-cared-for slaves also worked in the stone trades. Small-town stone workers built houses of unworked or partially worked fieldstones. In locations where the type of stone (like the basalt of the Galilee and Golan regions) allowed the creation of stone "beams" (usually no more than six feet long), the use of expensive timbers could be avoided (see *Figure 9.24*).

CARPENTRY—When we think of Joseph and Jesus, the carpentry trade comes immediately to mind. But wood was scarce in the area around tiny Nazareth and the nearby bustling city of Sepphoris, where they likely

Figure 9.24—Basalt beams, Chorazin (photos: John Witte Moore)

Figure 9.25—Chiusi Vase loom (photo: Steven Collins)

plied their trade as *tektonoi* (craftsmen). Therefore, it is possible that the family business, Joseph and Sons, worked as much in stone as with wood. Perhaps they built houses and made the furniture as well!

FLINT—For thousands of years, flint had provided the sharpest cutting edge for everything from skinning animals to performing delicate surgical procedures. For many tasks, a freshly knapped flint blade was still the tool of choice.

TEXTILES—While cottage-level spinning and weaving was widely practiced in small towns and rural areas, the large quantity of yarn and thread needed to create raw cloth, clothing, draperies, tapestries, and rugs demanded by the world's largest and wealthiest empire could only be met by large-scale production facilities. The type of loom used by Roman period weavers had been in service since the Neolithic Period. It was the upright, or warp-weighted, loom (as depicted on the famous Chiusi vase; see *Figure 9.25*). Warp-weighted looms keep the warp threads taut by using weights (modern looms do this with the beam). The threads were hung from a rectangular wooden frame supported by wooden poles. The poles could either be set into the ground or leaned against a wall. A shuttle carried the weft threads between the warp threads by moving a heddle (a stick) to which alternating warp threads were tied. After each shuttle pass, the weft threads were "beaten" with a reed, joining them with the completed portion of fabric.

GLASS—True glass production began as early as the third millennium BC in Egypt. But while glass items were prized during the Bronze and Iron Ages, they were costly and rare. In the Hellenistic period, glass production accelerated. In the Roman world, glass technology took off like a rocket. Glass vessels of every imaginable level of quality and artistry graced the homes and palaces of the elite, and simple glass vessels were used by common people as well (see *Figure 9.26*).

POTTERY—Late Hellenistic and Early Roman wares are virtually indistinguishable, except that pottery produced in the Roman period tended to be pinkish to reddish and had the look of what we today would call terra cotta (see *Figure 9.26*). Early Roman period

Figure 9.26—Early Roman pottery and glass (photos: Daniel Galassini, Steven Collins, David E. Graves, courtesy of Museum of Archaeology, Trinity Southwest University)

pottery was often produced with horizontal grooving or ribbing—thus the designation ribbed ware—which gave it a very practical nonskid surface. The Romans also produced a very expensive red sintered ware called terra sigillata (meaning clay with impressed designs).

TRADE—In Roman times, both maritime and overland commercial trade thrived. High demand for common and exotic materials and goods created shipping companies, broker/middlemen, port labor jobs, and haulers using the sea lanes and caravan routes. Ship builders and camel suppliers prospered as well. Insurance companies covered cargo shipments that were subject to storms and piracy on the seas and bands of thieves by land. But the Romans did their best to police the seas and road systems within their realm, all part of the *Pax Romana*. But materials and goods were not the only cargo to traverse the commercial routes of the empire. Ideas flowed freely from Spain to Persia, from Palestine to Rome. The Christian gospel was such a "cargo" (see *Breakout 9.15* and *Map 9.05*).

THE SPREAD OF CHRISTIANITY

Since the resurrection of Christ, the followers of Jesus (mostly Jews, slaves, and military initially) began to spread the gospel message in the same cities, towns, and villages in which they lived, and eventually (according to the book of Acts) this message spread throughout much of the Near East and Europe. These new followers would gather together in house-churches regularly on Sunday to engage in the learning of doctrine, fellowship, breaking of bread (communion), and prayers (Acts 2:42). That churches sprang up early in the Levant is attested by early twentieth-century exploration. While excavating at Dura-Europos (also Dura-Europus), situated in modern Syria on the banks of the Euphrates River, French and American teams unearthed the earliest known house-church, which dated to the early to mid-third century AD. Early structural renderings by the late Clark Hopkins (see *The Discovery of Dura-Europos*

and *MacMillan Bible Atlas*) reveal the church's structure complete with early Christian art (currently held at the Yale University Art Gallery), eucharistic documents, and baptistry.

With the spread of the message of Christ as King and a physical resurrection from the dead came persecution—sometimes from the Roman government, which viewed Christianity as a threat to the sovereign rule of the emperor (emperor worship), or from those holding the popular Platonist notion that the resurrection of a physical body was repugnant (Acts 17). While other theological assaults emerged from the Jewish religious leaders, these challenges would often lead to persecution, which did not end until the early

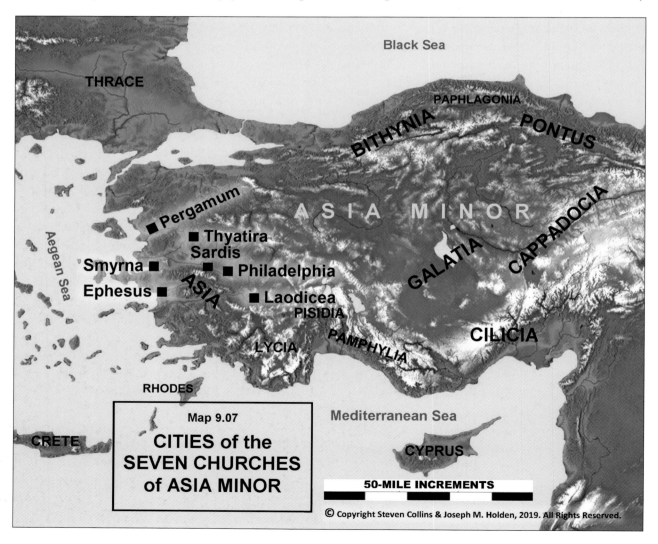

Map 9.07

CITIES of the SEVEN CHURCHES of ASIA MINOR

50-MILE INCREMENTS

BREAKOUT 9.12

CIRCUMCISION AND BAPTISM

Not every covenant has a sign or token connected with it, but some do. *Circumcision* was the sign or token of the Abrahamic covenant. It was to be performed only on males on the eighth day of life. This distinguished Hebrew circumcision from all other circumcisions practiced in ancient times. It also served as a reminder that this covenant was a blood covenant, and a sign of their unique identity as the chosen people of Yahweh. Failure to circumcise meant that the father would face the divine judgment of being cut off or executed. For this reason, Moses almost died for failing to circumcise his second son, and only when this act was completed was Moses's life spared (Exodus 4:24-26).

Circumcision was also prescribed by the Mosaic covenant (Leviticus 12:3), but the significance was not the same. Under the Abrahamic covenant it was mandatory for Hebrews only (and Gentiles living in a Hebrew or Israelite household) and was a sign of their unique identity as the people of Yahweh. Under the Law of Moses it was mandatory for all Israelites and for those Gentiles who converted to "the way of Yahweh" and wished to partake of the spiritual blessings of his covenants with Israel. Circumcision was the means of submission to the Mosaic Law, and it obligated one to keep the whole law (Galatians 5:3).

Galatians 3:15–4:7 points out that with the death of the Messiah the rule of the Law of Moses came to an end, and so in the present age there is no basis for circumcising Jews or Gentiles. However, the Abrahamic covenant is an ongoing covenant that includes the circumcision of Abraham's descendants, the Jewish people, and even Messianic Jews are still required to circumcise their sons. This explains why Paul refused to allow Titus to be circumcised yet initiated the circumcision of Timothy. Titus had no Jewish ancestry, while Timothy did (Acts 16:1-3; 21:17-26).

Already in the Hebrew Scriptures, the antitype of "circumcision of the flesh" was "circumcision of the heart," and this did not change in the New Testament.

Baptism was already a common Jewish practice long before it became a church practice. The key Hebrew word is *tvilah*, which means "immersion," and that was the only kind of baptism that was, and is, practiced in Judaism. The basic meaning was the concept of identification: to identify with a person or message or group. When a Gentile converted to Judaism he would undergo immersion, identifying with the God of Israel and the Jewish people. A new identity also meant a break from the old— namely, a break from polytheism and paganism.

Moving from Hebrew to Greek, two key words need to be noted. First, *bapto,* which means "to dip" or "to dye." This was the action of dipping a cloth into dye and thus changing its color— therefore, changing its identification. The second word is *baptizo,* which means "to immerse" and corresponds to the Hebrew *tvilah.* The meaning of the act is identification; the meaning of the term is immersion.

Is baptism the antitype to circumcision and does baptism replace circumcision? The answer is no. Circumcision shows the faith and obedience of the parents and not the child. Baptism shows the faith and obedience of the person undergoing the immersion, not the parents. There was no practice of infant baptism in the Hebrew Bible or in Judaism, nor is it found anywhere in the New Testament.

A. Fruchtenbaum

BREAKOUT 9.13

CRUCIFIXION

Jesus of Nazareth was tried, flogged, and crucified, suffering a terrible death that is almost beyond imagination. The Romans had perfected a form of execution used by Alexander the Great, perhaps originally introduced by the Persians. The practice was designed to produce a slow death with maximum pain and suffering.

Originally, the condemned was tied to a tree on the ground, naked and exposed to passers-by and wild animals. This was changed to the use of raised crosses in various configurations. It was customary for the condemned to carry the crossbar—which could weigh up to 125 pounds—to the execution site. Crucifixion was usually preceded by flogging, a form of scourging with either a small, multitailed *flagellum* (whip), or perhaps the much larger *flagrum*. The leather strips of the whip were embedded with pieces of bone or small lead weights that would tear the flesh on contact, causing tremendous pain as the condemned writhed against the rough wood of the cross.

The feet and hands were secured to the cross either by ropes or nails. The Romans seemed to prefer using nails. Church tradition has taught that the nails were inserted through the palms of Jesus' hands, but recent scholarship has shown that the nails were probably driven through the wrists (considered as part of the hand), a practice that would allow the arms to support the weight of a victim hanging on the cross. When the condemned slumped downward, body weight pulling against the nails caused excruciating pain.

Death would finally occur from asphyxia or shock. The crucified person, hanging from the arms, would experience increasing difficulty with breathing, and eventually would pass into unconsciousness and death. To prolong the ordeal, the Romans often provided a small "bench" upon which the condemned would sit, or a small platform for the feet. This would allow the individual to push upward each time he wanted to take a breath and thus survive a while longer.

The agonizing descent toward death often lasted for two or three days, but Jesus yielded up his spirit to the Father within hours. In fact, Pontius Pilate was surprised when, the very afternoon of the crucifixion, he was approached for permission to allow Jesus's dead body to be taken down (Mark 15:44).

Heel bone of a crucified man with nail intact, Israel Museum reproduction; crucifixion nails/spikes (photos: Daniel Galassini, courtesy of Museum of Archaeology, Trinity Southwest University)

Latin inscription with the name of "Pontius Pilatus," prefect of Judea, who presided over Jesus's crucifixion during the reign of Tiberieum (photo: Joseph Holden)

To assure that the condemned had indeed died on the cross, the soldiers would sometimes break the lower legs of the crucified. Without the support of the legs, the person would hang from severely weakened arms and suffocate within minutes. However, we are told that a spear was thrust into Jesus's side instead, and blood and fluids from the lungs flowed out, signaling that he was already dead.

Crucifixion was designed to inflict intense suffering for a prolonged period of time. It was an excruciating way to die. As an aside, our word *excruciating* derives from a Latin word that means "out of the cross."

J. Moore

fourth century AD with the Edict of Toleration and the Edict of Milan.

As the church spread throughout Asia Minor (Turkey) and Europe, it came into contact with rival religious belief systems such as emperor worship, the Roman mystery cults, polytheism, and the cult of Artemis along with their magical incantation formulas know as the *Ephesia Grammata* (Acts 19:28). Christians were pressed to defend the faith and develop an apologetic response that could both clearly distinguish Christianity from the cults and also withstand severe counterargument. Among these early apologists were the apostle Paul (Philippians 1:7, 17), Justin Martyr, Irenaeus, Tertullian, and eventually, Augustine.

However, as Christianity grew over the next few centuries, at the same time that its leaders clarified its doctrines, it was challenged by sophisticated philosophical and theological ideas emerging from Gnosticism (believed the creator god of the Old Testament is evil, matter is impure, and wrote false gospels of Christ), Arianism (Jesus did not have a divine nature), and from other heretics on the fringes of the church (for example, the teachings of Cerinthus, Valentinus, Arius, Eutychius, and Nestorius). Because Christianity grew up in this intellectually challenging environment of Hellenistic philosophy and Roman religious practice, believers understood the need to defend, clarify, and present the gospel in terms appropriate for the Greco-Roman age.

Jesus's Resurrection

That the Romans crucified (see *Breakout 9.13*) Jesus at the instigation of prominent Jewish leaders is a matter of historical record. But, as Jesus himself predicted, that was not the end of the story. The primary historical sources also report that Jesus rose from the grave—*physically*.

As much as many would like to, you cannot cut out any of the New Testament materials and hope to make sense of the rest of them. They all fit perfectly into a consistent historical account of Jesus's life. Certainly the resurrection of Jesus was a unique, supernatural event—call it a miracle if you like. But the fact remains that the collective witnesses to the resurrection did not call it a miracle—they presented it as *historical reality*.

We're dealing here with an event that happened in three-dimensional physical space and time in the real universe. Not a vision. Not a hallucination. Not some bizarre, mystical illusion beyond the five senses. The reports of the resurrection simply state that Jesus lived a real human life, died a real human death—blood, pain, sweat, and all that—and came back to life again. What's so strange about that? Except that he is the only person who ever successfully pulled off such a thing! But the eyewitnesses saw it. They

heard him. They ate with him. They touched him. They analyzed the situation. As strange as it may have seemed even to them, they called it like they saw it. He had been executed—dead as dead could be. But now he was alive—*again*. Even skeptical Thomas couldn't deny the material facts.

What else could they have reported? Men do not typically die for a fabricated story they know to be untrue. The tomb was empty. Jesus kept bumping into them (not by accident, to be sure!) time and time again. He was alive. Period.

Because the primary historical source materials containing the eyewitness accounts of Jesus's resurrection—found in the New Testament—were written in the same general location and within the same generation as the events themselves, and because a great number of eyewitnesses (both positive and hostile) were still living at the times of writing, the possibility for the development of legends surrounding the life, death, and resurrection of Jesus was nil.

Certainly myths and legends about Jesus did eventually show up, but not until the next century. The apocryphal literature of the church and the writings of other groups who claimed to follow Jesus, such as the Gnostics, had stories about the life of Jesus

that included mythological elements. But these were later developments far removed from the eyewitnesses of the resurrection events. The close time-proximity of the New Testament documents to the events they describe prevented this kind of mythologizing. "Jesus as myth" is a favorite theory of liberal critics, but facts show such views to be nonsensical.

All ancient and modern sources accept the fact of the empty tomb. Every theory attempting to counter Jesus's physical resurrection assumes that his tomb was empty, attempting to explain it away with historically absurd scenarios. Aside from the numerous physical appearances recorded in the historical documents, the fact of the empty tomb was a hard, tangible datum that the opposition had to account for or ignore. Without that gaping, empty grave, the resurrection of Jesus might be easier to dismiss.

Legally (and logically), *direct* (firsthand) *evidence* in support of a fact that cannot be successfully impugned, and that is capable of withstanding the full force of the rules of evidence, conclusively establishes that fact. Such is the case for Jesus's physical resurrection. In a legal context, because the evidence for the resurrection was thoroughly available to the five senses and firsthand in nature, it could not be contradicted by anything less than evidence of greater weight. Because all the theories against Jesus's resurrection are hearsay or worse, the direct evidence of the eyewitness reports of the resurrection cannot be overturned—*legally or historically.*

S. Collins, J. Holden

BREAKOUT 9.15

PAUL: ROMAN CITIZEN

The Bible records in Acts 23:25-28 that the apostle Paul was a Roman citizen. When Paul was about to be killed and some Roman soldiers came to his rescue, evidently he told the centurion, "I was born free"—that is, he was a citizen. This poses an interesting question: How was a man from an occupied nation in the Roman Empire born as a free Roman citizen?

Roman citizenship carried many privileges, including the right to vote and hold office, freedom to move about the empire unrestricted, protection from torture, the right to a legal trial, and the right to appeal to the highest court in the land—Caesar himself. A free noncitizen living within the Roman Empire was called a *peregrinus* (Latin, "foreigner, someone from abroad") and did not enjoy the same rights.

Citizenship was of utmost importance in the empire, documented by a birth registration much like our birth certificates. Roman citizens generally had three names—a first, middle, and last name—and only Roman citizens were allowed this right. Under Roman law, anyone else caught signing his signature with three names was charged with the crime of forgery. Interestingly, another way of being charged with forgery was for a noncitizen to wear a toga!

For citizens, a serious violation of Roman law could bring with it a sentence of exile. For noncitizens, the sentence was usually being thrown to wild beasts. Under Roman law, a citizen could not receive the death penalty for any crime save treason. A good biblical example of the difference between the legal punishment of a peregrinus versus a Roman citizen was in the sentencing of the apostle Paul versus that of the apostle Peter. Paul (a Roman citizen) was sentenced to beheading, whereas Peter (a Judean peregrinus) was sentenced to crucifixion.

There were a few ways a person could obtain Roman citizenship, and individuals were not automatically citizens just because they were born within the empire. If born within the empire, one was a citizen if both parents were citizens united in a lawful Roman marriage. Also, if a child was adopted by parents who were citizens and they had a lawful marriage, then the child was a citizen. Further, citizenship followed the bloodline of the mother. If the mother of a child was a Roman citizen but the father was unknown or a slave, the child was a citizen. However, if the father was a citizen and the mother a slave, the child was a slave. Citizenship could also be earned through 25 years of service in the Roman military. And finally, the emperor reserved the right to grant citizenship in special cases.

The Bible does not record how the apostle Paul, a man who could easily have been a peregrinus, was born free as a Roman citizen—we are simply told that he was. It is reasonable to think that before the apostle Paul was born, God had set in motion an intricate plan that would one day find his declaration of the gospel of Jesus Christ penetrating to the highest echelons of the Roman Empire—including the house of Caesar himself!

A. Everett, J. Holden

BREAKOUT 9.16

The First Jewish Revolt and Jerusalem Temple Destruction

The Holy Land was brought under Roman domination in 63 BC. Roman rule was relatively benign for the next several decades, including the reigns of Caesar Augustus and Tiberius, the first two emperors.

However, during the early years of the Christian movement after Jesus's crucifixion and resurrection (see *Breakouts 9.13, 9.14*), Rome was ruled by Caligula (AD 37–41), Claudius (AD 41–54), and Nero (AD 54–68). During this period, the region of Palestine was neglected by Rome and the various political appointees to the region were incompetent or corrupt. Their political abuses led to increasing social unrest, especially between the Greek (Hellenized) and Jewish populations. In AD 66, just a few years after Paul's departure for Rome, rioting erupted in several cities, resulting in thousands of Jewish deaths. Large groups of Jews opposed to the Roman occupation joined forces, eventually capturing the Roman garrison at Masada. They then marched to Jerusalem and took control of the Roman garrison at the Antonia Fortress

adjacent to the Temple Mount. At this point, the area was free of Roman soldiers for the first time in more than a century.

Emperor Nero sent an army under the command of Vespasian to put down the rebellion. Vespasian arrived in AD 67 and began, with great brutality, to devastate the countryside town by town. His final assault would be on Jerusalem. However, when Nero committed suicide in AD 68, three Roman generals attempted to claim the throne, each being quickly overthrown by the next contender. Vespasian put his siege of Jerusalem on hold pending the outcome of the power struggle back in Rome. But when his soldiers ultimately acclaimed Vespasian as emperor, he returned to Rome, assuming the throne in the summer of AD 69.

The Roman army resumed its attack on Jerusalem under the leadership of Titus, the son of Vespasian (who became the next emperor in AD 79). The siege commenced in early AD 70, and Jerusalem finally fell on September 8 of that same year. The entire city was razed to the ground. The surviving rebels were crucified, sent

to the mines as slaves, or taken to Rome to be marched in the Triumph of Titus, then executed or sent to the arenas. The Jewish temple was destroyed during the siege, but the temple treasures were taken to Rome and eventually used by Emperor Vespasian to fund construction of the Colosseum. A depiction of the temple treasures being displayed in the Triumph of Titus is found on the Arch of Titus in the Roman Forum.

Various rebel fortresses remained to be captured, and this task was given to generals Bassus and Silva. It was Silva who brought the rebellion to an end with the fall of Masada in either AD 73 or 74.

The events of the rebellion and the Roman response are detailed in the writings of Josephus ben Mathias, known to us as the historian Flavius Josephus (see *Breakout 9.17*). It should be noted that a second rebellion, the Bar Kochba Revolt (AD 132–135), resulted in the final expulsion of the Jewish people from Jerusalem, which was then rebuilt as the Roman city of Aelia Capitolina.

J. Moore

BREAKOUT 9.17

FLAVIUS JOSEPHUS

Flavius Josephus gives us one of the most important historical sources for illuminating the New Testament books. He was born in Jerusalem in AD 37 as Yosef ben Matityahu. His mother was a Hasmonean descendant, and his father was a priest named Matthias. He was well educated, and at a young age he studied all three of the Jewish sects: Sadducees, Essenes, and Pharisees. He became an Essene for three years, living in the desert, then returned to civilization to become a Pharisee for the remainder of his life. He was politically involved and connected, and in AD 64 traveled to Rome to intercede on behalf of some Jewish priests.

Due to the increasing tension between the Jews and Rome by AD 66, it was clear that war was imminent. The Jews appointed generals to organize armies, and Josephus was appointed general over the Galilee area. He raised an army of 100,000, whom he trained according to Roman military standards. When the cities of Galilee were taken by the Romans under the leadership of

Vespasian, Josephus was taken prisoner. During the rest of the Jewish war, which ended in AD 73/74, the Romans took advantage of Josephus's education, talents, and notoriety. He was able to reason with his people, encouraging them to surrender. He was also an eyewitness to the major battles in the war, including the siege and fall of Jerusalem. Josephus took Vespasian's family name, Flavius, for his own.

Josephus is best known for his historical writings. His first major book, *The Wars of the Jews*, starts with Antiochus Epiphanes taking Jerusalem in 168 BC and ends shortly after the fall of Masada in AD 73/74. It provides detailed accounts of the rise and fall of the Hasmonean kingdom, the Romans in Judea, and the Jewish war that he personally witnessed. It is said that he had access to the journals of Roman generals while writing the book. *The Wars* was completed between AD 75 and 79 and published immediately for the Roman population.

Josephus's second major work was *The Antiquities of the Jews*.

This book is his commentary on the Hebrew Scriptures (Old Testament) and gives a historical account of the Jews up to the start of the Jewish War in AD 66. In places where *Antiquities* covers the same events as *The Wars*, Josephus uses *Antiquities* to correct mistakes in *The Wars*. *Antiquities* was completed and published in AD 93/94.

These two works comprise the most important historical background material we have for the intertestamental and New Testament eras. Josephus's writings offer cultural information as well as the political backdrops, tensions, and conflicts during these periods. Of course, there are some mistakes in Josephus's writings and he is often accused of exaggerating what he reported. But keep in mind that when his books went into publication, some of the people he wrote about were still alive and would have been able to publicly refute and correct any inaccuracies in his works.

Josephus died in AD 95.

J. Bulot, S. Collins

PART 2

WHAT ARCHAEOLOGY HAS REVEALED TO US

CHAPTER 10

ARCHAEOLOGY AND THE BIBLE

WORDS OF CAUTION

By its very nature archaeology is a soft science. That is, while it often uses many of the hard sciences in archaeological analysis—disciplines like chemistry, physics, geology, astrophysics, zoology, and botany—the conclusions drawn on the basis of mostly mute artifacts and related data are, by nature, *interpretations*. Rarely do analyses of archaeological data support a *single* interpretation or conclusion.

Ideally, there should be an attempt to sift carefully through data sets and logically weigh evidences for or against a range of possible interpretations. But this *doesn't* always happen. Occasionally the preconceptions and biases of researchers complicate the process. Conventional wisdom and even one's worldview can slant an interpretation in a particular direction. Thus, on one hand, those tending toward an antibiblical bias adopt interpretations of archaeological data that they think *disprove* the Bible. On the other hand, scholars who favor the historical credibility of the Scriptures most often reach conclusions *favoring* the Bible. Yet both anti- and pro-Bible scholars are drawing from a *range* of interpretations. Overall, true objectivity is hard to come by!

Given these realities, there is a large amount of material from ANE studies and archaeology that intersects the study of the Hebrew Scriptures in particular. As interpreted by scholars, some of it corroborates pieces of biblical history, while some of it doesn't. But one thing is certain: The pro-Bible approach of mid-twentieth-century scholars like Nelson Glueck, William F. Albright, Millar Burrows, G. Ernest Wright, Merrill Unger, Joseph Free, and Mitchell

Dahood—"the Bible is confirmed by every turn of the spade"—is no longer believed by the vast majority of the archaeological community. Today, being called Albrightian is derisive, *not* a compliment. "Biblical archaeology" itself is, in most archaeological circles, a loathsome concept to be avoided. In fact, the death of biblical archaeology is commonly celebrated.

No better examples of the difference between outdated mid-twentieth-century biblical archaeology and the twenty-first-century world of ANE archaeology exist than what's found in many volumes about biblical archaeology—even recent ones! It is safe to say, although unfortunate, that there is a lot of material in many Bible dictionaries, Bible encyclopedias, and books on biblical archaeology that can't withstand the scrutiny of today's archaeological scholarship, whether agnostic or evangelical. So many advancements in archaeological science have happened in the past 25 years—highly accelerated since 1999—that quoting the views and conclusions of past scholars in support of the biblical text can be highly suspect, if not foolish. Today, when building a case for the Bible's historical credibility, we must focus on the more recent methodologies, data, and discoveries, being careful to use pre-1999 sources *only after meticulous reanalysis* in the light of more advanced technologies and the current state of knowledge.

There are glaring examples that are included in popular books dealing with the historical value of the book of Genesis. For example, some include an overzealous approach to the Ebla Tablets, which are said to offer confirmation of certain cities (Ur, Sodom, and Gomorrah) and names (Adam, Eve, and Noah), and to offer the oldest known creation accounts outside the book of Genesis.

The archaeological data for these claims come from the epigraphic work of Giovanni Pettinato in the 1970s. Suffice it to say that by 1995 virtually every biblical connection originally thought to exist in the Ebla archives had evaporated as knowledge of the Eblaite language advanced. By the year 2000, hardly a single reading proposed by Pettinato—much less those he connected to the Bible—remained valid. It appears that Pettinato misunderstood the language so profoundly that later scholars of Eblaitica dismissed the bulk of his translations out of hand.

Indeed, there was no so-called Ebla Geographical Atlas with the names of biblical cities like Sodom and Gomorrah. It was all a false alarm, an unfortunate mistake. Along the way, Pettinato was dismissed from the Ebla project and a new epigrapher was put in charge of the Ebla archives. But now Bible scholars had a big problem on their hands. They had made such a big deal about the Ebla/Bible connections—brandishing these "discoveries" in hundreds, even thousands, of publications—that it was impossible to get the proverbial toothpaste back into the tube. Still today, not a few evangelicals unversed in the state of Ebla scholarship naively tout the discredited Ebla/Bible links in books and articles. This kind of information disconnect can be a serious pitfall for biblical scholars—if not embarrassing!

The purpose of chapters 10 and 11 is to connect you with the best and most recent scholarship illuminating the proper place of archaeology in biblical studies, and vice versa. As far as is humanly possible, twenty-first-century biblical scholars must avoid the errors of their nineteenth- and twentieth-century counterparts.

This isn't to say that the biblical archaeology of the past—that of Albright, Wright, Free, and their contemporaries—is without value. Far from it. There remain many valid viewpoints and discoveries that *do* corroborate the biblical text in remarkable ways. We don't want to throw out the baby with the bathwater! But the issue today is the *relationship* between the Bible and archaeology. Clarifying the proper relationship

between biblical text and archaeological science begins by being careful with words such as *prove* and *proof* in favor of terms like *consistent with*, *corroborate*, and *commensurate with*.

The relationship between biblical studies and archaeology should be a two-way street. It has to be a dialogue in which each discipline legitimately complements the other. Both biblical and archaeological scholarship must go where the evidence leads. When archaeology clarifies a biblical passage, it does so because the world of the Bible is the same world that produced the material excavated by the archaeologist. The reverse can also happen when a biblical text provides a historical framework for an archaeological find. This is a relationship that should be encouraged, not discouraged!

But gone are the days when the most influential ANE archaeologists were people of faith—people who viewed the Bible, the Torah in particular, as real history—or at least as containing real history. In those days, the focus of ANE archaeology was "proving" the historicity of biblical narratives. Fortunately, in many ways, the new archaeological era, with its ever-emerging technologies and more advanced research paradigms, is poised to illuminate the biblical text as never before—*and already is doing this*.

Bible-respecting scholars in the archaeological community are well aware of the prevailing viewpoint that says, "Archaeologists shouldn't use the Bible as a principal focus"—they want archaeology for archaeology's sake. Regardless, we must also understand the importance of the Bible and other ancient texts that can provide a framework for finding and clarifying geographical locations, event horizons, and historical figures. Responsible archaeology uses *every* available resource to open windows into the past. It is well known that sites like Sodom, Heshbon, Aroer, Dibon, Nebo, Bethany beyond the Jordan, Jerusalem, Hazor, Megiddo, Lachish, Gath, and many others, are identified *because they appear in biblical narratives* with enough embedded geographical data to aid in locating them.

If rigorous scholarship and responsible, objective

archaeology can confirm links between biblical locations and archaeological sites, that is worthwhile. If the same approach leads to the conclusion that some connections are not justified, then so be it. But we can't avoid evidences because of bias one way or the other. As philosopher A.J. Ayer reminded us a long time ago, we must clearly state the criteria whereby any hypothesis can be verified or falsified, then follow the evidence wherever it leads. This is the strict method of science, and biblical archaeology must adhere to it.

On one hand, it's intellectually dishonest to categorically dismiss the Bible as a historical framework or a site-identification tool. It can't be denied that the Bible remains one of the best—arguably *the* best—historical and geographical sources surviving from the ancient world. And it's common for certain archaeological excavations to garner more attention than others simply because of possible biblical connections! This is perfectly reasonable.

On the other hand, pursuing archaeology *solely* from a biblical perspective may obscure the larger reality of Near Eastern cultural settings. A biblical bias—one derived from a particular theological or hermeneutical approach—could influence the interpretation of data which, ironically, could otherwise have illumined the Bible even more profoundly. In all archaeological endeavors, the fair goal is *objectivity*. Indeed, sites with no clear biblical connection are just as important for determining the history of the region. Archaeological importance should never be equated with biblical importance!

WRESTLING WITH OBJECTIVITY VS. SUBJECTIVITY IN BIBLICAL ARCHAEOLOGY

Why is it important to address the Bible's historical authenticity? The answer is simple: Any defense of biblical credibility in the historical arena must offer *evidence that a reasonable mind would accept as a demonstration of the fact*. In this regard, biblical archaeology is a risky business. This is because archaeology is a *science*, and belief or unbelief rises or falls on the basis of evidence (data). In science, it boils down to facts (that which corresponds to reality), not blind faith.

The Bible-respecting archaeologist is convinced that the Book has organic connections to three-dimensional space-time reality. It is neither myth nor fiction. Thus, this question is of utmost importance: If the nature of biblical narrative is fictional and not factual, then on the basis of what logic can its spiritual implications and theological truths be embraced? If both are *real*, text and ground should match up given a reasonable level of objectivity.

Reality is a seamless whole. History is anything but. History happens when fragments of reality experienced by the senses are stitched together into a comprehensible narrative. It is not possible for human beings, individually or collectively, to detect all the nuances of reality simply because much or most of it is unobservable. While a given chronicler may attribute a battle victory to military genius, a peek at the "underbelly" of the event might show that the defeated force was suffering from acute diarrhea and resultant dehydration! From this angle, we can't help but recall the plague of tumors (better, hemorrhoids!) that Yahweh inflicted on the Philistines after they captured the Ark of the Covenant from the Israelites. While a historian may attribute the loss of a battle to tactical failure, in reality it may have been an "act of God" (and such they are deemed in not a few twenty-first-century insurance policies!).

A historian might ask, "How can we wrap our writing of history around an act of God?" For reasons that are all too obvious, secular historians and archaeologists alike—not to mention a majority of philosophers and scientists—avoid mixing divine causes into their work. But even when people of faith write history, they have ways of stroking a reader's skepticism by weaving in threads of rationalism—for example, suggesting that events like the Israelites fleeing across the Re(e)d Sea involved a convergence of natural phenomena. Merely mentioning that God could have used wind and simple physics to "part the waters" introduces a comfort level for accepting what is, by all definitions, a miracle. But on the chance that God *does* exist, would he not be the most fundamental element of reality itself?

With that in mind, it seems odd that some historians and philosophers of science insist on categorically denying *any* involvement of deity in the physical dimensions. But why should we pretend that our pathetically sewn and tattered perception of history—or of science, for that matter—is at all a true representation of the reality it so feebly observes? Would not a divine perspective on history be infinitely superior? Of course it would. And that's precisely what the Bible gives us.

The tendency of historians to avoid the supernatural is understandable. Certainly, logic and reason should prevail when writing about the past. But we must exercise care in what passes for *logic* and *reason*. If God exists and *is* the Creator of all, and *is* actively involved in his universe, then it makes no sense to write him out of his own story. But in framing histories touching on the ANE, scholars can be illogical and unreasonable in their exclusion of biblical material not only by dismissing the divine element, but also by denying historicity of people and events—even certain cities, towns, and geographical locations—found in biblical texts. For example, not only do many disallow Moses's interactions with Yahweh, but they also reject the existence of Moses himself! This is a rather strange modus operandi when we consider just how ANE history is composed in general.

After serving as director of 14 excavation seasons at Tall el-Hammam/Sodom in Jordan, Steven Collins speaks to this crucial point:

> This kind of categorical dismissal of the historical character of the biblical narratives is, from a historiographical perspective, sheer nonsense. Such anti-biblical bias is clearly exposed when we realize how our understanding of history is pieced together from extant ancient Near Eastern records. The documents and inscriptions from which we derive such "histories" are all, without exception, set within a mythological context amidst gods, goddesses, and demons; yet historians are inclined to accept these ancient accounts as generally factual and their human characters as actual. If this were not the case, we would have no

histories of ancient Egypt, Anatolia, or Mesopotamia at all. The stories of great Egyptian pharaohs like Tuthmosis III and Rameses II are inextricably bound up with divine dimensions, yet no one denies the historical reality behind these characters who, by their own proclamations, wore the mantle of divinity.[1]

Alan Millard, Emeritus Rankin Professor of Hebrew and Ancient Semitic Languages, the University of Liverpool, weighs in on the same theme:

> [The] similarity between Israelite and other ancient Near Eastern reports has to be recognized…There is no difference in the type or result in these episodes…Each nation believed her own deity or deities acted on her behalf. Just as the Lord sent the hailstones on the Amorites, so that more died from them than from Israelite swords, so Adad finished off the enemy of Sargon of Assyria with thunder and hailstones. There need be no doubt that the Assyrian enemy's experience was as real as the Amorites', both being beaten down by heavy hail. Again, the historian and commentator is obliged to treat the reports as factual evidence of ancient events. At this point the secular historian may halt, however, and view the Hebrew histories as no different from the Assyrian or Hittite or Egyptian.[2]

Renowned ANE scholar Kenneth A. Kitchen asserts:

> [Assyrian] campaign reports contain a large amount of good firsthand information. Yet at intervals the Assyrian kings also attribute this or that success to the overwhelming splendor of their god Assur, or of this terrible weapon. In his campaign against Hezekiah of Judah and allies in 701, Sennacherib did just this, "trusting in Assur my lord." That he did so has no bearing whatsoever on the historicity of his main account, successively conquering Phoenicia…then Joppa and Ekron, and Lachish.[3]

Collins adds:

> [Often] when historians and archaeologists approach biblical stories, key characters—Abraham, Joseph, Moses, Joshua—and the accomplishments attributed to them are called fictional, non-historical, or mythical simply because of their relationship to Yahweh. The reality of the human characters in Egyptian records is uncritically accepted, while the existence of the Israelite heroes is readily dismissed. This is idiocy! Treating biblical characters in this manner is historiographically unjustified, illogical, and unreasonable. And further, we shouldn't be so irresponsible as to reject out-of-hand the interactions of Yahweh, the biblical God of history, with men and women of old. Indeed, the whirlwind may be the result of God's hand sweeping through reality, creating a vortex of observed phenomena that defies all our powers of observation and explanation. For human witnesses, reality may evidence all manner of chaos; whereas the Bible allows us to see that the whirlwind is often shaped like the hand of God—but only for those who, through Scripture, have enough "distance" to observe history from the divine perspective.[4]

Some scholars are compelled by antisupernatural bias to assign late Iron Age (IA; post-1000 BC; even post-600 BC) dates for the origin of Torah narratives. In doing so, they often multiply their error by refusing to be objective. One good example of this—there are many—is the use of *selective comparisons*. This happens when a piece of biblical narrative is laid alongside a cultural context considerably later in date than the timeframe demanded by reasonable biblical chronologies. Egyptologist James K. Hoffmeier observes the inherent weakness of J. Van Seters's comparison of the Israelite crossing of the Jordan River during flood stage with Neo-Assyrian (eighth–seventh centuries BC) accounts of Sargon II and Ashurbanipal's crossing of the Tigris and Euphrates during the spring high-water season. Hoffmeier counters:

> Van Seters's treatment of this matter fails on two points. First, the spring of the year was the traditional time for kings to go to war in Israel (cf. 2 Sam. 11:2) as well as in Mesopotamia...Spring is also when the rivers, the Jordan as well as the Tigris and Euphrates, are at their highest levels because of melting snow from the mountains to the north. Secondly, the seemingly miraculous crossing of raging rivers by a king is well attested in earlier Near Eastern sources [such as] Hattusili I (c. 1650 BC) [and] Sargon the Great (c. 2371–2316 BC). Consequently, there is no basis for Van Seters's assertion. The river crossing in Joshua 3 by Israel's forces accurately reflects the seasonal realities of military life in the Near East throughout the three millennia BC.[5]

Like Van Seters, some scholars compare Pentateuchal (Torah) narratives with later—usually late IA, after 1000 BC—ANE texts and cultural settings for the specific purpose of "proving" that stories about the biblical patriarchs and the origins of Israel were myths or pious fictions spun by Judahite priests as late as the Babylonian, Persian, or even Hellenistic periods. The failure to exercise even a modicum of objectivity by simply suggesting comparisons with earlier Bronze Age (BA) materials is a glaring deficiency in their methodology. Hoffmeier's more balanced approach includes making comparisons based on ANE texts and cultural backgrounds belonging to the third and second millennia BC when, according to reasonable biblical chronologies, the events actually took place.

We must recognize that presupposition and bias exist in the scholarly world. Often these predilections create blind spots and gaps in research and publication that are often difficult to identify. Because the anti-Bible bias is so strong in current academia, sticking to facts and reasonably interpreted data is crucial. We also have to allow changes in our thinking when better methods and new data point in a different direction than in the past.

On balance, the twenty-first-century world of archaeology is perhaps better able to demonstrate the historical authenticity of the biblical record in ways never imagined in the "Albrightian old days." As will become clear in the pages ahead, there are excellent reasons to trust the historical quality of the Old Testament. But it is as *the Word of God* that it carries the weight of the divine perspective. God will not turn up on the blade of a trowel, but his infinite conception of history provides a framework of *true narrative representation* that must not be ignored in the composition of ancient history.[6]

Collins assesses the importance of the Bible in historical understanding:

> Relative to the human task of writing conceptions of ancient Near Eastern history, a typical approach to the Bible—albeit typically with a good dose of anti-supernatural bias—has been to treat it as *patient* rather than *agent*. But because the Bible *is* God's representation of reality, and because the "perfections" of the true narrative case are everywhere in Scripture superior to all other representations, I am convinced (by substantial evidence) that biblical data must occupy the role of *agent* in our attempts to reconstruct any sequence of ancient Near Eastern events which overlaps the biblical narrative. Approaching Scripture critically as merely another collection of ancient Near Eastern texts may lend a tone of scholarship to the work of Bible scholars, but it is actually the death of real objectivity. As the divine perspective, the Bible must always be the corrective, never the corrected. If the Bible *is* God's representation of reality, then an objective assessment of all matters historical and archaeological must begin and end with Scripture [emphasis in original].[7]

THE PROPER RELATIONSHIP BETWEEN ARCHAEOLOGY AND BIBLICAL STUDIES

The influence of the Bible on ANE archaeology has been a mixed bag. While scholars with Christian roots or active personal faith have greatly advanced the discipline of ANE archaeology from its nineteenth-century beginnings to the present day, unfortunate examples of false leads, discredited theories, and even out-and-out fraud have dotted the landscape. As mentioned previously, in the 1970s, interpretations of texts from the cuneiform archives of Ebla in north Syria excited the world of biblical scholarship with claims of "map lists" mentioning Sodom and Gomorrah and numerous "authentications" of personal names and deities found in biblical stories. By the year 2000, all this had been dashed to the ground.

Because so many in the Christian community are naïve when it comes to biblical archaeology, they remain vulnerable to spurious claims, half-truths, and hoaxes. Year in and year out, fabricated "discoveries"—everything from the Ark of the Covenant to chariot wheels in the Red Sea to Mount Sinai in Arabia to giant human skeletons—capture the imagination of Christians the world over. And when, in the last third of the twentieth century, ANE archaeology began to turn its back on the Bible, an unfortunate situation resulted. Instead of countering with *legitimate* archaeology, much of Christendom developed an appetite for pseudo-archaeology and junk science offering sensational, Bible-supporting "discoveries."

Today, specious "Bible-proving" claims persist, and unsuspecting Christians continue to believe them. Thankfully, this kind of truth-twisting is avoidable, but only when the Christian community embraces and supports responsible archaeology. The historicity of the Bible does not need to be propped up by false "evidence." Proper, scientific archaeology is consistent with biblical history, and the archaeological pendulum *is* swinging back toward the historical authenticity of the Bible. Bible students are well advised to keep up with the pace of discovery in the legitimate archaeological arena.

If biblical archaeology is defined as the investigation of ancient material cultures with a view to illuminating biblical narratives, then it certainly deserves a place within the framework of ANE studies. However, for this relationship to thrive, the extremes of so-called minimalism and maximalism should be avoided in the pursuit of more productive discussion. Scholars on the extreme left generally disallow the Bible a voice in the pursuit of archaeology. Those on the extreme right tend to disregard archaeological data as a hermeneutical tool when interpreting biblical texts.

In order for both *text* and *ground* to serve the other in meaningful ways, each opposing viewpoint should encourage dialogue. When relevant, archaeology should take its rightful place in biblical interpretation. When applicable, the biblical text should influence the interpretation of archaeological data. Such interaction between archaeologists and biblical scholars is, unfortunately, rare. When it does happen, both disciplines are better for it.

THE HEYDAY OF BIBLICAL ARCHAEOLOGY (1885–1985): A THUMBNAIL HISTORY

It is impossible to appreciate the current state of affairs between archaeology and biblical studies without a sense of their mutual history. The following is a brief but necessary overview of the century-and-a-half—and often rocky—relationship between the two.

Near Eastern archaeology sprang from "Christian" roots. In the late nineteenth century, European and American theologians and Bible scholars saw the development of archaeology in Egypt, Mesopotamia, and the Levant (Canaan) as a new and intriguing means of providing historical background for the biblical text. Although New Testament scholars had long benefited from Greco-Roman classical studies, students of the Hebrew Scriptures operated in a virtual vacuum. While the threads of Old Testament stories were woven into the fabric of ANE kingdoms and empires, for nineteenth-century scholars the ANE world—the biblical world—remained hidden behind an almost-impenetrable fog of myth and mystery.

This began to change when Napoleon, along with an army of soldiers and scholars, arrived in Egypt near the beginning of the nineteenth century. In a variety of publications replete with drawings and descriptive narratives, the heretofore invisible world of the Old Testament was making headlines around the globe. Christian publishers were quick to take advantage of the excitement. A taste for all things oriental and biblical swept like wildfire through the Christian community. Although anything remotely resembling archaeology was still a half-century away, the flavor of exploration and discovery had whetted the appetites of Bible-oriented scholars and laymen alike. A new era of Bible fervor was born.

By the late nineteenth century, discoveries illuminating the Bible were coming fast and furious. It seemed as if Scripture-based scholars could find no end of new "proofs" of the Bible's historical underpinnings. Many in the Christian world gained confidence in the light of these new finds, which was especially encouraging given the recent rise of so-called higher biblical criticism in the academic institutions of Europe and America. On one hand, the higher critics were declaring that Moses had nothing to do with writing the Torah. Perhaps Moses never existed at all and was merely a literary convention. On the other hand, the Mesopotamian world of Abraham and the Egyptian world of Moses were making a big splash in the media. Higher criticism lived in its segregated world of literary analysis, little affected by the budding discipline of ANE archaeology. Biblical studies found renewed energy with its new ally, archaeology, often deemed biblical archaeology. It was inevitable, however, that higher criticism and biblical archaeology were on a collision course that would eventually reach critical mass toward the end of the twentieth century.

Biblical archaeology prospered on the cutting edge of ANE studies through most of the twentieth century. From the late nineteenth century until about two-thirds of the way into the twentieth century, ANE scholars were not put off by the term biblical archaeologist. Indeed, some relished it. But all the while, higher critical theory was gaining ground among the Old Testament crowd. In time, it dominated the study of the Hebrew Scriptures. While Old Testament scholars were busy carving up the Pentateuch and other Old Testament historical books into an evolutionary concoction of redacted literary strands prejudiced by ancient Israelite and Judahite sociotheological agendas, ANE researchers and biblical archaeologists were coming up with artifactual reasons for taking biblical history more or less at face value. However, the influence of higher criticism was slowly but surely making inroads into archaeological curricula. The tide was turning, and not in favor of the Bible.

By the dawn of the twenty-first century, cries for the elimination of biblical archaeology rang through the halls of many academic institutions. Soon thereafter, not a few scholars delighted over the "death" of biblical archaeology. Those who objected to the snubbing of the Book that, for a century, had provided significant impetus for ANE archaeology were now marginalized. The perception of past efforts by Christian scholars to substantiate theological beliefs with archaeological evidence—admittedly a non sequitur—became a common straw man against using the Bible as an archaeological tool. As so often happens in these kinds of debates, both sides could be accused of tossing out the opposite baby with the bathwater.

But this shift in thinking wasn't all bad. The simple truth is that such a historical adjustment was inevitable given that during ANE archaeology's first 100 years the biblical emphasis—a small subset of the larger discipline—was arguably the tail wagging the dog. In many ways the clamor against biblical archaeology wasn't so much a reaction against connecting archaeology with the Bible as it was a concern that the larger world of the ancient Fertile Crescent and adjacent regions was being obscured by an overemphasis on things biblical. Biblical archaeology was myopic. What scholars wanted was an opportunity to put things in their proper perspective. In the process, finds touted as proving elements of the biblical narrative suffered a kind of hyper-scrutiny to which they were not subjected in the earlier Bible-friendly climate.

To be fair, better archaeological methods, technologies, and research paradigms did result in overturning many of the views held by pro-Bible scholars like Garstang and Albright. But much remained. Although pushed to the fringes of archaeology in the new not-so-friendly-to-the-Bible environment, elements of ANE material culture were still inextricably bound together with biblical stories, and legitimately so. As much as

they tried, scholars opposing biblical historicity were unable to dislodge the Bible from its position as a collection of remarkable ANE documents. In many ways this was a typical pendulum swing. It reached its leftmost extreme in the late 1990s. Since then it has been moving decidedly back toward the center. This is because the Old Testament is a first-rate collection of ancient historical and geographical documents.

Millard makes this comment on the historical authenticity of the ancient Hebrew documents of the Old Testament:

> Comparing the Aramaic monuments with the records of Israel's history seems to indicate that both describe the same sort of politics and similar attitudes to events...With those, and other, ancient texts available, it is, surely, unscientific and very subjective to treat the Hebrew records from the start as if they are totally different creations.[8]

Collins comments:

> Since the beginning of the twenty-first century, significant work in both ANE studies and archaeology have led to dramatic corroborations of the OT's historical authenticity—not necessarily a reaffirmation of once-discredited data, but a new era in which more rigorous scholarship and scientific methodologies have placed the biblical text back alongside the trowel and patiche.[9]

It is a new day for biblical archaeology, one in which the Bible does not get a pass simply because it's fashionable or self-serving to do so. It's an environment in which every link between the Bible and archaeology is rigorously scrutinized and challenged. But within scientific disciplines, this is how it should be!

Joseph Holden and Norman Geisler recognize the importance of a proper scientific foundation for biblical archaeology:

> Archaeology…has its limitations. Although it deals with artifacts, features, measurements, and

tangible data, archaeology also involves many interpretive judgments and probabilities. Any interpretations and conclusions must be considered in light of human fallibility and the sparse nature of the data itself…this is compounded by the fact that only a small amount of the evidence has survived and can be either isolated or disconnected from its in-situ environment. Floods, fires, warfare, natural deterioration, burial, temperature, political climate and time, have all collaborated to make the discovery of biblical artifacts difficult. Therefore, archaeology cannot be classified as an "exact" science; but neither can any empirical science for that matter. Despite its limitations, archaeology is governed by generally accepted principles and methods as a forensic science and is a valuable tool in uncovering the past. Therefore, archaeology has become an indispensable discipline in the historian's tool belt to unearth data supporting the historical reliability of the Bible beyond a reasonable doubt.[10]

EARLY DIGGERS INTO THE BIBLICAL WORLD

Archaeology as a *scientific* discipline did not exist in the late nineteenth century. Yet several foundational figures contributed to what would, by the early twentieth century, morph into modern archaeology. In these early days, even the most famous of the explorer-scholars were little more than treasure hunters. Their main focus was to fill the museums of their home countries full to the brim with wondrous pieces of the biblical world. Even today, revered institutions like the Louvre and the British Museum have basements filled with huge nineteenth-century crates full of ANE artifacts—from cuneiform tablets to enormous stone statuary and architectural elements—that have never seen the light of day since they were packed and shipped from Mesopotamia and Egypt more than 10 years ago. Late nineteenth-century archaeology often masqueraded as science, but rarely rose to that level of rigor (at least in the present sense).

Space prevents a detailed presentation of the many personalities who participated in archaeology's embryonic stages, but the following are especially worthy of mention.

Paul-Émile Botta (1802–1870), of Italian and French heritage, and Englishman Austin Henry Layard (1817–1894) both came from Christian families. Their early work focused on Mesopotamia. Neither had any formal education in archaeology nor ANE history. Those disciplines simply didn't exist in their day. In terms of using the Bible in their work, Botta and Layard were equally neutral. While they seemingly took biblical stories at face value, proving the Bible was not their agenda. Most people in that era accepted the Bible as historically reliable, so there was no reason for them to press the issue. Between them they collected a massive volume of Mesopotamian antiquities for the Louvre and British Museum. In decades to come, scholars would come to view these treasures as windows into the world of the Genesis patriarchs.

When Englishman Sir William Matthew Flinders Petrie (1853–1942) focused his sights on excavating in the Near East, archaeology took its first steps in the direction of true science. A Christian and member of the Plymouth Brethren, he was also an impeccable scholar. Although many of his contemporaries were aggressive treasure hunters with few, if any, of the critical skills necessary for doing proper archaeology, Petrie had an eye for detail and a penchant for logic and reason. He put these to good use. His self-training in survey methods, philology, and Egyptology also stood him in good stead. Under Petrie's direction, excavation became meticulous and systematic.

It was Petrie's critical eye that first observed the importance of stratigraphy (successive material layers within an excavation site) in the archaeological process. He also observed that pottery forms changed from one stratum (a specific layer of material remains) to the next. With this discovery, ceramic typology was born. In time, Petrie formalized both stratigraphy and the study of ceramic forms, laying the foundation for all subsequent archaeology, particularly in the Levant. Because of these monumental contributions, Petrie is rightfully the father of modern archaeology. He also believed the Bible to be historically reliable. His term *proto-Sinaitic*—a chronological allusion to the law delivered to Moses at Mount Sinai—as a descriptor for the early Semitic alphabet is indicative of his biblical leanings. With Petrie, archaeology as science began with a healthy respect for biblical history.

BIBLICAL ARCHAEOLOGY'S GOLDEN AGE

With Petrie leading ANE archaeology from its nineteenth-century beginnings into the twentieth century, a global public had learned to anticipate, even expect, significant discoveries that widened the window on the world of Bible characters like Abraham, Moses, David, and Solomon. Even though most of the forthcoming archaeological data were of the more mundane kind, occasional biblical finds were enough to keep pace with public interest. And archaeologists were more than glad to feed the frenzy.

John Garstang (1876–1956), a professor of archaeology at the University of Liverpool from 1907 to 1941, had aggressively sought connections between his archaeological pursuits and the Old Testament. His excavations at Jericho during the 1920s upped the ante on biblically significant finds. The walls of Jericho that fell flat outward upon a trumpet blast from Joshua's army were the stuff of Sunday sermons and sacred songs. In the 1920s, when Garstang announced the discovery of those very walls, the news made headlines on every continent. The "proof" was in. The signature evidence of Joshua's conquest of Jericho was "on the books," and biblical archaeology had taken a substantial leap forward.

Nelson Glueck (1900–1971)—archaeologist, Jewish rabbi, and president of the Hebrew Union College in Cincinnati—believed that the documents comprising the Old Testament were highly important for the study of ANE history. In Glueck, Christian scholars found a noteworthy ally. However, he let it be known that he did not take a traditional, literal approach to the Bible. This notwithstanding, Glueck profoundly

reinforced the general historical character of Old Testament narratives, as witnessed in his sweeping geographical surveys identifying biblical sites throughout the Holy Land.

To say that William Foxwell Albright (1891–1971) was *the* most influential—indeed, most powerful—ANE scholar and archaeologist during the first two-thirds of the twentieth century is by no means an overstatement. In a word, he was a genius. The son of Evangelical Methodist missionary parents, Albright inherited a deep regard for the historical character of the Old Testament, including the Torah material ostensibly discredited by the higher critics. He earned his PhD from Johns Hopkins University, where he subsequently held a long professorship. With his then-unparalleled expertise in field methods (most notably at Gibeah, Tell Beit Mirsim, and Bethel), Semitic languages, ancient ceramics, and ANE studies, Albright was always a force to be reckoned with in both ANE and biblical archaeology.

Throughout his stellar career Albright was unwavering in his belief that the stories of the Pentateuch rose from a core of historical reality. In the archives of ancient Mesopotamia—Nuzi, Mari, and Nineveh among them—he saw what to him were undeniable evidences supporting the historical milieus of Abraham, Isaac, and Jacob. He observed the hand of Joshua in the Late Bronze Age (LBA) destruction layers of ancient Canaanite cities. In general, Albright saw no reason to doubt the historical outline of the Hebrew Bible. In terms of biblical archaeology as defined by evangelical Bible scholars, he was a veritable hero figure—*the* go-to-guy when arguing in favor of biblical historicity. In many ways Albright *was* biblical archaeology incarnate. Further, due to his notoriety, America became the epicenter of Levantine and biblical archaeology.

Satisfied with Albright's support of the Old Testament's historical authenticity, evangelicals were perfectly willing to overlook his doctrinal eccentricities. He was not an evangelical by any stretch of the imagination. Neither was he adverse to the basic tenets of Old Testament higher criticism. The means and timing of the codification of the Pentateuch were of little interest to Albright. A long period of oral transmission was reasonable, but it was the historical backdrop of the Old Testament that interested him. For him, the origins of the Pentateuch lay in the Bronze Age (BA), transmission and codification dynamics notwithstanding. In linking archaeological finds with the Bible, when Albright used phrases like *reasonably comparable*, *consistent with*, and *parallel to*, conservative Bible scholars spun them into *proof*, *proves*, and *proving*. Thus, many of Albright's evidences for biblical historicity were overstated. But biblical archaeology was riding high, and occasional critics were mostly ignored.

Albright's views were tempered and repackaged for Christian audiences by his protégé, George Earnest Wright (1909–1974). Wright was an excellent ANE scholar and archaeologist, and more theologically conservative than Albright. Through his writings dealing with archaeology and the Bible, he emerged as the darling of Bible-based publications such as commentaries, dictionaries, encyclopedias, and atlases. For Bible scholars, Wright was the wellhead of Albright's gushing spring of ANE knowledge. In light of the fact that it usually takes 30 to 40 years for new archaeological discoveries or conclusions to find their way into Bible-related publications, it is no wonder that when Bible scholars seek support for biblical historicity they still turn to W.F. Albright and G.E. Wright for definitive information and quotations—something no current ANE scholar or archaeologist would do, given that many of Albright's and Wright's parallels between archaeology and the Bible are now considered doubtful or discredited.

Beyond G.E. Wright, Albright launched or considerably influenced the careers of a generation of world-renowned ANE and biblical scholars—Frank Moore Cross, David Noel Freedman, Kathleen Kenyon, Merrill Unger, Yigael Yadin, Avriham Biran, Alan Millard, and Kenneth Kitchen among them. Each of these worked in what is considered the golden era of biblical archaeology, but also experienced the more recent escalation of antibiblical sentiment amongst ANE archaeologists. One of these scholars in particular contributed significantly to the "near death" of biblical archaeology.

Dame Kathleen M. Kenyon (1906–1978), daughter of the celebrated Sir Frederic Kenyon, was a pivotal figure in the evolution of archaeological field methods. From the perspective of biblical archaeology, she presided over a markedly negative turn in the dialogue regarding the Bible's historical veracity. Kenyon, equipped with better field methods, came away with different conclusions about the stratum Garstang had identified as belonging to the time of Joshua (a stretch of the LBA between c. 1400 BC and 1200 BC depending on one's date for the exodus). She dated that stratum to the end of the Middle Bronze Age (MBA), c. 1550 BC. The majority of archaeologists agreed with her assessment of the data. She, along with most scholars, also dated the Israelite exodus and conquest of Canaan to the thirteenth century BC, or during the reign of Rameses II. The implications for the biblical story were obvious: Jericho was not occupied in the time frame assigned to Joshua. The famous walls first discovered 30 years earlier were centuries older than Garstang thought. Unwittingly, Kenyon had dealt biblical archaeology a major blow.

Scholars unsympathetic to biblical historicity were quick to seize on Kenyon's Jericho conclusions. To them the truth was obvious: As mentioned in earlier chapters, the story of Joshua's conquest of Jericho was likely an etiological legend spun by Israelite/Judahite priests to explain the ruins of Tell es-Sultan (the site's modern Arabic name). Perhaps the higher critics were right in assigning the story to a post-seventh- to sixth-century BC strand of Judahite literature.

But the bad news and negative press were not over. The story of Joshua's campaign came under attack again—this time from a site 14 miles west-northeast of Jericho. It was the second town taken by the Israelites in the book of Joshua: Ai. One of the excavators of the traditional site of Ai (et-Tell), Joseph Callaway (1920–1988), was drawn into the debate over the historicity of the book of Joshua by no plan of his own. As a professor of Old Testament and biblical law/archaeology at Southern Baptist Theological Seminary (1958–1982), he approached the excavation of et-Tell (Ai) fully expecting to find evidence of Joshua's destruction of the town which, in line with a majority of archaeologists, he dated to the thirteenth century BC (LBA2b). But his expectations were not realized. Callaway's excavations confirmed that the site terminated abruptly toward the end of the Early Bronze Age (EBA), c. 2500 BC, and was not reoccupied until the IA, after c. 1200 BC, but only by an unwalled village. There was no evidence of architecture or pottery from the LBA. As at Jericho, there was no LBA town on the site for Joshua to conquer. Once again a famous battle overseen by Joshua was demoted from history to the realm of etiological lore.

The apparent incongruity between text and ground was unsettling for Callaway. His experience while excavating at Ai caused him to reconsider the nature of Bible history. Callaway abandoned his belief in the historical fidelity of the Hexateuch (Genesis through Joshua). How this affected his personal faith is still a matter of debate. It was little consolation to consider that et-Tell was likely the Ai (meaning "ruin" or "heap") of the Abraham narratives. Nor did he consider that a nearby namesake site may have served as the Ai of Joshua's account. In the minds of most scholars, Callaway's work at Ai confirmed what Kenyon found—or did not find—at Jericho. The historicity of the book of Joshua had suffered another major hit.

It didn't take long for the results of Kenyon's and Callaway's research at Jericho and Ai to sink in: The exploits of Joshua appeared to be a collection of etiological legends. This was the new conventional wisdom of mainstream archaeology. The Albrightian era that marked the heyday of biblical archaeology was over. Post-Albrightian archaeologists—steeped in Old Testament higher critical theory, if they had any training in the Hebrew Scriptures at all—relegated the patriarchal era of Abraham, Isaac, Jacob, and Joseph to the realm of religious fiction. Most seriously doubted the reality of Moses and Joshua, even David and Solomon. While some renowned archaeologists like Benjamin Mazar and Amnon Ben-Tor held to the general historical character of some Old Testament narratives, they still doubted the historicity of the Genesis accounts. General confidence in the historical quality of the Hebrew Scriptures, particularly the Torah, was beginning to fade.

A minority of conservative archaeologists held firm, however. For them, historicity was a matter of *interpreting* archaeological data, even biblical hermeneutics. But by the late 1980s, the gap between a more liberal majority and the minority of Bible-respecting archaeologists had widened even further. This gap would soon get much worse.

ATTACKS AGAINST BIBLICAL ARCHAEOLOGY (POST 1985) AND THE RISE OF MINIMALISM

By 1985, belief in the historical accuracy of the Hexateuch was a minority position. Immersed in nineteenth-century higher criticism—given new impetus by Old Testament scholars through the twentieth century—the larger community of Syro-Palestinian (Levantine) archaeologists were persuaded that the mutual verdict of fieldwork and emerging technologies was firm: The biblical archaeology of Albright and Wright had been dashed to the ground and categorically discredited. During the 1990s, the situation continued to deteriorate. Space prohibits a detailed accounting of all the players in this drama, but the following overview captures the essence of the struggle between the minimalists and maximalists during the first decade of the twenty-first century.

Minimalism holds that most of the Old Testament, especially the Torah and Joshua (the Hexateuch), is myth or religious fiction. Maximalism believes—in varying degrees—that the Old Testament is mostly or entirely factual. The current situation (2019) finds the maximalists in the extreme minority. As will be demonstrated, however, this is not due to the scientific nature of the case against biblical archaeology. Rather, it is attributable to a residual antibiblical bias still influencing the interpretation of archaeological data. A bit more history is in order.

The positions and opinions of William G. Dever have been critical to the debate between minimalism and maximalism. Considered by many as the dean of

Syro-Palestinian archaeologists in the United States, he is often credited with the "death" of biblical archaeology. He is fond of saying that while he did not actually kill it, he did "write the obituary." In a February 24, 2007 article in the *Wall Street Journal*, Dever stated, "No responsible scholar goes out with a trowel in one hand and a Bible in the other." He credits his drift from theologically trained evangelical clergyman to agnostic ANE scholar to his archaeological training and career. His contributions to archaeological science are remarkable, and his influence on the latest generation of Levantine archaeologists is substantial. Though he is now retired, he still writes extensively and continues to speak out for a less-extreme form of minimalism.

The career of Amihai Mazar, for decades a professor in the Institute of Archaeology at the Hebrew University in Jerusalem, has been remarkable to say the least. Among his excavations are Timnah, Bet Shan, and Rehov. Unlike some of his colleagues in Israel, he enjoys exceptional rapport among Christian and evangelical scholars. Because he is more or less a centrist in the dialogue concerning archaeology and the Bible, he occupies a key position in the minimalist/maximalist controversy. While he does see the Genesis patriarchal narratives as mythical and the remainder of the Torah as containing only kernels of historical memory, Mazar seeks a balanced approach to employing the Bible in archaeological contexts.

Since 1985, Israel Finkelstein has—perhaps by default—served as the most influential spokesman of biblical minimalism among Israeli archaeologists. Professor of the Archaeology of Israel at Tel Aviv University and codirector of the Megiddo excavations, he believes strongly that the Hebrew Bible is devoid of any factual information that might provide insights into the origins and history of ancient Israel. His position on the origins of Israel is often called *emergence theory*. In a nutshell, his view is this: There were no Hebrew patriarchs and there was no Moses; there was no Israelite sojourn in nor exodus from Egypt; there was no Joshua, and no conquest of Canaan—all of it is fiction or worse.

Finkelstein believes that sometime after c. 1000 BC

the Israelites evolved from the local Canaanite population, emerging—thus, emergence theory—as distinguishable clans of Yahweh enthusiasts who managed to create a kingdom for themselves in the central highlands. A political Israelite state coalesced under the leadership of fabled warrior-chieftains David and Solomon—perhaps historical figures, perhaps not. In the late IA (c. eighth–seventh centuries BC), Yahwistic priests in Israel, then Judah, edited through oral and written tribal traditions for the purpose of assembling a "national myth" justifying the divine right of the nation to occupy its expanding borders.

Finkelstein's views, originally considered radical by his Israeli colleagues, have gained increasing acceptance in many circles. Although hard to imagine, there are views of Israel's origins even to the "left" of Finkelstein. These facts should remind conservative and evangelical scholars that the pro-Bible archaeological culture of Albright's era is now a fading memory.

THE "DEATH" OF BIBLICAL ARCHAEOLOGY

By the year 2000 there was a near-consensus among Levantine archaeologists that biblical archaeology was finally dead and that the Torah, if not the entire Old Testament, was categorically mythical in nature. For certain, twentieth-century biblical archaeology was not going to return in its original form. In reality, the larger discipline of archaeological science has not returned to the Old Testament as a workable outline for constructing ANE history. The following quotations from ANE scholars are indicative of the growing antibiblical climate in the last quarter of the twentieth century. In many circles, these views are still in vogue today.

Thomas L. Thompson on biblical history:

> Salvation history is not a historical account of saving events open to the study of the historian. Salvation history did not happen; it is a literary form which has its own historical context. In fact, we can say that the faith of Israel is not a historical

faith, in the sense of a faith based on historical events; it is rather a faith within history.[11]

Dorothy Irvin on Israelite history:

Of these narratives [Davidic lore] as well as all the narratives of the Pentateuch, the historical problem is not so much that they are historically unverifiable, and especially not that they are untrue historically, but that they are radically irrelevant as sources of Israel's history.[12]

John Van Seters on Mosaic history:

There is no primary and secondary material, no ancient oral tradition behind the text. The plague narrative did not exist as a specific tradition before the Yahwist's work and is, therefore, no older than the exilic period.[13]

Gösta Ahlström on the Exodus:

Since the biblical text is concerned primarily with divine actions, which are not verifiable, it is impossible to use the exodus story as a source to reconstruct the history of the LBA and early Iron Age 1 (IA1) periods. The text is concerned with mythology rather than with a detailed reporting of historical facts. As soon as someone "relates" a god's actions or words, mythology has been written.[14]

Israel Finkelstein and Nadav Na'aman on the conquest:

Combination of archaeological and historical research demonstrates that the biblical account of the Conquest and occupation of Canaan [by the Israelites] is entirely divorced from historical reality.[15]

Niles P. Lemche on the Hebrew patriarchs:

The patriarchal narratives are...fiction, not reality. That world does not represent a real world. It

stands outside the usual representation of time and space. As a matter of fact...neither the narratives nor their world can be dated to any precise period.[16]

The silver lining in all this is that biblical archaeology was not as dead as the opposition thought. All through the transition from the Albrightian era to the current state of archaeology, astute Bible-respecting archaeologists—and other scholars as well—have continued in the field, in research and publication, and in the use of emerging technologies and methods of scientific analysis. Bible scholars need not be alarmed! A new biblical archaeology has emerged, and on a far better footing than Albright could have imagined.

Today the old regime of biblical archaeology is of little service to the Bible student. And the new order in biblical archaeology offers a wealth of solid data from the ANE, supported by better logic, critical thinking, superior methods, and more rigorous scholarship—with an active opposition mounting challenges all along the way. Iron sharpens iron.

THE PRESENT RESURGENCE AND FUTURE OF BIBLICAL ARCHAEOLOGY

Moderate and conservative reactions against Finkelstein and the minimalists have exploded into an avalanche of new and reinterpreted data from across the spectrum of ANE studies and archaeology corroborating the historical authenticity of Old Testament narratives. This material is even demonstrating the historical character of the Genesis patriarchal narratives—not echoing Albright's failed attempts in this vein, but with *historical synchronisms* and elements of *cultural specificity*.

The crux of the matter is data interpretation and this question: Is there reasonable correspondence and/or consistency between the biblical text and the archaeological data?

Professor Kitchen emphasizes that the two *are* compatible:

The Sinai covenant (all three versions, Deuteronomy included) has to have originated within a close-set period (1400–1200)—likewise other features. The phenomena of the united monarchy fit well into what we know of the period and of ancient royal usages. The primeval protohistory embodies early popular tradition going very far back, and is set in an early format. Thus we have a consistent level of good, fact-based correlations right through from circa 2000 B.C. (with earlier roots) down to 400 B.C. In terms of general reliability...the Old Testament comes out remarkably well, so long as its writings and writers are treated fairly and evenhandedly, in line with independent data, open to all.[17]

Collins's *dialogical approach* to archaeology and the Bible is most helpful:

I have observed that scholars on both extremes of what I often call the *Bible believe-o-meter* have adopted structurally similar, but opposite, approaches. Minimalists, to the extent possible, do not allow the Bible to intersect with their archaeology. Maximalists, as far as possible, throw out archaeological conclusions that challenge "traditional" interpretations of biblical texts, allowing only data that harmonize with their textual preconceptions...If both "sides" are willing to admit that no scholars are infallible or in possession of *all* the facts, then we can view points of correspondence (or lack thereof) between text *and* tell with better objectivity...In short, we need to *talk*! And we need to do so without thinking that we, individually, must come away with a victory for our own point of view. Has archaeology gone too far in throwing out the Bible? Yes! But have some scholars gone too far in throwing out archaeology? Yes! (emphasis in original).[18]

Collins's solution is straightforward:

...approach the subject of the Bible and arch-

aeology *dialogically*. In practical terms, it works like this: First, each "side" must give up the idea that those on the opposite end are "fringe lunatics." Scholars may never agree completely, but at the very least they need to understand and respect how others arrived at their positions...Second, minimalists [should] lay aside categorical rejection of the Bible at the level of history and geography [and] maximalists [must] disconnect biblical history and geography from theology...Third, scholars should learn to think *geographically*. Is anyone actually going to deny the importance of biblical texts in terms of geography?...Biblical texts are, at the geographical level, the product of ancient observers who lived on that terrain. They deserve respect and careful attention...Fourth, be open to cause-and-effect relationships between biblical and ancient history when reasonable observations from numerous data-sets—including the biblical text—converge. When levels of correspondence rise to statistically meaningful levels, do not ignore them merely because they contradict previously accepted ideas...Fifth, let both archaeology and the biblical text participate in the dialogue. Both have something to say...I could never understand how any scholar—regardless of "pet" theories about textual origins—could toss the Bible out of the repertoire of archaeological tools. Seriously?—eliminate an ancient text full of geographical and historical clues from the archaeological process? Because of what? Because Yahweh enacted a covenant with Abram? Because Moses had face-to-face conversations with Yahweh? Because the Israelites told stories that cast a less-than-flattering light on their (often enemy) neighbors? Really? On *this* basis we shall finally eliminate most everything we know about the ancient Near East. Archaeology cut loose from religiously-loaded texts? Good luck with that! (emphasis in original).[19]

One of the leaders of this resurgence of respect for biblical historicity is Egyptologist and ANE scholar

K.A. Kitchen (emeritus professor at the University of Liverpool). His propensity for logic and heavy documentation demonstrate convincingly that Abraham, Isaac, and Jacob authentically belong to the MBA (c. 1900–1550 BC) and could not have originated in the imaginations of late-IA Judahite priests as the proponents of Old Testament higher criticism insist. Kitchen further confirms that cultural elements found in the stories of Moses and Joshua match those of the LBA. That late-IA Judahite writers/editors and their priestly associates could have known or had access to BA historical and cultural details is essentially absurd. Again, Kitchen, in his inimitable style, aptly sums up the situation:

> The theories current in Old Testament studies, however brilliantly conceived and elaborated, were mainly established in a vacuum with little or no reference to the Ancient Near East, and initially too often in accordance with a priori philosophical and literary principles. It is solely because the data from the Ancient Near East coincide so much better with the existing observable structure of Old Testament history, literature and religion than with the theoretical reconstructions, that we are compelled—as happens in Ancient Oriental studies—to question or even to abandon such theories regardless of their popularity. Facts, not votes, determine the truth.[20]

BIBLICAL ARCHAEOLOGY IN THE TWENTY-FIRST CENTURY: BETTER SCIENCE, BETTER EVIDENCE

It is important here to at least identify some of the Bible-respecting field archaeologists working today and their ongoing contributions to the subject of biblical historicity. The following are selected because they are currently—or have since 2000—directing major excavations in the Southern Levant or are working with excavations and/or publishing in a significant area of expertise. None of them are without controversy

regarding their data interpretations and conclusions, nor do they always agree with each other. However, they are all active members of the community of ANE scholars and they are making significant contributions to a better understanding of the ancient Levant and how the Bible meshes with that world. They are among the ones to watch.

Steven Ortiz, who heads the archaeology program at Southwestern Baptist Theological Seminary, is a protégé of William Dever. He most recently directed the excavations at Tel Gezer in Israel. His career illustrates that scientific rigor and conservative biblical beliefs can, in fact, coexist harmoniously.

This is also true in the remarkable work of Leen Ritmeyer, widely recognized as the world's leading authority on the Temple Mount in Jerusalem. During two decades of working for Benjamin Mazar, he became the chief archaeological architect for the south Temple Mount excavations. He has produced technical and reconstruction drawings for dozens of the most important excavations in Israel and, among many other projects, is currently working with the Tall el-Hammam Excavation Project (Sodom) in Jordan. His work appears in hundreds of scholarly publications and his Temple Mount research is detailed in a recent book, *The Quest* (Carta/Lamb 2006).

Israeli archaeologist Eilat Mazar, granddaughter of Benjamin Mazar, exhibits a solid commitment to the historical underpinnings of the Old Testament. She currently directs excavations in the City of David south of Jerusalem's Old City. Although criticized in some quarters for her insistence that she has found the remnants of King David's palace by using information from relevant biblical texts, she continues to make a reasonable case for her discoveries. She stands in stark contrast to the minimalists and demonstrates that the reports of the death of biblical archaeology do not reflect the reality of the situation on the ground.

American archaeologist Bryant G. Wood, the chief archaeologist for the Associates for Biblical Research, is held in high esteem among Christianity's most conservative evangelicals. He has deftly carried the banner of *biblical literalism* throughout his career. His excavations at Khirbet el-Maqatir have challenged the traditional location of the site of Ai, which was destroyed by Joshua (see the discussion on J. Callaway earlier in this chapter). The contrast between Wood and other scholars within the Christian community—like Kitchen, Millard, Ortiz, Mullins, Collins, and Stripling—represents the fact that there is little consensus among even conservative archaeologists and ANE scholars on issues like the date of the exodus and the nature of biblical chronology, whether literal, honorific, or figurative.

The career of Robert A. Mullins, Professor of Archaeology and Old Testament at Azusa Pacific University, demonstrates that an archaeologist who also happens to be a Christian can make remarkable contributions to Levantine archaeology. His acumen in the typology of ancient ceramics and field archaeology shows the ability of a faith-oriented individual to accomplish impeccable, objective scientific work. Mullins's current excavation at the biblical site of Abel Beth Maacah in northern Israel shows how the Bible can be used responsibly in an archaeological context, particularly in terms of ancient geography.

One of the coeditors of this volume, Steven Collins, is Director of the School of Archaeology, Veritas International University, and currently directs the Tall el-Hammam Excavation Project in Jordan, which (at the time of this writing) is in its fifteenth season. The identification of Tall el-Hammam as biblical Sodom has opened up a historic discussion concerning the factuality of the Abrahamic narratives in Genesis. Collins's recent book (coauthored with L.C. Scott) *Discovering the City of Sodom* (Simon and Schuster/Howard Books 2013) documents his extensive research and excavations in the south Jordan Valley.

Scott Stripling directed the most recent excavations at Khirbet el-Maqatir (likely Joshua's Ai) and also served as a supervisor with the Temple Mount Sifting Project in Jerusalem. He is currently Director of Excavations at ancient Shiloh (since 2017). A wealth of new data is coming forth from Shiloh, and Stripling's work there will be extremely important for understanding Israel's early centuries. Stripling is currently Provost and Director of the Archaeology Institute at The Bible Seminary.

While space prevents a more comprehensive catalog of significant contributors to biblical archaeology in the twenty-first century, each of the scholars mentioned above has demonstrated that the disciplines of biblical studies and ANE archaeology have risen from the selfsame reality and have a meaningful relationship. Biblical archaeology is alive and well, and in good hands.

CHAPTER 11

ARCHAEOLOGICAL DISCOVERIES SUPPORTING THE AUTHENTICITY OF THE BIBLE

ARCHAEOLOGY AND ANE STUDIES VS. RADICAL OLD TESTAMENT CRITICISM

What can archaeology tell us about the Bible? Can archaeology prove that anything in the Bible is true? Not any more or less than it can prove the elements of any historical account true or false. But what it *can* do—and very effectively— is to illumine our understanding of the biblical text. It can also confirm—or call into question—the interpretation of a given Scripture passage. Archaeology can also demonstrate that the physical record preserved in the stratigraphy of tells (tels or talls; "layer cake" ruin mounds) is consistent with what's reported in historical documents like those comprising the Old Testament. Because the Bible arises from an ANE context—what Steven Collins calls its reality base—it only makes sense that archaeology can assist in revealing the biblical world and the elements of material culture comprising it.

Because the Bible is historically authentic, it should be no surprise when archaeological data connects, often remarkably, with the biblical text. Correspondences between the Bible and archaeology fall into two basic categories: *cultural specificity* and *historical synchronisms*.

Collins describes cultural specificity as

elements of culture existing uniquely in specific times and places. The concept is quite simple: cultures in given locations change dramatically through time as a result of both internal and external factors. For example, things like fad and fashion affect everything from pottery to weapons to jewelry. Changes brought about by the external pressures of migration and warfare are also common in the Near Eastern archaeological record. As a result of the fluid changes in culture over time, the elements of material culture in one period may be identifiably, even dramatically, different from the same elements of material culture in a subsequent period, say, two or three centuries later… elements of material culture often differ from region to region as well.[1]

Collins explains historical synchronisms as

points of correspondence between two (or more) parallel histories—say, Egypt, Mesopotamia, and Israel (the Bible)—in the same chronological period, for example, 1550–1400 BC. The more points of correspondence between the parallel histories, the more probable the relationship between them will be linked by multiple "shared" events or event horizons. For example, we have biblical history, as in the Pentateuch, and we have a chronologically parallel portion of Egyptian history. In order to "fine tune" the relationship between biblical and Egyptian history, we must look for shared events or potential cause-and-effect relationships between the two that can link the separate histories together. Because of the chronological uncertainties of both biblical and Egyptian history…Linking parallel histories together—like biblical history and the history of Egypt—is best done using *events*, not dates.[2]

Together, cultural specificity and historical synchronisms provide powerful evidence that biblical narratives ostensibly belonging to the Bronze Age (BA) actually *do* belong to that age. The logic is transparent. If, as Old Testament higher criticism purports, the Hexateuch (Pentateuch and Joshua) is a multilayered literary composition assembled from a variety of late Iron Age (IA; after c. 700 BC) sources, then we would expect those texts to contain elements of history, culture, and literary genre belonging to the late IA. In fact, one would be hard-pressed to imagine a means whereby *any* authentically BA material could find its way into the writings of late-IA Israelite and Judahite priests, a culture far removed from the archaic, pagan world of Middle Bronze Age (MBA) and Late Bronze Age (LBA) Canaan, and Egypt for that matter. If the higher critics are correct, then the stories of the Hebrew patriarchs, Moses, and Joshua should be chock-full of late-IA anachronisms. But exactly the opposite is true. The Hexateuch is packed with authentic BA elements.

K.A. Kitchen's expertise in this regard is unparalleled. He observes that

> the old Wellhausen-type view is ruled out by the horde of contrary facts unearthed since 1878 and 1886. We have here [in the Hexateuch] the Canaan of the early second millennium and *not* of the Hebrew monarchy period, in any wise. The oft-stated claim of a "consensus" that the patriarchs never existed is itself a case of self-delusion [given the previous and more recent ANE data]… We do not actually need firsthand naming of the patriarchs in ancient records; plenty of other historical characters are in the same case. The tombs of Early, Middle, and Late Bronze Canaan have yielded countless bodies of nameless citizens of Canaan; but their anonymity (no texts!) does not render them nonexistent. What is sauce for the goose is sauce for the gander.[3]

Even the structure of the Genesis stories militates against theories of piecemeal composition during the pre-exilic, exilic, and post-exilic Judahite world. Their complex literary construction is BA in nature and points to a unifying, single, composing hand.

Isaac M. Kikawada and A. Quinn, scholars in Near Eastern studies and rhetoric, respectively, at the University of California, Berkeley, identify extensive parallels—including chiasmic structures—between Genesis 1–11 and the MBA (c. eighteenth century BC) Akkadian Atrahasis Epic:

> If Genesis does follow the Atrahasis pattern, we would not only expect the three central episodes to be repetitive but also episode one (creation) and episode 5 (resolution) to be tied together [which they are, in a chiasmus]. We would expect to find features shared by these two stories, perhaps features not found in the central three episodes [which we do]. (Of course, the documentary hypothesis predicts differently, for the creation story and Tower of Babel are attributed to the Priestly and Yahwist sources respectively.)[4]

In the following thumbnail sketches are examples of reasonable correspondence between known ANE archaeological and anthropological observations and various biblical stories and texts. Selections are limited to known and well-studied archaeological data that are consistent with biblical materials. Conspicuously absent are things like the Garden of Eden, Noah's ark, and the Ark of the Covenant. Put simply, if an alleged biblical object cannot be physically examined, measured, photographed, sampled, tested, and published, it is not available to archaeological science and cannot rightly be included in a discussion of archaeology and the Old Testament.

Here are some elements of cultural specificity and historical synchronisms that clearly demonstrate the historical authenticity of the primeval BA and IA Scriptures.

ANCIENT KING LISTS AND PATRIARCHAL LONGEVITY (*See Chapter 2*)

Several "king lists" have survived from the ANE. Some of these lists seem to indicate that rulers lived and reigned for thousands of years, particularly the ones from the preflood period. For example, the Sumerian king list has reigns as long as 10,800 to 64,800 years. By comparison, the life spans of the early Genesis patriarchs are measured in hundreds of years. Do these parallels demonstrate that ANE peoples believed a period of great longevity existed in the distant past? Some scholars understand the Genesis life span numbers in a literal base-ten arithmetic sense, following the lead of Bishop Ussher (seventeenth century AD).[5]

Others see significant problems with the literal approach and suggest that the numbers are derived from an authentic Mesopotamian-style sexagesimal (base-sixty) number system, or are honorific (attributing status or character), or are formulaic (traditional number conventions with symbolic meanings, such as forty which represents a traditional generation).[6] It is also possible that two or more of these elements are integrated to create the large numbers in both the Bible and other ANE documents. The 110 death-age of Joseph is the same 110 years documented in numerous ancient sources as the "idealized" life span of a noble Egyptian.[7] Thus, regardless of the approach taken, the long life spans of the early Genesis patriarchs are authentic to their ancient Near Eastern context.

ARARAT, URARTU, AND THE NOAH STORY (*See Chapter 1*)

According to Genesis 8:4, Noah's ark "came to rest on the mountains of Ararat." Geographically, this is the Urartu region north of Mesopotamia, between the Black Sea and Caspian Sea.

This is the gateway to a special region on planet earth—the area comprising the epicenter of global human population expansion. In ancient times and through much of history, great waves of human migration expanded concentrically in all directions from that location, forcing the movement of people groups farther from that "Ararat epicenter"…the earliest evidences of developing civilizations are in that immediate neighborhood, i.e., the Fertile Crescent, and the farther from that area you go, the later civilization develops. For example, "high" civilization in the Indus Valley developed later than those of Mesopotamia and Egypt. Civilizations in China developed later than those in India. And the civilizations of the Western Hemisphere developed even later. So, we could ask the question: Why were the Aztecs and Incas in the fifteenth century *AD* doing what the Egyptians and Mesopotamians had done in 3000 BC? The answer: It's a long, long way from Mount Ararat! And the hub of all that human colonizing activity was the Urartu/Ararat region. We know this from modern anthropological studies; but how did the writer of Genesis know that?[8]

John G. Leslie—PhD in experimental pathology; MD, a practicing physician; PhD in archaeology and biblical history—demonstrates that the Noah narrative has all the earmarks of a "true narrative representation" (TNR):

The entire story is consistent with a true narrative account. It precisely described the ark's structure: length—300 cubits, breadth—50 cubits, and height—30 cubits. These are sea worthy dimensions. It was made of gopher wood and sealed with pitch—materials available to Noah…It has been shown that the number of animals taken onto the ark along with Noah and his family were feasible…There are at least nine literary devices that argue for a unified and thus a single composition of the Noah flood account…There are data in the various fields of science and anthropology that are consistent with what might be expected with a worldwide flood like the Noah flood account… Anthropological/archeological studies from throughout the world reveal information that is consistent with a common source for the story of a…flood and the origin and migration of early populations from the Middle East…The Noah Flood Story meets the criteria for a TNR, and can be reliably read as an accurate eyewitness account consistent with a worldwide flood. This has significant ethical/moral implications for mankind in this present age.[9]

BIBLICAL BABEL, THE MYSTERIOUS DEMISE OF CHALCOLITHIC CULTURE, AND THE SUBSEQUENT RISE OF FORTIFIED CITIES IN THE EARLY BRONZE AGE (*See Chapter 1*)

The events surrounding the Tower of Babel (Genesis 11) likely occurred during the late fifth millennium BC. Collins speaks to the subject:

> It's a well-known story, but I think the biblical account is a simplified version of a much larger socio-cultural catastrophe—the tip of the proverbial iceberg. The text indicates events that had global impact. Surely, the result of a sudden confusion of human language into multiple tongues would have wreaked havoc throughout human societies. But this may help to solve a problem that archaeologists have long considered a mystery: the demise of Chalcolithic civilization.[10]

The Chalcolithic Period (CP; meaning Copper-Stone Age) was an advanced sociocultural complex. For example, this civilization's settlement planning, agriculture, and metallurgy were some of the most advanced in antiquity. But toward the end of the fifth millennium BC, or perhaps the beginning of the fourth millennium BC, most CP settlements came to a screeching halt. Large and small villages across the

Fertile Crescent mysteriously ceased to exist—not destroyed by warfare, but simply abandoned. For several hundred years following, most of the population reverted to nomadism or seminomadism. Huge migrations of humanity pushed to the east and west.[11]

Around 3200 BC came the rise of urbanism. For the first time in the history of humanity great cities arose, surrounded by massive fortifications with thick walls, towers, and monumental gateways. But they were not frightened by some Hollywood-style monster! They were protecting themselves against attacks from neighboring cities and city-states.[12]

It appears that people were suddenly fighting among themselves and building great walled cities as an answer to the crisis. Could the division of languages have precipitated this new phenomenon of localized warfare?

Collins, who directs excavations in the Middle Ghor (south Jordan Valley), the location of the most populous Chalcolithic civilization in the south Levant, reasons:

> Historically, the greatest divider of humankind is language, not race or religion. There is little doubt in my mind that all these biblical and Near Eastern phenomena fold together. And, by the way, there is still no better explanation for the origin of diverse human languages than the story of Babel.[13]

THE TABLE OF NATIONS AND MODERN ANTHROPOLOGY (*See Chapter 1*)

In Genesis chapter 10 is a remarkable record often called the Table of Nations. It includes individual and family origins of ancient ethnolinguistic groups. Anthropological and archaeological studies worldwide support the cultural outline recorded in Genesis 10 (note: this is an ethnolinguistic outline and has little to do with genome tracking). The Genesis record also specifies that the area we call the Fertile Crescent was the cradle of civilization, which is a well-known fact. In reflecting the rise of urbanization, it also lists the names of Early Bronze Age (EBA) cities such as Erech (Uruk) and Accad (Akkad), which would have been entirely unknown to late-IA Judahite priests. Archaeology confirms this abundantly. Collins asks a key question: "Why would the Hebrew account in Genesis be so concerned about far-flung peoples and foreign places when the origin myths of other cultures focus narrowly on their own lands?"[14] The straightforward answer is that Genesis 10 is historically grounded.

ABRAM'S UR AND THE SEMITIC DOMINATION OF MESOPOTAMIA (*See Chapter 2*)

The descendants of Shem, or Semites, became the prevailing focus of the Genesis text after the Babel event (Genesis 11). Toward the end of the third millennium into the early second millennium BC, the Semitic ancestors of Abraham moved into south Mesopotamia, the region of ancient Sumer, also known as Shinar. Archaeology confirms this general picture. Toward the end of the third millennium and into the mid-second millennium BC, the Semitic population of Mesopotamia overwhelmed the Sumerian (non-Semitic) residents of south Mesopotamia. Semitic languages, particularly Akkadian, dominated the linguistic scene.[15]

TERAH'S AND ABRAM'S URGE TO MOVE AND THE MIGRATIONS OF THE EARLY SECOND MILLENNIUM BC (*See Chapter 2*)

In the biblical story of Genesis 11, after 1990 BC, Semitic clans such as the one led by Terah departed from Ur and traveled the length of Mesopotamia to the city of Haran in Syria. There they continued their seminomadic lifestyle as herders. Their religion was mainly tribal animism (referenced in Joshua 24).

K.A. Kitchen comments on the wide scope of travel during the MBA, the time of Terah and Abraham:

Terah and his family may have dwelled in the city proper. But if they were already pastoralists, they may equally have lived in rural settlements around Ur, like other such tribal people who gave their names to districts around major Babylonian cities, particularly in the early second millennium… Pastoralist tribal groups ranged far and wide in the early second millennium…Around Haran there may have been other such settlements that also reflect [the] names of Abraham's ancestors. But at present only the late name-forms survive; a Til-(sha)-Turakhi would represent the resettlement (ninth century) of an ancient Turakh or Tirakh (cf. Terah), a later Sarugi may reflect Serug, and so on…Thus Terah might have had family origins around Haran and Nakhur [reflecting Nahor], followed the common "drift" southeastward, in his case to Ur, and then returned north with his family.[16]

Again, archaeology confirms the world of Terah and Abraham. During Middle Bronze Age 2 (MBA2; 1900–1550 BC), mass migrations of nomadic and seminomadic peoples, primarily of Semitic extraction, traversed throughout the Fertile Crescent. As was Terah, they were tribal animists.[17]

ABRAM ENTERS MIDDLE BRONZE AGE CANAAN (*See Chapter 2*)

In the second millennium BC (MBA), Abram moved his family from north Syria/Mesopotamia into Canaan, where they continued to pursue a seminomadic lifestyle. According to Genesis 12, they pitched their tents between urban centers (such as Jerusalem and Shechem) and their satellite towns (such as Hebron and Bethel) and the uninhabited ruins of formerly great cities, as indicated by the term Ai (*ha'ay*), which means "the ruin." This is soundly confirmed by the archaeological record.

The amazing thing about the biblical statement that Abram "pitched his tent, with Bethel on the west and [*ha*] Ai ['the ruin'] on the east" is that we know where these cities are, and their respective occupational histories match the story perfectly. Bethel was a medium-sized walled town during MBA2. About two miles to the east lies the EBA site, called et-Tell today, which is obviously the site of Ai, and was, in fact, lying in ruins during Abraham's day, the MBA. All this is virtually a geographical given. But it also means that archaeologists know within a hill or two where Abram's original campsite was located.

Collins, who explored the area extensively while excavating with Bryant Wood at Khirbet el-Maqatir from 1995 to 2000, confirms this amazing piece of biblical geography:

> That ancient city [Ai in the Abra(ha)m narratives]—we don't know its original name—was one of the largest fortified cities of the Early Bronze Age west of the Jordan River; it was destroyed several hundred years before Abram was born…Thus, archaeology confirms that the great city to the east of Abram's camp was, in fact, a huge, impressive ruin in Abram's day—*ha'ay*, the Ruin—exactly as the Bible says! We have to understand how impressive this is. This is fine-tuned information from a remote, real world about which late Iron Age Judahite writers would have had absolutely no information.[18]

ABRAM SPEAKS FACE TO FACE WITH PHARAOH AND BATTLES A COALITION OF FOREIGN KINGS (*See Chapter 2*)

Abram was briefly welcomed into Egypt by the pharaoh himself (and later asked, not so politely, to leave), after which a coalition of Elamite, Mesopotamian, and (possibly) Hurrian or Hittite kings swept through the Levant (Canaan), wreaking havoc (Genesis 12; 14).

Archaeology shows that nomadic and seminomadic tribes routinely coursed between Canaan and Egypt during the MBA. Egypt, Hatti, and Mesopotamia

vied for control of Canaanite commerce, particularly olive oil and wine. As mentioned above, the Intermediate Bronze Age (IBA, before Abram's time) was often marred by violence as new sociopolitical entities sought to establish themselves in the region. During the MBA, and with increasing frequency, Canaan found itself to be a buffer between Egypt and the powers of Hatti and Mesopotamia, and it was often caught in the crossfire. Therefore, the story of a north-northeast coalition of kings (or kinglets) running raids into Canaan is quite reasonable.

But how could Abram, a nomadic chieftain, have had a face-to-face conversation with the pharaoh of Egypt without an interpreter? Liberal scholars often raise this question as a point of criticism. Well, the answer is quite simple. Remember, Abram was born and reared in the southern Mesopotamian city of Ur. The dominant language of that region was Akkadian, which means Abram's birth language was Akkadian. By that time, Akkadian had also become the Near East's *lingua franca* for international communication. Even the Egyptians used Akkadian for international correspondence, trade, and commerce on the larger Near Eastern scene. While Abram certainly adopted Canaanite (which later became Hebrew) as his new language when he entered Canaan, Akkadian, his birth language, continued to be a great asset to him. Thus, when he stood face to face with pharaoh in Egypt, they could easily converse in Akkadian. After all, Egyptian kings were highly educated and, without doubt, would have spoken the language of international diplomacy.[19]

There is also another possibility: Beginning around 1900 BC, climate change began to put stress on the populations of the Levant—so much so that large numbers of Semitic Asiatic peoples migrated to Egypt. By 1800 BC, they had taken over Egypt to the point of being in power during the Fourteenth and Fifteenth Dynasties—all Semitic (Canaanean) pharaohs! Because this was the period during which Abraham was in Egypt, he may have conversed with the Egyptian king in Canaanite!

GENESIS 13:1-12 LEADS TO THE MONUMENTAL DISCOVERY OF SODOM AND THE CITIES OF THE PLAIN (*See Chapter 2*)

In 2011, the director general of the Jordan Department of Antiquities stated on a Jordanian news broadcast, "The excavation of Tall el-Hammam/Sodom is perhaps the most important archaeological discovery of all time." The reason for the declaration was twofold: (1) the geographical and archaeological evidence for the identification of Tall el-Hammam as the infamous city of Sodom was about as good as it gets when trying to identify a biblical city; and (2) the very existence of Sodom and the Cities of the Plain—much less the story about God destroying them with burning stones and fire from the heavens—was seriously doubted by most scholars. For them, the story was out-and-out myth or fiction. If, therefore, Tall el-Hammam is, in fact, Sodom, it would perhaps constitute the most important confirmation of the historical reality of biblical narrative since the onset of Old Testament higher critical theory. And the evidence in support of this is strong.

Joseph Holden and Norman Geisler, who researched the discoveries at Tall el-Hammam (with Holden excavating for two seasons) for their recent book on biblical archaeology, explain:

> Many existing biblical sites have been confirmed based on much less geographical evidence than that offered for Tall el-Hammam. Indeed, after reviewing the still-increasing amount of archaeological, biblical, and geographical evidence, if one denies that Tall el-Hammam is the biblical city of Sodom, every biblical city that has been confirmed on less than epigraphical evidence must be called into question.[20]

It has been true for more than 100 years that the legitimate discovery of the Cities of the Plain, as the Bible calls them, would be compelling evidence that the historical fabric of Genesis is indeed *factual*. Further, if the archaeological evidence confirmed that these cities were, in fact, destroyed in a manner commensurate with the biblical description in Genesis 19, that would be a remarkable discovery indeed. For nearly a decade and a half, the Tall el-Hammam Excavation Project (TeHEP) has been unearthing the lost city of Sodom itself, a city-state and civilization that flourished for more than 2,500 years before it was (in reality!) destroyed by a violent, fiery catastrophe, likely of cosmic origin.

Collins, director and chief archaeologist of the Tall el-Hammam Excavation Project in Jordan, comments on the continuing work at the site:

> A decade of focused research and exploration into the location of Sodom by our team of archaeologists and supporting scientists has led to the discovery of a group of ancient sites that are, by far, the best candidates for the infamous Cities of the Plain (Genesis 13–19), the largest—Tall el-Hammam—fitting the biblical description of Sodom itself.[21]

The key to finding the actual location of Sodom was an intricate analysis of the biblical text. Collins explains,

> The three main biblical criteria for finding the Cities of the Plain are: *(1) geography*—the biblical text clearly indicates that they were located on the eastern edge of the Jordan Disk (= "Plain of the Jordan"; plain = Heb., *kikkar* = "circle" or "disk"), the well-watered circular plain of the southern Jordan Valley *N* of the Dead Sea (Gen. 13:1-12); *(2) chronology*—they must date from the Middle Bronze Age, the only possible timeframe for Abraham and Lot, with underlying strata from a previous era such as the Early Bronze Age (because the cities are also mentioned in Gen. 10); and *(3) stratigraphy*—their Middle Bronze Age destruction must be followed by at least a few centuries of inoccupation, because well after the time of Abraham, Moses found the area to be an uninhabited wasteland, as recorded in Numbers 21:20.[22]

Now in its fourteenth season, the Tall el-Hammam Excavations have unearthed many important elements of the city: more than 150 acres of occupational footprint; 62 acres enclosed within a massive fortification system surrounding both an upper and lower city with defensive ramparts nearly 100 feet thick in places and massive city walls; a monumental gateway system with plazas and towers; a temple complex; domestic and administrative structures; a large palace with exterior walls more than five feet thick; streets and roadways; weapons, jewelry, figurines, and implements supporting a large textile industry; and all or pieces of nearly 100,000 separate pottery vessels. It is a city worthy to be mentioned in Genesis 10 along with Babylon, Akkad, and Nineveh. Tall el-Hammam/Sodom was the largest city in the south Levant for much of its history and was the urban core of a major city-state with numerous satellite towns within its hegemony.

The only objection that some have raised is over the chronology. Some, like E.H. Merrill, place the career of Abraham, and thus the story of Sodom, between 2166 and 1991 BC, during the IBA (also called EB4). However, several scholars, including Collins, argue convincingly that Abraham belongs to the MBA2 period, *after* 1800 BC.

More than a dozen lines of evidence supporting a later date for Abraham, Collins asserts:

> Ussherians might try to make the case that it is not necessary to see [Jerusalem, Hebron, Dan, and Damascus of the Sodom narratives] as "formal" cities in the time of Abr(ah)am, and that the existence of open villages at those locations would suffice. But this cannot be said of Jerusalem which, in the time of Abr(ah)am (Genesis 14), sports a king who has a formal covenant with Abraham and a political relationship with the king of the Sodom city-state. No such socio-political condition existed at Jerusalem during IB2 or MB1. And even though there were minor occupations (likely seasonal) at all four sites during IB1 (c. 2500–2100 BCE), they were virtually abandoned during IB2 except perhaps for squatters (basically

undetectable). I repeat for emphasis: *There was no city or king at Jerusalem between 2200 and 1800 BCE; therefore, Melchizedek's Salem (Jerusalem) did not exist during Merrill's or Ussher's timeframe for Abraham* (emphasis in original).[23]

Although it usually takes 30 to 40 years for new archaeological discoveries to displace older, obsolete ideas, many Bible-based publications and documentary film producers are already beginning to recognize the probability that Tall el-Hammam is Sodom. This is due to the fact more than 15 years of rigorous research and on-ground exploration across 14 excavation seasons—and more than a decade and a half of vigorous scholarly interaction on the subject—have continued to reinforce that identification. Not only has Tall el-Hammam found its place in the scholarly literature because of the important position it occupies in the BA history of the south Levant, it is also being written into biblical history because of its fidelity to the Genesis criteria for Sodom.

The latest edition of the *Lexham Bible Dictionary* (Logos Bible Software/Lexham Press, 2015) and several other books have already incorporated the Hammam/Sodom data, and since 2012 at least five different documentary films about Hammam/Sodom have been produced for networks like National Geographic, the Discovery and History channels, and other media outlets. Articles about Tall el-Hammam/Sodom continue to appear in secular magazines like *Popular Archaeology* and *Biblical Archaeology Review*. During 2015 and 2018 major media coverage on the discovery of Sodom at Tall el-Hammam found its way into virtually every print and Internet media venue in the world, including Associated Press, Reuters, and Fox News, with articles showing up in major newspapers and magazines in North and South America, South Africa, Europe, Asia, and Australia, including *The Washington Post* and even the politically liberal *HuffPost*. Without a doubt, Tall el-Hammam/Sodom is presently the highest-profile excavation on the planet and is likely to continue as such for some time to come. This remarkable discovery has become a powerful public witness to the historical accuracy of the Genesis record.

THE DESTRUCTION OF SODOM: AN EXCLAMATION MARK FOR BIBLICAL HISTORICITY (*See Chapter 2*)

If finding the city of Sodom was exciting news, then the emerging evidence of its destruction has to be considered nothing short of spectacular. The excavation activity at Tall el-Hammam, and the meticulous exploration of the east Jordan Disk where the ruins of Sodom and its satellite towns are located, has produced substantial data related to the destruction not only of Sodom itself, but of the entire Land of the Kikkar (see Genesis 19:28). Laboratory analyses of samples taken at Tall el-Hammam and the surrounding Kikkar (southern Jordan Valley "plain, disk") by scientists from seven independent universities are confirming an astounding fact: Sodom and the entire 400 square kilometers of the east Jordan Kikkar/Disk were wiped out in an instant by the explosion of a meteoritic object that subjected the area to a catastrophic shockwave and heat blast in excess of 12,000° centigrade (21,632° F).

Phillip J. Silvia, who heads the multiuniversity research team and wrote his PhD dissertation on the subject, writes,

> The existence of a robust civilization occupying the entire Transjordan Middle Ghor [the eastern half of the Kikkar] during the Middle Bronze Age was unknown to early explorers of the region but has now been confirmed through a correlation of excavation reports published since the 1980s. Also revealed through these reports and ongoing excavations at Tall el-Hammam is the sudden, violent, and total destruction of the entire region during the second half of the Middle Bronze Age that brought an end to the occupying civilization and left the region uninhabited for nearly seven centuries.

The discovery and analysis of vitrified pottery sherds at Tall el-Hammam and a large melt rock consisting of glass-coated, fused sand suggest that the destruction event was explosive in nature and included an intense shock front and an extreme thermal profile. Based on the mineral content of these melt products, the temperature and exposure time profile required to create them was far beyond the technological capabilities of Middle Bronze Age people. The only known natural source of such an energy profile is a meteoritic airburst. A literal fire came down from the sky and destroyed the cities of the plain, burned every living plant as well as the ground itself, and poisoned what soil remained with a toxic brine of salts from the Dead Sea. This hypothesized event is also broadly consistent with the recorded and presumably eyewitness account in Genesis 19:22-28.

Without usable ground on which to grow crops, it was impossible for people to reestablish permanent settlements in the region immediately or soon after the destruction event. It took over six centuries for the ground to recover sufficiently to support agricultural use again. The city-state that existed in the region during the Middle Bronze Age was replaced during the Iron Age with a series of forts and military outposts of the relatively new kingdom of Israel. An entirely new civilization reoccupied the Transjordan Middle Ghor.[24]

Right place, right time, right stuff, and right story—these are confirmed at the actual location of Sodom northeast of the Dead Sea, where the Bible specifies that the Kikkar of the Jordan and the Cities of the Kikkar were located. From the great and powerful city of Sodom itself to the cosmic fireball from Yahweh that destroyed it, the reality of the Sodom narratives has turned Old Testament criticism on its ear.[25]

ABRAHAM, ISAAC, AND JACOB AND MIDDLE BRONZE AGE TREATIES (*See Chapter 2*)

Genesis records Abraham's covenant with Yahweh (chapters 15 and 17) and his treaties with Abimelech (chapter 21), with subsequent treaties enacted by Isaac (chapter 26) and Jacob (chapter 31). The covenants and treaties of the various archaeological periods—the Early Bronze Age (EBA; c. 3900–2500 BC), Intermediate Bronze Age (IBA; c. 2500–2100 BC), Middle Bronze Age (MBA; c. 2100–1550 BC), Late Bronze Age (LBA; c. 1550–1200 BC), and Iron Age (IA; c. 1200–332 BC)—are structured quite differently. The components—such as title/preamble, historical prologue, stipulations, depositing text, reading out, witness, and blessings and curses—are assembled variously in different periods; so much so that the covenants and treaties of one period do not resemble (structurally) anything like those in other periods.[26]

Thus, covenants and treaties of the MBA are dissimilar to those of the LBA and early IA, and they certainly don't look anything like covenants and treaties from the latter part of the IA—that is, the Persian period. The patriarchal treaties of Genesis reflect the covenant/treaty structure of the MBA, not any period before or after. Relative to Old Testament higher criticism and the so-called Documentary Hypothesis, the operative question is this: How would Israelite and/or Judahite writers living in the late IA possibly deduce the precise structure of MBA covenants/treaties? The answer is a simple one: They could not.[27] There were no means available to them whereby they could access such data; indeed, why would they care to do so?

The leading expert on ANE covenants, contracts, and treaties, K.A. Kitchen, comments on the period-specific nature of the patriarchal treaties.

> [In] Gen. 21:23-24 (Abram/Beersheba I), 21:27-33 (Abram/Beersheba II), 26:28-31 (Isaac/Gerar), and 31:44-54 (Jacob/Laban), we have very concise reports of the process of making four distinct and successive treaties between the three successive Hebrew patriarchs and Gerar (Abraham, Isaac) and Laban (Jacob). We are *not* given formal documents in extensor; we are just given brief accounts of the actual process of enactment, as often at Mari. Nevertheless, when tabulated, the content of these four treaties *does* correspond quite closely to what we find in both the process of enactment and the final documents at Mari and Tell Leilan, and *not* to what was current at other periods.[28]

ABRAHAM, ISAAC, AND JACOB GET RICH, AND THEIR NAMES FIT THE BILL (*See Chapter 2*)

According to Genesis, the Hebrew clans headed by warrior-chieftains Abraham, Isaac, and Jacob accrued great wealth while operating within the context of the Canaanite economy (Genesis 13–45). The time frame for this is very specific, according to the archaeological evidence: MBA2, c. 1900–1550 BC. After the collapse of EBA urbanism c. 2500 BC, much of the Southern Levant, especially the central highlands of Canaan, remained without cities and towns for the duration of the IBA (c. 2500–2100) and Middle Bronze Age 1 (MBA1; c. 2100–1900 BC).

While a few villages sparsely dotted the landscape of the highland spine between 2500 and 1800 BC, cities and towns like Hebron, Jerusalem, Shechem, and Laish/Lasha (Dan) remained mere piles of rubble covered by wind- and rain-borne sediments and were overgrown with vegetation. While some coastal locations like Ashkelon sprang back to life during MBA1, inland sites like Jerusalem, Hebron, and Dan did not rise again until the 1800s BC, the beginning of MBA2. Even the mighty Hazor of north Canaan remained abandoned until the beginning of MBA2.

Given all this, and the fact that the post-1550 BC LBA economic depression and radical population decline in Canaan was no place for the Hebrew patriarchs, the second half of the MBA is the *only* possible timeframe during which a large nomadic clan like Abraham's could be rich and prosperous amongst the highland city-states that bought their products and services.[29] Abraham himself became rich while operating in, around, and for Jerusalem and its ruler Melchizedek.

The archaeological record confirms that the MBA2 time frame was the high-water mark of Canaanite civilization, and Levantine products were in demand in both Egypt and Mesopotamia. Trade in and through the Levant was at an all-time high. The city-states prospered, and so did the nomadic groups that coursed around and between them.

On another note, the names of the ancient Hebrew patriarchs reflect the popularity of the Amorite imperfective—names beginning with *ya/yi* (such as Ishmael, Isaac, Jacob, and Joseph)—as was common during the MBA. This name style diminished in frequency through the LBA and became rare by the time of the IA. The biblical text follows this same pattern. Kitchen observes:

> For many decades it has been noticed that some of the names in the families of the patriarchs were patterned on a particular model, what experts in the field have commonly called an "Amorite Imperfective"…In this type we have a verbal form with prefixed pronoun element *ya/yi*. And likewise, it was noted that very many of these names are found in the Mari archives of the eighteenth century. Among our patriarchs, such names include Jacob, Isaac, Ishmael, and Joseph…That it is so emerges from a thoroughgoing study of the entire collected corpus of West Semitic personal names of "Amorite" type (better, West Semitic)… The results are striking. While such names are readily found in use at all periods, their popularity in the early second millennium cannot be paralleled at *any other period* (emphasis in original).[30]

THE HEBREW PATRIARCHS AND CANAANITE PRACTICES (*See Chapter 2*)

While Yahweh was the principal deity of the Hebrew clans, many also venerated the household (animistic) gods (spirits) of the local Canaanites (Genesis 31). The archaeological record and the text of Genesis are entirely consistent in this regard. As revealed by the proliferation of high places and fertility images in this period, local Canaanite gods were worshipped in sacred precincts in both city and hilltop sites. The Hebrews/Israelites gravitated toward the same kinds of practices for the bulk of their history. Such an undesirable past for the Israelite and Judahite ancestors is difficult to imagine as a late literary invention, as suggested by higher critical theory.[31]

FAMINE IN CANAAN DRIVES JACOB'S CLANS INTO EGYPT (*See Chapter 2*)

During the early years of MBA2, in the 1800s BC, a climatological downturn hit Syria and Canaan. This led to the migration of large numbers of people—particularly from the northern regions—into Egypt. Eventually these Semitic migrants took over Egypt and ruled as the so-called Hyksos for about 250 years beginning around 1800 BC. The Genesis text mirrors this situation with remarkable fidelity. The (Semitic) Hebrew clans led by Jacob also migrated from Canaan to Egypt and were thus welcomed by a Hyksos (Semitic!) pharaoh (Genesis 46–47). The climatological scenario that precipitated these migrations did not exist during MBA1 (a wet period) prior to the nineteenth century BC, placing the stories of Abraham, Isaac, and Jacob during MBA2 when Semitic migrations to Egypt *did* occur, with dire consequences for the native Egyptians.[32]

Collins, whose work on synchronisms between the collapse of Egypt's Eighteenth Dynasty and the exodus events is critical to this discussion, writes,

> By the seventeenth century BCE, a long-lasting influx of Asiatic Semites (probably Amorites) into the Nile Delta region culminates in the domination of Lower Egypt by the Hyksos kings of the Fourteenth and Fifteenth Dynasties. Powerless to resist the Asiatics, the Theban Seventeenth

Dynasty often pays tribute to the Hyksos regime, which apparently has formed an alliance with the Nubians to the south of the Theban realm.[33]

This general scenario—in MBA2 Canaan—is amply supported by archaeological excavations throughout the area of ancient Canaan. No doubt the burgeoning Canaanite population put a great deal of pressure on the land. And with a touch of drought, a near disaster befell the Southern Levant. The transition from MBA1 to MBA2 was marked by instability in Canaan, possibly brought about by these climate changes. As a result, hordes of Asiatic Semites moved from the Levant and settled in the Nile Delta region (Lower Egypt)…Mazar sees the transition from MBA1 to MBA2 in Canaan as rather uneventful, which fails to explain the movement of Canaanites into the Nile Delta region.[34]

THE PRICE OF SLAVES IN ANTIQUITY: JOSEPH AND MOSES (*See Chapters 2 and 3*)

In Genesis 37, Joseph's brothers sell him into slavery for 20 shekels of silver. According to historical data, this occurred during the MBA2 period. An investigation of ANE trade documents shows that the average price of a slave in this period was, in fact, 20 shekels. The cost of a slave in the Mosaic Law, during the LBA, was 30 shekels of silver (Exodus 21:32)—a bit of ancient inflation! Ancient trade documents confirm that the average price of a slave during the LBA was also 30 shekels—not likely a mere coincidence.

When compared with the IA price of 90 and 120 shekels, an obvious question arises: Given the assumptions of Old Testament higher criticism, how was it possible for late-IA Judahite priests not only to get the period prices right, but also to reflect the actual inflationary curve from a millennium or more before their time? It makes more sense that the prices are accurate because the biblical record is historically accurate.[35]

JOSEPH SERVES A PHARAOH WHO RIDES IN CHARIOTS (*See Chapter 2*)

Jacob's son Joseph rose to the position of pharaoh's administrative head (vizier) of Egypt and was formally presented as such to the Egyptian populace by means of a royal chariot processional (Genesis 41:42-45). This picture is strikingly authentic and, for a variety of reasons, can only belong to the Semitic Hyksos period in Egypt (c. 1800–1550 BC). The Hyksos pharaohs (as Manetho later called them) were themselves Asiatic Semites, making the high appointment of the Semitic Joseph entirely reasonable. Such an appointment during the previous Middle Kingdom would be problematic, likewise in the following New Kingdom that was explicitly anti-Semitic/anti-Asiatic. And the Semitic Hyksos, who took control of Lower Egypt during MBA2—the Fourteenth and Fifteenth Dynasties—are a perfect fit for the Joseph story for another reason: *The Hyksos introduced the horse and chariot into Egypt.* Chariots are entirely missing from Egypt prior to the rise of the Hyksos.[36]

THE BEGINNING OF EGYPT'S EIGHTEENTH DYNASTY: THE ISRAELITES IN BONDAGE (*See Chapters 2 and 3*)

Along with other Semitic groups from the Southern Levant, the clans derived from the sons of Jacob settled and prospered in Lower Egypt—that is, until the beginning of the highly anti-Asiatic Eighteenth Dynasty. At this time, according to the Bible, a pharaoh "arose…over Egypt, who did not know Joseph" (Exodus 1:8). In other words, a king came to power who either loathed or had negative memories of the great Semitic leader. This biblical scenario is completely supported by the archaeological and historical record toward the beginning of the LBA and makes little sense elsewhere.

While Asiatics had dominated the Nile Delta region during the Hyksos period—the Semitic regime of Lower Egypt that had embraced Joseph and his relatives—their rule came to a sudden end about 1550 BC. At that time, Ahmosis—founder of Egypt's Eighteenth Dynasty and ruling from Thebes in Upper Egypt—overthrew the Hyksos and drove their surviving military from Lower Egypt back into Canaan, thereby unifying the Black Land (Egypt's name for itself) for the first time in more than two centuries. The exploits of the native Egyptians, led by Pharaoh Ahmosis, against the hated Hyksos set the stage for the Tuthmossid Eighteenth Dynasty. As a reaction against the Hyksos debacle (allowing Semites to rule Egypt), Ahmosis set in motion a policy of hatred against and enslavement of Asiatic Semites—a policy that would last until the dynasty collapsed in the fourteenth century BC.[37]

PHARAOH'S PARANOIA OVER THE ISRAELITES IN GOSHEN (*See Chapter 3*)

The biblical text reports that at the time of Moses's birth (likely the late fifteenth century BC) the reigning Egyptian king developed a kind of paranoia against the growing population of Israelites in the Nile Delta region (surely the Egyptians made no fine distinction between Israelites and Semitic Asiatics in general) and viewed them as a potential threat to the national security of a newly unified Egypt (Exodus 1). Once again, the historical facts fit the biblical story perfectly. The kings of the early- to mid-Eighteenth Dynasty—Ahmosis, Amenhotep I, Tuthmosis I, Tuthmosis II, Hatshepsut, and Tuthmosis III—all followed an aggressive policy of dominating over and enslaving the Semitic population of the Nile Delta region.[38] Collins provides pertinent details:

> After several failed attempts by the Theban Seventeenth Dynasty to overthrow the Hyksos regime of Lower Egypt, a powerful Pharaoh named Ahmosis ascends to the Theban throne in the early to mid-sixteenth century BCE. Ahmosis, the first king of the Eighteenth Dynasty, successfully routs the Hyksos from Lower Egypt, reunifying the Black Land and reinforcing Egypt's eastern

border against further Asiatic incursions. Having chased the hated Hyksos armies back to Canaan from whence they had originally come, Ahmosis sets in motion a state policy of hatred against Asiatic Semites that becomes a standard for Eighteenth Dynasty administrations. From this point on, the enslavement of Delta region Asiatics by the Eighteenth Dynasty is pursued with vigor, including incursions into the central hill country of Canaan to capture more slaves. As a result of this policy, the population of central Canaan is severely depleted. But as would be expected, Ahmosis's primary focus is to increase the overall stability of Egypt through administrative, economic, and military development.[39]

MOSES FLEES WHILE EGYPT SUBJECTS CANAAN TO AN IRON-FISTED HEGEMONY (*See Chapter 3*)

The biblical account says that after Moses had killed an Egyptian supervisor, he fled Egypt. Then after the death of an unnamed Egyptian king, under orders from Yahweh, Moses returned to Egypt to free the Israelites who remained in bondage in the Nile Delta region (Exodus 2). Indeed, under Tuthmosis III, Amenhotep II, and Tuthmosis IV, Egypt maintained a firm grip on its slaves in Lower Egypt as well as its dominance over its provinces in Canaan and Syria all the way to the Euphrates River. Thus, it would make no historical sense for Moses to flee to Canaan, the land of his ancestors, which he did not. Instead, he traveled eastward toward Midian. The political situation in the region during the Eighteenth Dynasty is entirely consistent with this portion of the Moses narrative.[40]

MOSES AND THE LATE BRONZE AGE LAW CODES (*See Chapter 3*)

When you examine the structure of the Mosaic covenant, there is no doubt that it belongs only to the LBA—specifically, it is formulated like Hittite covenants/treaties of the same period. Moses lived during the LBA—what else would you expect? And the Mosaic codes look nothing like covenants/treaties from the IA. Therefore, one must ask the same question asked earlier: How would someone living and writing in the late IA possibly guess the precise structure of LBA Hittite covenants/treaties? Again, it is impossible! No late-IA storyteller would care about that kind of precision.[41]

Kitchen's knowledge of ancient covenant/treaty structures is unparalleled; he observes:

> The basic correspondence between Sinai and the [Late Bronze Age] Hittite corpus (reaching into Egypt!) is clear beyond all doubt; the order and magnitude of blessing (short) and curses (long) in Sinai goes back to the earlier law-"code" tradition…Other very minor variations…occur also inside the Hittite corpus itself, and are directly comparable with the Sinai data…all these are common to [Hittite] phase V and Sinai and… not to any other phase at all! Sinai and its two renewals—especially the version in Deuteronomy—belong squarely within phase V, within 1400–1200, *and at no other date* (emphasis in original).[42]

Needless to say, the presence of a LBA Hittite treaty structure in the legal sections of the Pentateuch is devastating to a LBA Hittite kingdom disappeared from history well before the onset of the IA—the era of the very different Neo-Hittites such as David's Uriah—it approaches credulity to think that late-IA Israelite/Judahite writers could come up with such material.

THE MOSAIC LAW HAS A HITTITE PATTERN, BUT HOW SO? (*See Chapter 3*)

In answering this question, a remarkable historical synchronism comes to light. During the early Eighteenth Dynasty, Egypt and Hatti were already negotiating a treaty with each other and had traded ambassadorial envoys. The same was true between Egypt and Mittani of northern Mesopotamia. An Egyptian treaty with Mittani would effectively cut off Hatti from the lucrative Mediterranean seaports of the north Levant. An Egyptian treaty with Hatti would all but eliminate Mittani's access to the coastal trade routes. Thus, whatever the Egyptians did, someone was going to be very unhappy!

Egyptian royals (this would have included Moses) were typically assigned to priestly duties, regional political appointments, and the diplomatic corps. The Egyptians and Hittites worked for decades on a potential treaty between the two superpowers, and this occurred during Moses's early adulthood years while a member of the royal family. It is thoroughly reasonable to suggest that Moses—whose very name was a component (*mose/mosis*) of the common Eighteenth Dynasty name Tuthmosis—may have served in a diplomatic position working with Hittite envoys on an Egypto-Hattian treaty agreement. Perhaps he even spent time in the Hittite homeland for the same purpose. How else might we explain Moses's familiarity with Hittite treaty formats? It makes perfect sense and brings the biblical text and the historical setting together in a splendid manner.

Collins outlines this remarkable historical context:

> The height of Egyptian hegemony and presence in Canaan and Syria occurred during the fifteenth century BCE during the reigns of Tuthmosis III, Amenhotep II, and Tuthmosis IV—a father-son-grandson sequence that prided itself in its Euphrates northern border. The final stage of Egypt's Levantine domination, and the peak of their strength in Asia, occurred during the reign of Tuthmosis IV when he succeeded in making a treaty with Artatama, king of Mittani (northern Mesopotamia). The Mittani king was now guardian and guarantor of Egypt's Euphrates border, while combined Egyptian and Mittani strength secured Mittani's corridor to the Mediterranean through northern Syria. It was a perfect setup for both "brothers." However enraged the Hittites

were by this "snub" from Egypt (Mittani was a perennial enemy of the Hittites), there was nothing Hatti could do to pursue its interests in acquiring a Mediterranean corridor of its own in the face of the new Egypto-Mittanian alliance. For the meantime, the Hittites were just sadly out of luck.[43]

The decades leading up to this historical moment were the perfect setting for a Moses-Hittite intersection. Of course, this kind of rationality is toxic to higher criticism.

MOSES MAKES DEMANDS, BUT PHARAOH RESISTS (*See Chapter 3*)

According to biblical narrative, Moses was in the "second generation" of his life ("eighty years old") when he stood before pharaoh to demand freedom for the Israelites (Exodus 7:7). The previous pharaoh was dead (Exodus 2:23). The new king whom Moses confronted was arrogant, defiant, and unwilling to relinquish the sizable labor pool of Israelite slaves who supported the Egyptian economy. If pharaoh had allowed the Hebrews to cross the border into the Sinai Wilderness—setting a potentially dangerous precedent—Lower Egypt would suffer (Exodus 5–7). As long as pharaoh saw the Israelites as advantageous to his Delta administration, in Goshen they would remain.

The pulse of the historical context is described as follows:[44]

> Having forced the Semitic Hyksos out of Lower Egypt and back into Asia, and having subdued the Nubians to extend the southern border of Upper Egypt, it was incumbent upon Eighteenth Dynasty Pharaohs to maintain control of their vast kingdom and provinces stretching southward into Nubia and northward to the Euphrates River. Most problematic were the Asiatic provinces which had a penchant for rebellion against their Egyptian overlords. Typically, upon the death of an Egyptian king, vassal city-state kings of Canaan and Syria tested the new Pharaoh's

resolve by staging revolts against Egyptian hegemony. As each of his predecessors had done, Tuthmosis IV, through military and diplomatic successes, retained a firm grip on the provinces of both Asia and Nubia. Maintaining a strong economy and military presence in the Delta region was critical for controlling the Asiatic provinces (Canaan and Syria).[45]

PHARAOH BEGINS TO LOSE HIS GRIP (*See Chapter 3*)

According to the Bible, Egypt's Delta region was devastated by plagues. The plague of the firstborn (better, "primal son") convinced pharaoh to release the Israelites to worship Yahweh in the desert. Pharaoh even asked Moses to bless him—that is, *to make an appeasement sacrifice to Yahweh on pharaoh's behalf* (Exodus 12). According to the text, the Israelites plundered the Egyptians of the Delta region (the area of Goshen), taking large amounts of silver, gold, and fine clothing (Exodus 12–14).

Factually, without a strong Delta economy and military presence, Egypt could not have sustained its hegemony in the Levant. Any economic failure or military depletion in Lower Egypt would open an opportunity for the city-states of Canaan and Syria to rid themselves of Egyptian interference. Up to this point in history, Tuthmosis III, Amenhotep IV, and Tuthmosis IV—representing the ascendant pinnacle of the New Kingdom Empire period—had successfully preserved their stranglehold on both Nubia and the Asiatic provinces. In order to keep the Black Land safe and prosperous, the pharaohs pursued several means of appeasing the gods of other peoples (even enemies) through rituals and by erecting worship centers for them.[46]

After the untimely death of Tuthmosis IV (dated variously from 1416 to 1386 BC, depending on the Egyptian chronology used), Egypt mysteriously withdrew from the Levant, which it had controlled for more than a century, and fell into a precipitous decline that resulted in the demise of the once-great Eighteenth Dynasty. But perhaps the collapse of the Eighteenth

Dynasty is not so much of a mystery after all when considered in light of the exodus event.

PHARAOH CAVES, AND THE EIGHTEENTH DYNASTY TAKES A NOSEDIVE (*See Chapter 3*)

According to Exodus 14, between the plagues, the plundering of wealth, and a substantial loss of slave labor, pharaoh had second thoughts about his agreement to let the Israelites go. He readied his personal chariot to pursue his departed "property." According to the biblical account, the Egyptian force included 600 select chariots and other chariots, foot soldiers, and a full complement of officers (staged from the Delta region). Pharaoh's army caught up with the Israelites at their camp near Baal-zephon, "between Migdol [a fortress] and the sea" (likely one of the large bitter lakes along Egypt's western border—Exodus 14:2).

By means of a strong eastern wind, Yahweh opened up a walkable pathway through the *yam suph* (Sea of Reeds), and the Israelites crossed through to the other side. Led by their chariot-driving pharaoh, the Egyptian army drowned as the waters returned and trapped them (Exodus 14). It is reasonable to conclude from the story that a significant portion of Egypt's Delta-based military force was destroyed in this event. The text further implies that pharaoh himself died with his troops (Psalm 136:15). The Israelites then departed for Mount Sinai, safe from the Egyptians who had pursued them.

An identification of parallels on the Egyptian side of history during the same period is instructive:

> Egyptian history impressively mirrors the biblical story. Tuthmosis IV, strong and courageous, was highly skilled in the arts of hunting, war, and personal combat. He was a master charioteer "whose horses were fleeter than the wind," and he depicted himself as an expert archer, shooting lions from his moving chariot. But while the Eighteenth Dynasty kings before him reigned for an average of 25 years (his grandfather, Tuthmosis III, ruled for 54 years, and his father, Amenhotep II, for 26 years), and his son, Amenhotep III, ruled for 38 years, Tuthmosis IV was mysteriously dead after ruling for only eight to ten years. The mummy of Tuthmosis IV reveals a handsome, young, and virile Pharaoh in the prime of life. When his son (but not firstborn), Amenhotep III, ascended the throne, the Black Land seemed at the height of its glory. But while the official records of Egypt typically don't admit any problems, there are definite signs that the empire of Egypt was in serious trouble relative to its Asiatic provinces.[47]

Is it mere coincidence that Tuthmosis IV was the last pharaoh of the Eighteenth Dynasty to conduct military engagements in Canaan and Syria? In the decades after Tuthmosis IV's death, Egypt's relationships with the Levantine cities attempt only to address existing diplomatic relations. Yet even *those* ties began to unravel. The Egyptian situation continued to slide downhill with increasing velocity during the reigns of Amenhotep III and Akhenaten (who abandoned the traditional gods of Egypt and created a monotheism of his own). While Amenhotep III retained control over Nubia, he was either unwilling or unable to launch military responses into the former Levantine territories that were now openly flaunting rebellion.

Why did Amenhotep III not mount a single military campaign to quell Asian revolts? It is logical that if he could have done so, he would have. The answer appears obvious: He did not because he *could not*. Disastrous economic and military setbacks in Egypt's Delta region—the only staging area from which Asian campaigns could be supported—would explain Amenhotep's reluctance to act.[48]

The Eighteenth Dynasty's problems were not temporary—they were terminal.

The synchronisms between the history of the Eighteenth Dynasty and the story of the Israelite exodus from Egypt seem irresistible. One might simply ask: If the events of the exodus story—ten horrific plagues, the plundering of Egyptian wealth, the severe labor and military losses, and the death of pharaoh himself—actually occurred as the Bible describes, what would have happened to the reigning dynasty? The answer is singular: That dynasty would likely have collapsed. It is notable that during the history of the New Kingdom (Eighteenth and Nineteenth Dynasties), including all possible dates for the exodus, there is only one such episode: the collapse of the Eighteenth Dynasty after the death of Tuthmosis IV, c. 1390+/– BC. The two parallel histories have no other point of intersection.

Just how low did the once-great Eighteenth Dynasty sink? The answer is nothing short of startling:

Why did the powerful Tuthmosid Dynasty crumble into oblivion? What would cause the internal affairs of Egypt to deteriorate so completely that a sonless, widowed queen [Ankhesenamun, wife of Tutankhamun, great grandson of Tuthmosis IV] would invite a foreign (enemy!) king [Suppiluliuma of Hatti] to make his son [Zidanza] Pharaoh of the Black Land? Bizarre? Yes; but reality nonetheless. Yet, I think there is a perfect explanation for the demise of the Eighteenth Dynasty: the five core events of the Exodus narrative that, according to the biblical accounts, wreaked havoc in Lower Egypt—plagues, plundering, huge labor losses, severe military losses, and the death of Pharaoh himself (Tuthmosis IV). Regardless of its level of power and wealth, such occurrences would have sent Egypt into the kind of crisis situation described in the ancient records. And is it possible that the plagues suffered by Egypt during the Amarna Age (a strain of "plague"? influenza? smallpox?), and subsequently contracted by the Hittites, were the epidemic result of lingering and/or mutating pathogens carried over from the plagues of the Exodus story? Not only is it possible, but I think it is highly probable.[49]

THE ISRAELITES DEPART FROM EGYPT AND FIGHT IN THE SINAI WILDERNESS (*See Chapter 3*)

On their way to Sinai, the Israelites fought against the Semitic Amalekites and defeated them (Exodus 17). Archaeology confirms that numerous groups of nomadic and seminomadic Semitic peoples thrived and operated in the Sinai Peninsula.[50]

MOSES GOES TO THE SACRED MOUNTAIN (*See Chapter 3*)

Moses led the Israelites to Mount Sinai, perhaps a mountain of long-standing sacredness to the Midianites and, no doubt, to other Semitic peoples in the region (Exodus 19). But how far was Mount Sinai/Horeb from Goshen? Without getting into a prolonged discussion on the proper location of Mount Sinai, suffice it to say that according to the text of Exodus, it was a three-day journey from the Israelite enclave in Goshen (Exodus 3:18), or perhaps from Egypt's eastern border (draw a line from the Gulf of Suez north to the Nile's Pelusiac confluence with the Mediterranean). The distance is reiterated several times in the text. And this is a computation of *distance*, which has nothing to do with time. A three-day journey is the distance that a moderately equipped army can travel in three days. Essentially, the distance can be no farther than 60 miles, which is probably much too generous; 60 kilometers is more like it. If you read the story carefully, it is apparent that Moses and Aaron traveled between Goshen and Mount Sinai several times, suggesting Mount Sinai's relatively close proximity to Egypt.

From every angle, the traditional location of Sinai/Horeb is problematic. It must be admitted that the location of the actual holy mountain is not known with any degree of certainty. However, a site in the north-central Sinai Wilderness—called Har Karkom—is a good example of such a sacred mountain. This site is near several water sources and includes more than 70,000 pieces of rock art (including a depiction of a double tablet divided into ten sections), ancient altars, and sacred precincts. These indicate that Har Karkom was a holy mountain for thousands of years. Such holy mountains existed in the Sinai Wilderness in ancient times, and this is certainly consistent with the exodus story.[51]

EXODUS, CONQUEST, AND NEW KINGDOM EGYPTIAN MAP-LISTS (See Chapter 3)

The books of Numbers and Joshua list the cities and locations through which the Israelites traveled. These sites are confirmed by Egyptian map-lists belonging to New Kingdom pharaohs such as Tuthmosis III, Amenhotep III, and Rameses II (fifteenth through thirteenth centuries BC). The biblical lists in Numbers 33 (Iyyin, Dibon-gad, Almon-diblathaim, Nebo, Abel-shittim, Jordan) and Joshua 15 (Janum-Apheqeh-Hebron) are in all respects similar to the Egyptian lists of the same period. With only minor variations, both the biblical and Egyptian lists include the same cities/locations *in the exact same order.*

Clearly, these matching biblical and Egyptian map-lists follow from the ancient Egyptian tradition of identifying key locations along important routes in geographical order as if one is traveling *from Egypt.* One remarkable point about these lists is that they soundly refute claims that certain biblical cities, such as Dibon in Numbers 33 and Hebron in Joshua 15, were not occupied during the LBA. Yet these locations are confirmed by both the Bible and the Egyptians! Why would late-IA Israelite/Judahite writers care about Egyptian-like geographical precision? It is doubtful that they would simply because they had no need to go to that extent to create a collection of simple stories about Israelite origins. It would be ancient literary overkill—that is, unless they are authentic historical accounts of a complex journey. These stories flow with the LBA in every detail.[52]

MOSES: CAPABLE AUTHOR AND LINGUIST (See Chapter 3)

According to the biblical story, Moses wrote in detail about the early history and law of the Israelites. But what writing system did he use? One must remember that Moses was educated in Egypt. This means that if he worked with documents (as previously suggested) as an official of some kind, it is likely that he was not only fluent in Egyptian and the regional languages of his day—such

as Canaanite and Akkadian—but he also knew how to read and write the associated scripts: hieroglyphics (Egyptian), cuneiform (Akkadian and Amorite), and the emerging Semitic linear alphabet (Canaanite). It is well documented that the Amarna Tablets of the Eighteenth Dynasty have among them clay tablets written to pharaoh—never by name, as in the Pentateuch!—in cuneiform script in both Akkadian and Canaanite dialects. And the Egyptians answered their foreign correspondence in Akkadian on cuneiform clay tablets.

So it is altogether possible, even probable, that Moses finally completed his five books using the linear Semitic alphabet to write an early form of the Hebrew language (basically, Canaanite "cooked" in isolation in Egypt for several centuries). Unlike the early days of nineteenth-century Old Testament higher criticism, during which scholars thought that the linear alphabet did not exist until around 1000 BC, current ANE scholarship has traced the beginnings of the Semitic alphabet back as early as the eighteenth/seventeenth centuries BC in Egypt itself. That's correct: The proto-Semitic alphabet began *in Egypt* as a reduction of selected hieroglyphic signs into simple linear letters that could be written with minimal strokes. That same alphabet—always morphing, of course—found its way into the Sinai Peninsula in the fifteenth/fourteenth centuries BC, there identified by Sir Flinders Petrie as proto-Sinaitic, by others as proto-Canaanite, and by still others as proto-Semitic. By the end of the LBA, the Semitic alphabet was used throughout the Levant, eventually replacing cuneiform as the preferred script.[53]

The implications are obvious. The origin of the Semitic alphabet follows the biblical movements of the Hebrew patriarchs and Israelites beginning with Jacob and Joseph in Egypt, then into the Sinai Peninsula with Moses, then into Canaan with Joshua. Is this another coincidence? We think not!

THE HORRORS OF CANAANITE RELIGION AND THE MOSAIC LAW (See Chapter 3)

The relevant Old Testament passages accurately

depict the religious context of the Southern Levant throughout the biblical periods. As biblical texts report, the Baal cults of the LBA represent some of the most degenerate features of Canaanite civilization. Besides offerings of wine, oil, firstfruits, and firstlings of the flock, the Baal cult temples had special chambers occupied by *kedeshim* (male prostitutes) and *kedeshoth* (female prostitutes). Worshippers at the Baal temples, as well as in the sacred spaces of other deities, were ritually "joined with" cult prostitutes in acts of fertility worship.

Such cultic sexual practices were strictly forbidden by the law that Moses received from Yahweh. Consider Numbers 25:5: "Moses said to the judges of Israel, 'Each of you kill those of his men who have yoked themselves to Baal of Peor.'" Archaeology confirms that Baal cults identified locally with various Canaanite cities and towns. In addition to Baal of Peor, there were Baal-gad (Joshua 11:17), Baal-hazor (2 Samuel 13:23), Baal-zephon (Numbers 33:7), and others. Leviticus 18:21 and other passages warn against the practices of the Molech cult in which children were often made to pass through or into a furnace or fire. Archaeological confirmation of human sacrifice has been unearthed all over the Levant. Such vile acts were specifically forbidden in the Mosaic Law (Leviticus 20:1-5). Judahite priests living in the late IA, particularly in the post-exilic era, would have had no means to write with such accuracy regarding the practices of a long-extinct Canaanite culture.[54]

ISRAELITES READ THE "BILLBOARDS" (*See Chapter 3*)

When the Israelites had safely crossed over into the land, Moses commanded the people to "set up large stones and plaster them" and "write on them all the words of this law" (Deuteronomy 27:2-3). The Israelites' ability to not only write text on stelae (an upright engraved stone monument) but also to read such text is amply supported by archaeology. The invention of the Semitic alphabet (described earlier) occurred while the Israelites were living in Egypt, and they obviously

took it with them all the way to Canaan. In Deuteronomy 27, God was, in essence, demanding public literacy for the first time in the history of the ANE. The compact, linear Semitic alphabet was easy to learn and enhanced people's ability to read and write. The volume of ancient graffiti on pottery (known as ostraca) and other surfaces attests to this fact. Writing on plastered stelae was a common practice in the ANE world, so Deuteronomy 27 is in perfect harmony with the realities of the LBA.[55]

THE PEOPLES OF LATE BRONZE AGE CANAAN (*See Chapter 3*)

Toward the end of Late Bronze Age 1 (LBA1) or early in Late Bronze Age 2 (LBA2; c. late fifteenth to early fourteenth centuries BC), the Israelites arrived at Kadesh-barnea, and from there commissioned spies to reconnoiter the Promised Land. The spies reported, "The cities are fortified and very large...The Amalekites dwell in the land of the Negev. The Hittites, the Jebusites, and the Amorites dwell in the hill country. And the Canaanites dwell by the sea, and along the Jordan" (Numbers 13:28-29).

Archaeology reveals that the ethnolinguistic, sociocultural setting of Canaan at the end of LBA1 was precisely as described in Numbers 13: Semitic tribes in the Negev (Amalekites and others), Semitic Amorites (Jebusites and others) dominating the hill country, non-Semitic Hittites pressing into the north hill country, and Canaanites in control of the coastal regions and the Jordan Valley. This was the precise situation in the Levant (the Promised Land is the Levant from the Euphrates to the river of Egypt). But how would late-IA priests and chroniclers know the ethnogeographic details of BA Canaan? If higher critical documentary theories are true, these details would be solely attributable to them. The better explanation is that detailed LBA information derives from the LBA.[56]

JOSHUA AND THE FOURTEENTH-CENTURY BC GEOPOLITICS OF CANAAN'S CENTRAL HILL COUNTRY (*See Chapter 3*)

According to the book of Joshua, when the Israelites entered Canaan, two main city-states occupied the central hill country: Shechem and Jerusalem. Likely due to ancestral roots reaching back to the Hebrew patriarchs, Joshua allied himself with the city of Shechem (Joshua 8; 24). The Amorite (Jebusite) city of Jerusalem and its allied cities were targeted for takeover (Joshua 10–12). The biblical record also recounts the failure of the Israelites to take Jerusalem, which stayed in Jebusite hands (Joshua 15). Archaeological excavations in these same highlands of Canaan reveal that, in fact, *only* two major city-states occupied that area during the time of the conquest in the fourteenth century BC: Shechem and Jerusalem—precisely as the text of Joshua describes.[57]

Collins, who has investigated and written extensively on this subject, recounts the remarkable parallels between Joshua's account and the situation in Canaan during the fourteenth century BC:

> In the Amarna Letters, it is revealed that the king of the Shechem city-state, Lab'ayu, was accused by other regional city-state rulers of aligning himself with the Habiru, and Lab'ayu's sons were accused of the same offense. Evidently, the Habiru had encamped around Shechem in great numbers and were, indeed, on friendly terms with Lab'ayu and his family. This was all happening early in Akhenaten's reign, and the timing is interesting. With Tuthmosis IV as the Pharaoh of the Exodus, Joshua could have launched the Conquest of Canaan while Lab'ayu was king of Shechem. And by what other term would Canaanite city-dwellers have referred to Joshua's Israelites, since they had all grown up as nomads in the wilderness and would have been perceived as nothing more or less than the marauding rabble they called "Habiru"? Although many scholars have disallowed—on quite flimsy grounds, I think—a

relationship between the terms "Habiru" and "Hebrew," there is no doubt about the linguistic similarity of the two terms. It is also worth noting that, according to the biblical text, the Israelites never attacked Shechem or any town belonging to the Shechem city-state. And might not the Akkadian name, Lab'ayu—which in Hebrew is *Leba'-Ya* = lion of Yahweh—suggest that the king of Shechem was, in some fashion, a worshipper of Yahweh, the God of Joshua (Heb. *Yehosua'* = Yahweh saves), revealing a possible religious affinity between the two leaders? Although written from radically different points of view, the biblical story of Joshua's association with Shechem as well as the Canaanite perception of Habiru ties to Lab'ayu's Shechem coalition as reflected in the Amarna correspondence seem to me far more than coincidental.[58]

The timing and elements of specificity between the careers of Joshua and Lab'ayu of Shechem are alluring. The fact that the biblical record of Joshua's exploits reflects with precision the geopolitical state of affairs in the land of Canaan during the fourteenth century BC—the biblical timeframe of the conquest—is compelling. No twist or permutation of Old Testament higher criticism can possibly account for this level of correspondence.

HOW CAN ISRAEL GET A PROMISED LAND FREE OF EGYPTIANS? (*See Chapter 3*)

The LBA1 era is known as the time of Egyptian domination over Canaan. During the reigns of Tuthmosis III, Amenhotep II, and Tuthmosis IV—the father-son-grandson serial triumvirate (three simultaneous rulers functioning jointly) that ruled Egypt at the height of the golden age of the New Kingdom—Egypt subjugated the Levant (Canaan and Syria) with an iron fist. Consciously controlling the population of Canaan with the stench of the Hyksos debacle still in their royal nostrils, the big three launched systematic military operations and slave raids into Canaan in order to keep the Semitic population under control. This aggression lasted for 100 years and succeeded in dropping the LBA Canaanite population by 75 percent as compared to the previous period, the MBA. During the 1500–1400 BC time frame, a heavy-handed Egyptian administrative and supporting military presence dominated Canaan.[59]

It is important to note that Egyptians are *never* mentioned in Joshua's Canaan campaigns. This fact is highly significant for establishing a precise time frame for Joshua's conquests. Collins explains:

> In the mid-fifteenth century BC…during the time of Moses, the three most abundant ethno-linguistic elements of the Levantine population were "the Canaanite and the Hittite and the Amorite…" (Exo. 3:8). Yahweh also implied that the Israelites would occupy that territory without Egyptian interference—the Egyptians aren't named in any of these predictions, nor are they mentioned in the book of Joshua as an enemy to be defeated. The precision of this situation is abundantly supported by the archaeological and historical record. The LBA1–2 Cisjordan Levant was indeed populated by Canaanites, Hittites, and Amorites. But while that territory was under powerful Egyptian hegemony through the reign of Tuthmosis IV, it wouldn't remain so for long. By the time Joshua and the Israelite army entered Canaan—about the second year of Akhenaten's reign—the Egyptians had completely lost their hold on the region.[60]

Egypt's withdrawal from Canaan began in the reign of Amenhotep III, son of Tuthmosis IV, during the decline and collapse of the Eighteenth Dynasty. Tuthmosis IV was the pharaoh of the exodus, and the wilderness wanderings lasted 38 years (Deuteronomy 2:14), after which Moses and Joshua made a beeline for the Jordan Valley, crossing into Canaan in the fortieth year after leaving Egypt. The exact duration of Amenhotep III's reign was also 38 years, during which the Egyptian presence in Canaan dropped virtually

to zero. A mere 2 years into Akhenaten's reign—the year Joshua crossed the Jordan River—Canaan was an "Egyptian-free" zone! Joshua mopped up what Egypt had left behind.[61] Astonishing? Indeed.

JOSHUA TAKES ON CANAAN (*See Chapter 3*)

Upon their return from reconnoitering the land of Canaan, the Israelite spies reported: "The cities are fortified and very large" (Numbers 13:28). An earlier passage gives an accounting of Bashan (north Transjordan) during the same period: "All these cities were fortified with high walls, gates, and bars, besides very many unwalled villages" (Deuteronomy 3:5). This is exactly the archaeological context of Canaan during the LBA. Recent statistical analysis of excavated Cis- and Transjordan LBA sites reveals that more than 60 percent were fortified, with smaller unwalled towns and villages interspersed throughout the region.[62] In addition, of the 19 cities specifically cited in Joshua as fortified, 16 were indeed fortified, while 2 (Beth Shan and Lachish) were positioned topographically such that they did not require substantial fortifications. However, they would appear fortified to any approaching army. (Data from the one remaining city is inconclusive.) Yet another historical synchronism.[63]

Once again, the Joshua narrative's fidelity to the sociopolitical and cultural setting of LBA Canaan is on target.

JOSHUA INVADES CANAAN, TAKES JERICHO (*See Chapter 3*)

In the fourteenth century BC, during the early years of Akhenaten in Egypt, Joshua and the Israelites crossed over the Jordan River and approached Jericho, a fortified Canaanite city, which they ultimately destroyed (Joshua 6). The conquest of the land of Canaan had begun. Archaeology reveals that although Jericho was unoccupied during LBA1 (1550–1400 BC), a town site did reappear within the old MBA walls shortly after the turn of the fourteenth century

BC. It is likely that the inhabitants reused and refurbished the older defenses, but not to the standards or quality of the master fortification builders of the previous period. It is also probable that their town wall, of typical LBA mudbrick construction, was simply built atop the old MBA ramparts without a stone foundation, thus its vulnerability to earth tremors. Built on the outer edge of the sloping ramparts, the mudbrick walls collapsed outward at critical locations, allowing the Israelites to charge into the town.[64]

The theory that the destruction of MBA Tell es-Sultan (Jericho's Arabic name) could be lowered to 1400 BC and thus make it the town Joshua conquered—espoused by Bryant G. Wood (1990) and John J. Bimson (1981)—has serious problems and is rejected by a majority of Levantine archaeologists, even most conservatives. Thus, a fourteenth-century BC (LBA2a) Jericho destruction, which does actually exist, is the more likely scenario. Archaeologically, *when put in the proper time frame*, the Jericho story rings true.

JOSHUA AT AI (*See Chapter 3*)

After Jericho, the Israelites turned their attention to a small hill country border fortress called Ai, which probably guarded the northern frontier of the Jebusite city-state centered at Jerusalem (Joshua 7–8). The location of a possible site for LBA2a Ai—Joshua's Ai—was unknown until recently, and the story was consigned to the genre of myth and legend. However, a site called Khirbet el-Maqatir, which matches the detailed geographical, topographical, and tactical details of the Ai conquest recorded in Joshua 7–8, has been excavated and identified by archaeologist Bryant G. Wood as the Ai of Joshua. Some agree; most do not. Admittedly, the evidence is thin.[65]

However, Collins, who disagrees with Wood's analysis of Jericho on the basis of excavations across the river at Tall el-Hammam/Sodom, *does* support Wood's conclusions about Maqatir as Ai. Collins states:

> Having analyzed much of the pottery from Khirbet el-Maqatir myself, along with excavating

there for six seasons, I have a better take on it than scholars who do not have firsthand experience with the site. There is LBA pottery there, and there are some stone foundations that may date to that period. But the site was heavily robbed out by later occupants, nearly obliterated. I must add, however, that the geographical evidence is compelling. The book of Joshua says Ai was very small, an insignificant place, probably nothing more than a fortified garrison of just a few acres. Maqatir is consistent with the biblical description of Ai, and all the associated geographical details. Therefore, I think Wood's identification is reasonable.[66]

JOSHUA'S BATTLE ACCOUNTS AND THE CHRONICLES OF TUTHMOSIS III (*See Chapter 3*)

Joshua's recounting of the battle of Ai is highly similar in structure and topical content to the battle of Megiddo account of Tuthmosis III (also spelled Thutmose and Thothmes). A.K. McLaughlin outlines the points of comparison: (1) war tactics and failure of command, (2) intelligence gathering, (3) divine campaign purpose, (4) time of year for the campaign, (5) deterioration of detail, (6) the mention of an alliance of local leaders, (7) literary motif of military leader, (8) literary motif of portraying the enemy as foolish, and other notable similarities.[67]

From these literary parallels, McLaughlin concludes that viewing the conquest of Ai as an etiological legend or fiction is entirely unwarranted.

> [Research demonstrates] quantitatively that conclusions of historicity of ancient Near Eastern texts, specifically with regards to an account found in the Bible, were subjectively reached and sometimes inappropriate. When a congruent bar was applied independently to two [nearly] contemporaneous battle accounts, a different conclusion was reached: inasmuch as the account of the Siege of Megiddo was historical, using the

same method, the account of the Battle of Ai was historical.[68]

Again, what the Old Testament radical critics have declared as late-IA myth or fiction, better and more rigorous analysis confirms as period-specific authentic history belonging to the LBA.

CANAAN AFTER THE CONQUEST
(*See Chapters 3 and 4*)

According to biblical reckoning (using a base-ten arithmetic understanding of 1 Kings 6:1), the conquest of Canaan by the Israelites began about 1406 BC (Masoretic Text) or 1366 BC (Septuagint)—the latter is preferable in light of phenomena associated with the collapse of Egypt's Eighteenth Dynasty, as noted earlier. Joshua and the Israelite forces entered Canaan, attacking major city centers and sites of strategic importance. By the end of the book of Joshua, the Israelites and accompanying tribes held a permanent but tenuous position in Canaan. Archaeology corroborates this biblical picture. Egypt's loss of control in Canaan and Syria during the Amarna period threw that region into veritable chaos. City-states warred against each other. Marauding Habiru (*'Apiru*) threatened many cities. Egypt was unable to maintain order even at the request of notable city-state kings who wrote letters to Egypt requesting military and financial assistance— which they never received. It was the perfect time for Joshua to be in Canaan.[69]

ISRAEL: A PEOPLE GROUP IN CANAAN DURING THE TIME OF THE JUDGES (*See Chapter 4*)

The book of Judges reveals that in the years following the death of Joshua, the Israelites did not entirely dominate in the land. Although Joshua succeeded in gaining a general occupation, Israel's hold on the land was far from secure. At the time of Joshua's death, Canaan was still dominated by local peoples. In fact, the tribes of Israel ended up adopting the Canaanite material culture, lifestyles, and even their pagan religions. For about 350 years, Israel was numerically a force to be reckoned with among the inhabitants of Canaan, but more often than not, the Jewish people failed to follow the true religion of Yahweh as prescribed by Moses. They were Canaanite in practice and Israelite in name only.

The biblical story fits perfectly with the historical and archaeological record. Archaeologically, there is no specific means of distinguishing between the Israelite and Canaanite cultures until well into the IA (after c. 1200 BC), but this is predictable given the fact that, virtually without exception, conquering peoples in the ANE were prone to adopting the culture of the conquered (as the Semitic Hyksos had adopted the culture of Egypt). But as Canaanite-like as the Israelites were, Pharaoh Merneptah, in about 1210 BC, recorded on a stele, "The princes are prostrate, saying Mercy! No one raises his head among the Nine Bows…Israel is laid waste, his seed is not…" By this time, Israel was sufficiently established in Canaan to be recognized by Merneptah as one of the perennial enemies (Nine Bows) of Egypt. And Israel was designated (by a linguistic determinative) on the Merneptah Stele as a people, not a nation with a king, which was accurate.[70]

ISRAEL VERSUS THE PHILISTINES (*See Chapter 4*)

Israel established a strong presence in the central highlands (Judges 21; 1 Samuel 1–7) during Iron Age 1 (IA1; 1200–1000 BC). Although the Israelite tribes were not entirely unified, their presence in the hill country was formidable; thus, the strength and numbers of the original inhabitants of Canaan began to wane. The Philistines dominated the Southern Levantine coast, occupying five major cities: Ashdod, Gaza, Ashkelon, Gath, and Ekron (1 Samuel 6). Israel and Philistia vied for control of the cities in the Shephelah (1 and 2 Samuel), which lay between the coast and the highlands.

Archaeology provides the same picture. Excavations at Ashdod, Gaza, Ashkelon, Gath, and Ekron reveal that they were distinctively Philistine and were the main cities of what many call the Philistine coalition. What can be described as distinctively Israelite culture in terms of architecture and artifacts is visible for the first time in IA1 in the archaeological record of the central highlands. The Shephelah cities, such as Beth Shemesh and Gezer, passed back and forth between the Israelites and the Philistines. Again, the biblical picture is confirmed.[71]

SAMSON AND PHILISTINE TEMPLE ARCHITECTURE
(*See Chapter 4*)

Judges 16 tells the story of Israel's most famous strongman, Samson, which many critics assign to the genre of myth and legend allegedly written during late Iron Age 2 (IA2; c. 600 BC). At the end of his tragic life, blinded and held captive by the Philistines at Gaza, Samson was taken to a temple and made to "stand between the pillars" (verse 25). Samson was able to push the pillars apart, causing the roof of the temple to collapse and kill himself along with a host of Philistine nobility. Most critics think it inconceivable that the dislocation of one or two pillars could collapse an entire building. But not so fast.

Archaeology provides a solid confirmation of the historical authenticity of this story. While Gaza remains mostly unexcavated, a Philistine city (a site known as Tell Qasile) with a temple similar in construction to that described in Judges 16, lies several miles to the north. The roof was supported by two closely spaced central cedar pillars resting on cylindrical limestone bases. This style of Philistine architecture has no close parallels elsewhere in the Levant but does resemble temples in Mycenae and in the Aegean region, the original homeland of the Philistines. Because the Philistines were virtually wiped out in the eighth century BC by the Assyrian invasion of the Levant, later Judahite writers would have had no way of knowing of the structure of Philistine temples. And why would they care? This is an incidental detail that mere fiction writers would have missed altogether.[72]

THE BIBLICAL PHILISTINES AND HOMER (*See Chapter 4*)

According to the biblical account (1 Samuel 5–6), the Philistines captured the Israelite Ark of the Covenant as a trophy of war, whereupon Yahweh, the Israelite God, sent a plague upon the Philistines (tumors or hemorrhoids). In an attempt to appease the anger of Yahweh, an assembly of the Philistine chiefs and people was held in each city. Priests and diviners were also called upon. The Philistines determined that the ark must be returned with guilt offerings. They fashioned tumors and mice out of gold. The ark and gold offerings were placed on a cart that was driven by cows toward Beth Shemesh. Philistine chiefs followed the ark on its journey. Upon the ark's arrival, the cows were sacrificed by the Israelites.

A careful study of the biblical text reveals that the original homeland of the Philistines was the Aegean region and several island locations, including Caphtor (Crete). Archaeology also affirms that the Philistines came from the Aegean area during the Homeric Bronze Age and settled on the southern coast of Canaan. And now the plot thickens.

From Homer's *Iliad* (lines 10-446 as summarized by Neal Bierling) we read that the Achaeans captured the daughter of Cryses, a priest of Apollo. Apollo inflicted a deadly plague on the Achaeans. An assembly of troops and chiefs was called. They called for a priest/prophet or an interpreter of dreams. They decided that the daughter of Cryses must be returned with holy offerings. Apollo was also known as Smintheus, the mouse god. Oxen for an offering were placed aboard ship (Cryses lived on an island). A chief and select crew accompanied Cryses's daughter. Upon arrival, the oxen were sacrificed.[73]

Even a casual comparison of Homer's *Iliad* with the biblical text reveals a remarkable preservation of an ancient Sea-People protocol for appeasing an angry god. To suggest that Judahite priests living in the latter centuries of the IA could have invented such a story is beyond reason. Why would they go to so much trouble to insert this authentic tidbit from the ancient Aegean culture? The biblical narrative is historically authentic in every way because it happened. That is the most logical explanation.

THE MINI-EMPIRE OF DAVID AND SOLOMON (*See Chapter 5*)

Near the end of IA1 (c. 1000 BC), Israel appointed its first king, Saul. Upon Saul's death, David assumed the throne and thus began the Davidic Dynasty (House of David) of Judahite kings (2 Samuel). The Philistines remained entrenched along the Southern Levantine coast while David consolidated his hill-country kingdom and proceeded to expand his territory. Solomon picked up where David left off and further expanded the kingdom in the early part of IA2.

There are some, however, who deny the historicity of the biblical figures David and Solomon and the kingdom they built. K.A. Kitchen counters this denial by pointing out that removal of the reality of an Israelite nation (what he calls a mini-empire) from the Levant leaves a significant void in the Levantine landscape. The politics of the Levantine region between Egypt and Mesopotamia make no sense at all without a reasonably powerful kingdom firmly established between them. If you cut the mini-empire of David and Solomon out of the picture, there remains a blank space on the map right where such a power should be.[74]

There is, however, ample positive evidence for the existence of the Davidic Dynasty as a substantial entity in the Levant during IA2. Three ninth-century BC inscriptions bear witness to the Davidic kingdom. An Aramaic inscription from Tel Dan (most probably placed by Hazael the Aramean—2 Kings 8) states that "a king of Israel of the House of David [*bytdvd*]" was defeated. The Tel Dan stele mentions the Israelite king Jehoram and the defeated king of the House of David, Ahaziah. The Mesha Stele, which mentions the Israelite king Omri, may also refer to the House of David (*bytd--*). An Egyptian monumental inscription from approximately the same period refers to the "heights of David." It is now very clear from the mounting volume of extrabiblical physical evidence that the House of David—the Israelite kingdom of David and Solomon and the later kingdom of Judah—is a cultural necessity for a complete picture of the Near East during IA2.[75]

SOLOMON'S WEALTH FINDS ITS WAY TO EGYPT (*See Chapter 5*)

Scripture tells us that Solomon collected tributes totaling more than 20 tons of gold annually (1 Kings 10). During the reign of Solomon's son Rehoboam, King Shishak of Egypt plundered Jerusalem and "took away the treasures of the house of the LORD and the treasures of the king's house" back to Egypt (1 Kings 14:26). Shishak also captured the fortified cities of Judah, including Jerusalem (2 Chronicles 12).

Although many biblical critics call into question the great wealth allegedly amassed by Solomon, archaeology confirms that the amount of gold attributed to him is commensurate with what is known of ANE kings during the IA. Egyptian inscriptions paralleling this biblical account also provide an interesting historical twist: Pharaoh Shoshenq I (biblical Shishak) died within a year of his plundering Jerusalem (c. 925 BC). After his death, Shoshenq's son, Osorkon I, took the throne. Within just over three years he made spectacular gifts to the gods and goddesses of Egypt, including more than 383 tons of silver and gold. Osorkon later buried his coregent son, Shoshenq II, in a solid silver coffin.[76]

Osorkon was a mediocre Egyptian king who reigned during a relatively depressed era of Egyptian history, yet his recorded actions reveal great personal wealth. From what source, then, did he acquire such riches? Clearly, it came as an inheritance from his father Shoshenq's financially lucrative campaign against Judah/Israel, which is recorded on his triumphal relief at the Karnak temple of Amun in Thebes. When Shoshenq died, all that wealth passed into the hands of his son, Osorkon, and the Solomon/Osorkon connection testifies to the cultural authenticity of the Bible as a historical record.[77]

ON THE ACCURACY OF DANIEL (*See Chapter 7*)

For years, critics of the Old Testament have denied the authenticity of the book of Daniel because of its references to Belshazzar, king of Babylon. Secular sources, such as the Greek historian Herodotus, knew nothing of this person in the line of Babylonian kings. As far as the critics were concerned, Belshazzar was a fabrication. No one knew of a Belshazzar outside the book of Daniel in the Hebrew Scriptures.[78]

According to Daniel, Belshazzar was the last reigning king before Babylon fell to the Medes and Persians, yet all other historical sources listed Nabonidus (Nabuna'id) as the last ruler of Babylon, with no mention of a Belshazzar. However, excavations at the site of ancient Ur have uncovered an interesting inscription by king Nabunaid (Nabonidus), which includes a prayer for himself and for his firstborn son, Bel-shar-usur (Belshazzar). Such prayers were written only for reigning monarchs. Also discovered were cuneiform documents that record how this Belshazzar made sacrifices at the temple of Sippar as "an offering of the king."[79]

Other information about Nabonidus reveals that he preferred travelling and battle to staying home in Babylon. Thus, Nabonidus made his son, Belshazzar, coregent and put him in charge of the city of Babylon. Daniel served under Belshazzar in Babylon, and even recorded that after he had deciphered the handwriting on the wall, the best that Belshazzar (who was the second highest ruler in the kingdom) could offer him was "third ruler in the kingdom" (Daniel 5:29).

For centuries the Bible had been the only surviving historical record of King Belshazzar. The discovery of archaeological evidence regarding Nabonidus and Belshazzar did not satisfy the critics, however, because Daniel refers to Belshazzar as the son of Nebuchadnezzar (Daniel 5:2, 11, 13, 18, 22). Since, according to the archaeological evidence, Belshazzar was the son of Nabonidus and not Nebuchadnezzar, they claimed that Daniel still had some of his facts wrong. Against this claim, several scholars note that Nabonidus probably married a daughter of Nebuchadnezzar in order to legitimize his claim to the throne, a common practice of that age. Such an action would effectively make the son of Nabonidus the grandson of Nebuchadnezzar. Thus, because the Aramaic words translated "son" and "grandson" are the same, Daniel could simply be referring to this relationship. Nabonidus named

another of his sons after Nebuchadnezzar, suggesting the high probability that Nabonidus wanted to draw on the widely known greatness of Nebuchadnezzar for his own purposes.[80]

There is also the fact that in the ANE, the terms father and son are also used to refer to political relationships, not just family relationships. For example, Jesus was called the son of David. Since Nebuchadnezzar was the greatest of all Babylonian kings, to be called his son would have been a good term to use for political pull. Egypt's Horemheb styled himself as the son of Amenhotep III—skipping over Akhenaten and Tutankhamun—simply because he despised the impotence of the other Amarna period pharaohs! Therefore, the fact that Daniel referred to Nebuchadnezzar and Belshazzar as father and son was a culturally accepted practice and presents no inaccuracy. To the contrary, in this instance and throughout the book, Daniel preserves important cultural and political information about the Near Eastern empires of the sixth century BC.[81]

PARTING COMMENTS:
THE TIP OF ICEBERG

These aforementioned bits and pieces of the Hebrew Scriptures reveal the fine-tuned nature of their historical and cultural acuity. They are lethal to higher critical theory. That Judahite priests living in Jerusalem during the late IA could have assembled the text of the Hexateuch (Genesis through Joshua) with its rich cultural diversity and specificity would be a miracle greater than the exodus plagues or the crossing of the Re(e)d Sea! The rest of the Old Testament follows suit.

Although in recent years the Old Testament—particularly Genesis through Joshua—has been attacked for its historical record, the facts of history and archaeology synchronize with the biblical narratives to a high degree. Thus, to doubt the historicity of the Bible is to step on very thin ice.

Professor Kitchen sums up the essence of this chapter:

In the last few years increasingly extreme views about the Old Testament writings have been trumpeted loudly and proclaimed ever more widely and stridently; in the service of these views, all manner of gross misinterpretations of original, first-hand documentary data from the ancient Near East itself are now being shot forth in turn, to prop up these extreme stances on the Old Testament, regardless of the real facts of the case. Ideological claptrap has also interfered with the present-day situation. It has been said that "political correctness" has decreed a priori that the Old Testament writings are historically unreliable and of negligible value. Even if this judgment were proved correct, it is no business whatsoever of the politically correct to say so, merely as an ideology. Such matters can *only* be assessed by expert examination of the available facts, and not by the ignorant pronouncements of some species

of neo-Nazi "thought police." It has also been rumored that, in turn, such things as hard facts, objective fact, and (above all) absolute truth have been discarded by resort to the dictates of "postmodernism"…But individual absolute truths in the shape of objective fact, "hard facts" that exist independently of what any human being may choose to wish or think—these abound around us in their hundreds of thousands in everyday life, and (quite simply) cannot be gainsaid or wished away…And so, we must firmly say to philosophical cranks (politically correct, postmodernist, or whatever else)—"Your fantasy agendas are irrelevant in and to the real world, both of today and of all preceding time back into remotest antiquity. Get real or (alas!) get lost!"[82]

Bibliography

CHAPTER 1 SOURCES

Aling, C.F. *Egypt and Bible History: From Earliest Times to 1000 B.C.* Grand Rapids: Baker Books, 1981.

Ben-Tor, A. "The Early Bronze Age," in A. Ben-Tor, ed. *The Archaeology of Ancient Israel.* New Haven: Yale University Press, 1992.

Bryce, T. *The Kingdom of The Hittites.* Oxford: Oxford University Press, 2005.

Crawford, H. *Sumer and the Sumerians,* Second Edition. London: University Printing House, 2011.

Dornemann, R.H. *The Archaeology of the Transjordan in the Bronze and Iron Ages.* Milwaukee: Milwaukee Public Museum, 1983.

Finegan, Jack. *Handbook of Biblical Chronology: Principles of Time Reckoning in the Ancient World and Problems of Chronology in the Bible.* Revised Edition. Peabody: Hendrickson, 1998.

Garfinkle, S.J. "Ancient Near Eastern City-States," in P.F. Bang and W. Scheidel, eds. *The Oxford Handbook of the State in the Ancient Near East and Mediterranean.* Oxford: Oxford University Press, 2016.

Glueck, N. "Exploration in Eastern Palestine, IV," in *The Annual of the American Schools of Oriental Research* 25–28. New Haven: American Schools of Oriental Research, 1951.

Hallo, William W., and K. Lawson Younger, Jr., eds. *The Context of Scripture.* 3 vols. Leiden/Boston: Brill, 2003.

Kemp, B.J. "Old Kingdom, Middle Kingdom and Second Intermediate Period c. 2686–1552 BC," in B.G. Trigger, et al., eds. *Ancient Egypt: A Social History.* Cambridge: Cambridge University Press, 1983.

_____. *Ancient Egypt: Anatomy of a Civilization.* New York: Routledge, 1991.

Kitchen, K.A. *On the Reliability of the Old Testament.* Grand Rapids: Eerdmans, 2003.

Mazar, Amihai. *Archaeology of the Land of the Bible 10,000–586 B.C.E.* NY: Doubleday 1990.

Postgate, J.N. *Early Mesopotamia.* London: Routledge, 1992.

Sasson, J.M. *From the Mari Archives, an Anthology of Old Babylonian Letters.* Winona Lake: Eisenbrauns, 2017.

Walton, John H. *Ancient Near Eastern Thought and the Old Testament: Introducing the Conceptual World of the Hebrew Bible.* Grand Rapids: Baker Academic, 2006.

CHAPTER 2 SOURCES

Ackroyd, P.R., and Evans, C.F., eds. *The Cambridge History of the Bible.* 3 vols. London: Cambridge University, 1970.

Aharoni, Y. *The Land of the Bible: A Historical Geography.* Revised Edition. Philadelphia: Westminster, 1980.

Albright, W.F. *Yahweh and the Gods of Canaan.* Winona Lake: Eisenbrauns, 1994.

Aling, C.F. *Egypt and Bible History: From Earliest Times to 1000 B.C.* Grand Rapids: Baker Books, 1981.

Allis, O.T. *The Five Books of Moses.* Nutley: Presbyterian & Reformed, 1949.

Archer, G.L. *A Survey of Old Testament Introduction.* Revised Edition. Chicago: Moody, 1976.

Avner, U. "Mazzebot Sites in the Negev and Sinai and Their Significance," in A. Biran et al., eds. *Biblical Archaeology Today.* Jerusalem: Israel Exploration Society, 1993.

Beek, M.A. *Atlas of Mesopotamia: A Survey of the History and Civilisation of Mesopotamia from the Stone Age to the Fall of Babylon*. New York: Thomas Nelson, 1962.

Belmonte, J.A. "Mediterranean Archaeotopography and Archaeoastronomy: Two Examples of Dolmenic Necropolices in the Jordan Valley," in *Archaeoastronomy 22* (supplement to *Journal for the History of Astronomy*, Vol. 28), (1997).

Boslough, M.B.E., and D.A. Crawford. "Low-Altitude Airbursts and the Impact Threat," in *International Journal of Impact Engineering* 35 (2008).

Bourke, S., Hua, Q., Lawson, E., Lovell, J., Zoppi, U., and M. Barbetti. "The Chronology of the Ghassulian Chalcolithic Period in the Southern Levant: New ^{14}C Determinations from Teleilat Ghassul," in *Radiocarbon* 43.3 (2001).

Boyer, G. "*ARMT*, VIII, No. 10, lines 1-4," in A. Parrot and G. Dossin, eds. *Archives Royales de Mari, transcrites et traduites*, 1958.

Bryce, T. *The Kingdom of The Hittites*. Oxford: Oxford University Press, 2005.

Bull, L. "Ancient Egypt," in Denton, et al., eds. *The Idea of History in the Ancient Near East*. New Haven: Yale University, 1955.

Burke, A.A. *"Walled up to Heaven": The Evolution of Middle Bronze Age Fortification Strategies in the Levant*. Winona Lake: Eisenbrauns, 2008.

Butler, Trent C., ed. *Holman Bible Dictionary*. Nashville: Holman Bible Publishers, 1991.

Cassuto, U. *Biblical and Oriental Studies*. 2 vols. Jerusalem: Magnes, The Hebrew University, 1973.

Chang-Ho, C., and J.K. Lee. "The Survey in the Regions of ʿIraq al-Amir and Wadi al-Kafrayn, 2000," in *Annual of the Department of Antiquities of Jordan* 46 (2002).

_____. *The Documentary Hypothesis and the Composition of the Pentateuch*. Jerusalem: Magnes, The Hebrew University, 1983.

Clayton, L.A., and I. Alkawamleh. "A-Salaam Archaeological Project," in *American Journal of Archaeology* III.3 (2007).

Collins, S. *The Defendable Faith: Lessons in Christian Apologetics*. Albuquerque: TSU Press, 2012.

Collins, S. "A Chronology for the Cities of the Plain," in *Biblical Research Bulletin* II.8. Albuquerque: Trinity Southwest University, 2002.

_____. "Explorations on the Eastern Jordan Disk," in *Biblical Research Bulletin* II.18. Albuquerque: Trinity Southwest University, 2002.

_____. "The Geography of the Cities of the Plain," in *Biblical Research Bulletin* II:1. Albuquerque: Trinity Southwest University, 2002.

_____. "A Response to Bryant G. Wood's Critique of Collins's Northern Sodom Theory," in *Biblical Research Bulletin* VII.7 (2007).

_____. "Where Is Sodom? The Case for Tall el-Hammam," in *Biblical Archaeology Review* 39.2 (2013).

Collins, S. "Tall el-Hammam Is *Still* Sodom: Critical Data-Sets Cast Serious Doubt on E.H. Merrill's Chronological Analysis," in *Biblical Research Bulletin* XIII.1 (2013).

_____. "Christian Contributions to Archaeology," in George T. Kurian and Mark A. Lamport, eds. *The Encyclopedia of Christian Education*, Vol. 1. Lanham: Rowman & Littlefield Publishers, 2015.

_____. *The Search for Sodom and Gomorrah*. Albuquerque: Trinity Southwest University Press, 2008.

Collins, S., and H. Aljarrah et. al. "Tall al-Ḥammām Season Six, 2011: Excavation, Survey, Interpretations and Insights," in *Annual of the Department of Antiquities of Jordan* 55 (2011).

Collins, S., and L. Scott. *Discovering the City of Sodom*. New York: Simon & Schuster, 2013.

Collins, S., and P.J. Silvia, eds. *Tall al-Ḥammām, Jordan: Exploration, Survey, Excavation, Interpretations, and Insights from Seasons One through Twelve*, Vol. 1. Albuquerque: Trinity Southwest University Press, 2017.

_____, eds. *Tall al-Ḥammām, Jordan: Exploration, Survey, Excavation, Interpretations, and Insights from Seasons One through Twelve*, Vol. 2. Albuquerque: Trinity Southwest University Press, 2017.

_____, eds. *The Kikkar Dialogues*. Albuquerque: TSU Press, 2019.

Crawford, H., *Sumer and the Sumerians.* Second Edition. London: University Printing House, 2011.

Dale, Robert D. "Measurement Devices of the Bible," in William H. Stephens, ed. *Biblical Illustrator* (Winter 1982).

Darnell, J.C., and D. Darnell. "1994-95 Annual Report," in *The Luxor-Farshut Desert Road Project.* Chicago: Oriental Institute, University of Chicago, 1997.

Davis, J.J., and J.C. Whitcomb. *A History of Israel from Conquest to Exile.* Grand Rapids: Baker Books, 1980.

Dever, W.G. "From the End of the Early Bronze Age to the Beginning of the Middle Bronze Age," in J. Aviram et al., eds. *Biblical Archaeology Today* (1985).

Dornemann, R.H. *The Archaeology of the Transjordan in the Bronze and Iron Ages.* Milwaukee: Milwaukee Public Museum, 1983.

Dubis, E. and M. Gorniak. "Funerary Sites in the Vicinity of Tell El-Umeiri, 1996 Season of the Madaba Plains Project," in *SAAC* 8 (1997).

Falconer, S.E. "The Middle Bronze Age," in R.B. Adams, ed. *Jordan: An Archaeological Reader.* London: Equinox, 2008.

Falconer, S.E., P.L. Fall, and J.E. Jones. "Life at the Foundation of Bronze Age Civilization: Agrarian Villages in the Jordan Valley," in T.E. Levy, P.M.M. Daviau, R.W. Younker, and M. Shaer, eds. *Crossing Jordan: North American Contributions to the Archaeology of Jordan.* London: Equinox, 2007.

Finegan, J. *Archaeological History of the Ancient Near East.* San Diego: Westview, 1979.

_____. *Handbook of Biblical Chronology: Principles of Time Reckoning in the Ancient World and Problems of Chronology in the Bible.* Revised Edition. Peabody: Hendrickson, 1998.

_____. *Light from the Ancient Past.* 2 vols. Princeton: Princeton University, 1974.

_____. *Myth and Mystery: An Introduction to the Pagan Religions of the Biblical World.* Grand Rapids: Baker Books, 1989.

Finkelstein, I., and R. Gophna. "Settlement, Demographic and Economic Patterns in the Highlands of Palestine in the Chalcolithic and Early Bronze Periods and the Beginning of Urbanism," in *Bulletin of the American Schools of Oriental Research* 289 (1993).

Galli, P. "Active Tectonics along the Wadi Araba-Jordan Valley Transform Fault," in *Journal of Geophysical Research* 104. B2 (1999).

Grant, M. *The History of Ancient Israel.* New York: Scribner's Sons, 1984.

Graves, David E. *Key Facts for the Location of Sodom: Navigating the Maze of Arguments.* Moncton: D.E. Graves, 2014.

Grimal, N. *A History of Ancient Egypt.* Oxford: Oxford University Press, 1992.

Hallo, William W., and K. Lawson Younger, Jr., eds. *The Context of Scripture.* 3 vols. Leiden/Boston: Brill, 2003.

Harrison, R.K. *Introduction to the Old Testament.* Grand Rapids: Eerdmans, 1969.

_____. *Old Testament Times.* Grand Rapids: Eerdmans, 1970.

Harrison, T. "Shifting Patterns of Settlement in the Highlands of Central Jordan during the Early Bronze Age," in *Bulletin of the American Schools of Oriental Research* 306 (1997).

Herr, L.G., L.T. Geraty, O.S. LaBianca, and R.W. Younker. "Madaba Plains Project: The 1989 Excavations at Tell el-'Umeiri and Vicinity," in *Annual of the Department of Antiquities of Jordan* 35 (1991).

Hoerth, A.J. *Archaeology and the Old Testament.* Grand Rapids: Baker Academic, 1998.

Hoerth, Mattingly, and Edwin Yamauchi, eds. *Peoples of the Old Testament World.* Grand Rapids: Baker Books, 1994.

Hoffmeier, J.K. "Current Issues in Archaeology: The Recently Discovered Tel Dan Inscription: Controversy and Confirmation," in *Archaeology in the Biblical World* 3:1 (1995).

Höflmayer, F. "Dating Catastrophes and Collapses in the Ancient Near East: The End of the First Urbanization in the Southern Levant and the 4.2kaBP Event," in L. Nigro, Capriotti G. and M. Sala, eds. *Reading Catastrophes: Methodological Approaches and Historical Interpretation: Earthquakes, Floods, Famines, Epidemics between Egypt and Palestine— 3rd–1st Millennium BC* [Rome] *Studies on the Archaeology of Palestine and Transjordan 11.* Rome: La Sapienza University, 2014.

Höflmayer, F., J. Kamlah, H. Sader, M.W. Dee, W. Kutsch-era, E.M. Wild, and S. Riehl. "New Evidence for Middle Bronze Age Chronology and Synchronisms in the Levant: Radiocarbon Dates from Tell el-Burak, Tell el-Dabʿa, and Tel Ifshar Compared," in *Bulletin of the American Schools of Oriental Research* 375 (2016).

Homès-Fredericq, D., and H.J. Franken. *Pottery and Potters—Past and Present: 7000 Years of Ceramic Art in Jordan.* Ausstellungskataloge der Universität Tübingen, Nr. 20, 1986.

Ibrahim, M., K. Yassine, and J.A. Sauer. "The East Jordan Valley Survey 1975 (Parts 1 and 2)," in K. Yassine, ed. *The Archaeology of Jordan: Essays and Reports.* Amman: Department of Archaeology, University of Jordan, 1988.

Kagan, E. J., D. Langgut, E. Boaretto, F.H. Neumann, and M. Stein. "Dead Sea Levels During the Bronze and Iron Ages," in *Radiocarbon* 57.2 (2015).

Kemp, B.J. *Ancient Egypt: Anatomy of a Civilization.* New York: Routledge, 1991.

_____. "Old Kingdom, Middle Kingdom and Second Intermediate Period c. 2686–1552 BC," in B.G. Trigger et al., eds. *Ancient Egypt: A Social History.* Cambridge: Cambridge University Press, 1983.

Kempenski, A. et al., eds. *The Architecture of Ancient Israel.* Jerusalem: Israel Exploration Society, 1992.

Kenyon, F.G. *The Bible and Archaeology.* New York: Harper Brothers, 1940.

Kenyon, K.M. *Amorites and Canaanites.* Oxford: Oxford University, 1966.

Khouri, R.G. *The Antiquities of the Jordan Rift Valley.* Amman: Al Kutba, 1988.

Kikawada, Isaac M., and Arthur Quinn. *Before Abraham Was: The Unity of Genesis 1–11.* Nashville: Abingdon Press, 1985.

Kitchen, K.A. *Ancient Orient and Old Testament.* Leicester: InterVarsity Press, 1966.

_____. *The Bible in Its World.* Downers Grove: InterVarsity Press, 1978.

_____. "The Patriarchal Age: Myth or History?," in *Biblical Archaeology Review* 21:2 (1995).

_____. "The Patriarchs Revisited: A Reply to Dr. Ronald S. Hendel," in *Near East Archaeological Society Bulletin* 43 (1998).

_____. "A Possible Mention of David in the Late Tenth Century BCE, and Deity Dod as Dead as the Dodo?," in *Journal for the Study of the Old Testament* 76 (1997).

Kitchen, K.A. and P.J.N. Lawrence. *Treaty, Law and Covenant in the Ancient Near East*, Vol. 3. Wiesbaden: Harrassowitz Verlag, 2012.

Langgut, D., I. Finkelstein, T.E. Litt, F.H. Neumann, and M. Stein. "Vegetation and Climate Changes During the Bronze and Iron Ages (~3600–600 BCE) in the Southern Levant Based on Palynological Records," in *Radiocarbon* 57.2 (2015).

Lawrence, D., G. Philip, H. Hunt, L. Snape-Kennedy, and T.J. Wilkinson. "Long Term Population, City Size and Climate Trends in the Fertile Crescent: A First Approximation," in *PLOS ONE* 11(3) (2016).

Leonard, A. "The Jordan Valley Survey, 1953: Some Unpublished Soundings Conducted by James Mellaart," in *Annual of the American Schools of Oriental Research* 50. Winona Lake: Eisenbrauns, 1992.

Letesson, Q. "Minoan Halls: A Syntactical Genealogy," in *American Journal of Archaeology* 117.3 (2013).

_____ and C. Knappett, eds. *Minoan Archaeology and Urbanism: New Perspectives on an Ancient Built Environment.* Oxford: Oxford University Press, 2017.

Longman III, Tremper. "Genealogies," in Paul Copan et al., eds. *Dictionary of Christianity and Science: The Definitive Reference for the Intersection of Christian Faith and Contemporary Science.* Grand Rapids: Zondervan, 2017.

MacDonald, B. *East of the Jordan: Territories and Sites of the Hebrew Scriptures.* Boston: American Schools of Oriental Research, 2000.

Matheney, M. Pierce. "Weights and Measures," in Trent C. Butler, ed. *Holman Bible Dictionary.* Nashville: Holman Bible Publishers, 1991.

Matthiae, P. *Studies on the Archaeology of Ebla 1980–2010*, F. Pinnock, ed. Wiesbaden: Harrassowitz, 2013.

Mazar, A. *Archaeology and the Land of the Bible 10,000–586 BCE.* New York: Doubleday, 1990.

McAllister, S.S. *Middle Bronze Age Fortifications in the Southern Levant: Systems Analysis and Quantitative Survey.* Doctoral dissertation, College of Archaeology and Biblical History, Trinity Southwest University, 2008.

McEnroe, J. *Archaeology of Minoan Crete: Constructing Identity in the Aegean Bronze Age.* Austin: University of Texas Press, 2010.

Melott, A.L., B.C. Thomas, G. Dreschhoff, and C.K. Johnson. "Cometary Airbursts and Atmospheric Chemistry: Tunguska and a Candidate Younger Dryas Event," in *Geology* 38.4 (2010).

Mendenhall, G.E. "Law and Covenant in Israel and the Ancient Near East" reprint (1955) in *Biblical Archaeologist* 17 (1954).

Millard, Alan R. "Israelite and Aramean History in Light of Inscriptions," in *Tyndale Bulletin* 41 (1990).

Najjar, M. "The Jordan Valley (East Bank) During the Middle Bronze Age in the Light of New Excavations," in M. Zaghloul, K. 'Amr, F. Zayadine, R. Nabeel, and N. Rida-Tawfiq, eds. *Studies in the History and Archaeology of Jordan* IV. Amman: Department of Antiquities of Jordan, 1992.

Neev, D. and K.O. Emery. *The Destruction of Sodom, Gomorrah, and Jericho: Geological, Climatological, and Archaeological Background.* Oxford: Oxford University Press, 1995.

Nigro, L. *Khirbet al-Batrawy II.* Rome: La Sapienza Expedition to Palestine and Transjordan (Rosapat) 06, 2008.

_____. "The Archaeology of Collapse and Resilience: Tell es-Sultan/Ancient Jericho as a Case Study," in L. Nigro, ed. *Overcoming Catastrophes: Essays on Disastrous Agents Characterization and Resilience Strategies in Pre-Classical Southern Levant.* [Rome] *Studies on the Archaeology of Palestine and Transjordan* 11. Rome: La Sapienza University, 2014.

Nigro, L., G. Capriotte, and M. Sala. "Reading Catastrophes: Methodological Approaches and Historical Interpretation: Earthquakes, Floods, Famines, Epidemics between Egypt and Palestine, 3rd–1st Millennium BC," in L. Nigro, G., Capriotti and M. Sala, eds. *[Rome] Studies on the Archaeology of Palestine and Transjordan* 11. Rome: La Sapienza University, 2014.

Naveh, J. *Early History of the Alphabet.* Second Revised Edition. Jerusalem: Magnes, The Hebrew University, 1987.

Oates, J. *Babylon.* London: Thames & Hudson, 1986.

Olson, Craig. *A Proposal for a Symbolic Interpretation of the Patriarchal Lifespans.* PhD dissertation, Dallas Theological Seminary, 2017.

_____. "How Old Was Father Abraham? A Reexamination of Patriarchal Lifespans," in Steven Collins, ed. *The Kikkar Dialogues.* Albuquerque: TSU Press, 2019.

Postgate, J.N., *Early Mesopotamia.* London: Routledge, 1992.

Prag, K. "The Intermediate Early Bronze–Middle Bronze Age: An Interpretation of the Evidence from Transjordan, Syria and Lebanon," in *Levant* 6 (1974).

_____. "Preliminary Report on the Excavations at Tell Iktanu and Tell al-Hammam, Jordan, 1990," in *Levant* 23 (1991).

_____. "The Dead Sea Dolmens: Death and the Landscape," in S. Campbell and A. Green, eds. *The Archaeology of Death in the Ancient Near East.* Oxford: Oxbow Monograph 51, 1995.

_____. "Water Strategies in the Iktānū Region of Jordan," in F. al-Khraysheh, R. Harahsheh, Q. Fakhoury, H. Taher, and S. Khouri, eds. *Studies in the History and Archaeology of Jordan IX.* Amman: Department of Antiquities of Jordan, 2007.

Parr, P.J. "The Origin of the Rampart Fortifications of Middle Bronze Age Palestine and Syria" in *Zeitschrift des deutschen Palästina-Vereins* 84 (1968).

Pritchard, J.B. *Ancient Near Eastern Texts Relating to the Old Testament.* Princeton: Princeton University Press, 1955.

Pritchard, J.B. *The Ancient Near East: An Anthology of Texts and Pictures.* 2 vols. Princeton: Princeton University, 1973.

Rainey, A.F., and R.S. Notley. *The Sacred Bridge.* Jerusalem: Carta, 2015.

Regev, J., P. de Miroschedji, R. Greenberg, E. Braun, E. Greenhut, and E. Boaretto. "Chronology of the Early Bronze Age in the Southern Levant: New Analysis for a High Chronology," in E. Boaretto and N.R. Rebollo Franco, eds. *Proceedings of the 6th Annual International Radiocarbon and Archaeology Symposium: Radiocarbon,* Vol. 54 Nr. 3–4. Tucson: University of Arizona, 2012.

Richard, S. "The Early Bronze Age: The Rise and Collapse of Urbanism." in *Biblical Archaeologist* 50 (1987).

Rosen, A.M. *Civilizing Climate: Social Responses to Climate Change in the Ancient Near East*. Lanham: AltaMira Press, 2007.

Roaf, M. *Cultural Atlas of Mesopotamia and the Ancient Near East*. Oxford: Oxford University, 1990.

Sasson, J.M. *From the Mari Archives, An Anthology of Old Babylonian Letters*. Winona Lake: Eisenbrauns, 2017.

Schath, K., S. Collins, and H. Aljarrah. "The Excavation of an Undisturbed Demi-Dolmen and Insights from the Ḥammām Megalithic Field, 2011 Season," in *Annual of the Department of Antiquities of Jordan* 55 (2011).

Schaub, T. "An Early Bronze IA-1B Tomb from Bâb edh-Dhrâ," in *Bulletin of the American Schools of Oriental Research* 210 (1973).

_____. "Mud-Brick Town Walls in the EB I–II Southern Levant and their Significance for Understanding the Formation of New Social Institutions," in F. al-Khraysheh, R. Harahsheh, Q. Fakhoury, H. Taher, and S. Khouri, eds. *Studies in the History and Archaeology of Jordan IX*. Amman: Department of Antiquities of Jordan, 2007.

_____ and M.S. Chesson. "Life in the Earliest Walled Towns on the Dead Sea Plain: Bab adh-Dhra' and an-Numayra," in T.E. Levy, P.M.M. Daviau, R.W. Younker, and M. Shaer, eds. *Crossing Jordan: North American Contributions to the Archaeology of Jordan*. London: Equinox, 2007.

Stekelis, M. "The Megalithic Necropolis/Burial-field of Ala-Safat, Transjordan," in *Mongrafias I*. Barcelona: Diputacian de Barcelona, 1961.

Shaw, I., and P. Nicholson, eds. *The Dictionary of Ancient Egypt*. London: British Museum, 1995.

Stern, E., ed. *The New Encyclopedia of Archaeological Excavations in the Holy Land*. Jerusalem/NY: IEJ/Simon & Schuster, 1993.

Thompson, Thomas L. *The Historicity of the Patriarchal Narratives*. Berlin: de Gruyer, 1974.

Thomsen, M.L. *The Sumerian Language*, Vol. 10, in *Copenhagen Studies in Assyriology*. Copenhagen: Academic, 1984.

Thomson, W.M. *The Land and the Book: Southern Palestine and Jerusalem*. New York: Harper and Brothers, 1882.

Tristram, H.B. *The Land of Moab Travels and Discoveries on the East Side of the Dead Sea and the Jordan*. Second Edition. Piscataway: Gorgias Press, 1874.

Warner, D. *The Archaeology of the Canaanite Cult: An Analysis of Canaanite Temples from the Middle and Late Bronze Age in Palestine*. Saarbrücken: VDM Verlag Dr. Müller Aktiengesellschaft & Co., 2008.

Weiss, H., and R. S. Bradley, "What Drives Societal Collapse?," in *Science* 291 (2001).

Wiseman, D.J., ed. *Peoples of Old Testament Times*. London: Oxford University, 1973.

Wood, L., and D.E. O'Brien. *A Survey of Israel's History*. Grand Rapids: Zondervan, 1986.

Wright, G.E. *Biblical Archaeology*. Revised Edition. Philadelphia: Westminster, 1962.

Yadin, Yigael. *The Art of Warfare in Biblical Lands*. Transl. by M. Pearlman. Jerusalem: International Publishing, 1963.

Yamauchi, Edwin. *The Stones and the Scriptures*. Philadelphia: J.B. Lippincott, 1972.

Zayadine, F., M. Najjar, and J.A. Greene. "Recent Excavations on the Citadel of Amman (Lower Terrace)," in *Annual of the Department of Antiquities of Jordan* 31 (1987).

Zohar, M. "Megalithic Cemeteries in the Levant," in O. Bar-Yosef and A. Khazanov, eds. *Pastoralism in the Levant: Archaeological Materials, Anthropological Perspectives, Monographs in World History* 10. Madison: Prehistory Press, 1992.

CHAPTER 3 SOURCES

Aharoni, Y. *The Land of the Bible: A Historical Geography*. Revised Edition. Philadelphia: Westminster, 1980.

Ahlström, Gösta. *Who Were the Israelites?* Winona Lake: Eisenbrauns, 1986.

Albright, W.F. *Yahweh and the Gods of Canaan*. Winona Lake: Eisenbrauns, 1994.

Aldred, C. *Akhenaten, King of Egypt*. London: Thames & Hudson, 1988.

Allen, Ronald B. "Numbers," in Tremper Longman III, and David E. Garland, eds. *Expositor's Bible Commentary, Numbers–Ruth*. Vol. 2. Grand Rapids: Zondervan, 2012.

Anati, Emmanuel. *The Mountain of God: Har Karkom*. New York: Rizzoli, 1986.

Archer, Gleason L. *A Survey of Old Testament Introduction*. Revised Edition. Chicago: Moody, 1976.

Ashley, Timothy R. "The Book of Numbers," *New International Commentary on the Old Testament*. Grand Rapids: Eerdmans, 1993.

Avner, U. "Mazzebot Sites in the Negev and Sinai and Their Significance," in A. Biran et al., eds. *Biblical Archaeology Today*. Jerusalem: Israel Exploration Society, 1993.

Ben-Tor, Amnon, ed. *The Archaeology of Ancient Israel*. New Haven: Yale, 1992.

Bimson, J. *Redating the Exodus and Conquest*. Sheffield: Almond Press, 1981.

Breasted, J.H. *Ancient Records of Egypt: Vol. 2, The Eighteenth Dynasty*. Transl. Revised. Chicago and Urbana: University of Illinois Press, 2001. Original edition, University of Chicago Press, 1906.

Briggs, P. *Testing the Factuality of the Conquest of Ai Narrative in the Book of Joshua*. Albuquerque: TSU Press, 2009.

Bryan, Betsy M. *The Reign of Thutmose IV*. Baltimore: Johns Hopkins University, 1991.

Campbell, E.F. *The Chronology of the Amarna Letters*. Baltimore: Johns Hopkins University, 1964.

Collins, S. *Let My People Go: Using Historical Synchronisms to Identify the Pharaoh of the Exodus*. Albuquerque: TSU Press, 2005.

_____. *The Defendable Faith: Lessons in Christian Apologetics*. Albuquerque: TSU Press, 2012.

_____. "Has Archaeology Gone Overboard in Throwing Out the Bible?," in *The Ancient Near East Today*. American Schools of Oriental Research, online ASOR.org. Accessed October 15, 2013.

_____. "Christian Contributions to Archaeology," in George T. Kurian and Mark A. Lamport, eds. *The Encyclopedia of Christian Education*, Vol. 1. Lanham: Rowman & Littlefield Publishers, 2015.

Darnell, J.C., and D. Darnell. "1994-95 Annual Report," in *The Luxor-Farshut Desert Road Project*. Chicago: Oriental Institute, University of Chicago, 1997.

Desroches-Noblecourt, C. "Le 'Bestiaire' Symbolique du Liberateur Ahmosis," in *Festschrift W. Westenforf*. Gottingen: Gottingen University, 1984.

Finkelstein, Israel, and Nadav Na'aman. *From Nomadism to Monarchy*. Jerusalem: Israel Exploration Society, 1994.

Flavius Josephus. *The Antiquities of the Jews* in *The Works of Josephus*. New Updated Edition. Transl. by W. Whiston. Peabody: Hendrickson, 1987.

Fouts, David M. "A Defense of the Hyperbolic Interpretation of Large Numbers in the Old Testament," in *Journal of the Evangelical Theological Society* 40, no. 3 (1997).

_____. "The Use of Large Numbers in the Old Testament with Particular Emphasis on the Use of 'elep." ThD dissertation. Dallas Theological Seminary, 1992.

Grimal, N. *A History of Ancient Egypt*. Oxford: Oxford University, 1992.

Hallo, William W., and K. Lawson Younger, Jr., eds. *The Context of Scripture*. 3 vols. Leiden/Boston: Brill, 2003.

Hansen, David G. *Evidence for Fortifications at Late Bronze I and IIA Locations in Palestine*. PhD dissertation. Newburgh: Trinity Theological Seminary, 2000.

Harrison, R.K. *Introduction to the Old Testament*. Grand Rapids: Eerdmans, 1969.

Harrison, R.K. *Old Testament Times*. Grand Rapids: Eerdmans, 1970.

Hayes, W.C. "Egypt: Internal Affairs from Tuthmosis I to the Death of Amenophis III," *Cambridge Ancient History*, Vol. II.1. Cambridge: Cambridge University, 1973.

Hoerth, A.J. *Archaeology and the Old Testament*. Grand Rapids: Baker Academic, 1998.

Hoerth, Mattingly, and E. Yamauchi, eds. *Peoples of the Old Testament World*. Grand Rapids: Baker Books, 1994.

Hoffmeier, James K. *Israel in Egypt: The Evidence for the Authenticity of the Exodus Tradition*. New York/Oxford: Oxford University Press, 1996.

Holden, Joseph M., and Norman Geisler. *The Popular Handbook of Archaeology and the Bible*. Eugene: Harvest House, 2013.

Irvin, Dorothy. "The Joseph and Moses Narratives," in J.H. Hayes and J.M. Miller, eds. *Israelite and Judaea History*. Philadelphia: Westminster, 1977.

Kikawada, Isaac M., and Arthur Quinn. *Before Abraham Was: The Unity of Genesis 1–11*. Nashville: Abingdon Press, 1985.

Kenyon, K.M. *Digging Up Jericho*. New York: Praeger, 1957.

_____. *Amorites and Canaanites*. Oxford: Oxford University Press, 1966.

_____. *Excavations at Jericho,* Vol. 3. Jerusalem: British School of Archaeology, 1981.

Kitchen, K.A. *Ancient Orient and the Old Testament.* Downers Grove: InterVarsity Press, 1966.

_____. *On the Reliability of the Old Testament.* Grand Rapids: Eerdmans, 2003.

Kozloff, A., and B. Bryan. *Egypt's Dazzling Sun: Amenhotep III and His World*. Cleveland: Cleveland Museum of Art and Indiana University, 1992.

Krahmalkov, Charles R. "Exodus Itinerary Confirmed by Egyptian Evidence," in *Biblical Archaeology Review* 20.5 (1994).

Lemche, Niels Peter. *Prelude to Israel's Past*. Peabody: Hendrickson, 1998.

Mazar, Amihai. *Archaeology and the Land of the Bible 10,000–586 BCE.* New York: Doubleday, 1992.

McLaughlin, Amanda K. *The Battle of Ai and the Siege of Megiddo: Using Legal Theory to Evaluate Conclusions of Historicity in Bronze Age Battle Accounts of the Near East.* PhD dissertation, Trinity Theological Seminary, 2005.

Mendenhall, G.E. "Law and Covenant in Israel and the Ancient Near East," in *Biblical Archaeologist* 17 (1954).

Moran, W.L. *The Amarna Letters.* Baltimore: Johns Hopkins University, 1992.

Murray, M.A. *The Splendor That Was Egypt.* New York: Praeger, 1969.

Naveh, J. *Early History of the Alphabet.* Second Revised Edition. Jerusalem: Magnes, The Hebrew University, 1987.

Nibbi, A., ed. *The Archaeology, Geography and History of the Egyptian Delta During the Pharaonic Period.* Oxford: Oxford University, 1986.

Pritchard, J.B. *Ancient Near Eastern Texts Relating to the Old Testament.* Princeton: Princeton University, 1955.

_____. *The Ancient Near East in Pictures, Relating to the Old Testament.* Princeton: Princeton University, 1969.

_____. *The Ancient Near East: An Anthology of Texts and Pictures.* Princeton: Princeton University, 1973.

Quirke, S. *Ancient Egyptian Religion.* London: British Museum, 1992.

Redford, Donald B. *History and Chronology of the Eighteenth Dynasty: Seven Studies.* Toronto: University of Toronto, 1967.

Redford, Donald B. *Akhenaten: The Heretic King.* Princeton: Princeton University, 1984.

_____. *Egypt, Canaan, and Israel in Ancient Times.* Princeton: Princeton University, 1992.

_____. *The Wars in Syria and Palestine of Thutmose III: Culture and History of the Ancient Near East* 16. Boston: Brill, 2003.

Roberts, J.J. *The Earliest Semitic Pantheon.* Baltimore: Johns Hopkins University, 1972.

Schulman, A.R. "Chariots, Chariotry and the Hyksos," in *Journal of the Society for the Study of Egyptian Antiquities* 10 (1980).

Shaw, I., and P. Nicholson, eds. *The Dictionary of Ancient Egypt.* London: British Museum, 1995.

Simons, J. *Handbook for the Study of Topographical Lists Relating to Western Asia.* Leiden: Brill, 1937.

Stern, E., ed. *The New Encyclopedia of Archaeological Excavations in the Holy Land.* New York: Simon & Schuster, 1993.

Stripling, S. "The Israelite Tabernacle at Shiloh," in *Bible and Spade* 29.3 (Fall 2016).

_____ and S. Lattimer. "Go Now to Shiloh," in *Popular Archaeology* 29 (Winter 2018).

Van Seters, John. "The Plagues of Egypt: Ancient Tradition or Literary Invention?," in *Zeitschrift für die Alttestamentliche Wissenshaft* 98 (1986).

Waltke, B.K. "Palestinian Artifactual Evidence Supporting the Early Date for the Exodus," in *Bibliotheca Sacra* 129 (1972).

Waterhouse, S.D. "Who are the Habiru of the Amarna Letters?," in *Journal of the Adventist Theological Society* 12/1 (2001).

White, J.E.M. *Ancient Egypt: Its Culture and History.* New York: Dover, 1970.

Wiseman, D.J., ed. *Peoples of Old Testament Times.* London: Oxford University, 1973.

Wood, Bryant G. "Did the Israelites Conquer Jericho?," in *Biblical Archaeology Review* 16.2 (1990).

Wood, Bryant G. "The Walls of Jericho," in *Bible and Spade* 12.2 (1999).

_____. "The Search for Joshua's Ai: Excavations at Kh. el-Maqatir," in *Bible and Spade* 12.1 (1998).

Wood, L., and D.E. O'Brien. *A Survey of Israel's History.* Grand Rapids: Zondervan, 1986.

Wright, G.E. *Biblical Archaeology.* Revised Edition. Philadelphia: Westminster, 1962.

Yadin, Yigael. *The Art of Warfare in Biblical Lands.* Transl. M. Pearlman. Jerusalem: International Publishing, 1963.

CHAPTER 4 SOURCES

Aharoni, Y. *The Land of the Bible: A Historical Geography.* Revised Edition. Philadelphia: Westminster, 1980.

Ahlström, Gösta. *Who Were the Israelites?* Winona Lake: Eisenbrauns, 1986.

Albright, W.F. *Yahweh and the Gods of Canaan.* Winona Lake: Eisenbrauns, 1994.

Archer, Gleason L. *A Survey of Old Testament Introduction.* Revised Edition. Chicago: Moody, 1976.

Archer, G.L. *Encyclopedia of Bible Difficulties.* Grand Rapids: Zondervan, 1982.

Avner, U. "Mazzebot Sites in the Negev and Sinai and Their Significance," in A. Biran et al., eds. *Biblical Archaeology Today.* Jerusalem: Israel Exploration Society, 1993.

Ben Tor, A., ed. *The Archaeology of Ancient Israel.* New Haven: Yale University Press, 1992.

Bergen, Robert D. *1, 2 Samuel.* Vol. 7. *New American Commentary.* Nashville: Broadman & Holman, 1996.

Bierling, N. *Giving Goliath His Due: New Archaeological Light on the Philistines.* Grand Rapids: Eerdmans, 1992.

Chamberlain, Gary Alan. *The Greek of the Septuagint: A Supplemental Lexicon.* Peabody: Hendrickson, 2011.

Collins, S. *Let My People Go: Using Historical Synchronisms to Identify the Pharaoh of the Exodus.* Albuquerque: TSU Press, 2005.

Craigie, Peter C. *The Problem of War in the Old Testament.* Grand Rapids: Eerdmans, 1978.

Dever, W.G. *What Did the Biblical Writers Know & When Did They Know It?* Grand Rapids: Eerdmans, 2001.

Dothan, T. *The Philistines and Their Material Culture.* Jerusalem: Israel Exploration Society, 1982.

Dothan, T. "The Arrival of the Sea Peoples: Cultural Diversity in Early Iron Age Canaan," in S. Gitin and W.G. Dever, eds. *Recent Excavations in Israel: Studies in Iron Age Archaeology.* The Annual of the *ASOR* 49. Winona Lake: ASOR, 1989.

Finegan, J. *Light from the Ancient Past.* Princeton: Princeton University, 1974.

_____. *Myth and Mystery: An Introduction to the Pagan Religions of the Biblical World.* Grand Rapids: Baker Books, 1989.

Finkelstein, I. *The Archaeology of the Israelite Settlement.* Jerusalem: Israel Exploration Society, 1988.

_____, and Nadav Na'aman. *From Nomadism to Monarchy.* Jerusalem: Israel Exploration Society, 1994.

_____, and N.A. Silberman. *The Bible Unearthed: Archaeology's New Vision of Ancient Israel and the Origins of Its Sacred Texts.* New York: Free Press, 2001.

Goetze, A. "The Struggle for the Domination of Syria (1400–1300 B.C.)," in *CAH* II.2 (1975).

Hallo, William W., and K. Lawson Younger, Jr., eds. *The Context of Scripture.* 3 vols. Leiden/Boston: Brill, 2003.

Harrison, R.K. *Introduction to the Old Testament.* Grand Rapids: Eerdmans, 1969.

_____. *Old Testament Times.* Grand Rapids: Eerdmans, 1970.

Hoerth, A.J. *Archaeology and the Old Testament.* Grand Rapids: Baker Academics, 1998.

Hoerth, Mattingly, and E. Yamauchi, eds. *Peoples of the Old Testament World.* Grand Rapids: Baker Books, 1994.

Holden, Joseph M., and Norman Geisler. *The Popular Handbook of Archaeology and the Bible.* Eugene: Harvest House, 2013.

Kempenski, A., et al., eds. *The Architecture of Ancient Israel.* Jerusalem: Israel Exploration Society, 1992.

Kitchen, K.A. *On the Reliability of the Old Testament.* Grand Rapids: Eerdmans, 2003.

_____. *The Bible in Its World: The Bible and Archaeology Today.* Eugene: Wipf & Stock Publishers, 1977.

Lohfink, N. "ḥāram; MᵉrEj ḥērem," in G. Johannes Botterweck and Helmer Ringgren, eds. *Theological Dictionary of the Old Testament.* Grand Rapids: Eerdmans, 1986.

Mazar, A. *Excavations at Tell Qasile: Part 1, The Philistine Sanctuary: Architecture and Cult Objects.* Qedem 12. Jerusalem: Israel Exploration Society, 1980.

_____. *Excavations at Tell Qasile: Part 2, The Philistine Sanctuary: Various Finds, the Pottery, Conclusions, Appendices.* Qedem 20. Jerusalem: Israel Exploration Society, 1985.

_____. *Archaeology and the Land of the Bible 10,000–586 BCE.* New York: Doubleday, 1992.

_____. "Excavations at Tell Qasile, 1982–1984: Preliminary Report," in *Israel Exploration Journal* 36, no. 1/2 (1986): 1-15. http://www.jstor.org/stable/27926005. Accessed: September 28, 2018.

Metzger, Bruce M., and Herbert G. May, eds. *The New Oxford Annotated Bible with the Apocrypha, an Ecumenical Study Bible.* Revised Standard Version, Second Edition of the New Testament. New York: Oxford University Press, 1977.

Naveh, J. *Early History of the Alphabet.* Second Revised Edition. Jerusalem: Magnes, The Hebrew University, 1987.

Pederson, J. *Israel: Its Life and Culture.* 2 Vols. New York: Oxford University Press, 1926-40.

Pritchard, J.B. *Ancient Near Eastern Texts Relating to the Old Testament.* Princeton: Princeton University, 1955.

_____. *The Ancient Near East in Pictures, Relating to the Old Testament.* Princeton: Princeton University, 1969.

_____. *The Ancient Near East: An Anthology of Texts and Pictures.* Princeton: Princeton University, 1973.

Rhalfs, Alfred, and Robert Hanhart, eds. *Septuaginta.* Stuttgart: German Bible Society, 2007.

Ritmeyer, Leen. *A Cutaway Elevation Reconstruction Drawing of the Philistine Temple at Tel Qasile, Israel.* Ritmeyer Archaeological Design, 2010.

Rudolf, Wilhelm, and Karl Elliger, eds. *Biblia Hebraica Stuttgartensia (BHS).* Transl. Karl Elliger. Stuttgart: Deutsche Bibelgesellschaft, 2006.

Wood, Leon. *Distressing Days of the Judges.* Grand Rapids: Zondervan, 1975.

Wright, G.E. *Biblical Archaeology.* Revised Edition. Philadelphia: Westminster, 1962.

Yadin, Yigael. *The Art of Warfare in Biblical Lands.* Transl. M. Pearlman. Jerusalem: International Publishing, 1963.

Youngblood, Ronald F. "1, 2 Samuel," in Tremper Longman III and David E. Garland, eds. *Expositor's Bible Commentary.* Revised Edition. Grand Rapids: Zondervan, 2012.

CHAPTER 5 SOURCES

Aharoni, Y. *The Land of the Bible: A Historical Geography.* Revised Edition. Philadelphia: Westminster, 1980.

Avner, U. "Mazzebot Sites in the Negev and Sinai and Their Significance," in A. Biran, et al., eds. *Biblical Archaeology Today.* Jerusalem: Israel Exploration Society, 1993.

Bahat, D. *Carta's Historical Atlas of Jerusalem.* Jerusalem: Carta, 1983.

Ben-Tor, Amnon, ed. *The Archaeology of Ancient Israel.* New Haven: Yale, 1992.

Bolen, Todd. "Identifying King David's Palace: Mazar's Flawed Reading of the Biblical Text," in *The Bible and Interpretation* (blog), September 2010, http://www.bibleinterp.com/opeds/ident357928.shtml.

Cahill, Jane M. "Jerusalem at the Time of the United Monarchy. The Archaeological Evidence," in Andrew G. Vaughn and Ann E. Killebrew, eds. *Jerusalem in Bible and Archaeology: The First Temple Period. SBL Symposium Series 18.* Atlanta: SBL, 2003.

Faust, Avraham. "Did Eilat Mazar Find David's Palace?," in *Biblical Archaeology Review* 38, no. 5 (2012).

Finkelstein, I. *The Archaeology of the Israelite Settlement.* Jerusalem: Israel Exploration Society, 1988.

_____, and Nadav Na'aman. *From Nomadism to Monarchy.* Jerusalem: Israel Exploration Society, 1994.

_____, Singer-Avitz, Lily, David Ussishkin, and Ze'ev Herzog. "Has King David's Palace in Jerusalem Been Found?," in *Tel Aviv* 34, no. 2 (2007).

Foakes Jackson, F.J., *Josephus and the Jews: The Religion and History of the Jews as Explained by Flavius Josephus.* Grand Rapids: Baker Books, 1977.

Garfinkel, Yosef. "Christopher Rollston's Methodology of Caution," in *Biblical Archaeology Review* 38, no. 5 (2012).

Hallo, William W., and K. Lawson Younger, Jr., eds. *The Context of Scripture.* 3 vols. Leiden/Boston: Brill, 2003.

Harrison, R.K. *Major Cities of the Biblical World.* Nashville: Thomas Nelson, 1985.

Harrison, R.K. *Introduction to the Old Testament.* Grand Rapids: Eerdmans, 1969.

Herzog, Ze'ev, Aharoni Miriam, Anson F. Rainey, and Shmuel Moshkovitz. "The Israelite Fortress at Arad," in *Bulletin of the American Schools of Oriental Research*, no. 254 (1984).

Hoerth, A.J. *Archaeology and the Old Testament.* Grand Rapids: Baker Academic, 1998.

Hoffmeier, J.K. "Current Issues in Archaeology: The Recently Discovered Tel Dan Inscription: Controversy and Confirmation," in *Archaeology in the Biblical World,* 3:1 (1995).

Holden, Joseph M., and Norman Geisler. *The Popular Handbook of Archaeology and the Bible.* Eugene: Harvest House, 2013.

Janeway, Brian "Cultural Transition in the Northern Levant during the Early Iron Age as Reflected in the Aegean-Style Pottery at Tell Tayinat." PhD dissertation, University of Toronto, 2013.

Kempenski, A. et al., eds. *The Architecture of Ancient Israel.* Jerusalem: Israel Exploration Society, 1992.

King, P. "Jerusalem" in David Noel Freedman, ed. *The Anchor Bible Dictionary.* New York: Doubleday, 1992.

Kitchen, Kenneth A. "A Possible Mention of David in the Late Tenth Century BCE, and Deity Dod as Dead as the Dodo?," in *Journal for the Study of the Old Testament* 76 (1997).

Kitchen, K.A. *On the Reliability of the Old Testament.* Grand Rapids: Eerdmans, 2003.

Lemaire, A. "'House of David' Restored in Moabite Inscription," in *Biblical Archaeology Review* (May/June 1994, w/ reply Nov/Dec 1994).

MacAlister, Robert A.S., and J.G. Duncan. *Excavations on the Hill of Ophel, Jerusalem 1923–1925. PEF Annual 4.* London: Palestine Exploration Fund, 1926.

Mazar, Amihai. "Archaeology and the Biblical Narrative: The Case of the United Monarchy," in Reinhard Gregor Kratz and Hermann Spieckermann, eds. *One God—One Cult—One Nation: Archaeological and Biblical Perspectives.* BZAW 405. Berlin: De Gruyter, 2011.

_____. "The Divided Monarchy: Comments on Some Archaeological Issues," in Israel Finkelstein and Brian B. Schmidt, eds. *The Quest for the Historical Israel. Archaeology and Biblical Studies* 17. Atlanta: SBL, 2007.

Mazar, Eilat. "Did I Find King David's Palace?," in *Biblical Archaeology Review* 32, no. 1 (2006).

_____. "Excavate King David's Palace," in *Biblical Archaeology Review* 23, no. 1 (1997).

_____. *Preliminary Report on the City of David Excavations 2005 at the Visitors Center Area.* Jerusalem: Shalem Press, 2008.

_____. *The Palace of King David Excavations at the Summit of the City of David: Preliminary Report of Seasons 2005–2007.* Jerusalem: Shoham Academic Research and Publication, 2009.

Mazar, Eilat, David Ben-Shlomo, and Shmuel Ahituv. "An Inscribed Pithos from the Ophel, Jerusalem," in *IEJ* 63, no. 1 (2013).

Millard, Alan R. "Story, History, and Theology," in A.R. Millard, J.K. Hoffmeier, and D.W. Baker, eds. *Faith, Tradition, and History.* Winona Lake: Eisenbrauns, 1994.

Mykytiuk, Lawrence J. *Identifying Biblical Persons in Northwest Semitic Inscriptions of 1200–539 B.C.E. SBL Academia Biblica* 12. Atlanta: SBL, 2004.

Na'aman, Nadav. "The Interchange Between Bible and Archaeology: The Case of David's Palace and the Millo," in *Biblical Archaeology Review* 40, no. 1 (2014).

Petrovich, Douglas. "The Ophel Pithos Inscription: Its Dating, Language, Translation, and Script," in *PEQ* 147, no. 2 (June 2015).

Pritchard, J.B. *Ancient Near Eastern Texts Relating to the Old Testament.* Princeton: Princeton University Press, 1955.

_____. *Solomon and Sheba.* London: Phaidon Press, 1974.

_____. *The Ancient Near East: An Anthology of Texts and Pictures.* 2 vols. Princeton: Princeton University, 1973.

_____. *The Ancient Near East in Pictures, Relating to the Old Testament.* Princeton: Princeton University, 1969.

Rainey, Anson. "The 'House of David' and the House of the Deconstructionists," in *Biblical Archaeology Review* 20:6 (1994).

Ricks, S. "Sheba, Queen of," in David Noel Freedman, ed. *The Anchor Bible Dictionary.* New York: Doubleday, 1992.

Steiner, Margreet L. "The 'Palace of David' Reconsidered in the Light of Earlier Excavations: Did Eilat Mazar Find King David's Palace? I Would Say Not," in *The Bible and Interpretation* (blog), September 2009, http://www.bibleinterp.com /articles/palace_2468.shtml.

Thiele, E.R. *The Mysterious Numbers of the Hebrew Kings.* Revised Edition. Grand Rapids: Zondervan, 1994.

Yadin, Yigael. *The Art of Warfare in Biblical Lands.* Transl. M. Pearlman. Jerusalem: International Publishing, 1963.

CHAPTER 6 SOURCES

Aharoni, Y. *The Land of the Bible: A Historical Geography.* Revised Edition. Philadelphia: Westminster, 1980.

Archer, Gleason L. *A Survey of Old Testament Introduction.* Revised Edition. Chicago: Moody, 1976.

Arnold, Bill T., and Bryan E. Beyer, *Readings from the Ancient Near East: Primary Sources for Old Testament Study.* Third Edition. Grand Rapids: Baker Books, 2005.

Ben-Tor, Amnon, ed. *The Archaeology of Ancient Israel.* New Haven: Yale, 1992.

Bruce, F.F. *Israel and The Nations.* Grand Rapids: Eerdmans, 1963.

Finegan, J. *Light from the Ancient Past.* Princeton: Princeton University, 1974.

Finegan, J. *Myth and Mystery: An Introduction to the Pagan Religions of the Biblical World.* Grand Rapids: Baker Books, 1989.

Finkelstein, I. *The Archaeology of the Israelite Settlement.* Jerusalem: Israel Exploration Society, 1988.

Forrest, Brandy A. *A Reassessment of the Bull Motif in the Ancient Near East and Its Affect on the Bulls of Tall el Hammam.* Doctoral Dissertation. Trinity Southwest University, 2018.

Hallo, William W., and K. Lawson Younger, Jr., eds. *The Context of Scripture.* 3 vols. Leiden/Boston: Brill, 2003.

Harrison, R.K. *Introduction to the Old Testament.* Grand Rapids: Eerdmans, 1969.

_____. *Old Testament Times.* Grand Rapids: Eerdmans, 1970.

Hess, Richard S. *Israelite Religions: An Archaeological and Biblical Survey.* Grand Rapids: Baker Academic, 2007.

Kempenski, A., et al., eds. *The Architecture of Ancient Israel.* Jerusalem: Israel Exploration Society, 1992.

Kitchen, K.A. "Shishak's Military Campaign in Israel Confirmed," in *Biblical Archaeology Review* 15:3 (1989).

_____. "Where Did Solomon's Gold Go?," in *Biblical Archaeology Review* 15:3 (1989).

_____. *On the Reliability of the Old Testament.* Grand Rapids: Eerdmans, 2003.

_____ and P.J.N. Lawrence. *Treaty, Law and Covenant in the Ancient Near East*, Vol. 3. Wiesbaden: Harrassowitz Verlag, 2012.

Mazar, Amihai. *Archaeology and the Land of the Bible 10,000–586 BCE.* New York: Doubleday, 1990.

Naveh, J. *Early History of the Alphabet.* Second Revised Edition. Jerusalem: Magnes, The Hebrew University, 1987.

Oates, J. *Babylon.* London: Thames & Hudson, 1986.

Pritchard, J.B. *Ancient Near Eastern Texts Relating to the Old Testament.* Princeton: Princeton University, 1955.

Pritchard, J.B. *The Ancient Near East in Pictures, Relating to the Old Testament.* Princeton: Princeton University, 1969.

Pritchard, J.B. *The Ancient Near East: An Anthology of Texts and Pictures.* Princeton: Princeton University, 1973.

Rice, Michael. *The Power of the Bull.* London: Routledge, 1998.

Sharpes, D.K. *Sacred Bull, Holy Cow: A Cultural Study of Civilization's Most Important Animal.* New York: Peter Lang Publishing, 2006.

Thiele, E.R. *The Mysterious Numbers of the Hebrew Kings.* Revised Edition. Grand Rapids: Zondervan, 1994.

Yadin, Yigael. *The Art of Warfare in Biblical Lands.* Transl. M. Pearlman. Jerusalem: International Publishing, 1963.

CHAPTER 7 SOURCES

Arnold, Bill T., and Bryan E. Beyer. *Readings from the Ancient Near East: Primary Sources for Old Testament Study.* Third Edition. Grand Rapids: Baker Books, 2005.

Barber, James L. "Hosea: The Depths of the Hesed for His Bride." A paper presented during a series of lectures concerning the Old Testament prophets at Hardin-Simmons University, Corpus Christi, TX, March 2013.

_____. "A Nation Gone A-Whoring: The Implications of YHWH's Command That Hosea Marry a Prostitute." A paper presented during a series of lectures concerning the Old Testament prophets at Hardin-Simmons University, Corpus Christi, TX, March 2013.

Bedford, Peter R. "Diaspora: Homeland Relations in Ezra-Nehemiah," in *Vetus Testamentum* 52, no. 2 (2002).

Ben-Tor, A., ed. *The Archaeology of Ancient Israel.* New Haven: Yale University Press, 1992.

Brettler, Marc Zvi. "Judaism in the Hebrew Bible? The Transition from Ancient Israelite Religion to Judaism," in *The Catholic Biblical Quarterly* 61, no. 3 (1999).

Brisco, Thomas V., ed. *Holman Bible Atlas.* Nashville: Broadman & Holman, 1999.

Chamberlain, Gary Alan. *The Greek of the Septuagint: A Supplemental Lexicon.* Peabody: Hendrickson, 2011.

Dever, W.G. *What Did the Biblical Writers Know & When Did They Know It?* Grand Rapids: Eerdmans, 2001.

Dozeman, Thomas B. "Geography and History in Herodotus and in Ezra-Nehemiah," in *Journal of Biblical Literature* 122, no. 3 (2003).

Finkelstein, I., and N.A. Silberman. *The Bible Unearthed: Archaeology's New Vision of Ancient Israel and the Origins of Its Sacred Texts.* New York: Free Press, 2001.

Flavius Josephus. *The New Complete Works of Josephus.* Revised and Expanded. Trans. William Whiston and Paul L. Maier. Grand Rapids: Kregel Publications, 1999.

Gadd, C.J. "Inscribed Prisms of Sargon II from Nimrud," in *Iraq* 16, no. 2 (1954).

Geisler, Norman L. *A Popular Survey of the Old Testament.* Grand Rapids: Baker Books, 2007.

Ghirshman, R. "The Ziggurat of Tchoga-Zanbil," in *Scientific American*, Vol. 204 (1961).

Hallo, William W., and K. Lawson Younger, Jr., eds. *The Context of Scripture*. 3 vols. Leiden/Boston: Brill, 2003.

Hays, J. Daniel, and Tremper Longman III. *Message of the Prophets: A Survey of the Prophetic and Apocalyptic Books of the Old Testament*. Grand Rapids: Zondervan, 2010.

Horeth, A.J. *Archaeology and the Old Testament*. Grand Rapids: Baker Books, 2006.

Kitchen, K.A. *On the Reliability of the Old Testament*. Grand Rapids: Eerdmans, 2003.

Knowles, Melody D. "Pilgrimage Imagery in the Returns in Ezra," in *Journal of Biblical Literature* 123, no. 1 (2004).

Koldewey, Robert. *The Excavations at Babylon*. London: Macmillan, 1914.

Lau, Peter H.W. "Gentile Incorporation into Israel in Ezra-Nehemiah?," in *Biblica* 90, no. 3 (2009).

Maier, Paul L. *Josephus, the Essential Writings*. Grand Rapids: Kregel Publications, 1988.

Mazar, A. *Archaeology of the Land of the Bible: 10,000–586 BCE*. New York: Doubleday, 1992.

Merrill, Eugene H. *A Kingdom of Priests: A History of Old Testament Israel*. Second Edition. Grand Rapids: Baker Books, 2008.

Metzger, Bruce M., and Herbert G. May, eds. *The New Oxford Annotated Bible with the Apocrypha, an Ecumenical Study Bible*. Revised Standard Version, Second Edition of the New Testament. New York: Oxford University Press, 1977.

Murphy, Frederick James. *Early Judaism: The Exile to the Time of Jesus*. Grand Rapids: Baker Academic, 2010.

Rawlinson, George. *The Kings of Israel and Judah*. First published by Anson D.F. Randolf and Company. Latest edition published by Molinarius Press, 2017.

Rhalfs, Alfred, and Robert Hanhart, eds. *Septuaginta*. Stuttgart: German Bible Society, 2007.

Rudolf, Wilhelm, and Karl Elliger, eds. *Biblia Hebraica Stuttgartensia (BHS)*. Trans. Karl Elliger. Stuttgart: Deutsche Bibelgesellschaft, 2006.

Thiele, E.R. *The Mysterious Numbers of the Hebrew Kings*. Revised Edition. Grand Rapids: Zondervan, 1994.

Weinberg, Saul S., "Post-Exilic Palestine: An Archaeological Report," in *The Israel Academy of Sciences and Humanities Proceedings* 4 (1969).

CHAPTER 8 SOURCES

Abegg, Jr., G. Martin G., Michael O. Wise, and Edward M. Cook. *The Dead Sea Scrolls: A New Translation*. Revised Edition. New York: HarperCollins, 2005.

Ben Tor, A., ed. *The Archaeology of Ancient Israel*. New Haven: Yale University Press, 1992.

Bonani, Georges, et al., "Radiocarbon Dating of Fourteen Dead Sea Scrolls," in *Radiocarbon* 34, no. 3 (2006).

_____. "Radiocarbon Dating of the Dead Sea Scrolls," in *Tigot* 20 (1991).

Brisco, Thomas V., ed. *Holman Bible Atlas*. Nashville: Broadman & Holman, 1999.

Budge, E.A. Wallis. *Rosetta Stone in the British Museum*. London: British Museum Press, 1913.

_____. *The Decrees of Memphis and Canopus: The Rosetta Stone*, Vol. 1. 3 vols. London: Kegan, Paul, Trench, Trübner & Co., 1904.

Chamberlain, Gary Alan. *The Greek of the Septuagint: A Supplemental Lexicon*. Peabody: Hendrickson, 2011.

Charlesworth, James H. *The Dead Sea Scrolls: Hebrew, Aramaic, and Greek Texts with English Translations*. Louisville: Westminster/Knox, 2000.

Cohen, Rudolf, and Yigal Yisraeli. "The Excavations of Rock Shelter XII/50 and in Caves XII/52-53," in *Atiqot* 41, no. 2 (2002).

Crawford, Sidnie White. "Has Every Book of the Bible Been Found Among the Dead Sea Scrolls?," in *Bible Review* 12 (October 1996).

De Troyer, Kristin. "Once More, the So-Called Esther Fragments of Cave 4," in *Revue de Qumrân* 19, no. 3 (75) (June 2000).

Dever, W.G. *What Did the Biblical Writers Know & When Did They Know It?* Grand Rapids: Eerdmans, 2001.

Dines, Jennifer Mary, and Michael Anthony Knibb. *The Septuagint.* New York: T&T Clark, 2004.

Donoughue, Carol. *The Mystery of the Hieroglyphs: The Story of the Rosetta Stone and the Race to Decipher Egyptian Hieroglyphs.* Oxford: Oxford University Press, 2002.

Doudna, G. "Dating the Scrolls on the Basis of Radiocarbon Analysis," in Peter W. Flint and James C. VanderKam, eds. *Dead Sea Scrolls After Fifty Years*, Vol. 1. Leiden: Brill, 1999.

Eisenman, Robert H., and James M. Robinson. *A Facsimile Edition of the Dead Sea Scrolls.* Washington, DC: Biblical Archaeology Society, 1992.

Eisenman, Robert H., and Michael O. Wise. *The Dead Sea Scrolls Uncovered: The First Complete Translation and Interpretation of 50 Key Documents Withheld for over 35 Years.* Rockport: Element, 1992.

Evans, Craig A. *Ancient Texts for New Testament Studies: A Guide to the Background Literature.* Grand Rapids: Baker Academic, 2005.

Finkelstein, I., and N.A. Silberman. *The Bible Unearthed: Archaeology's New Vision of Ancient Israel and the Origins of Its Sacred Texts.* New York: Free Press, 2001.

Freeman, Philip. *Alexander the Great.* New York: Simon & Schuster, 2011.

Golden, Peter B. *Central Asia in World History.* New York: Oxford University Press, 2011.

Green, Peter. *Alexander of Macedon, 356–323 B.C.: A Historical Biography.* Berkeley: University of California Press, 1991.

Hallo, William W., and K. Lawson Younger, Jr., eds. *The Context of Scripture.* 3 vols. Leiden/Boston: Brill, 2003.

Hammond, N.G.L. *Alexander the Great: King, Commander and Statesman.* Bristol: Bristol Classical, 2001.

Harrison, R.K., and Martin G. Abegg, Jr. "Dead Sea Scrolls," in Merrill C. Tenney and Moises Silva, eds. *The Zondervan Pictorial Encyclopedia of the Bible.* 5 vols. Grand Rapids: Zondervan, 2009.

Heckel, Waldemar, and Lawrence A. Tritle, eds. *Alexander the Great: A New History.* Malden: Wiley-Blackwell, 2009.

Kitchen. K.A. *On the Reliability of the Old Testament.* Grand Rapids: Eerdmans, 2003.

Magness, Jodi. *The Archaeology of Qumran and the Dead Sea Scrolls.* Grand Rapids: Eerdmans, 2003.

Maier, Paul L. *Josephus, the Essential Writings.* Grand Rapids: Kregel Publications, 1988.

Marcos, Natalio Fernández, and Wilfred G.E. Watson. *The Septuagint in Context: Introduction to the Greek Version of the Bible.* Leiden: Brill, 2000.

Martínez, Florentino García. *The Texts of Qumran and the History of the Community: Proceedings of the Groningen Congress on the Dead Sea Scrolls (20-23 August 1989).* Paris: Gabalda, 1990.

Mazar, A. *Archaeology of the Land of the Bible: 10,000–586 BCE.* New York: Doubleday, 1992.

Metzger, Bruce M., and Herbert G. May, eds. *The New Oxford Annotated Bible with the Apocrypha, an Ecumenical Study Bible.* Revised Standard Version, Second Edition of the New Testament. New York: Oxford University, 1977.

Müller, Møgens. *The First Bible of the Church: A Plea for the Septuagint.* Sheffield: Sheffield Academic Press, 2009.

Murphy, Frederick James. *Early Judaism: The Exile to the Time of Jesus.* Grand Rapids: Baker Academic, 2010.

Niskanen, Paul. "Daniel's Portrait of Antiochus IV: Echoes of a Persian King," in *The Catholic Biblical Quarterly* 66, no. 3 (2004).

Parkinson, R.B., Whitfield Diffie, Mary Fischer, and R.S. Simpson. *Cracking Codes: The Rosetta Stone and Decipherment.* Berkeley: University of California Press, 1999.

Patrick, Sean. *Alexander the Great: The Macedonian Who Conquered the World.* Clearwater: Oculus, 2013.

Prevas, John. *Envy of the Gods: Alexander the Great's Ill-Fated Journey Across Asia.* Cambridge: Da Capo, 2005.

Price, J. Randall. *The Dead Sea Scrolls: The Discovery Heard Around the World.* Torrance: Rose, 2005.

Price, J. Randall, and H. Wayne House. *Zondervan Handbook of Biblical Archaeology: A Book by Book Guide to Archaeological Discoveries Related to the Bible.* Grand Rapids: Zondervan, 2018.

Ray, J.D. *The Rosetta Stone and the Rebirth of Ancient Egypt.* Cambridge: Harvard University Press, 2007.

Rhalfs, Alfred, and Robert Hanhart, eds. *Septuaginta.* Stuttgart: German Bible Society, 2007.

Roisman, Joseph. *Alexander the Great: Ancient and Modern Perspectives: Problems in European Civilization.* Lexington: Heath, 1995.

Salt, Henry, Jean-François Champollion, and Thomas Young. *Essay on Dr. Young's and M. Champollion's Phonetic System of Hieroglyphics: With Some Additional Discoveries.* London: Londman, Hurst, Rees, Orme, Brown & Green, 1823.

Scolnic, Benjamin. "Antiochus IV as the Scorned Prince in Dan 11:2," in *Vetus Testamentum* 62, no. 4 (2012).

_____. "The Milesian Connection: Dan 11:23 and Antiochus IV's Rise to Power," in *Vetus Testamentum* 63, no. 1 (2013).

Shutt, R. James H. "Letter of Aristeas," in David Noel Freedman, Gary A. Herion, David F. Graf, and John David Pleins, eds. *Anchor Bible Dictionary.* New York: Doubleday, 1996.

Silva, Moisés, and Karen Jobes. *Invitation to the Septuagint.* Grand Rapids: Baker Academic, 2005.

Stoneman, Richard. *Alexander the Great: A Life in Legend.* New Haven: Yale University Press, 2008.

Sáenz-Badillos, Angel. *A History of the Hebrew Language.* Trans. John Elwolde. Cambridge: Cambridge University Press, 1996.

Schiffman, Lawrence H. ed., *Archaeology and History in the Dead Sea Scrolls: The New York University Conference in Memory of Yigael Yadin,* JSOT/ASOR Monographs Vol. 2, *Journal for the Study of the Pseudepigrapha Supplement Series 8.* Sheffield: JSOT Press, 1990.

Schoville, Keith N. "Top Ten Archaeological Discoveries of the Twentieth Century Relating to the Biblical World," in *Stone-Campbell Journal* 4, no. 1 (2001).

Talmon, Shemarayahu. "Was the Book of Esther Known at Qumran?," in *Dead Sea Discoveries* 2, no. 3 (November 1995).

Tigchelaar, Eibert J.C. and Florentino García Martínez. *The Dead Sea Scrolls.* Study Edition. 2 Vols. Grand Rapids: Eerdmans, 1999.

Tov, Emanuel. "A List of the Texts from the Judean Desert," in Peter W. Flint and James C. VanderKam, eds. *The Dead Sea Scrolls After Fifty Years: A Comprehensive Assessment,* Vol. 2. Leiden: Brill, 1999.

VanderKam James C., and Peter W. Flint. *The Meaning of the Dead Sea Scrolls: Their Significance for Understanding the Bible, Judaism, Jesus, and Christianity.* San Francisco: Harper, 2002.

Vanderkam, James C., *The Dead Sea Scrolls Today.* Grand Rapids: Eerdmans, 2010.

Wace, Henry. *A Dictionary of Christian Biography: And Literature to the End of the Sixth Century A.D. with an Account of the Principal Sects and Heresies.* Peabody: Hendrickson, 1994.

Walbank, F.W. *The Hellenistic World.* New York: HarperCollins, 2017.

Yenne, Bill. *Alexander the Great: Lessons from History's Undefeated General.* New York: Palgrave Macmillan, 2010.

Zacharia, Katerina, ed. *Hellenisms: Culture, Identity, and Ethnicity from Antiquity to Modernity.* London: Routledge, 2016.

CHAPTER 9 SOURCES

Aufderheide, Arthur C. *The Scientific Study of Mummies*. Cambridge: Cambridge University Press, 2003.

Aviam, Mordechai. "Regionalism of Tombs and Burial Customs in the Galilee During the Hellenistic, Roman and Byzantine Periods," in Mordechai Aviam, ed. *Jews, Pagans and Christians in the Galilee: 25 Years of Archaeological Excavations and Surveys: Hellenistic to Byzantine Periods. Land of Galilee 1*. Rochester: University of Rochester Press, 2004.

Bagatti, Bellarmino, and Józef Tadeusz Milik. *Gli Scavi Del "Dominus Flevit": Monte Oliveto-Gerusalemme*. Vol. 2. Jerusalem: Tipografia dei PP. Francescani, 1958.

Bagshawe, Richard W. *Roman Roads. Shire Archaeology*. Buckinghamshire: Shire Publications, 2000.

Bahat, Dan. "Does the Holy Sepulchre Church Mark the Burial of Jesus?," in *Biblical Archaeology Review* 12, no. 3 (1986).

Barkay, Gabriele, and Amos Kloner. "Burial Caves North of Damascus Gate, Jerusalem," in *IEJ* 26 (1976).

Biddle, Martin. *The Tomb of Christ*. Stroud: Sutton, 1999.

Brisco, Thomas V., ed. *Holman Bible Atlas*. Nashville: Broadman & Holman, 1999.

Broshi, Magen. "Qumran and the Essenes: Purity and Pollution, Six Categories," in *Revue De Qumrân* 22, no. 3 (87) (2006).

Bruce, F.F. *Israel and The Nations*. Grand Rapids: Eerdmans, 1963.

Byers, Gary A., Scott D. Stripling, and Bryant G. Wood. "Excavations at Khirbet el-Maqatir: the 2009–2011 Seasons," in *Judea and Samaria Research Studies,* Vol. 25, no. 2 (2016).

Burns, Joshua Ezra. "Essene Sectarianism and Social Differentiation in Judaea after 70 C.E.," in *The Harvard Theological Review* 99, no. 3 (2006).

Cancik, Hubert, and Helmuth Schneider, eds. *Brill's New Pauly*. Antiquity Volumes Online. Transl. Christine F. Salazar and Francis G. Gentry. 22 Vols. Leiden: Brill, 2006.

Chamberlain, Gary Alan. *The Greek of the Septuagint: A Supplemental Lexicon*. Peabody: Hendrickson, 2011.

Corbo, Virgilio C. *Il Santo Sepolcro Di Gerusalemme, Aspetti Arceologici Dalle Origini Al Periodo Crociato. Parts I–III*. Jerusalem: Franciscan, 1982.

Cross, Frank Leslie, and Elizabeth A. Livingstone, eds. *The Oxford Dictionary of The Christian Church*. Oxford: Oxford University Press, 2005.

Davies, Hugh E.H. "Designing Roman Roads," in *Britannia* 29 (1998).

Eakins, J. Kenneth. "Herod's Fortress Palaces In Israel," in James McLemore, ed. *Biblical Illustrator* (Winter 1997).

Evans, Craig A. *Jesus and the Ossuaries: What Burial Practices Reveal About the Beginning of Christianity*. Waco: Baylor University Press, 2003.

_____. "The Family Buried Together Stays Together: On the Burial of the Executed in Family Tombs," in Craig A. Evans, ed. *The World of Jesus and the Early Church: Identity and Interpretation in Early Communities of Faith*. Peabody: Hendrickson, 2011.

Feder, Kenneth L. *Encyclopedia of Dubious Archaeology: From Atlantis to the Walam Olum*. Santa Barbara: Greenwood, 2010.

Flavius Josephus, *Antiquities of the Jews,* in *The New Complete Works of Josephus*: Revised and Expanded Edition, Transl. W. Whiston. Grand Rapids: Kregel Publications, 1999.

Foakes Jackson, F.J. *Josephus and the Jews: The Religion and History of the Jews as Explained by Flavius Josephus*. Grand Rapids: Baker Books, 1977.

Forbes, Robert J. *Studies in Ancient Technology,* Vol. 2. Leiden: Brill, 1993.

Geisler, Norman L., and Joseph M. Holden. *The Popular Handbook of Archaeology and the Bible*. Eugene: Harvest House, 2013.

_____. "Burials: Ancient Jewish," in David Noel Freedman, Gary A. Herion, David F. Graf, and John David Pleins. *Anchor Bible Dictionary*. New York: Doubleday, 1996.

Graves, David E., and D. Scott Stripling. "Re-Examination of the Location for the Ancient City of Livias," in *Levant* 43, no. 2 (2011).

Hachlili, Rachel. "Burial Practices at Qumran," in *Revue de Qumrân* 16, no. 2 (1993).

_____, and Ann E. Killebrew. "Jewish Funerary Customs during the Second Temple Period in Light of the Excavations at the Jericho Necropolis," in *PEQ* 115 (1983).

Hagen, Victor W. Von. *The Roads That Led to Rome.* New York: World Publishing, 1967.

Hallo, William W., and K. Lawson Younger, Jr., eds. *The Context of Scripture.* 3 vols. Leiden/Boston: Brill, 2003.

Hargreaves, G.H. "Road Planning Operations of Roman Surveyors," in BA dissertation. London: University College London, 1990.

Hays, J. Daniel, and Tremper Longman III. *Message of the Prophets: A Survey of the Prophetic and Apocalyptic Books of the Old Testament.* Grand Rapids: Zondervan, 2010.

Hirschfeld, Yizhar. *Qumran in Context: Reassessing the Archaeological Evidence.* Peabody: Hendrickson, 2004.

Josephus, Flavius. *The New Complete Works of Josephus.* Revised and Expanded Edition. Trans. William Whiston and Paul L. Maier. Grand Rapids: Kregel Publications, 1999.

Kelhoffer, James A. "Did John the Baptist Eat Like a Former Essene? Locust-Eating in the Ancient Near East and at Qumran," in *Dead Sea Discoveries* 11, no. 3 (2004).

Kelly, Robert L., and David Hurst Thomas. *Archaeology.* Boston: Cengage Learning, 2012.

Laurence, Ray. *The Roads of Roman Italy: Mobility and Cultural Change.* New York: Routledge, 1999.

Mare, W. Harold. "The Place of Christ's Crucifixion and Burial," in *Bible and Spade* 3, no. 2 (1974).

McRay, John. *Archaeology and the New Testament.* Grand Rapids, Baker Books, 1997.

McRay, John. "Tomb Typology and the Tomb of Jesus," in *Archaeology and the Biblical World* 2, no. 2 (1994).

Magness, Jodi. *The Holy Land Revealed* (Great Courses). Chantilly: The Teaching Company, 2010.

_____. *The Archaeology of Qumran and the Dead Sea Scrolls* (Studies in the Dead Sea Scrolls and Related Literature). Grand Rapids: Eerdmans, 2002.

_____. *Stone and Dung, Oil and Spit: Jewish Daily Life in the Time of Jesus.* Grand Rapids: Eerdmans, 2011.

Metzger, Bruce M., and Herbert G. May, eds. *The New Oxford Annotated Bible with the Apocrypha, an Ecumenical Study Bible.* Revised Standard Version, Second Edition of the New Testament. New York: Oxford University, 1977.

Murphy, Frederick James. *Early Judaism: The Exile to the Time of Jesus.* Grand Rapids: Baker Academic, 2010.

Murphy-O'Connor, Jerome. "Sites Associated with John the Baptist," in *Revue Biblique (1946–)* 112, no. 2 (2005).

Netzer, Ehud. "Herod's Building Projects: State Necessity or Personal Need?," in Lee Levine, ed., *The Jerusalem Cathedra.* Detroit: Wayne State University Press, 1981.

Quilici, Lorenzo. "Land Transport, Part 1: Roads and Bridges," in John Peter Oleson, ed. *The Oxford Handbook of Engineering and Technology in the Classical World.* Oxford: Oxford University Press, 2009.

Rahmani, L.Y. *A Catalogue of Jewish Ossuaries: In the Collections of the State of Israel.* Jerusalem: Israel Academy of Sciences and Humanities, 1994.

_____. "Ancient Jerusalem's Funerary Customs and Tombs: Part Four," in *The Biblical Archaeologist* 45, no. 2 (1982).

_____. "Jewish Rock-Cut Tombs in Jerusalem," in *Atiqot* 3 (1961).

Rebuffat, R. "Via Militaris," in *Latomus* 46 (1987).

Regev, E. "Family Burial, Family Structure, and the Urbanization of Herodian Jerusalem," in *PEQ* 136 (2004).

Rhalfs, Alfred, and Robert Hanhart, eds. *Septuaginta.* Stuttgart: German Bible Society, 2007.

Ritmeyer, Leen. "Quarrying and Transporting Stones for Herod's Temple Mount," in *Biblical Archaeology Review* (Nov/Dec 1989).

Rudolf, Wilhelm, and Karl Elliger, eds. *Biblia Hebraica Stuttgartensia (BHS).* Transl. Karl Elliger. Stuttgart: Deutsche Bibelgesellschaft, 2006.

Sabin, Philip, Hans van Wees, and Michael Whitby. *The Cambridge History of Greek and Roman Warfare: Volume 1, Greece, The Hellenistic World and the Rise of Rome.* Cambridge: Cambridge University Press, 2007.

Schwartz, Joshua. "Lessons from Inter-Communal Conflict During the Second Temple Period," in *Jewish Political Studies Review* 12, no. 3/4 (2000).

Seland, Torrey. "Saul of Tarsus and Early Zealotism Reading Gal 1,13-14 in Light of Philo's Writings," in *Biblica* 83, no. 4 (2002).

Singer, Samuel. *Lexikon der Sprichwörter des romanisch-germanischen Mittelalters.* Berlin: de Gruyter, 2000.

Smith, William, ed. *Dictionary of Greek and Roman Antiquities.* London: Murray, 1875.

Stager, Larry. "The Archaeology of the Family in Ancient Israel," in *Bulletin of the American Schools of Oriental Research* 260 (1985).

Thiele, E.R. *The Mysterious Numbers of the Hebrew Kings.* Revised Edition. Grand Rapids: Zondervan, 1994.

Ussishkin, David. "The Necropolis from the Time of the Kingdom of Judah at Silwan, Jerusalem," in *The Biblical Archaeologist* 33, no. 2 (May 1970).

Vermès, Géza, ed. *The Complete Dead Sea Scrolls in English.* New York: Allen Lane/Penguin Press, 1997.

Vörös, Győző. "Machaerus: The Golgotha of Saint John the Baptist," in *Revue Biblique (1946–)* 119, no. 2 (2012).

Wiseman, T.P. "Roman Republican Road-Building," in *Papers of the British School at Rome* 38 (1970).

Wood, Bryant G. "Jerusalem Report: Israeli Scholars Date Garden Tomb to the Israelite Monarchy," in *Bible and Spade* 11, no. 1 (1982).

Yizhar Hirschfeld *The Palestinian Dwelling in the Roman-Byzantine Period.* Jerusalem: Franciscan, 1995.

Zeitlin, Solomon. "The Essenes and Messianic Expectations. A Historical Study of the Sects and Ideas during the Second Jewish Commonwealth," in *The Jewish Quarterly Review* 45, no. 2 (1954).

CHAPTERS 10 AND 11 SOURCES

Aharoni, Y. *The Land of the Bible: A Historical Geography.* Revised Edition. Philadelphia: Westminster, 1980.

Ahlström, Gösta. *Who Were the Israelites?* Winona Lake: Eisenbrauns, 1986.

Albright, W.F. *Yahweh and the Gods of Canaan.* Winona Lake: Eisenbrauns, 1994.

Aldred, C. *Akhenaten, King of Egypt.* London: Thames & Hudson, 1988.

Allis, Oswald T. *The Old Testament: Its Claims and Critics.* Nutley: Presbyterian & Reformed, 1972.

Anati, Emmanuel. *The Mountain of God: Har Karkom.* New York: Rizzoli, 1986.

Archer, Gleason L. *A Survey of Old Testament Introduction.* Revised Edition. Chicago: Moody, 1976.

Archer, G.L. *Encyclopedia of Bible Difficulties.* Grand Rapids: Zondervan, 1982.

Avner, U. "Mazzebot Sites in the Negev and Sinai and Their Significance," in A. Biran et al., eds. *Biblical Archaeology Today.* Jerusalem: Israel Exploration Society, 1993.

Ayer, A.J. *Language, Truth and Logic.* New York: Dover, 1946.

Beek, M.A. *Atlas of Mesopotamia: A Survey of the History and Civilisation of Mesopotamia from the Stone Age to the Fall of Babylon.* New York: Thomas Nelson, 1962.

Ben-Tor, Amnon, ed. *The Archaeology of Ancient Israel.* New Haven: Yale, 1992.

Bierling, Neal. *Giving Goliath His Due: New Archaeological Light on the Philistines.* Grand Rapids: Eerdmans, 1992.

Bimson, John J. *Redating the Exodus and Conquest.* Sheffield: Almond Press, 1981.

Biran, Avraham. Interview (1996) in J. Randall Price, *The Stones Cry Out.* Eugene: Harvest House, 1997.

Breasted, J.H. *Ancient Records of Egypt: Vol. 2, The Eighteenth Dynasty*, Transl. and Revised. Chicago and Urbana: University of Illinois Press, 2001. Original edition, University of Chicago Press, 1906.

Briggs, P. *Testing the Factuality of the Conquest of Ai Narrative in the Book of Joshua.* Albuquerque: TSU Press, 2009; based on Briggs's PhD dissertation, Trinity Theological Seminary.

Bryan, Betsy M. *The Reign of Thutmose IV.* Baltimore: Johns Hopkins University, 1991.

Campbell, E.F. *The Chronology of the Amarna Letters.* Baltimore: Johns Hopkins University, 1964.

Collins, S. *Let My People Go: Using Historical Synchronisms to Identify the Pharaoh of the Exodus.* Albuquerque: TSU Press, 2005.

_____. "A Response to Bryant G. Wood's Critique of Collins's Northern Sodom Theory," in *Biblical Research Bulletin* VII.7 (2007).

_____. *The Defendable Faith: Lessons in Christian Apologetics.* Albuquerque: TSU Press, 2012.

_____. "Where Is Sodom? The Case for Tall el-Hammam," in *Biblical Archaeology Review* 39.2 (2013).

_____. "Tall el-Hammam Is *Still* Sodom: Critical Data-Sets Cast Serious Doubt on E.H. Merrill's Chronological Analysis," in *Biblical Research Bulletin* XIII.1 (2013).

_____. "Christian Contributions to Archaeology," in George T. Kurian and Mark A. Lamport, eds. *The Encyclopedia of Christian Education*, Vol. 1. Lanham: Rowman & Littlefield Publishers, 2015a.

_____. Personal communication with the chapter author. January 2015.

_____, Carroll M. Kobs, and Michael C. Luddeni. *The Tall al-Hammam Excavations,* Vol 1. Winona Lake: Eisenbrauns, 2015.

_____, and J.W. Oller, Jr. "Is the Bible a True Narrative Representation?," in *Biblical Research Bulletin* I.3 (2001). (A version of this article first appeared in the *Global Journal of Classical Theology,* Vol. 2, No. 2, August 2000. This version is revised and updated from the earlier version.)

_____, and Latayne C. Scott. *Discovering the City of Sodom.* New York: Simon & Schuster, 2013.

_____, and Phillip J. Silvia, eds. *The Kikkar Dialogues.* Albuquerque: TSU Press, 2019.

Craig, William Lane. *Reasonable Faith: Christian Truth and Apologetics.* Wheaton: Crossway Books, 2008.

Custance, Arthur C. *The Doorway Papers.* 10 Vols. Grand Rapids: Zondervan, 1975.

Darnell, J.C., and D. Darnell. "1994–95 Annual Report," in *The Luxor-Farshut Desert Road Project.* Chicago: Oriental Institute, University of Chicago, 1997.

Desroches-Noblecourt, C. "Le 'Bestiaire' Symbolique du Libérateur Ahmosis," in *Festschrift W. Westenforf.* Gottingen: Gottingen University, 1984.

Dever, William G. "From the End of the Early Bronze Age to the Beginning of the Middle Bronze Age," in J. Aviram et al., eds. *Biblical Archaeology Today*, 1985.

Dothan, T. *The Philistines and Their Material Culture.* Jerusalem: Israel Exploration Society, 1982.

Dothan, T. "The Arrival of the Sea Peoples: Cultural Diversity in Early Iron Age Canaan," in S. Gitin and W.G. Dever, eds. *Recent Excavations in Israel: Studies in Iron Age Archaeology. The Annual of the ASOR* 49. Winona Lake: ASOR, 1989.

Finegan, J. *Light from the Ancient Past.* Princeton: Princeton University, 1974.

_____. *Myth and Mystery: An Introduction to the Pagan Religions of the Biblical World.* Grand Rapids: Baker Books, 1989.

Finkelstein, I. *The Archaeology of the Israelite Settlement.* Jerusalem: Israel Exploration Society, 1988.

_____, and Nadav Na'aman. *From Nomadism to Monarchy.* Jerusalem: Israel Exploration Society, 1994.

Giles, F.J. *The Amarna Age: Western Asia, ACES 5.* Warminster: Aris and Phillips, 1997.

Goedicke, Hans. *The Battle of Megiddo.* Baltimore: Halgo, 2000.

Graves, David E. *Key Facts for the Location of Sodom: Navigating the Maze of Arguments.* Moncton, NB: D.E. Graves, 2014.

Grimal, N. *A History of Ancient Egypt.* Oxford: Oxford University, 1992.

Hansen, David G. *Evidence for Fortifications at Late Bronze I and IIA Locations in Palestine.* PhD dissertation. Newburgh: Trinity Theological Seminary, 2000.

Harrison, R.K. *Introduction to the Old Testament*. Grand Rapids: Eerdmans, 1969.

_____. *Old Testament Times*. Grand Rapids: Eerdmans, 1970.

Hayes, W.C. "Egypt: Internal Affairs from Tuthmosis I to the Death of Amenophis III," in *Cambridge Ancient History*, Vol. II.1. Cambridge: Cambridge University, 1973.

Hoerth, A.J. *Archaeology and the Old Testament*. Grand Rapids: Baker Academic, 1998.

Hoerth, Mattingly, and Edwin Yamauchi, eds. *Peoples of the Old Testament World*. Grand Rapids: Baker Books, 1994.

Hoffmeier, J.K. "Current Issues in Archaeology: The Recently Discovered Tel Dan Inscription: Controversy and Confirmation," in *Archaeology in the Biblical World*, 3:1 (1995).

Hoffmeier, James K. *Israel in Egypt: The Evidence for the Authenticity of the Exodus Tradition*. Oxford: Oxford University Press, 1996.

Holden, Joseph M., and Norman Geisler. *The Popular Handbook of Archaeology and the Bible*. Eugene: Harvest House, 2013.

Irvin, Dorothy. "The Joseph and Moses Narratives," in J.H. Hayes and J.M. Miller, eds. *Israelite and Judaea History*. Philadelphia: Westminster, 1977.

Jacobsen, T. *The Treasures of Darkness: A History of Mesopotamian Religion*. New Haven: Yale University, 1976.

Janssen, J.M.A. *Oudheidkundige Mededelingen uit het Rijksmuseum van Oudheden te Leiden* 31 (1950).

Kikawada, Isaac M., and Arthur Quinn. *Before Abraham Was: The Unity of Genesis 1–11*. Nashville: Abingdon Press, 1985.

Kempenski, A. et al., eds. *The Architecture of Ancient Israel*. Jerusalem: Israel Exploration Society, 1992.

Kenyon, Kathleen M. *Digging Up Jericho*. New York: Praeger, 1957.

_____. *Amorites and Canaanites*. Oxford: Oxford University, 1966.

_____. *Excavations at Jericho*, Vol. 3. Jerusalem: British School of Archaeology, 1981.

_____. *Ancient Orient and Old Testament*. Chicago: InterVarsity Press, 1966.

_____. *Ramesside Inscriptions*. Oxford: Oxford University, 1979.

_____. "Shishak's Military Campaign in Israel Confirmed," in *Biblical Archaeology Review* 15:3 (1989).

_____. "Where Did Solomon's Gold Go?," in *Biblical Archaeology Review* 15:3 (1989).

_____. "The Patriarchal Age: Myth or History?," in *Biblical Archaeology Review* 21:2. 1995.

_____. "A Possible Mention of David in the Late Tenth Century BCE, and Deity Dod as Dead as the Dodo?," in *Journal for the Study of the Old Testament* 76 (1997).

_____. "The Patriarchs Revisited: A Reply to Dr. Ronald S. Hendel," in *Near East Archaeological Society Bulletin* 43 (1998).

_____. *On the Reliability of the Old Testament*. Grand Rapids: Eerdmans, 2003.

_____, and P.J.N. Lawrence. *Treaty, Law and Covenant in the Ancient Near East*, Vol. 3. Wiesbaden: Harrassowitz Verlag, 2012.

Kozloff, A., and B. Bryan. *Egypt's Dazzling Sun: Amenhotep III and His World*. Cleveland: Cleveland Museum of Art and Indiana University, 1992.

Krahmalkov, Charles R. "Exodus Itinerary Confirmed by Egyptian Evidence" *Biblical Archaeology Review* 20.5 (1994).

Lemaire, A. "'House of David' Restored in Moabite Inscription," in *Biblical Archaeology Review* (May/June 1994, w/ reply Nov/Dec 1994).

Lemche, Niels Peter. *Prelude to Israel's Past*. Peabody: Hendrickson, 1998.

Leslie, John G. *Evaluation of the Noah Flood Account as a True Narrative Representation*. PhD dissertation, Trinity Southwest University, 2012.

Manley, B. *The Penguin Historical Atlas of Ancient Egypt*. London: Penguin, 1996.

Mazar, Amihai. *Excavations at Tell Qasile: Part 1, The Philistine Sanctuary: Architecture and Cult Objects. Qedem 12*. Jerusalem: Israel Exploration Society, 1980.

_____. *Excavations at Tell Qasile: Part 2, The Philistine Sanctuary: Various Finds, the Pottery, Conclusions, Appendices. Qedem 20.* Jerusalem: Israel Exploration Society, 1985.

_____. *Archaeology and the Land of the Bible 10,000–586 BCE.* New York: Doubleday, 1990.

McDowell, Josh. *Daniel in the Critics' Den.* San Bernardino: Campus Crusade, 1979.

McLaughlin, Amanda K. *The Battle of Ai and the Siege of Megiddo: Using Legal Theory to Evaluate Conclusions of Historicity in Bronze Age Battle Accounts of the Near East.* PhD dissertation, Trinity Theological Seminary, 2005.

Mellaart, J. *The Chalcolithic and Early Bronze Ages in the Near East and Anatolia.* Beirut: Beirut University, 1966.

Mendenhall, G.E. "Law and Covenant in Israel and the Ancient Near East," in *Biblical Archaeologist* 17 (1954).

Merrill, Eugene H. "The Lifespans of the EB–MB Patriarchs: A Hermeneutical and Historical Conundrum," in *Southwestern Journal of Theology* 57.2 (Spring 2015).

Millard, Alan R. "Israelite and Aramea history in Light of Inscriptions," in *Tyndale Bulletin* 41 (1990).

Millard, Alan R. "Story, History, and Theology," in A.R. Millard, J.K. Hoffmeier, and D.W. Baker, eds. *Faith, Tradition, and History.* Winona Lake: Eisenbrauns, 1994.

Moran, W.L. *The Amarna Letters.* Baltimore: Johns Hopkins University, 1992.

Murray, M.A. *The Splendor That Was Egypt.* New York: Praeger, 1969.

Naveh, J. *Early History of the Alphabet.* Second Revised Edition. Jerusalem: Magnes, The Hebrew University, 1987.

Nibbi, A., ed. *The Archaeology, Geography and History of the Egyptian Delta During the Pharaonic Period.* Oxford: Oxford University, 1986.

Oates, J. *Babylon.* London: Thames & Hudson, 1986.

Oller Jr., J.W., and S. Collins. "The Logic of True Narrative Representations," in *Biblical Research Bulletin* I.2 (2001). (A version of this article first appeared in the *Global Journal of Classical Theology*, Vol. 2, No. 2, August 2000. This version is revised and updated from the earlier version.)

Olson, Craig. *A Proposal for a Symbolic Interpretation of the Patriarchal Lifespans.* PhD dissertation, Dallas Theological Seminary, 2017.

Olson, Craig. "How Old Was Father Abraham? A Reexamination of Patriarchal Lifespans," in S. Collins, ed. *The Kikkar Dialogues.* Albuquerque: TSU Press 2019.

Oren, E., and I. Gilead. "Chalcolithic Sites in Northeastern Sinai," in *Tel Aviv* 8 (1981).

Pederson, J. *Israel: Its Life and Culture.* 2 Vols. New York: Oxford University Press, 1926-40.

Pritchard, J.B. *Ancient Near Eastern Texts Relating to the Old Testament.* Princeton: Princeton University, 1955.

_____. *The Ancient Near East in Pictures, Relating to the Old Testament.* Princeton: Princeton University, 1969.

_____. *The Ancient Near East: An Anthology of Texts and Pictures.* Princeton: Princeton University, 1973.

Quirke, S. *Ancient Egyptian Religion.* London: British Museum, 1992.

Rainey, Anson. "The 'House of David' and the House of the Deconstructionists," in *Biblical Archaeology Review* 20:6 (1994).

Redford, Donald B. *History and Chronology of the Eighteenth Dynasty: Seven Studies.* Toronto: University of Toronto, 1967.

Redford, Donald B. *Akhenaten: The Heretic King.* Princeton: Princeton University, 1984.

_____. *Egypt, Canaan, and Israel in Ancient Times.* Princeton: Princeton University, 1992.

_____. *The Wars in Syria and Palestine of Thutmose III: Culture and History of the Ancient Near East* 16. Boston: Brill, 2003.

Richard, Suzanne. "Toward a Consensus of Opinion on the End of the Early Bronze Age in Palestine-Transjordan," in *Bulletin of the American Schools of Oriental Research* 237 (1980).

Roaf, M. *Cultural Atlas of Mesopotamia and the Ancient Near East.* Oxford: Oxford University, 1990.

Roberts, J.J. *The Earliest Semitic Pantheon.* Baltimore: Johns Hopkins University, 1972.

Schulman, A.R. "Chariots, Chariotry and the Hyksos," in *Journal of the Society for the Study of Egyptian Antiquities* 10 (1980).

Shaw, I., and P. Nicholson, eds. *The Dictionary of Ancient Egypt*. London: British Museum, 1995.

Silvia, Phillip J. *The Middle Bronze Age Civilization-Ending Destruction of the Middle Ghor*. PhD dissertation. Albuquerque: Trinity Southwest University, 2015.

_____. *The Destruction of Sodom: What We Have Learned from Tall el-Hammam and Its Neighbors*. Albuquerque: TSU Press, 2016.

Simons, J., *Handbook for the Study of Topographical Lists Relating to Western Asia*. Leiden: Brill, 1937.

Stern, E., ed. *The New Encyclopedia of Archaeological Excavations in the Holy Land*. New York: Simon & Schuster, 1993.

Thompson, Thomas L. *The Historicity of the Patriarchal Narratives*. Berlin: de Gruyer, 1974.

Thomsen, M.L. *The Sumerian Language*, Vol. 10, in *Copenhagen Studies in Assyriology*. Copenhagen: Academic, 1984.

Valbelle, D. *Les Neufs Arcs*. Paris: Sorbonne, 1990.

Van Seters, John. "The Plagues of Egypt: Ancient Tradition or Literary Invention?," in *Zeitschrift für die Alttestamentliche Wissenshaft* 98 (1986).

Waltke, B.K. "Palestinian Artifactual Evidence Supporting the Early Date for the Exodus," in *Bibliotheca Sacra* 129 (1972).

Waterhouse, S.D. "Who Are the Habiru of the Amarna Letters?," in *Journal of the Adventist Theological Society* 12/1 (2001).

White, J.E.M. *Ancient Egypt: Its Culture and History*. New York: Dover, 1970.

Wilson, R.D. *A Scientific Investigation of the Old Testament*. Chicago: Moody, 1959.

Wiseman, D.J., ed. *Peoples of Old Testament Times*. London: Oxford University, 1973.

Wood, Bryant G. "Did the Israelites Conquer Jericho?," in *Biblical Archaeology Review* 16.2 (1990).

_____. "The Walls of Jericho," in *Bible and Spade* 12.2 (1999).

_____. "The Search for Joshua's Ai: Excavations at Kh. el-Maqatir," in *Bible and Spade* 12.1 (1999).

Wood, L. and D.E. O'Brien. *A Survey of Israel's History*. Grand Rapids: Zondervan, 1986.

Wright, G.E. *Biblical Archaeology*. Revised Edition. Philadelphia: Westminster, 1962.

Yadin, Yigael. *The Art of Warfare in Biblical Lands*. Transl. M. Pearlman. Jerusalem: International Publishing, 1963.

INDEXES

INDEX OF BREAKOUTS

INDEX OF FIGURES

Index of Maps

Notes

Note: There are no endnotes for chapters 1-9. The resources used for those chapters are listed in the Bibliography section beginning on page 361.

CHAPTER 10—ARCHAEOLOGY AND THE BIBLE

1. Collins, Steven, *The Defendable Faith: Lessons in Christian Apologetics* (Albuquerque: TSU Press, 2012), 309-10.

2. Millard, Alan R., "Story, History, and Theology," in A.R. Millard, J.K. Hoffmeier, and D.W. Baker, eds., *Faith, Tradition, and History* (Winona Lake: Eisenbrauns, 1994), 63-64.

3. Kitchen, Kenneth A. *On the Reliability of the Old Testament* (Grand Rapids: Eerdmans, 2003), 48.

4. Collins, *The Defendable Faith,* 215.

5. Hoffmeier, James K, *Israel in Egypt: The Evidence for the Authenticity of the Exodus Tradition* (New Oxford: Oxford University Press, 1996), 40.

6. See Oller, Jr., J.W., and Steven Collins, "The Logic of True Narrative Representations," in *Biblical Research Bulletin* I.2. 2001.

7. Collins, *The Defendable Faith,* 216.

8. Millard, Alan R. "Israelite and Aramean History in Light of Inscriptions," in *Tyndale Bulletin* 41 (1990), 275.

9. Collins, Steven, Carroll M. Kobs, and Michael C. Luddeni. *The Tall al-Hammam Excavations,* Volume 1 (Winona Lake: Eisenbrauns, 2015), 59.

10. Holden, Joseph M. and Norman Geisler, *The Popular Handbook of Archaeology and the Bible* (Eugene: Harvest House, 2013), 200–01.

11. Thompson, Thomas L., *The Historicity of the Patriarchal Narratives* (Berlin: de Gruyer, 1974), 328-29.

12. Irvin, Dorothy, "The Joseph and Moses Narratives," in J.H. Hayes and J.M. Miller, eds., *Israelite and Judaea History* (Philadelphia: Westminster, 1977), 212.

13. Van Seters, John, "The Plagues of Egypt: Ancient Tradition or Literary Invention?," in *Zeitschrift für die Alttestamentliche Wissenshaft* 98 (1986), 38.

14. Ahlström, Gösta, *Who Were the Israelites?* (Winona Lake: Eisenbrauns, 1986), 46.

15. Finkelstein, Israel and Nadav Na'aman, *From Nomadism to Monarchy* (Jerusalem: Israel Exploration Society, 1994), 13.

16. Lemche, Niels Peter, *Prelude to Israel's Past* (Peabody: Hendrickson, 1998), 39.

17. Kitchen, *On the Reliability of the Old Testament,* 500.

18. Collins, Steven, "Has Archaeology Gone Overboard in Throwing Out the Bible?," in *The Ancient Near East Today* (American Schools of Oriental Research), accessed online ASOR.org. October 15, 2013.

19. Collins, "Has Archaeology Gone Overboard in Throwing Out the Bible?"

20. Kitchen, *On the Reliability of the Old Testament,* 172.

CHAPTER 11—ARCHAEOLOGICAL DISCOVERIES SUPPORTING THE AUTHENTICITY OF THE BIBLE

1. Collins, *The Defendable Faith: Lessons in Christian Apologetics* (Albuquerque: TSU Press, 2012), 217-18.

2. Collins, *The Defendable Faith,* 229.

3. Kitchen, *On the Reliability of the Old Testament* (Grand Rapids: Eerdmans, 2003), 372.

4. Kikawada, Isaac M., and Arthur Quinn, *Before Abraham Was: The Unity of Genesis 1–11* (Nashville: Abingdon Press, 1985), 69.

5. See Merrill, Eugene H., "The Lifespans of the EB–MB Patriarchs: A Hermeneutical and Historical Conundrum," in *Southwestern Journal of Theology* 57.2 (Spring 2015), 267-80.

6. Kitchen, *On the Reliability of the Old Testament*, 351-52; Collins, Steven, "Tall el-Hammam Is *Still* Sodom: Critical Data-Sets Cast Serious Doubt on E.H. Merrill's Chronological Analysis," in *Biblical Research Bulletin* XIII.1. 2013c; see Olson, Craig, *A Proposal for a Symbolic Interpretation of the Patriarchal Lifespans*, PhD dissertation, Dallas Theological Seminary (2017); see Olson, Craig, "How Old Was Father Abraham? A Reexamination of Patriarchal Lifespans," in Steven Collins, ed., *The Kikkar Dialogues* (Albuquerque: TSU Press 2019).

7. Kitchen, *On the Reliability of the Old Testament*, 351-52; Janssen, J.M.A., *Oudheidkundige Mededelingen uit het Rijksmuseum van Oudheden te Leiden* 31 (1950), 33-41.

8. Collins, *The Defendable Faith*, 233.

9. Leslie, John G., *Evaluation of the Noah Flood Account as a True Narrative Representation*. PhD dissertation, Trinity Southwest University (2012), 130, 192, 262, 264.

10. Collins, *The Defendable Faith*, 233-34.

11. Aharoni, Y., *The Land of the Bible: A Historical Geography*, rev. ed. (Philadelphia: Westminster Press, 1980), 134-35; Ben-Tor, Amnon, ed., *The Archaeology of Ancient Israel* (New Haven: Yale, 1992), 40-80, 81-125; Mazar, Amihai, *Archaeology and the Land of the Bible 10,000–586 BCE.* (New York: Doubleday, 1990), 59-89, 91-143.

12. Kempenski, A., et al., eds., *The Architecture of Ancient Israel* (Jerusalem: Israel Exploration Society, 1992), 51-2; Mellaart, J., *The Chalcolithic and Early Bronze Ages in the Near East and Anatolia* (Beirut: Beirut University, 1966), 9-57; Oren, E., and I. Gilead, "Chalcolithic Sites in Northeastern Sinai," in *Tel Aviv* 8 (1981), 25-44.

13. Collins, *The Defendable Faith*, 234.

14. Collins, *The Defendable Faith*, 219.

15. Hoerth, A.J., *Archaeology and the Old Testament* (Grand Rapids: Baker Academic, 1998), 31-74; Manley, B., *The Penguin Historical Atlas of Ancient Egypt* (London: Penguin, 1996), 72-89; Oates, J., *Babylon* (London: Thames & Hudson, 1986), 9-59; Thomsen, M.L., "The Sumerian Language," Vol. 10, in *Copenhagen Studies in Assyriology* (Copenhagen: Academic, 1984), 19-33.

16. Kitchen, *On the Reliability of the Old Testament*, 316-18.

17. Beek, M.A., *Atlas of Mesopotamia: A Survey of the History and Civilisation of Mesopotamia from the Stone Age to the Fall of Babylon* (New York: T. Nelson, 1962), 138; Ben-Tor, *The Archaeology of Ancient Israel*, 126-58; Finegan, J., *Myth and Mystery: An Introduction to the Pagan Religions of the Biblical World* (Grand Rapids: Baker Books, 1989), 19-38; see Jacobsen, T. *The Treasures of Darkness: A History of Mesopotamian Religion* (New Haven: Yale University, 1976) and Roberts, J.J., *The Earliest Semitic Pantheon* (Baltimore: Johns Hopkins University, 1972).

18. Collins, *The Defendable Faith,* 235; see Ben-Tor, *The Archaeology of Ancient Israel*, 81-125; Mazar, Amihai, *Archaeology and the Land of the Bible 10,000–586 BCE,* 141-43, 151-71; Richard, Suzanne, "Toward a Consensus of Opinion on the End of the Early Bronze Age in Palestine-Transjordan," in *Bulletin of the American Schools of Oriental Research* 237 (1980), 5-34.

19. See Dever, William G., "From the End of the Early Bronze Age to the Beginning of the Middle Bronze Age," in J. Aviram et al., eds., *Biblical Archaeology Today* (1985); Mazar, *Archaeology and the Land of the Bible 10,000–586 BCE*, 141-43, 151-71.

20. Holden and Geisler, *The Popular Handbook of Archaeology and the Bible*, 219.

21. Collins, *The Defendable Faith,* 236.

22. Collins, Steven, "Where Is Sodom? The Case for Tall el-Hammam," in *Biblical Archaeology Review* 39.2 (2013). 70-71; see also Collins, *The Defendable Faith*, 236-37; Collins and Scott, *Discovering the City of Sodom*; Collins, Kobs and Luddeni. *The Tall al-Hammam Excavations*; Collins and Silvia, eds. *The Kikkar Dialogues.*

23. Collins, "Tall el-Hammam Is *Still* Sodom: Critical Data-Sets Cast Serious Doubt on E.H. Merrill's Chronological Analysis," 14.

24. Silvia, Phillip J., *The Middle Bronze Age Civilization-Ending Destruction of the Middle Ghor.* PhD dissertation (Albuquerque: Trinity Southwest University, 2015), 187-88; Silvia, Phillip J., *The Destruction of Sodom: What We Have Learned from Tall el-Hammam and Its Neighbors* (Albuquerque: TSU Press, 2016), 171.

25. For a detailed account see Collins and Scott, *Discovering the City of Sodom.*

26. Kitchen, *On the Reliability of the Old Testament,* 283ff; Kitchen, K.A., and P.J.N. Lawrence, *Treaty, Law and Covenant in the Ancient Near East*, Vol. 3 (Wiesbaden: Harrassowitz Verlag, 2012), 31-74.

27. Kitchen, Kenneth A., *Ancient Orient and Old Testament* (Chicago: InterVarsity Press, 1966), 90-102; Kitchen, *On the Reliability of the Old Testament,* 283ff; see also Kitchen, Kenneth A. "The Patriarchal Age: Myth or History?" *Biblical Archaeology Review* 21:2 (1995); Kitchen, Kenneth A. "The Patriarchs Revisited: A Reply to Dr. Ronald S. Hendel," *Near East Archaeological Society Bulletin* 43 (1998); Kitchen, K.A. and P.J.N. Lawrence, *Treaty, Law and Covenant in the Ancient Near East*, Vol. 3 (Wiesbaden: Harrassowitz Verlag, 2012), 31-74; cf. Mendenhall, G.E., "Law and Covenant in Israel and the Ancient Near East," in *Biblical Archaeologist* 17 (1954), 26-46, 50-76.

28. Kitchen, *On the Reliability of the Old Testament*, 323.

29. Ben-Tor, *The Archaeology of Ancient Israel*, 159-210; Mazar, *Archaeology and the Land of the Bible 10,000–586 BCE*, 174-226.

30. Kitchen, *On the Reliability of the Old Testament*, 341-42.

31. Albright, W.F., *Yahweh and the Gods of Canaan* (Winona Lake: Eisenbrauns, 1994), 53-152; Avner, U., "Mazzebot Sites in the Negev and Sinai and Their Significance," in A. Biran et al., eds., *Biblical Archaeology Today* (Jerusalem: Israel Exploration Society, 1993), 166-81; Ben-Tor, *The Archaeology of Ancient Israel*, 159-210; Finegan, J., *Myth and Mystery: An Introduction to the Pagan Religions of the Biblical World* (Grand Rapids: Baker Books, 1989), 119-54; Mazar, *Archaeology and the Land of the Bible 10,000–586 BCE*, 174-226.

32. Ben-Tor, *The Archaeology of Ancient Israel*, 179; Lemche, Niels Peter, *Prelude to Israel's Past* (Peabody: Hendrickson, 1998), 42, 119-21; Manley, B., *The Penguin Historical Atlas of Ancient Egypt* (London: Penguin, 1996), 39-41; Mazar, *Archaeology and the Land of the Bible 10,000–586 BCE*, 191-92.

33. Collins, Steven, *Let My People Go: Using Historical Synchronisms to Identify the Pharaoh of the Exodus* (Albuquerque: TSU Press, 2005), 34.

34. Collins, *The Defendable Faith*, 238.

35. Boyer, G. *ARMT*, VIII, No. 10, lines 1-4, in A. Parrot and G. Dossin, eds., *Archives Royales de Mari, transcrites et traduites* (1958), 23; Kitchen, *On the Reliability of the Old Testament*, 52-53, 344ff; see also Kitchen, "The Patriarchal Age: Myth or History?"; Kitchen, "The Patriarchs Revisited: A Reply to Dr. Ronald S. Hendel."

36. Manley, *The Penguin Historical Atlas of Ancient Egypt*, 39-41; Schulman, A.R., "Chariots, Chariotry and the Hyksos," in *Journal of the Society for the Study of Egyptian Antiquities* 10 (1980), 105-53; Shaw, I., and P. Nicholson, eds., *The Dictionary of Ancient Egypt* (London: British Museum, 1995), 63-64.

37. See Desroches-Noblecourt, C., "Le 'Bestiaire' Symbolique du Libérateur Ahmosis," in *Festschrift W. Westenforf* (Gottingen: Gottingen University, 1984); Grimal, N., *A History of Ancient Egypt* (Oxford: Oxford University, 1992), 193-202; Murray, M.A., *The Splendor That Was Egypt* (New York: Praeger, 1969), 29-30; Shaw and Nicholson, eds., *The Dictionary of Ancient Egypt*, 18-19; White, J.E.M., *Ancient Egypt: Its Culture and History* (New York: Dover, 1970), 160-65; see also Collins, *Let My People Go*.

38. Grimal, *A History of Ancient Egypt*, 199-292; White, *Ancient Egypt: Its Culture and History*, 164-68.

39. Collins, *Let My People Go*, 34-45.

40. Collins, *Let My People Go*, 132; Grimal, *A History of Ancient Egypt*, 199-292; Shaw and Nicholson, eds., *The Dictionary of Ancient Egypt*, 41; see also Hayes, W.C., "Egypt: Internal Affairs from Tuthmosis I to the Death of Amenophis III," in *Cambridge Ancient History*, Vol. II.1. (Cambridge: Cambridge University, 1973); Nibbi, A., ed., *The Archaeology, Geography and History of the Egyptian Delta During the Pharaonic Period* (Oxford: Oxford

University, 1986); Redford, Donald B., *History and Chronology of the Eighteenth Dynasty: Seven Studies* (Toronto: University of Toronto, 1967); Roaf, M., *Cultural Atlas of Mesopotamia and the Ancient Near East* (Oxford: Oxford University, 1990).

41. Kitchen, *Ancient Orient and Old Testament*, 90-102; Kitchen, *On the Reliability of the Old Testament*, 283ff; Kitchen, "The Patriarchal Age: Myth or History?"

42. Kitchen, *On the Reliability of the Old Testament*, 287-88.

43. Collins, *Let My People Go*, 132.

44. Bryan, Betsy M. *The Reign of Thutmose IV* (Baltimore: Johns Hopkins University, 1991); Grimal, *A History of Ancient Egypt*, 199-292; Hayes, "Egypt: Internal Affairs from Tuthmosis I to the Death of Amenophis III,"; Nibbi, *The Archaeology, Geography and History of the Egyptian Delta During the Pharaonic Period*; Redford, Donald B., *Egypt, Canaan, and Israel in Ancient Times* (Princeton: Princeton University, 1992), 167-68, 192-213; Redford, *History and Chronology of the Eighteenth Dynasty: Seven Studies*; White, *Ancient Egypt: Its Culture and History*, 164-69.

45. Collins, *The Defendable Faith*, 240.

46. Bryan, *The Reign of Thutmose IV*; Hayes, "Egypt: Internal Affairs from Tuthmosis I to the Death of Amenophis III," 313-400; Pritchard, J.B., *The Ancient Near East in Pictures, Relating to the Old Testament* (Princeton: Princeton University, 1969), 249-50; see also Quirke, S., *Ancient Egyptian Religion* (London: British Museum, 1992).

47. Collins, *The Defendable Faith*, 241; see also Collins, *Let My People Go*.

48. Aharoni, Y., *The Land of the Bible: A Historical Geography*, rev. ed. (Philadelphia: Westminster, 1980), 169-76; Grimal, *A History of Ancient Egypt*, 199-292; Hayes, "Egypt: Internal Affairs from Tuthmosis I to the Death of Amenophis III," 313-416; Shaw and Nicholson. eds., *The Dictionary of Ancient Egypt*, 29; White, *Ancient Egypt: Its Culture and History*, 169-71.

49. Collins, *Let My People Go*, 129.

50. Finegan, *Light from the Ancient Past*, 148, 162-63, 165; Mazar, *Archaeology and the Land of the Bible 10,000–586 BCE*, 275-76; Stern, E., ed., *The New Encyclopedia of Archaeological Excavations in the Holy Land* (New York: Simon & Schuster, 1993), 1388-96.

51. See Anati, Emmanuel, *The Mountain of God: Har Karkom* (New York: Rizzoli, 1986); Hoerth, *Archaeology and the Old Testament*, 164-70; Pritchard, J.B., *Ancient Near Eastern Texts Relating to the Old Testament* (Princeton: Princeton University, 1955), 227-29, 254, 259; Pritchard, *The Ancient Near East in Pictures*, 295, 376, 385.

52. Kitchen, Kenneth A., *Ramesside Inscriptions* (Oxford: Oxford University, 1979); Krahmalkov, Charles R., "Exodus Itinerary

Confirmed by Egyptian Evidence," in *Biblical Archaeology Review* 20.5 (1994), 55-62; Pritchard, *Ancient Near Eastern Texts Relating to the Old Testament*, 242-43; see also Simons, J., *Handbook for the Study of Topographical Lists Relating to Western Asia* (Leiden: Brill, 1937).

53. See Darnell, J.C., and D. Darnell, "1994-95 Annual Report," in *The Luxor-Farshut Desert Road Project* (Chicago: Oriental Institute, University of Chicago, 1997); Mazar, *Archaeology and the Land of the Bible 10,000–586 BCE*, 275-76; Naveh, J., *Early History of the Alphabet* (Jerusalem: Magnes, 1987), 23-28; Stern, *The New Encyclopedia of Archaeological Excavations in the Holy Land*, 1388-96.

54. See Albright, W.F., *Yahweh and the Gods of Canaan* (Winona Lake: Eisenbrauns, 1994); Archer, Gleason L., *A Survey of Old Testament Introduction*, rev. ed. (Chicago: Moody, 1976); Harrison, R.K., *Old Testament Times* (Grand Rapids: Eerdmans, 1970), Kitchen, *Ancient Orient and Old Testament*; Pederson *Israel: Its Life and Culture*.

55. Mazar, *Archaeology and the Land of the Bible 10,000–586 BCE*, 275-76; Naveh, *Early History of the Alphabet*, 23-28.

56. Hoerth, Mattingly, and Edwin Yamauchi, eds., *Peoples of the Old Testament World* (Grand Rapids: Baker Books, 1994), 127-82; see Kenyon, Kathleen M., *Amorites and Canaanites* (Oxford: Oxford University, 1966); Mazar, *Archaeology and the Land of the Bible 10,000–586 BCE*, 232–291; Wiseman, D.J., ed., *Peoples of Old Testament Times* (London: Oxford University, 1973), 29-52, 100-133, 197-228.

57. Ben-Tor, *The Archaeology of Ancient Israel*, 211-57; Hoerth, *Archaeology and the Old Testament*, 216-19; Pritchard, J.B., *The Ancient Near East: An Anthology of Texts and Pictures* (Princeton: Princeton University, 1973), 262-77; Wright, G.E., *Biblical Archaeology*, rev. ed. (Philadelphia: Westminster, 1962), 38, 45-47.

58. Collins, *Let My People Go*, 76–77; see also Moran, W.L. *The Amarna Letters* (Baltimore: Johns Hopkins University, 1992), particularly EA 237, EA 244, EA 245, EA 246, EA 249, EA 250, EA 252, EA 253, EA 254, EA 255, EA 263, EA 280, EA 287, and EA 289; also see Waterhouse, S.D., "Who Are the Habiru of the Amarna Letters?," in *Journal of the Adventist Theological Society* 12/1 (2001), 31-42; Giles, F.J., *The Amarna Age: Western Asia, ACES 5* (Warminster: Aris and Phillips, 1997).

59. See Bryan, *The Reign of Thutmose IV*; Hayes, "Egypt: Internal Affairs from Tuthmosis I to the Death of Amenophis III"; Hoerth and Yamauchi, eds., *Peoples of the Old Testament World*, 127-82; see Kenyon, Kathleen M., *Amorites and Canaanites* (Oxford: Oxford University, 1966); Mazar, *Archaeology and the Land of the Bible 10,000–586 BCE*, 232-91; Redford, *History and Chronology of the Eighteenth Dynasty*; Wiseman, *Peoples of Old Testament Times*, 29-52, 100-133, 197-228.

60. Collins, *The Defendable Faith*, 239.

61. See details in Collins, *Let My People Go*; see also Grimal, *A History of Ancient Egypt*, 199-292; Hayes, "Egypt: Internal Affairs from Tuthmosis I to the Death of Amenophis III," 313-416; see Kozloff, A., and Bryan, B., *Egypt's Dazzling Sun: Amenhotep III and His World*. (Cleveland: Cleveland Museum of Art and Indiana University, 1992); see Redford, Donald B., *Akhenaten: The Heretic King* (Princeton: Princeton University, 1984); Shaw and Nicholson, eds., *The Dictionary of Ancient Egypt*, 20-21; White, *Ancient Egypt: Its Culture and History*, 169-75.

62. See Hansen, David G., *Evidence for Fortifications at Late Bronze I and IIA Locations in Palestine*, PhD dissertation (Newburgh: Trinity Theological Seminary, 2000).

63. Ben-Tor, *The Archaeology of Ancient Israel*, 217-18; Mazar, *Archaeology and the Land of the Bible 10,000–586 BCE*, 241-44.

64. Hoerth, *Archaeology and the Old Testament*, 209-10; see Kenyon, Kathleen M., *Digging Up Jericho* (New York: Praeger, 1957); see Kenyon, Kathleen M., *Excavations at Jericho*, Vol. 3 (Jerusalem: British School of Archaeology, 1981); Wood, Bryant G., "Did the Israelites Conquer Jericho?," in *Biblical Archaeology Review* 16.2 (1990), 44-58; Wood, Bryant G., "The Walls of Jericho" in *Bible and Spade* 12.2 (1999), 35-42.

65. Wood, Bryant G., "The Search for Joshua's Ai: Excavations at Kh. el-Maqatir," in *Bible and Spade* 12.1 (1999), 21-30; see Briggs, P., *Testing the Factuality of the Conquest of Ai Narrative in the Book of Joshua* (Albuquerque: TSU Press, 2009); based on Briggs's PhD dissertation (Trinity Theological Seminary); Ben-Tor, *The Archaeology of Ancient Israel*, 211-57.

66. Personal communication, January 2015; see also Briggs, *Testing the Factuality of the Conquest of Ai Narrative in the Book of Joshua*.

67. McLaughlin, Amanda K., *The Battle of Ai and the Siege of Megiddo: Using Legal Theory to Evaluate Conclusions of Historicity in Bronze Age Battle Accounts of the Near East*, PhD dissertation (Trinity Theological Seminary, 2005), 99-105.

68. McLaughlin 123; see also Yadin, Yigael, *The Art of Warfare in Biblical Lands*, trans. M. Pearlman (Jerusalem: International Publishing, 1963), 102; Goedicke, Hans, *The Battle of Megiddo* (Baltimore: Halgo, 2000), 25, 28; see Redford, Donald B., *The Wars in Syria and Palestine of Thutmose III: Culture and History of the Ancient Near East* 16 (Boston: Brill, 2003); Breasted, J.H., *Ancient Records of Egypt: Vol. 2, The Eighteenth Dynasty*, transl. revised (Chicago and Urbana: University of Illinois Press, 2001). Original edition, University of Chicago Press, 1906), 165, 178, 180.

69. Aldred, C., *Akhenaten, King of Egypt* (London: Thames & Hudson, 1988), 183-94; see Campbell, E.F., *The Chronology of the Amarna Letters* (Baltimore: Johns Hopkins University, 1964); Moran, W.L., *The Amarna Letters* (Baltimore: Johns Hopkins

University, 1992); Waltke, B.K., "Palestinian Artifactual Evidence Supporting the Early Date for the Exodus," in *Bibliotheca Sacra* 129 (1972); White, *Ancient Egypt: Its Culture and History*, 170-73.

70. Ben-Tor, *The Archaeology of Ancient Israel*, 258-301; Hoerth and Yamauchi, eds., *Peoples of the Old Testament World*, 271-83; see Kitchen, Kenneth A., *Ramesside Inscriptions* (Oxford: Oxford University, 1979); Mazar, *Archaeology and the Land of the Bible 10,000–586 BCE*, 287-323; Pritchard, *Ancient Near Eastern Texts Relating to the Old Testament*, 376-78; Shaw and Nicholson, eds., *The Dictionary of Ancient Egypt*, 203; see Valbelle, D., *Les Neufs Arcs* (Paris: Sorbonne, 1990).

71. Ben-Tor, *The Archaeology of Ancient Israel*, 258-301; see Bierling, Neal, *Giving Goliath His Due: New Archaeological Light on the Philistines* (Grand Rapids: Eerdmans, 1992); Dothan, Trudy, "The Arrival of the Sea Peoples: Cultural Diversity in Early Iron Age Canaan," in S. Gitin and W.G. Dever, eds., *Recent Excavations in Israel: Studies in Iron Age Archaeology. The Annual of the ASOR* 49 (Winona Lake: ASOR, 1989); Dothan, T., *The Philistines and Their Material Culture* (Jerusalem: Israel Exploration Society, 1982); Finkelstein, I., *The Archaeology of the Israelite Settlement* (Jerusalem: Israel Exploration Society, 1988); Kempenski, et al., *The Architecture of Ancient Israel*, 191-301; Mazar, *Archaeology and the Land of the Bible 10,000–586 BCE*, 295-363.

72. Bierling, *Giving Goliath His Due: New Archaeological Light on the Philistines*, 113-119; Mazar, Amihai, *Excavations at Tell Qasile: Part 1, The Philistine Sanctuary: Architecture and Cult Objects. Qedem 12* (Jerusalem: Israel Exploration Society, 1980); Mazar, A., *Excavations at Tell Qasile: Part 2, The Philistine Sanctuary: Various Finds, the Pottery, Conclusions, Appendices. Qedem 20* (Jerusalem: Israel Exploration Society, 1985).

73. Bierling, *Giving Goliath His Due: New Archaeological Light on the Philistines*, 71-76.

74. Kitchen, *On the Reliability of the Old Testament*, 98-107.

75. Biran, Avraham, interview (1996) in Randall Price, *The Stones Cry Out* (Eugene: Harvest House, 1997), 165-70; Hoffmeier, J.K., "Current Issues in Archaeology: The Recently Discovered Tel Dan Inscription: Controversy and Confirmation," in *Archaeology in the Biblical World* 3:1 (1995); Kitchen, Kenneth A., "A Possible Mention of David in the Late Tenth Century BCE, and Deity Dod as Dead as the Dodo?," in *Journal for the Study of the Old Testament* 76 (1997); Lemaire, A., "'House of David' Restored in Moabite Inscription," in *Biblical Archaeology Review* (May/June 1994, w/ reply Nov/Dec 1994); Rainey, Anson, "The 'House of David' and the House of the Deconstructionists," in *Biblical Archaeology Review* 20:6 (1994).

76. See Kitchen, Kenneth A., "Shishak's Military Campaign in Israel Confirmed," in *Biblical Archaeology Review* 15:3 (1989); Kitchen, Kenneth A., "Where Did Solomon's Gold Go?," in *Biblical Archaeology Review* 15:3 (1989).

77. Pritchard, *Ancient Near Eastern Texts Relating to the Old Testament*, 118, 263-64.

78. See Allis, Oswald T., *The Old Testament: Its Claims and Critics* (Nutley: Presbyterian & Reformed, 1972); Archer, *A Survey of Old Testament Introduction*.

79. See relevant sections in Archer, *A Survey of Old Testament Introduction*.

80. See McDowell, Josh, *Daniel in the Critics' Den* (San Bernardino: Campus Crusade, 1979).

81. See relevant sections of Harrison, *Introduction to the Old Testament*; Wilson, R.D., *A Scientific Investigation of the Old Testament* (Chicago: Moody, 1959); Wood, L., and D.E. O'Brien, *A Survey of Israel's History* (Grand Rapids: Zondervan, 1986).

82. Kitchen, *On the Reliability of the Old Testament*, xiv.

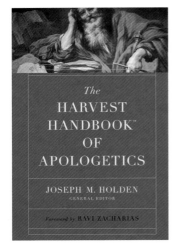

THE HARVEST HANDBOOK™ OF APOLOGETICS
Joseph M. Holden, General Editor

Scripture calls every believer—including you—to be prepared to defend the faith.

From the preacher to the churchgoer, the teacher to the student, *The Harvest Handbook™ of Apologetics* is the comprehensive resource all believers need in a world full of uncertainty and relentless criticism. This collection of well-reasoned, Scripture-based essays comes from respected Christian apologists and Bible scholars, including...

Norman L. Geisler	Walter C. Kaiser Jr.	John Warwick Montgomery
Stephen C. Meyer	Josh McDowell	Ron Rhodes
William A. Dembski	Randall Price	Gary R. Habermas
Edwin M. Yamauchi	Randy Alcorn	Ed Hindson

What is the evidence for Jesus's existence? How can you address the seeming contradictions in the Bible? How can you best explain the relationship between science and faith? You'll discover concise and convincing responses to these questions and many more.

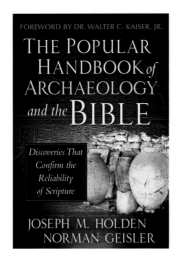

THE POPULAR HANDBOOK OF ARCHAEOLOGY AND THE BIBLE
Joseph M. Holden and Norman Geisler

From two leading Christian apologists, here is a fascinating survey of the most important Old and New Testament archaeological discoveries through the ages.

Biblical archaeology has always stirred excitement among believers and curiosity among unbelievers. The evidence dug up with a spade can speak volumes—and serve as a powerful testimony of the reliability of Scripture.

Norm Geisler and Joe Holden have put together an impressive array of finds that confirm the biblical people and events of ages past.

To learn more about Harvest House books and
to read sample chapters, visit our website:

www.harvesthousepublishers.com

HARVEST HOUSE PUBLISHERS
EUGENE, OREGON

TIMELINE

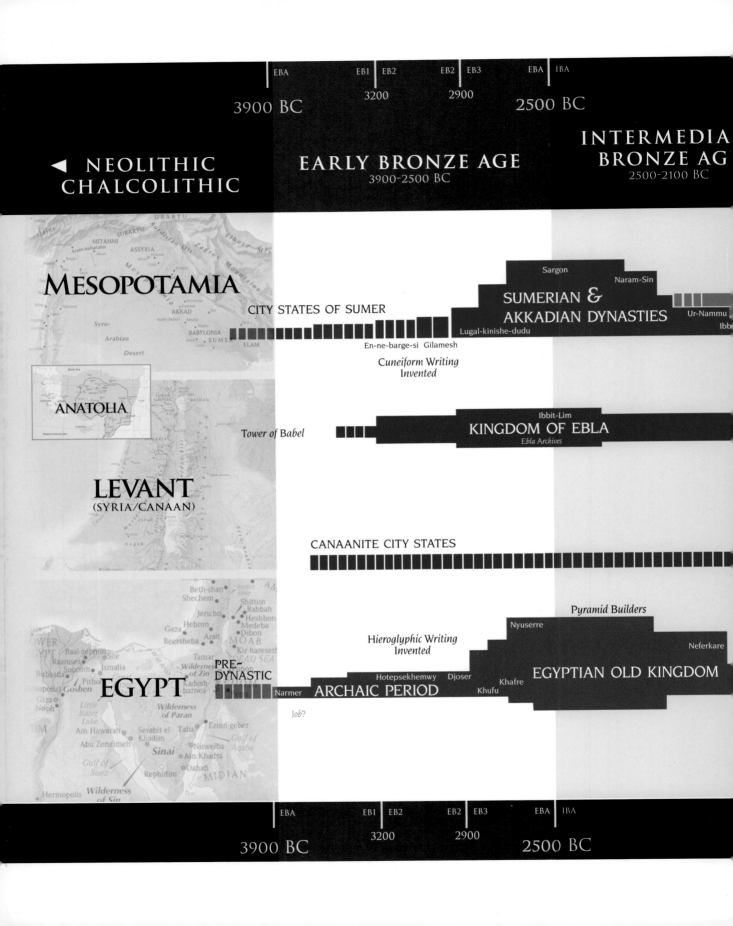

| EBA | | EB1 | EB2 | | EB2 | EB3 | | EBA | IBA |

3900 BC   3200   2900   2500 BC

◄ NEOLITHIC
CHALCOLITHIC

EARLY BRONZE AGE
3900-2500 BC

INTERMEDIA
BRONZE AG
2500-2100 BC

MESOPOTAMIA

CITY STATES OF SUMER

Sargon

Naram-Sin

SUMERIAN &
AKKADIAN DYNASTIES

Ur-Nammu

Lugal-kinishe-dudu

Ibb

En-ne-barge-si   Gilamesh

*Cuneiform Writing
Invented*

ANATOLIA

Ibbit-Lim

KINGDOM OF EBLA

Tower of Babel

Ebla Archives

LEVANT
(SYRIA/CANAAN)

CANAANITE CITY STATES

EGYPT

Pyramid Builders

Nyuserre

Neferkare

*Hieroglyphic Writing
Invented*

Hotepsekhemwy   Djoser

EGYPTIAN OLD KINGDOM

PRE-
DYNASTIC

Narmer   ARCHAIC PERIOD

Khafre

Khufu

Job?

IRON AGE
1200-332 BC

H

Comi
Ale
th

Nabopolassar

Tiglath Pileser III

Cyrus Cylinder

Xerxes I

Darius II   Artaxerxes II

NEO~BABYLONIAN
EMPIRE

Cyrus II   MEDO-PERSIAN EMPIRE   Darius III

k Obelisk   Shalmaneser IV

tter'
Inve

Shalmaneser V

Darius I

ASSYRIAN
EMPIRE

539 Babylon
Falls

Prism of Sennacherib

Elisha

Essarhaddon

Nebuchadnezzar

am   Sennacherib
ram Jehu
Jehoahaz   609 Assyria
Jehoash   Sargon II   Falls to
Jeroboam II   Babylon
Zechariah
Shallum
Menahem
Pekahiah
Pekah
Hoshea

Ashur-banipal

Ashur-uballit II

722 Fall of Samaria   Library at
Nineveh

Lachish   Nabonidus
Letters   Belshazzar   Zerubbabel   Ezra   Nehemiah

haziah Athaliah   Manasseh Amon Josiah Jehoahaz Jehoiakim Jehoiachin Zedekiah   Rebuilding of Jerusalem & Temple
         Joash   Amaziah Uzziah Jotham Ahaz Hezekiah   Destruction of
                                                                                 Jerusalem & Temple

Mesha Stele   Siloam Inscription   586 Jews Exiled
                                                                   to Babylon

Necho II

Tirhakah

Psammetichus III

ediat

Joel   Amos   Hosea   Zephaniah Habakkuk Ezekiel   2 Kings   Daniel   Haggai   Ezra   Nehemiah   Malachi
                  Jonah Micah Isaiah Nahum   Jeremiah   1 Kings Lamentations Zechariah Esther 1 Chronicles 2 Chronicles

ELLENISTIC PERIOD
332-63 BC

EARLY ROMAN PERIOD
63 BC – AD 180

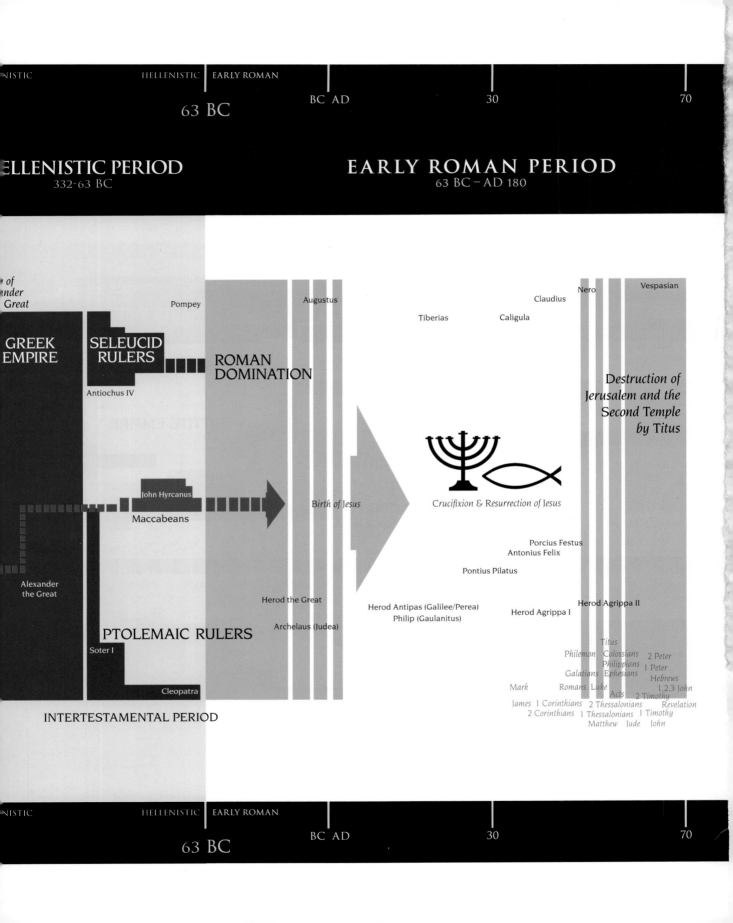

of
nder
Great

Pompey

Augustus

Nero

Vespasian

Claudius

Tiberias

Caligula

GREEK EMPIRE

SELEUCID RULERS

ROMAN DOMINATION

Antiochus IV

Destruction of Jerusalem and the Second Temple by Titus

John Hyrcanus

Crucifixion & Resurrection of Jesus

Maccabeans

Birth of Jesus

Porcius Festus
Antonius Felix

Pontius Pilatus

Alexander the Great

Herod Antipas (Galilee/Perea)
Philip (Gaulanitus)

Herod Agrippa II

Herod Agrippa I

Herod the Great

PTOLEMAIC RULERS

Archelaus (Judea)

Soter I

Titus

Philemon Colossians   2 Peter
Philippians 1 Peter
Galatians Ephesians   Hebrews
Mark   Romans Luke   1,2,3 John
Acts   2 Timothy
James 1 Corinthians 2 Thessalonians   Revelation
2 Corinthians 1 Thessalonians 1 Timothy
Matthew   Jude   John

Cleopatra

INTERTESTAMENTAL PERIOD